ASTROLOGY OF THE WORLD

VOLUME II:

Revolutions & History

TRANSLATED & EDITED BY
BENJAMIN N. DYKES, PHD

The Cazimi Press
Minneapolis, Minnesota
2014

Published and printed in the United States of America

by The Cazimi Press
515 5th Street SE #11, Minneapolis, MN 55414

© 2014 by Benjamin N. Dykes, Ph.D.

All rights reserved. No part of this publication may be reproduced, stored in or introduced into a retrieval system, or transmitted, in any form or by any means (electronic, mechanical, photocopying, recording or otherwise), without the prior written permission of both the copyright owner and the above publisher of this book.

The scanning, uploading, and distribution of this book via the Internet or via any other means without the permission of the publisher is illegal and punishable by law. Please purchase only authorized editions and do not participate in or encourage electronic piracy of copyrighted materials. Your support of the author's rights is appreciated.

ISBN-13: 978-1-934586-41-9

Acknowledgements

I would like to thank the following friends and colleagues, in alphabetical order: Benno van Dalen, and Philip Graves.

Also available at www.bendykes.com:

Designed for curious modern astrology students, *Traditional Astrology for Today* explains basic ideas in history, philosophy and counseling, dignities, chart interpretation, and predictive techniques. Non-technical and friendly for modern beginners.

The first volume of the new medieval mundane series, *Astrology of the World I: The Ptolemaic Inheritance* describes numerous techniques in weather prediction, prices and commodities, eclipses and comets, and chorography, translated from Arabic and Latin sources.

Two classic introductions to astrology, by Abū Ma'shar and al-Qabīsī, are translated with commentary in this volume. *Introductions to Traditional Astrology* is an essential reference work for traditional students.

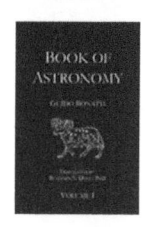

The classic medieval text by Guido Bonatti, the *Book of Astronomy* is now available in paperback reprints. This famous work is a complete guide to basic principles, horary, elections, mundane, and natal astrology.

This first English translation of Hephaistion of Thebes's *Apotelesmatics* Book III contains much fascinating material from the original Dorotheus poem and numerous other electional texts, including rules on thought-interpretation.

The largest compilation of traditional electional material, *Choices & Inceptions: Traditional Electional Astrology* contains works by Sahl, al-Rijāl, al-'Imrānī, and others, beginning with an extensive discussion of elections and questions by Benjamin Dykes.

The famous medieval horary compilation *The Book of the Nine Judges* is now available in translation for the first time! It is the largest traditional horary work available, and the third in the horary series.

The Search of the Heart is the first in the horary series, and focuses on the use of victors (special significators or *almutens*) and the practice of thought-interpretation: divining thoughts and predicting outcomes before the client speaks.

The Forty Chapters is a famous and influential horary work by al-Kindī, and is the second volume of the horary series. Beginning with a general introduction to astrology, al-Kindī covers topics such as war, wealth, travel, pregnancy, marriage, and more.

The first volume of the *Persian Nativities* series on natal astrology contains *The Book of Aristotle*, an advanced work on nativities and prediction by Māshā'allāh, and a beginner-level work by his student Abū 'Ali al-Khayyāt, *On the Judgments of Nativities*.

The second volume of *Persian Nativities* features a The second volume of *Persian Nativities* features a shorter, beginner-level work on nativities and prediction by 'Umar al-Tabarī, and a much longer book on nativities by his younger follower, Abū Bakr.

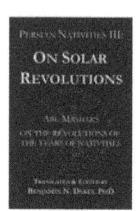

The third volume of *Persian Nativities* is a translation of Abū Ma'shar 's work on solar revolutions, devoted solely to the Persian annual predictive system. Learn about profections, distributions, *firdārīyyāt*, transits, and more!

This compilation of sixteen works by Sahl b. Bishr and Māshā'allāh covers all areas of traditional astrology, from basic concepts to horary, elections, natal interpretation, and mundane astrology. It is also available in paperback.

Expand your knowledge of traditional astrology, philosophy, and esoteric thought with the *Logos & Light* audio series: downloadable, college-level lectures on MP3 at a fraction of the university cost!

Enjoy these new additions in our magic/esoteric series:

Astrological Magic: Basic Rituals & Meditations is a basic introduction to ritual magic for astrologers. It introduces a magical cosmology and electional rules, and shows how to perform ritual correctly, integrating Tarot and visualizations with rituals for all Elements, Planets, and Signs.

Available as an MP3 download, *Music of the Elements* was composed especially for *Astrological Magic* by MjDawn, an experienced electronic artist and ritualists. Hear free clips at bendykes.com/music.php!

Nights is a special, 2-disc remastering by MjDawn of the album GAMMA, and is a deep and powerful set of 2 full-disc MP3 soundtracks suitable for meditation or ritual work, especially those in *Astrological Magic*. Hear free clips at bendykes.com/music.php!

Aeonian Glow is a new version of the original ambient work mixed by Steve Roach, redesigned by MjDawn and Vir Unis from the original, pre-mixed files. This MP3 album is entrancing and enchanting: hear free clips at bendykes.com/music.php!

TABLE OF CONTENTS

Book Abbreviations vi
Table of Figures vii
INTRODUCTION 1
§1: Structure of the book & suggested reading 2
§2: Historical vs. episodic mundane astrology 4
§3: Thumbnail sketch of world-years, the Flood, & mean conjunctions ... 6
§4: World years, Flood dates, & a controversy 10
§5: Mean conjunctions, triplicity shifts, & types of year 18
§6: Māshā'allāh's mundane astrology 28
§7: Al-Battānī: an under-reported alternative 30
§8: Saturn-Mars conjunctions in Cancer 32
§9: Time lords & techniques in historical astrology 35
§10: Mundane Lots, & Saturn-Jupiter as Lots 40
§11: Julian days & key data for Islamic historical astrology 43
§12: How to interpret an ingress chart 46
§13: Special Arabic vocabulary 52
PART I: SHORT SUMMARIES & PRINCIPLES 58
Section I.1: Al-Qabīsī on Mundane Profections 58
Section I.2: Al-Qabīsī on Mundane Lots 63
Section I.3: Al-Kindī's *Forty Chapters* 68
Section I.4: 'Umar on Mundane Directions 71
Section I.5: 'Umar-Kankah, *The Universal Book* 74
Section I.6: Al-Qabīsī (*attr.*), *On Conjunctions in the Signs* 82
PART II: MĀSHĀ'ALLĀH & HIS DERIVATIVES 86
Section II.1: Māshā'allāh's Historical Astrology 86
Section II.2: Māshā'allāh, *On the Revolutions of the Years of the World* 99
  Chapter 1: On the places of the luminaries from the Ascendant 100
  Chapter 2: On the triplicities 101
  Chapter 3: On the division of the earth 102
  Chapter 4: When it is necessary to revolve the quarters of the years . 103
  Chapter 5: On discovering the lord of the year 104
  Chapter 6: On the portions & testimonies of the planets, from which the lord of the year is identified 104
  Chapter 7: On the luminaries, if they were in the angles 105
  Chapter 8: When the lord of the year hands rulership to another 105
  Chapter 9: On the strength of the lord of the year 106
  Chapter 10: When the lord of the Ascendant is made into the lord of the year 106
  Chapter 11: What things must be looked at in judgments about kings & the rustics 107
  Chapter 12: When the lord of the year is falling [away from the Ascendant] 108

Chapter 13: On the strength & weakness of the lord of the year 109
Chapter 14: On the adversary of the king 110
Chapter 15: On the impediment of the king.. 112
Chapter 16: On the place of the lord of the year 113
Chapter 17: On the signification of Mercury & the Moon................. 113
Chapter 18: On the strength of the luminaries.................................... 114
Chapter 19: On the planet to which the lord of year is being joined . 115
Chapter 20: When the lord of the year & the significator of the king are retrograde 118
Chapter 21: On war... 118
Chapter 22: On the signification of the three superiors...................... 119
Chapter 23: On a year to be feared.. 121
Chapter 24: On the signification of the Head & Tail of the Dragon of the Moon 121
Chapter 25: On the signification of a planet in the signification of wars if it was slow, retrograde, or direct... 122
Chapter 26: On the condition of the king when his significator is entering into burning 123
Chapter 27: Whether there is going to be war, & who would attain victory.. 125
Chapter 28: On the impediment of the citizens of that clime 126
Chapter 29: On the enemies of the king... 126
Chapter 30: On the power of the luminaries 127
Chapter 31: On the division of the world according to the three superior planets... 128
Chapter 32: On the division of the climes 129
Chapter 33: On the nature of the winds & triplicities 130
Chapter 34: On the number of cities in each clime 130
Chapter 35: When the Sun hands over his own management to the Moon 130
Chapter 36: On the signification of Mars & the other planets in the angles, if they were lords of the year... 131
Chapter 37: On the calamities of the year 133
Chapter 38: On the signification of a planet when it enters burning or goes out from it 133
Chapter 39: On the signification of Saturn when he is in his own exaltation... 134
Chapter 40: On an eclipse, if there were one in that same year.......... 134
Chapter 41: When the Sun is made the significator of the king 135
Chapter 42: On the condition of the king in that same year.............. 137
Chapter 43: On the impediment of the rustics.................................... 139
Chapter 44: On the detriment of the king... 140
Chapter 45: On the signification of Mars [in the triplicities].............. 141
Chapter 46: On the signification of Saturn in the triplicities 142

Contents

Section II.3: Māshā'allāh, *Letter on Eclipses* 144
    Chapter 1: On the system of the circle of the stars, & how they operate in this world 146
    Chapter 2: On the diversity of the work of the stars in the regions of the earth 147
    Chapter 3: On the natures of the signs 147
    Chapter 4: On the revolution of years 148
    Chapter 5: On the eclipse of the Moon, & its being 149
    Chapter 6: On the changing of the seasons by the changing of the planets (namely, the heavy ones) 149
    Chapter 7: On the eclipse of the Sun & its signification 150
    Chapter 8: On the conjunction of the planets & their effect 151
    Chapter 9: On the conjunction of the superior planets 152
    Chapter 10: On the greater conjunction 153
    Chapter 11: On the middle conjunction 154
    Chapter 12: On the lesser conjunction 155
Section II.4: Māshā'allāh's *Book of Conjunctions* 156
    Chapter 1: Introduction, & the Flood 159
    Chapter 2: Conjunction #121, the shift indicating the Flood 160
    Chapter 3: Conjunction #122, shift for the year of the Flood 162
    Chapter 4: Conjunction #289, indicating Christ 165
    Chapter 5: Conjunction #290, containing the nativity of Christ 166
    Chapter 6: Aries ingress for Christ's nativity (13 BC) 168
    Chapter 7: Conjunctions #320-322, shift indicating Islam & Muhammad's birth & early career 169
    Chapter 8: Conjunction #323, indicating the victory of the Muslims (630 AD) 174
    Chapter 9: Conjunction #324, fall of the Sassanians (650 AD) 177
    Chapter 10: Conjunction #329, rise of the 'Abbasids (749 AD) 180
    Chapter 11: Conjunction #332, the shift to fire & Caliph al-Ma'mūn (809 AD) 183
    Chapter 12: Conjunction #333, 2nd fiery conjunction (828 AD) 189
    Chapter 13: Conjunction #334, 3rd fiery conjunction (848 AD) 191
    Chapter 14: Conjunction #335, 4th fiery conjunction (868 AD) 193
    Chapter 15: Conjunction #336, 5th fiery conjunction (888 AD) 195
    Chapter 16: Conjunction #337, 6th fiery conjunction (908 AD) 197
    Chapter 17: Conjunction #338, 7th fiery conjunction (rise of the Buwayhids, 928 AD) 200
    Chapter 18: Ibn Hibintā's true conjunction, Sagittarius (928 AD) 202
Section II.5: Abū Ma'shar, *Scito horam introitus* 205
Section II.6: "Abū Ma'shar," *Book of Tested Things* 294
PART III: ABŪ MA'SHAR'S *FLOWERS* 301
    Book I: The Lord of the Year 304
    Book II: The Indications of the Planets by Themselves 316

Book III: Prices, Weather, War, Disasters..................324
Book IV: The Malefics in the Signs & Places 330
Book V: On the Fixed Stars.......................................333
Book VI: On the Direction of the Superior Planets in the Signs 342
Book VII: On the Nodes & Comets 351

PART IV: AL-RIJĀL, *THE BOOK OF THE SKILLED* VIII 356
Section IV.1: Introduction 356
Section IV.2: *The Book of the Skilled* VIII 358
    Chapter VIII.0: Invocation & Prologue..........................358
    Chapter VIII.1: On mentioning the introductory things, from [which] the knowledgeable person will seek aid..........................358
    Chapter VIII.2: On years indicating fertility & sterility.............361
    Chapter VIII.3: On years signifying unrest & wars................363
    Chapter VIII.4: On the knowledge of the lord of the year.........370
    Chapter VIII.5: On the conjunction [of the planets], by Hermes.......384
    Chapter VIII.6: The matter of the populace & the citizens 390
    Chapter VIII.7: The indications of the planets in their arrival in the Ascendant & the remaining houses..................398
    Chapter VIII.8: On knowing the place of the earth in which the event happens 412
    Chapter VIII.9: On the indications of the planets.................417
    Chapter VIII.10: On knowing the places of what happens 419
    Chapter VIII.11: Likewise on the revolution of the year............421
    Chapter VIII.12: On the judgments of the Lots in the houses 426
    Chapter VIII.13: On the indications of war......................426
    Chapter VIII.14: On the survival of kings & their conditions............430
    Chapter VIII.15: On the knowledge of the [king's] accession & its period..................431
    Chapter VIII.16: On the death of kings 434
    Chapter VIII.17: On the changing of kings 439
    Chapter VIII.18: On kings & their lifespans.....................444
    Chapter VIII.19: On the knowledge of the death of kings from the revolution of the year of the world 445
    Chapter VIII.20: On the amount of the king's longevity, from the year of his accession 445
    Chapter VIII.21: On a question about the matters of kings 446
    Chapter VIII.22: On considering the revolution of the year of the world for the accession of the acceder 448
    Chapter VIII.23: On the overlooking of the planets................453
    Chapter VIII.24: On the unions of the planets....................456
    Chapter VIII.25: On the connection of the planets 458
    Chapter VIII.26: On the consideration of the events of the weather & the variation of the atmosphere, the times, & their behavior with respect to heat & cold..................466

Chapter VIII.27: On rains, thunders, lightning bolts, & winds 469
Chapter VIII.28: On the opening of doors of rains, & other things . 471
Chapter VIII.29: On the foundations 472
Chapter VIII.30: On the time in which rain is hoped for 473
Chapter VIII.31: On epidemics, health, drought, & fertility 475
Chapter VIII.32: On the times of the occurrence of evil, civil unrest, fire, & submersion 477
Chapter VIII.33: On prices 480
Chapter VIII.34: On what belongs to the signs & the planets, of the regions & countries 489
Chapter VIII.35: On the knowledge of cities belonging to the signs . 492
Chapter VIII.36: What regions & villages belong to the planets 495
Chapter VIII.37: On the longitudes of countries & their latitudes, based on what Habs mentioned in his *Zīj* 497
Chapter VIII.38: On the knowledge of the procedure of the two Lots, [and] in it are two differing accounts 499
Chapter VIII.39: On the knowledge of the sign of the terminal point from the Ascendant of the shift of the transit indicating the religion [of the Arabs] 504
Chapter VIII.40: On the knowledge of the terminal points & the distribution 507
Chapter VIII.41: On falling stars 508
Appendix A: Tables of Mean Conjunctions 510
Appendix B: Saturn-Mars Conjunctions in Cancer 519
Appendix C: Chart Examples from Sahl 527
Appendix D: Table of Turns (Mighty *Fardārs*) 541
GLOSSARY 544
BIBLIOGRAPHY 566
SELECT INDEX 569

Book Abbreviations

AW1-3	Various	*Astrology of the World Vols. 1-3*
BOA	Guido Bonatti	*The Book of Astronomy*
BRD	Abū Ma'shar	*The Book of Religions and Dynasties (On the Great Conjunctions)*
Conjunctions	Māshā'allāh	*Book on Conjunctions (in present volume)*
Flowers	Abū Ma'shar	*The Flowers of Abū Ma'shar (in present volume)*
ITA	Abū Ma'shar et al.	*Introductions to Traditional Astrology: Abū Ma'shar & al-Qabīsī*
Judges	Various	*The Book of the Nine Judges*
PN1-3	Various	*Persian Nativities vols. 1-3*
RYW	Māshā'allāh	*On the Revolutions of the Years of the World (in present volume)*
Scito	Abū Ma'shar	*Scito Horam Introitus (in present volume)*
Skilled	Al-Rijāl	*The Book of the Skilled in the Judgments of the Stars*
WSM	Sahl b. Bishr & Māshā'allāh	*Works of Sahl & Māshā'allāh*

TABLE OF FIGURES

Figure 1: Idealized triplicity shifts 8
Figure 2: 2000 Ingress, with mean & true conjunctions..................................9
Figure 3: Flood-Kaliyuga, 3102 BC (Fagan-Bradley sidereal).......................13
Figure 4: Revolutions in 360,000 years: Āryabhata & Abū Ma'shar...............14
Figure 5: Illustrated mean period of Jupiter 19
Figure 6: Mean tropical cycle of Jupiter..20
Figure 7: Contemporary values for years & mean periods............................21
Figure 8: Complete table of mean conjunctions & distances 22
Figure 9: Illustration of mean conjunctional period 24
Figure 10: Eleven tropical mean conjunctions in the fiery triplicity............25
Figure 11: Tropical & sidereal triplicity shifts compared 26
Figure 12: Abū Ma'shar's parameters for Saturn-Jupiter conjunctions 27
Figure 13: Mean tropical conjunction of 1901...28
Figure 14: Māshā'allāh's parameters for Saturn-Jupiter conjunctions............30
Figure 15: Modern version of al-Battānī's triplicity shift 32
Figure 16: 2004 Aries ingress for Indonesia...33
Figure 17: Version of al-Kindī's ingress for the Hijrah, 622 AD..................34
Figure 18: 1941 ingresses for Washington, DC and Tokyo..........................38
Figure 19: Mundane Lots in *AW2*..42
Figure 20: Saturn & Jupiter as First & Second Lots.....................................42
Figure 21: Julian dates for key astrological events..44
Figure 22: Julian dates for key calendar/event dates....................................44
Figure 23: Mundane significations of planets...49
Figure 24: Six ways for a planet to "fall" in Arabic......................................53
Figure 25: Table illustrating al-Kindī's profection from 571 AD 61
Figure 26: Two "greatest Lots" for Wilhelm II (al-Qabīsī 5.17)......................66
Figure 27: Direction of Mars to MC: "Axis of Evil" speech.........................73
Figure 28: Cancer-Mercury *Fardār*, Aries ingress 940 AD (tropical) 80
Figure 29: 'Umar-Kankah: Epoch, Flood, Mighty *Fardārs*..........................81
Figure 30: Māshā'allāh's Zoroastrian Thousands 88
Figure 31: Table of Māshā'allāh's Thousands..90
Figure 32: Māshā'allāh's parameters for Saturn-Jupiter conjunctions............91
Figure 33: Māshā'allāh's mean conjunctions, recalculated 93
Figure 34: Ibn Hibintā's true conjunction #338...93
Figure 35: Māshā'allāh's "accurate" triplicity shifts......................................95
Figure 36: Māshā'allāh's "divergent" triplicity shifts....................................96
Figure 37: Illustration of tropical excess of revolution.................................96
Figure 38: Lord of year (Venus) handing management to Mars 106
Figure 39: Saturn reflecting Jupiter's light to the Ascendant.......................109
Figure 40: Thief age, superior planets (Heph. III.45, 13).............................111
Figure 41: Thief age, inferior planets (Heph. III.45, 15)..............................111

viii   ASTROLOGY OF THE WORLD II: REVOLUTIONS & HISTORY

Figure 42: The Sun as significator of the people & the king 136
Figure 43: Aries ingress #121, the shift indicating the Flood (3381 BC).....161
Figure 44: Aries ingress for #122, the Flood (3361 BC)..................163
Figure 45: Aries ingress for #289, indicating Christ (46 BC) 166
Figure 46: Conjunction of nativity of Christ (26 BC) 167
Figure 47: Aries ingress for year of Christ's nativity (13 BC) 168
Figure 48: Ingress for watery shift (#320) indicating Islam (571 AD).......170
Figure 49: Third watery conjunction, #322 (609 AD).....................174
Figure 50: Aries ingress for #323, victory for Muslims....................175
Figure 51: Aries ingress for #324, the fall of the Sassanians..............177
Figure 52: Ingress for #329, the rise of the 'Abbasids 180
Figure 53: Ingress for #332, shift to fire & Caliph al-Ma'mun (809 AD)...183
Figure 54: Ingress for #333, the 2nd fiery conjunction (829 AD).........190
Figure 55: Ingress for #334, the 3rd fiery conjunction (848 AD) 192
Figure 56: Ingress for #335, the 4th fiery conjunction (868 AD).........193
Figure 57: Ingress for #336, the 5th fiery conjunction (888 AD).........195
Figure 58: Ingress for #337, the 6th fiery conjunction (907 AD).........197
Figure 59: Ingress for #338, the 7th fiery conjunction (928 AD).........200
Figure 60: Ibn Hibintā's true conjunction for #338 (October 8, 928) 203
Figure 61: Thief age, superior planets (Heph. III.45, 13)..................233
Figure 62: Thief age, inferior planets (Heph. III.45, 15)..................233
Figure 63: Version (from MS) of Sahl's Example #1, 656 AD..............278
Figure 64: Sahl's Example #1, 656 AD (modern tropical) 278
Figure 65: Zodiacal direction for Sahl's Example #1 285
Figure 66: The fiery, eastern triplicity 311
Figure 67: The earthy, southern triplicity 311
Figure 68: The airy, western triplicity 311
Figure 69: The watery, northern triplicity 311
Figure 67: Saturnus 316
Figure 68: Jupiter..318
Figure 69: Mars..319
Figure 70: Sol 320
Figure 71: Venus 321
Figure 72: Mercurius...322
Figure 73: Luna..323
Figure 74: Motion of Sun over longitudes in 12h (al-Rijāl VIII.8, 2-3) 414
Figure 75: Finding terrestrial longitude of the misfortune (VIII.8, 7-9)........415
Figure 76: Al-Kindī's directions for fighting 451
Figure 77: Al-Rijāl's proposed correction to al-Kindī.....................452
Figure 78: 'Umar's foundations of the Moon (*Skilled* VIII.29) 472
Figure 79: A Persian *Thema Mundi* (al-Rijāl Ch. VIII.35)................494
Figure 80: Illustration of "two Lots" version 2 (*Skilled* VIII.38, 3-4) 500
Figure 81: Illustration of "two Lots" version 3 (*Skilled* VIII.38, 5-14) 502
Figure 82: Table of tropical mean Saturn-Jupiter conjunctions 514

Figure 83: Table of sidereal mean Saturn-Jupiter conjunctions 518
Figure 84: Table of tropical mean Saturn-Mars in Cancer conjunctions 523
Figure 85: Table of sidereal mean Saturn-Mars in Cancer conjunctions 526
Figure 86: Version (adapted from Vat.) of Sahl's Example #2 (657 AD) ... 531
Figure 87: "Preferred" tropical version of Sahl's example #2 531
Figure 88: Version (adapted from MS) of Sahl's Example #3 (692 AD) 536
Figure 89: Sahl's Example #3 (692 AD), tropical zodiac 536
Figure 90: Version (adapted from MS) of Sahl's Example #4 (719 AD) 539
Figure 91: Sahl's Example #4 (modern tropical) 539
Figure 92: Table of Turns (mighty *fardārs*) 543

INTRODUCTION

I am happy to present *Astrology of the World Volume II: Revolutions & History* (hereafter, *AW2*). This is the second volume of my medieval mundane series, to be followed in 2015 by a translation of Abū Ma'shar's *Book of Religions and Dynasties* (*BRD*), often known by its Latin name, *On the Great Conjunctions*. This book contains numerous works essential for medieval mundane astrology, with some major portions translated from Arabic instead of the Latin sources which have comprised most of my translations since 2007. While *BRD* is in preparation, I will proceed with an Arabic series, a Renaissance/Early Modern Latin series, and continue to manage a Hellenistic Greek series.

I had originally planned to release this book earlier, but several things inevitably delayed it. One important issue was the fact that I had to learn essential concepts in conjunctional theory and geocentric astronomy, which are barely known even by most scholars today. Unfortunately, the learned treatises by people like Pingree, Kennedy, and others, are very difficult for the beginner. I was helped immeasurably by Evans's *History and Practice of Ancient Astronomy* (1998). But even then, my research required working through unfamiliar equations, scholarly disputes, and creating extensive Excel spreadsheets I never imagined I would need.

In order to make this material accessible for the beginner, I have included numerous explanations, diagrams (lacking in most scholarly articles), and tables. I beg the reader's patience in working through these, as the information in this Introduction in particular will be invaluable for understanding what follows. Modern astrology programs base their calculations on accurate, contemporary values for things like the length of the year, but this data was not available to medievals, who often borrowed and adapted data from numerous authors and civilizations. For example, the sidereal year is currently calculated as 365.256363 days, but most Arabic-speaking astrologers employing a sidereal zodiac used a year of 365.259 or 365.2590278 days: this might not make a difference from one year to the next, but because mundane astrologers calculated charts for thousands of years in the past, these small differences can add up—not to mention the differences in their planetary parameters. So in many cases I have provided a contemporary sidereal or tropical chart, with explanations in my *Comments* or footnotes to make it clear how the modern chart diverges from the values in the manuscripts.

§1: Structure of the book & suggested reading

Most readers nowadays will be interested in mundane ingresses and Saturn-Jupiter conjunctions (and especially, in the tropical zodiac). But many authors in this book also discuss mundane time lord techniques, such as mundane profections, something called a Turn, and other things. Most also introduced or accepted a Flood date into their chronologies. Without going into the details here, I want to make a summary statement about two streams of thought in these texts, which can be conflated if one does not pay attention:

Stream 1: Māshā'allāh. Māshā'allāh's historical astrology has Saturn-Jupiter conjunctions embedded within a Zoroastrian theory of "Thousands," whereby each planet in turn acts as a time lord for the whole world, for 1,000 sidereal years. Although Māshā'allāh uses transits and mundane profections, he is not really interested in any other time-lord system (and barely even discusses the Thousands). His Flood is dated to 3361 BC.

Stream 2: Abū Ma'shar. Abū Ma'shar, perhaps drawing on 'Umar al-Tabarī and Kankah, embeds his conjunctions in numerous other time-lord systems, particularly the Turn and mundane directions. The texts in this book provide key dates for the transition from one time lord to the next, but apart from that they are hardly used in any interpretive context. (*BRD* has much more on these.) His Flood is dated to 3102 BC.

This book is divided into four Parts, each with Sections, and the pieces in each Section have numbered sentences in boldface. The Parts are as follows:

Part I: Short Summaries & Principles. These works provide overviews of basic concepts, a few mundane Lots, types of conjunctions to observe, and include some of the key time-lord dates I just mentioned. Al-Kindī (Section I.3) has some brief instructions of his own on how to interpret an ingress chart.

Part II: Māshā'allāh & his Derivatives. This Part contains a lengthy analysis of Māshā'allāh's historical astrology, followed by a well-known work on interpreting ingresses, types of conjunctions and brief notes on eclipses, and a detailed analysis of numerous mundane charts which I have newly translated from Arabic. (It had already been translated in a rather confusing edition by Pingree and Kennedy in 1971.) Following these are a work attributed to Abū Ma'shar but highly dependent on Māshā'allāh, with traces of Sahl and others in it, and finally a brief *pastiche* comprised entirely of excerpts from Māshā'allāh and some of Abū Ma'shar's *Flowers*.

Part III: Abū Ma'shar's Flowers. Here I have newly retranslated the *Flowers of Abū Ma'shar*, a medieval Latin translation of an Arabic work by Abū Ma'shar. In this I was helped by an Arabic manuscript of the original text, but I limited my corrections of the Latin so as to save my own Arabic translation for a future time. *Flowers* is a brisk and pretty complete guide to ingresses, with valuable sections on fixed stars and other things.

Part IV: The Book of the Skilled, Book VIII. Finally, I provide the first modern translation of the whole of Book VIII of al-Rijāl's (Haly Abenragel's) *The Book of the Skilled in the Judgments of the Stars*, which covers all areas of mundane astrology (but focusing on ingresses). Al-Rijāl is valuable for providing the views of numerous authors (not always explicitly named), and especially includes sections which are either taken from *BRD* or (since their vocabulary and wording often differs) from their common source.

Finally, let me provide a suggested course of reading for those who are new to—or even somewhat experienced in—this area of astrology. The list of texts is roughly in their order of complexity:

Conjunctional Theory *& Time Lords*	Ingresses
• This Introduction • Al-Qabīsī, Section I.1 • Appendices A-B • 'Umar-Kankah, Section I.5 • Section II.3, Māshā'allāh's *Letter* • Section II.1, *Comment* on Māshā'allāh • Section II.4, Māshā'allāh's *Conjunctions* • Part IV.2, al-Rijāl's *Skilled* VIII.39-40	• This Introduction • Section I.3, al-Kindī • Section II.2, Māshā'allāh's *RYW* • Part III, *Flowers* • Section II.5, *Scito* • Part IV.2, al-Rijāl *Skilled* • Appendix C • Section II.1, *Comment* on Māshā'allāh • Section II.4, Māshā'allāh's *Conjunctions* • Lots: Section I.2 (al-Qabīsī) • and *Skilled* VIII.38

§2: Historical vs. episodic mundane astrology

In *Astrology of the World Volume I: The Ptolemaic Inheritance* (or *AW1*) we looked at the side of mundane astrology I am now calling "episodic," which was largely based on Ptolemy: predicting weather, prices, and other things based on seasonal and monthly ingress charts, the charts of New and Full Moons, and eclipses (and sometimes, comets). It also included chorography, the assigning of regions of the earth to the planets and signs. I call this family of techniques "episodic," because to a great extent there is nothing intrinsic that connects one event to another. For example, given some particular eclipse, Ptolemy teaches how to interpret it and determine how long its effects will last. But the eclipse, its events and period, form an isolated episode rather than being part of a larger story.[1] The same is relatively true of New and Full Moons: Ptolemy said to examine the lunation that most immediately preceded every seasonal ingress, and to continue using that kind of lunation until the next season arrived. For example, if the lunation prior to the Aries ingress was a Full Moon, then we should use the Full Moon charts through-

---

[1] It is true that solar eclipses fall into groups, such that the paths of eclipses in certain Saros series will reappear in roughly the same places of the earth after a certain time; but this was not how Ptolemy thought about eclipses, and traditionally they do not form part of a larger historical structure.

out the spring; when the Cancer ingress arrives, see what kind of lunation immediately precedes *it*, and so on. But each season, and in a sense each lunation, could be seen as an episode not particularly related to others. Finally, annual ingresses themselves are somewhat episodic, since traditionally there are few conceptual links between one and another. But as we will see in this volume, the Persian astrologers above all embedded ingresses into a larger framework of "historical" astrology. The use of ingresses here is largely political and social, as opposed to concerns about weather and prices often found in episodic approaches.

Traditional Mundane Astrology

Episodic	**Historical**
• Ingresses	• Conjunctions
• Lunations	• Time lords
• Eclipses	• Ingresses (political)

Historical astrology (a term coined by scholars such as Pingree and Kennedy) aims to make broader periods of history intelligible, and focuses on astrological indications for all areas of politics and culture. Unlike episodic mundane astrology, time periods retain a certain character even when apparently nothing astrological is happening—this is also characteristic of natal methods that divide life up into periods ruled by time lords, not to mention normal historical ways of dividing history up into "centuries," "decades," or "ages." An important difference between academic history and historical astrology is that the latter uses periods actually grounded in nature, namely the motions of the planets.

This branch can be traced to post-Hellenistic Persian and Indian ideas, and I describe it here as a tiered approach with two levels:

- At the broadest level, it applies time-lord systems to bracket periods of history, particularly using mundane directions or distributions through the bounds, mundane *fardārs*, and mundane profections. Some of these methods cover spans of hundreds of years. It is the least developed approach in the literature, and in some senses it is the least practical. We will deal with it in a more theoretical way.

- Within this framework (and sometimes apparently separate from it) is the use of regular planetary conjunctions as structuring devices for smaller periods of history. The most important type is the "mean" conjunction of Saturn and Jupiter every 20 years or so, but al-Kindī and Abū Ma'shar also mention the conjunction of Saturn and Mars in Cancer (every 30 years), and Māshā'allāh mentions others.[2] (And some astrologers rejected the mean conjunction in favor of true conjunctions: see below.)[3] The Saturn-Jupiter conjunctions have a two-fold structure. On the one hand, their conjunctions happen every 20 years, in the same triplicity (such as the watery signs). But after about 12 of such conjunctions over about 240 years, they shift into the next triplicity and signal broad changes in culture and politics.

When using mean conjunctions, astrologers analyzed them using Aries ingresses[4] (and occasionally the other movable signs), so there is much lore about interpreting ingresses. For example, it might be of interest that the Ascendant of some ingress is also the sign of the most recent Saturn-Jupiter conjunction.

Mundane astrology requires the knowledge of both historical details and numerous mundane techniques. In what follows, I will first give a short, thumbnail sketch of the basics. Then I will go into much greater detail concerning all of these topics, dealing especially with Abū Ma'shar and Māshā'allāh, probably the two most important figures in this field. In addition, we will have to cover some points of traditional astronomy.

§3: Thumbnail sketch of world-years, the Flood, & mean conjunctions

Here I provide a brief overview of the central ideas in conjunctional astrology, with reference to time-lord systems that will be addressed in further detail below. I defer any citations until later.

Ancient philosophers and astrologers posited that the world undergoes certain cycles or "world-years," which coincide with certain planetary align-

---

[2] See his *Letter* (in Section II.3 of this book).
[3] These include al-Battani, ibn Ezra (Sela, p. 53), and ibn Labbān (II.11, **3**).
[4] Theophilus (quoted in Pingree 2001, p. 16) says that the Persians use the Aries ingress as the beginning of their year, as do Critodemus, Valens, Dorotheus, Timocharis, "and their associates."

ments; sometimes these cycles and events refer to the creation and destruction of the world, sometimes to other events such as the great Flood. World-years can stretch from thousands to millions of years. In the medieval period, the Flood itself was assigned two dates, based on different astronomical systems: February 18, 3102 BC (Abū Ma'shar's "Persian" system) or July 30, 3361 BC (Māshā'allāh). Abū Ma'shar's Flood date was supposed to coincide with certain rare planetary conjunctions, while Māshā'allāh's had another rationale.

Against this general background of world-years, astrologers divided history into smaller but still lengthy periods ruled by time lords, such as Māshā'allāh's "Thousands" (periods of 1,000 years, each ruled by a single planet), various kinds of *fardār*s, profections, and so on. These periods are more symbolic and tend not to coincide with particular configurations of planets.

At the next level down, astrologers used certain patterns found within the conjunctions of the traditional outer planets (Saturn, Jupiter, and Mars). The Saturn-Jupiter conjunctions are the most important, and occur every 19.8 years (rounded up to 20 years).[5] They have a peculiar characteristic, because of the motions of these planets: once a conjunction happens at the beginning of the sign of some triplicity, successive conjunctions take place within that same triplicity. But the degree of the conjunction in each sign slowly creeps forward, so that after an idealized 12 conjunctions, they shift into the following triplicity (fire, then earth, air, water, then back to fire). These changes are called "triplicity shifts."[6]

The entire 240-year period of a particular triplicity (12 x 20 years) is meant to describe changes in world power and politics, while individual conjunctions every 20 years show lesser changes within the general theme. There are various rules to tell when events predicted by the conjunctions will take place. The following diagram shows the basic structure of these shifts, taking the fiery triplicity as an example:

---

[5] The Saturn-Mars conjunctions in Cancer (approximately every 30 years) were considered important by al-Kindī (although he probably did not invent them): they are then used or described by Abū Ma'shar and ibn Hibintā, among others.
[6] Actually, in Arabic they are called by other names, such as the "shift of the transit." But "shift" is the most important term.

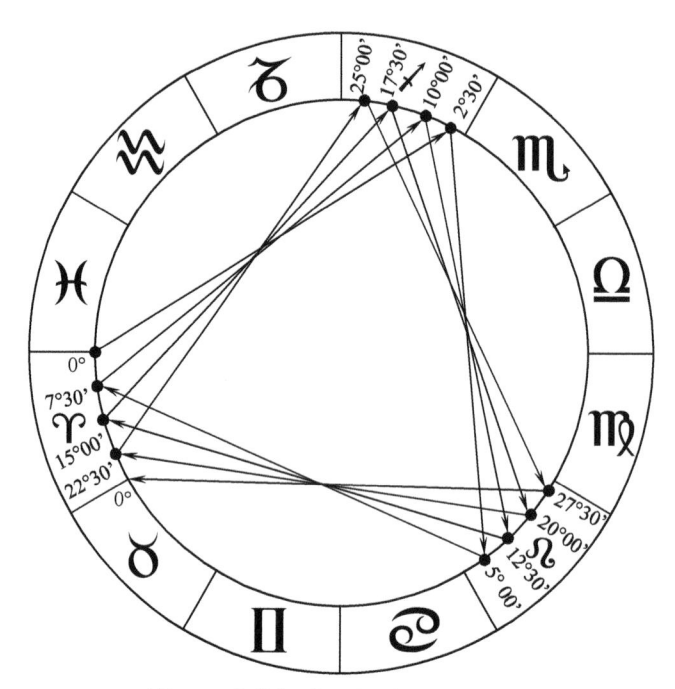

Figure 1: Idealized triplicity shifts

These conjunctions are "mean" conjunctions (described below), not "true" conjunctions as we find them in the ephemeris.

Finally, when casting a mundane chart, most astrologers did not cast the chart for the mean conjunction, but for the Aries ingress for the seasonal year *in which* a mean conjunction took place—from March to March. So for example, if a mean conjunction occurred in October, they would cast the ingress chart for the previous March; likewise, for a conjunction in February 2014, they would still cast the previous year's Aries ingress (2013), because the 2014 ingress had not happened yet. For their interpretations of these charts, they especially relied on one or two important planets, which can be called "victors":[7] the lord of the year (which summarized the theme of the year), and often the "significator" or "indicator" of the king (describing the affairs of the political authority).

The chart below illustrates the mean and true Saturn-Jupiter conjunctions in 2000 AD, at the mean triplicity shift into air. The chart is cast for the Aries

---

[7] See the Glossary.

ingress in March, 2000; in May there was a true conjunction of their bodies at 22° Taurus, and in November their mean conjunction fell at 0° Gemini.

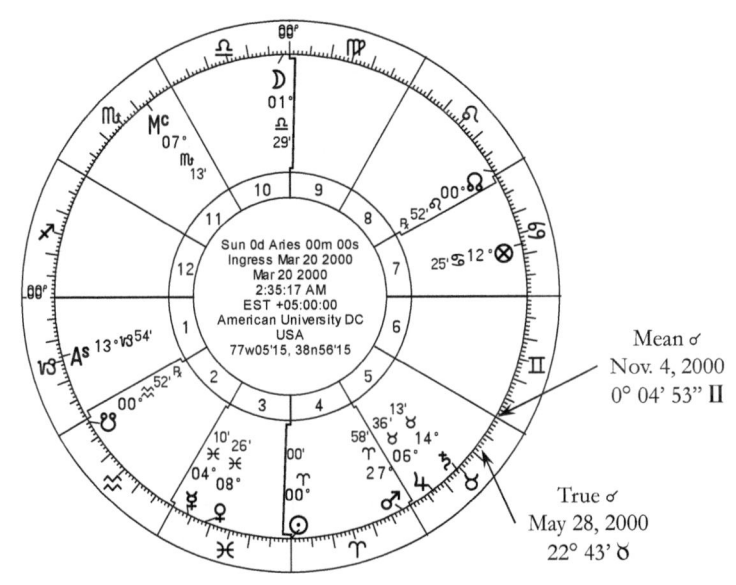

Figure 2: 2000 Ingress, with mean & true conjunctions

So much for the brief description. Before moving to some details, it is important to note three key points about actual medieval practice:

- The numbers of conjunctions and the length of their periods in the "standard" account are idealized. In order to get a series of exactly 12 conjunctions in each triplicity every time, the degrees of the conjunctions can only creep forward by exactly 2.5° every time within the signs. But there is no astronomical system in which this is true, due to the actual mean motions of Saturn and Jupiter. So, the length of a triplicity period will vary between 10-13 conjunctions, depending on whether one is using a sidereal or tropical zodiac (see below).
- Sometimes, medieval astrologers paired an Aries ingress with an *earlier* mean conjunction, contrary to what the theory dictates. The most important example was the Scorpio conjunction in December

570: it should have been paired with the 570 ingress, but was considered with the later ingress of 571, *not* the 570 conjunction.[8]
- Although most astrologers used these ingress charts for interpreting mean conjunctions, one notable dissenter was al-Battānī (see below). He disdained mean conjunctions in favor of (1) eclipses which happened to coincide closely with (2) *true* conjunctions. In this, he was consciously following a Ptolemaic model focused on actual planetary configurations.

In Appendices A and B I provide contemporary parameters for calculating mean conjunctions (both tropical and sidereal), along with handy tables. Below I will also provide similar information, but with explanations.

§4: World years, Flood dates, & a controversy[9]

Let us return to the bigger picture and discuss the concept of world-years, Floods, and a contention between Pingree and van der Waerden.

The idea of periodic planetary returns and conjunctions denoting meaningful epochs and catastrophes (or even eternal recurrences) is old—at least as old as Plato[10] and an apocryphal report about Aristotle,[11] not to mention the Pythagoreans. The Babylonian astrologer Berossus speaks of periodic floods when planets conjoin in Capricorn, and conflagrations in Cancer; this view is repeated by Firmicus Maternus as late as the 4th Century.[12] The length of these astronomically or astrologically-defined world years varied from author to author, but usually were multiples of 12, such as 10,800 years (Heraclitus) or 3,600,000 years (Cassandrus). In Indian astrology these types of periods go under the name of yogas or yugas, and sources for them can be traced back to the 2nd Century AD; they are reported in the Laws of Manu and the Mahābhārata. The fact that some of the Babylonian and Indian values are the same, intuitively suggests a historical connection between them, although the numerical values are often derived in different ways.[13] Van der

---

[8] Another example is Māshā'allāh's #333, which was in 828 AD but paired with the 829 AD ingress (see *Conjunctions* Ch. 12).
[9] Much of this section is based on van der Waerden 1978.
[10] *Tim.* 39c-d.
[11] Van der Waerden 1978, p. 359.
[12] *Mathesis* III.2 (Holden's translation).
[13] Van der Waerden 1978, p. 362.

Waerden suggests that the Babylonians inspired the Indian values.[14] But whatever the precise details, the Greeks, Babylonians, and Indians were already talking about these matters prior to any Persian astrological sources we know of: this is important to know, since the Persians (and from them, the Arabs) were largely credited with the development of the complex astro-historical schemes we find in historical astrology.

The belief in the Flood, and that it may have taken place during a conjunction in a specific sign (such as Capricorn) motivated attempts to date it. Al-Bīrūnī recognizes several attempts to do this, and notes that while it is hopeless to determine its date by the Torah or Christian Bible, astrologers have attempted to find it using Saturn-Jupiter conjunctions.[15] Now in point of fact, there was no great planetary conjunction on these dates, nor in surrounding centuries, even though many of the planets' true sidereal positions were in the rough area of 0° Aries in Abū Ma'shar's system (see figure below). So the first thing to understand is that the search for a Flood within this period is a red herring: it relies on inaccurate data.[16] But the sources of this view and Abū Ma'shar's data have been the subject of some scholarly controversy and speak to Abū Ma'shar's own integrity, so we must address that here.

There were two primary views about the date of the Flood. The first is the Flood-Kaliyuga (so-called by modern scholars) of February 18, 3102 BC, associated with Abū Ma'shar and his sources. The second is Māshā'allāh's (July 30, 3361 BC) which I will discuss in a separate section below. Al-Sijzī (a follower of Abū Ma'shar) described three sources of the Flood-Kaliyuga:[17]

1. Certain Indians who follow the tables of the *Sindhind*. Their world-year (called a *kalpa*) is 4,320,000,000 years long, and the date in 3102 BC identifies the beginning of a shorter sub-period, the Kaliyuga (hence, the Flood-Kaliyuga). According to this view all seven plan-

---

[14] Van der Waerden 1978, p. 363.
[15] Van der Waerden 1978, p. 364; see also al-Bīrūnī 1983, pp. 27-29.
[16] As van der Waerden points out (1978, p. 377), the *reason* for the inaccuracy in Abū Ma'shar's case is that Saturn moves faster than the Persian system assumed: namely, 26" per year faster. When projecting back to the Flood date, this gives an error of about 26° off, as the diagram suggests.
[17] Van der Waerden 1978, pp. 367-69.

ets, *and* their apogees, *and* their nodes,[18] conjoin at exactly 0° sidereal Aries.

2. Followers of Arjabhaz (Ar.) or Āryabhata (Sanskrit),[19] who uses a period of 4,320,000 years (called a Mahāyuga or Caturyuga). This shorter yuga likewise begins in 3102 BC. Āryabhata actually had two systems, one in which the conjunction took place at midnight on February 18 (called the "midnight system"),[20] and one at sunrise (the "morning" system). Apparently, the morning system is slightly more accurate for the lifetime of Āryabhata.[21]

3. Persians (and perhaps some Babylonians), including Abū Ma'shar and a *zīj* called the *Arkand*.[22] This world year is 360,000 Persian years long (131,493,240 days).[23] The 3102 BC date above was exactly in its middle, at 180,000 years of the world year. Rather than marking a yuga, it marked the Biblical/Qur'ānic Flood.

So all systems have some kind of conjunction on the same day, but while the Indians and Āryabhata make this the *beginning* of a period, Abū Ma'shar makes this the *middle* of his world year, and accompanied by a Flood.

As to the relationships between these three systems, they are obviously close; in fact, it seems that some may derived from the others, though there is disagreement on this point. According to Pingree,[24] the *Arkand* in (3) above was really another name for the midnight system of Āryabhata (2), and van der Waerden further says (following al-Bīrūnī)[25] that the *Arkand* probably comes from a Sanskrit work of Brahmagupta, the *Khandakhādyaka* (which also follows this midnight system).[26] Furthermore, the *Zīj al-Shāh* was based

---

[18] This is an extremely demanding requirement: thus all planets will be *exactly* on the ecliptic, at *exactly* 0° Aries (sidereal), and the center of their epicycles will be *exactly* on their apogees.
[19] Āryabhata was born in about 476 AD (van der Waerden 1978, p. 368).
[20] This version was developed ca. 500 AD.
[21] Van der Waerden 1978, p. 370.
[22] Van der Waerden 1978 (p. 366) suggests that Abū Ma'shar got his value of 360,000 years from the *Zīj al-Shāh*, which of course was translated into Arabic from Persian.
[23] That is, 360,000 * a Persian sidereal year of 365.259 days (this is perhaps rounded slightly down from Māshā'allāh's sidereal year, 365.2590278 days).
[24] Pingree 1968, p. 28.
[25] See al-Bīrūnī 2002, p. 755.
[26] Van der Waerden 1978, p. 371. The *Khandakhādyaka* was written in 665 AD. But Sachau, the translator of al-Bīrūnī's *India* (2002, p. 755) doubts this equating of the two works.

in part on the *Arkand*.[27] Although the *Zīj al-Shāh* did not use the same date for the Flood-Kaliyuga (putting it instead at 00:00 on Thursday the 17th), Āryabhata was aware of the Thursday value. Van der Waerden (like Pingree) argues that it comes from an earlier tradition.[28] Finally, the old *Sūryasiddhānta* (early centuries AD) is also based on the midnight system used by Āryabhata: the number of years in its lunar period is 180,000, and the number of its revolutions in that time is the same as Abū Ma'shar's Persian system.

Thus in terms of parameters, there is an agreement between several key aspects of (1) Indian sources, (2) Āryabhata's midnight system, and (3) Abū Ma'shar's Persian sources.

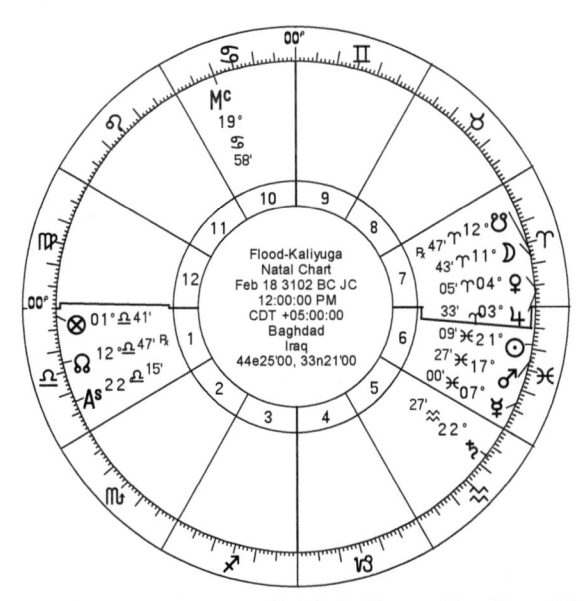

Figure 3: Flood-Kaliyuga, 3102 BC (Fagan-Bradley sidereal)

Since pretty much all of the later historical astrology seems to have been based on Abū Ma'shar (and to a lesser extent on Māshā'allāh, see below), let us focus on him for the details of this Flood-Kaliyuga date, and begin with the number of revolutions each planet makes in his world year. This is important, because for the planets to experience a mean conjunction at 0°

---

[27] Van der Waerden 1978, pp. 370-71.
[28] For details, including the length of Ārybhata's year which could explain the Thursday-Friday distinction, see van der Waerden 1978 (p. 372).

Aries, the centers of their epicycles must coincide, which further means that they must have completed an integer (or "whole") number of revolutions: for, every time they return to 0° Aries, by definition they must have each made a complete revolution since the last time.

Now, Abū Ma'shar's great year is 360,000 Persian sidereal years of 365.259 days apiece, and he believes that there was a conjunction of all of the planets at its beginning, and then again at exactly one-half of that (180,000 years), on the Flood-Kaliyuga date in 3102 BC. And indeed, his list of planetary revolutions provides integer numbers for all of the planets. However, we face a problem in understanding the origins of his numbers, because the other sources listed above do not have integer numbers in 360,000 years—and therefore will not have them at after 180,000 years, either. The table below (excerpted from Pingree 1968, p. 32) illustrates this point:

	Āryabhata	Abū Ma'shar
Saturn	12,214 – 1/3	12,214
Jupiter	30,352	30,352

Figure 4: Revolutions in 360,000 years: Āryabhata & Abū Ma'shar

As the table shows, according to the sunrise system of Āryabhata, in 360,000 years Saturn completes 12,214 *minus* 1/3 revolutions (or 12,213.66666); by definition then, at exactly one-half this time (180,000 years, the Flood-Kaliyuga), he will only have completed 6,106.8333 revolutions—not an integer number as would be required in Abū Ma'shar's "Persian" system. But Abū Ma'shar gives Saturn a full 12,214 revolutions.

Before discussing the values themselves, I should mention two famous criticisms of Abū Ma'shar by al-Bīrūnī.[29] First, that Abū Ma'shar *assumed* a great conjunction of planets every 180,000 years only after getting an *approximate* result for the Flood at the end of Pisces in 3102 BC. Second, that Abū Ma'shar had only relied on "Persian" measurements for his values; and by "Persian," al-Bīrūnī probably meant the *Zīj al-Shāh*, a famous book of tables but not the only available one. Al-Bīrūnī specifically points out the differences I mentioned above, that Abū Ma'shar's integer numbers of revolutions differed from other well-established *zīj*es.

---

[29] Al-Bīrūnī 1983, p. 29.

With these criticisms in mind, there are two interpretations of what Abū Ma'shar did. The first is stated by Pingree,[30] namely that Abū Ma'shar started with the Indian values, but because they did not give him the integer number of revolutions he wanted, he simply rounded them up and down. Since these calculations would not have matched observations, such an approach would have required the addition of certain corrections:[31] as a result, Abū Ma'shar had to claim that at the Flood-Kaliyuga, the planets (or perhaps their mean positions) were *between* 27° Pisces and 1° Aries.[32] (As one may see from the chart above, the accurate positions were even farther afield than this.) So, this interpretation accuses Abū Ma'shar of dishonesty.

The second interpretation is more charitable, and is suggested by van der Waerden: that Abū Ma'shar's numbers of revolutions were indeed *Persian to begin with*. That is, Indian scholars separately incorporated their own larger periods like the *kalpa* into their astronomy, which "enabled the Hindu astronomers to construct better and more flexible astronomical systems."[33] But since their parameters were not based on a 360,000 year period in the first place, it is not surprising that their systems do not yield integer numbers of revolutions every 180,000 years. So according to this interpretation, Abū Ma'shar found his Persian world year and integer number of revolutions in solely Persian sources, acquitting him of dishonesty even though the values were inaccurate anyway.

Van der Waerden reminds us of four points which support the *Persian* source of Abū Ma'shar's numbers.[34] First, the Persians had been making new observations in 450 and 610 AD, the earlier ones being revised during the reign of Khusro Anūshīrvān[35] (ca. 560). So, they had already been at work constructing their own Persian tables. Second, al-Bīrūnī and ibn Yūnis each explicitly say that Abū Ma'shar's system was based *only* on the "observations of the Persians." Third, the Indian systems themselves say nothing about the Flood, but only speak in terms of their own yugas. The Flood only appears in

---

[30] Pingree 1968, p. 31-33.
[31] Van der Waerden suggests that these values may have come from Brahmagupta.
[32] Van der Waerden 1978, p. 370. Van der Waerden points to al-Bīrūnī (1983, p. 29), but al-Bīrūnī's point is that Abū Ma'shar made an assumption about where the conjunction would be, and that his values differ from other well-established *zīj*es.
[33] Van der Waerden 1978, p. 375.
[34] Van der Waerden 1978, p. 375.
[35] Also spelled: Kisrā Anūshīrwān.

Persian and Hellenistic sources. So the Indian sources were not involved at all in the content or meaning of Abū Ma'shar's Flood-based world year.

The fourth argument goes directly to the question of astronomical values. If we assume that Abū Ma'shar's integer numbers are accurate (though they are not), then we should expect calculations for planetary positions in any century to be accurate. But in fact, they are only rather accurate for the 6th Century AD: for positions in previous centuries, the errors in the longitudes of Saturn and Jupiter get worse and worse as one goes back in time, increasing by about 1° per century. If the Persian system had been invented in Indi-Indian sources many centuries earlier, these errors would have been obvious and unacceptable. So if we allow a maximum acceptable error of about 1°-2°, then the Persian system of Abū Ma'shar could not have been invented before the 5th Century, when contemporary calculations would have been rather accurate.

If van der Waerden is right, then it means the following for Abū Ma'shar and the immediate origin of the Persian world year he promoted: it was based on Persian observations and theories around the 5th Century AD, which were closer to calculations like that of the midnight system of Āryabhata, but not identical to it. Abū Ma'shar's values may have been wrong, but they were not the result of cheating or rounding numbers off to fit his own idiosyncratic theory.

This more charitable interpretation also mitigates al-Bīrūnī's criticisms. Abū Ma'shar may have been wrong to assume that there would be a Flood every 180,000 years, but he may have been directed to the 180,000 year theory by some Persian text which used the inaccurate values. And he may have not have assumed the Flood itself out of nowhere, but again from some Persian, or Babylonian, or Hellenistic tradition. Therefore, the differences between his integer numbers of revolutions and those of the Indian systems were not due to dishonestly rounding the numbers up and down, but because this other, Persian system was simply different from (and perhaps less precise than) the Indian cycles of millions of years.

As a supplement to his interpretation, van der Waerden offers a few reasons why the Persian system and Flood date probably had a Hellenistic origin:[36]

---

[36] Van der Waerden 1978, pp. 377-82.

- The Flood date was calculated backwards rather than being observed. But to do this, one needs a conception of "mean longitudes" derived from planetary cycles, which does not appear in older Babylonian sources (e.g. among the Seleucids). Only the Hellenistic Greeks used mean longitudes accompanied by equations to provide corrections for finding true longitudes.
- Manuscripts of Abū Ma'shar's BRD[37] attribute the calculation of the Flood date from the birth of Adam to an Anynūs or Ab.th.nūs,[38] an obviously Greek name which is tempting to associate with Abydenos, a Greek historian who wrote on Babylonian history and chronology, "partly based on" Berossus—the Babylonian astrologer who also wrote on the Flood and the great year (see above). Even if this is not the correct Greek personage, Abū Ma'shar used the transliteration of a Greek name in identifying one of his sources of the Flood date. A similar name (*Anianus*) is mentioned by al-Bīrūnī in exactly this context.[39]
- In a review of Arabic and Greek astrological and astronomical references to "the Chaldeans," "the Egyptians," and "the Babylonians," van der Waerden found that they could all be traced to Greek-language Hellenistic sources or favorably compared with them: these include Greek summaries of Babylonian concepts (partially excerpted in Geminus) and the now barely-extant textbook of Nechepso-Petosiris. According to his analysis, "Chaldeans" refers to early Hellenistic texts, and "Babylonians" to later ones. Van der Waerden suggests that the source of these later attributions to the Babylonians, were really references to Teucer of Babylon. It is known that Teucer's work was translated into Pahlavi and used by Abū Ma'shar in his *Great Introduction*.

The upshot of this proposal by van der Waerden, is that Abū Ma'shar got his "Persian" system of 360,000 years through the Pahlavi translation of

---

[37] Escurial, Bibl. Real, 937 fol. 5r. See *BRD* I.1, **26**.

[38] ابثنوس. Other manuscripts give ملبوس and اسوس.

[39] Al-Bīrūnī 1983, p. 25. The translator Sachau also suggests اثنيوس (Athenaios), p. 374. As van der Waerden rightly points out, these apparently divergent spellings in English or Greek are only due to a difference in the dots over letters in the Arabic (which are frequently missing or sloppily jotted down).

Teucer, who however did not invent it but only reported it. Van der Waerden concludes, "The man who discovered the conjunction of 3102 BC must have been an astronomer who calculated conjunctions in the past and found an approximate conjunction of all planets near 0° Aries in the year 3102. Only after this discovery was it possible to set up an astronomical theory based upon the assumption that this conjunction took place in the middle of a 'Great Year' of 360,000 years."[40]

In the next section we will look at the actual parameters needed for constructing a conjunctional theory, and compare the accurate values with Abū Ma'shar's.

§5: Mean conjunctions, triplicity shifts, & types of year

As I mentioned above, Saturn-Jupiter conjunctions, and their grouping by triplicities, formed the backbone of historical astrology. The basic approach, and the roles the conjunctions played within larger periods like the world years were already well in place by the time of Māshā'allāh; but Abū Ma'shar seems to have been the one who really popularized and regularized the approach followed by astrologers after the 9th Century AD. In order to understand how these conjunctional cycles work, both in theory *and* practice, we need to introduce some terminology.

First of all, the whole apparatus of this conjunctional astrology was structured on *mean conjunctions*. What is a mean conjunction? Astrologers tend to use "true" conjunctions, which are the conjunctions of the planets *as they appear to us*. (In Ptolemaic astronomy, a "true" position is one as seen from earth.) Thus, if we see in the ephemeris or a computer program that Saturn and Jupiter are conjoining at 15° Capricorn, we expect to be able to look up in the heavens, and see the actual bodies of the planets together, within the degree of 15° Capricorn. And as we know, sometimes Saturn and Jupiter make three true conjunctions: once when the quicker Jupiter goes past Saturn, then when he retrogrades back across him, and then finally after he goes direct again.

But a "mean" conjunction in Ptolemaic astronomy happens at precise, regular intervals. It is based on the average length of each planet's cycle in the zodiac, which is nothing more than the cycles we are familiar with today: the 12-year cycle of Jupiter is actually a rounding-up of the more accurate

---

[40] Van der Waerden 1978, p. 383.

cycle of 11.86 years. Likewise, the period of the "Saturn return" is 29.4 years. But in Ptolemaic astronomy this period has a technical meaning: it is the length of time it takes for the *center of a planet's epicycle* to revolve exactly once around the zodiac. The position of the center of the epicycle is its "mean" position as it revolves at a constant or mean rate. As one might surmise, since planets also rotate on their epicycles, their true positions will usually not coincide with this point when it returns, but they will be direct or retrograde on one or another side of it. The diagram below illustrates what I mean:

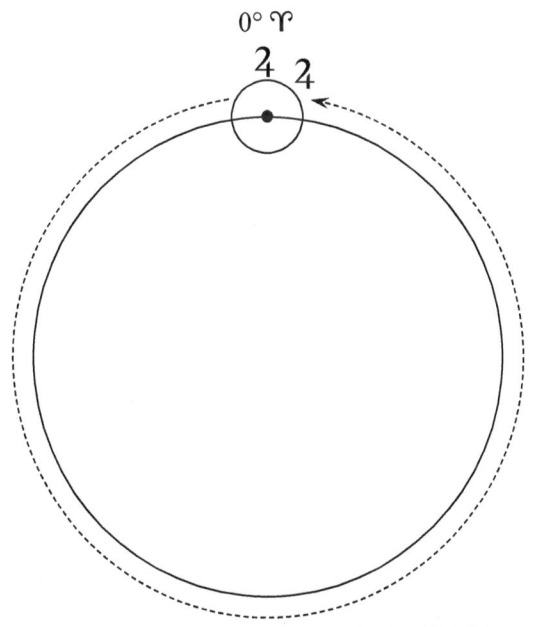

Figure 5: Illustrated mean period of Jupiter

In the diagram, Jupiter starts out with the center of his epicycle (his "mean" position) at 0° Aries, and I have assumed that his body itself is also there (his "true" position). As time goes on, the epicycle moves counter-clockwise around the zodiac, as does his own position on it. After 11.86 years, the center of the epicycle reaches 0° Aries again, completing his mean period. But note that because he moves on his epicycle at a different rate, at the end of the mean period his body will have rotated the equivalent of about

308°, not a full circuit. So at the end of the period his true position will appear to be earlier in the zodiac than 0° Aries.

From this we can easily see what the definition of a mean conjunction between two planets is: it is the conjunction of the centers of their epicycles. This concept may seem out of date nowadays, but in fact we *need* this type of astronomy in order to determine when and where to place our Saturn-Jupiter conjunctions within the triplicities. Or rather, we need to know only one of them: after that, we can project the mean conjunctions forward and backward into history and construct our triplicity series.

Now, in order to construct a series of mean conjunctions, we need three pieces of information: (1) the type of year and zodiac, whether tropical or sidereal; (2) the length of the mean periods; and (3) the precise time and location of one mean conjunction. Let me discuss each of these in turn, especially since medieval texts often differ from modern values and assumptions. Below I will also provide a table of accurate planetary values, and one may consult Appendices A and B to see fuller tables of conjunctions and triplicity shifts.

(1) Tropical and sidereal years and zodiacs. The tropical year and zodiac refers to the return of the Sun to 0° Aries or the equinoctial point, which is defined as the intersection of the celestial equator and ecliptic. But because the equinoctial points precess "backwards" against the fixed stars, by the time the mean Sun or any planet returns to its tropical position in a given year, it will have traveled slightly less than the full 360° from the previous time. This means that the tropical year, as well as any tropical cycles, will be slightly shorter in time and distance than their sidereal equivalents. Let's look more closely at Jupiter's mean cycle to see how this works, removing the epicycle for the sake of simplicity.

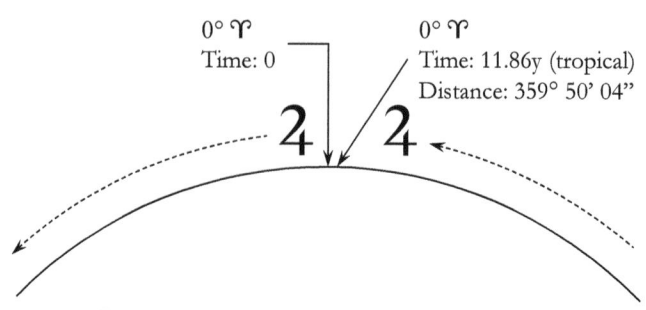

Figure 6: Mean tropical cycle of Jupiter

In this figure, Jupiter begins his cycle at 0° Aries. The rate of precession is 50.28" per tropical year. So, by the time he approaches his original position 11.86 years later, the point of 0° Aries will have precessed backwards by 9' 56": thus Jupiter's "return" to the new tropical 0° Aries is actually not a full 360°, but 359° 50' 04".

Now, in a sidereal year and zodiac there is no precession. Instead, 0° Aries (or whatever point you like) is defined in a fixed way relative to the stars: thus for Jupiter to return to 0° Aries really means moving a full 360°, to precisely the same point. Traveling this extra distance takes more time, so both the distance and time involved is longer in sidereal systems. The sidereal year is about 1.000038804 times longer than a tropical year. In the case of Jupiter, his sidereal period is about 1.9 days longer than the tropical one.

Māshā'allāh, as well as Abū Ma'shar (or at least in his mundane astrology) *used a sidereal zodiac.*[41] Most medieval Latins, as well as al-Battānī, used a tropical one. The choice of zodiac is up to you, but it is important to know that *only* a sidereal system will yield 12 conjunctions per triplicity—I will return to this below.

(2) Mean periods and triplicity shifts. Using contemporary data, it is easy to derive the mean periods for both Saturn and Jupiter. The tropical period is the number of days in the planet's tropical cycle, divided by the length of the tropical year; the sidereal period is the days in the sidereal cycle, divided by the sidereal year. I have used data given by NASA.[42] Following are the contemporary values:

NASA Tropical Year: 365.24219 days	
NASA Sidereal Year: 365.256363 days	
Tropical Period in Trop. Years:	*Sidereal Period in Sid. Years:*
Saturn: 29.4241473	Saturn: 29.45662578
Jupiter: 11.85677646	Jupiter: 11.86177556

Figure 7: Contemporary values for years & mean periods

---

[41] For Māshā'allāh, see the section on his astrology below.
[42] The Jupiter Fact Sheet is available at: nssdc.gsfc.nasa.gov/planetary/factsheet/jupiterfact.html. The Saturn Fact Sheet is at: nssdc.gsfc.nasa.gov/planetary/factsheet/saturnfact.html. Both sheets only calculate the length of the periods and years to 3 decimal points, which is slightly less accurate than one would like.

According to the table, the sidereal year is about 00:20:25 longer than the tropical year. The periods are measured in their respective years, as well. For instance, the tropical period of Jupiter is 11.85677646 *tropical years*: so, this value multiplied by the length of the tropical year makes his mean period 4330.595 days long. The same can be done with the other values.

Once we know the lengths of the year and periods, it is easy to determine precisely how often mean conjunctions will take place, as well as exactly how far apart they will be. Following are the two formulas we need:

Length of a conjunctional period:
(Period 1 * Period 2) / (Period 1 − Period 2)

Distance between conjunctions:
((Conjunctional period − shorter period) / shorter period) * 360

By inserting the period values into the equations, we get the following:

NASA Tropical Year: 365.24219 days NASA Sidereal Year: 365.256363 days			
	Conjunctional period (years)	Conjunctional distance	Conj. per triplicity
Tropical Period/Years: Saturn: 29.4241473 Jupiter: 11.85677646	19.85929143	242.9754326° = advance of 2° 58' 32"	10-11
Sidereal Period/Years: Saturn: 29.45662578 Jupiter: 11.86177556	19.8585313	242.6982412° = advance of 2° 41' 54"	11-12

Figure 8: Complete table of mean conjunctions *&* distances

As we can see, in a tropical system, mean Saturn and Jupiter will conjoin every 19.85929143 tropical years (or 7253.45109 days), what I am calling their "conjunctional period." The sidereal conjunctional period is 19.8585313 sidereal years, or 7253.454917 days, which is a fraction of a day more. Now, at first this suggests that the choice of zodiacs will affect the conjunctional period. But actually it does not: *the planets will conjoin at exactly the same time, no matter what kind of zodiac you use*. The conjunctional periods are equal, because the conjunctional period is based purely on the constant rate of the planets. Put differently, look at the length of the tropical period and that of the sidereal period: you will see that the tropical *period* is slightly longer, but the tropical *year* is slightly shorter. The reverse is true for the sidereal values. Thus, the longer period of the shorter year (tropical) is equivalent to the shorter period of the longer year (sidereal). The apparent difference between these periods is due to the fact that the NASA website only calculates to 3 decimal places, so when we solve our equations it will seem as though the sidereal period lasts 5.5 minutes longer than the tropical. In reality the periods are equal, and if you use this data it will take about 5,184 years or almost 262 mean conjunctions before there is a 1-day difference between them.

However, the choice of zodiacs *does* determine the conjunctional *distance*. Both systems make each successive conjunction take place in roughly a clockwise or backwards trine from the previous one. In a tropical system, the distance between successive conjunctions is 242.9754323° or 242° 58' 32". Sidereally, the distance is 242.6982412° or 242° 41' 54".

To illustrate how these mean conjunctions work, consider the figure below. I have removed the epicycles in order to show the idealized mean motion of the planets.

In these figures, the mean positions of Jupiter Saturn (i.e., without their epicycles) begin at some degree (here labeled 0°). After one-half of Jupiter's period (5.9 years), he will have traveled around one-half of the circle (at 180°), while Saturn will have traveled only 72°. When Jupiter completes his period (11.86 years, at 360°), Saturn will only be at 144°. Finally, after about 7.9 years more (or 19.8 total), Saturn will have made it to 242°, where Jupiter finally catches up to him and makes the mean conjunction. The sidereal and tropical values are not the same, but they are so close that the figure illustrates both well enough.

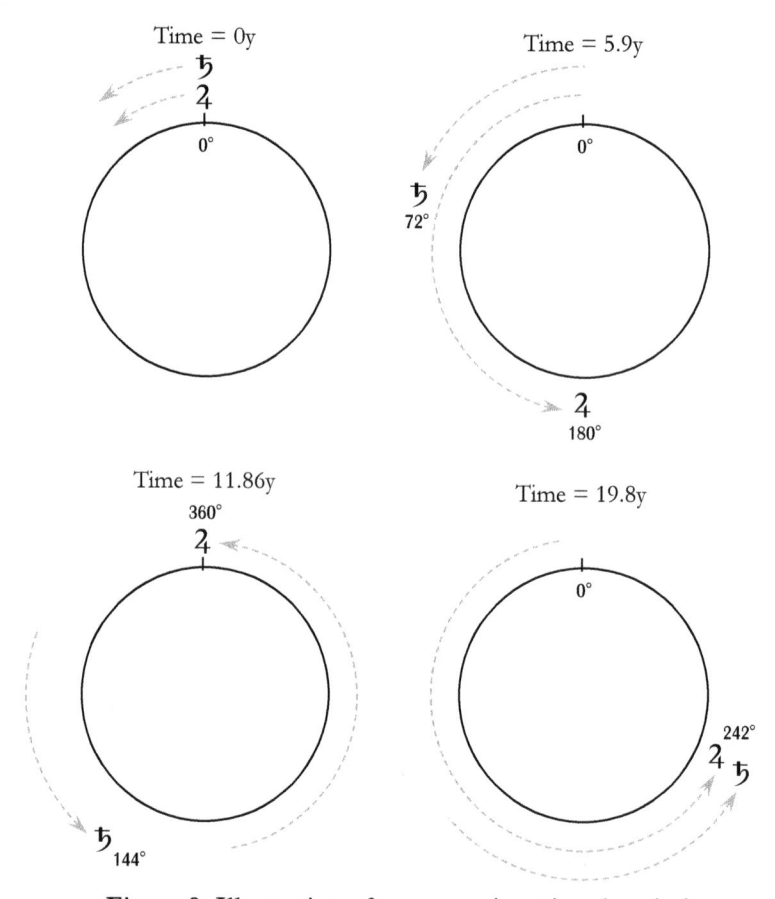

Figure 9: Illustration of mean conjunctional period

Now, earlier I related the standard version of the conjunctional series: every successive conjunction advances by a little over 242°, which is a little less than a backwards trine from the previous position. This means that successive conjunctions will take place within the same triplicity, but because an exact triangle would be 240°, the actual degrees within each sign will slowly advance until the conjunctions enter a new triplicity. The number of mean conjunctions in each triplicity is idealized at 12, but how many are there, really? If there were always exactly 12, then the conjunctional distance could only be 242° 30', advancing by 2° 30' within each sign (see the diagram in §3). Abū Ma'shar's own parameters gave something a bit less: 242° 25' 17": this makes 12 but sometimes 13 conjunctions in each triplicity. Māshā'allāh's value was 242° 25' 35", also 12-13 conjunctions.

The table above shows the accurate values: in a tropical system, there will be 10 or 11 conjunctions, and in a sidereal system 11 or 12. The figure below shows this visually, in the tropical system.

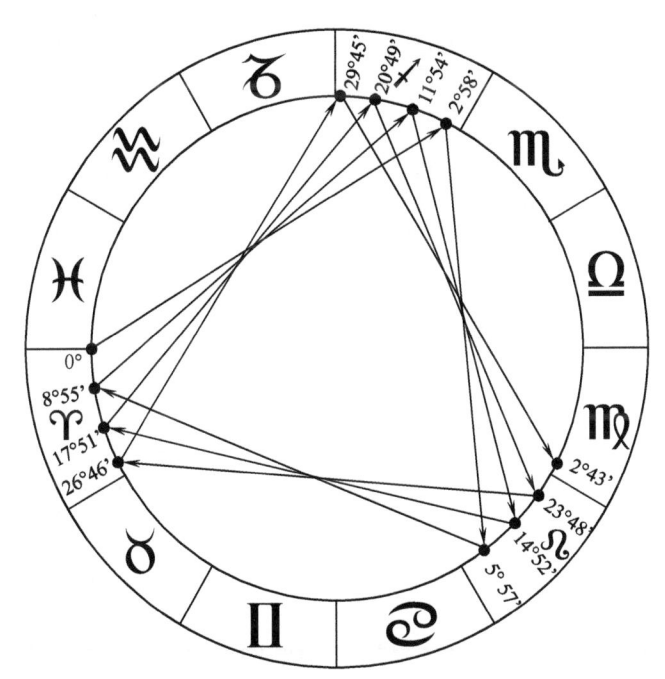

Figure 10: Eleven tropical mean conjunctions in the fiery triplicity

Every mean conjunction advances by 242° 58' 32" of the circle, or 2° 58' 32" in the actual degrees of the signs. If conjunction #1 is at 0° of a sign (here, Aries), then #2 will be at about 2° 58' 32" of Sagittarius, #3 at 5° 57' 04" Leo, and so on, always moving in a backwards or clockwise trine. But then #11 will be at 29° 45' 20", the last of the triplicity: the next conjunction will be a triplicity shift into the earthy triplicity, at 2° 43' 52" Virgo. The differences between the tropical and sidereal series may then be illustrated this way:

Tropical Series	Distance	Sidereal Series	Distance
Fire (1)	0°	Fire (1)	0°
2	2.975°	2	2.698°
3	5.951°	3	5.396°
4	8.926°	4	8.095°
5	11.902°	5	10.793°
6	14.877°	6	13.491°
7	17.853°	7	16.189°
8	20.828°	8	18.888°
9	23.803°	9	21.586°
10	26.779°	10	24.284°
11	29.754°	11	26.982°
Earth (1)	2.730°	12	29.681°
2	5.705°	Earth (1)	2.379°
3	8.681°	2	5.077°
4	11.656°	3	7.775°
5	14.631°	4	10.474°
6	17.607°	5	13.172°
7	20.582°	6	15.870°
8	23.558°	7	18.568°
9	26.533°	8	21.267°
10	29.509°	9	23.965°
		10	26.663°
		11	29.361°

Figure 11: Tropical & sidereal triplicity shifts compared

Beginning at 0° of some sign for their mean conjunction #1, the tropical series will have 11 conjunctions before shifting into earth for 10 conjunctions. The sidereal series will have 12 conjunctions before shifting into earth for 11 conjunctions. In this way we can see that the idealized system of 12 conjunctions per triplicity is not correct.

As a point of interest, I append here Abū Ma'shar's own parameters.[43] Māshā'allāh's are given in §6.

- Sidereal year: 365.259 days.[44]
- Sidereal period of Saturn: 29.47437367 sidereal years.
- Sidereal period of Jupiter: 11.86083289 sidereal years.
- Conjunctional period: 19.84783327 sidereal years (7249.599731 days).
- Conjunctional distance: 242.4214356° (242° 25' 17").
- Number of conjunctions in each triplicity: 12-13.

Figure 12: Abū Ma'shar's parameters for Saturn-Jupiter conjunctions

(3) A recent mean conjunction.

As an example, the tropical periods of Saturn and Jupiter dictate that a mean tropical conjunction occurred on July 20, 1901, at 15° 12' Capricorn; but on that day, their true positions were 12° 00' and 5° 42' Capricorn, respectively.

Although none of the ancient and medieval astronomers had the more precise values for the year and periods which we have today, you should not think that this difference between mean and true conjunctions was a flaw in the theory itself. Nor are these periods merely rough or approximate: given an accurate length of the year and each of the planets' periods, a mean conjunction can be timed down to the hour or even minute. The regular, mean conjunctions played a *structuring* role in large spans of historical astrology. (But the fact that the mean and true conjunctions happened at different times and degrees means that we need to make some astrological choices when we cast their charts and make interpretations.) The difficulty in interpreting the calculations in medieval conjunctional theory has more to do with the fact (a) the length of their periods and years were not the same from author to author, and (b) some used tropical periods and a tropical zodiac, others sidereal.

---

[43] See for example Kennedy 1963, and van der Waerden 1978 (p. 376).
[44] This might actually be 365.2590278 days, as with Māshā'allāh (see Section II.1 below).

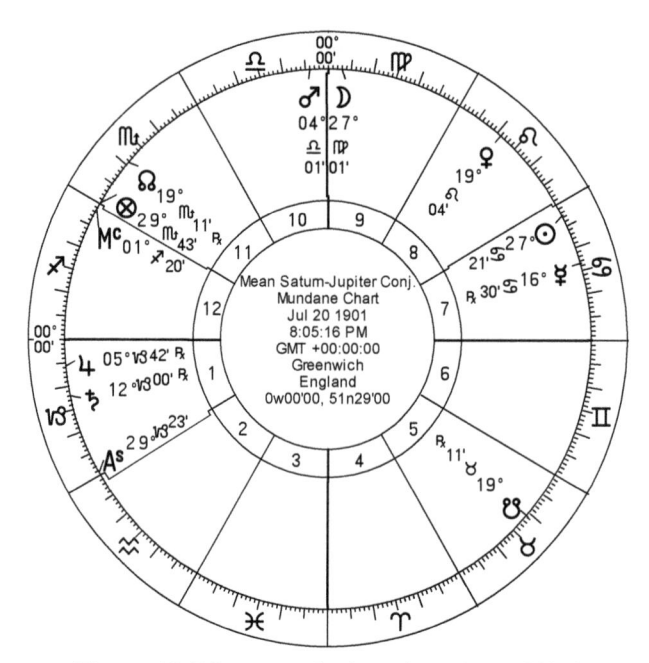

28   *Astrology of the World II: Revolutions & History*

Figure 13: Mean tropical conjunction of 1901

§6: Māshā'allāh's mundane astrology

The Persian Jewish astrologer Māshā'allāh wielded great influence over later mundane writers. This volume presents three works, two translated from Latin (as the Arabic originals have been lost), and a third translated from an Arabic version with commentary by ibn Hibintā. I will describe these in Section II.1 in my longer introduction to Māshā'allāh, and only summarize a few points here.

Like Abū Ma'shar, Māshā'allāh uses a sidereal zodiac and parameters derived from a version of the *Zīj al-Shāh*; like everyone else he uses mean Saturn-Jupiter conjunctions, and he also has a Flood date and time lords. However, his Flood theory and time lords are different:

Flood date and "indicator" conjunction. Earlier, we saw that Abū Ma'shar claimed a Flood date on February 18, 3102 BC, on which day there was also a conjunction of all planets at approximately 0° Aries. So, the conjunction happened at the Flood itself. Māshā'allāh however, claimed that the Flood was first "indicated" by a mean Saturn-Jupiter conjunction in Scorpio on September 23, 3381 BC, and that the Flood took place on or around the following conjunction in Cancer, July 30, 3361 BC. (Māshā'allāh does not explicitly state that the Flood was actually on the day of the conjunction, but he may have meant that.) So, about 259 years separate the two Floods.

Thousands. In addition, Māshā'allāh does not seem to be interested in, or even know about, Abū Ma'shar's array of time lords such as the mundane directions, mighty *fardārs* or Turns, and so on—although he does use mundane profections. Instead, Māshā'allāh embeds his series of Saturn-Jupiter conjunctions within a framework of Thousands: periods of 1,000 years, each ruled by a different planet in turn. His initial conjunction begins near the middle of the Mars Thousand (6292-5292 BC), and his Flood occurs in the Venus Thousand (4292-3292 BC). In Māshā'allāh's system (which derives from Zoroastrianism), we would currently be living in the Sun Thousand.

The discrepancy between the two Floods may have bothered Arabic commentators, as there were attempts to coordinate the two systems using the Turns and mundane directions: for example, 'Umar-Kankah (Section I.5) affirms Abū Ma'shar's Flood, but points out the number of years between the two Floods and makes his time lords (mundane directions and Turns) begin with Māshā'allāh's indicator conjunction. Unfortunately, Abū Ma'shar's Flood has nothing to do with Māshā'allāh's chronology. Māshā'allāh's own Saturn-Jupiter conjunction in Aries is a full 1.5 years earlier than Abū Ma'shar's, in August 3103 BC, and within these time-lord systems there are no changes marking Abū Ma'shar's Flood.

Errors in Māshā'allāh's chronology. I will deal with Māshā'allāh's errors in more detail in Section II.1; for now, I will simply list some important ones. Perhaps the most important one for the issue of chronology is the Islamic conjunction in Scorpio itself. Arabic writers took it as a given that the mean conjunction on December 12, 570 AD was a triplicity shift into water. However, this is impossible even given their parameters. Māshā'allāh himself identifies the conjunction as being in 4° 02' Scorpio: but because conjunctions can only creep forward about 2° 30' at a time, it is impossible that *any* triplicity shift could happen this far into a sign. Indeed, the triplicity shift into water could only have happened in the previous conjunction, in Pisces, on February 5, 551 AD. It is surprising to me that I haven't found any 20th Century scholar who points this out. (Māshā'allāh is also wrong about other shifts, too.)

A second error which affects the working astrologer, is Māshā'allāh's misuse of the "excess of revolution," which is used to determine the Ascendant of solar revolutions (or here, annual Aries ingresses) every year. To put it simply, instead of advancing the Ascendant using equatorial degrees, Māshā'allāh adds the amount in zodiacal degrees: this means that his Ascendants are unusable, for any year, for the location he wants. Therefore, we cannot cast the charts in modern software because the location required to get his false Ascendant at that time might be in the middle of the ocean, or in North America, *etc.* The working astrologer must instead be content to observe only his theory of interpretation and prediction.

Following is a table of Māshā'allāh's basic parameters, to mirror Abū Ma'shar's above. Section II.1 will have more tables of data for understanding his chronology.

- Length of (sidereal) year: 365.2590278 days.
- Sidereal period of Jupiter: 11.86194263 sidereal years.
- Sidereal period of Saturn: 29.47677147 sidereal years.
- Conjunctional period: 19.84985351 years (7250.338194 days).[45]
- Conjunctional distance: 242.4263889° (242° 25' 35").[46]
- Number of conjunctions in each triplicity: 12-13.

Figure 14: Māshā'allāh's parameters for Saturn-Jupiter conjunctions

§7: Al-Battānī: an under-reported alternative

So far we have seen that astrologers tended on the one hand to follow Ptolemy in casting charts for lunations and eclipses, and on the other hand to cast charts for ingresses and mean (not true) conjunctions. But unlike Ptolemy they tended to use a sidereal zodiac. Moreover, they did not seem to connect the Persian conjunctional theory with lunations and eclipses.

An important exception to this rule was the famous astronomer al-Battānī (d. 929), a follower of Ptolemy who wrote a tropical *zīj* called the *Zīj al-Sābi'* (*The Sabian Tables*). Around 900 AD, al-Battānī wrote his own astrological history of Muhammad's career and the early Caliphates, a genre of astrological writing that includes Māshā'allāh's own *Conjunctions*.[47] Al-Battānī sniffs at

---

[45] According to the text, this is 19 sidereal years, 10 months (of 30 days apiece), 10 days, and 10 hours. (At one point the text has 11 hours.)
[46] Māshā'allāh's text is not always precise as to the seconds.
[47] See Kennedy et al. 2009-10 for a critical edition, translation, and analysis of al-Battānī's work.

the use of ingress charts as well as the mean Saturn-Jupiter conjunctions, saying they have no foundation or explanation. Instead, he casts charts for eclipses, emphasizing those which occur close to *true* Saturn-Jupiter conjunctions.[48] As he was a follower of Ptolemy we may guess why. Ptolemy's theory of astrology was naturalistic and causal, so that mundane effects really flow directly or indirectly from the physical interactions of the planets and their effects of cooling, heating, drying, and moistening. Thus in *Tet.* II Ptolemy does not advocate casting the charts of seasonal ingresses, but rather the New and Full Moons which precede them, as having a greater physical effect. Indeed, the centerpiece of Ptolemy's entire mundane astrology is the use of eclipses, which are nothing more than special cases of New and Full Moons (albeit the most dramatic ones).

So we can guess that al-Battānī would make the following claims. (a) Ingresses do not have causal power, or else Ptolemy would have used them. (b) Mean conjunctions are irrelevant, because the effects of Saturn and Jupiter are conferred by the signs they are actually in and the causal powers of their bodies, not the mathematical convergence of the centers of their epicycles. (c) Conjunctions and ingresses do not really have anything to do with each other, anyway: what could the relationship really be between any mean or even true conjunction in September, and the Sun's ingress into Aries in March? Therefore, it is better to focus on the actual behavior of planetary events with causal power: eclipses and true conjunctions, especially when an eclipse occurs close to the true conjunction of Saturn and Jupiter. Even if one does not have a naturalistic, causal view of astrology, this approach is attractive because it neatly sidesteps troubling questions about the overall role of mean conjunctions, how many there ought to be, why ingresses matter, and so on.

In the future I hope to write more about al-Battānī, but for the moment I offer here a modern tropical version of one of his charts, representing the birth and career of Muhammad. I have cast the chart for the appropriate day and for al-Battānī's Ascendant (his planetary values are not exactly the same as in modern software, especially since at the time he was using the *Mumtaḥan zīj*). The chart is cast for a lunar eclipse, as the reader may see, and only a few degrees from the eclipse are the bodies of Saturn and Jupiter, which have just recently made a true conjunction (in al-Battānī's calculations, there is less

---

[48] See Kennedy et al. (*ibid.*), and *Skilled* VIII.1, **13**.

than 30' separating them). Please note also that because he does not use mean conjunctions, al-Battānī is entitled to say that his conjunction was indeed a triplicity shift into water: the true conjunction of 551 was still in air.

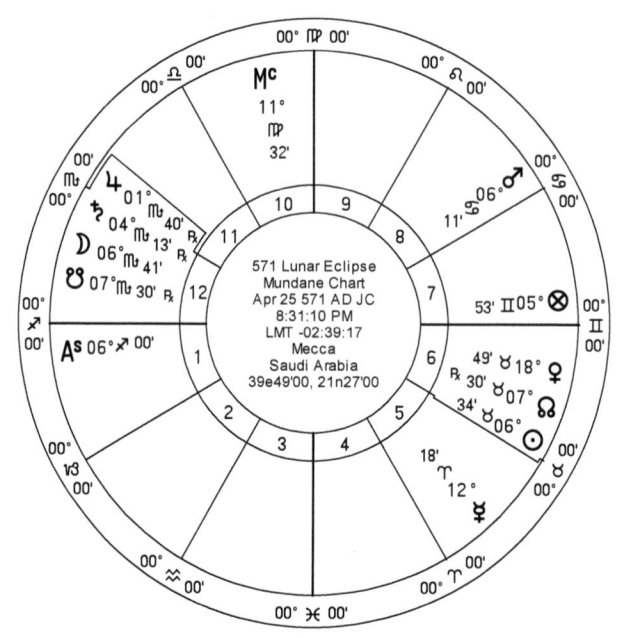

Figure 15: Modern version of al-Battānī's triplicity shift & eclipse for Islam

§8: Saturn-Mars conjunctions in Cancer

Although Saturn-Jupiter conjunctions dominated Persian conjunctional theory, authors occasionally mention the Saturn-Mars conjunction in Cancer. Their mean conjunction occurs near the beginning of Cancer every 30 years (see Appendix B), and is occasionally accompanied by a second conjunction almost 2 years later: since Mars's tropical and sidereal periods are about 1.88 years long, Saturn (or rather the center of his epicycle) will sometimes still be in Cancer by the time Mars returns for a second conjunction.

So far as we know, these conjunctions were invented by al-Kindī and then passed on to Abū Ma'shar, who popularized them. Māshā'allāh does indeed mention Saturn-Mars conjunctions in his *Letter* Ch. 11, but does not specifically mention Cancer. Al-Kindī on the other hand uses the Cancer conjunction extensively in his analysis and prediction of the length of Arab rule.[49]

Saturn is in his detriment in Cancer, and Mars is in his fall, so we should expect their conjunction to indicate something destructive. If we go by the normal logic of mean Saturn-Jupiter conjunctions, we might consider the 2004 Indonesian Tsunami, which occurred on December 26, 2004. In Indonesia (capital Banda Aceh), the Ascendant of the Aries ingress was Cancer, with Saturn in it, something which already looks threatening particularly since he is the lord of the eighth. But it so happens there was a mean and true conjunction of Saturn-Mars in Cancer soon after this: the mean conjunction on April 28 was at 12° Cancer, and the true conjunction on May 24 was at 11° Cancer. Both of these degrees are in the rising sign, just a few degrees from the ingress Ascendant. So, we might expect something destructive this year. I also note that on December 26, the directed Ascendant of the revolution was just entering the bound of Saturn at 25° Aries, a degree exactly squared by transiting Saturn from 25° Cancer.

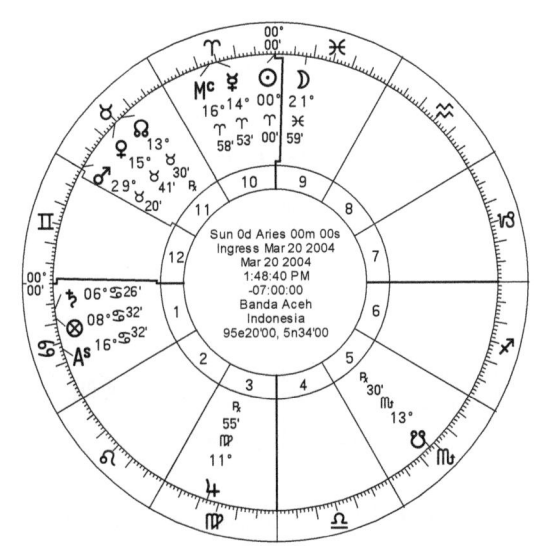

Figure 16: 2004 Aries ingress for Indonesia

---

[49] See Appendix III of Burnett and Yamamoto's *BRD*, vol. 1.

In his work on the length of Arab rule, al-Kindī argues that Cancer was the Ascendant of the Aries ingress in the year of the Hijrah (622 AD), when Muhammad fled to Medina, with the Saturn-Mars conjunction in it.[50] But *because* Jupiter was in aversion to Cancer, his moderating influence was absent from the conjunction, and so it spelled destruction for the rule of the Persians, who still ruled from Iraq at the time. Moreover the Moon, who was the victor over the degree of the conjunction (according to al-Kindī), was applying to an exalted Venus in the ninth, from Taurus: this indicated that the impetus of the events would be transferred to Venus in the ninth, indicating the Arabs (who are traditionally ruled by Venus) and a prophet (the ninth). The chart below represents this situation in the tropical zodiac according to modern calculations:

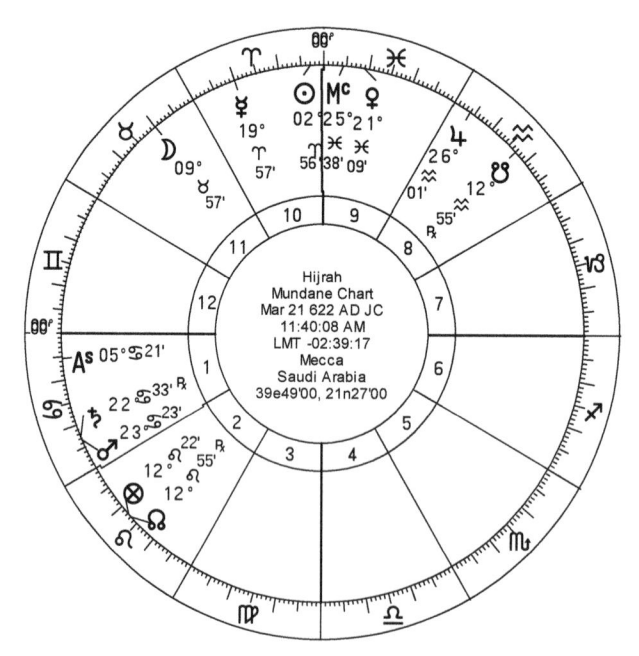

Figure 17: Version of al-Kindī's ingress for the Hijrah, 622 AD

In several other examples, al-Kindī argues that the aversion or configuration of Jupiter, as well as the application of the Moon, shows how destructive or complete the transfer of power will be, in addition to who will rule next.

---

[50] *Ibid.*

In Appendix B I provide tables for both mean and true Saturn-Mars conjunctions in Cancer. As with the Saturn-Jupiter conjunctions, I think the practicing astrologer should keep an open mind about how these are to be used. By themselves, they may not indicate precisely a war, but only shifts in power. For example, there was a conjunction in 1915 when WWI was already underway, and in 1946 after WWII was already complete: but both might indicate a reconfiguration of politics *after* these wars.

§9: Time lords & techniques in historical astrology

Saturn-Jupiter conjunctions are not only the *primary* structuring devices for astrological history, they are also *primarily* structuring devices. There are a couple of exceptions, such as in Māshā'allāh's *Letter* Ch. 10. In **7**, Māshā'allāh says that the quality of the conjunction is partly based on which of the two planets (Saturn or Jupiter) is the victor, which seems to mean the one which is closer to the apogee of its epicycle—at least, this is how ibn Labbān II.11, **4** understands it.[51] And in **10**, Māshā'allāh says that the angularity of the mean conjunction will indicate the birth of prophets or kings.

But numerous other techniques are used to understand history and predict events, some playing a structuring role like the triplicity shifts, others being used more concretely to identify and characterize periods and events. The easiest to understand are those which are simply direct applications of natal techniques, while others—even if inspired by natal techniques—are a bit more exotic. Let us begin with some of the more familiar ones from natal astrology.

Mundane profections. Once we have established some important sign for a period, we can perform annual profections in order to get a year-by-year understanding of how the period unfolds. Our texts list at least four types of profection, with some indication as to what distinguishes them:

1. From the Ascendant of the Aries ingress associated with a triplicity shift—such as the Libra Ascendant of 571 AD, which was commonly taken as the ingress for the 570 Saturn-Jupiter conjunction of

---

[51] See Bibliography.

Islam. This profection shows what occurs to the people or adherents of that culture or religion.[52]

2. From the MC or tenth of that same ingress. This shows the "matter" (or perhaps command) of the culture/religion, and its authority.[53]
3. From the sign of the conjunction itself—such as profecting from Scorpio, the sign of the 570 conjunction. This profection shows what happens to the culture or faith itself (increase, decrease, good condition, corruption). The lord of the profection indicates what happens to the elite and dynastic inheritors of the culture/religion.[54]
4. From the Ascendant of the Aries ingress of any other Saturn-Jupiter conjunction.[55]

Pingree (1968, p. 60) pointed out that this kind of mundane profection is the smallest type, of which there were larger ones added by people like Abū Ma'shar (remember that these are given in Abū Ma'shar's incorrect sidereal years):

- Mighty (12,000 years): 1 sign / 1000 solar years of 365.259 days (= 1 sign / 365,259 days).
- Big (1,200 years): 1 sign / 100 solar years of 365.259 days (= 1 sign / 36,525.9 days).
- Middle (120 years): 1 sign / 10 solar years of 365.259 days (= 1 sign / 3,652.59 days).
- Small (12 years): 1 sign / 1 solar year of 365.259 days. This is the normal annual profection.

Pingree understood these to be continuous profections: that is, not jumping from sign to sign as units, but moving smoothly and proportionately through each sign in accordance with the time passed since the beginning of Abū Ma'shar's world year in 183,102 BC. My own view is that it is a waste of time to pay much attention to all but the "small" or annual profection. In the first place, they are based on both Abū Ma'shar's false Flood date and his false world year—if one could actually find a day with such a powerful set of

---

[52] *Skilled* VIII.39, **16** and **21**.
[53] *Skilled* VIII.39, **17** and **22**.
[54] *Skilled* VIII.39, **18-19** and **23-24**.
[55] Al-Qabīsī 4.10, **3**, in Section I.1.

conjunctions of all the planets, then it might be worth looking at them. In the second place, expanding the simple and effective annual profection seems artificial and obsessive rather than actually being informative. Why not invent an even "mightier" profection of 120,000 years?

Directions/distributions of the ingress Ascendant or MC. Just as we can direct the Ascendant or other points around the solar revolution of a nativity, so we may direct the Ascendant of an ingress for the year as a whole or for the people, and the MC for the king or leader.[56] In Section I.4 I give an example of directing Mars to the MC (or the MC to Mars, depending on how one looks at it). But the same can be done with the Ascendant. Following are two ingress charts, one for Washington DC, the other for Tokyo, Japan, both indicating December 7, 1941 as a direction of the Ascendant to Mars or his opposition (i.e., the day of the Japanese attack on Pearl Harbor). It is important to note that many medieval authors (probably following 'Umar al-Tabarī) calculated these directions incorrectly: rather than directing by ascensions (or even, following Ptolemy, using right ascension, oblique ascensions, and proportional semi-arcs), they simply divided the 360° of the circle by 365.25 days, and assigned a day to each 59' 08". But this is a complete distortion of the principles of directing, and treats directions as though they are continuous profections. Since the signs do not all arise on the horizon at the same rate (hence the crooked and straight, or short and long signs), they are not worth the same amounts of time. But using ascensions, one may often use solar revolution charts to time events down to the very day, as we see here.

---

[56] See 'Umar in Section I.4, and *Skilled* VIII.21, **2-7**.

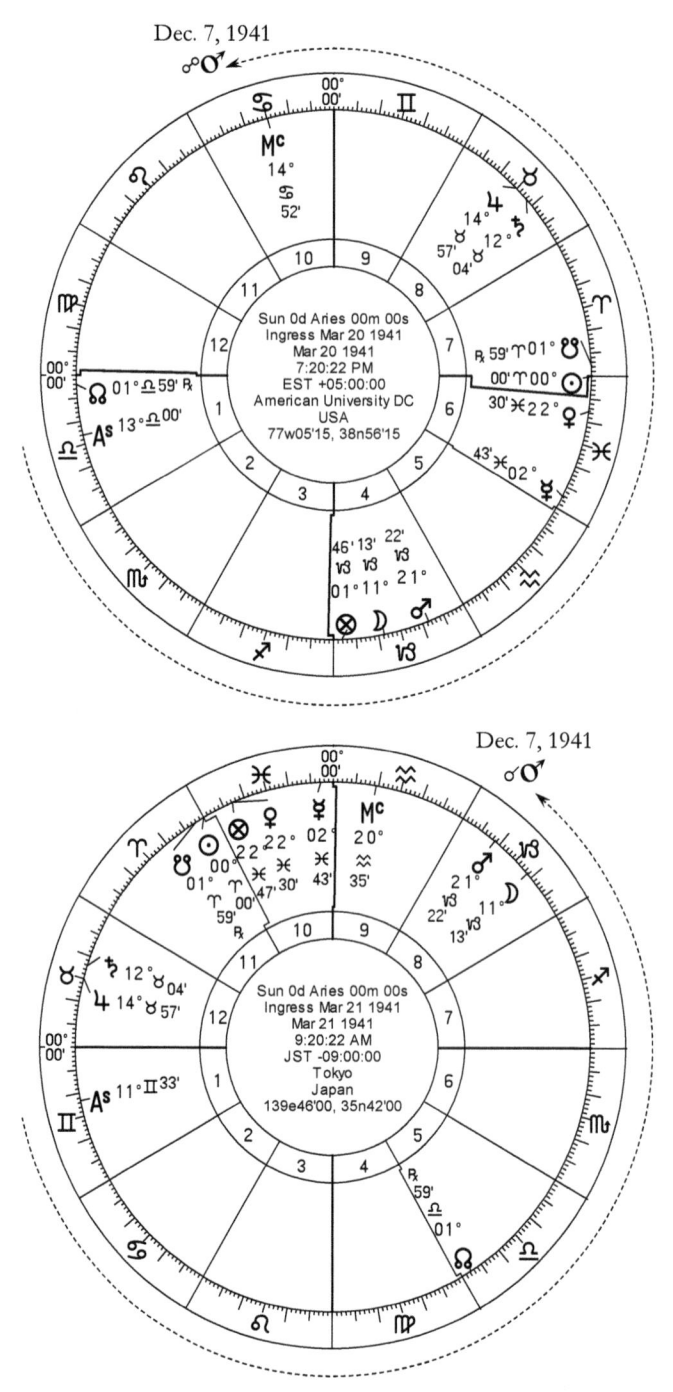

38 ASTROLOGY OF THE WORLD II: REVOLUTIONS & HISTORY

Figure 18: 1941 ingresses for Washington, DC and Tokyo

Just as with the mundane profections, Pingree (and Kennedy before him) listed several other types of mundane directions or distributions described by Abū Ma'shar:[57]

- Mighty (360,000 years): 1° / 1000 solar years of 365.259 days (= 1° / 365,259 days).
- Big (36,000 years): 1° / 100 solar years of 365.259 days (= 1° / 36,525.9 days).
- Middle (3,600 years): 1° / 10 solar years of 365.259 days (= 1° / 3,652.59 days).
- Small (360 years): 1° / 1 solar year of 365.259 days (= 1° / 365.259 days).[58]

As is stated many times in this book, astrologers using the "small" mundane direction began a 360-year cycle at 0° Aries in the year of Māshā'allāh's "indicator" conjunction for his Flood, 3381 BC (although Māshā'allāh himself seems not to have done this). For more on this direction in particular, see Section I.5.

Thousands. The Zoroastrian Thousands are a series of 12 periods of 1000 years apiece, each ruled by a single planet. In my brief introduction to Māshā'allāh above, and in Section II.1, I describe these in detail as well as how Māshā'allāh may have used (or misused) them.

Turns. The Turns (Ar. *dawr*) are a time-lord system in which a sign and planet are paired, beginning with Aries-Saturn, then Taurus-Jupiter, and so on, each lasting for 360 sidereal years—therefore, each Turn lasts as long as a mundane direction of 360 years as mentioned above. According to some, Māshā'allāh's indicator conjunction in 3381 BC was taken to be the start of the Cancer-Saturn Turn; for others, it was Abū Ma'shar's Flood in 3102 BC. In Appendix D I have included a table of Turns, with the number of (sidereal) days allotted to each one, so that the reader may experiment with beginning the Turns at any desired time. See also Section I.5.

---

[57] Pingree 1968, p. 59.
[58] This is equivalent to a natal distribution, using Ptolemy's timing key—but using a sidereal year.

Other mundane fardārs. The Turn is actually one of a set of periods called *fardār*s, which is Abū Ma'shar's spelling for what is otherwise known as the *firdārīyyāt* in natal astrology. In addition to the Turn, which is known as a "mighty" *fardār* (where each period is 360 years), Abū Ma'shar adds:

- Big (78 years). This assigns a descending number of years to each of the signs, in order (Aries has 12, Taurus has 11, and so on). The sum of all the years is 78 solar years of 365.259 days apiece, so 1 cycle of big *fardārs* is 28,490.202 days.
- Middle (675 years total). This series assigns 75 sidereal years apiece to the planets and Nodes, but in order of their *exaltations*. So, since the Sun is exalted in Aries, he gets 75 years; the Moon is exalted in Taurus, so she gets 75 years; then the Head (for Gemini), Jupiter (for Cancer), Mercury (for Virgo), Saturn (for Libra), the Tail (for Sagittarius), Mars (for Capricorn), and Venus (for Pisces). One entire cycle is 675 solar years of 365.259 days apiece, or 246,549.825 days. (Note that this period is longer than the "big" *fardār* above!).
- Small (75 years total). This is identical to the natal *firdārīyyāh* (a total of 75 years), along with its sub-periods. This mundane version uses the order of exaltations (see above). Apparently there is no diurnal-nocturnal distinction, so that the periods always begin with the Sun.

Again, since the world-years and Flood dates of Māshā'allāh and Abū Ma'shar are not accurate in any case, I do not see the point of these time-lord systems; but I include them here for the interested reader.

Quarters. Finally, in BRD Abū Ma'shar describes a systems of Quarters, each of which is 90 years long. I will describe this further in my own translation of *BRD*.

§10: Mundane Lots, & Saturn-Jupiter as Lots

This book contains numerous mundane Lots, a few of which already appeared in *AW1* for weather prediction. In almost every case we have calculations for them, along with instructions; in a few cases they are only listed by name or have no instructions. In the table below I organize them according to type. Afterwards, I deal briefly with Saturn and Jupiter as being the "First" and "Second" Lots.

For the most part, if a Lot is projected from the Ascendant, I omit mention of the Ascendant; otherwise I try to include as much of the formula as is possible—some Lots are rather complicated and have various exceptions and special rules. My way of describing the formulas is as follows, inserting an arrow between the first two points to indicate their interval, and a comma before the point from which it is projected. So a Lot of the Father cast from the Sun to Saturn, and projected from the Ascendant, would be: ☉ → ♄, Asc. Also, I ignore any nocturnal-diurnal distinctions.

Weather		
Rain	☽ → ♀, ☉	*Scito* Ch. 1, **4**.
Air & winds	☿ → his lord	*Skilled* VIII.26, **20-24**.
Days	☉ → ♄, ☽	*Skilled* VIII.26, **25-26**.

Rulership & Authority		
Rulership & authority	☽ → ♂	Section I.2, al-Qabīsī 5.17, **2**; *Skilled* VIII.17, **21-24**.
"	ASC of ♂ → ♂	Section I.2, al-Qabīsī 5.17, **3**; *Skilled* VIII.17, **43**.
"	☉ → MC, ♃	Section I.2, al-Qabīsī 5.17, **4**.
"	☉ → ♄	*Skilled* VIII.17, **42**.
Rulership or accession	☉ → 15° ♌ ☽ → 15° ♋	Section I.2, al-Qabīsī 5.17, **5**.
"	♃ → ♄	Section I.2, al-Qabīsī 5.17, **6**.
Work & authority	♃ → MC[59]	*Skilled* VIII.22, **20** and **25**.
Kingdom or rulership	*No calc. given*	*Scito* Ch. 1, **4**; *Skilled* VIII.17, **14-15, 19-20, 25-28, 33, 37, 40**.
Lot of the transit	*No calc. given*	*Conjunctions* Ch. 3, **16**.

---

[59] But see the footnotes to this Lot for alternative calculations.

War & Peace		
Peace-making	☉ → Desc	*Skilled* VIII.3, **15-18**.
Fighting	♂ → ☽, ☉	*Skilled* VIII.3, **15-18**.
War, courage, conquering, victory	No calc. given	*Skilled* VIII.4, **101**.
Highness, victory, flourishing	Spirit → ♃	*Skilled* VIII.17, **3-4**.

Pairs of Lots		
Greatest Lots	(Complicated)	Section I.2, al-Qabīsī 5.18, **2-9**.
"Two Lots" #1	☉ → ♄, ♃ ☉ → MC, ♃	*Skilled* VIII.38, **2**.
" #2	♄ → ♃, ♂ ♃ → ♄, ♂	*Skilled* VIII.38, **3-4**.
" #3	(Complicated)	*Skilled* VIII.38, **5-14**.
" #4	(Complicated)	*Skilled* VIII.38, **17**.

Figure 19: Mundane Lots in *AW2*

Finally, it is an unusual fact that Arabic texts sometimes refer to Saturn as a "First Lot" and Jupiter as a "Second Lot." The earliest references in this book come from Māshā'allāh and 'Umar al-Tabarī, so I suspect this was a designation inherited from the Sassanian Persians. There must be some deeper lore involved which explains their being called "Lots," but we will have to wait for further translations before making any firm conclusions. In all of these cases, the two planets are treated as a pair, often looking at the distance between them. Following are all of the texts here which treat them as Lots:

Saturn & Jupiter as First & Second Lots
• *Conjunctions* Ch. 7, **19** (Māshā'allāh).
• *Scito* Ch. 38, **16-18**, with possible inclusion of Mars in **21** (uncertain).
• *Scito* Ch. 96, **28** and **28** (from Sahl?).
• *Skilled* VIII.14, **4** and **14** (maybe 'Umar).
• *Skilled* VIII.15, **14-15** ('Umar).
• *Skilled* VIII.16, **33** (uncertain).
• *Skilled* VIII.20, **5-11** ('Umar).

Figure 20: Saturn & Jupiter as First & Second Lots

§11: Julian days & key data for Islamic historical astrology

In this section I provide an explanation of Julian days (which are used extensively throughout this book) and some key reference dates in Islamic historical astrology. Although it's unreasonable to memorize Julian days, the reader should at least memorize the month and years of the events below, as they are mentioned again and again in the texts. After the tables, I briefly mention the Islamic Ascendant for 571 AD.

At a minimum, you should absolutely memorize the date and degree number of the assumed mean conjunction for Islam:

- December 12, 570 AD
- 4° Scorpio
- Triplicity shift into water (allegedly)

Julian days

Julian days (JD) were developed by astronomers as a handy way of counting individual days (and fractions of days) across large spans of time. This was necessary both because of leap days added in our conventional Gregorian calendar, but because calculating dates with traditional calendars can be a nightmare. Older cultures often kept calendars based on regnal dates: that is, the day that a given ruler assumed the throne. Over time, it meant having to explain a certain date by means of several calendars—one can even find this in Ptolemy's *Almagest*. For example, in the so-called *Universal Book* in Section I.5 of this book, a commentator identifies the date of a chart by calculating it in three different calendars: those of the Muslims, Alexander the Great, and the Persians. In Islamic historical astrology, it was common to list dates in the Yazdijird calendar, which is nothing more than a calendar of days deriving from the day that Yazdijird III, the last Sassanian Persian king, ascended the throne.

Julian days are based on mean noon UT, i.e., noon at Greenwich. So, any JD that ends in .0 is exactly noon, while any that ends in .5 is exactly midnight. By convention, astronomers decided that JD 0.0 is equivalent to noon on January 1, 4713 BC. There are websites and formulas for converting dates to JD, and vice versa.[60] Following are some key dates used frequently in the texts—the JD in a few cases might be off by .5 (i.e., 12 hours), depending on how it was calculated.

Astrological dates

Description	JD	Calendar Date
Māshā'allāh's conjunction #0	-390512.2221	November 2, 5783 BC
Ingress for Māshā'allāh's "indicator" conjunction / Cancer-Saturn Turn	486553.5	February 11, 3381 BC
Māshā'allāh's "indicator" conjunction	486778.6994	Sept. 23, 3381 BC
Māshā'allāh's Flood conjunction	494029.0375	July 30, 3361 BC
Abū Ma'shar's Flood-Kaliyuga	588465.5	February 18, 3102 BC
Islamic conjunction (Scorpio)	1929596	December 12, 570 AD
Islamic Aries ingress	1929693	March 19, 571 AD
Gemini-Venus Turn	1932981	March 19, 580 AD

Figure 21: Julian dates for key astrological events

Calendar/event reference dates

Description	JD	Calendar Date
Hijrah	1948439	July 15, 622 AD
1st of Yazdijird calendar	1952063	June 16, 632 AD

Figure 22: Julian dates for key calendar/event dates

Throughout this book, I will provide JDs as much as possible. They are very handy for calculating lengths of time, especially long series of Saturn-Jupiter conjunctions. In several cases, it was useful to have them because some authors group time into unusual periods: for example, taking long lengths of time as years of exactly 365 days, and then grouping the remaining days into months of 30 days.

---

[60] For positive JDs, I have used either the US Naval Observatory's site (http://aa.usno.navy.mil/data/docs/JulianDate.php), or Excel formulas based on Duffett-Smith 1988 (pp. 6-9). For the few negative JDs in this book, I have used a different site (http://www.stevegs.com/utils/jd_calc/jd_calc.htm).

Ascendants for Islam

Of key importance in historical astrology is the use of mundane profections, which in Arabic are called "terminal points" because profections are interpreted according to where they terminate or stop. One of the key profections mentioned in these texts is the profection from the Ascendant of the Aries ingress for Islam, in 571 AD. But because some astrologers used a sidereal zodiac, others not, and at any rate people used different tables, there were different opinions on what the Ascendant was. Following are four views, who held them, and their sources:

- Libra. This was the most common view, held by Māshā'allāh,[61] Sahl,[62] and Abū Ma'shar.[63]
- Gemini, according to al-Kindī.[64]
- Aries, according to the *Sindhind* tables or some version of them.[65]
- Cancer, according to the *Mumtahan* tables.[66]

One thing that accounts for these differences (apart from the sidereal-tropical distinction), is that charts were not all cast for the same location. Māshā'allāh's charts in *Conjunctions* seem to be cast for Baghdad, while others were apparently cast for 'Ujjain (a city in India at 23° 10' N, 75° 46' E), which was thought to be in the middle of the inhabitable world (see for example *Skilled* VIII.8), or perhaps even on the equator or cities thought to be on the equator.[67] The choice of location and zodiac must also be made by modern astrologers.

---

[61] *Conjunctions* Ch. 7.
[62] *Scito* Ch. 95, and Appendix C Example #2.
[63] *BRD* VIII.2, **4**.
[64] *Skilled* VIII.39, **5**; also al-Qabīsī's report in Ch. 4.9 of Section I.1 of this book.
[65] *Skilled* VIII.39, **6**.
[66] *Skilled* VIII.39, **7**.
[67] See Pingree 1977, p. 12 n. 14; Pingree 1968, p. 45; Burnett and Yamamoto's *BRD*, vol. 1 p. 559, n. 12).

§12: How to interpret an ingress chart

In this section I collect key texts from this book in order to guide the reader in the interpretation of ingress charts. Please note that I am not drawing on any practical expertise of my own, nor am I acting as referee between different points of view. Likewise, there are not the only texts in the subjects listed here, but only those which seemed more important, astrologically obvious, repeated across authors, and so on.

Number and location of charts. The first question is: how many charts do we need? Authors are generally agreed that this depends on the Ascendant of the Aries ingress. If it is fixed, then only one chart is needed, that of the Aries ingress itself. If common or mutable (such as Gemini), then we need two: *both* the Aries *and* the Libra ingress charts. If it is movable or cardinal (such as Cancer), we need the ingress chart for all four movable signs or seasons: Aries, Cancer, Libra, Capricorn. Māshā'allāh (*RYW* Ch. 4) adds that these extra charts are especially needed if the lord of the year at the Aries ingress is also in a sign of that particular type. For example, if the Ascendant of the Aries ingress was Sagittarius, and the lord of the year was in Pisces, it really emphasizes the common-sign nature of the ingress, and the need for two charts that year. But in all cases, the Aries ingress chart is still foundational for everything.

One thing rarely discussed in the literature is the *location* of the chart. In some cases (but none I have actually seen), astrologers used a position on the equator or in India which was taken to be in the middle of the inhabitable world (see *Skilled* VIII.8). In others, astrologers used a politically important city, regardless of whether it was the center of events (such as Māshā'allāh's use of Baghdad in *Conjunctions*). Others used the city in which important events actually occurred when doing retrospective interpretations (such as Sahl: see Appendix C). Probably the consensus among astrologers is that the capital city of a nation or empire is best for appraising the country as a whole—but one can easily understand an interest in casting regional charts as well. For example, it makes sense that during the British Empire one would cast charts for London, but why not for locations in India as well, in order to diagnose regional issues?

The lord of the year: identifying. The next typical step in these texts is the identification of the lord of the year. This is a victor,[68] and a version of what I call a victor "among places." That is, we look at the planets which rule the various dignities of the Ascendant, along with the luminaries (especially the sect light), and see which of them is in the most powerful houses of the chart: whichever of these candidates appears to be the best, is the most authoritative and powerful planet, and is the lord of the year which gives the best overall indications of what the year is going to be like for the nation as a whole. To this, some authors add such things as planets in the Ascendant or the planet receiving the most applications (or "testimonies"). The rationale for the latter is that when one planet connects with or "pushes" to another, the one receiving the pushing comes to be in charge of the matter: thus, any planet receiving multiple applications will have more responsibility in the year, and is a good candidate for being the lord of the year.

For example, suppose the Ascendant of the year is Pisces, and the chart is nocturnal. Let its domicile lord Jupiter be in the tenth, well-dignified in his own domicile. But let its exalted lord Venus be in the eleventh (Capricorn), with the Moon applying to her. We might say that Venus is a better candidate for being the lord of the year, because even though she is not in as powerful a house as Jupiter, she is the nocturnal benefic and is receiving the application of the sect light (the Moon). This is just a simple example, and most charts are not so clear-cut.

Following are key texts on finding the lord of the year:

- *RYW* Chs. 5-8 and 12.
- *Conjunctions* (my introductory *Comment*).
- *Scito* Chs. 2-4.
- *Flowers* Ch. I.1; see also III.8, **8-12**.
- *Skilled* Ch. VIII.4, **2-16**.

The lord of the year: interpreting. Since the lord of the year is a victor that sums up much of the meaning of the year, normal astrological rules should apply to its interpretation: for example, its planetary nature, angularity, dignities, and how it relates to other planets. An exalted Venus in the eleventh and in aversion to the malefics, should be a very different lord of

---

[68] See the Glossary.

the year than Saturn in detriment in the ninth, squared by Mars and in aversion to the benefics. In Abū Ma'shar's *Flowers*, benefic aspects from other planets to the lord of the year mean that the people and topics indicated by those planets will have good effects on the year; squares indicate tension and disagreements involving those people, and oppositions signify open hostility and even war. Following are key texts with advice on interpreting the lord of the year:

- *RYW* Chs. 13-17, 19-20, and 23, **3**.
- *Scito* Chs. 18-19, 33 (**1-10**), 37, 53, 55, 57, 62.
- *Flowers* I-II (all), V.1-V.2.
- *Skilled* VIII.4, **17-22** and **31-35** and **52-55**; VIII.5, **47-50** and **55-61**; VIII.6, **25-40** and **48-75**; VIII.7; VIII.8.

The significator of the king: identifying. Just as there is a lord of the year, some texts insist on a significator of the king for interpreting the actions and condition of the king: this was almost always identified with the lord of the Midheaven or a planet in the tenth. Following are standard rules for finding it:

- *RYW* Chs. 11; 19, **3-7**; 41.
- *Scito* Chs. 6-7.

The significator of the king: interpreting. Numerous texts provide rules for interpreting the significator of the king, such as:

- *RYW* Chs. 11, 13-15, 17, 19-20, 23 (**3**), 26, 29, 42 (**8-39**).
- *Scito* Chs. 13 (**4**), 18, 33 (**1-10**), 35, 37, 49-52, 54-58, 62, 70 (**27**), 71 (**5-14**), 73 (**25**), 74 (**26-27**), 77 (**1-4**).
- *Skilled* VIII.4, **36-45** and **52-55** and **97**.

Mundane significations of planets. In traditional texts, interpreting planets depends on reducing their many significations to classes of people, especially social and political classes. (I omit here geographical indications, such as treating planets in the Ascendant as indication people from the east, or the Sun as the significator of the fourth clime). Following is a table of key mundane significations of the planets, from sources in this book:[69]

♄	The current and lawful king, religious men of faith, the wealthy, old men, sheikhs, farmers and rural people, household managers.
♃	Nobles, magnates, ministers (or the chief minister), those close to the king, consuls, [social] leaders, respectable people, judges, bishops, rebels.[70]
♂	Soldiers, generals, kings' allies, rebels against the king.
☉	Kings, the wealthy, honorable men.
♀	Women, women of the king, singers,[71] people causing delight and fun.
☿	Businessmen, scribes and writers, astrologers, teachers, sages, children (esp. boys), governmental ministers.
☽	Common people/masses, merchants, women, legates/legations.
Asc	Common people/masses, merchants.
MC	Kings, the wealthy.

Figure 23: Mundane significations of planets

Indications of war. Following is a list of primary material on how to identify wars in charts, or information about the enemy; below I summarize a few of the more important indications.

- *Letter* Ch. 4, **8**.
- *RYW* Ch. 14; Ch. 21; Ch. 22, **4-6** and **14**; Ch. 24, **8**; Ch. 25, **2-7**; Ch. 27.
- *Scito* Ch. 28, **2**; Ch. 34; Ch. 36; Chs. 38-39; Ch. 45; Ch. 48; Ch. 59; Chs. 66-68; Ch. 77, **1-5**.
- *Flowers* III.3.

---

[69] See *RYW* Ch. 30, **4**; Ch. 43, **7-8**; *Scito* Ch. 12; Ch. 17, **1**; Ch. 25; Ch. 26, **1**; Ch. 27, **1**; Ch. 28, **1** and **3**; Ch. 32; Ch. 41; Ch. 71, **6-14**; *Flowers* Book II; *Skilled* Ch. VIII.21, **2-7**.

[70] The indication of rebels for Jupiter is probably because rebellion is often stirred up by other wealthy powerful interests in society. In *Skilled* VIII.6, **57-58**, Jupiter means rebellion specifically when considered in relation to Saturn, who tends to indicate the current, lawful king.

[71] Or perhaps the artistic class in general.

- *Skilled* VIII.3, **2-26** and **37**; VIII.4, **39** and **46-50** and **177-78** and **191** and **197**; VIII.5, **35**; VIII.6, **16**; VIII.13, **2-18** and **32-56**; VIII.16, **20-21**.

There is some overlap between these passages (which sometimes advise when fighting will begin or end, or who will win). Following are some of the more notable and easy to grasp, sometimes involving a combination of several passages above. But please note that these lists are not exhaustive: for example, it makes sense that the list emphasizes the indications of Mars, but in some of Sahl's examples the lord of the year being an exalted Saturn in the 10th in a nocturnal chart is enough to indicate violence. Moreover, I omit many of the possible indications that might come about through time lords or directions.

- Mars strong and angular (esp. in the 4th), esp. if lord of the year.
- Mars conjoining or squaring Tail.
- Mars squaring Saturn and Jupiter.
- Mars signifies direct hostility, Saturn cunning.
- Mars peregrine, joined to a strong Saturn.
- Mars squaring or opposing the Sun in a diurnal revolution.
- Mars in the eighth.
- Mars as lord of the year, retrograde in a bad or peregrine place, in aversion to benefics.
- Malefics lords of the year, in aversion to benefics.
- Malefics in an assembly or hard aspect, especially in an angle, especially in human signs.
- Malefic in the angles (especially the Ascendant or Midheaven), especially if retrograde.
- Jupiter and Saturn squaring or opposed at the revolution.
- Slow planets suggest war, retrograde planets suggest flight or disintegration of the war, and direct planets indicate peace.
- When the year reaches the place of Mars at the triplicity shift.[72]

Speaking of Mars, several texts relate his cycle to the performance and intensity of the war: if direct, the fighting is strong and allies reliable;

---

[72] This is no doubt a mundane profection.

retrograde, the fighting is quick because allies are unreliable; stationing, the fighting is very intense.

One might very well ask how likely it is that any or several of these will always indicate actual war. Indeed, as I mentioned above, sometimes war is seen by other indications. But I think we can respond in two ways. On the one hand, many conflicts in the past that might have been settled by threats and war, are now carried out by legalistic and economic means—such as when we speak of a trade war, or sanctions against nations. So these indications of Mars and such above (or even, the Saturn-Mars conjunctions in Cancer) may be better understood through those kinds of events. On the other hand, we should recall that it is especially easy for "civilized" and "peace-loving" nations to carry out proxy wars and bomb other nations from far away while claiming not to be at war. For example, in 2014 Barack Obama became the fourth U.S. President in a row to believe that peace will occur in Iraq only if it continues to be bombed. If we agree that one country dropping bombs on another, along with exchanges of firepower, are military and warlike actions, then one could well argue that the U.S. has been at war in Iraq since 1991. So "war" does not have to fit into a narrowly-defined image of formal declarations of war followed by mustachioed generals in epaulettes personally leading troops into battle.

Fixed stars. Hardly any of the texts in this book address the matter of fixed stars, the notable exception being *Flowers* V. Its rules may be summarized as follows: if a malefic fixed star falls on either the lord or cusp of a house, then the people, things, and bodily limbs attributed to that house will be affected accordingly. (For these purposes, Abū Ma'shar seems to treat the lord of the year and lord of the Ascendant as interchangeable.) This also affects children born that year, whose Ascendants are that very sign: for example, if a malefic fixed star is on the cusp of the 2nd, Gemini, then children born that year with Gemini rising will be adversely affected, especially with respect to their finances.

§13: Special Arabic vocabulary

Since the Middle Ages, readers of traditional astrology have encountered specialized jargon from Arabic and Persian, usually transliterated so that their straightforward meaning was unknown. And modern scholars and translators have often been tempted to maintain this mystery. For several years I kept transliterating words like *hyleg/hīlāj* or *almuten/mubtazz* because I thought it led to a more "authentic" experience of reading these texts, like the medieval and Renaissance Latins might have had. Contemporary academic scholars often continue to transliterate these same words. Considerations like "authenticity" might also lie behind the tendency among practitioners of *jyotish* or Indian astrology to substitute complicated Sanskrit terms for what must in many cases be simple, everyday, and ultimately more revealing words. In the past few years, I have decided to stop transliterating and switch over to a carefully considered, standardized English vocabulary. For example, I now call a *mubtazz* a "victor," because that is basically what the word means in Arabic: it was a translation of the Greek *epikratētōr*, which also means to win out, predominate, and so on.

Following, then, are a few of the thematic word groups which seemed especially relevant in this book, and how I propose to translate them:

Whole-sign houses and quadrant divisions. At least the early part of the Arabic period was one of mixture between these two approaches to houses. Both Māshā'allāh and Sahl appear to use whole signs as their basis, but when it suits them they are willing to change to quadrant divisions (such as Porphyry or Alchabitius Semi-Arc houses) if it will put a planet in a more interesting house. Māshā'allāh and al-Rijāl provide the vocabulary that distinguishes planets in a house by whole sign or by quadrant division:

- "Number" (Ar. *ʿadad*):[73] houses counted by whole sign, namely as pre-given, individual units to be counted from the Ascendant.
- "Division" (Ar. *qismah*)[74] or "equation" (Ar. *taswiyah*):[75] houses gotten by *dividing* the region between the horizon and meridian into smaller ones according to a formula.

---

[73] See *Conjunctions* Ch. 7, **17-18**; *Skilled* VIII.16, **43**.
[74] See *Conjunctions* Ch. 2, **5**; Ch. 7, **17**; Ch. 17, **2**.
[75] See *Conjunctions* Ch. 17, **5**; *Skilled* VIII.16, **43**.

Types of "falling." Hellenistic astrology already had at least two ways in which a planet may be said to "fall": being in a "declining" (Gr. *apoklima*) place, i.e., a cadent place, such as the third or ninth, and being in its own "fall" (Gr. *hupsōma*), i.e., the opposite of exaltation, such as the Moon in Scorpio. As medieval Latin translators began to translate Arabic texts, they encountered still more types of falling, but tended to translate all of them indifferently using some form of *cado* ("to fall, decline"). Obviously this can lead to misunderstanding, especially when one does not know about one important traditional concept, "aversion" (Gr. *apostrophē*). Aversion means that a planet is in a sign which is not configured to some other by a classical aspect: for example, a planet in Gemini is in aversion to any planet in Cancer, because Gemini and Cancer (being adjacent signs) do not form a classical aspect with each other. Instead, Gemini is configured to Leo and Aries by sextiles, Virgo and Pisces by squares, and so on. So if we follow the Latin approach and say that the Moon is *cadens* from, or "cadent" from the malefics, what does this mean? We might be tempted to say that "cadent" means being "in the third house or sign" from something, just as the third house from the Ascendant is cadent, the twelfth (being the third from the tenth) is a cadent house, and so on. But no: falling away from the malefics is an idiomatic Arabic phrase meaning aversion, and Arabic texts use slightly different wording when speaking of being in a declining or cadent place.

The following diagram illustrates *six* ways in which Jupiter could be described as "falling." The degree of the Midheaven is in early Aquarius (the tenth sign), with Mars in it. Jupiter is in late Capricorn, the ninth sign.

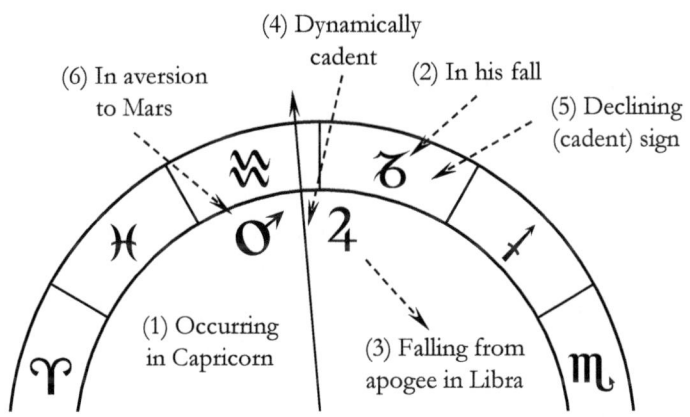

Figure 24: Six ways for a planet to "fall" in Arabic

Verb 1: waqaʿa

(1) "Occur." First, Jupiter is "falling" by simply being in Capricorn, since this verb colloquially means " to occur, happen." This may seem trivial, but suppose he was in Pisces: we can imagine a Latin text remaining literally faithful to the Arabic and saying that he "was falling" (*fuerit cadens*) in the eleventh, which sounds like he is either cadent or in his fall, neither of which is true. Still, this is the least astrologically interesting type of falling.

Verb 2: habaṭa

(2) "Fall, descension, downfall." Because Jupiter's exaltation is in Cancer, he is also in its counter-dignity in Capricorn, his "fall" (Lat. *casus*) or "descension" (Lat. *descensio*) or "downfall." For the most part, I try to keep calling this "fall" when the meaning is clear, but sometimes have used "downfall" or "descension" when the context makes these terms the clearer ones. This is the *only* time I used these two latter words.

(3) "Coming down" from the apogee. It so happens that in Ptolemaic astronomy, the large circle on which Jupiter travels (his deferent or eccentric circle) is displaced so that his apogee (where he is farthest away from earth) is currently in Libra. So as he moves forward in the signs away from Libra, he is "coming down" from that height and closer to the Earth. My use of this phrase is provisional, as Arabic has numerous verbs for decreasing, going down, falling, etc. (and the contrary), which are used in a variety of astronomical scenarios, and I am not yet confident that I will stick with this phrase. (This verb can also indicate decreasing in zodiacal latitude.) In this book, I generally add a footnote to explain what astronomical scenario I believe an author is talking about.

Verb 3: saqaṭa[76]

(4) "Falling" (dynamic cadence, by quadrant division). Since Jupiter is in an earlier degree than the Midheaven (and let us insist that he is more than 5° away) he is cadent and so dynamically weaker—as opposed to being angular or succeedent. "Cadent" translates the Latin *cadens*, which simply means "fall-

---

[76] I believe that the Latin verb *labor* would have been a better translation of this verb, but it was almost always translated using *cado*.

ing, declining." Now, for those who use house systems based on quadrant divisions (Porphyry, Placidus, etc.), this region of falling or dynamic cadence is also nothing less than the ninth house itself, since in those systems the degree of the Midheaven defines the beginning of the tenth house. In quadrant systems, these regions define both house topics and planetary intensity; but here I am confining myself only to the question of intensity or strength, hence "falling" means "earlier than the axial degree" and "dynamically weak." *However*, it is not always clear in the Arabic texts whether by "falling" the author means (5) instead, or even sometimes (6): so this term is sometimes ambiguous.

(5) "Declining" (cadence by whole sign). Because Jupiter is in the ninth *sign*, Jupiter is also in a sign that is "declining" from the angular sign Aquarius. This is a whole-sign concept, in which the angular signs are the first (where the degree of the Ascendant is), fourth, seventh, and tenth signs. So, the cadent signs are the third, sixth, ninth, and twelfth signs. Since Arabic authors of at least the first century or so of this period tended to favor whole signs, it is often clear that when a planet is "falling" it means it is "declining," or in a cadent sign.

(6) "Falling away from" (in aversion to). Finally, because Capricorn itself is not configured to Aquarius by any classical aspect, the signs are in aversion, and Jupiter in Capricorn cannot see either Aquarius or anything in it (Mars). So Jupiter is "falling away" from (*saqaṭa ʿan*) Mars, which might be thought of as falling away *from his view*. This sense of falling is always easy to spot. First, it is accompanied by the preposition *ʿan* ("away, from"), and is commonly found in two idiomatic phrases: falling away from the benefics/malefics, and falling away from the Ascendant—that is, being in aversion to the benefics/malefics, and being in aversion to the Ascendant.

Conjoining, uniting, connecting (Ar. *qārana, ʾiqtarana, ʾittaṣala*). Traditional literature has numerous ways to speak of how planets connect and combine with one another; this is made more complicated by the fact that Arabic is very flexible in its verb forms, and we do not always know what word a Latin author is translating from, or the scenario he has in mind. Following are the ways I translate these special terms from Arabic—note that several come from the same root verb, *qarana*:

- *Assembly* (Ar. *muqāranah* [from *qārana*, Form III pass. part.]). This refers to two or more planets being in the same sign, and is the same as the Hellenistic "co-presence."
- *Connect, connection* (Ar. ʾ*ittaṣala*, ʾ*ittiṣāl*). This refers to two or more planets being connected by degree (whether by body or aspect), and not simply being related by sign.
- *Conjoin, conjunction* (Ar. *qārana*, *qirān* [Form III, and verbal noun]). The noun *qirān* normally refers specifically to *mean conjunctions* (such as the mean Saturn-Jupiter conjunctions). The verb is sometimes used on its own, and it is unclear to me whether it always denotes a mean conjunction, or is equivalent to a *connection* (above).
- *Unite, be united, union* (Ar. ʾ*iqtarana*, ʾ*iqtarān*, Form VIII). It is unclear to me whether this has a technical meaning; in most cases it is probably just a synonym for a *connection*, as ibn Hibintā uses it in his commentary to Māshā'allāh's *Conjunctions* Ch. 18, **2** (in Section II.4 of this book). But al-Qabīsī Ch. 4.2 (in Section I.1) uses it as a synonym for mean conjunctions.

Advancing vs. retreating and withdrawing. Arabic has a specialized vocabulary relating to how strong or weak planets are, understood in terms of angularity. Unfortunately, I think we cannot say definitively yet how uniform this vocabulary is across different authors, among other things. The terms fall into two groups: one which is ideally moving by diurnal motion toward the axial degrees, and the other ideally moving past and away from them.

- *"Advancing"* (Ar. ʾ*iqbāl*, *muqbil*, *zā'id*). These three terms all refer to a planet which is angular or succeedent. For the first two terms, this is certainly understood in dynamical terms (i.e., by quadrant houses or divisions), but possibly being in an angular or succeedent sign would be acceptable. The third term is certainly understood dynamically. So, in the diagram above, Mars is absolutely advancing in every sense: by whole sign as well as by being in a later degree than the MC, moving by diurnal motion towards it.
- *"Retreating"* (Ar. ʾ*idbār*), *"withdrawing"* (Ar. *zā'il*). These two terms express the contrary of the other three. "Retreating" should probably be understood in dynamical terms, but may refer to whole signs as well. "Withdrawing" is certainly dynamical, even within an angu-

lar or succeedent sign: thus if the IC were in the fourth or fifth sign, and a planet were in that sign but in an earlier degree, it would be still be "withdrawing." This book contains several chart examples of withdrawal, such as *Conjunctions* Ch. 8, **6**, or sentence **A9** of Sahl's mundane Example #1, in *Scito* Ch. 95. In the diagram above, Jupiter is retreating or withdrawing in every sense.

Portions and shares. Arabic, following (in part) Greek, has some unfamiliar words which in the Latin tradition became simply "degree" and "dignity." The word "portion" or "section" or "piece" (Ar. *juz'*) normally means the "degree" where something is, but in some cases may actually indicate the *bound* or term in which something is. In this book, "portion" usually translates the Arabic, but I will not use it in this technical way in my own commentaries, and in the case of Latin translation, I cannot always be sure that *portio* or *pars* mean the same as "degree." In many cases it is obvious it does not, such as when speaking of "portions of the earth" or similar phrases.

The word "share" (Ar. *ḥazza*) is synonymous with "dignity," such as a planet being in one of its own dignities or "shares."

PART I:
SHORT SUMMARIES & PRINCIPLES

SECTION I.1:
AL-QABĪSĪ ON MUNDANE PROFECTIONS

Comment by Dykes. These excerpts from al-Qabīsī's *Book of the Introduction to the Craft of the Judgments of the Stars* (translated by me from Arabic) present a basic outline of conjunctional theory, with some Islamic chronology using mundane profections. My source text was Burnett and Yamamoto's critical edition of al-Qabīsī (2004).

Ch. 4.2. The excerpts begin with a brief list of types of conjunctions, all of which I have discussed in my Introduction. I remind the reader that the lengths of the mean conjunctional periods (e.g., 20 years between Saturn-Jupiter conjunctions, 30 years between Saturn-Mars conjunctions in Cancer) are all according to the idealized theory promoted by Abū Ma'shar. Not only does Abū Ma'shar use slightly incorrect sidereal values (and it also matters a great deal whether one is using a tropical or sidereal zodiac), but the time until the return to Aries or between individual shifts depends on exactly where in a sign a conjunction lands.

Ch. 4.9. Here, al-Qabīsī introduces mundane profections in the context of some key dates and calendrical points of his day. He begins with the view of al-Kindī, who believed that the Ascendant of the Aries ingress in 571 AD was Gemini (**1-2**). From there, the profection to Muḥammad's flight or Hijrah to Medina in 622 reached Virgo (**2**). From Virgo in 622, the profection continued to Cancer in 632 AD (**3-6**), the year of the accession of Yazdijird III (June 16, 632). This is only interesting because it was a common reference point in calendrics, and in Ch. 4.10 al-Qabīsī states some of his intervals of years in the Yazdijird calendar.

Ch. 4.10. However, the more common view of the Ascendant of 571 was that it was Libra, and al-Qabīsī duly begins to report from Abū Ma'shar's *BRD*, which represents this view (**1**). He points out that one may also profect from the sign of the conjunction of Islam itself, Scorpio (**2**). But then Abū Ma'shar does something interesting: instead of profecting endlessly from the Libra Ascendant of 571 AD, he allows that one may profect from the Ascendants of certain other conjunctions: for example, he says that the Ascendant of 749 AD (the beginning of the 'Abbasids) was Virgo (**3**), and the Ascendant of 809 AD (the shift into the fiery triplicity) was Leo (**4**).

ಬಿ ಜಿ ಲ

Introduction Ch. 4.2: [Types of conjunctions]

1 And the first [of the technical terms] is the conjunction: and the types[77] indicating alterations (and other things) in this world from the conjunctions are six:[78]

2 The most powerful of them is the union of Saturn and Jupiter at the beginning of Aries, and that comes to be every 960 years.

3 And the second is their union at the beginning of every triplicity, and that is every 240 years; and they unite in 12 conjunctions in every triplicity, then their union shifts to the next triplicity which follows it.

4 And the third is the union of Saturn and Mars at the beginning of Cancer, and that is every 30 years.

5 And the fourth, the union of Saturn and Jupiter in sign [after] sign, and that is every 20 years.

6 And the fifth, the alighting of the more powerful luminary into the point of the vernal equinox, and that is every solar year.[79]

7 And the sixth, the union of the two luminaries or their opposition, and that is every one-half of a lunar month.

8 And when "the Ascendant of the conjunction" is stated, indeed what is intended by it is "the Ascendant at the Sun's entrance into the point of the vernal equinox at the beginning of the year in which the conjunction is."

---

[77] الامور.
[78] Al-Qabīsī's list is based on *BRD* I.1, **12-20**.
[79] The phrase "solar year" implies a sidereal zodiac.

Introduction Ch. 4.9: [Al-Kindī's mundane profections]

[Profection from the 571 AD ingress to the Hijrah (622 AD)]

1 And as for the terminal point from the years of the world, indeed al-Kindī reported that between the year of the conjunction indicating the religion and the Hijrah, there were 52 solar years.[80] **2** And the Ascendant of the year of the conjunction of the religion was Gemini, and the year in which the Prophet of God fled (the prayers and peace of God be upon him!), reached Virgo.[81]

[Profection from the Hijrah to the accession of Yazdijird III (632 AD)]

3 And between the Hijrah and Yazdijird, was 3,624 days.[82] **4** And if you wanted knowledge of that,[83] then take the years of Yazdijird, and expand them into days, just as was made clear to you in the *Zīj*, and add on top of that what is between the Hijrah and Yazdijird (in days), and divide that by 365 ¼ days; and what comes out is the solar years, and what is left over is of the months and days of the incomplete year. **5** And what is summed up in years are the solar years since the Hijrah. **6** So find one sign for every year, and begin with Virgo, and where your counting of the signs terminates, that is the sign which the year of the world has reached from the Ascendant of the conjunction of the religion.[84]

---

[80] If we count 571 AD (the Aries ingress used for the 570 AD conjunction) as year #1, then the Hijrah in 622 AD is year #52. But the number of elapsed years is only 51 (622 – 571 = 51).

[81] Most sources treat the Ascendant of the 571 ingress as being Libra (see my Introduction), but al-Kindī views it as being Gemini: according to *Skilled* VIII.39, **5**, al-Kindī used Ptolemaic tables to draw this conclusion. If 571 AD is Gemini, then by annual profection 622 AD is Virgo. See the table below.

[82] The Hijrah took place on July 15, 622 (JD 1948438.5), and the first day of Yazdijird was June 16, 632 (JD 1952062.5): the difference is 3,624 days.

[83] That is, the profection from the Hijrah (in Virgo) to Yazdijird.

[84] The time between the Hijrah and Yazdijird is 9.92 years (3,624 days / 365.25 or 365.259 = 9.92). But we did not really need to do this, since the annual profection from March 571 AD (Gemini) to June 632 AD comes to Cancer. But al-Qabīsī might be thinking of profections in a continuous way, so that each degree of the zodiac is worth a certain amount of time: in that case, the exact number of days and zodiacal position would matter.

SECTION I.1: AL-QABĪSĪ ON MUNDANE PROFECTIONS

♈		581	593	605	617	629
♉		582	594	606	618	630
♊	571	583	595	607	619	631
♋	572	584	596	608	620	**632**
♌	573	585	597	609	621	
♍	574	586	598	610	**622**	
♎	575	587	599	611	623	
♏	576	588	600	612	624	
♐	577	589	601	613	625	
♑	578	590	602	614	626	
♒	579	591	603	615	627	
♓	580	592	604	616	628	

Figure 25: Table illustrating al-Kindī's profection from 571 AD

Introduction Ch. 4.10: [Abū Ma'shar's mundane profections]

[Profection from 571 to Yazdijird]

1 And as for [others] besides al-Kindī, it was thought that one should add 61 solar years, 2 months, 12 days, and 16 hours (Persian) on top of the completed years of Yazdijird, and expand them into days, and turn them back into solar years, just as we made clear, and you begin the projection from the sign of Libra.)[85]

---

[85] This is a bit confusing, and al-Qabīsī's report of this value from Abū Ma'shar conceals how Abū Ma'shar got his value (*BRD* VIII.2, **8**). Abū Ma'shar uses "Persian" years of 365 days, grouping leftover days into months of 30 days. First, Abū Ma'shar takes the 3,624 days between the 571 ingress and the Hijrah and converts them into his "Persian" years: 9y 11m 9d. Then, he adds to this 51y 3m 3d 16h – which should be 18,708.66 days. If we add the days together, we get 22,332.66, which is about 37 days fewer than the actual amount (22,370 days). What has happened? Well, one problem is that when Abū Ma'shar adds his intervals together he converts groups of 12 months (of 30 days) into a year, ignoring the fact that he is now missing 5 days (12 * 30 = 360 days, not 365). But there may also be a transcription error: according to Burnett and Yamamoto (2000, p. 501 n. 16), al-Sijzī has 3 months instead of Abū Ma'shar's 2. This extra month, plus the 5 missing days, would give us 22,367.66 days, almost exactly the correct amount. At any rate, the profection from Libra in 571 AD would reach Capricorn in 632 AD.

2 And if you wanted the terminal point from the sign of the conjunction of the religion, then the projection is from Scorpio.[86]

[Profection from the 'Abbasids (749 AD)]

3 And if you wanted the terminal point from the Ascendant of the ['Abbasid] dynasty, then subtract 117 Persian years from the completed years of Yazdijird, and turn them back into solar years just as we did before, and begin the projection from Virgo.[87]

[Profection from the shift into fire (809 AD)]

4 And if you wanted the terminal point from the Ascendant of the shift of the transit from the watery triplicity to the fiery triplicity, then subtract 176 years from the complete years of Yazdijird, and turn the remainder into solar years, and you begin the projection from Leo.[88] **5** And where the counting ends, then it is the sign of the terminal point from every one of the beginnings which we described before.

---

[86] In other words, you may profect from the sign in which the conjunction happened.
[87] According to Abū Ma'shar (*BRD* VIII.2, **5**), the Ascendant of the Aries ingress of 749 AD was Virgo, in year 117 of Yazdijird.
[88] According to Abū Ma'shar (*BRD* VIII.2, **6**), the Ascendant of the Aries ingress of 809 AD was Leo, in year 176 of Yazdijird.

SECTION I.2: AL-QABĪSĪ ON MUNDANE LOTS

Comment by Dykes. These excerpts from al-Qabīsī reproduce rather faithfully several mundane Lots described by Abū Ma'shar in *BRD*. In some cases neither al-Qabīsī nor Abū Ma'shar explain how to use the Lots, nor where they come from (though some must come from the Sassanian Persians). At the end of this section, I illustrate a couple of Lots with an example.

Note that for the two "greatest" Lots, one Lot is calculated using positions in the most recent triplicity shift, while the other uses the most recent, lesser Saturn-Jupiter conjunction. In this way, the Lots are meant to link the current regime to the general trend of the entire triplicity shift—although the precise use of the Lots is unclear and ought to be analyzed in a full historical example.

ಠ ಞ ಆ

Introduction Ch. 5.17: [Several mundane Lots]

1 Since we have finished with these Lots which occur in particular matters,[89] we will follow them up with the Lots which occur in the revolution of the years of the world and the conjunctions indicating the matters of the king,[90] and how long the king will remain.

[Three Lots of rulership and authority]

2 And belonging to that is [1] a Lot known as the Lot of rulership and authority, employed in the revolution of the year of the world, taken from Mars to the Moon and projected from the Ascendant of the conjunction indicating the shift of the religion.[91]

3 It is used in another respect: [2] it is taken from the degree of the Ascendant of the conjunction to the degree of the conjunction, and projected from the degree of the Ascendant of the revolution.[92]

---

[89] That is, the Lots of individual houses from previous chapters. See *ITA* VI.
[90] "King" in this sentence could also be read as "rulership."
[91] See *BRD* I.4, **6**. This Lot and its lord are used to describe the values and spiritual focus of the people who define the culture of the new dynasty or religion.
[92] See *BRD* I.4, **8**. This Lot is also used to appraise the character and future of the culture of the new religion.

4 And [3] it is also used by taking from the degree of the Sun to the Midheaven of the revolution, and projected from the degree of Jupiter.[93]

[Two Lots of the period of rulership]

5 The Lot of the period of rulership is taken [1] at the time of the accession of the king, from the Sun to the 15th degree of Leo, and projected from the Moon; then it is taken from the Moon to the 15th degree of Cancer and projected from the Sun.[94]

6 Another Lot for the period of the accession of the king is taken [2] at the time of the accession of the king, by day from Jupiter to Saturn, and by night the contrary, and is projected from the Ascendant of the revolution of the year in which the king accedes. **7** And if Jupiter was in a sign having two bodies, and the revolution was diurnal, and Jupiter was declining from the stakes, then let it be taken from Saturn to Jupiter, and on top of that one adds 30°, and it is projected from the Ascendant. **8** And if Saturn and Jupiter were opposed and they were both falling away from the Ascendant, then let what emerges between them be halved and projected from the Ascendant. **9** And if Jupiter was in his own exaltation, and the revolution was nocturnal, then let it be calculated from him to Saturn and projected from the Ascendant.[95]

---

[93] See *BRD* I.4, **8**, which presents this Lot as an alternative to [2]. But Abū Ma'shar measures from "the degree of the Midheaven of the Sun" to the Midheaven of the revolution, which seems a bit too imaginative or unusual to be an accepted Lot. (Of course, other mundane Lots are even more exotic.)

[94] See *BRD* II.4, **12**, where this Lot is instead used to determine the activity and interests (or perhaps policies) of the king according to the lord of the Lot. Moreover, I suspect that by day one should only use the Sun portion of the calculation, and by night the Moon portion, but Abū Ma'shar seems to want to calculate both at once. For him, the

[95] See *BRD* II.5, **14**. This is a "lifespan" Lot, and Abū Ma'shar says to watch the Sun's ingress into the sign of the Lot, as well as the profection from the Sun to the Lot (plus other rules).

Introduction Ch. 5.18: [*The two "greatest" Lots*][96]

1 The operation of the two "greatest" Lots: from them is the extraction of the period of the accession of the king. **2** The first of them is that you look, at the time of the accession of the king, at where the year has reached from the conjunction of the triplicity which indicated the religion, by calculating a year for every 30°, and a month for every 2.5°.[97] **3** And if you came to know that (in which sign and degree [it is]), then preserve that, for it is the position from which the first Lot is equated.[98] **4** So if you wanted its equation, then establish the Ascendant of the revolution of the year in which the king acceded. **5** Then take from the planet (from among Saturn and Jupiter) eastern from the Sun in that year, to the degree of the equation of the first Lot which you preserved, and project it from the Ascendant of the revolution: and where it ends, that is the position of the first Lot.

6 The second Lot of the two: from the conjunction in which the king acceded, see which sign and degree the year has reached (with a calculation of a year for every 30°), on the day and month in which the king accedes, for it is the position of the equation of the second Lot. **7** So preserve it, then take from the planet (from among Saturn and Jupiter) western from the Sun to the position of the equation of the second Lot which you preserved, and project it from the Ascendant of the revolution: and where it ends, that is the position of the second Lot. **8** And if they were both eastern or western, then take the first one from Saturn, and the second one from Jupiter.

9 These are the Lots which indicate the matters of the rulership and its duration.[99]

---

[96] Or, "most powerful." See *BRD* II.5, **15**.

[97] In other words, this is a continuous profection from the ingress of the triplicity shift to the *very time* of the accession itself, *not* to the ingress of the year of the accession.

[98] Or rather, "calculated exactly." In traditional astronomy, a position is "equated" if it is converted from its provisional assumed position to its final, correct position, by adding some amount called an "equation."

[99] Abū Ma'shar then gives other instructions for determining the length of rule, totally ignoring the Lots he has just described.

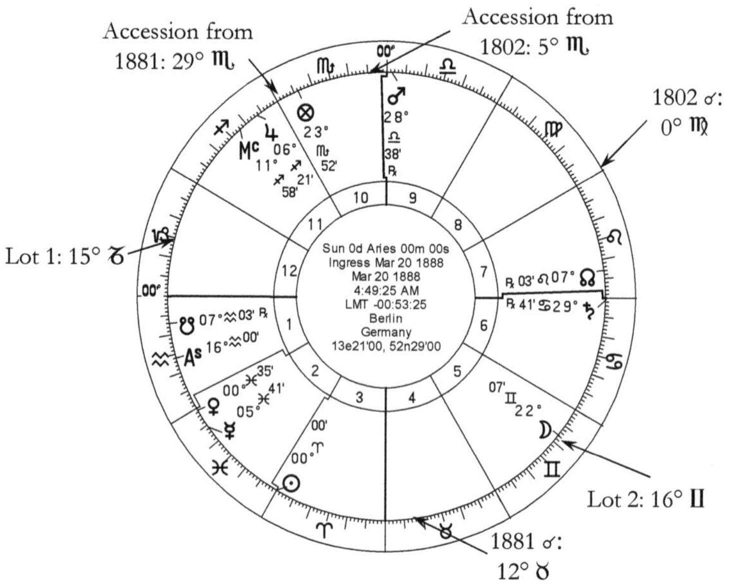
Accession from
1881: 29° ♏
Accession from
1802: 5° ♏
1802 ☌:
0° ♍
Lot 1: 15° ♑
Lot 2: 16° ♊
1881 ☌:
12° ♉
Sun 0d Aries 00m 00s
Ingress Mar 20 1888
Mar 20 1888
4:49:25 AM
LMT -00:53:25
Berlin
Germany
13e21'00, 52n29'00

Figure 26: Two "greatest Lots" for Wilhelm II (al-Qabīsī 5.17)

Comment by Dykes. Let us calculate these "greatest" Lots in an example. This is the figure of the Aries ingress for Kaiser Wilhelm II's accession, which was on June 15, 1888. Let us assume that the triplicity shift to earth on April 3, 1802 (at 0° 20' Virgo) was a change of "religions." The conjunction period he was in, was the conjunction at 12° 14' Taurus on November 9, 1881. The values in the figure are rounded.

Lot 1:

1802 ♍ conjunction (0° 20'):	150° 20'
Time from conjunction to accession	(86y 2m)
Value in degrees:[100]	65° 00'
Sum (= first "equation"):	215° 20' (5° 20' ♏)

100 Profections returns to themselves every 12 years. The total years are 86, but because 84 is a multiple of 12, we can omit 84 years, leaving 2y 2m left. The profection proceeds 60° in 2 years to 0° 20' Scorpio, with the final two months being 5°. So the total amount we will add to the 1802 conjunction is 65°, which reaches 5° 20' Scorpio.

Eastern planet (♃) to first equation:	328° 59'
ASC of 1888 ingress (16° ♒)	316° 00'
Sum:	644° 59' (-360° = 284° 59')
Position of 1st Lot:	14° 59' ♑

Lot 2:

1881 ♉ conjunction (12° 14'):	42° 14'
Time from conjunction to accession	(6y 7m)
Value in degrees:[101]	197° 30'
Sum (= second "equation"):	239° 44' (29° 44' ♏)

Western planet (♄) to second equation:	120° 03'
ASC of 1888 ingress (16° ♒)	316° 00'
Sum:	436° 03' (-360° = 76° 03')
Position of 2nd Lot:	16° 03' ♊

---

[101] The 6 years are 180° (6 * 30°), while the 7 months are 17° 30' (7 * 2.5° = 17° 30'), for a total of 197° 30'.

SECTION I.3: AL-KINDĪ'S *FORTY CHAPTERS*

Comment by Dykes. What follows is part of my translation of al-Kindī's *Forty Chapters*, a work on astrological principles, questions, elections, and mundane analysis. For my edition of the full Latin *Forty Chapters* (2010), I relied primarily on Hugo of Santalla's Latin translation, but occasionally drew on that of his colleague, Robert of Ketton. I am grateful to Charles Burnett for the use of his private Latin edition of their translations.

This particular chapter is mainly a discussion of ingresses—or rather, because al-Kindī often follows Ptolemy when he can (see *AW1*), it is on how to analyze the New/Full Moon which precedes the ingress. The primary consideration is the Moon and the planet to which she applies just after the lunation: the angularity, dignity, and other conditions pertaining to them (al-Kindī lists five variations on this situation). There is no house or topical analysis. However, al-Kindī does make a brief mention of what seem to be mundane profections connected to Saturn-Jupiter conjunctions (§692): so he is at least gesturing at conjunctional theory.

As with so many other chapters from al-Kindī, al-Rijāl reproduces his own version (*Skilled* Ch. VIII.6), so the reader should consult that as well.

ಬಿ ಬಿ ಡ

Chapter 40: *On the revolution of the years of the world*[102]

§688 In revolutions of the years of the world, the east[103] of the conjunction or opposition (namely the one preceding the solar ingress into Aries) and the rest of the pivots must be established with the most subtle computation, and also the places of the stars. Then, one must note to what kind of star the Moon would apply after that conjunction or opposition: namely to a lucky or unlucky one, strong or weak. For, the nature of that [star] has an indication over the future things which will happen to the people.

§689-690 If therefore [1] the Moon, being in an advancing[104] [place and] obtaining some dignity there, commingled herself with a lucky [planet], strong in an advancing [place] and in one of its own dignities, a fertile year

---
[102] This chapter is only in Robert.
[103] That is, the Ascendant.
[104] That is, "angular." See my Glossary and the Introduction for this term.

and abundant sustenance will befall the people, and their happiness will follow happiness, and they will advance themselves to one good from another. That conjunction being made with Jupiter, the people will pursue faithfulness, cleanliness, and good moods in that year, and will make many offspring and will rejoice in good health. With Venus, abundance and joy will come to pass, and the people will be devoted to[105] fornication and much ornamentation, [and] will even enter into marriage.

§691 But [2] the Moon being remote, nor applying in some dignity of hers, [but] applying to a lucky one in an advancing [place] in one of its own dignities, what was said before about good fortune will [indeed] happen, except that [the people] will incur the luckiness from a calamity, and [the year] will be first weak, then strong.

But an inversion of this will happen if [3] the Moon is advancing and obtaining some dignity, [and] she applied to a lucky [but] remote star outside of [any] dignity.

But [4] each one[106] being remote and outside [any] dignity, [then] a change will happen: just as from a good status to a corresponding one before, so here [it would be] from a bad one to a corresponding one—but with the health of the body as a companion.[107]

§692 If [5] the Moon, being weak and peregrine, commingled herself with an unlucky, strong [planet] holding onto an advancing [place], [then] evil, degradation, weakness, slight sustenance, and manifold disease will happen to the people.[108] And if that unlucky one would rule the eighth from the Moon, or it would even obtain a strong power in her eighth (even though it is not its lord), frequent death will follow; and likewise even if it is not unlucky [but] if, ruling the eighth of the Moon, it regards her. Indeed, with the unlucky one being Saturn, Saturnian diseases will happen (namely melancholic) which will be the occasion of the death. But it being Mars, acute and hot diseases will follow, and at the same time a pouring out of blood, and slaughter.

[With the infortune] holding a human sign—but especially if the year applied[109] either [*a*] to that place which Mars was allotted at the beginning of

---

[105] *Militabit*.
[106] Namely, the Moon and the fortunate planet to which she applies.
[107] In other words, the year will be difficult but at least people will have good health.
[108] The other relationships with malefics, corresponding to the benefics above, are mentioned briefly in §693 below.
[109] This paragraph undoubtedly describes three different mundane profections, probably from the Ascendant of the last triplicity shift. The three places are as follows: (*a*) the place

that people, or [*b*] to the place where [the Saturn-Jupiter conjunction] changed its trigon,[110] or [*c*] to his[111] own place in the conjunction[112] which most recently preceded the revolution—that year will abound in battles and the pouring out of blood in the direction of the lands corresponding to the sign which Mars is allotted in that year and in the above-listed places, the end of which will happen in that year when Mars will incur his own burning or fall, or Jupiter [would incur] burning.

§693 Then the place of Mars must be noted, namely whether he is eastern or western, right or left. For, his direction will attain victory,[113] by the command of God.

And if Mercury were putting on[114] the nature of the corrupting Mars, mortality will fall upon the year. But with Mercury wearing the nature of Saturn in an earthy sign at the revolution of the year, an earthquake will shatter islands and seacoasts, cliffs and rocky places.

Finally, every manner between the Moon and a lucky one indicated above (namely with respect to remoteness and advancing, strength and weakness, and the rest of that kind), should be considered here between the Moon and an unlucky one, and a change of this kind should be judged according to this: from evil into something similar, or into the contrary.

---

of Mars at the ingress of the triplicity shift which indicated the people in question. (*b*) The sign of the mean Saturn-Jupiter conjunction at the triplicity shift. (*c*) The place of Mars at the ingress of the last mean Saturn-Jupiter conjunction, even if it was only one of the lesser ones every 19.8 years. In the case of the 570 AD conjunction indicating Islam, the Ascendant of the Aries ingress was widely taken to be Libra: (*a*) would be to Gemini, (*b*) to Scorpio, and (*c*) would vary.

[110] That is, "triplicity."
[111] Tentatively reading "his" (Mars) instead of the more neutral "its."
[112] *Alkiren*, a transliteration of Ar. *al-qirān*.
[113] That is, the people in or from that direction.
[114] This probably means that Mercury is closely aspecting Mars by degree. Arabic texts sometimes speak of a planet being "clothed" by another planet when their indications become mixed or conditioned through a conjunction or aspect.

SECTION I.4:
'UMAR ON MUNDANE DIRECTIONS

Comment by Dykes. The information below comes from Chapter II.3 of *Three Books on Nativities*, the Latin edition of 'Umar al-Tabarī's book on nativities, which I published in *PN2*. Caution should be used in 'Umar's approach, because as I have remarked elsewhere he mistakenly treats the direction of points in the revolution as though they are incremental profections. That is, 'Umar divides the zodiacal circle by 365 days, yielding 59' 08" of the circle per day. This might be fine if one is doing certain kinds of profections, but directions are based on ascensions—ascensional times, right ascension, oblique ascension. The signs and points in them do not all rise at the same rate, so not every degree will be worth the same amount of time. If anything, the *equatorial* circle must be measured at 59' 08" per day.[1]

☼ ☼ ☽

[Chapter II.3: How mundane directions differ from the revolutions of nativities]

The direction for knowing the condition of the king, and for knowing for how long he will be in charge of the kingdom, and for [knowing] the revolution of the year of the world or of the year of the native:

> Now, for either the direction of the king or the wealthy, you will direct for them from the degree of the Midheaven by means of the ascensions of the right circle,[2] one day for every 59' 08", until it reaches the bad ones or the fortunes.

> And for knowing the condition of the king's body, in the soundness and infirmity of it,[3] you will direct likewise from the degree of the Ascendant to the bad ones [and] the fortunes.

---

[1] Instructions for directing or distributing the Ascendant like this, in both nativities and solar revolutions, can be found at www.bendykes.com/audio/astrologylectures.php.
[2] That is, by right ascensions (not oblique ascensions, as when directing the Ascendant).
[3] Omitting *corporis*.

And [for knowing the condition] of the vulgar and the rustics, in the revolution of the world you will direct from the degree of the Ascendant to the bad ones and the fortunes, one day for every 59' 08".

And for knowing the condition of the king, you will direct from the degree of the Midheaven to the fortunes and the bad ones, [one day] for every 59' 08".

And for knowing the condition of the native's years in the revolution of the years of nativities, you will direct from the degree of the Ascendant to the fortunes and the bad ones, one day for every 59' 8".

And when the advancement[4] reached the good ones of the sign, [it signifies] soundness and prosperity and success. And when it reached the bad ones, it signifies infirmity and loss and the commixture[5] of his condition, if God wills.

ಲ ಲ ಲ

Comment by Dykes. I provide here an example picked at random, the Aries ingress for the USA in 2001. I wanted to direct the Midheaven to some aspect of Mars to investigate the "condition" or action of the leader. In this chart, the RAMC is 303.7394°, and the RA of Mars himself is 255.034° or 254.95°.[6] The clockwise arc from the body of Mars to the MC is therefore about 311.2°, which equates to about 315.8 days, or January 29-30, 2002. President Bush made his famous and saber-rattling "axis of evil" speech on January 29, specifically targeting Iraq (with consequences we are all aware of).

---

[4] Reading *profectio* for *perfectio*. In context I take this to refer to the advancement of the directed point, but it is possible that 'Umar is now making a brief statement about profections (in which case, *perfectio* translates the standard Arabic term for the "terminal point" of the profection).
[5] This probably means "confusion."
[6] The first number takes the latitude of his body into account, the second only the zodiacal degree. The difference is insignificant.

SECTION I.4: 'UMAR ON MUNDANE DIRECTIONS   73

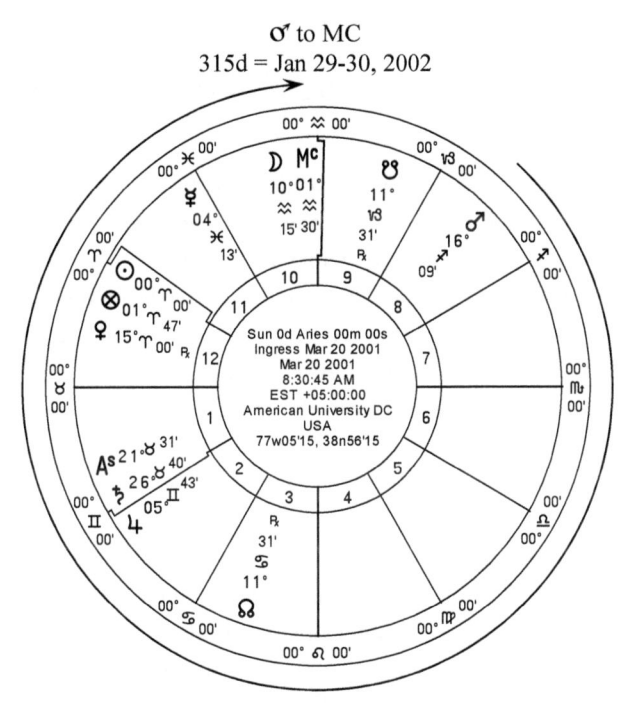

Figure 27: Direction of Mars to MC: "Axis of Evil" speech

SECTION I.5:
'UMAR-KANKAH, *THE UNIVERSAL BOOK*

Comment by Dykes. The *Universal Book* (or *Liber Universus*) is a condensed Latin work on chronology in 15 sentences, translated from an otherwise unknown Arabic work attributed to 'Umar al-Tabarī and Kankah the Indian (both 8th Century AD). If genuine, it would have been written in the late 700s AD. For my Latin source text, I relied on Pingree 1977 and the Appendix of Burnett and Yamamoto's edition of *BRD* (volume 2). However, not only is the Arabic source unknown, but even the character of the Latin translation, and its title, is a bit misunderstood. Let us first look at this.

In some of the manuscripts of 'Umar's Latin *Book of Nativities* (later, *Three Books on Nativities*),[1] is a short work translated by John of Seville[2] between 1125-1140 AD and attributed to 'Umar: the *Liber Universus* (*The Universal Book, The Whole Book*).[3] Or at least, this is its assumed title and attribution. For as Burnett and Yamamoto point out,[4] in the Latin manuscripts 'Umar's *Book on Nativities* first ended with a short *explicit*, followed by some other passages (including, apparently, this work), and then finally ended with a full *explicit* naming John of Spain as the translator and saying that "the whole [*universus*] book" of 'Umar's had been completed. Thus, over time the description "whole book" (referring to the entire set of works) became the title of only this short piece (and perhaps others at the end): *The Universal Book*. This confusion must have been supported by the fact that the Latin *universus/universum* can mean both "whole, universal" and "world, universe," and mundane astrology is precisely the topic of this work. Burnett and Yamamoto simply call it by its *incipit*, which explicitly attributes it to Kankah the Indian (*Dixit Kankaf Indus*, "Kankah the Indian said"). I will call it *The Universal Book* rather than by its *incipit*, until perhaps we can discover what Kankah himself called it, or what work of his it is from.[5]

---

[1] I have translated this from the Latin version for my *PN2* (Arabic edition forthcoming).
[2] Or John of Spain, according to the *explicit*.
[3] Some later works even quote *The Universal Book* within the *Three Books on Nativities* (Pingree 1977, p. 9).
[4] In *BRD* vol. 2, p. 342.
[5] Pingree (1977, p. 9) says that he was wrong to attribute *The Universal Book* to Kankah, because it also appears appended to a Latin translation of certain tables by al-Jayyānī (who lived in the 11th Century), and al-Jayyānī could not have included a later Latin work into his own Arabic. This explanation makes no sense to me, since the Latin translations post-

As Burnett and Yamamoto point out, the doctrines and terminology of *The Universal Book* are very close to Abū Ma'shar's *BRD*, but with some slight fictions and misleading references. The whole point of the piece is to determine what time lords are in effect at the time of the conjunction of Islam (570 AD) and in the author's own era. The text uses the mighty *fardārs* (which pair a sign and planet together), and the mundane direction of the Ascendant: both a single *fardār* and a complete cycle of the Ascendant around the zodiac take 360 "solar" or Persian sidereal years of 365.259 days. The chronology begins virtually at Māshā'allāh's "indicator" conjunction, the Saturn-Jupiter conjunction of 3381 BC which foreshadowed his own Flood (in 3361 BC). In this year Kankah begins the *fardārs* with Cancer-Saturn (64 *fardārs* into the series), and the mundane Ascendant at 0° Aries.

There are three misleading references in the text:

- The epoch year (3381 BC) matches Māshā'allāh's Flood chronology, but Kankah takes pains to count the 279 years from it to Abū Ma'shar's Flood-Kaliyuga in 3102 BC (**1-2**, also **11**). This is misleading because the latter plays no role in the changing of these time lords (nor does Kankah even mention what the time lords are during it). So apart from indicating it for a curious reader, all references to the Flood-Kaliyuga or periods of 279 years are a distraction.
- Likewise, Kankah wants to let his contemporaries know where the upcoming changes fit into a common calendrical system of his day, the Yazdijird calendar (**8, 11**). This does not help a modern reader, but it must be understood in order to appreciate certain calculations made by astrologers of the time.
- Finally, although Kankah calculates the interval between the earlier dates (3381 BC, 3102 BC) and the mean Saturn-Jupiter conjunction of December 570 AD, he then omits three months between that conjunction and the Aries ingress of 571 (**8**). This was typical of astrologers writing chronologies of the Islamic era, who should have used the 570 ingress but used 571 instead. This rather vitiates his careful calculation, down to the hour, of the period between the ingress and Yazdijird's enthronement, because those three months are left out of the entire period from the Flood dates.

---

date both al-Jayyānī and Kankah. Burnett and Yamamoto (*ibid.*, p. 342, n. 4) charitably ignore it.

Since this piece is rather tricky in its calculations, and cramped in its exposition, the following is a summary as divided into sentences:

1: Kankah begins with an epoch date of February 11, 3381 BC (= JD 486553.5),[6] when the Cancer-Saturn Turn or mighty *fardār* begins, and his mundane Ascendant is at 0° Aries. He points out that this date is 279 years[7] before the Flood-Kaliyuga on February 18, 3102 BC (JD 588465.5).

2-7: Kankah introduces some confusing mathematical instructions. His only point is that, since we have a beginning or epoch date (in 3381 BC, see above), we can know what the mighty *fardār* is for any other date. For example, suppose we take the number of years since the epoch date, and divide that by 360, since each *fardār* is 360 years long (**2**). If we get no remainder, that is, if the number of years is a multiple of 360, then a *fardār* has just ended and a new one is beginning; but if there is a remainder, it means that we are partway through the current *fardār* (**3**). Obviously there will be one new *fardār* every 360 years, which will advance through the pairings of signs and planets (**4-6**). And since the mundane distribution goes around the zodiac every 360 years, the mundane Ascendant will either have returned to 0° Aries (if there is no remainder) or will be somewhere else in the zodiac (if there is a remainder), one degree for every year (**7**).

For example, suppose 521 solar/sidereal years have passed since the epoch date. Since each *fardār* lasts for 360 years, this means the first *fardār* (Cancer-Saturn) has expired and we are 161 years into the next one, Leo-Jupiter (521 − 360 = 161). Likewise, since the mundane distribution takes 360 years, one full cycle has expired and we are 161° into the next one, which equates to 11° Virgo.

8: Kankah wants to know what the *fardār* and distribution is for his own era, and so he begins by identifying a recent event, the Saturn-Jupiter triplicity shift into water (i.e., Scorpio). The mean conjunction in Scorpio occurred in December, 570 AD, which is 3,671 years after the Flood-Kaliyuga in 3102 BC (**8**). Put differently, 570 AD is 3,950 years after the epoch date itself in 3381 BC: dividing 3,950 by 360 gives us 10.972, which means that at the time of the Scorpio conjunction, almost 11 *fardārs* have elapsed. So we know that

---

[6] This was virtually Māshā'allāh's indicator conjunction (the Saturn-Jupiter conjunction which *foreshadowed* his own Flood), which occurred according to Māshā'allāh on September 23, 3381 BC (JD 486778.6994)—Pingree calculated this as September 25 (Pingree 1968, p. 41). For Māshā'allāh, see my Introduction and my comment to *Conjunctions* (Section II.4 below).

[7] Or rather, 279 years and about 4 days.

the Scorpio conjunction occurred near the end of the 11th *fardār*, Taurus-Sun, and is about to change into the next one, Gemini-Venus, about 10 years later.

Kankah now takes a detour by speaking of the period between the mean conjunction and the beginning of the reign of Yazdijird III (the last Sassanian king, overthrown by the Muslims), and in so doing employs a little fiction. For the mean conjunction was in December 570, but Islamic astrologers always used the 571 AD Aries ingress for their chart. So Kankah skips ahead by three months to the ingress on March 19, 571, or JD 1929692.5 (**8**). Now, Yazdijird came to the throne on June 16, 632 AD (= JD 1952062.5), which was 22,370 days after the 571 ingress. For calendrical purposes Kankah treats each calendar year as having 365 days, and each month as having 30 days: so, 22,370 days equals 61 years, 3 months, 15 days, and some odd hours (**8**).[8] It is important to note that the only reason to bring up Yazdijird was that many ancient peoples numbered their calendars according to the number of years in a particular king's reign. Otherwise, we get no useful information from it.

9-10: Now that Kankah has reminded us where the mean conjunction (or its associated Aries ingress) is relative to Yazdijird III, he returns to his chronology. Again, there were 3,950 years between the epoch date in 3381 BC and the conjunction of 570. Both the mighty *fardār* and a complete direction of the mundane Ascendant last 360 years, which mean we have completed 10.972 *fardārs* and complete cycles around the zodiac (3,950 / 360 = 10.972). For the direction of the Ascendant, this remainder of .972 equals 350° or 20° Pisces, so in the year of the mean conjunction in 570 AD, the mundane Ascendant was at 20° Pisces (**9**). Likewise, there have been 10.972 mighty *fardārs*: 10 *fardārs* have elapsed and we are 350 years into the eleventh (Taurus-Sun). Therefore the *fardār* will change to Gemini-Venus in 10 years or 580 AD (**10**), which is the *fardār* in which Kankah is writing. In that year the Ascendant will have returned to 0° Aries.

11-14: Now it is easy to see when the *fardār* and distribution will change again: namely, 360 years later or the Aries ingress of 940 AD. This is 4,041 years after the Flood-Kaliyuga (**11**), which is an unhelpful bit of information: why not just omit the Flood-Kaliyuga and advance in multiples of 360 from the epoch date in 3381 BC, in which case the Aries ingress of 940 AD is 4,320 years or 12 cycles after it? At any rate, the change to Cancer-Mercury

---

[8] According to Pingree the extra hours have to do with measuring the actual hour of Yazdijird's enthronement.

will happen at or around March 21, 940 AD, or JD 2064472.5 (remember that Kankah skipped 3 months and is now measuring the years between Aries ingresses), and the mundane Ascendant at 0° Aries will be in the bound of Jupiter (**14**). Kankah expresses this date in several calendars (**11**), and an interpolator refers to a later set of tables by al-Khwārizmī (**12-13**).[9]

Based on this sidereal time-lord system, the year 2014 is 5,394 years after the epoch year of 3381 BC, so 14.983 cycles have passed since the beginning of Cancer-Saturn. This means we are currently in the *fardār* of Virgo-Saturn and the mundane Ascendant is at 24° Pisces. In 2020 AD we will change to the Libra-Jupiter *fardār*, with a 0° Aries Ascendant. But as I pointed out in my Introduction, this is all based on a presumed Flood in about 3361 BC, using incorrect sidereal parameters.

ಏ ಏ ಔ

1 Kankah the Indian said that the beginning of the Turn[10] was 279 years before the Thursday which was the beginning of the years of the Flood,[11] and Saturn and the sign of Cancer were in charge of that Turn; and that at the beginning of that same Turn, the distribution and direction[12] arrived at the first degree of the sign of Aries.

2 If therefore you wanted to know when that same Turn will be completed, take the years of the Flood, and add 279 years on top of them, and project what was collected [by] 360 years (that is, divide by 360 years).[13] **3** If the number were at an end, the Turn is already completed; and if something remained, the years [which are] passing by will be from the Turn which is not at an end. **4** And when you project the 360 [years], know how many times

---

[9] Pingree notes that because the text claims that the tables of al-Khwārizmī was used, these sentences could not have been written by ʿUmar or Kankah (p. 10).

[10] In the Latin, *orbis*; but as Burnett and Yamamoto point out (*ibid.*, p. 343, n.6), *orbis* is the same word used in *BRD* to translate *dawr*. I will follow Arabic usage here for the sake of clarity. Pingree 1977 (p. 11, n. 2) believes that *orbis* here translates *fardār*, since we're talking about the *fardār*s.

[11] The Flood-Kaliyuga was midnight on the night of Thursday (or the morning of Friday), February 18, 3102 BC (JD 588465.5). So, the earlier epoch date is in 3381 BC.

[12] Pingree (1977, p. 11, n. 4) believes this latter is a mundane profection; but Burnett and Yamamoto (*ibid.*, p. 343 n. 11) believe it is a primary direction. I am inclined to think that Pingree is correct, because mundane distributions are precisely primary directions already.

[13] See my *Comment*. This odd phrasing seems to be because the author wants to both (a) determine by division how many years have already passed at the time of writing, and (b) continue to project in periods of 360 from whatever starting point we have already found.

SECTION I.5: 'UMAR-KANKAH, THE UNIVERSAL BOOK

you have projected this number, and project one sign for every time. **5** And begin from Cancer, and where the numbering was finished, that sign will be a lord of the Turn. **6** And if you projected a planet for every time (and you began from Saturn), the planet at which the advancement arrived will be a lord of the Turn. **7** And if you took the years of the Flood, and on top of them you added 279 years, and you projected those Turns (that is, you divided them by 360 years), and a number remained to you, project that number from the beginning of Aries, a year for every degree: where the number reached in terms of degrees, it is that degree to which the direction and distribution has come.

8 And know that 3,671 solar years were completed [from] the Flood until the conjunction was changed from the airy signs to the watery signs (and this was in Scorpio),[14] and this[15] was 61 years and 3 months and 15 days and 12 1/3 hours before Yazdijird, the king of the Persians. **9** And the direction and distribution in this year [of the mean conjunction] arrived at the twentieth degree of Pisces. **10** And 10 solar years after this change [of triplicities] (that is, 3,681 years [after] the Flood), 11 cycles were already completed from the cycle which was 279 years before the Flood: and this is the revolution of the year of the Blessed One,[16] of the year (that is, the cycle) in which we are.[17]

11 And it was this[18] at the completion of 12 cycles: from the cycle which was before the cycle of the Flood by 279 years, namely at the completion of the solar year 4,041 of the Flood,[19] and there were on top [of that] 2 hours and 5/6, and 1/5 of 1/6 of an hour, at the city of 'Ūjjaīn,[20] on the Saturday which was the ninth day of Jumādā II[21] (namely the sixth lunar month), in

---

[14] There is a little fudging in this sentence. The conjunction in Scorpio was December 12, 570 AD; subtracting 3,671 yields 3102 BC, the year of the Flood. But the calculation in the rest of the sentence is taken from the *571* Aries ingress.
[15] The 571 AD ingress.
[16] The Islamic Prophet Muhammad, whose name means "the praised/praiseworthy one."
[17] The author is telling us that the triplicity shift heralding Islam (570 AD) occurred only ten years before a new mighty *fardar* (i.e., to Gemini-Venus). The triplicity change of 570 AD, plus 10 years, is 580 AD, which is 3,681 years after the Flood-Kaliyuga. From the epoch date (3381 BC) to 580 AD is 3,960 years. Again, at a rate of 1°/year in the zodiac from 0° Aries, 3960° is exactly 11 cycles around the zodiac.
[18] The text is referring to a chart which does not appear (see diagrams below).
[19] That is, 12 mighty *fardārs* is 4,320 years total. Projected from the epoch date (3381 BC) is 940 AD, which is 4,041 years from the Flood (3102 BC).
[20] Lat. *Arim* or *Arin* (Pingree 1977, p. 12 n. 14). 'Ūjjaīn (a city in India at 23° 10' N, 75° 46' E) was a standard place from which to cast mundane charts: see Pingree 1968, p. 45. But in Pingree 1977, he says that this chart is really cast for Baghdad.
[21] Following Pingree instead of "Last Jumādā" (Lat. *ultimi Gumedi*).

the year 328 of the Arabs, which is the 21st day of the month of March in the year 1,251 of Alexander the Great, and it is the day <27>[22] of Isfandārmudh (which is the twelfth month of the Persians), in the year 308 of King Yazdijird. **12** And the Ascendant and the planets were equated by the *Zīj* (that is, by a book of courses) of al-Khwārizmī, a master of the Indians, at the center of the world, as we said.[23] **13** And for the city of Cordoba they are 10 and 2/3 hours of the night of the aforewritten Saturday.[24] **14** The lord of the Turn from the signs [is] Cancer, the lord of the planets Mercury, the degree to which the direction has arrived is the first degree of Aries, and the distributor Jupiter.

15 The whole book of ʿUmar ibn al-Farrukhān al-Ṭabarī is completed (with praise to God and for His aid), which Master John of Spain, and at Limia, translated from Arabic into Latin.

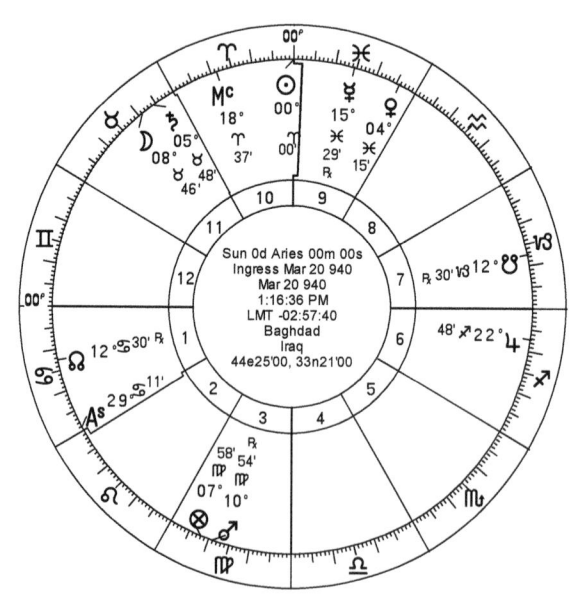

Figure 28: Cancer-Mercury *Fardār*, Aries ingress 940 AD (tropical)[25]

---

[22] Adding with Pingree.
[23] Again, at 'Ujjaīn.
[24] This would be 10:40 PM on Friday, March 20, 940 AD (Pingree 1977, p. 10).
[25] The astronomical commentator in **11-13** has apparently calculated the ingress in the tropical zodiac using medieval tables; the chart here is calculated in modern software.

SECTION I.5: 'UMAR-KANKAH, THE UNIVERSAL BOOK

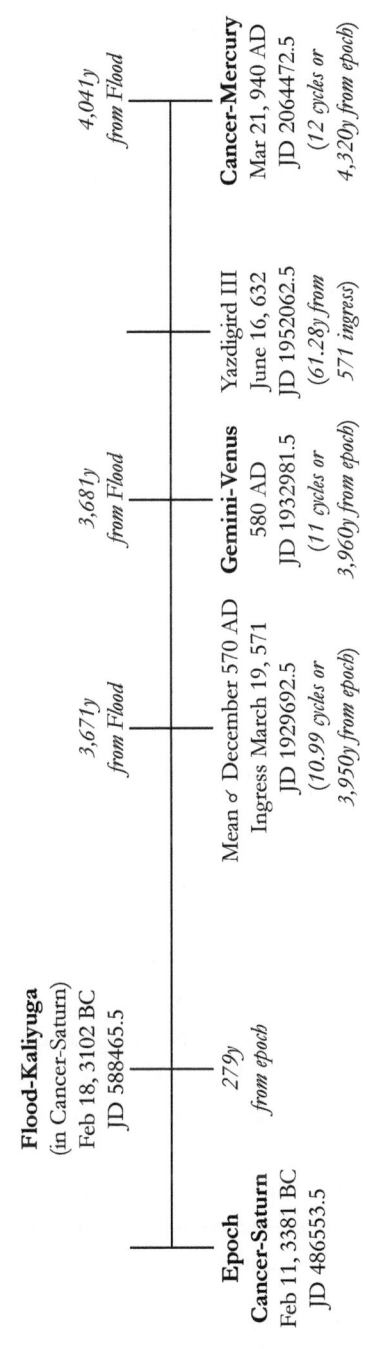

Epoch Cancer-Saturn
Feb 11, 3381 BC
JD 486553.5

279y from epoch

Flood-Kaliyuga (in Cancer-Saturn)
Feb 18, 3102 BC
JD 588465.5

3,671y from Flood

Mean ♂ December 570 AD Ingress March 19, 571
JD 1929692.5
(10.99 cycles or 3,950y from epoch)

3,681y from Flood

Gemini-Venus
580 AD
JD 1932981.5
(11 cycles or 3,960y from epoch)

Yazdigird III
June 16, 632
JD 1952062.5
(61.28y from 571 ingress)

4,041y from Flood

Cancer-Mercury
Mar 21, 940 AD
JD 2064472.5
(12 cycles or 4,320y from epoch)

Figure 29: 'Umar-Kankah: Epoch, Flood, Mighty *Fardārs*

SECTION I.6: AL-QABĪSĪ (*ATTR.*), *ON CONJUNCTIONS IN THE SIGNS*

Comment by Dykes. In Section II.11 of *AW1*, I translated paragraphs **1-3** of a Latin text attributed to al-Qabīsī: *On the Conjunctions of the Planets in the Twelve Signs*, edited by Burnett in Appendix III of his edition of al-Qabīsī's *Introduction to Astrology* (2004). I present the remaining paragraphs (**4-17**) here, which are on planetary combinations in the signs at the Aries ingress.

Burnett notes (p. 375) that this text probably derives from a Western source, since references throughout the piece appear to treat Arabs as enemies (**4**) and point to other Western titles and references (**4-5, 11**). But it could only have been augmented by (not created by) a Western source, since virtually all of the basic combinations and interpretations may be seen in *Skilled* VIII.5 (in Section IV.2 of this book), attributed to Hermes. Here, I have followed Burnett by numbering only the paragraphs.

ಠ ಠ ಠ

¶4 On the signification of the conjunction of the planets in Aries. If however you made a figure, and you saw Saturn and Jupiter being conjoined together in Aries, or appearing near [it],[1] they will signify a new, future sect. But if Jupiter, Venus, Mercury, the Sun, and the Moon (or at least three) were in that same [sign], there will be fertility, and men will be good, much rain and hail, writers will make profit, beasts will be had for a cheap price, and fresh waters will have an increase. But if Jupiter and the Moon were in one and the same degree of that same sign in the east, then it will be signified that the king will do justice and [make] the right judgment, and his mastery will be good. But if Saturn and Mars, or Mars and Jupiter, or Mars and Mercury, or Mars and Venus, were in that same place in the east, war will happen,[2] and much blood of Arabs will be shed in the temples, and they will be overthrown, and their soldiers captured and dragged away.

¶5 On the signification of the conjunction of the planets in Taurus. If Venus and Mars were conjoined in one degree of Taurus, women will initiate

---

[1] *Prope.* This probably means, "near the *beginning*" of Aries, perhaps so that they could be conjoined in the last degree or so of Pisces as well.
[2] Or perhaps, "if [they] were in that same place, war will happen *in the east*."

seditions against [their] men, demanding illicit sex from them, and animals will die. When however Mars was in Taurus, war will come to be towards the south, and great winds, so that the fruits of trees will fall to the ground and the majority of them will perish and be dried out. If however Mars and Jupiter, Venus and the Moon, or three of them, were in that same place, men will be extreme liars[3] and the greatest uproar will even happen between them; those who are more beautiful will even die in that year, because Jupiter and Venus signify the beautiful, but Mars will kill [if] joined with them in the same degree or remaining steady[4] in [that] sign. Much rain will happen and the water of the sea and springs will be abundant. Men will go out from the southern side, desiring to kill their own lord, nor will they be able to achieve it. But if Saturn, Jupiter, and Mars were in the same degree of Taurus, then emperors and kings will lose their empires and kingdoms, or they will die thoroughly terrified by excessive fear, and monks and canons will desert the habit[5] of the religion or will die. But if Saturn and Mars stood[6] there, women will become infirm in the breasts and throat or groin, and men in the testicles and bladder.

¶6 On the signification of the conjunction of the planets in Gemini. If the Sun and Mercury, Venus and the Moon, were together in Gemini, writers will profit little, and slaves will disdain obeying [their] masters, there will be much grain in the land, and the roads will be made troublesome by robbers. But if Mars and Saturn, or Mars and Jupiter, were there, there will be a war in the land of Armenia: for enemies will rush in upon them, and Moabites initiating war will kill their own elders, and they will go to the mountainous areas, trusting in the divinations of seers,[7] and a great wind will rush in from the direction of the east.

¶7 On the signification of the conjunction of the planets in Cancer. If Saturn, Jupiter, Mars, the Sun, and the Moon were in Cancer, panic and fear will surround the peoples, which will stir up outrages, and some men will harass others with annoyances, and even then signs will be seen in the sky (like comets and torches flying in the air), there will be an earthquake, not

---

[3] Or, "most/extremely false" (*mendacissimi*).
[4] This probably means "stationing."
[5] *Habitus*, which refers broadly to the entire style, manner, and custom in something.
[6] *Steterint*. Normally this is used to indicate a planetary station, but here the Latin writer may mean that they "are" there.
[7] *Vates*. This can also mean "bards," which is how Burnett and Yamamoto take it.

much water, fruits will be laid waste, sailors will be endangered on the sea, and cities and forts and country homes built on the shore of the sea will be disturbed by a horrible fear, and the north wind will be very harmful in that year.

¶8 On the signification of the conjunction of the planets in Leo. If Saturn, Jupiter, Mars, and the Moon were in Leo, the eastern people will make war amongst themselves, and men will be vexed by pains of the belly and stomach and intestines. But if Jupiter, Mars, and the Sun were there, merchants will fear lest [their] masters would do them injustice, wind will rush in coming from the east, and the Arabs will have fear.

¶9 On the signification of the conjunction of the planets in Virgo. If Saturn and Mars and Mercury were conjoined in Virgo, virtually all seed of the earth will perish, being laid waste by locusts. But if Saturn and the Sun were obscured there,[8] and the Tail and Mars were there, then war and sedition will arise between the poor and the rich in the land of the Nubians and in the south. But if Saturn and Jupiter were there, then there will be much rain, and wind will come from the south, virtually all things (and more so the grain and wine) will be expensive.

¶10 On the signification of the conjunction of the planets in Libra. If Mars and Jupiter were in Libra, the sky will be red, which is a sign of the infirmity of men and the shedding of blood. But if the Sun and Jupiter and the Moon were there, women will die and there will be much rain. If however Mars and Saturn were there, there will be war and robbers will besiege the roads.

¶11 On the signification of the conjunction of the planets in Scorpio. If Saturn and Mars and Venus were joined in Scorpio, they will signify that the king will be killed by poison, and some of the lords will detract from others and will bear bad will towards each other. And if the Moon were with any of these, so much rain will come to be that the world will seem to be virtually overwhelmed by the rains of Deucalion. If Jupiter and Saturn were in any degree of this sign, understand generally through all of these things that false prophets are going to come, sowing a new sect.

¶12 On the signification of the conjunction of the planets in Sagittarius. If Mars and Jupiter were in Sagittarius, war will come to be next to the sea. But

---

[8] *Obscurati.* Meaning unclear: probably Saturn would be obscured by the Sun's rays, but why would the Sun be obscured? One possibility is that there is a solar eclipse, since the next clause assumes that the Tail is there.

if Saturn, Jupiter, and Mercury, and the Moon were there, the world will virtually perish through flooding, and the rivers and seas will receive an increase on account of the inundations of waters, and scribes, medical doctors, astrologers, and priests will be multiplied in the world and will be honored by the people. But if Saturn and Mars were there, robbers will plunder the rustics and country estates, and pirates will harass ships on the sea. But if Mars and Venus were there, prostitutes will snatch away boys and girls, leading them away into captivity.

¶13 On the signification of the conjunction of the planets in Capricorn. If the Sun, Mars, and Mercury were in Capricorn, many lords will die and then there will be much infirmity and men will burn harvests and homes, and there will be excessive wind, little grain will be recovered, [and] thieves will possess both the sea and land. Which if Saturn and Mars were there, there will not be so much evil, war will be minimal, and the race of men will fear God.

¶14 On the signification of the conjunction of the planets in Aquarius. If Saturn and Mars and the Moon were in Aquarius, little rain will come to be, all things will be dried, but the waters of springs will be sufficiently abundant, and the roads will be harassed by robbers, the sky will be disturbed by clouds (however it will not give rain), [and] then a man will be born about whom there will be great joy among the people, to whom many clans will be subjected, every monastery will be affluent, and there will be many monks, and men will be fearing God.

¶15 On the signification of the conjunction of the planets in Pisces. If Jupiter were in Pisces, there will be much religion in men.

¶16 Therefore, whatever true judgment you wanted to give concerning any year (what there would be in it), you should examine the conjunctions, complexions, and significations of the planets subtlely, both through these things which have been written, and through the skill of your mind (likewise, with the natures of the signs in which the planets were having been inspected), and you would be able to make certain judgments about things to come, if God wills.

¶17 Al-Qabīsī on the significations of the conjunction of the planets in each of the signs in the revolutions of the years of the world, translated by John of Spain, ends.

PART II:
MĀSHĀ'ALLĀH & HIS DERIVATIVES

SECTION II.1:
MĀSHĀ'ALLĀH'S HISTORICAL ASTROLOGY

This Part contains three works by Māshā'allāh (Sections II.2-4), followed by two others known only in Latin, which derive directly from them. The fourth work is *Scito horam introitus* (Section II.5), attributed to Abū Ma'shar, and the fifth is *Liber experimentorum* (Section II.6), comprised of almost verbatim excerpts from *Latin* translations, but which has traces of a Jewish editor. The three works of Māshā'allāh are as follows:

(1) On the Revolutions of the Years of the World (RYW), in Section II.2. This work in 46 shortish chapters describes in detail how to interpret Aries ingress charts, and focuses especially on how to select two key planets: the lord of the year and the indicator or significator of the king. It is notable that *RYW* presents a straightforward method without concrete examples, while his extensive work on conjunctions (see [2] below) provides numerous examples which do not conform to any simple method. It is likely that the instructions in *RYW* are meant primarily as a set of guidelines following typical astrological principles, rather than laws set in stone. This work was relied on by Abū Ma'shar in his own works, as I point out in my *Comment*.

(2) Letter on Eclipses (Letter), in Section II.3. The title of this short work in 12 chapters is rather misleading, as it has very little to do with eclipses. The title in one of the Latin sources is *On the Roots of Revolutions*, which is more appropriate. After a short series of chapters on general principles concerning weather, ingresses, and eclipses, it concludes with a general theory of planetary conjunctions, focusing on the three superior planets. Of these conjunctions, a conjunction of all three is the "greatest," that of Saturn-Jupiter the "greater," that of Saturn-Mars is the "middle," and that of Jupiter-Mars is the "lesser." This vocabulary stands apart from the usual designations, which call the return of the Saturn-Jupiter conjunction to Aries the greater conjunction, the triplicity shifts the middle, and the 20-year conjunctions within them the lesser.

(3) The Book of Conjunctions (Conjunctions), in Section II.4, which may be the same as a *Book of Conjunctions, Religions, and Peoples*. This work is especially valuable as it presents both Māshā'allāh's own example charts and evidence of the kind of planetary parameters and historical theory Māshā'allāh actually operated with. In this, Māshā'allāh departs a great deal from Abū Ma'shar's Persian theory of conjunctions and the Flood.

Conjunctions requires the most exegesis and analysis, and I will devote the rest of these introductory comments to it.

Māshā'allāh's Thousands & Flood Date

First, let us recall from the Introduction how Māshā'allāh differs from Abū Ma'shar. Abū Ma'shar's Persian doctrine claims that the planets are conjoined every 180,000 years, so twice in a world-year of 360,000 years.[1] The most recent conjunction, which was approximate and not exact, was supposed to be his own Flood-Kaliyuga, on February 18, 3102 BC.

By contrast, Māshā'allāh nests his Saturn-Jupiter conjunctions into a Zoroastrian "millennial" theory, or theory of Thousands, in which the world as a whole is governed by each planet for 1,000 sidereal years, up to a maximal cosmic period of 12,000 years. Māshā'allāh's conjunction #0 begins in 7° Taurus on November 2, 5783 BC (JD -390512.2221),[2] a few years after the middle of the Mars Thousand, which itself began in 6292 BC (see below).

In this series, the Flood itself was *indicated* by the triplicity shift to Scorpio in 3381 BC (#121), but the Flood itself took place during the very year of the following Cancer conjunction, which took place on July 30 or 31, 3361 BC (#122). According to Kennedy and Pingree 1971 (hereafter, KP), this was the day of the Flood (although Māshā'allāh does not expressly say so, hinting only that it was around that date).[3]

So Māshā'allāh's conjunctions (1) begin at an asymmetrical point within the Thousands, his Flood (2) does not happen during a shift but is "indicated" by a preceding one, and (3) the date corresponds only with a Saturn-Jupiter conjunction, not one of all the planets. There are 279 years between his indicator conjunction (#121) and Abū Ma'shar's Flood, and 259 between

---

[1] Again, these are all in his "Persian" sidereal years of 365.259 or 365.2590278 days.
[2] Kennedy and Pingree date this to November 3.
[3] See *Conjunctions* Ch. 3, **3**.

his Flood conjunction and Abū Ma'shar's. But the two schemes *have nothing to do with one another.*

In order to understand Māshā'allāh's Thousands, and how he may well have altered the original scheme, let us look at the diagram below.

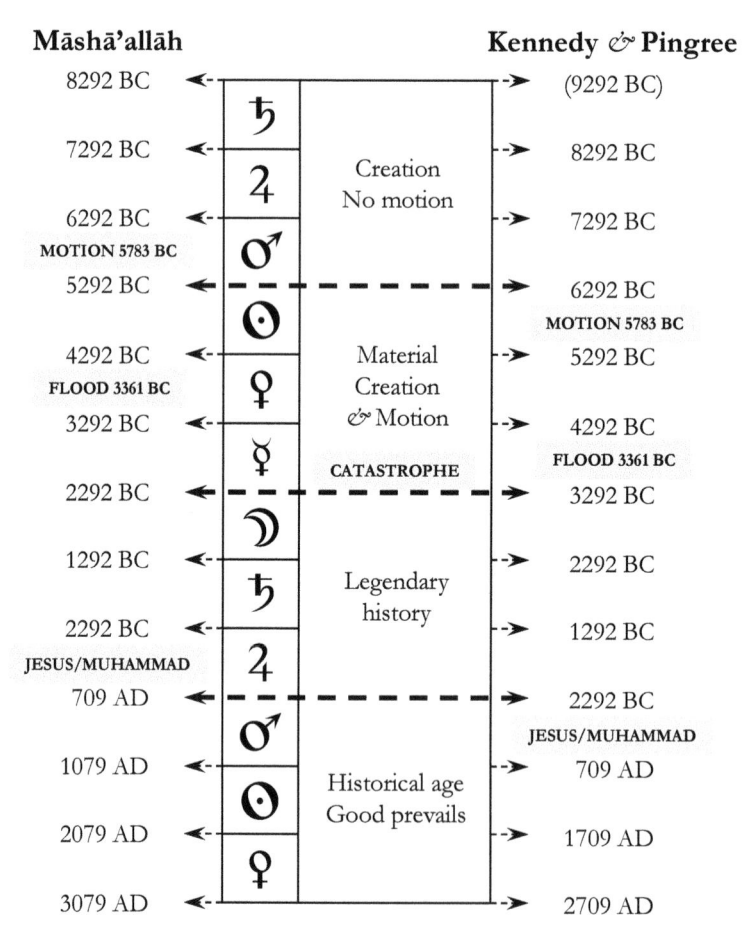

Māshā'allāh		Kennedy & Pingree
8292 BC	♄	(9292 BC)
7292 BC	♃ Creation	8292 BC
6292 BC	No motion	7292 BC
MOTION 5783 BC	♂	
5292 BC	- - - - - -	6292 BC
	☉	MOTION 5783 BC
4292 BC	Material	5292 BC
FLOOD 3361 BC	♀ Creation	
3292 BC	& Motion	4292 BC
	☿	FLOOD 3361 BC
2292 BC	CATASTROPHE	3292 BC
1292 BC	☽	2292 BC
	♄ Legendary history	
2292 BC		1292 BC
JESUS/MUHAMMAD	♃	
709 AD	- - - - - -	2292 BC
	♂	JESUS/MUHAMMAD
1079 AD	Historical age	709 AD
	☉ Good prevails	
2079 AD		1709 AD
	♀	
3079 AD		2709 AD

Figure 30: Māshā'allāh's Zoroastrian Thousands

According to Zoroastrian theory, the world lasts for 12,000 years, grouped into four ages of 3,000 years apiece. Astrologically, we can assign (as Māshā'allāh does) the first Thousand to Saturn, the next to Jupiter, and so on. The first age is one of creation, but it is non-material and without motion in the heavens. The second age is material creation, and near its end is a catastrophe. The third comprises legendary history, an age of myth and heroes.

The last age involves regular history and the appearance of several Saviors, with the last one ushering in a state of goodness at the end.

Now, on the left is Māshā'allāh's own chronology. The world begins with the Saturn Thousand in 8292 BC, and Māshā'allāh identifies the "beginning of the motion" of the heavens (mentioned several times in *Conjunctions*) with conjunction #0, just after the middle of the Mars Thousand. This puts his Flood (3361 BC) in the Venus Thousand, and Jesus and Muhammad in the Jupiter Thousand, the last part of the third age. According to this scheme, we are in the Sun Thousand now.

However, it is easy to see that there is something wrong here. First of all, material creation is not supposed to begin until the second age, but Māshā'allāh has put it in the first. Second, while Jesus and Muhammad might be associated with Jupiter because they are religious figures, historical prophets are not supposed to start appearing until the fourth age, and Māshā'allāh has put them in the third. For this reason, KP suggest that we shift the Thousands down by one notch: then (1) the world and the Saturn Thousand will begin in 9292 BC, (2) the beginning of motion actually falls into the second age, (3) the Flood is now a catastrophe occurring at the end of the second age, and (4) Jesus and Muhammad appear at the beginning of the last age, that of Prophets and recorded history. In this way, Zoroastrian theory and Māshā'allāh's chronology match up well.

Nevertheless, this does not explain certain puzzling features of the series, namely the astrological features. The oddest one, perhaps, is that Māshā'allāh does not even begin his motion (conjunction #0) with a triplicity shift, and not even symmetrically within the Mars Thousand. The middle of the Mars Thousand was August 9, 5792 BC (JD -393883.5534), but conjunction #0 was 9 years, 2 months, and 23 days (or 3371.33125 days) later, on November 2, 5783 BC (JD -390512.2221). Moreover, #0 is assigned to 7° 42' Taurus, not even a triplicity shift. And why Taurus? Why in the Mars Thousand? KP suggest that the use of Taurus was due to "the role played by the sacrifice of the Primordial Bull in the creation of the material world" (p. 90), but this does not explain why #0 is not at a triplicity shift. And as for the Mars Thousand, KP suggest that perhaps Māshā'allāh or someone else wanted to associate the evil influence of Ahriman (the principle of darkness and evil), who initiated hostilities against Ahura Mazda (the principle of light and good), with Mars, immediately before or around the beginning of material creation. But this could easily be done by putting the attacks first, in the Mars Thousand, while still beginning motion in the Sun Thousand.

Finally, what is even the *astrological* significance of the Flood being in the Venus Thousand (Māshā'allāh) or Mercury Thousand (KP)? Again, in ibn Hibintā's long excerpt there is no analysis of this. I do note however that, based on Māshā'allāh's parameters, the beginning of the Jupiter Thousand took place only 8 months after a triplicity shift into Pisces[4]—given that Jupiter rules Pisces, this may be significant. But it seems like a large price to pay to put the entire Zoroastrian scheme off by 1,000 years, or avoid associating a triplicity shift with something like the beginning of motion.

Anyhow, Māshā'allāh's Thousands are as follows, and as one may see from the table we are currently living in Māshā'allāh's Sun Thousand—but if KP are right, then we are in the Venus Thousand, only 7 centuries from the Zoroastrian End Times!

Thousand	Begins on JD:	Date:
♄	-1307031.1229	7/18/8292 BC
♃	-941772.0951	7/27/7292 BC
♂	-576513.0673	8/5/6292 BC
☉	-211254.0395	8/14/5292 BC
♀	154004.9883	8/23/4292 BC
☿	519264.0161	9/1/3292 BC
☽	884523.0439	9/10/2292 BC
♄	1249782.0717	9/19/1292 BC
♃	1615041.0995	9/28/292 BC
♂	1980300.1273	10/7/709 AD
☉	2345559.1551	10/27/1709 AD
♀	2710818.1829	11/13/2709 AD

Figure 31: Table of Māshā'allāh's Thousands

Māshā'allāh's parameters

Now let us consider the parameters used by Māshā'allāh in calculating his year and the mean annual motions of Saturn and Jupiter, which generate the length of their conjunction period and its placements.

---

[4] This would be conjunction #-76, on March 18, 7291 BC (JD -941537.9248240).

Like Abū Ma'shar, Māshā'allāh used a sidereal zodiac and sidereal year. If we assume that the tropical and sidereal zodiacs diverged in about 150 AD, then by 800 AD (approximately at the time Māshā'allāh was writing), the original sidereal positions would have diverged about 9° from the tropical ones. But since Māshā'allāh was using the *Zij al-Shāh* in the version of Kisrā Anūshirwān (r. 531-579 AD),[5] the divergence from tropical values after those 400 years (up to 550 AD) would only have been about 5°. This is indeed what we find in Māshā'allāh's *Book on Reception*, where Māshā'allāh's planetary positions are earlier than the tropical ones by an average of about 5° throughout.[6]

Next, we must understand that Māshā'allāh's calculations are only as good as his tables (apart from a number of mistakes he himself makes). Following are his basic parameters:

- Length of (sidereal) year: 365.2590278 days.
- Sidereal period of Jupiter: 11.86194263 sidereal years.
- Sidereal period of Saturn: 29.47677147 sidereal years.
- Conjunctional period: 19.84985351 years (7250.338194 days).[7]
- Conjunctional distance: 242.4263889° (242° 25' 35").[8]
- Number of conjunctions in each triplicity: 12-13.

Figure 32: Māshā'allāh's parameters for Saturn-Jupiter conjunctions

Obviously then, Māshā'allāh's shifts and other values will differ from the more accurate ones available today. In dating his mean conjunctions, I have assumed that KP were correct in assigning the conjunction of 570 AD to December 12, since this conjunction was of the greatest interest to Muslim astro-historiographers. Using an Excel spreadsheet, it is easy to project dates and intervals backwards and forwards. However, KP themselves may have engaged in a little bit of rounding up and down themselves, since my exact

---

[5] KP 1971, pp. *vii-viii*. The epoch date used in this *zīj* was the date of his accession.
[6] See Hand's calculations of these divergences in his translation (1998, pp. 85-88). For my translation, see my *WSM*.
[7] According to the text, this is 19 sidereal years, 10 months (of 30 days apiece), 10 days, and 10 hours. (At one point the text has 11 hours.)
[8] Māshā'allāh's text is not always precise as to the seconds.

periods of time, converted directly into Julian and Gregorian dates,[9] do not always match theirs: sometimes our dates diverge by a few days.

Speaking of dates and chronology, the reader of *Conjunctions* will note that large numbers of days and years are sometimes converted in unusual ways. Sometimes large numbers of days are converted directly into Māshā'allāh's sidereal year, with the remaining days treated in terms of a year of 12 months of 30 days. For example, if we divide the conjunctional period in days (7250.338194) by Māshā'allāh's sidereal year (365.2590278 days), we get 19.84985351 sidereal years (see above). This becomes 19y plus a fraction, which is multiplied by the days in the sidereal year to get 310.416 days, or 10m (of 30 days) plus 10d, and some hours. This is purely for the sake of convenience. However, when ibn Hibintā adds different periods of time together, he sometimes forgets that he is working with years of 365 days, and misses the extra 5. As much as possible, I will provide the number of JDs in the footnotes, converting them into years and months by dividing the days by Māshā'allāh's sidereal year, then multiplying the remainder by 365 and then grouping them into 30-day months.

Māshā'allāh's mean conjunctions:

As I mentioned before, Māshā'allāh's mean conjunctions do not fit symmetrically into his Thousands. Conjunction #0 begins 3371.33125 days after the *middle* of the Mars Thousand—that is, days after its middle. This number occasionally plays tricks on the reader, as dates are sometimes calculated from the middle, sometimes simply from #0 itself. In addition, the calculations are not always correct.

Following is a table of all of the mean conjunctions *explicitly* dealt with by Māshā'allāh, beginning with the middle of the Mars Thousand (for others, see below). The boldface values are Māshā'allāh's own, which he has rounded up and down, but the positions of the other conjunctions, as well as all JDs and calendar dates, were calculated based on the Islamic conjunction #320.

---

[9] I have used the US Naval Observatory's site (aa.usno.navy.mil/data/docs/JulianDate.php), or my own Excel spreadsheets based on Duffett-Smith 1988. For negative JDs, I have used a different site (www.stevegs.com/utils/jd_calc/jd_calc.htm).

SECTION II.1: MĀSHĀ'ALLĀH'S HISTORICAL ASTROLOGY   93

Conj. #	Mean Position	Julian Day	Date[10]
Middle of Mars Thousand		-393883.5534	8/09/5792 BC
0	**7° 42' Taurus**	-390512.2221	11/02/5783 BC
121	**1° 24' Scorpio**	486778.6994	9/23/3381 BC
122	**3° 40' Cancer**	494029.0375	7/30/3361 BC
289	**18° 55' Sagittarius**	1704835.516	8/03/46 BC
290	21° 27' Leo[11]	1712085.854	6/09/26 BC
320	**4° 02' Scorpio**	1929596	12/12/570
323	**11° 19' Scorpio**	1951347.015	7/01/630
324	**13° 42' Cancer**	1958597.353	5/07/650
329	26° 05' Scorpio	1994849.044	8/07/749
332	3° 21' Sagittarius	2016600.058	2/24/809
333	5° 47' Leo	2023850.397	12/31/828
334	8° 13' Aries	2031100.735	11/07/848
335	10° 38' Sagittarius	2038351.073	9/13/868
336	13° 04' Leo	2045601.411	7/20/888
337	15° 29' Aries	2052851.749	5/27/908
338	17° 55' Sagittarius	2060102.087	4/02/928

Figure 33: Māshā'allāh's mean conjunctions, recalculated

In addition, the text contains two other charts. The last is for the *true* conjunction of #338, as calculated and partially described by ibn Hibintā (Ch. 18):

Conj. #	True Position	Julian Day	Date
338 (true)	16° 41' Sagittarius	2060291[12]	10/8/928

Figure 34: Ibn Hibintā's true conjunction #338

---

[10] I provide the Gregorian dates as calculated by my spreadsheets; negative JDs were calculated by a website (http://www.stevegs.com/utils/jd_calc/jd_calc.htm); KP's dates diverge by a few days here and there.

[11] Actually, ibn Hibintā's text gives this as 11° 20' Leo. But since the previous conjunction (#289) was said to be in 18° Sagittarius, it cannot be 11° Leo, but rather 21°. The value here is my own.

[12] JD given for noon; this chart cannot be exactly calculated using ibn Hibintā's methods because we do not have a copy of the *zīj* he used (see Ch. 18).

The second extra chart is cast for the Aries ingress of 13 BC (on 3/14/13 BC), allegedly the ingress for the birth of Christ (Ch. 6). This chronology puts Christ's birth rather early, while later (Ch. 7, **1**) the chronology implies a more standard date of 2 BC. As KP put it (p. 12), "Māshā'allāh has clumsily jammed together two chronological systems...without regard for their fundamental incongruence."

Māshā'allāh's triplicity shifts

Following is a table of Māshā'allāh's triplicity shifts, as generated from my spreadsheet. It is divided into two sections: (1) above, my "accurate" calculation of his positions and dates, and (2) below, Māshā'allāh's "divergent" positions and dates. As above, these calculations were based on the mean position given by Māshā'allāh for Islamic conjunction #320 (4° 02' Scorpio), on 12/12/570 AD. Boldface dates represent Māshā'allāh's own values.

Part (2) of the table, or the "divergent" conjunctions, represent Māshā'allāh's *mistaken* triplicity shifts. That is, even within his parameters, some of his shifts did not occur when he believed they did (and I am surprised that KP never pointed this out, especially the mistaken Islamic conjunction). For example, based on statements within *Conjunctions*, Māshā'allāh believed that #308 was a shift to air, #320 a shift to water, and #332 a shift to fire. But if we suppose that Māshā'allāh was even roughly correct about the position of conjunction #320 (at 4° 02' Scorpio), then *none* of these conjunctions could have been triplicity shifts, as all of them fall too far into their signs. Since in Māshā'allāh's system conjunctions can only advance by 2° 25' 35" at a time, it is impossible that any shift could land as far as 4° 02', for example. So, in part (2) I list what Māshā'allāh *believed* the shifts for these conjunctions were, as well as what the position actually was, based on his own calculations (again, using the Islamic conjunction #320's day and position as the standard).

Let me emphasize, too, that my "accurate" positions would change slightly depending on where there were measured from: if the position of conjunction #0 had been taken as the basis, the values for all conjunctions would be slightly different, and this would have resulted in several other triplicity shifts being rather off. The lesson is simply that, given Māshā'allāh's parameters, a few shifts would change no matter which conjunction we used as our standard. But in no way could the shift into water have happened at the Scorpio conjunction of 570 AD.

Section II.1: Māshā'allāh's Historical Astrology

(1) Māshā'allāh's Triplicity Shifts (calculated from #320)				
Conj. #	Triplicity	Shift at:	Julian Day	Gregorian Date
-3-9	Earth	0° 37' ♉	-412263.2367	4/15/5842 BC
10-21	Air	2° 09' ♒	-318008.8401	5/04/5584 BC
22-33	Water	1° 16' ♓	-231004.7818	7/18/5436 BC
34-46	Fire	0° 23' ♈	-144000.7235	9/30/5108 BC
47-58	Earth	1° 56' ♑	-49746.3270	10/21/4850 BC
59-70	Air	1° 03' ♒	37257.7314	1/03/4611 BC
71-83	Water	0° 10' ♓	124261.7897	3/18/4373 BC
84-95	Fire	1° 42' ♐	218516.1862	4/07/4115 BC
96-108	Earth	0° 49' ♑	305520.2445	6/20/3877 BC
109-120	Air	2° 22' ♎	399774.6411	7/11/3619 BC
121-132	Water	1° 24' ♏[13]	486778.6994	9/23/3381 BC[14]
133-145	Fire	0° 36' ♐	573782.7577	12/07/3143 BC
146-157	Earth	2° 08' ♍	668037.1542	12/26/2885 BC
158-169	Air	1° 15' ♎	755041.2126	3/11/2646 BC
170-182	Water	0° 22' ♏	842045.2709	5/24/2408 BC
183-194	Fire	1° 55' ♌	936299.6674	6/14/2150 BC
195-206	Earth	1° 02' ♍	1023303.7257	8/27/1912 BC
207-219	Air	0° 09' ♎	1110307.7841	11/10/1674 BC
220-231	Water	1° 42' ♋	1204562.1806	11/29/1416 BC
232-244	Fire	0° 49' ♌	1291566.2389	2/12/1177 BC
245-256	Earth	2° 21' ♉	1385820.6354	3/4/919 BC
257-268	Air	1° 28' ♊	1472824.6938	5/17/681 BC
269-281	Water	0° 35' ♋	1559828.7521	7/31/443 BC
282-293	Fire	2° 08' ♈	1654083.1486	8/19/185 BC
294-305	Earth	1° 15' ♉	1741087.2070	11/02/54
306-318	Air	0° 22' ♊	1828091.2653	1/15/293
319-330	Water	1° 54' ♓	1922345.6618	2/5/551
331-342	Fire	1° 01' ♈	2009349.7201	11/20/789
(343)	(Earth)	0° 08' ♉	2096353.7785	7/4/1027

Figure 35: Māshā'allāh's "accurate" triplicity shifts

---

[13] By calculation (as calculated using the 570 conjunction), this should be 1° 29'.
[14] KP date this to 9/25/3381 BC.

(2) Māshā'allāh's Divergent Triplicities				
Conj. #	Triplicity	Shift at:	Julian Day	Gregorian Date
308-319	Air	5° 13' ♎	1842591.9417	9/28/332
320-331	Water	4° 02' ♏	1929596	12/12/570
332	Fire	3° 27' ♐	2016600.0583	2/24/809

Figure 36: Māshā'allāh's "divergent" triplicity shifts

Māshā'allāh's calculation errors

In their commentary on *Conjunctions*, KP point out numerous errors of calculation in Māshā'allāh's charts. The most important one to note is Māshā'allāh's misuse of the *excess of revolution*, which means his Ascendants are totally wrong.

The excess of revolution is nothing more than the number of equatorial degrees that the heavens turn every year, beyond 365 days. For example, the tropical year is 365.24219 days long. This means that after 365 rotations, the heavens turn on the equator .24219 more of the circle before the year actually ends. This extra .24219, multiplied by 360° (or, 87° 11' 18"), is the value of the tropical excess. In a tropical system, the excess of revolution used by older astrologers is always around 87-89°, because the tropical year is shorter. Sidereal excesses are always around 92-93°. Following are three sets of excesses:

- Accurate modern tropical excess: 87° 11' 18".
- Accurate modern sidereal excess: 92° 17' 26".
- Māshā'allāh's sidereal excess: 93° 15'.

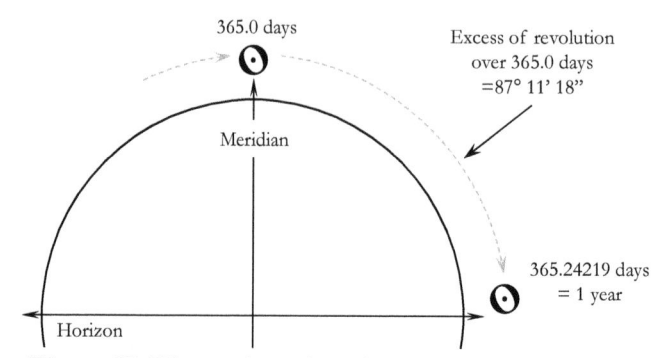

Figure 37: Illustration of tropical excess of revolution

The excess is very useful because it allows us to calculate the Ascendants of any solar revolution (whether natal or mundane) very quickly without a computer. You may have noticed that when you cast successive solar revolutions for yourself, the Ascendant jumps by about a square in the zodiac each year—this distance represents the excess of revolution, *as converted into zodiacal degrees*. The distance on the equator is always the same, but because the zodiac is askew from the equator, some signs are worth more or fewer equatorial degrees than others because they rise more slowly or quickly; moreover, the values are sensitive to latitude on the earth. The value of a sign in equatorial degrees is precisely what is meant by the phrase "ascensional times."

If you know how to use a table of ascensional times,[15] it is easy to take the excess, apply it to the ascensions at your latitude, and in less than a minute get your next year's Ascendant. So if the Ascendant of your tropical solar revolution this year was at 15° Gemini, next year's Ascendant will not be 87° 11' 18" away, in 12° 11' 18" Virgo—it will fall somewhat short of that or further away, depending on your hemisphere and latitude.

Unfortunately, Māshā'allāh continually made precisely this mistake, adding his sidereal excess to the previous year's Ascendant as though it was already in zodiacal degrees. Normally, he multiplies his excess by the number of years between conjunctions, and immediately applies the resulting degrees directly onto the zodiac, with complete disregard to ascensions, latitude, and so on. Thus if the Ascendant of one Aries ingress was 15° Gemini, Māshā'allāh would have simply added his 93° 15' excess and gotten 18° 15' Virgo for the next year. This is completely incorrect, and the upshot is that *Māshā'allāh's Ascendants are impossible* for Baghdad (or rather, Babylon), which is where he calculated the charts for. It is useless to try to cast his charts in a modern format and see what the "more exact" chart would be, because his use of the excess of the revolution gives completely false Ascendants. Unfortunately, we must simply look at his own interpretive *method* to understand his astrology, and pretend that the charts are accurate.[16]

Finally, there is one other important error in Māshā'allāh's chronology, which I have mentioned before but went oddly by KP. For astrologers in the

---

[15] I have a free, updated table calculated using Duffett-Smith 1988, on my website (www.bendykes.com/reviews/study.php).
[16] Nevertheless I have calculated Māshā'allāh's Midheavens for the location of Baghdad (in grey dotted lines), since Māshā'allāh was working there and used the Babylon System A ascensions, which assume such a location.

Islamic world, it was highly significant that the Saturn-Jupiter conjunction in 570 AD (#320), which heralded Islam and Muhammad, was a triplicity shift (into Scorpio, to be precise). But in working out *all* of Māshā'allāh's conjunctions, it is absolutely clear that the shift into water was not in 570 at all, but at the previous conjunction in Pisces in 551 AD (#319). This can be proven not only by calculating all of his dates and conjunctional positions, but simply through the fact that Māshā'allāh's conjunctions advance at a rate of only 2° 25' 35" for each successive sign. Māshā'allāh's Scorpio conjunction in 570 was 4° 02' into Scorpio, far more than 2° 25' 35". So the previous one could not have been an airy conjunction at the end of Aquarius: rather, conjunction #318 was at about 29° Gemini, #319 was the shift into 1° Pisces, and #320 was the *second* watery conjunction, in 4° Scorpio. This fact greatly disturbs the entire framework of Māshā'allāh's chronology of the early Islamic period within the watery triplicity. So we must practice caution when interpreting, or rather taking for granted, Islamic conjunctional chronologies: not only do they usually use a sidereal zodiac (which most Western astrologers do not), and in addition their sidereal year and measurements are not completely accurate, but they even assign a shift into water 20 years too late.

SECTION II.2:
MĀSHĀ'ALLĀH, *ON THE REVOLUTIONS OF THE YEARS OF THE WORLD*

Comment by Dykes. This Latin work (henceforth *RYW*) on interpreting annual ingresses is the only version that survives of Māshā'allāh's Arabic.[1] It was evidently rather popular in Arabic circles, as numerous passages from it can be found in Sahl's work on revolutions (forthcoming) as well as *Scito*, which borrows from it heavily (in Section II.5 below). Passages from *BRD* and *Flowers* can also be traced back to the Arabic *RYW*. For my edition, I have used the following:

- Heller, Nuremberg 1549.
- Madrid Lat. 10053 (13th Cent.), 132ra-135vb.
- Paris BN Lat. 16204 (13th Cent.), 391-404.
- Burnett and Yamamoto's edition of Chs. 45-46, which they edited based on *BRD* and put into their edition of *BRD* (pp. 345-47). For these chapters, my added material based on their reconstruction is found in the pointed brackets < >.
- *Scito*, which sometimes helps to correct difficult readings here (and *vice versa*).

ಙ ಙ ಛ

The book of Māshā'allāh on the revolutions of the years of the world, begins

[Prologue]

2 May God watch over you, and increase life for you; may God raise you up and lay open for you the revolution of years, the knowledge and arrangement of which is that you should know when the Sun enters the first minute of the sign of Aries. **3** And when you knew this, you will establish the Ascendant and the four angles, and the rest of the places of the celestial figure by degrees and minutes, and you should establish the places of the

---

[1] See Sezgin, p. 105, #7.

planets in the signs by degrees and minutes, and their being according to the order of the circle (namely by their direct motion and by retrogradation, slowness and[2] quickness, and their elevation and latitude, and the projection of their rays). **4** And know that a retrograde planet has no strength over good, until it goes direct.

5 After these things, look at the Ascendant and its lord, and at the lord of the exaltation of the Ascendant (if there was an exaltation of some planet in that sign), and the lord of the bound and of the triplicity, and the place of the lord of the hour[3] from the Ascendant, and see of what kind are their places relative to each other, and how they are in a place of enmity of the Ascendant, and which in a place of friendship. **6** For if the lord of the Ascendant appeared in an inimical or hostile place from the Ascendant, it signifies the detriment of that same clime, in accordance with the hostility or contrariety of the lord of the Ascendant with the Hour-marker. **7** And if it were in the sixth place, there will be infirmity; if it were in the eighth, there will be death; if it were in the twelfth, there will be enmity or discord, according to the nature of the sign in which the lord of the Ascendant is. **8** Likewise if the lord of the bound, and the lord of the exaltation, and triplicity, were in the said places [that are] inimical to the Ascendant—but this will be below what is signified by the lord of the Ascendant.

Chapter 1: On the places of the luminaries from the Ascendant

2 After these things, look at the places of the luminaries from the Ascendant, and from the lord of the Ascendant. **3** Because if the revolution were in the day, and the Sun looked at the Ascendant or[4] its lord, and the Sun was free from the bad ones, it signifies the strength and attainment or victory of the citizens of that clime—and better than that if the Sun gave up his management[5] to the lord of the Ascendant, and if he was received in the place in which he was. **4** Because if it was just as we have said, the wealthy and powerful of that clime will be humbled by and subjected to the master

---

[2] Following Paris for the rest of this paragraph.
[3] This is ambiguous. On its face, it seems to mean the lord of the planetary hour. But in Greek-language astrology, it was not uncommon to speak of the *lord of the Ascendant* as the "lord of the Hour," i.e., the Hour-marker. For examples of this, see Hephaistion's *Apotelesmatics III: On Inceptions* (2013).
[4] Reading *aut* for *ut*.
[5] This is probably a pushing of management (see *ITA* III.18).

of that clime, and prosperity and peace will be bestowed upon him, and health, with a good condition, by the will of God. **5** And likewise the Moon, if she bore herself toward the Ascendant and its lord just as we stated regarding the Sun, if the revolution were in the night. **6** And if the lords of the luminaries (or one of them) were looking at them from a strong place, and received them, there will not be detriment in men, nor any disturbance, but they will be secure and calm, seeking justice, and judging by means of it.

7 But if it were the reverse concerning the Sun, Moon, and the lords of the Ascendant, and the lords of the luminaries, say everything to the contrary, and turn the good things which we have said, into bad. **8** And[6] look at the reception of the planets toward each other, and their hostilities, and pronounce according to what you saw regarding lands and areas which they were in charge of.

Chapter 2: On the triplicities

2 Know that the signs signify parts of the world through their own natures, not through their places. **3** Wherefore if a part of the world agreed with the nature of its sign,[7] what is signified will be stronger for it.

4 Aries and its triplicity (Leo and Sagittarius) are signs of the east: which if they came together with the Ascendant,[8] their signification will be stronger.

5 Taurus and its triplicity (Virgo and Capricorn) are signs of the south: wherefore if they came together with the sign[9] of the Midheaven, their signification will be greater.

6 Gemini and its triplicity (Libra and Aquarius) are signs of the west: which if they came together with the sign of the angle of the west, what is signified by them will be stronger.

---

[6] Following primarily Paris.
[7] That is, with the triplicity of the sign on the angle in question. See below.
[8] *Convenerint.* That is, if one of them actually was the rising sign; and so in what follows.
[9] Reading singular here and in the next paragraph.

7 Cancer and its triplicity (Scorpio and Pisces) are signs of the north: wherefore if they came together with the angle of the earth, what is signified by them will be stronger.

8 On the other hand, these things which we have said are even applied to[10] the planets appearing in these places.[11]

Chapter 3: On the division of the earth

2 Know that the earth has two divisions: the east and the south is one, because they agree in heat; and the west and the north is the other, because they agree in cold.

3 After these, the earth is divided by the seven divisions of the seven planets in the climes, according to the order of the circles. **4** Therefore, the climes are known from the circle according to the order of the planets, just as with the lords of the hours. **5** For the first clime is Saturn's, the second Jupiter's, the third Mars's, the fourth the Sun's, the fifth Venus's, the sixth Mercury's, the seventh the Moon's.[12] **6** But the climes are according to the nature of the circle.[13]

7 After that is a well-known thing belonging to each sign, in terms of lands and cities;[14] and likewise for the bounds. **8** Because perhaps there will be a city belonging to some sign, and the bound of some planet of that sign conquers in [that city]. **9** Like Iraq, for example, which is said to belong to Cancer, and its planet is Jupiter, since the place of Iraq is in the place of the Jupiterian bound, from the nineteenth degree of Cancer up to its twenty-seventh, which is the bound of Jupiter.[15] **10** And the alighting[16] of the for-

---

[10] *Accommodantur.*
[11] That is, planets in fiery signs or the east signify the east, and so on.
[12] It is unclear to me whether Māshā'allāh is working numerically upwards, or geographically downwards. That is, if Saturn gets the first Ptolemaic clime, then Saturn's clime is closer to the equator and the Moon's is closer to the arctic circle. But if he is working geographically downwards, then Saturn really has the seventh clime higher in the north, and the Moon has the first clime closer to the equator.
[13] Perhaps this refers to geographic latitude.
[14] That is, the climes are derived astronomically from the order of planetary circles, while individual countries and cities are then associated with each zodiacal sign as a whole.
[15] The bound of Jupiter in Cancer actually runs from 19°—25° 59' (i.e., up to 26°). The *Liber Experimentorum* (Section II.6 below) has it correct.

tunes onto this place signifies fitness around Iraq in particular, and likewise the alighting of the bad ones onto the same place signifies evil around Iraq. **11** Likewise you will know this from the alighting of the fortunes and the bad ones in the rest of the bounds, as we have already expounded this to you.[17] **12** Therefore, know them just as I have told you, because if you did this, it will not be concealed from you which sign or which bound a city belongs to.

Chapter 4: When it is necessary to revolve the quarters of the years

2 After this, look at whether the ascending sign is fixed, movable, or common, and look likewise at the lord of the year. **3** Because if the Ascendant of the year were a movable sign, revolutions of the quarters in the year will be necessary, and more so if the lord of the year was in a movable sign. **4** And if it was a common sign, there will be exactly two revolutions necessary in the year (that is, at the beginning of Aries and Libra) and more so if the lord of the year was in a common sign: therefore do even with the entrance [of the Sun] into the first minute of Libra as with the beginning of the year. **5** And with the movable [signs], do likewise through all the quarters of the year. **6** But if the Ascendant was a fixed sign, the revolution of the year will be the one prevailing [over] all the quarters of the year, and more strongly so if the lord of the year was in a fixed sign. **7** But if the lord of the year was in a movable sign, the abundance or want which it signified will be only in the first quarter of the year—unless [such a] distinction is even in the second, third, and fourth [quarters]: then it will be according to what that same quarter signified, in terms of abundance or want.[18]

---

[16] Here and throughout, reading for *descensio* ("descending, dismounting"), which undoubtedly translates the Arabic *nazūl*.

[17] Unfortunately, this bound of Jupiter in Cancer is the only well-known example of associating bounds with cities; therefore, we do not know how Māshā'allāh or his sources might have assigned other ancient cities.

[18] The lord of the year being in a movable sign will tend to limit or intensify its effect in *that* particular quarter of the year.

Chapter 5: On discovering the lord of the year

2 Therefore, if you wished to know the lord of the year, look in the hour of the revolution at the planet which was stronger than the rest in its own place, and which had more testimonies, and make that one the lord of the year in the clime in which you are. **3** After this, give to the seven climes (from out of the clime in which you are),[19] according to what I told you before, in terms of the seven planets.[20] **4** And I will explain to you the portions of the planets and their testimonies, so you may know the lord of the year.

Chapter 6: On the portions[21] & testimonies of the planets, from which the lord of the year is identified

2 Know that the stronger of the planets is that one which is in the Ascendant, not remote from the angle nor falling,[22] or the one which was thus in the Midheaven; but in the setting [angle] and the angle of the earth it will be lower than [what] I told you regarding strength, by one-fourth. **3** And the eleventh sign is below the setting [angle] and the angle of the earth; and the ninth [sign] below the eleventh, and the fifth [sign] below the ninth, and the third [sign] below the fifth.

4 If the lord of the Ascendant were in the Hour-marker,[23] namely by 3° in front of or behind its cusp, not falling nor remote from the angle of the Ascendant, it will not be necessary with it to look at another planet. **5** Likewise the lord of the exaltation of the ascending sign, if it was in the degrees of its exaltation. **6** But the lord of the triplicity, if it was in the Ascendant, will have one-third of the strength of the lord of the Ascendant. **7** Also the lord of the bound has one-fifth of the strength, and this [is] in proportion to their strength in the signs. **8** And the lord of the hour has one-seventh.

---

[19] *Ex climate in quo fueris*. The function of this is unclear to me.
[20] Māshā'allāh is probably referring to Ch. 3, in which various cities and peoples receive planetary attributions. But Paris says *ex plagis 7* ("of/from the areas") instead of "of the seven planets." Cf. *Conjunctions*, where in addition to the lord of the year Māshā'allāh makes predictions about individual climes—particularly for the fourth clime (Babylon, Iraq) based on the Sun.
[21] This probably means "roles" or "dignities."
[22] *Cadens* ("cadent"). This seems to mean, "not very far from the Ascendant in *later* degrees (remote) nor being cadent in *earlier* degrees (see **4** below).
[23] *Horoscopo*.

9 And know that this comes to be if they were in the Ascendant or the Midheaven. **10** But if they were in the west or in the angle of the earth, their strength will be decreased; likewise if they were in the eleventh, the ninth, and the fifth, it will be decreased more.

Chapter 7: On the luminaries, if they were in the angles

2 Know that the luminaries, if they were in any of the angles, will be the lords of the year—unless the one which was in an angle was impeded (which if it were so, it will signify the impediment and weakness of that same clime which is subject to that sign). **3** And better than that [is] if the Sun in the day were in an angle, and the Moon in the night in an angle. **4** And likewise the nocturnal stars[24] thrive in the night, and the diurnal ones in the day. **5** Therefore, once you have established the revolutions of the years, begin afterwards with the consideration of the strengths, according to what I have told you.

Chapter 8: When the lord of the year hands over rulership[25] to another

2 And if the lord of the year appeared to you, see if perhaps it would hand over its own management to another: that is, like if it is in the house of another planet, and that planet appears in an optimal place from the Ascendant, and the lord of the year is also conjoined to it. **3** Because if it were so, the one who is the lord of that sign in which you found the governor of the year, is made the lord of the year, because it receives [the original lord of the year] from its own house; and better than that, if the luminaries looked at it, or [if] the lords of [the luminaries'] signs (in which they were found) did. **4** But if it did not[26] hand over its own management to the lord of its own house, see whether it has strength in its own place on top of the manage-

---

[24] Planets.
[25] *Commitat dominium.* This chapter goes on to use "disposition" or "management" (*dispositio*) rather than rulership (*dominium*). But the definitional statement (**2**) make it clear that this is what Abū Ma'shar calls "pushing nature" (*ITA* III.15), provided that the planet receiving the aspect is also configured to the Ascendant. In point of fact, this is the kind of situation that Māshā'allāh prefers when identifying the significators in, and interpreting, question charts: see *WSM* (the *Book on Reception*), and Ch. 12 below.
[26] Paris lacks this "not" (*non*).

ment (which will be its strength just as I designated to you in the sixth chapter).

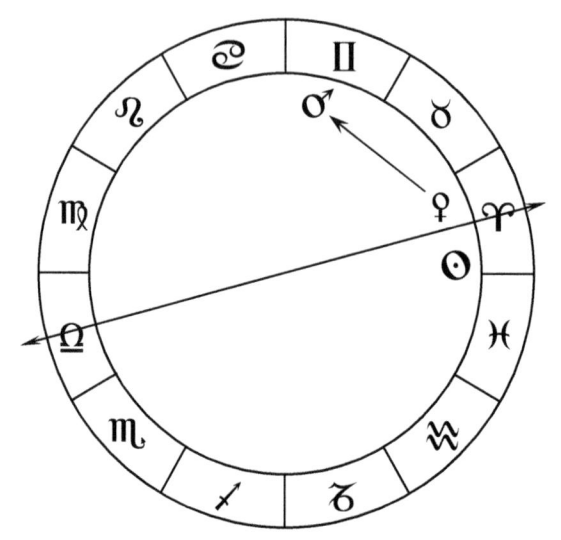

Figure 38: Lord of year (Venus) handing management to Mars[27]

Chapter 9: On the strength of the lord of the year

2 If planets were joined to the lord of the year, and they handed over their own management to it, joy will come to that clime from every direction, according to the arrangement[28] and strength of the planets.

Chapter 10: When the lord of the Ascendant is made into the lord of the year

2 If the luminaries (or one of them) handed over their own management to the lord of the Ascendant, it will not be necessary to look at another with this, because it itself is the lord of the year without a doubt.

---

[27] In this example of Ch. 8, I have made Libra rising at the time of the Aries ingress. Venus is the lord of the Ascendant and powerful in an angle, and I take her to be the lord of the year. She is closely applying by sextile to Mars, who rules her sign, and he is in a good place from the Ascendant.

[28] *Dispositionem.* Here, I take the Latin translator to refer to their positions and condition, rather than their management in the sense of ruling.

Chapter 11: What things must be looked at in judgments about kings & the rustics

2 You will also look, for the rustics and their condition, from the lord of the year and its place, and from the aspect of the planets toward it. **3** But for the king of the clime, you will judge from the lord of the Midheaven and from the Sun (namely from one [of these]),[29] and from the conjunction and the separation of the planets from them. **4** And of the Sun and the lord of the Midheaven, you will choose the stronger one according to the strength of the places, and you will put down the conquering one as the significator of the king.

5 And if you knew the significator of the king, his condition with the rustics (in terms of good and evil) and whatever will come out for him in that same year (in terms of difficulty[30] and abundance and want) will not lie hidden from you, by the command of God—namely, about every matter of his empire: that is, about his rustics, and his assets, about his children too and his women, and about his health and infirmity, about a foreign journey, and his strength and weakness, or about his ruin.

6 And know that this chapter on the king is clearer than the chapter on the lord of the year and the condition of the rustics, because you are looking for the king as an individual, and the rustics as a group.[31]

7 And if you knew the lord of the year and the significator of the king of that same region, see who looks at it, and what kind of strength belongs to the one looking at it, and whether they are in their own light or in the light of another,[32] and whether it is necessary that they look at their own places. **8** Because perhaps the lord of the year will be strong, not in need, or perhaps it will be weak and in need.[33] **9** But how this happens, I will explain to you in the following chapters.

---

[29] This parenthetical remark added from Paris.
[30] Reading *districtione* with Paris for *distractione*.
[31] *Regi singulariter, et rusticis universaliter.*
[32] Being "in its own light" probably refers to the phrase as defined by al-Qabīsī (*ITA* II.9), that a planet is out of the Sun's rays and not currently connected to another planet.
[33] See the next chapter.

Chapter 12: When the lord of the year is falling [away from the Ascendant][34]

2 If the lord of the year were falling [away] from the Ascendant, not looking at the Ascendant (in the eighth, sixth, second, or twelfth sign), then it will be in need, and therefore weakness will befall it, because it fell into a place removed from the Ascendant: and therefore it needs a planet to which it would be joined, which would reflect its light[35] upon[36] the Midheaven—and [this other planet] would strengthen it. **3** Because if a planet had more testimonies and it was the lord of the year, and it was in the eighth place, then it would need a planet which would see it from out of the Midheaven. **4** And every planet which does not see the Ascendant *does* see the Midheaven from a trine or sextile aspect), except the one which was in the third sign, where it is weakened and does not see the Midheaven.

---

[34] In this chapter (and in *Scito*, Ch. 3, **3-7**), Māshā'allāh imagines that the lord of the year is in aversion to (or "falling [away]" from) the Ascendant, which is unfortunate precisely because it cannot see the rising sign from such a position. Thus, we need another planet (here, one in the Midheaven or rather the tenth sign) to reflect the light from the sign in aversion, to the Ascendant. This is wholly in line with Māshā'allāh's approach to question charts: in questions, Māshā'allāh prefers that if the lord of the Ascendant or the Moon are in aversion to the Ascendant, we want them to be able to apply to some other planet which *does* see the Ascendant (see his *Book on Reception* in *WSM*). So the whole point of the discussion is that if the lord of the year is in a place which does not see the Ascendant, it needs a planet *in* the tenth, to reflect its light there. The trouble is that both while both *RYW* and *Scito* affirm that they are talking about places in aversion to the Ascendant, each concludes by mentioning the "third," which either seems irrelevant (*RYW*) or redundant (*Scito*). (1) *RYW* **4** speaks of the third sign from the Ascendant, which is a new topic: it is true that it is a weaker house and does not look at the Midheaven, but because it does look at the Ascendant, it seems irrelevant. But it could be made relevant by adding a phrase to the effect that we *also do not want* the lord of the year in the third: for like the averse places it is indeed weak, but *because* it cannot see any the tenth, it cannot be helped by any reflecting planet there. The problem with this solution, is that Māshā'allāh himself explicitly allows the lord of the year to be in the third, even though it is the least preferable (*RYW* Ch. 6, 3). (2) But *Scito* **7** explicitly names the third *from the tenth*, namely the twelfth (a comment probably added by the Latin translator), which is weakened and does look—that is, does not look at the Ascendant. But this is puzzling and redundant, since it was precisely such a place that needed reflection from the tenth. Perhaps this could be improved by saying that the twelfth is *too weak* to be helped in any case, *even though* it does see the Midheaven—but then, why doesn't the text simply say that? I have left both texts as they are on this point, and probably only identifying the original Arabic (which is probably in Sahl) will solve the problem.

[35] *Reddat lumen suum.*

[36] *Ad.* Normally this means "to," but the point is that while the aspect is indeed going to a planet in the Midheaven, it is then being reflected from there: so the reflection could be seen as being "upon" the Midheaven.

5 And if the planet which was strong out of the Midheaven was the lord of the sign in which the governor of the year (to whom more testimonies were joined) appeared, and the lord of the year itself was joined to him, [the planet in the Midheaven] will receive the management of the year and its signification, and it will be the lord of the year.[37] **6** But I have already expounded to you this topic before at the beginning of this book, and how the lord of the Ascendant will be made strong in its own place by the lord of its house, or by another.[38]

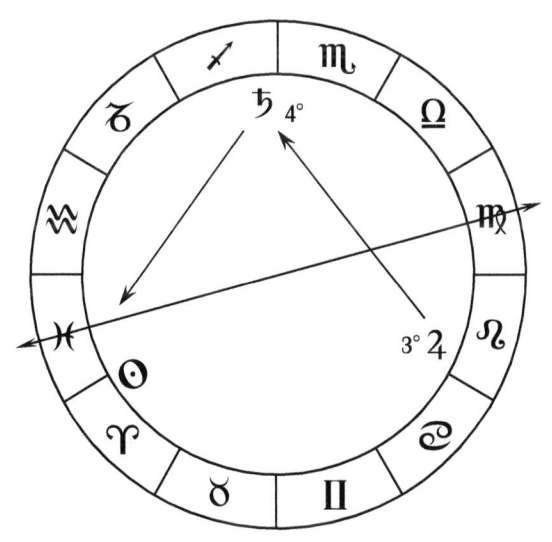

Figure 39: Saturn reflecting Jupiter's light to the Ascendant[39]

Chapter 13: On the strength & weakness of the lord of the year

2 After this, look at the one which is looking at the lord of the year, and pronounce what it would signify according to the quality of its place, in

---

[37] This is an example of just the kind of reception that Māshā'allāh prefers when reflecting the light. Again, see his *Book on Reception*. It is also an example of Ch. 8, **2** above.
[38] See Ch. 8.
[39] In this example based on Ch. 12, Jupiter is the lord of the Ascendant and the Sun is applying to him; but Jupiter is weak and in aversion to the Ascendant because he is in the sixth sign. He applies next to Saturn in the tenth, who—because he is able to see the rising sign—can reflect the light into Pisces via the tenth and thereby help Jupiter.

terms of good and evil; [and] if it were strong, strongly; and if it were weak, weakly.⁴⁰

3 Know that the aspect of the opposition signifies discord and contention, and likewise the square; but the trine or sextile aspect [signifies] friendship and concord. **4** If the bad ones looked at the significator of the year or the significator of the king from the opposition, the impediment will be from enemies. **5** And if they looked from a square aspect, it will be from certain people who are thought to be peacemakers, whose enmity was previously concealed. **6** And if it was from the trine or sextile aspect, it will be from friends.

7 After this, see whether the impediment would enter upon the king or upon the rustics. **8** Which if it entered upon the king, look to see whether the rustics will help him or not; but if it entered over the rustics, see whether the king would help them or not. **9** But whether [they do or not] can be known from the state of their significators.

Chapter 14: On the adversary of the king

2 After this, look at the house in which there was a bad planet, to see whether the significator of the king or the lord of the year had some testimony in it: which if it came out [like that], there will be enmity from that clime, in accordance with that testimony. **3** Look even to see if perhaps the lord of the year were in charge, and the significator of the king was not in charge:⁴¹ because if it were so, the enemy will be from that same clime, but the king will be weakened, and another will be led into his place. **4** But if the significator of the king were in charge, and the lord of the year was not in charge, the enemy will not be from his clime, nor from his kingdom: but the king will bring them under his sway, and he will subjugate them.

5 But once you have completed this, look at the place of the bad planet, to see what kind of direction it is [in]: because the destruction will be from that direction, from the city or clime, or from the clime of that same sign.

6 The age of the general and the princes⁴² is also known from the place of the bad one from the Sun: which if it were eastern, it will be a young man;

---

⁴⁰ *Forte...debile.* This could also be translated as, "and if it were strong, [its signification is] strong; and if it were weak, [its signification is] weak."
⁴¹ *Praeerit.* Māshā'allāh might be suggesting that we choose the victor between the two.
⁴² Reading *principum* for *principium* ("beginning").

and if it were western it will be an old man; and pronounce in this what there is between them according to what the place of the planet was, from the conjunction[43] of the Sun up to its burning.[44]

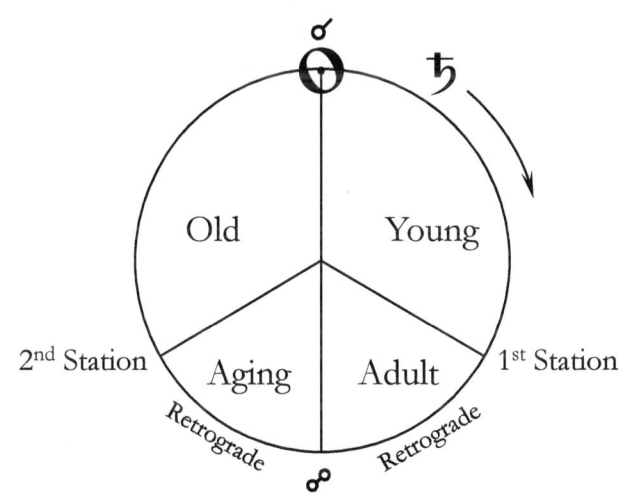

Figure 40: Thief age, superior planets (Heph. III.45, 13)

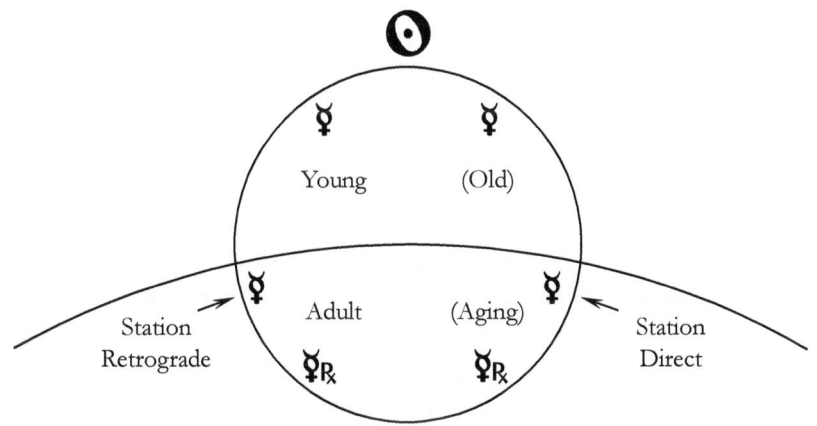

Figure 41: Thief age, inferior planets (Heph. III.45, 15)

---

[43] This should probably read, "opposition."
[44] Probably the best way to understand this use of easternness and westernness is from Dorotheus, as described by Hephaistion (*Apotel.* III.45, **13-15**). See diagrams.

7 Also, if a bad one were in the Midheaven, and it impeded the lord of the year,[45] this [trouble] will enter among all men. **8** And if it were in the east, the evil will be from the direction of the east; and if it were in the west, it will be from the direction of the west; and likewise in the north and south, if it were in the angle of the earth or the Midheaven.

9 And know that nothing is worse for the state of the citizens of the land, and the city which belongs to that same sign in the bad one was, than if it is retrograde in the revolution of a year; and more strongly than that if the bad one were in an angle.

Chapter 15: On the impediment of the king

2 After this, look at the bad one which is looking at the lord of the year or at the significator of the king: because if it looked from the Ascendant, it signifies that the impediment is common [to all];[46] and if it were in the second, it will be in connection with assets; if it were in the third, it will be in connection with brothers; and if it were in the fourth, it will be in connection with fathers and real estate; and if it were in the fifth, it will be in connection with children; and if it were in the sixth, it will be in connection with infirmities; and if it were in the seventh, it will be because of war and contention; and if it were in the eighth, it will be in connection with death. **3** And if the bad one was in a common sign, it is feared concerning the king, if his significator looked at it just as I told you before. **4** And if the lord of the year was not the significator of the king, it is feared concerning the rustics, because there will be mortality in them. **5** And if it were in the ninth, in connection with foreign travel; and if it were in the tenth, it will be in connection with the king and his rulership; and if it were in the eleventh, in connection with friends; and if it were in the twelfth, in connection with enemies. **6** And speak likewise concerning the good which it signified, by the will of God.

7 Say likewise in the revolution of the years of a native, just as you have spoken in the revolution of the years of the world.[47]

---

[45] *Scito* Ch. 29, **1** has "lord of the Ascendant."
[46] Madrid says it is "in the body" (*in corpore*), as does *Scito* Ch. 29, **4**.
[47] Madrid says simply, "And speak likewise in a revolution of the years of the world," which is unhelpful because that is precisely the topic we are addressing.

Chapter 16: On the place of the lord of the year

2 After this, look at the lord of the year to see in whose house it receives the year, and in what bound, and in what exaltation or triplicity. **3** Then look at what kind its place is, out of those which I have said before. **4** Because if [its lords] looked at it and received it, it will be stronger.

5 After this, look at the sign in which the significator of the year is, whose clime it is, or whose city: because the master of that clime will be stronger, and will have happier successes, beyond the rest of the climes.

6 Then, put down a planet for each clime:[48] nor will it be concealed from you, by the will of God, what will come about for the king of that clime. **7** And know that the stronger of the kings will be the one whose city or clime belongs to the lord of the year. **8** Then look at the one which follows by succession: and everyone who was born under that same sign in that land, or under the sign of the lord of the year, will be fit for the good, and there will be trust in it—unless it was impeded. **9** And when you have done this, look at which one is making a peace agreement with or is turned against it, with respect to the places of the planets and their aspects (the opposition, and the square, the trine, and the sextile aspect), and with respect to the houses out of which they are looking.

10 And know that a planet which is under the rays is like one suffering: for when it enters under the solar rays, its strength recedes, and when it goes out from under the rays it signifies increase and progress.[49]

Chapter 17: On the signification of Mercury & the Moon

2 Know that, of the seven planets, there are none for which fortune or misfortune varies[50] more quickly than for the Moon and Mercury: and this comes to be on account of the multitude of their diversity and burning.[51] **3** Because a planet, if its burning was abundant, signifies evil, and especially

---

[48] I believe this means must judge the condition of each clime based on the planet assigned to it: for instance, a bad Saturn will mean something bad for the clime ruled by Saturn, *etc.*
[49] *Profectum.* Or, "profit," "success."
[50] Madrid reads, "is enjoyed" (*fruatur*).
[51] That is, because they undergo burning and changes in their cycles so frequently.

every planet which was under the Sun:[52] if one of them were the lord of the year or[53] the significator of the king, and one of the bad ones was looking at it, then the condition of the year and the king will be worse in this way than it [ever] could be.

4 And if a diurnal planet were in his rays in a revolution of the day (and a nocturnal planet in a revolution of the night), the Sun signifies the king, because then he[54] receives the strength of the planets. **5** And if the lord of the house of the Ascendant were under the rays of the Sun, [he will be][55] more worthy for the annual rulership. **6** And look well[56] at the places of the luminaries, and at the aspects of the lords of their houses to them, and their own aspects[57] to each other.

Chapter 18: On the strength of the luminaries

2 Consider even whether their aspect had strength:[58] because[59] a planet will be stronger by aspect if it were looking from out of its own house, or its own exaltation, or triplicity, or bound, or from out of a place of strength, or it was the lord of the Lot of Fortune,[60] and in addition to what I said it was eastern or direct: for then it will be stronger than it could [ever] be.

3 Look also at the Lot of Fortune and its lord, and at their places of the signs, because these [places][61] strengthen the lord of the year and the significator of the king. **4** Which if they[62] were impeded, look at them and their

---

[52] This must mean the inferior planets.
[53] Madrid reads "and," suggesting that they are the same planet.
[54] Madrid reads, "the planet." If this is the correct reading, it suggests that (a) the planet is the putative lord of the year because it is being applied to by other planets, etc.; but (b) by being under the rays, the Sun takes over its role. Māshā'allāh does indeed use this approach of favoring a planet being applied to, in his *Conjunctions*.
[55] I take this to refer to the Sun. Madrid is clearer, saying "…is under the rays, the Sun will be more worthy…".
[56] *Optime*.
[57] Or perhaps, the aspects "of them" (*eorum*) to each other, suggesting the lords of their places and not the luminaries themselves (*suorum*). Madrid has, "of the lords of their own houses to them, and the aspects of [the luminaries, *earum*] to each other."
[58] Referring to **6** in the previous chapter.
[59] Reading *quia* for *qua*.
[60] A partly illegible note above this phrase in Madrid seems to read, "[and it was] looking at it," referring to the Lot of Fortune.
[61] According to *Scito* Ch. 49, **2**, this is the place of a fortune.
[62] I am not sure whether this refers to the two significators (of the year and the king), or to the Lot and its lord.

places in the signs: because the Lot of Fortune is the strength of the luminaries. **5** But if the said significators were made fit in the place of a fortune,[63] they signify good and fitness; and if they were impeded under the rays, they signify detriment and loss according to the essence of the signs in which they are.

Chapter 19: On the planet to which the lord of the year is being joined

2 After this, look at the lord of the year to see to whom it is being joined: because trust and fear will be in connection with this. **3** Look also to see if perhaps the significator of the king were the lord of the year—and I will explain to you by what means[64] this could come about. **4** Namely, so that if the lord of the year [was] having testimony in the Midheaven, or if the lord of the exaltation of the Midheaven or the lord of the Midheaven[65] handed over its own management and its own strength[66] to [the lord of the year], or if the lord of the Midheaven was in its[67] domicile, looking at it. **5** For if it were so, the lord of the year will be the significator of the king. **6** And if you knew this in a revolution of years, know even the significator of the king from the lord of the year, and know his condition with respect to[68] the condition of the rustics. **7** Which if the Sun[69] were the lord of the year, look just as I have told you in the first chapter.

8 Look even at the lord of the Midheaven: if it were under the rays, entering into burning, this signifies the death of the king. **9** And if it has already gone out from burning, and is not yet appearing, the Sun will be more worthy than it in the signification of the king.

---

[63] Indicating a benefic (and reading with *Scito*), rather than "Fortune" (which suggests the Lot).
[64] *Ratione*. Or, "argument, reasoning," *etc.*
[65] Adding "or the lord of the Midheaven" with Madrid.
[66] This is perhaps Abū Ma'shar's "pushing power," *ITA* III.16.
[67] I.e., the lord of the year (reading with Heller). But Madrid says, "in its *own* [*sua*] house." If Heller is right, it is a case of "pushing nature" (*ITA* III.15); if Madrid is right it is "pushing power" (*ITA* III.16).
[68] *De*. Or perhaps, "from."
[69] Adding "the Sun" with Madrid, for the indeterminate "it" implied in Heller.

10 After this, see to whom the significator of the king is being conjoined. **11** Because if it is being conjoined to the lord of the year, he[70] will hand over his management to the rustics; and if it was separated from the lord of the year, and was joined to a bad planet which is inimical to the Ascendant, he will go on his knees regarding them,[71] and the king will send in detriment upon them.[72] **12** And if the significator of the king were joined to some planet in the eighth or in the seventh, from the opposition or square aspect, death will be feared for the king in that same year. **13** Likewise if it were joined to the lords of [the eighth or seventh, they being] outside of these places which I told you: and more strongly so if they[73] were joined to the bad ones. **14** And infirmity will be feared for him if it were joined to a planet in the third[74] or sixth house, or to their lords (just as I told you in the beginning).[75] **15** Likewise, you look, on every day of [the revolution] in this way.[76]

16 And I have said these things if the lord of the Midheaven handed over its management to the lord of the year. **17** But if the lord of the Midheaven did not hand it over to it, [the lord of the Midheaven] will be more worthy in this which I have said.

18 Look even in the twelve places of the region[77] in terms of difficulty and abundance, and in terms of fear and sorrow, and look likewise regarding the general regions of the climes and the directions.[78]

19 After this, consider who is the lord of the house of the lord of the year. **20** Which if it looked at [the lord of the year], and received [it], joy and security will find them; and if it did not look at it, fear and trouble will find them. **21** Which if the lord of the year handed over management to the significator of the king, it will send in difficulties upon [the rustics] on account

---

[70] In some of the following, there is an overlap in meaning between what the planet is doing, and what the king is doing. Thus the significator of the king may be handing over its management, but this is also what the king will be doing.

[71] *Supplicabitur super eos.*

[72] I think this means that the king will be very weak, and through this weakness will be disastrous for the country.

[73] This must refer to the lords of the seventh and eighth, or planets in them.

[74] Perhaps this should be, "twelfth."

[75] See the *Prologue*, **7**; also Ch. 12, **2**.

[76] This implies that the handing over of management is not simply a one-time event to be evaluated at the beginning of the year, but must be monitored throughout the year. But **15** does not seem to appear in Madrid.

[77] Reading *regionis* for *regioni*.

[78] For example, the benefics will indicate good things in the directions in which they are in the chart, and conversely.

of the acquisition of assets if the handing over[79] was from the square aspect or the opposition; but if it was from the trine or sextile aspect, it signifies the rendering of provisions[80] without the coming of difficulty upon the rustics. **22** And if it handed over its own management without an aspect,[81] this will be without the king's knowledge. **23** And[82] if it looked at the lord of its house,[83] the king will extract assets in that same year; and if it did not look, he will extract assets without bad intentions.

24 After this, look at the assets of the king: from the eleventh if the significator of the king were the lord of the Midheaven, and from the second if it was the lord of the year. **25** And look at the condition of the soldiers toward the king, from the lord of the sign in which it was, and from the lord of the bound or face.

26 And[84] assist these through the Lot of Fortune and its lord: because if the significator of the king looked at it or was with it,[85] it signifies the good fortune of the king. **27** Judge likewise[86] in the same way for the rustics, from the lord of the year.

28 And know the condition of the king from his significator, but that of the powerful and the nobles, from the lord of the year. **29** Because if you did this, their condition will not be concealed [from you], as well as what is going to come about for them in the year (of good or of evil), and in what way or for what reason, if God wills.

---

[79] Reading *commissio* with Madrid, for Heller's *commixtio* ("commixture").
[80] *Census*, referring broadly to the system of agricultural provisions and tax assessments collected by the king.
[81] I am not sure what Māshā'allāh means here; perhaps he means their light is reflected or collected or transferred through some third planet.
[82] Note the similarity between this sentence and *Skilled* VIII.17, **33-35** (and its source in *BRD* II.4, **11**), which specifically brings the second house into play.
[83] Madrid adds, "that is, of the sign in which it was."
[84] For this paragraph, see *Skilled* VIII.5, **67** and *Scito* Ch. 56, **5-6**.
[85] There is confusion in the pronouns as to whether the significator of the king is supposed to have this relation to the Lot, or to its lord.
[86] Reading with Madrid for "clearly."

Chapter 20: When the lord of the year & the significator of the king are retrograde

2 After this, look at the lord of the year and at the significator of the king, to see if they were retrograde: they signify the loss and weakness of the king, and of the citizens of that same kingdom. **3** But if they were both retrograde (or one of them), see in whose bound it is retrograde, namely whether it is in the bound of a fortune or a bad one, and pay attention to it[87] in your work—and likewise the lords of the houses [they are in]. **4** Because if a planet were retrograde in the house of a fortune, it will be better than in the house of a bad one or in the bound of a bad one. **5** The retrogradation of the significator of the king signifies the weakness of the king, and the retrogradation of the lord of the year signifies the weakness of his rulership.[88]

Chapter 21: On war

2 After this, look at war from the direction [of movement] in which Mars was: which if he were direct, it will be because of eager men who do not want to flee; and if he were retrograde, the war will be with robbers who do not rest in one place, and will not advance to war.[89]

3 But Saturn signifies the distress[90] of the cities of the region in which he was, according to the essence of the sign in which he appeared, and according to the essence of his place in the houses through succession (like the Ascendant, and the house of assets, until it arrives at the twelfth). **4** And if he were retrograde, it will be just as I told you about Mars, and this will be more severe from the conjunction. **5** And[91] if he were joined to the lord of the year, it will be more severe for the king from the lands in which [Saturn] was (of[92] the clime).

---

[87] *Mitte eum.* Here and below, I take this to be the continued use of medieval meanings of *mitto* to translate the Arabic *wajuha*, "direct, guide, channel, face, confront," as in Sahl's *On Elect.* §36. Clearly we are supposed to "use" this planet, but it is unclear whether it is allowed to overrule the signification of the retrograde planet.
[88] *Scito* Ch. 57, **3** speaks of the citizens suffering, not the king's own rulership.
[89] *Scito* Ch. 36 then adds that if Mars is in his station, the war will be stronger.
[90] *Districtionem.* This word has the sense of confinement and difficulty, as opposed to the violence of Mars.
[91] See *Scito* Ch. 37, **1-2**, which distinguishes the lord of the year and the significator of the king here.
[92] Reading *ex* with Madrid for Heller's "and" (*et*).

6 After this, look at the attainment and victory from the stronger one of the planets, because it signifies the multitude of the soldiers and their strength, just as you otherwise look at the testimony of the planets and their strength in their own places.

7 After this,[93] look at the quickness of the victory (or its slowness) from Jupiter, Saturn, and the testimonies of their conjunction, and the nature of their profection in the root, according to the course of the circle in the greater years (in which the middle conjunction comes to be, which is changed from triplicity into another triplicity).[94] **8** The lesser one, which comes to be from their profection in the root, [signifies] a change[95] of sects and kingdoms. **9** For this signifies what I have told you regarding their conjunction in three ways, which I will reveal to you in the following chapter.

Chapter 22: On the signification of the three superiors

2 If you sought concerning this, do just as you do in the revolution of the years of a native based on[96] the root of the nativity, because you will take the signification of sects and kingdoms from the conjunction of Saturn and Jupiter, and their change from triplicity to triplicity. **3** Look even at the presence of the three planets which are above the Sun, and at their places in the fixed and movable signs, and the common ones, and pay attention to it[97] in the hour of the destruction of things, as I will reveal to you concerning the course of Saturn and Mars, and I will explain all of these things.

4 Know that if the bad ones (namely Saturn and Mars) were in a sign [made] in the image of men, and one bad one was joined to the other, and it was direct or retrograde, from the conjunction and the square aspect or the

---

[93] In this paragraph, Māshā'allāh labels the conjunctions differently than in his *Letter* (Section II.3, Chs. 10-12).
[94] I am not sure what conjunctions and profections Māshā'allāh is describing here; it is also possible that the correct word here is not "profection," but "presence" (as in the next chapter, **3**).
[95] Reading *[significat] mutationem* for *mutatio*.
[96] *Super*, probably translating the Ar. ʿalā.
[97] *Mitte eam.* See note above. *Eam* is feminine and so could refer to the "presence" or "signification"; but presumably we should pay attention to everything mentioned.

opposition, there will be pestilences in men. **5** But if it were retrograde, it will be more insidious[98] and faster.

6 And it is good for you to see whether the aspect or conjunction is from any angle: which if it were so, it will be more insidious and strong. **7** Look then to see in which angle it is. **8** But if it was Saturn who is slower, in the fourth or in the Midheaven, and the retrograde planet which is being joined to him [is] in the seventh, this evil will come from the direction of the west, and the king will be made great, and will be extended and strengthened. **9** And if the slower one were in the west,[99] and the retrograde one which is being joined to him [were] in the fourth, this will begin in the region which I will tell you, until it comes to the west.

10 After this, look at the manner of the inception [of the evil] from the direction of[100] the quicker planet which is being joined to the heavier one, and know that evil will come about when the quick planet arrives at[101] the place of the heavier and slower one. **11** And know that the retrograde and conjoined one (that is, the one which is being joined to the heavier one), if it were in a common sign, there will be death from war or from killing; and in fixed and movable[102] ones it will be according to what the stronger of the bad ones signified in its own places. **12** If the stronger one were Mars, it will be from war or an infirmity which is hot; which if Saturn were stronger, there will be death from every infirmity which was of the likeness of Saturn. **13** And commingle the strength of Mars to him. **14** And if what we said before was outside the angles, [the evil] will be small, [and] afterwards it will be dissolved.

---

[98] *Calidius*, reading as the comparative of *callidus*. But this might be the comparative of *calidus* ("hot"), in which case it suggests the doctrine found in al-Kindī in which retrograde planets cause heat (see *AW1*).
[99] I.e., in the seventh.
[100] *Parte*. This could either mean from the spatial direction (as above), or simply "in connection to, in relation to."
[101] Reading *perveniet* with Madrid for *proveniet* ("proceeds to").
[102] Reading *mobilibus* with Madrid for *immobilibus* (which is probably a misread for *in mobilibus*).

Chapter 23: On a year to be feared

2 If you wished to turn the years of the world[103] in which one should have fear, see whether there is a conjunction of Saturn and Jupiter[104] in that same year: which if there were one, it will be more evil; and if there were not one, it will be easier. **3** Likewise the lord of the year or the significator of the king, if they transited past a slow and bad planet in an angle, then it will be feared because of its signification, just as I told you concerning destruction and death.

4 Also, look at the bad ones to see if they were in such a condition as we have described above in their place of the night or day. **5** Because Saturn in a diurnal and masculine sign impedes less, and Mars in a feminine sign[105] and place of the night is of lesser impediment. **6** After this, look to see whether they are received in their places or not. **7** Because if they were received their impediment will be less, and if there were an infirmity in that same year, [people] will not die (except for a few). **8** And if they signified killing, there will not be wounds and there will not be killing (except for a little bit), and men will feel pity for each other.

Chapter 24: On the signification of the Head *&* Tail of the Dragon of the Moon

2 Know[106] that the Head of the Dragon corresponds to the fortunes, and the Tail aids the bad ones.[107] **3** And so, look at the conjunction of the Head and Saturn, because it signifies the essence of the sign in which they are conjoined, just as it signifies in an eclipse of the luminaries. **4** For if it were in Aries and its triplicity in the way that I told you, it will be in beasts and wolves according to the essence of the sign in which they are being conjoined. **5** And if it were in Taurus and its triplicity, it will be in trees and

---

[103] That, is casting an Aries ingress chart.
[104] Adding *et Iovis* with Madrid.
[105] This should probably read "masculine," as Mars is a masculine planet.
[106] For 2-7, see *Scito* Ch. 64, **1-5** and *Skilled* VIII.5, **26-30**.
[107] The view that the Head is like the benefics and the Tail like the malefics is a common medieval one. Another approach is to say that the Head aids both because its nature is to increase, and the Tail harms both because its nature is to decrease: that is, the Head will magnify any planet's good or evil, and the Tail will diminish it.

herbs, and there will be few rains and provisions. **6** And if they were conjoined in the airy signs, men and birds will find impediment, and the winds will blow. **7** And in watery signs, rain and water will be multiplied, and fish and cold, and locusts, and the creeping things of the earth will be multiplied.

8 And look for the square aspect of Mars[108] and the Tail, and their conjunction, because they would signify a powerful war and famine, and a multitude of fear, and there will be great cold, and a multitude of evil. **9** And if Saturn were joined with the Tail, it signifies famine and a scarcity of good, and the strength of the cold, and the destruction of trees, and it will be in the direction in which he is. **10** And if the Sun burned up a planet in that direction, this will be stronger in that [direction] than in the rest of the directions.

Chapter 25: On the signification of a planet in the signification of wars if it was slow, retrograde, or direct

2 Know that a slower planet signifies war, and a retrograde one signifies flight. **3** But a direct one signifies peace, and especially if a fortune looked at it from the Midheaven. **4** And if the lord of its house (or the lord of the triplicity, or the lord of the bound, or the lord of its exaltation) was looking at that planet, it signifies a multitude of allies from relatives and others, in accordance with what I have told you.[109]

5 Look[110] even at the condition of the master of the army from the planets from which the signification[111] is taken. **6** Because if it were in its own house, he will be from the household members of the king, and is well-known; and if it were in its own exaltation, he will be noble and advantageous to the kingdom;[112] and if it were in the triplicities,[113] he will be below what I said (but he will be well-known), and he is below them. **7** But if it

---

[108] Reading *Mars* with *Scito* (Ch. 64, **6**) for "a bad one" (*malus*).
[109] Māshā'allāh means the interpretation of the aspect according to its type: i.e., sextiles mean one thing, squares another, and so on.
[110] For this paragraph, cf. also Ch. 29 below.
[111] Madrid reads, "significator" (*significator*).
[112] This probably means he is *worthy* of a kingdom: this stock phrase is frequently repeated in the medieval astrological literature.
[113] Or rather, in *its own* triplicity.

were not any of these, he will not be noted nor of good stock,[114] and perhaps it will be said about him that he was born from fornication.

8 And[115] know that the diurnal planets are the Sun, Saturn, and Jupiter, and [they are] masculine in the day, and feminine in the night. **9** And the nocturnal planets [are] the Moon, Mars, and Venus, and they are feminine in the day, masculine in the night. **10** But Mercury is masculine with the masculine ones, feminine with the feminine ones, also nocturnal with the nocturnal ones, diurnal with the diurnal ones.[116]

Chapter 26: On the condition of the king when his significator is entering into burning

2 If[117] the significator of the king is entering into burning in the revolution of the year, the king of that region will die in that same year. **3** And if it was at the extremity of the rays, grief and sorrow will enter upon him—but if a fortune was looking at it, he will escape. **4** And if what I told you was the case, and it has already crossed over the burning, anger and contention will enter upon him, [but] afterwards he will be released from it, and his condition will be made fortunate—unless a bad one is looking at it, because then it signifies the prolongation of those things which I said, and their difficulty,[118] and it will be feared concerning him according to the nature of the sign—whether it was an infirmity or death. **5** Therefore, look at the hour of that signification from the time of the significator of the evil.[119] **6** And likewise,

---

[114] Reading *generosus* with Madrid for *gratiosus* ("influential, obliging").
[115] For **8** and **9**, Māshā'allāh is trying to communicate a sense of sect, which is not altogether successful. It is true that the diurnal principle is considered more masculine, and the nocturnal one feminine. But a planet's relation to the sect of the chart is typically a matter of fitness and temperate operation. So by day, diurnal planets are *of* the sect and act more fitly and temperately in the native's life, while nocturnal ones are *contrary* to the sect and not as comfortably suitable to it. See *ITA* III.2.
[116] A Hellenistic view which seems to make more sense is Ptolemy's (*Tet.* I.7), also reflected in Porphyry (Schmidt 2009, p. 87), that Mercury is diurnal when he rises before the Sun, and nocturnal when he rises after the Sun. But authorities generally agree that Mercury's benefic or malefic qualities derive from his configurations and aspects.
[117] For al-Rijāl's Arabic version of the first few sentences, see his Ch. VIII.16, **9-12**. For Abū Ma'shar's, see *BRD* II.7, **6**.
[118] *Districtionem*. Madrid reads, "destruction" (*destructionem*).
[119] Reading *significatoris mali* with Madrid for *significator et mali*. By the "time," Māshā'allāh means changes in a planet's condition by transit: see **7**. For other lists, see Sahl's *On Times*

if a bad one looked at the significator of the king from the opposition or the square aspect, or from the conjunction, it will be feared concerning him, if what I said were in an angle. **7** And the time of the evil will be at the burning of the significator, and at the arrival of that same bad one to the place of the significator or to the Midheaven, or to the Ascendant, unless a fortune would relieve it by an aspect, and thus this same bad one would be an ally in nature. **8** And if the bad one (whichever one it was) were the significator of the king, destruction will enter upon men from the direction of the king, and more strongly so if it were in an angle: then it signifies that he will not be bothered[120] by their destruction.

9 And[121] if [the bad one] were in the Midheaven (in addition to what I told you),[122] there will be difficulty from certain strangers. **10** And this will be wholly in the place of the bad one[123] if it were in the east, and likewise if it were in the west. **11** And if it were in the Midheaven, it will be generally in the rest of men, and especially in the area of *Banāt na‘sh*[124] (that is, Ursa Major, through which the north is signified).[125] **12** And if it was in the direction of the angle of the earth, it will be in the direction of the east and al-Zanj,[126] that is, of the blacks.

13 And the fortunes likewise will bear significations. **14** Therefore, examine the directions in which they were, unless the fortunes were retrograde and in a bad place (that is, in their descensions, or in the oppositions of their own houses): because these places belong to their unluckiness,[127] in which they are weakened.

(in *WSM*), and my discussion of times in *Choices & Inceptions*. Typical examples include a planet stationing, or coming out of the rays, etc.

[120] *Fatigabitur.*

[121] Sentences **9-12** are unclear to me, and I cannot really see how to make sense of the angles and directions Māshā'allāh describes. There may be some confusion in the transmission of the Latin translation, but the parallel passage in *Scito* Ch. 52 is also confusing. See also *Skilled* VIII.4, **176** and VIII.7, **137**.

[122] That is, given the situation with the significator of the king described above.

[123] *In loco mali*. I am not sure what Māshā'allāh means here.

[124] *Benetnaas*. Lit., "daughters of the bier/coffin," the grouping of stars Ursa Major *α—η*, especially *η* (who is also known as Alkaid). See Kunitzsch and Smart 2006, p. 57.

[125] Omitting "and if you said in the northern direction" (Madrid seems to read, "if they say").

[126] *Accenden*. Al-Zanj (whence we get names like Zanzibar) refers to the southeastern part of Africa south of (and including part of) modern Somalia, Kenya, Tanzania, Mozambique, *etc*. But it also refers to the slave population of southern Iraq, which had been from that part of Africa. Finally, there is also a Zanjān province in Iran, east of Iraq, implied by the *–en* ending. Compare this passage with *Scito* Ch. 47, **4** and Ch. 52, **4**.

[127] Or, "unhappiness" (*infoelicitatis*). Madrid reads, "enmity" (*inimicitiae*).

15 And[128] look at the planet from which the king and his condition is signified, and pronounce according to the being of the planets and their advancement through individual days, concerning difficulty and want or abundance, concerning good or evil. **16** After this, look for the receiving of light and its pushing, because this signifies what is going to come about for the rustics.

Chapter 27: Whether there is going to be war, *& who would attain victory*

2 And if you were asked about war,[129] whether there was going to be one, and who would achieve victory, look for the one (for whom you wished to look) to see what kind of condition [his significator] would have in that year, and how the significator of the king and the lord of the year look at it. **3** Which if it were strong by place, and the significator of the king did not look at it, and the lord of the year *did* look at it, it will be a grave matter for the owner of the interrogation,[130] and the king will not help him, but there will be allies from the household members of the king. **4** And if the significator of the king did look at it, predict the aid of the king towards him, according to the aspect in terms of strength and weakness. **5** Which if it[131] were of the nature of an enemy, say he is going to be affected by an injury from him; and if it were of the nature of making peace, judge according to what you found. **6** And therefore I have indicated this to you so that you may imitate it, and you may know how you should look at his topic:[132] because something will not be concealed from you by this method in the description of it.

---

[128] The Arabic version of **15-16** is in *Skilled* VIII.16, **15-16**.
[129] This chapter seems to describe something like a question chart asked in the context of the mundane revolution. Here, Māshā'allāh apparently wants us to identify a planet in the chart which represents the querent, and then see how the lord of the year and significator of the king are configured with it. But which planet should represent the querent? Possibly a universal significator (such as Jupiter for a noble or wealthy person, *etc.*) or else the lord of the Ascendant of a separate question chart. This chapter may be derived from material by Theophilus, who specialized in questions about war. An edition of his surviving works will be published by me in 2015.
[130] That is, the querent. Madrid reads, "the king will be severe to him."
[131] It is unclear whether this is the aspect, or the significator of the king. A marginal note in Madrid clarifies that this is the significator of the king, but I am not sure if this is a scribal note or part of the original translation.
[132] *Capitulum*.

7 And know [this] rationally from its defects[133] just as I have told you before in the chapter on the revolution, and you should not lose [sight of] the destruction nor fitness without looking at it, and you would see in addition the aid of the planets toward him according to the essences of the houses, through the longness and shortness of their houses.[134]

Chapter 28: On the impediment of the citizens of that clime

2 Know that a planet which was under the rays impedes the citizens of that clime, and destroys their condition, so they may acknowledge themselves to be subdued and to be subjects; and more strongly than that if it were in an angle at the revolution, or [if] a bad one looked at it. **3** Because if it were just as I have told you, under the rays, and it was at the end of the sign in which it is, and a bad one looked at it from the front part, and another bad one from the back part,[135] this clime will suffer according to the aspect of the bad one. **4** But if it was a conjunction in one sign, the whole of them will suffer; and if it was an opposition, half of them; but if it were from the square aspect, one-fourth of them. **5** But if Saturn went before it and Mars were after it, they will be taken captive, and only a few of them will be killed. **6** But if Mars went before him and Saturn were after him, the whole of them will be killed.

Chapter 29: On the enemies of the king

2 For[136] these people, look at the bad one which looks at the significator of the king. **3** If it looked at it from out of a sign in which the [significator of the] king had testimony, the enemy will be from his land, in accordance with the testimony.[137] **4** And if it looked at it from out of the house of the significator of the king, the enemy will be from his household members. **5**

---

[133] Reading with Madrid for Heller's "And know his departure rationally."
[134] Reading *domorum* with Madrid for Heller's *dominorum* ("lords"). Māshā'allāh seems to be referring to signs of long and short ascension, probably with the sense that aspects from signs of long ascension will be more effective.
[135] This must refer to besieging by degree (*ITA* IV.4.2). In this situation, the planet would be both besieged and in the bound of a malefic.
[136] For this paragraph, cf. Ch. 25 above.
[137] See the following sentences.

And if it looked at it from [the significator's] own exaltation, he will be of the nobles, from those who are like him, and of his rank. **6** But the triplicity and the bound signify the citizens of his domination.

7 And know that the trine and sextile aspects signify relatives. **8** And the opposition [signifies] enemies, and the first square aspect[138] signifies the house of the father, but the second square signifies influential people and those well-born, similar to the king, and of those who are fit for a kingdom. **9** For the conjunction, look to the sign about which we have spoken: because if [the significator of the king] had testimony in it,[139] he will be of those relatives who were nourished with him; and if it did not have testimony, their lineage will be one.[140] **10** Observe this chapter very well.

Chapter 30: On the power of the luminaries

2 After this, look at the places of the luminaries, and at their strength, and at their separation and conjunction, likewise to whom they are being joined,[141] or by the same token being separated: because the conjunction of the sextile or trine aspect is weak, but the opposition, square, and [bodily] conjunction strong. **3** Observe this chapter very well, because it signifies the quantity of their strength; and I will indicate to you generally the work of the seven planets, and their signification.

4 The Sun signifies the king, the Moon the generality of the common people, Jupiter signifies nobles, Mars signifies warriors, Saturn signifies the religious men of faith, Venus signifies women, Mercury signifies businessmen and boys. **5** Therefore see if one of these was a significator, whether it has a portion[142] of rulership in that year. **6** Because if it had a portion in that year, destruction and detriment will enter in upon [the people] which I said. **7**

---

[138] This aspect is cast forward in the order of signs, into a later degree (such as from Taurus to Leo). The second square aspect is cast backward against the order of signs, into an earlier degree (such as from Leo to Taurus). Here Māshā'allāh is saying that if the malefic falls on the fourth from the significator (the "first" square), then it pertains to the father; on the tenth, it pertains to an authority.

[139] Madrid has "they," referring both to the significator of the king and the malefic.

[140] That is, of the same lineage but not of the same household.

[141] Madrid says, "*namely*, to whom they are joined," thus omitting the consideration of the luminaries' relation to each other.

[142] This probably refers to playing a role by having a rulership, here and in the next sentence.

And its "portion" is that it would be in the Ascendant or in the Midheaven by its own degree and sign, except for Venus and the Moon: because these, if they were in their own houses in the west or in the angle of the earth, they signify a strong impediment, since these two are of the same nature.[143] **8** And Mars likewise is nocturnal, but he is below them [in strength]. **9** But Jupiter and Saturn and the Sun will be of their nature,[144] and more strongly than that if the Ascendant and the Midheaven is in their houses. **10** Every masculine planet will be stronger in the east, and likewise [in] their houses, and likewise if they were eastern. **11** And the feminine planets in the west are even stronger, and it will be better than that if they were southern,[145] and likewise in their houses.[146]

Chapter 31: On the division of the world according to the three superior planets

2 Know that the world is divided into three divisions according to the natures of the three planets which are above the Sun (namely according to their essences and complexions). **3** Therefore, the upper part of the world belongs to Saturn, and the middle part of the world belongs to Jupiter (and it is the temperate part, like the essence of Jupiter); but the lower part belongs to Mars, which is the hot part, and it is according to the essence of Mars.

4 And the Moon participates with Saturn in his part, because her sign is opposite the sign of Saturn. **5** Therefore from the quality of the mind[147] of the citizens of this part, there is a scarcity of wisdom and customs, a cutting-off of piety, and forgetfulness. **6** Also, their colors are red and white, but the

---

[143] That is, by sect. The Ascendant and Midheaven are conceived of as being masculine and diurnal.
[144] That is, of the nature of the Ascendant and Midheaven, diurnal.
[145] This might refer to southern ecliptical latitude.
[146] Māshā'allāh is drawing together the planets and the angles by the analogy of sect and elemental qualities. In other words, if a given planet is aspecting the luminaries, then that type of person will be affected most during the year; and if they are in angles appropriate to themselves, and especially if their domiciles are on those angles, then the significations will be even more relevant and powerful. So if Venus (a feminine, nocturnal planet) is in the seventh or fourth (both signifying a loss of light, and akin to femininity), and especially if Taurus or Libra is on that (or an) angle, then the people she signifies will even more certainly be affected.
[147] Reading with Madrid for Heller's "quality of the intemperate years."

whiteness is like leadenness.[148] **7** The complexion of them and of their air is even of the darkness of the earth.

8 And Mercury participates with Jupiter, because his house is opposed to his house. **9** Also,[149] the quality of the mind of the citizens of this part is wisdom, and certainty, and religion, and truth, and the kinship[150] of piety, and even sharpness of the mind. **10** And their colors are of a diverse complexion, namely commingled in whiteness and blackness and redness, because their houses are commingled from the cold of the earth and the heat of the air. **11** Therefore the division of these is more worthy and more valuable than the rest of the divisions, and their land (the land of the philosophers and the wise) is better than the other lands.

12 And Venus participates with Mars, because her house is opposed to his house, just as we have said before. **13** Also, from the quality of the mind of its citizens it is a part of the shamefulness and desire of Venus, and drinking parties and games, according to the places of its planets. **14** And their colors are commingled from the heat of the earth and the air.

15 And the Sun participates with Jupiter and Mercury in their parts.

Chapter 32: On the division of the climes

2 Also, the climes are divided according to these ways, in worldly quality and colors of bodies, according to the order of the circle in its latitude. **3** After this the climes are even divided over the twelve signs, which are the parts[151] of the circle; and in these are 360 lesser segments divided by the degrees of the Sun, which make 21,600 minutes. **4** But the lesser minutes are not necessary, except in a revolution of the years of the world, and namely in a revolution of the year pertaining to the topic of the Sun.[152] **5** Understand

---

[148] *Livido*. This word can also mean "black-and-blue."
[149] Reading this sentence with Madrid.
[150] Reading *communio* from Madrid's abbreviation.
[151] Madrid seems to read, "portals" or "doors" (*portae*).
[152] *In capitulis Solis*. I am uncertain what this means. It could refer to the direction of the Ascendant of a solar revolution (either of the world or a nativity) around the chart, as described by 'Umar al-Tabarī in *PN2* or in my audio workshop on this same topic (www.bendykes.com/audio/astrologylectures.php).

likewise in the equation of the Sun, so that the degree of the Ascendant and the quarters may not be concealed from you.[153]

Chapter 33: On the nature of the winds & triplicities

2 Moreover, the east and its wind is hot and dry, the west and its wind is cold and moist, the south and its wind is hot and moist, the north and its wind is cold and dry.

3 And likewise Aries and its triplicity is hot and dry, Taurus and its triplicity is cold and dry, Gemini and its triplicity is hot and moist, Cancer and its triplicity is cold and moist.

Chapter 34: On the number of cities in each clime

2 Also, they described that in the seven climes which is the world, there are cities and castles and villages according to the number of the twelve signs of heaven. **3** Likewise, the cities [are] just like the twelve signs, which are great cities, of which there are two in every clime: namely two of Saturn, two of Jupiter, two of Mars, two of Venus, one of the Sun, one of the Moon, two of Mercury.[154] **4** And I will reveal to you how many cities, villages and castles they said there were in the seven climes. **5** For[155] in the first clime they said there were 3,100; and in the second clime, 1,713; in the third, 1,077; in the fourth, 2,944; in the fifth, 3,006; in the sixth, 3,408; in the seventh, 3,300.

Chapter 35: When the Sun hands over his own management to the Moon

2 Therefore, look at the revolution in which, if the Sun hands over the management to the Moon (that is, if the revolution were in the night), look at the Moon and her place from the Ascendant, [to see] if it was consistent

---

[153] This seems simply to mean that one must be careful in calculating the exact time of the Sun's ingress.
[154] In other words, there are twelve great cities altogether.
[155] These numbers in Heller do not add up to 21,600 as claimed (nor do the slightly different numbers in Madrid). See the alternate values attributed to Hermes, described by al-Rijāl in his Ch. VIII.34, **16-18** (*AW1*, Section IV.4).

with her being the lord of the management. **3** [Then] look at the lord of her house, and the aspect of the planets to it,[156] and speak according to what you saw concerning the aspect of the bad ones and the fortunes, and their conjunction. **4** And look at her place from Saturn, what kind it is (namely whether she is being joined to him or being separated from him).[157] **5** Moreover, look for the increase or decrease of her light.

6 Also, look at whether an eclipse would happen to her in that year, or not.[158] **7** After this,[159] look at the eclipse of the Moon, and at its place, and at the eclipse of the Sun, and at its place, and at the aspect of the planets to it.

8 And know that if the lord of the Ascendant were impeded in that year, the king will send in detriment upon the rustics, and their condition will be made severe according to the essence of that sign, in that same land which belonged to that sign. **9** For example, if the Ascendant of the year was Libra, and Venus was falling,[160] or retrograde, or under the rays, the land of Libra will be destroyed, and infirmities and pestilence will befall it.

10 After this, look to every sign according to the being of its lord, and its place from it, and their fitness and detriment will be according to the aspect: and speak concerning this according to what you saw. **11** And if you made good concerning these things, look at the second sign and its lord, then at the third and its lord, just in the way I have told you, until you complete the twelve signs. **12** And you will look better in the signs of the angles, because they have a strength beyond the rest of the signs.

Chapter 36: On the signification of Mars & the other planets in the angles, if they were lords of the year

2 Know that if Mars were in the Midheaven at the hour of the revolution,[161] this will signify that the king will put some people in the gibbet. **3**

---

[156] This may be her lord, but as the Moon is masculine in Arabic, Māshā'allāh might mean the Moon (which makes a bit more astrological sense).
[157] This is probably because he is the malefic of the diurnal sect, and so is more problematic in a nocturnal chart.
[158] See also Ch. 40 below.
[159] I.e., if indeed an eclipse *would* happen.
[160] *Cadens.* This means being cadent, but I am not sure if Māshā'allāh means it by whole sign or quadrant divisions.
[161] In *Scito* and Sahl, Mars must also be in Gemini.

And if he were in the Ascendant or in the angle of the west, he will cut off the hands of some people of his rulership. **4** And in the angle of the earth, he will kill [them].

5 And if Saturn were in the Ascendant,[162] it signifies famine, death, infirmities, and vehement and harmful winds.

6 And if Mercury were the lord of the year and the lord of the Ascendant,[163] and he was free from the bad ones, and the fortunes were looking at him, the year will be good and useful for the wise, merchants, and boys. **7** And better than that if he were received by the lord of the house in which he was. **8** But if you found contrary things, say the contrary.

9 And if the Moon was in the Ascendant [and was] the lord of the year,[164] and she was free from the bad ones, rains will be multiplied, and rivers and cold will overflow, and men will find good and joy—and better than that if she were received.

10 And if Jupiter were in the Ascendant [and was the lord of the year], it will be a year of security, and the matters of men and the wealthy will be made fit, and they will be successful.[165] **11** And if he was received, the generality of the common people will find good from the king, and will esteem their king.

12 And if Mars were in the Ascendant [and was] the lord of the year,[166] there will be an earthquake in that land, and the rain will be little, and there will be [only] modest war.[167]

13 And if the Sun were in the Ascendant, and he was the lord of the year, and free from the bad ones, the wealthy will rejoice and good will overflow, and matters will be successful; but if he was impeded, everything that I said will be to the contrary.

---

[162] We should add, "and was lord of the year," as below. Cf. also *Scito* Ch. 79, **12**.
[163] Adding "and the lord of the Ascendant" with Madrid; but this should probably read simply, "And if Mercury were *in* the Ascendant," to parallel the other statements below.
[164] Adding "lord of the year" with Madrid.
[165] Or perhaps, "profitable" (*proficient*).
[166] Adding "lord of the year" with Madrid.
[167] For Venus, see *Scito* Ch. 79, **10-11**.

Chapter 37: On the calamities of the year[168]

2 Know that the condition of the year will be made severe if the bad ones were in the part of the upper circle, and in the northern part,[169] and especially if Mars handed over his own management to Saturn: because Saturn signifies severe things, and long-lasting ones, concerning the appearance of detriment in the earth, and the weakness of the king, and the taking away of faith and religion; and robberies will be multiplied, and contentions, and especially if one of the bad ones were in the Midheaven.

3 And in addition, look at the Moon: because if she handed over her own management to Saturn from the lower part of the circle, from under the earth, it signifies tribulation and detriment and the changing of the kingdom. **4** And if the Moon pushed her light to Saturn, and she was with him [in the same sign] or in the square aspect or in the opposition, it will be that much worse.

5 And look likewise at the Sun just as you have looked at the Moon:[170] because if he were received, it signifies the taking away[171] of the evil.

6 And know that the fortunes would signify the loosening of evil, and the taking away of it, if they were strong in their place, having good testimony. **7** And if they were direct, they signify good and fitness.

Chapter 38: On the signification of a planet when it enters burning or goes out from it

2 Know that when a planet goes out from under the rays and burning, it will be just like a boy who advances and is increased—so long as the bad ones did not look at it. **3** And likewise when it enters under the rays and burning, it will be like a worn-out old man. **4** Therefore, consider this chapter very well.

---

[168] For an alternative version of this chapter, see *Scito* Ch. 76, **1-8**.
[169] This may be something of a misread. My sense is that this means both (1) in the upper parts of their epicycles and/or deferents (toward their apogees) and (2) in northern ecliptical latitude. See *Scito* Ch. 76 for a lengthier version of this, and a different interpretation.
[170] This probably means, "the Sun's relationship to Mars," since Mars is the luminary of the nocturnal sect and so contrary to the Sun's (just as Saturn is of the diurnal sect and contrary to the Moon's).
[171] Reading *ablationem* with Madrid for Heller's "fitness" (*aptationem*).

Chapter 39: On the signification of Saturn when he is in his own exaltation

2 Consider the entrance of each planet into its own exaltation—and particularly Saturn, because then he is stronger. **3** And in addition, [see] what he would have in terms of testimony and strength: look even to see if he received management, because it will signify great things. **4** And likewise Jupiter and the rest of the planets.

5 And while the year is being revolved, look at the fortunes and the bad ones: if they were looking from out of a fixed sign, what they signified in terms of good or evil will be prolonged. **6** And if they looked from a movable sign, this will be modest; but if they looked from a common sign, it will be something in the middle.

Chapter 40: On an eclipse, if there were one in that same year

2 After this, look at the subject of an eclipse, if you knew that there would be an eclipse in that same year.[172] **3** And so, look in that year at the lord of the sign in which the eclipse will be, what its condition is, and what kind of place it has with the lord of the Ascendant of the eclipse, and what kind of condition it has from the lord of the year and the significator of the king, and how the fortunes or bad ones look at it. **4** Because if it[173] were impeded by the aspect of the bad ones, what it signified will be made worse[174] and multiplied, and more strongly so if the lord of the house of the eclipse was the significator of the king. **5** Because if it was the significator of the king, and there were bad ones looking at it, it will be feared concerning [the king] when the Sun arrives at the Midheaven of the eclipse. **6** And if it was the lord of the year, it will be feared concerning the rustics when the Sun arrives at the Ascendant of the eclipse, according to the judgment[175] of the nature of the Ascendant.

---

[172] See also Ch. 35 above.
[173] Despite **7** below, this is probably the lord of the sign of the eclipse.
[174] Reading *aggravabitur* with Madrid for Heller's more vague *exasperabitur* ("irritated").
[175] *Rationem*.

7 If it[176] was according the image of a man, there will be impediment in men; and if it was according to the essence of animals, it will be in animals; and if it was under the essence of water, it will be in waters, in accordance with the essence of the ascending sign.

8 And know that, of the hours of the eclipse of the Moon, there is a dividing up of one month to every hour; and for the eclipse of the Sun, a year for every hour.

9 After this, look at the bad ones: if they were in the Ascendant or closer to the Ascendant, there will be impediment in the middle part of the earth (which we said belongs to Jupiter and Mercury). **10** And if the bad ones were in the Midheaven, or closer to the Midheaven, it will be in the upper part of the orb[177] (which we have said belongs to Saturn and the Moon). **11** But in the west, or closer to the west, it will be in the lower part of the earth (which belongs to Mars and Venus).

Chapter 41: When the Sun is made the significator of the king

2 And if the Sun were the lord of the Ascendant in the revolution (wherefore Venus is then the lord of the Midheaven),[178] and were Venus under his rays, then the Sun will be the significator of the king.[179]

---

[176] Heller's sentence makes it seem like this is the Ascendant, but a marginal note in Madrid clarifies that this is the sign of the *eclipse*—which makes more sense in the context of Ptolemy's method. But as the medievals tended to focus more on the Ascendant of the eclipse and its lord, it may be that instead.

[177] "Of the orb" omitted in Madrid. See Ch. 31 above. Since Māshā'allāh is judging *visible* eclipses (as in Ptolemy), there are only three angles it can be on and so three regions of latitude: the fourth or lower Midheaven (the IC) is invisible, below the earth.

[178] This assumes Leo rising and Taurus as the 10th house. For present purposes Māshā'allāh is ignoring issues of whether the Sun is fit to be the lord.

[179] Sahl's version of **2** (and **7**) explains with a bit more detail: "And if the Sun was the lord of the Ascendant and Venus under his rays, then the Sun is first in the indication of the public and the king. And likewise if Venus was at the end of *its stake*, then she would also push power to the Sun, and the lord of the Midheaven would not be the indicator of the king, except in what I mentioned to you, that the lord of the Midheaven is pushing the management to the lord of the Ascendant" (Beatty Ar. 5467, fol. 157 lines 2-8). What does not quite make sense is "its stake," which could grammatically refer either to the Sun or Venus. But *Scito* Ch. 10, **1** makes it seem as though this "stake" or "angle" relates to her position in her epicycle. Nevertheless the Latin version here makes more sense, since it opposes being under the rays (**2**) with being out of them (**7**). To be in its "own light" means that Venus is out of the rays and not already connected to another planet. For parallel passages, see *Scito* Chs. 9-10.

3 Then, look at the condition of the king through his place from the bad ones and the fortunes, and from his strength in his own place, and from the aspect of the lords of the houses to him, according to what I have explained to you concerning their testimonies and aspects, until he completes[180] the twelve signs. **4** Therefore, look at which of the planets is in an optimal place, and which of them is impeded, and which burned up, or which is remote from the angle and the house, and pronounce the strength of evil from the bad ones, and the fitness of the good from the fortunes. **5** On the other hand, if the Sun was northern in his latitude, or he handed over his management to a northern bad one from the opposition or conjunction or the square aspect, or a trine or sextile, his signification will not be concealed from you. **6** And likewise if the[181] bad one handed over its own management to a planet in the sixth, it will signify infirmity, and likewise in the eighth it will signify death, and in the twelfth sorrow, distress, captivity, and enmities.

7 But if Venus had gone out from under the Sun's rays, in her own light, she will be more worthy for the signification of the king, and better than that if she were in the Midheaven.

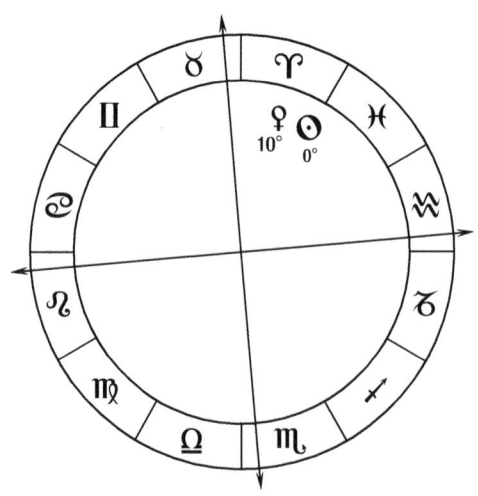

Figure 42: The Sun as significator of the people & the king

---

[180] This sounds like we are to make note of his transits throughout the year. But Madrid reads *explens* or perhaps *expleveris*, which is an instruction to the *astrologer* to complete an *analysis* of all the signs. I suspect Madrid is correct.

[181] I take this to be the malefic mentioned in the previous sentence, not just "a" malefic in general.

Chapter 42: On the condition of the king in that same year

2 Indeed if you knew [it] through what I said, and it was revealed to you concerning the signification of the king and the nobles and the rustics, see what will be concerning the king's condition in that same year: whether he will be made free not, and what kind of being he will have with his rustics, and whether he will have a faraway or nearby foreign journey, or war, or what will be concerning his matters.[182] **3** But look at this[183] from the lord of the house of foreign travel at the hour of the revolution, and from its place in the circle: because if it was direct or[184] received in its place, he will go leisurely[185] and by roaming; and if it was slow and in its station, it signifies slowness on the foreign journey. **4** And if it was retrograde and received, he will go out and turn back quickly; and if it were retrograde without reception, it signifies detriment in the king's foreign journey, and it will not be completed.

5 After this, look at the house[186] of foreign travel. **6** If its lord were retrograde, seeing its own house from the square aspect or the opposition, he will go to battle [with] an enemy. **7** And if it looked from the trine or sextile aspect, he will to go make peace.[187]

8 After this, look for his being safe[188] on his foreign journey and the condition of his body, and to his significator. **9** If it were free from the bad ones and from its enemies (of the planets), and the lord of the house of foreign travel is not in the house of infirmity or in a place of impediment, the king will be kept safe on his foreign journey. **10** Which if the significator of the king were free from those things which I said, and the lord of the house of foreign travel was impeded, it signifies difficulty for the king on the journey, and grief and infirmity, according to the quality of the essence of the sign. **11** And if the lord of the house of foreign travel was free from the malefics and

---

[182] Reading *rebus* for *re*.
[183] That is, foreign travel.
[184] Madrid reads, "and," which is probably correct.
[185] Reading *spaciatum* with Madrid for Heller's puzzling *exaciatum*.
[186] Reading *domum* for *dominum* ("lord").
[187] This seems to be related to the idea that the type of aspect shows the type of person or purpose; the key here is not that the lord is aspecting its own domicile, but what kind of aspect it is. And this seems different than speaking of whether the malefics are aspecting: the lord of the 9th represents not just the foreign travel, but the king's control over it, and his intentions; so if the lord aspects, it shows actual control and intention, and the type of aspect shows the purpose.
[188] Here and below ("kept safe") the noun/verb pair is *salvatio/salvo*, which has connotations both of being saved (including in the religious sense), safe, and healthy.

[the king's] significator was impeded, what he was fearing will happen to him from hindrance or infirmity.

12 After this, look at the lord of the house of foreign travel. **13** If it were in the second, he will go out to gather assets. **14** And if it were in the third (because it is in the opposition of its house) he will go out to the contention of war. **15** And if it were in the fourth, it will signify that the foreign travel will be bad, and death will be feared concerning him in that year.[189] **16** And if a bad one looked at it from the square aspect or the opposition or conjunction, what is signified by the matter will be more severe, and it will be feared concerning him.[190]

17 And if the significator of the king were in the Ascendant at the hour of the revolution, it signifies tranquility, and he will not go on a foreign journey. **18** But if it was remote from the Ascendant, and another planet [was] in the Ascendant with it, not remote,[191] look at who that planet is. **19** Because if it was an enemy of the significator, he will go out regarding him who seeks his kingdom, and he contends with him in it. **20** And if it was a friend, he will hand over his kingdom to the man whose significator that planet is, and he will be put in charge of that kingdom.[192]

21 And if the significator of the king was in the second from the Ascendant, he will seek assets in that same year. **22** But if a bad one was with it, or looked at it from the square aspect or the opposition or the conjunction, he will squander his assets, and will extract his treasures. **23** And if it was in the third, he will multiply his cavalry, and he will desire a foreign journey. **24** And if it was in the fourth, he will not go on a foreign journey but he will desire quiet. **25** And if it was in the fifth, he will have a son, and he will long for[193] him. **26** And if it was in the sixth, infirmity will befall him. **27** And if it was in the seventh, his sexual intercourse will be multiplied. **28** And if it was in the eighth, death will be feared concerning him. **29** And if it was in the ninth, he will go on a foreign journey. **30** And if it was in the tenth, he will be strengthened in his kingdom. **31** And this is so known from its condition in its direct motion and retrogradation and station: because directness signifies

---

[189] The fourth is the eighth (death) from the ninth.
[190] For the remaining houses, see *Scito* Ch. 70, **7-19**.
[191] I believe this means that both planets are in the rising sign, but the significator of the king is far away from the degree of the Ascendant in an earlier degree, while the other planet is in a later degree.
[192] This must mean that he will set up a friend to rule the kingdom in his absence while he is abroad.
[193] *Desiderabit*. This could perhaps be a scribal error for *diliget*, "he will love/esteem" him.

fitness, and retrogradation signifies detriment, and its first station is just like retrogradation, and its second station is just like being direct. **32** And if [it] was in the eleventh, it signifies fitness, esteem, piety, liberality and expenses: because this house is the second from the house of the king. **33** And if it was in the twelfth, it signifies searching for his enemies,[194] and his purpose in that. **34** Which if then the significator of the king looked at the lord of his house, he will win victory [over] them, if God wills.

35 And say likewise if the significator of the king handed over management to the lords of these houses which I said: for it will signify the same for him[195] as it would signify if it was in their houses. **36** And if the significator of the king were joined to a planet appearing in the ninth or the third, it signifies a foreign journey. **37** And likewise, a conjunction with the lord of the house of infirmity or with the lord of the house of death signifies the infirmity or death of the king. **38** And if the significator of the king was under the rays or near them by 12°, it will be feared concerning the king,[196] and this will be at the hour of its burning.[197] **39** And likewise the lord of the ninth: if it was falling or in a bad place, it will be feared for him on his foreign journey.[198]

Chapter 43: On the impediment of the rustics

2 And if the lord of the Ascendant were burned in an angle, impediment will enter in upon the rustics. **3** And if it was burned in the Midheaven, this impediment will be in connection with the king. **4** And if the Sun was the lord of the Midheaven, and the lord of the Ascendant burned, men will find difficulty from the king, because it is under the rays. **5** If the burning were in the fourth angle (which is the angle of the earth), it signifies that death will fall on men.

---

[194] Reading *inquisitionem* with Madrid for Heller's *acquisitionem* ("the acquisition of his enemies").
[195] Reading *ei* with Madrid for Heller's *ibi* ("there").
[196] Omitting a redundant "at the hour of its burning."
[197] *Scito*'s muddled version of this sentence (Ch. 73, **25**) suggests that each degree between the significator and the Sun should be considered as one month of time.
[198] That is, if the significator of the king was joined with a lord of the ninth who was in such a condition.

6 Which if the Ascendant was a feminine sign this will be in women, and if it was masculine this will be in men. **7** And if Mercury was the lord of the Ascendant this will be in boys; and if it was Venus or the Moon it will be more in women; and if it was Jupiter or Saturn it will be in middle-aged people;[199] and if it was the Sun or Mars they signify young men. **8** And if [the lord] was eastern it will be in boys and youths; and if it was western it will be in old men and little old ladies.[200]

Chapter 44: On the detriment of the king

2 Look for the king (at the hour of the revolution) from the Sun. **3** Which if Mars looked at him or was joined to him, killing will be feared concerning him; and if he was joined to Saturn, difficulty and poison will be feared for him.

4 And if the lord of the Ascendant of the year was burned up in the Midheaven, what I said will be feared in the same ways, and it will be in his own region in which he is, and it will not be outside of that land. **5** And if the burning was in the angle of the earth or in the opposite [of the Ascendant], that is, the seventh, what I told you will be from someone who will come outside the land in which he is. **6** And in this subject, the opposition of the bad ones and their square aspect is more severe than their conjunction.

7 And if the Sun were the significator of the king, and he looked at Jupiter from the opposition, the king will become angry with[201] his household members, and he will hold them in suspicion, and he will be burdened by them. **8** And likewise if the lord of the Ascendant was opposed: he will get angry[202] with his rustics, he will mistrust them badly, and will impede them. **9** Finally, know the reception of the planets with one another, and the projection of their lights. **10** And know the agreement or disagreement[203] of the Ascendant and its lord.

---

[199] *Mediocribus.*
[200] Reading *anibus* with Madrid for Heller's *vetulis* ("poor old ladies"). *Cf.* Ch. 14 for a similar statement about ages.
[201] Madrid reads, "will be inimical to."
[202] Again, Madrid has "will be inimical to."
[203] Madrid has, "friendship and enmity" of the Ascendant and its lord, which suggests good and bad aspects to them.

Chapter 45: On the signification of Mars [in the triplicities][204]

2 Know that each bad one (namely Saturn and Mars), if one of them were in an angle in the revolution of the year, <it will have indications based on its position and direct or retrograde motion>.[205]

3 And [if] Mars were direct in earthy signs <and angular>, it signifies the destruction of trees and the death of animals. **4** And if Mars looked at the significator of the king, <what he indicates is particular to the king>. **5** And [if] Mars was commingled with the light of Saturn, <it is more intense>. **6** <If Mars is retrograde>, it signifies contention and the shedding of blood.

7 And if he were in an airy sign, <angular and direct>, it signifies <fighting and bloodshed because of justice and seeking truth; but if retrograde, it is because of> injuries and enmities. **8** But if he was not in an angle, and he looked at the Ascendant, it signifies infirmity from winds and blood,[206] and more severely in every land in whose sign his light was [by body] or the opposition, or a square aspect. **9** Which if he were retrograde, it signifies pestilence. **10** And if he were in a sign which does not look at the Ascendant, and he was direct, it will signify <burning and> infirmity, and the detriment of seeds. **11** But if he were retrograde, it will signify death and infirmity and blood.

12 And if Mars was the lord of the year, and he was in fiery signs, and he was in an angle, direct, he signifies a hot and dry infirmity, and the powerful will contend with each other. **13** And if he were retrograde this will be more severe, and destruction and robberies will be multiplied. **14** But if he were in fiery signs outside an angle, and he did not look at the Ascendant <but was direct>, men will afflict each other with injuries, and this will be more severe in the sign in which his square aspect or opposition is. **15** <If he is retrograde, it is stronger.> **16** <If he does not look at the Ascendant and is direct, it indicates heat.> **17** <If retrograde, it is more intense>, and the impediment which I told you <about will affect the countries of the signs which he

---

[204] For this chapter, cf. *BRD* II.8, **21, 25, 27, 23**.
[205] Based on the parallel passages in Abū Ma'shar's *BRD*, we are generally assuming that the malefic is also the lord of the year—even though in some cases the text has the malefic angular (or in some other place) and looking at the lord of the year instead.
[206] This must be related to ancient and medieval notions of the passage of air into the blood through the lungs. See *On Sig. Planet.* Ch. 7, in *WSM*.

sees from the square and opposition, and it> will be according to the essence of that same sign, and the nature of the planet.[207]

Chapter 46: On the signification of Saturn in the triplicities[208]

2 If Saturn were the lord of the year, and he was in Aries and its triplicity, and he was direct in an angle, it will signify many rains, and the contentions of the wealthy, and more strongly so if he received the management of Mars and his strength: because it signifies that the rustics would contend with the king. **3** And if he were retrograde, the condition of men will be burdened. **4** And if he were remote from the angle [but] looking at the Ascendant, difficulty will enter in on top of the nobles if he were direct; but if he were retrograde, he will destroy the houses of assets. **5** And if he received management from Mars and the Moon, it signifies a severe cold and the death of animals, along with what I told you about wars and conflicts. **6** And if he was falling and did not look at the Ascendant, and he was direct, the cold of winter will be made severe; but if he were retrograde <and Mars is looking at him>, there will be contention and rebellion among the rustics.

7 And if Saturn were the lord of the year in earthy signs, in an angle, direct, it signifies contention and war, and the death of animals, particularly in that land in whose sign he was. **8** And if he were retrograde, it will destroy harvests and seeds, and youths will die, and more strongly so if he were in the Midheaven. **9** And if he were remote from the angle, looking at the Ascendant, <and is direct, plants will not be corrupted.> **10** <If he were retrograde>, seeds will be destroyed, and youths will die, and the harvests will be little. **11** But if he did not look at the Ascendant, <and is direct>, the evil will be modest.

12 And if Saturn were the lord of the year and was in Gemini and its triplicity, and he was in an angle of the Ascendant of the year, <direct>, northern winds will be burdensome, and they will be strong and harmful, and an infirmity of the essence of Saturn will befall the rustics, and there will be war and contention and the shedding of blood in men. **13** And if he were

---

[207] The Latin texts omit Mars in the watery signs, corresponding to *BRD* II.8, **29**.
[208] For this chapter, cf. *BRD* II.8, **22, 24, 26, 28**. The sentences here are in a different order than in *BRD*, so that it is difficult to know whether and how to rearrange them.

retrograde, it signifies the contention of the wealthy and the nobles, and[209] if he were in the angle of the earth, and he was the lord of the year in this triplicity, it signifies earthquake. **14** And if he was not the lord of the year, and he received the management of the lord of the Ascendant, and he was in this place, men will die in an earthquake. **15** And if he received the management of the lord of the Midheaven, it signifies contention and battle in the acquisition of the kingdom. **16** And if he were remote from the angle and was direct, <looking at the Ascendant>, severe winter cold and winds will arise. **17** And if he were retrograde and remote, it signifies infirmity and winds. **18** And if he were falling, and did not look at the Ascendant, and he was direct, <the blowing of winds will be cold, with much coldness in the countries of the sign in which he is.> **19** <If he is retrograde>, the southern winds and infirmities will be multiplied, and this will be collectively in low-class persons.

20 And if Saturn were the lord of the year, and he was in watery signs, in an angle, <and Mars is falling from him>, the cold will be severe, and locusts will be multiplied. **21** And if he were retrograde, there will be the greatest battle and powerful death. **22** But if he were remote from the angle, <but is looking at the Ascendant and is direct>, rains and waters will be multiplied. **23** And[210] if a planetary fortune is joined to him, it decreases the said hardships. **24** And if he were falling, not looking at the Ascendant, <and direct, and Mars is falling from him, there will be peace rather than evil.> **25** <But> it signifies the infirmity of the citizens of the sign in which he is, <even though they will be cured>. **26** But if he were retrograde, <and Mars looks at him, and the fortunes are falling from him>, the cold will be severe, and locusts will be multiplied.

---

[209] The rest of this sentence, through **15**, appeared near the end of the paragraph in the Latin, but I have replaced them up here so as to be in accord with *BRD*.

[210] This sentence was originally the last in the paragraph, but I have put it here so as to be in accord with *BRD*.

Section II.3:
Māshā'allāh, *Letter on Eclipses*

Comment by Dykes. The Arabic original of this work is lost, and only Hebrew and Latin versions survive. In the Latin it is often called the *Letter on Eclipses* (hereafter, *Letter*), but in light of the lengthier Hebrew title (which I have used below), "eclipses" was probably only the beginning of its title. Hervagius (below) adopts part of the first sentence for his title.

The earliest complete Hebrew manuscript version is dated 1367 AD (Sela, p. 236), and it is close to John of Seville's 12th Century Latin.[1] The Hebrew translation has been attributed to ibn Ezra himself, but Sela argues (pp. 237-38) that the Hebrew translation was made by someone who nevertheless was familiar with ibn Ezra's style and idiosyncratic vocabulary (and seems to have had access to *both* the Arabic and John's Latin). Sela's argument is that ibn Ezra usually identifies himself as the author (but does not do so here), and moreover never refers to this work in his two Hebrew mundane books, even though he does often cite Māshā'allāh. The Hebrew also includes technical terms which ibn Ezra does not use, and includes Latin transliterations and loanwords which ibn Ezra tends to avoid.

Letter is a brief introductory work on eclipses, some weather and other mundane indications, and conjunctional theory. Unlike in other works, Māshā'allāh has four types of conjunctions here, which Sela (p. 236) says was never used by other Arabic-speaking astrologers, nor ibn Ezra nor Abraham bar Hiyya. They are:

- Greatest conjunction: a conjunction of all three superiors (Ch. 9).
- Greater conjunction: Saturn-Jupiter (Ch. 10).
- Middle conjunction: Saturn-Mars (Ch. 11).
- Lesser conjunction: Jupiter-Mars (Ch. 12).

For this translation from Latin, I have used the following:

- Paris BNF lat. 16204 (13th Cent.), ff. 387-91, which labels this work "On the Roots of Revolutions."
- Hervagius 1533 (printed edition).

---

[1] Sela points out that the earliest partial copy known to him can be dated to 1257 (p. 236).

- Heller 1549 (printed edition).
- Sela 2010, pp. 235-59 (critical edition of the Hebrew).

℘ ℘ ℘

On eclipses of the Moon and the Sun, the conjunctions of the planets, & the revolutions of years

2 The first chapter is on the system[2] of the circle and stars, and how they operate in this world.

The second chapter: on the diversity of the footprints: that is, of the work of the stars in the regions of the earth.

The third chapter: on the signs and their natures (namely, the hot and cold), and that, of them, there are the fixed or movable, diurnal, or nocturnal.

Fourth: on the revolution of years.

Fifth: on the eclipse of the Moon, and its signification.

Sixth: on the changing of weather through the alteration of the planets (namely, of the heavy ones).

Seventh: on the eclipse of the Sun, and its signification.

Eighth: on the conjunction of the planets, and its work.

Ninth: on the conjunction of the higher planets.

Tenth: on the greater[3] conjunction.

Eleventh: on the middle conjunction.

Twelfth: on the lesser conjunction.

---

[2] *Ratione.* This might also be read as, "doctrine, calculation," *etc.*
[3] Reading *maiori* for *maiorum*.

Chapter 1: On the system of the circle of the stars, & how they operate in this world

2 Māshā'allāh said:[4] The Lord Most High has made the earth in the likeness of a sphere, and He made the higher circle[5] be spinning in the circumference[6] of the same, and He placed the earth fixed and immobile, and in the middle of the circle, not declining to the right nor to the left, and He placed the four elements [as being] mobile (that is, He made them be moved by the motion of the seven planets). **3** But the Head of the Dragon, and the signs, and all of the stars, participate with the seven planets in their works and natures. **4** And therefore the work of the planets in this world is like the magnet stone and iron:[7] because just as iron is attracted to this stone[8] from a known distance, so every creature and everything which is upon the earth is brought about by the motion of the planets and all things which are above the earth—both that of seeds and animals—namely, fortune or impediment. **5** Also, fitness or destruction comes to be from the motions of the planets in their works, the greatest indication of which matter is the diversity of men in their conditions, and in fortunes and misfortunes. **6** And since we see certain rational men deprived of goods, but certain stupid men enjoying goods to the fullest, [we must ask] whether[9] this does not have any cause signifying that fortune and misfortune would come to be apart from the decision and will of those who undergo fortunes or impediments. **7** And all of this, by the will of God, is the work of the planets, and their fortune and misfortune.[10]

---

[4] Omitting *quia*, which may have originally been written as *quod*, which is the sense of the Hebrew.
[5] That is, the outer heavens.
[6] *Circuitu*.
[7] Compare with Sahl's *On Elections* §10b, in my *Choices & Inceptions*.
[8] Reading *ad* for *ab*.
[9] *Numquid hoc*.
[10] This is a rough attempt at a theodicy, using the planets and God's will as an explanation as to why the wicked flourish and the virtuous suffer. (See also Bonatti's slightly more extended take on this in the *Book of Astronomy* pp. 637-38.) Māshā'allāh is saying that while we would expect people to get what they deserve through their own merit and choices, planetary effects (which have been put into motion by God) sometimes override this, bringing benefit to the undeserving and withholding it from the deserving.

Chapter 2: On the diversity of the work of the stars in the regions[11] of the earth

2 Māshā'allāh said: Know that the planets have diverse work according to the diversity of the climes. **3** Because in certain climes certain planets come to be fortunes, and certain ones bad—in another clime, in different arrangements.[12] **4** And in fact every rational being ought to understand the reasons for the climes and regions: like the land of the Ethiopians, in which there is always heat, and the land of the Slavs, among whom there is always cold. **5** And if the planets signified overflowing cold for the citizens of Ethiopia, their air is tempered;[13] and if the planets signified this for the Slavs, their air will be corrupted, and their habitation will be ruined. **6** And because of this, the knowledge of the reason[14] for the climes and regions and air is necessary.

7 And know that the knowledge of the stars is very serious, and that the most worthy thing can be known from it: that is, namely, every general thing and what pertains to many,[15] as are the revolutions of years and eclipses—understand the significations of these. **8** And this is not known except by an acquaintance with the natures of the signs and whatever each one of them signifies in terms of regions and provinces and universal matters. **9** And we have already said this before in our books, but now let us state briefly a part of these matters, and let us begin (with the aid of God).

Chapter 3: On the natures of the signs

2 Māshā'allāh said: The signs are twelve, in individual [signs are] 30°, in a degree 60', in a minute 60", and thus up to the quantity of a point,[16] up to the infinite. **3** And these are their names: Aries, Taurus, Gemini, Cancer, Leo, Virgo, Libra, Scorpio, Sagittarius, Capricorn, Aquarius, Pisces.

4 And they have significations over fire, and air, water, and earth.[17] **5** Of them, three are fiery: namely Aries, Leo, and Sagittarius. **6** And three earthy

---

[11] Reading *plagis* in the classical sense.
[12] *Ordinibus*. That is, planets that are benefic in one region, may be malefic in another.
[13] *Temperatur*, lit. "combined properly."
[14] *Rationis*.
[15] *Plurale*.
[16] Omitting *primi*.
[17] Adding with 1533 (and the Hebrew).

ones: Taurus, Virgo, and Capricorn. **7** And three airy ones: Gemini, Libra, and Aquarius. **8** And three watery ones: Cancer, Scorpio, and Pisces.

9 The fiery and airy signs are masculine, the earthy and watery ones feminine. **10** And all of the [masculine] ones are diurnal, and the feminine ones nocturnal.

11 Also, four of the signs are movable (namely, in which the weather is moved), which are Aries, Cancer, Libra, and Capricorn. **12** And four [are] fixed (in which the weather is fixed), namely Taurus, Leo, Scorpio, and Aquarius. **13** Also, four are bicorporeal or common (in which two bodies[18] are joined):[19] which are Gemini, Virgo, Sagittarius, and Pisces. **14** These are the natures of the signs.

Chapter 4: On the revolution of years

2 Māshā'allāh said: If you want to know what would happen in the world from winds and from rains, and the rest, establish the Ascendant at the hour of the Sun's entrance into the first point of Aries, and establish the seven planets for that same hour. **3** And, the figure having been made, consider which of them is in charge of it.[20] **4** Which if it were a fortune, the season will be made fit; but if it was a bad one or impeded, the world will be corrupted. **5** And do likewise in the quarters of the year and its months.

6 And know that if many planets were conjoined in watery signs at the revolution of the year, they will signify a multitude of rain; and in fiery signs, an overflowing of heat and dryness or the sterility of the land;[21] and in the airy ones, a multitude of winds; and in the earthy ones, frost and snows. **7** And likewise in the quarters of the year: if the planets were in cold signs, they will signify the severity of the cold and the decrease of heat.

8 Also, know that if Mars and Saturn were in charge of [the year], and the fortunes did not look at them, they will signify a multitude of war, and the destruction of the world. **9** Thus even if Mars were the lord of the summer quarter, and he was in one of the houses of Mercury, it will signify a multitude of rains and pestilences. **10** And you should know that the severity of

---

[18] Following Paris. 1533 reads, "seasons," which was evidently meant to parallel the above statements about weather).
[19] The Hebrew adds: "because weather becomes mixed" when the Sun is in them.
[20] See Māshā'allāh's general rules in *RYW*, Prologue and Ch. 6 (Section II.2 of this book).
[21] The Hebrew adds, "high prices."

the dryness and the sterility of the earth, or the dearth of the grain supply, does not come to be except from the conjunction of the planets in the fiery signs. **11** Understand this, and test it, and you will discover.

Chapter 5: On the eclipse of the Moon, & its being

2 Māshā'allāh said: It behooves you to consider the eclipses of the year (both the lunar ones and the solar ones), and to know the Ascendant of the middle of the eclipse,[22] and the one who is in charge of that same Ascendant and of its figure. **3** Which if it were a bad one, it will signify impediment and destruction. **4** But if it was a fortune, it will signify fitness.

5 And know that the eclipse of the Moon, if it were in the cold signs, signifies the severity of the cold, and in watery ones the severity of rains, if the season supported it (that is, if it were winter). **6** But if it was summer, it will signify the temperateness of the air. **7** Understand and test the rest thusly. **8** You should understand that if the fortunes looked at the Moon and received her, [the eclipse's] signification will be with respect to those things which they signify concerning good and profit.[23]

Chapter 6: On the changing of the seasons by the changing of the planets (namely, the heavy ones)

2 Māshā'allāh said: If you wished to know the variation of the season with respect to the diverse things of the corruptible world, know the signs of the heavy planets (namely, whether they are hot or cold). **3** Which if they were hot, it will signify heat in the summer, [but] the temperateness of the air in the winter. **4** And if they were in the cold signs, it will signify cold in the winter and temperateness in the summer.

5 Likewise, if the planets were conjoined in watery signs it will signify overflowing rains (and the corruption of the air by those same rains)[24] in the

---

[22] That is, the time of the eclipse's center.
[23] *Proficuum*. This should be taken broadly, to include whatever is beneficial or profitable (including good weather).
[24] Adding a parenthetical remark from 1533, to reflect the Hebrew (which has "bad weather").

winter, and the good mixture of the air in the summer and a multitude[25] of dew. **6** And test according to this, because you will not go astray.

7 But the heavy planets are Saturn, Jupiter and Mars, and you ought to combine the Sun with them, too.[26] **8** In short, know that the heavy planets, if they were in the direction of any of the regions, they will signify dryness and the sterility of the earth; but if they were elongated from it, they will signify a multitude of rains. **9** By "nearness" I want it to be understood that they are in northern signs, and by "distance," in southern ones.[27]

10 Know also that the heavy planets, if they were all western,[28] they signify a multitude of rains in the winter and the good mixture of the air in the summer. **11** And likewise, in arising[29] they signify the good mixture of the air in the winter and excessive dryness in the summer.

Chapter 7: On the eclipse of the Sun & its signification

2 Māshā'allāh said:[30] Know that in an eclipse of the Sun, it cannot come to be but that some great event would be signified, according to the size of the eclipse—that is, that it comes to be from one-fourth of the Sun's body, and [what is] above that.[31] **3** But the knowledge of those things which happen from the eclipse of the Sun, is that you should know the Ascendant of the middle of the eclipse, and the planets conquering over[32] the figures of the eclipse. **4** Which if [the victors] were bad ones, they will signify the hin-

---

[25] Reading *multitudinem* for *similitudinem*.
[26] That is, include the Sun along with them when looking at the signs.
[27] As Sela points out (p. 251, n. 22), Māshā'allāh probably means that planets in signs of northern declination will be closer to the climes of the northern hemisphere (which were the primary inhabitable ones). Thus, the southern signs were considered to be more distant. Compare this with al-Kindī's doctrines in *AW1*, and note that when the Sun in particular is in the northern signs, it is spring and summer (hotter) in the northern hemisphere.
[28] That is, sinking under the rays or rising after the Sun in a later degree.
[29] That is, being eastern of the Sun or rising out of the rays in degrees preceding him.
[30] Reading **2** and **3** with 1533, which matches the Hebrew more closely. Paris combines the first two sentences, saying: "**2** Māshā'allāh said: Know that in an eclipse of the Sun, it cannot be but that some great event would be signified, according to the size of the eclipse and the planets conquering over the sign of the eclipse."
[31] Māshā'allāh seems to be referring to the notion that the more the Sun is eclipsed, the greater the extent of the effects: see Ptolemy's view in *AW1*, Section III.2 (from *Tet.* II.7, **13**).
[32] This refers to victors, i.e., planets which have the most rulership and authority.

drance and corruption of kings and the wealthy; and if they were fortunes, they will signify the good fortune and fitness of the being of things.

5 And you should know that the eclipse of the Sun, if it were in Aries, will signify the ruin[33] of kings and the wealthy, and dryness or the sterility of the earth, and famine; and thus in the rest of the fiery signs. **6** But in the watery ones, it will signify a multitude of rains, and detriment from them. **7** Understand also that if the fortunes were looking [at the eclipse], they will subtract evil. **8** But if the bad ones were looking, they will amplify [the evil] and will subtract fortune.

9 Know even that if the Sun or the Moon were [someone's][34] releaser or house-master,[35] and it was [the one] obscured [in the eclipse], it will signify great danger or a serious infirmity for him whose releaser or house-master it was, unless the fortunes were looking [at it].[36]

Chapter 8: On the conjunction of the planets & their effect

2 Māshā'allāh said: The conjunction of the planets signifies the accidents of this world and its matters, which must thus be considered at the time of the conjunction of the higher and lower planets.[37] **3** Because the fortunes signify good fortune and a good effect, if they conquered over the figure of the conjunction. **4** But if the bad ones conquered, they will signify evil and the effecting of evil. **5** Wherefore, [if] you even knew [that the bad ones] were conjoined in any one of the signs, they will signify detriment and a multitude of evil according to the essence of that same sign. **6** That is, if the conjunction were in watery signs, it will signify the detriment of the rains, and thusly in the rest of the signs. **7** If however they were conjoined in femi-

---

[33] *Interitum*, which can also mean "death," but I take it that the translator would have used *mortem* if he had meant death.
[34] Adding with 1533.
[35] *Hyleg vel alcochoden*, also known as the *hilāj* and *kadukhudāh*, two of the primary indicators of longevity in Perso-Arabic natal astrology.
[36] In other words, see if your natal releaser or house-master is a luminary: when that luminary undergoes eclipse in real time, it indicates difficulties unless the benefics aspect it. But Māshā'allāh does not say whether these are the transiting benefics' aspects to the natal luminary, or to the eclipse itself, or they are the natal benefics' aspect to the position of the real-time eclipse, or what.
[37] This is very close to statements about the "opening of the doors" in weather prediction: see similar quotes by Māshā'allāh and 'Umar in *AW1*: Section I.5 (Ch. 82, **18**), and Section I.7, **32**.

nine signs, they will signify pestilences and the death of animals of the feminine sex (and the same is said concerning masculine [signs and sexes]).

8 And know that the conjunctions [of the planets][38] and the eclipse of the luminaries, if they were in fixed signs, will signify the lastingness of evil and its detriment; and if they were in movable signs, they will signify the smallness of the lastingness of the evil and its detriment; but if they were in common signs, they will signify mediocre evil. **9** And say thus about the good.

Chapter 9: On the conjunction of the superior planets

2 Māshā'allāh said: Know that the greatest things, and those to be marveled at, happen from the conjunction of the superior planets, and this comes to be on account of the slowness of their motion. **3** And if these three were conjoined in one bound or face, and the Sun looked at them, they will signify the destructions of sects and kingdoms, and the changing of them [from one place to another], and the greatest matters, in accordance with the stronger of them, and of the one conquering over their signs.[39] **4** And this is their greatest conjunction, which signifies prophets[40] and the destruction of certain climes, and the greatest matters, and especially of any of the inferior planets gave aid to them. **5** And you should know that the one stronger than the rest will be the significator: which if it were a fortune, it will signify good fortune; and if it were a bad one, it will signify evil and tribulation.

6 Understand even that these planets, if they were conjoined in their own exaltations, they will signify good and the fitness of the weather, and a multitude of the stirring-up of wars, and the demonstration of miracles. **7** But if they were conjoined in their falls, they will signify the detriment and dryness and sterility of the earth, and famine, unless they are made fortunate.[41] **8** Wherefore, [if] you knew [that] they were conjoined in a fiery sign, they will even signify the sterility of the earth; and in a watery sign, they will signify a multitude of rain; in an airy one, the strength of the winds; and in an earthy

---

[38] Probably of the malefic planets, as in the previous sentences.
[39] That is, of the most significant planet among the three themselves, as well as the victor over their position. See **5** below.
[40] Reading with the Hebrew, for "prophecies."
[41] Sela's translation of the Hebrew has, "benefic."

one, the overflowing of cold and detriment. **9** And if they were conjoined in masculine signs, they will signify the detriment of masculine animals; and thus with the feminine ones.

Chapter 10: On the greater conjunction

2 Māshā'allāh said: We have already stated that the [most] principal[42] things happen from the greatest[43] [kind of] conjunction, which is that of the superior planets. **3** But these superior planets have other conjunctions, even ones signifying greater events. **4** For the conjunction of Saturn and Jupiter is the greater conjunction, and it signifies [great] events and sects. **5** But the knowledge of the events from this is had by looking at the Ascendant, and at the planets at the hour of their conjunction,[44] and which of them rules in the figure. **6** Which if [the ruler or victor] were a fortune, it will signify good and the fitness of the times; and if it was a bad one, [it will signify] detriment and dryness, and moreover the sterility of the earth, and wars. **7** And know also that if Jupiter were stronger than Saturn, it will signify good in that same conjunction; but if Saturn will be in charge, it will signify detriment and tribulation.

8 And know that their conjunction in the fiery and airy signs signifies dryness and the sterility of the earth, and moreover the severity of the cold; and in earthy ones, the destruction of seeds, and famine. **9** In watery ones it will signify the excessiveness of rains and of pestilence, under the condition that they are impeded. **10** Finally,[45] if they were made fortunate, they will signify the increase of goods in all things signified by them; and if bad, decrease.

11 Moreover, know that the greater conjunction, if it were in any of the angles (and especially in the angle of the Midheaven), it will signify the ap-

---

[42] The Hebrew has, "momentous."
[43] *Maiori*, but reading in the superlative to distinguish it from the "great" or "greater" conjunction of Saturn-Jupiter, discussed below.
[44] This may be preferable in theory, but most texts cast the chart for the Aries ingress of the year in which the *mean* conjunction occurs, not the true conjunction (see my Introduction). At any rate, medievals like Māshā'allāh would not have been able to calculate the true conjunction accurately enough to get the right Ascendant.
[45] The Hebrew version connects this to the previous sentence, so that Māshā'allāh is continuing to speak of their good or bad condition in the watery signs.

pearance of a king or a prophet from the direction of that same sign.[46] **12** But if that sign itself were made fortunate, and its lord of a good condition, this will signify his triumph and domination; but if [the sign] and its lord were impeded, it will signify his ruin and dejection. **13** And the conjunction will have to be [determined][47] after the noted years of that conjunction, which we have brought up elsewhere.

Chapter 11: On the middle conjunction

2 Māshā'allāh said: The middle conjunction is namely the conjunction of Mars and Saturn, and it signifies the happening of wars and the contrarieties of battles. **3** If you wished to know the events, know the one ruling in the figure of their conjunction:[48] which if it were a fortunate one, it will signify good and its fitness; and if it were a bad one, it will signify evil and its impediment.

4 Know even that their conjunction in the signs of men signifies the multitude of their infirmities. **5** And their conjunction in any of the angles of the year[49] signifies the contrariety of the wealthy or the kings, and a multitude of battles, and the matter will last until they are joined the next time.[50] **6** And their conjunction in fiery signs signifies the dryness (namely the sterility) of the earth; and in airy ones, winds; in watery ones, a multitude of rains; in earthy ones, frost and snows, and a multitude of cold spells. **7** Know even that if the fortunes were looking, they subtract evil, and the bad ones will increase [it]. **8** Test[51] this in the way I have described for you, and you will discover it, if God wills.

---

[46] This may means from the south for earthy signs, the east for fiery signs, *etc*. But the Hebrew reads as though it is regions *ruled by* the sign, which is a matter of chorography (see *AW1*, Part IV).

[47] The Latin seems to read *meruenda* or perhaps *metuenda*, suggesting a misspelling for either "win, deserve" or "measure." But the sentence itself does not make sense to me, nor does it appear in the Hebrew. I suggest that it means, "the *time* of the *event* should be determined as being after [a certain number of] known years after the conjunction," using a timing method such as mundane profections. See his *Conjunctions* (in Section II.4 of this book).

[48] That is, the "victor of" the chart, known as the lord of the year.

[49] The Hebrew has, "turning points." I am not sure if this simply means an angular place in the Aries ingress, or in one of the movable signs, or what.

[50] Since the mean tropical period of Mars is about 1.88 years, it will tend to be slightly longer than that.

[51] This sentence appears only in 1533.

Chapter 12: On the lesser conjunction

2 Māshā'allāh said: The lesser conjunction is the conjunction of Jupiter and Mars, and this signifies occurrences which come to be in rains and clouds, and the corruption of the air, and war. **3** But if a fortune conquered in their conjunction, it will signify good fortune; and if a bad one, evil. **4** And know that Jupiter and Mars, if they were conjoined in the Ascendant of the year or in any of its angles,[52] they will signify the stirring-up and differences [between] kings, unless the good ones were looking.

5 Know even that however often a fortune was conjoined with a bad one, the nature[53] of the stronger of them will appear. **6** And if a bad one were joined to a bad one, evil will abound, unless the one who is in charge of the conjunction is a fortune: understand [this].

7 And this is the last thing of those which we have brought forth in this book, and it is of the secrets of the knowledge of the stars.

And [the book] of Māshā'allāh translated by John of Spain (in Lunia), from Arabic into Latin, is completed.

---

[52] I believe this means: if their *future* conjunction (after the Aries ingress) happens in any of the angles of the Ascendant of the Aries ingress.
[53] Reading *natura* with 1533 for *fortuna*.

SECTION II.4:
MĀSHĀ'ALLĀH'S *BOOK OF CONJUNCTIONS*

Comment by Dykes. The following is my own translation of the portion of Māshā'allāh's *On Conjunctions, Religions, and Peoples* (hereafter, *Conjunctions*)[1] which was excerpted in ibn Hibintā's Arabic *Al-mughnā fī aḥkām al-nujūm*.[2] So far as I know, ibn Hibintā's excerpt is the only remaining record of this work (which was originally in 21 chapters or books, according to Sezgin). It was translated by Kennedy and Pingree in 1971 (hereafter known as KP), but my own translation provides some clearer readings along with my own chapter divisions and subsection titles. My commentary draws on KP's extensive notes and calculations.

Throughout, ibn Hibintā inserts his own commentary, usually on chronology and time lords. For example, Māshā'allāh shows little or no interest in time-lord systems beyond the Zoroastrian Thousands (and some mundane profections), but ibn Hibintā often reminds the reader where the directed mundane Ascendant is. Also inserted in two places of the text (Chs. 11 and 17-18) are comments by ibn Hibintā about the bloody transition from the 'Abbasids to the Buwayhids in Iraq. KP believe that ibn Hibintā presents a "sycophantic" version of the events in Ch. 18, **7-13**, while providing his more honest opinion in Ch. 11, **21-23**. But this seems to be overstated. Ibn Hibintā is plain about the violence and unrest which hollowed out the 'Abbasids' authority in both chapters, and it was no secret that the Buwayhids came to power via violence.

In my Introduction, I explained various errors in Māshā'allāh's calculations, particularly in his Ascendants: namely, that the Ascendants are unusable. But what is of interest are his methods, so let us turn to those now. One should note that Māshā'allāh normally employs whole-sign houses (houses by "number"), but sometimes refers to quadrant-based houses (houses by "division").

---

[1] See Sezgin p. 103, #2, although KP (p. 89) are not certain it is the same work.
[2] The manuscript was originally Munich Cod. Arab. 852, ff. 214v-233v, but reprinted in a facsimile edition by Fuad Sezgin (1987). Some pages are out of order in the Arabic: the correct order is: 214v-215v, 226r-233v (234v is blank), then 216r-225v.

Māshā'allāh's lord of the year

KP frequently identify the planet which they believe is Māshā'allāh's significator of the king, but Māshā'allāh himself never uses this phrase (although he does so quite a bit in *RYW*). Instead, great emphasis is put on finding the lord of the year. For the most part, these follow standard astrological principles found elsewhere in this volume and my Introduction: various lords of the Ascendant, angular planets, the sect light, and so on. Following is a list showing the types of considerations Māshā'allāh actually uses. Only the first few items are mentioned multiple times, the majority being mentioned only once:

- Lords of the Ascendant (by domicile, exaltation, triplicity, or bound).
- Lords of a luminary, preferably the sect light (by domicile, triplicity, or bound).
- A planet in the Ascendant, or even entering into the rising sign by transit.
- A planet to which a luminary applies (perhaps preferably, the sect light).
- A planet with many "testimonies" or "witnessing," which refers both to possessing dignities where it is, and having the application of multiple planets to it.
- Being well dignified and in a powerful place.
- Perhaps, being the sect light itself.

Notable interpretive principles and timing. Māshā'allāh employs angularity, profections, and transits in his timing methods:

- Angular significators show something happening sooner, e.g., during the period of the conjunction in question.[3]
- When the Ascendant of a triplicity shift is a common or mutable sign, the events indicated will not happen during that conjunction, but in the second conjunction of the series. Fixed and movable As-

---

[3] Ch. 3, **8-9**; Ch. 5; Ch. 7, **19** (possibly).

cendants show that the events will happen during the first period, that of the shift itself.[4]

- When the Ascendant of some ingress profects to (1) the sign of the conjunction itself,[5] or to the ingress position of the malefics.
- The profection of a problematic ingress planet, to the Ascendant.[6]
- The transit of a notable planet (especially Saturn) to some position (especially to the Sun). For example, in Ch. 9, **4-8**, The Sun in Aries applies to Saturn in Cancer; the events take place after 9 years, when transiting Saturn opposes the position of the Sun.
- By repetition: predicted events may happen (1) when the rising sign of a previous ingress repeats later on, and (2) when the Saturn-Jupiter conjunction returns to the same sign. For example, triplicity shifts often show changes of dynasty; but the shift to Muslim rule did not take place during the (alleged) triplicity shift to water and the sign of Scorpio, but during the period of the *next* Scorpio conjunction.[7]

Speaking of the principle of repetition, in Ch. 11 Māshā'allāh (or perhaps ibn Hibintā, in what may be his own comment) also points to an intriguing interpretive method. Again, triplicity shifts often show important changes in dynasties and power. But when the ingress of one shift (such as the shift into fire, #332) repeats important features of rulership from the previous one (such as #320 into water), then while there might be some kind of dynastic change, it will not be complete. In the case of the shift into fire, the rise of 'Abbasid Caliph al-Ma'mun (who was half Persian) showed increased Persian influence in the 'Abbasid dynasty, but still with great continuity of rule.[8]

Finally, a note on dates and chronology. In my Section II.1, I provided Māshā'allāh's parameters for his chronology: the length of the year, conjunctional period, and so on. In Māshā'allāh's text and ibn Hibintā's chronology, periods are often given in year-month-day form, but are either incorrect or grouped misleadingly into 30-day months (which are then occasionally add-

---

[4] Chs. 2, **6-9**; 7, **19-20**.
[5] Ch. 3, **14-17**.
[6] Chs. 8, **11**; Ch. 11, **22**; probably Ch. 11, **6**.
[7] Ch. 8.
[8] Actually, at the 7th fiery conjunction, which happened to be a return to Sagittarius as in #332, 'Abbasid power was hollowed out and largely gave way to the Buwayhids, who were rather different.

ed, disregarding the fact that the year has 365 calendar days). In my footnotes, I will provide the correct values where I can, in the following way. First, I will (a) give the actual number of Julian days in the period. Then, I will (b) divide by the sidereal year (365.2590278 days). I will then multiply the remainder by 365 calendar days, and group the result into 30-day months.

৪০ ৪০ ৫৪

[Chapter 1: Introduction, & the Flood]

1 In the name of God the Merciful, the Compassionate: Lord, lead the way[9] by Thy mercy. **2** God be praised, the Praiseworthy, the Glorious, the Tutor,[10] the Doer of what He desires, Creator of night and day, and Knower of what is on the land and seas, and Revealer of what is concealed in wisdom and the secrets as an indicator for His worshippers of His majesty, and guidance for them to His wisdom, and urging them to His worship alone; [none] participates with Him, nothing is like Him,[11] and He is the Creator of all things, and He is the Almighty, the Wise.

3 Next,[12] some of our statements have already preceded, as well as what we have gathered from the sciences in the craft of astrology, in the first two parts which have been concluded of this, our book. **4** And we are reporting in this part what Māshā'allāh arranged of the appointed times of the conjunctions coming to be between Saturn and Jupiter, and their shift in the triplicities, and what he gave with it of the form of the celestial sphere in the famous times of them and the recorded events which happened in them in terms of the virtuous prophecies[13] and dazzling wonders, and what he judged in it about everything of that, and [what] he explained of its evidence, and what Hermes and others besides him reported of the judgments about the conjunctions and the revolutions of the years of the world, with what the ancients said in the judgments of the years of nativities (and other things

---

[9] Lit., "set [this account] in motion," "make it begin" (نسيّر). KP read, "make smooth the way."
[10] المعيد, which is sometimes understood as "restorer"—both tutoring and restoring have to do with repetition and returning to the same thing.
[11] Reading as كمثل. KP seem to read كميل ("complete").
[12] Reading this sentence somewhat loosely, as the exact wording would be very awkward in English.
[13] Reading النبوءات with KP, but the text has النبوّات, "prophethoods."

besides this), [and] what follows upon this of the periods of kings and governors, and the times of wars (and he mentions the condition of prices), so that one may attain to the highest honors, with the assistance of God and the excellence of his fulfillment.

5 Māshā'allāh reported in his book on conjunctions that the first conjunction between Saturn and Jupiter took place at the start of the motion (509 years, 2 months, and 24 days having elapsed of the Thousand of Mars), and that it was located at 7° 42' Taurus.[14] **6** And after that he mentioned the conjunctions taking place in this earthy triplicity, conjunction after conjunction, adding degrees for the position of every conjunction on top of the position of the conjunction which was before it: 2° 25', without explaining the deficiency in that.[15] **7** Then, the conjunctions [proceed] in triplicity by triplicity, the period of each conjunction being 19 years, 10 months, and 11 days, until it reaches the shift of the transit in Libra and its triplicity,[16] [then] to Scorpio and its triplicity,[17] after 2,412 years, 6 months, and 26 days [from the middle of the Mars Thousand]:[18] and that is the one in which the Flood took place.

[Chapter 2: Conjunction #121, the shift indicating the Flood]

1 And the first of the conjunctions of this transit was in 1° 24' Scorpio,[19] and its period [was] 19 years, 10 months, and 10 days [and 10 hours].[20] **2** And the form of the celestial circle at the Sun's entrance into Aries for the year in which this first conjunction of the shift of the transit happened, is based on what Māshā'allāh reported of it, according to this image.

---

[14] See Section II.1 for the dating of conjunction #0 and the middle of the Mars Thousand.
[15] Ibn Hibintā may be referring to the fact that the actual interval is slightly more, 2° 25' 35".
[16] Conjunction #109.
[17] Conjunction #121.
[18] Opposite this is a marginal note: "Years: 2412, Days: 206." The correct interval between conjunctions #0 and #121 was 877290.9215 days, or 2401y 10m 3.780167d.
[19] This should be 1° 14' Scorpio, since the next conjunction was at 3° 40' Cancer: the difference between these is 2° 26', which is closer to the proper interval of 2° 25' 35".
[20] Adding to clarify the proper length.

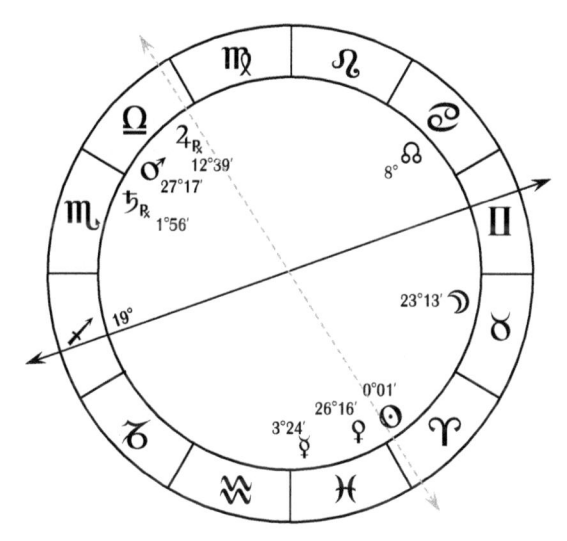

Figure 43: Aries ingress #121, the shift indicating the Flood (3381 BC)

3 Māshā'allāh said that he did not find a more suitable [planet] in this year than (1) Jupiter,[21] because he is the lord of the Ascendant and the lord of the triplicity of the Sun, and [the Sun's] bound,[22] and [the Sun] is pushing his power to [Jupiter];[23] and (2) Venus, because she is the lord of the house of the Moon, and she is in her own exaltation; and [the Moon] is in the sixth, received from her place.[24] **4** And Saturn is in the twelfth, retrograde. **5** And Jupiter and Mars in the eleventh [by sign] ([but] they are both in the tenth by division); and they are both retrograde. **6** So the retrogradation of the three planets at the revolution of this transit, in the Midheaven and a spiritual

---

[21] In this paragraph, Māshā'allāh identifies *both* Jupiter and Venus as being suitable for being lords of the year (introducing each with the preposition من, used to denote comparison). But KP (p. 40) evidently took the second occurrence of من in its usual sense (meaning "from"): thus, since the text speaks about the Sun pushing *to* Jupiter, KP thought the Sun was receiving it *from* Venus. But as the chart shows, the Sun is in aversion to Venus and is in no position to receive rays from her. Now, it is true that after crossing the sign boundary she will indeed connect with the Sun, but this is usually reserved for the Moon (as in Ch. 12, **3**), and the text does not actually say the Sun *receives* it from her, nor that *she* is pushing it.
[22] The Sun is at the beginning of Aries, the bound of Jupiter (in the Egyptian system, 0° - 5° 59').
[23] For "pushing power," see *ITA* III.16.
[24] The Moon is applying by sextile to her domicile lord, Venus.

sign,[25] indicates the spiritual disaster of the earth in the second conjunction from this transit—because the Ascendant is a sign having two bodies. **7** Likewise, look in the shift of the transits from [one] triplicity to the next: for if you saw the transit announcing miracles or disaster or the births of prophets, then you consider the Ascendant of the year of the shift. **8** And if it was one having two bodies (and especially Sagittarius), there will not be anything in the first conjunction, and from the second conjunction is known the report of the event. **9** And if the sign were fixed or movable, then the time of the event is in the first conjunction of the shift of the transit. **10** And if the Moon (who is the lord of the light of the night in this year) had been corrupted, there would have remained nothing of the [lower] world, because her being safe indicates growth and increase after the disaster.

[Chapter 3: Conjunction #122, shift containing the year of the Flood]

1 And the occurrence of the second conjunction from this transit, in which the Flood was, was in 3° 40' Cancer. **2** And the form of the celestial sphere at the time of the Sun's entrance into Aries for the year in which it took place, is based on what is established in this image, according to what Māshā'allāh described of it. **3** And the Flood took place in the fifth month from it.[26]

4 Māshā'allāh said: I looked, in the time of the earth's disaster (which the retrogradation of the superior planets had indicated at the time of the shift of the transit to the watery triplicity), based on [the fact] that it was in the second conjunction from it.[27] **5** And I found Jupiter to be the most suitable of the planets in this year, because he is the lord of the Ascendant and the lord of its bound, and of the triplicity of the Sun.[28] **6** And [the Sun] and Venus (the lord of the exaltation of the Ascendant) are assembled.

---

[25] That is, a human sign (Libra). Libra is often classed as human, along with the other airy signs. See Ch. 3, **14**. Note that only two planets (Jupiter and Mars) are in both the tenth by quadrant divisions and a spiritual sign.

[26] Therefore the Flood took place in about July of 3381 BC. KP (who time the Flood to July 30-31) say that the Sun would have been in Leo at the time: this would have allowed the Moon to be in Cancer, just as in the *Thema Mundi* which was the chart of the birth of the world: see *ITA* III.6.2.

[27] See Ch. 2, **6-8**.

[28] This seems to be an error. Māshā'allāh must mean he is the lord of the *bound and triplicity* of the Sun, which can be gotten by removing the possessive pronoun (حدّه) and leaving حدّ.

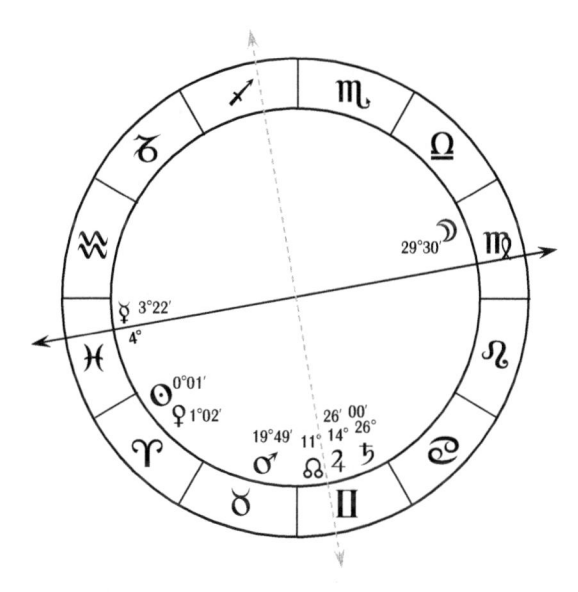

Figure 44: Aries ingress for #122, the Flood (3361 BC)

7 And [Jupiter] is in the stake of the earth,[29] in a sign not appropriate for him,[30] with Saturn, and that [Jupiter] is not connecting with him in it, and the lord of [Jupiter's] house is in the Ascendant: that indicates that what was described before about the disaster is in *this* year, in the fifth month of it, at the easternness of Saturn and [the position of] Jupiter in Cancer.[31] **8** and if [this] was not the place of Jupiter and the lord of his house, and [the place of] the Moon (who owns the light of the night) in the stakes, the event would have been in the fifth *year* from the conjunction. **9** However, their place in the stakes made it earlier, and appointed it in the fifth month of the first year of it.[32] **10** So, understand this.

For the bound of the Ascendant itself is ruled by Venus. KP take this to mean there is a separate set of nocturnal bounds (since the chart is nocturnal).
[29] Jupiter is in the fourth sign, but at Baghdad the IC would also be in the few degrees just prior to him, thus putting him in the fourth by quadrant divisions as well.
[30] Jupiter is peregrine, in Gemini.
[31] According to KP, the date of the chart is February 12: by June-July Saturn will have made his heliacal rising; likewise, Jupiter will have entered Cancer.
[32] Māshā'allāh seems to mean something like the following. (1) We know that the Flood will take place during the period of #122, because the Ascendant of #121 was a common sign. Now we need to know *when* during #122 it will be: during this first year, or later? (2) The lord of the year, its lord, and the Moon, are all angular, which means the Flood will happen in this *first* year. (3) If they had not been angular, it would happen in some later

11 And know that if you saw the superior planets (which are above the Sun) retrograde at the revolution of the shift of the transit from [one] triplicity to the next, or the revolution of the year of one of the conjunctions, they indicate the disaster is by means of heavenly misfortunes. **12** And if the two planets which are lower than the Sun are both retrograde in it, that is by earthly misfortunes. **13** And if all of them were retrograde, they indicate heavenly and earthly misfortunes: so look accordingly.

14 If they were in spiritual, human signs (and they are Gemini and Virgo and Libra, and the first half of Sagittarius, and all of Aquarius), the misfortunes will be in the people. **15** And if they were in other signs, [such as] animals, the misfortunes will be in the types [of things] attributed to those signs. **16** And if you wanted to know what the class of the misfortune and suffering is, then look, with the shift of the conjunctions from [one] conjunction to another, at the Lot of the transit[33] and which sign it falls in. **17** For if it fell in a fiery sign, the misfortune is from fire; and in a watery sign the misfortune is from water; and in an airy sign the suffering is by means of wind; and in a sign of earth it is from tremors or earthquakes or the falling of rocks.

18 What there is from the indication in the transit,[34] indicates powerful things which will happen in the conjunctions; and what there is from it at the time of the conjunction[35] indicates what will happen in its year; and what there is from it at the time of any of the revolutions of the year of the world,[36] indicates what will happen in the months of it. **19** And every one of these stages is easier than what was before it.[37]

---

year. All that remains is to determine the time units—how many months (of the first year) or years (later in the period) could the event be? I suggest that what Māshā'allāh means is this: (4) *since* the degree of the mean conjunction is in Cancer, then a profection from the Ascendant (Pisces) to Cancer indicates 5 time units. Since the Flood happens this year, it must be 5 months. Finally, (5) this is confirmed by the fact that in five months both Saturn and Jupiter will be doing something significant: Saturn will be making a heliacal rising, and Jupiter will have ingressed into the location of the mean conjunction; both will be in Cancer.

[33] This probably refers to the degree of the mean conjunction itself, since Saturn and Jupiter are typically called the "First" and "Second" Lots.
[34] That is, the triplicity shift.
[35] That is, the Aries ingress for the year of a mean conjunction.
[36] That is, Aries ingresses for any other year in a 20-year period.
[37] To me this sounds like a statement about the types of charts just described (and not a statement to students about how this will get easier). For the word "stage" (منزلة) comes from a verb that especially means to step or go downwards, suggesting that the ingress charts for triplicity shifts are the "highest" and most powerful and ominous; the ingresses

[Chapter 4: Conjunction #289, indicating Christ]

1 And between the time of the first conjunction of Saturn and Jupiter (at the start of the motion) and the month of the Flood (after omitting the 9 years and 2 months and 24 days of increase over the 500 years Māshā'allāh mentioned had elapsed of the Thousand of Mars),[38] because Māshā'allāh had performed it in the calculation and its method that 2,423 years, 6 months, and 12 days are put down.[39]

2 And Māshā'allāh arranged the conjunctions in order after that, triplicity by triplicity, until he reached the fiery triplicity, which was the birth of Christ (upon him be peace), in the ninth conjunction of it.[40] **3** And it is the triplicity of Leo, so the eighth conjunction from this transit was in Sagittarius, 18° 55'.[41] **4** And its period of time [was] 19 years, 10 months, 10 days [and 10 hours]. **5** And the beginning of it was at the completion of 5,749 years, 5 months, 8 days from the beginning of the conjunctions.[42] **5** And the form of the celestial sphere at the Sun's entrance into Aries at the time of the revolution of the year of the world in which it took place, is according to what is established in this image.

6 And Māshā'allāh reported that when he looked in it, he did not find a planet stronger than the Sun, for he was in the Ascendant, and is the lord of its exaltation, pushing his management to Saturn. **7** And [Saturn] is in the ninth, the place of prophethood. **8** And likewise the Moon and Mercury:[43] that indicates that a prophet will be born: God will illuminate the darkness through him, and give understanding from blindness.[44]

---

for individual conjunctions less so, and the other annual ingresses are the lowest and least momentous.

[38] In other words, between conjunctions #0 and #122—although the "month of the Flood" was in July and the mean conjunction a few months earlier.

[39] This is ibn Hibintā's calculation. The correct value between #0 and #122 is 884541.2597 days, or 2421y 8m 8.97d.

[40] The triplicity shift to Leo was #282 (185 BC). The "indicator" conjunction was #289 (46 BC), the eighth in the series. The mean conjunction *during which* Māshā'allāh says he was born, was #290 (26 BC), the ninth in the series.

[41] A better value would be 19° 01'.

[42] The correct value between conjunctions #0 and #289 is 2095347.738 days, or 5736y 7m 11.797d.

[43] Māshā'allāh seems to mean that both the Moon and Mercury push management to Saturn (see **9**); but only Mercury does so, not the Moon (since she is separating from his trine, not applying).

[44] Or, "give sight to the blind" (KP), though the Arabic has "blindness." The difficulty is the preposition من ("of, from"), which makes for an awkward interpretation of the verb.

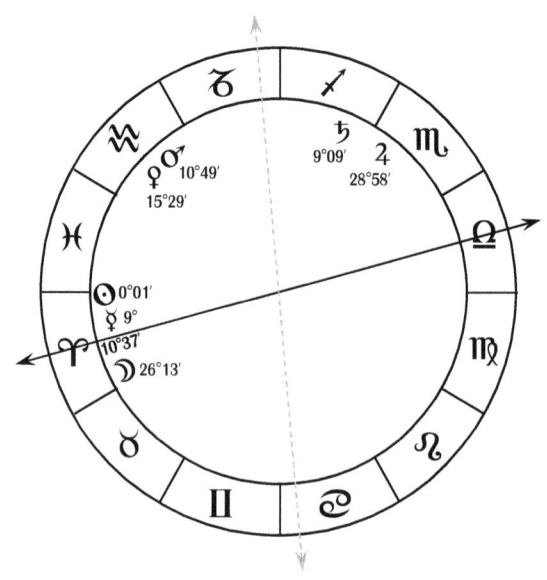

Figure 45: Aries ingress for #289, indicating Christ (46 BC)

9 And because Saturn in Sagittarius is the receiver of the power of the luminaries from the Ascendant, it indicates that his birth is in the second conjunction from this conjunction.[45] **10** And because the aspect is from the trine, it indicates his kindness and gentleness. **11** And because of the place of Saturn from the lord of his house, it indicates what violence he will encounter from his people.[46]

[Chapter 5: Conjunction #290, containing the nativity of Christ]

1 And the ninth conjunction (in which the Christ was born, in the thirteenth year from it),[47] was in 11° 20' Leo,[48] and the form of the celestial

---

KP point out that according to Māshā'allāh's own *Letter* (see Ch. 10, **11-12**), that a Saturn-Jupiter conjunction indicates a king or prophet if it is in an angle (especially the tenth).
[45] Earlier, Māshā'allāh had said that this would be the case if the *Ascendant* was a common sign; but now he extends it to the planet receiving the management or impetus of the year (here, Saturn).
[46] The lord of Sagittarius (Jupiter) is in the twelfth (enemies, secret enemies) from Saturn.
[47] Mean conjunction #290 is in 26 BC, and according to the scheme below Christ will be born 13 years later, in 13 BC (see below).
[48] This should be 21° 20', since 18° 55' (Māshā'allāh's value for #289) + 2° 25' = 21° 20'.

circle at the Sun's entrance into Aries for the year in which it took place, is according to this image.

2 Māshā'allāh reported that when he looked in this image, he found the Sun (the luminary of the day) and Mercury (the lord of the house of the Moon) both pushing their management to Saturn (the lord of the seventh and eighth from the Ascendant). **3** And [Saturn] is received in his place, increasing [his] direct motion: that indicates that the prophet (whose birth the first conjunction indicated would be in this conjunction)[49] will be born at the completion of the thirteenth year from it.[50]

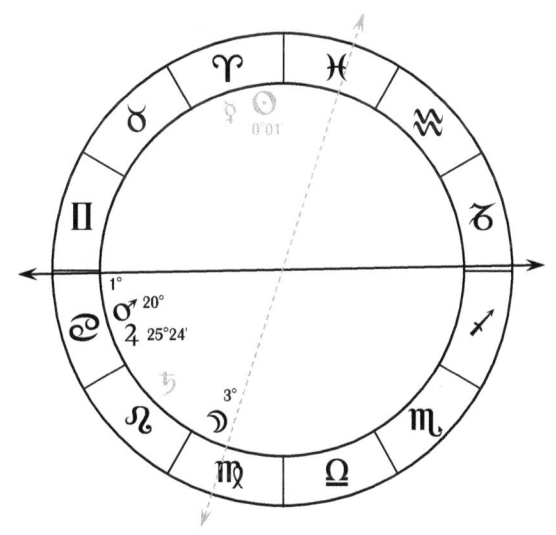

Figure 46: Conjunction of nativity of Christ (26 BC)

---

[49] By "first" conjunction we should expect that Māshā'allāh means the shift into triplicity (#282), which is not described in the text. But perhaps we should read this as the "prior" conjunction, referring to the indicator conjunction for Christ, #289 above.
[50] Māshā'allāh does not explain how the motion of Saturn determines that the birth will be in the 13th year (viz. 13 BC). It is unclear to me what "this" is, which indicates that it must be the 13th year (13 BC). But the profected Ascendant will reach Leo in 13 years, and Leo is the very sign of this mean conjunction.

[Chapter 6: Aries ingress for Christ's nativity (13 BC)][51]

1 And [he said] that he found the form of the celestial sphere at the time of the revolution of the year of the world in which the Christ was born (peace be upon him), and it is the thirteenth [year], based on this image.

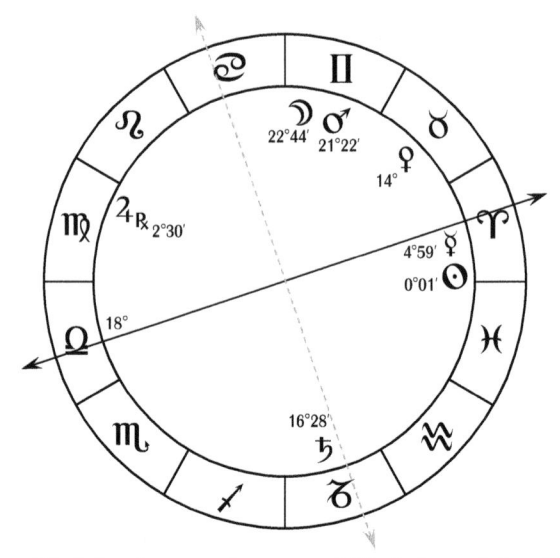

Figure 47: Aries ingress for year of Christ's nativity (13 BC)

2 And when he looked at the places of the planets, he found the lord of the year to be Saturn, because of his strength and the abundance of his testimony, and because all of the stars (except Mars and the Moon) were pushing their management to him. **3** And, he is in his own house, and the Ascendant is his exaltation and his triplicity. **4** And the lord of the Ascendant is pushing her management to him from her own house, the eighth:[52] that indicates that he is born [in] 10 months of this year.[53] **5** And because the rev-

---

[51] As KP remark (p. 72), Māshā'allāh combines two different chronological systems when dealing with the birth of Jesus. For this ingress, his chronology has 13 BC; but later, when measuring up to the mean conjunction indicating the birth of Muhammad (#321), he more correctly uses 2 BC as the birth year.

[52] Reading "eighth" for "second" (an addition of one letter). It does not make sense to me that Taurus would be her "second" house, and at any rate she is indeed in the eighth.

[53] Again, it is unclear to me what "that" refers to in particular. But if we take the first month to extend from the Ascendant into 18° Scorpio, and so on, then the tenth month does indeed terminate in Leo, the place of the mean conjunction. We could get the same result by looking at the tenth quadrant division (i.e., the division from the MC to the cusp

olution is by night, and the Moon is with Mars in the ninth, it indicates the violence he will encounter, and killing will be feared from him in an elevated place, because they are assembled in the highest of the signs.[54]

6 So between the time of (1) the first conjunction at the start of the motion, and (2) the year in which the Christ (upon him peace) was born (and that is the thirteenth [year] from this conjunction), after the subtraction of the 9 years and months of increase on top of the 500 years [which] transpired of the Thousand of Mars (since Māshā'allāh had performed it in the calculation—and it is not the path one should pursue in it), there came to be 5,773 years, and 24 days.[55]

7 And between (1) the time of the Flood and (2) the end of the year in which the Christ was born, was 3,349 solar years, 6 months, and twelve days.[56]

[Chapter 7: Conjunctions #320-322, shift indicating Islam & Muhammad's birth & early career]

1 And the conjunctions continued after that in a continuous succession of them, until the transit shifted from the airy triplicity ([and] it is Gemini and what belongs to it), to Cancer and its triplicity, in which the state of the Arabs was, at the completion of 6,345 years and 3 months, and 20 days. **2** In it we put the additional 9 years and months on top of the 500 years elapsed

---

of the eleventh house). KP (p. 97) believe this refers to the ten signs between the Sun and Saturn; they are probably including the fact that the Sun will have entered Capricorn itself at that time.

[54] The Moon is the sect light; she is conjoined with the malefic Mars in Gemini, high in the chart (and, with Cancer, having the most northern declination). There is a widespread tradition of Mars in Gemini in the Midheaven indicating hangings and crucifixions: see *Scito* Ch. 74, **29**; *BRD* VIII.1, **18**; *Skilled* Ch. VIII.13, **38**; cf. *RYW* Ch. 36, **2-4**. By mentioning that they are in the ninth, Māshā'allāh might be pointing out religious reasons for the death.

[55] The correct value is closer to 5769 years, 2 months, 20 days.

[56] This would yield 3/11/11 BC, about a year off from Māshā'allāh's dating. Adjacent to this sentence is a marginal note: "Between the Flood and the birth of the Christ (upon our prophet and upon him peace), was 3,349 solar [years]" (although to me the *49* is hard to recognize). KP remark that this is in different handwriting, but it is hard to know since it is so cramped. Besides, the text displays hashmarks indicating that the note fits here, so it may very well belong to the ibn Hibintā text, added later by the same scribe who originally skipped it. Whatever the case, the originator of the comment was undoubtedly a Christian.

170   *AW2 PART II: MĀSHĀ'ALLĀH & HIS DERIVATIVES*

from the Thousand of Mars. **3** So, there remained 6,336 years, and 26 days from the time of the conjunction taking place at the start of the motion.[57]

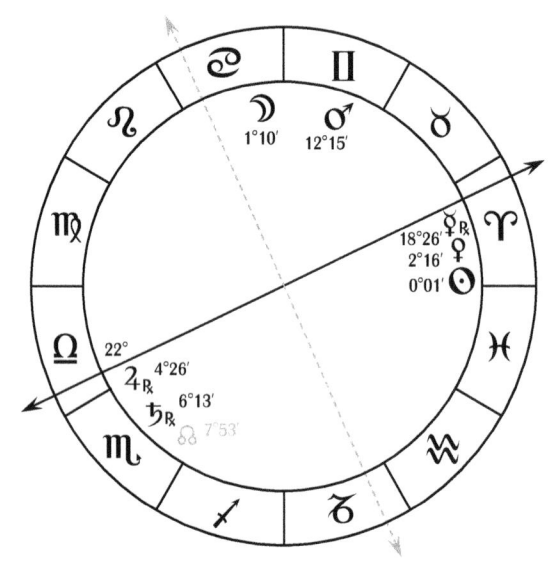

Figure 48: Ingress for watery shift (#320) indicating Islam (571 AD)

4 And the first of the conjunctions of this triplicity taking place, is in 4° 02' of Scorpio, and it is the conjunction of the religion [of Islam], and in the second year from it[58] was born the Prophet Muhammad (may the prayers of God be upon him and his family, and peace). **5** And Māshā'allāh and others of the scholars besides him reported that the revolution of the year of the world in which this conjunction took place was in the second hour of the night whose morning was the 23rd of Bahman, but there is no date apart from what was already stated about the start of the motion, because there are not any years to base it on.[59] **6** And the form of the celestial sphere was according to this image.

---

[57] Ibn Hibintā is measuring from conjunction #0 to #320. From the middle of the Mars Thousand to #320 is 6345 years, 3 months, 20 days. He subtracts the amount between the middle and #0 (9 years, 2 months, 24 days) to get 6336 years, 0 months, 26 days. Nevertheless, the period from #0 to #320 was 2,320,108.222 days, or 6351y 11m 17.89d.

[58] Or perhaps, the second year "of" it: if we profect the Libra Ascendant to Scorpio, this is the second year of the period.

[59] عمل على. According to KP (p. 98), ibn Hibintā means that Māshā'allāh does not provide a proper calendrical basis for determining the date (since he uses Persian months). But KP argue for 3/19/571, with further remarks on the *Zīj al-Shāh*.

SECTION II.4: MĀSHĀ'ALLĀH'S BOOK OF CONJUNCTIONS

[Ibn Hibintā's (?) comment on time-lords and chronology][60]

7 And indeed it reached Libra from the conjunction of the Flood,[61] and Gemini from the sign of the terminal point of the Turn.[62] **8** So from here started the Turn of the Arabs, [which] belongs to Venus and Mercury,[63] of which this year is the first one, and the length of its period is 360 years.

9 And from the place of the conjunction of Saturn and Jupiter at the time of the Flood, Sagittarius.[64]

10 And from the distribution (which puts down one year for every degree of equality) [it reaches] the end of 19° Pisces and the beginning of 20° Pisces, the beginning of every Turn.[65]

11 And between the Sun's entrance into Aries in this year, and the first day of the year of the Hijrah (in Persian years) was 51 years, 3 months, 8 days, 16 hours. **12** And from the first day of the Hijrah to the day of the rulership of

---

[60] What follows (**7-16**) seems to be a set of comments inserted by ibn Hibintā, about how this conjunction fits into other mundane time-lord systems (mighty *fardārs*, Turns, profections, and distributions). KP make this suggestion, which I agree with—but I do not agree with their interpretation of **9**. Two good reasons for believing this is by ibn Hibintā, are: (1) Māshā'allāh does not mention these other systems, except for profections (which we have already seen him use); (2) the following statements interrupt the usual sequence of sentences, in which the declaration "…according to this image" is immediately followed by "And Māshā'allāh said" (**6, 17**).

[61] KP (1971, p. 99) suggest that this refers to a mighty profection (see introduction), which begins with Aries in the Mars Thousand. Indeed, if we pair Mars-Aries, Sun-Taurus, etc., then this conjunction #320 (in the Jupiter Thousand) is during the Libra mighty profection.

[62] The Turns were said to begin in 3381 BC with Cancer-Saturn (see Introduction), which means that they changed to Gemini-Venus in 580 AD—which later astrologers associated with Muhammad and the mean conjunction of 570. See 'Umar's *Universal Book* above.

[63] Gemini is ruled by Mercury.

[64] To me this sounds like an annual profection. If Māshā'allāh or ibn Hibintā is profecting in 30-degree increments, then the profection of the conjunction of the Flood itself (#122, in 3° 40' Cancer) will make the 30-increment end in Sagittarius in 580 AD. (The same is true if one profects from the Scorpio position from #121.) KP (pp. 99-100) propose the unlikely solution that ibn Hibintā is already speaking of the next technique (directions or distributions), which the text does not introduce until the next sentence.

[65] The "small" mundane directions or distributions (see Introduction) give one year to each degree of the zodiac, thus going around the chart in 360 years. If the distribution reached 20° Pisces in 580 AD, then by the successive subtraction of 360 years we can see it was likewise there in the year of Māshā'allāh's indicator-conjunction #121 (3381 BC), the same year in which the Cancer-Saturn Turn begins. This distribution would have put the mundane Ascendant in 10° Aries in the year of Māshā'allāh's Flood (#122), 9° Cancer at the middle of the Mars Thousand, and 18° Cancer at Māshā'allāh's conjunction #0.

Yazdijird the king, is 9 years, 11 months, and 9 days (Persian). **13** The total of that is 61 years, 2 months, 17 days, and 16 hours.[66]

14 And there came to be from the time of the Flood to the first conjunction of the religion, 3,912 years, 6 months, and 14 days.[67]

15 And from the time of the Flood to the beginning of the rulership of Yazdijird was 3,974 years, 9 months, and 1 day.[68] **16** But Abū Ma'shar reported that it was 3,733 years, 2 months, 26 days, 9 minutes, and 10 seconds.[69]

[Māshā'allāh's interpretation]

17 And Māshā'allāh said that when he looked in this image [at] the places of its planets, he found the strongest of them and the greatest of them in testimony, to be Saturn: because he was entering into the Ascendant,[70] and he is the lord of its exaltation, and the Moon (the lord of the light of the night) is pushing her management to him from the tenth (by number) and the ninth (by division), the place of prophethood, and Jupiter is pushing his management to her. **18** And he found Mars in Gemini (and it is the ninth by

---

[66] In **11-13**, ibn Hibintā is trying to measure between the date of the Aries ingress of 571 and the 1st day of Yazdijird. But he is using the wrong Hijrah date for the first calculation, and his years are rendered in years of 365 days, not the proper sidereal years of 365.2590278 days we have been using so far. The Aries ingress was on 3/14/571 (JD 1929693), the Hijrah on 7/15/622 (JD 1948439), and the 1st of Yazdijird's reign on 6/16/632 (JD 1952063). According to ibn Hibintā, from the ingress to the Hijrah was 51y 3m 8d 16h, or 18713 days (it should be 18746 days); from the Hijrah to Yazdijird is 9y 11m 9d, or 3624 days (correct). If we add his years up in columns, carrying over the excess months into the year column yields 61y 2m 17d 16h. However, ibn Hibintā has made a mistake, since his years are 365-day years, and his months are 30-day months. Thus we need to move 5 more days over to create the extra year: 61y 2m *12d* 16h. At any rate, the correct number of days from the ingress to Yazdijird is 22370, or 61y 2m 29.136d.

[67] This is completely wrong, and results from ibn Hibintā's other erroneous calculations. As KP point out (1971, p. 100), ibn Hibintā believes that from #0-320 was 6366y 0m 26d, and that from #0-122 was 2423y 6m 12d. The difference between them (#122-320) is indeed the number given here: 3912y 6m 14d. But #122 was on JD 494030, and #320 on JD 1929596: the difference is 1435566 days, or 3930y 3m 7.951d.

[68] Ibn Hibintā is trying to measure from #122 to the 1st of Yazdijird. But he is actually adding his erroneous value for #122-320 (3912y 6m 14d) to his erroneous value from the Aries ingress of 571 to the 1st of Yazdijird (61y 2m 17d 16h). Adding these in columns yields 3973y 9m 1d 16h, one year short of the value given above. The correct value between #122 and the 1st of Yazdijird is 1458033 days, or 3991y 9m 14.018d.

[69] Ibn Hibintā is comparing Māshā'allāh's Flood conjunction with Abū Ma'shar's Flood-Kaliyuga. Abū Ma'shar uses the proper sidereal years, which makes this value come to JD 1363597.96 (or 1363598), the day of Abū Ma'shar's Flood on February 18, 3102 BC.

[70] That is, he is retrograding into Libra.

number), in the highest [part] of the belt, climbing to its highest point,[71] receiving the management of the Sun, Venus, and Mercury (through his retrogradation).

19 So all of that, as well as the First Lot (and it is Saturn) [being] in Scorpio, and his lord in the house of faith, indicates that a prophet will be born in Tihāmah (the land of the Arabs) in the second year from this conjunction: and that is because of the place of the First Lot in Scorpio, and the Moon's connection with Venus.[72] **20** And if the Ascendant had been a sign having two bodies, and Saturn in a sign having two bodies, I would have said that his birth was in the second conjunction.

21 And because of the reception of Venus and Mars in their places,[73] and the place of the Moon in the Midheaven,[74] it indicates that he will be safe from killing. **22** And because Venus has already been close to burning[75] ([Māshā'allāh] wants [to say] "emergence from the rays"),[76] it indicates that he will encounter hardships and go into hiding; then he will make connections and be strengthened and be talked about, and will rule the people of his religion.[77] **23** Because of the place of the Moon in the Midheaven,[78] and because of Mars in the house of faith, it indicates that he will seek faith, and the establishment of it, by fighting. **24** And because the Moon is connecting with Venus, the nature of Venus is in the people of his religion, and her ethics. **25** And the people of Tihāmah will encounter distress from enemies in the second year from this conjunction,[79] until they flee and are dispersed in the countries.[80] **26** And it was thus because this year was the Year of the Ele-

---

[71] Mars is in the middle of Gemini, advancing towards the solsticial point at 0° Cancer, the most northern zodiacal point in declination.
[72] Māshā'allāh has already said that a fixed or movable Ascendant means the events will happen in the period of the first mean conjunction (Ch. 2, **9**). The fact that it is in the next year may be due to a profection: if the Libra Ascendant is the current year, then Scorpio (the place of the mean conjunction) would be the next year.
[73] Venus is in Aries, and is applying to her lord, Mars, from a sextile; Mars is in Gemini, and his lord Mercury is applying to him from a sextile.
[74] That is, by whole signs or by "number."
[75] KP read "escaped," which is not true because she is still under the rays.
[76] This ibn Hibintā's comment. Māshā'allāh may be pointing out that she has previously approached the Sun and undergone burning, but is in the process of going out of the rays.
[77] This could also be read as, "and the people of his religion will rule," as KP have it.
[78] This would qualify her as being the significator of the king (see *RYW*).
[79] Again, this is probably the profection I suggested in **19** above.
[80] "Country" (بلد) can also mean smaller civil units like communities and cities.

174   *AW2 PART II: MĀSHĀ'ALLĀH & HIS DERIVATIVES*

phant, in which the Prophet (the prayers of God be upon him and his family, and peace), was born.[81]

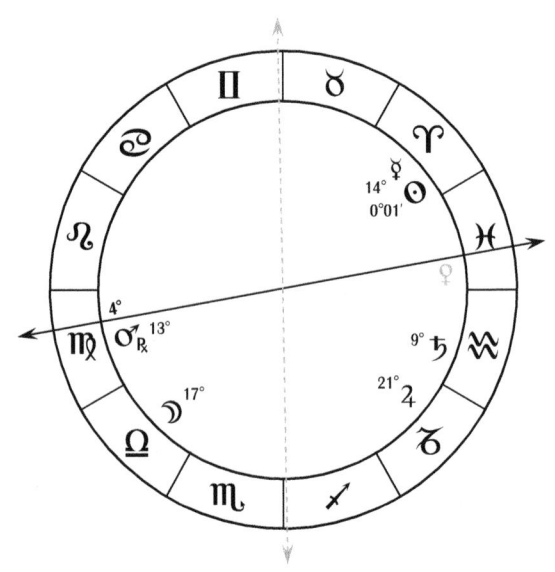

Figure 49: Third watery conjunction, #322 (609 AD)[82]

[Chapter 8: Conjunction #323, indicating the victory of the Muslims (630 AD)]

[Comment by ibn Hibintā on chronology]

1 Then, the years of the first conjunction elapsed (and it is 19 years, 10 months, and 10 days), and the years of the second conjunction, and the years of the third conjunction. **2** And all of that came to 59 years and 7 months,[83] [and] the end of it was before the time in which Yazdijird ruled, by 1 year, 9 months, 17 days, and 16 hours.[84]

---

[81] Māshā'allāh takes Muhammad's birth to be 2/7/572 (KP, p. 127). The "Year of the Elephant" refers to about 570 AD, in which the Christian ruler of Yemen (a vassal of Ethiopia) waged war on Mecca with war elephants.

[82] Māshā'allāh does not provide this chart; KP (p. 103) have gotten it from other sources. It lacks an interpretation.

[83] In ibn Hibintā's 365-day years, this would be 59y 7m 3d.

[84] This is incorrect, due in part to calendrical issues described by Kennedy (1971 p. 102). According to KP, #323 was on 7/4/630, JD 1952063, which makes the proper sidereal

[Māshā'allāh's interpretation]

3 And the fourth conjunction fell in Scorpio, 11° 19'. **4** Māshā'allāh reported that the form of the celestial sphere at the Sun's entrance to Aries [in] the year in which this conjunction took place, was according to this image.

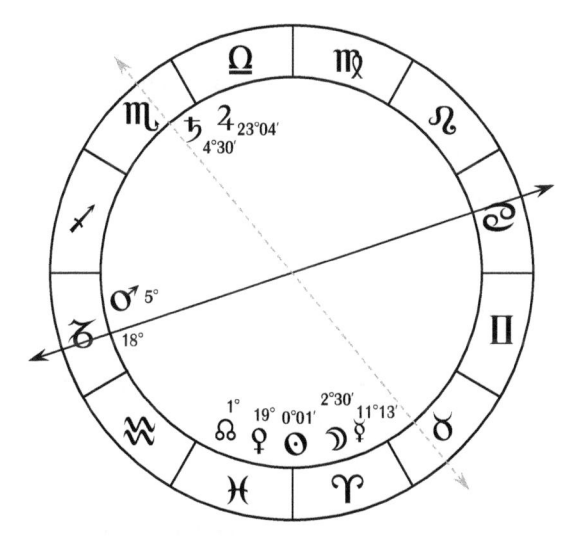

Figure 50: Aries ingress for #323, victory for Muslims (4th watery conjunction, 630 AD)

5 So he looked at its Ascendant and the places of its planets when the conjunction returned to the sign of the root which indicated the birth of the Prophet (the prayers of God be upon him and his family, and peace). **6** And [so], the place of the two infortunes in the two stakes,[85] and the withdrawal of the Sun and the Moon and Jupiter from the stakes, and the strength of Saturn in this conjunction, and the abundance of his testimonies, and his coming to be in the sign of the Arabs, indicates the strength of the Arabs in

---

value between it and Yazdijird 1y 11m 12.7d. My calculation puts it on 7/6/630, JD 1951347.015, yielding 1y 11m 20.477d.

[85] This is a bit puzzling. Mars is indeed withdrawing from the degree of the Ascendant, but perhaps being in the rising sign is enough to make him strong and angular. As for Saturn, he is not in an angular sign, so Māshā'allāh must think that the degree of the MC is in an earlier degree than Saturn's, or Saturn is so close to it that he partakes of its strength. At any rate, neither Mars nor Saturn is withdrawing to the extent that the other planets are.

it, and their victory over one who is superior to them. **7** And the pushing of the management of Mars (who is the lord of the exaltation of the Ascendant) to [Saturn], that is, in this conjunction, and the reception of one of them by the other,[86] indicates civil unrest and the spilling of much blood, and the ruin of the king of the fourth clime,[87] and the victory of the rabble over the king. **8** And because Mars is in the Ascendant, it indicates the departure of its king toward[88] the east, and his ruin there.[89]

9 And because Saturn is in the Midheaven, it indicates the misery of the tribulation and misfortune. **10** And because he is in the sign of the Arabs, and Venus is with the Head in her exaltation, it indicates the strength of the Arabs and their seeking the kingdom. **11** And because of the place of the position of Saturn from the Ascendant (which is his house), it indicates the fear of the people of the house of the Prophet (the prayers of God be upon him, and peace) in the three years elapsing from this conjunction.[90] **12** And because the revolution is nocturnal, and the Moon is under the rays, and the Sun made unfortunate, and they are both withdrawing from the fourth, entering into the third,[91] it indicates what misfortune will befall the people of Babylon, and their dispersal in the countries, and the victory of their enemies over them and their king.

13 And this conjunction is the one in which the Arabs conquered the king of Persia and his countries, and sent him away from them, and possessing it without him. **14** And the banishment of Yazdijird from the Two Cities was

---

[86] Māshā'allāh might be referring to the mutual reception between them (although the aspect from Mars is separating).

[87] Māshā'allāh assigns the fourth clime to the Sun (*RYW* Ch. 3, **5**), and KP say the fourth clime is usually taken to be Babylon (p. 103); this connection seems to be confirmed below in Ch. 9, **3-4**. So Māshā'allāh must be referring to the Sassanian Persians. KP say that no significant Persian king went far eastward during the tumult of the late 620s and early 630s (in which multiple assassinations finally ended with Yazdijird III becoming the last king on 6/16/632). But Yazdijird himself *did* flee ever eastward, suffering military disaster after disaster. He finally ended up in Merv or Marw, where he was killed in 651. Astrologically, his "ruin" must refer to the fact that the Sun is withdrawing, and applying to Mars (who is overcoming him by a superior square). The "rabble" here might also be Mars, representing the people by being in the Ascendant.

[88] Reading الى for "by means of" or "with" (ب).

[89] Māshā'allāh might be considering Mars to be the significator of the king (which is the opinion of KP). Being in the Ascendant, he indicates the east.

[90] This seems to be a profection from Saturn himself to Capricorn: counting Scorpio as the first year, he reaches Capricorn in the third year.

[91] That is, the third quadrant division or quadrant house. But they are clearly already in it.

after 3 years of it had elapsed, and at the completion of 4 years and a little more of his own reign.[92]

[Chapter 9: Conjunction #324, the fall of the Sassanians (650 AD)]

1 Then, after that was the fifth conjunction, and its period was 19 years, 10 months, and 11 days, in 13° 42' Cancer. **2** And the form of the celestial sphere at the revolution of the year of the world in which it took place, was according to this image.

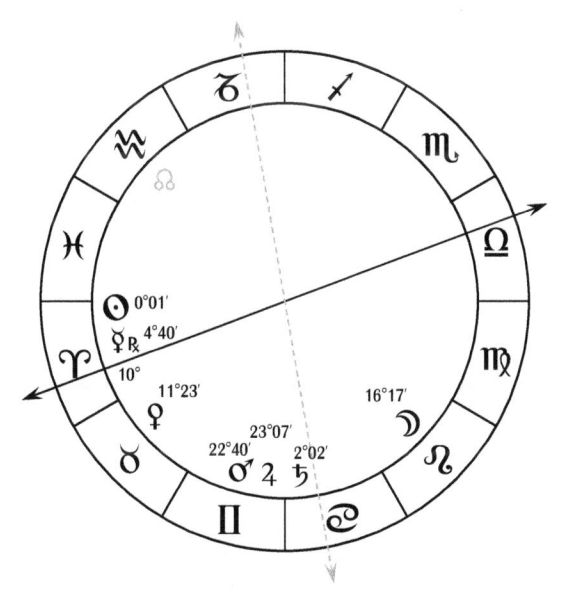

Figure 51: Aries ingress for #324, the fall of the Sassanians (5th watery conjunction, 650 AD)

3 And Māshā'allāh reported that he looked in this revolution at the Ascendant and the places of the planets, and the lord of the year was the Sun,[93] and he is pushing his management to Saturn from a square. **4** And that indi-

---

[92] The Muslims began to invade the Sassanians with multiple, quick victories in 633 AD; they took the Sassanian capital in June 637.
[93] Probably because he is the sect light, in the rising sign, and is the exalted lord of the Ascendant.

cated the ruin of the king of Babylon,[94] and his annihilation in the fourth year of it,[95] and the occurrence of civil unrest at the end of the ninth year,[96] and corruption and much spilling of blood, because Saturn (who is the manager or the Sun from the square) is opposing him, in his own exaltation, and contends with [the Sun] for the kingdom. **5** And if the Sun (and he is the lord of the year) had not been pushing his management to Saturn, he would not have signified fighting and wars after the annihilation of the king of Persia. **6** However, he did push the management to him, so since [Saturn] came to be in his own exaltation, opposed to [the Sun], he contended with [the Sun] for the kingdom, and [the Sun] indicated what I mentioned. **7** And it will not cease to be like that until he goes out from his exaltation and arrives in Scorpio. **8** And the Sassanian[97] will die in the region of the east,[98] and it will corrupt the crops in the first and second years.[99]

9 And since the great conjunction was being changed from Gemini to Cancer, and from Libra to Scorpio, and from Aquarius to Pisces, it indicated that there will remain (of the issue of this doomed king and his kin) one who is in the land which Pisces is in charge of, in Tabaristān and what borders on it.[100]

10 And because of Jupiter's falling away from the stake, and his being in Pisces with Mars, and the corruption of the Sun by Saturn and the Moon by the Tail, it indicates the ruin of the kings of people as well as the eminent

---

[94] Not only is the square from the Saturn in detriment hostile, but by pushing to Saturn, the Sun puts his matter into Saturn's hands.

[95] This is the profection from the Sun (or the Ascendant) to Saturn.

[96] KP point out (1971, p. 108) that this refers to a *transit* of Saturn (see the following sentences). Over 9 years, Saturn's mean motion will bring him about 108° forward, into Libra (actually, close to the very degree of his exaltation). When he is in Libra, he will oppose the Sun, who has pushed the management into his hands. This indicates contention until Saturn exits Libra (see **7**). The period from about 656-661 AD was very bloody as various Muslim factions vied for power, and included the Battle of the Camel (for a chart of this and a description, see *Scito* Ch. 95).

[97] الصسان, which should probably be spelled الساسان. KP do not translate this word, but identify it as Yazdijird.

[98] The Sun, which here indicates Yazdijird, is in the east; he was killed in 651 AD.

[99] That is, until Saturn exits Cancer and enters Leo; see Māshā'allāh's *Letter*, Ch. 10, L9.

[100] It is true that some members of Yazdijird's family survived, and possibly in Tabaristān (KP, p. 107). As for Pisces, it does rule Tabaristān (see *AW1* Section IV.5), but the meaning here is unclear. Conjunctions in Scorpio have indicated Arabs, and in this conjunction (Cancer), we see that Yazdijird flees to Khurāsān and Merv (ruled by Cancer); so something else of these matters (i.e., a surviving member of the Sassanians) continues on in places like Tabaristān (ruled by Pisces). Unfortunately, Māshā'allāh or ibn Hibintā omits any description of the other conjunctions in Cancer and Pisces.

people of them, and much spilling of blood in the land of Cancer (which is the fourth clime).[101]

[Comment by ibn Hibintā on chronology]

11 And after this [is] the sixth conjunction, and its period is 19 years, 10 months, and 11 days.[102] **12** And [then] the seventh conjunction,[103] and its period is like that, and likewise the eighth conjunction.[104] **13** And the ninth conjunction is just like that in [its] period of time.[105] **14** And all the years of these conjunctions came to 119 years, 2 months, and 6 days.[106] **15** Of these, before Yazdijird took hold of the kingdom, [was] 1 year, 9 months, and 17 days, and [so] the remainder of the years of Yazdijird was 117 years, 6 months,[107] and 19 days.[108]

---

[101] Māshā'allāh mentions dividing the climes according to the signs in *RYW* Ch. 32, **3**. But I am not sure exactly why Cancer is being identified with the fourth clime: if we divided the northern latitudes into 12 regions, the Cancer region would not overlap the region of the Sun (which is also the fourth clime).
[102] Conjunction #325 in Pisces, according to KP on 3/18/670 (JD 1965844), but by my calculation 3/14/670 (JD 1965847.691).
[103] Conjunction #326 in Scorpio, according to KP on 1/22/690 (JD 197310), but by my calculation 1/18/690 (JD 1973098.029).
[104] Conjunction #327 in Cancer, according to KP on 11/30/710 (JD 1980719), but by my calculation on 11/24/710 (JD 1980348.367).
[105] Conjunction #328 in Pisces, according to KP on 10/5/729 (JD 1987603), but by my calculation on 10/1/729 (JD 1987598.706).
[106] Ibn Hibintā or Māshā'allāh is combining the periods of the six conjunctions #323-328 (the fourth through ninth watery conjunctions), using the conjunctional period 19y 10m 11d, but ignores the extra 5 days at the end of the year. The proper period is 43502.02916 days, or 119y 1m 6.179d.
[107] This should be 4 months, as a calculation in the margin shows. The note further remarks, "And that is in Rabi' I, 132 AH."
[108] To put this rather useless bit of information more simply, conjunction #323 took place on JD 1951359 (KP) or JD 1951347 (Dykes); the 1st day of Yazdijird was JD 1952063; therefore the time between Yazdijird and conjunction #329 (the tenth watery conjunction) was 42790 days (KP) or 42786.044 (Dykes), which is a little over 117 years.

[Chapter 10: Conjunction #329, the rise of the 'Abbasids (749 AD)][109]

1 And the tenth conjunction (in which was the dynasty of the 'Abbasids and the extinction of the Banī 'Umayyah)[110] was in Scorpio, and it is the sign of the religion [of Islam]. **2** And the year of the world was revolved for this conjunction at the end of the 12th hour of the day of the 17th of Bahram, which is 117 years[111] of Yazdijird.[112] **3** And the form of the celestial sphere in the opinion of what Māshā'allāh stated of it, was according to this image.

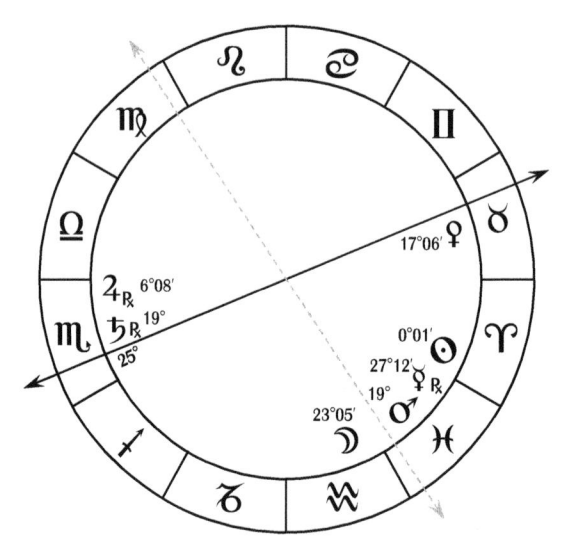

Figure 52: Ingress for #329, the rise of the 'Abbasids
(10th watery conjunction, 749 AD)

[Comment by ibn Hibintā on chronology]

4 And[113] the fourth year[114] from the conjunction of the religion arrived at Cancer, and from the place of the conjunction to Leo, and from the degree

---

[109] In this chapter, Māshā'allāh is referring to the demise of the 'Umayyads (considered more "western") at the hands of the 'Abbasids (from the east). This officially began in 750, but certain battles continued for several more years.
[110] That is, the 'Umayyads.
[111] Reading for 119, following KP.
[112] A marginal note reads, "And that is on the 6th of Sha'bān, 131 AH." See the end of the previous chapter for this dating.
[113] KP's interpretation of the first part of this sentence makes little sense, and it seems to me that there have been some errors in transmission. I propose the following: (1) If we

of the distribution taking place at the beginning of each Turn [that is], 20° Pisces), to 19° Virgo.[115] **5** And in it is the rays of Mars and Mercury (through his retrogradation).[116]

[Māshā'allāh's interpretation]

6 And Māshā'allāh reported [that] he looked in the revolution of this year, in which the conjunction returned to Scorpio, and it is the sign which had indicated the birth of the Prophet (the prayers of God be upon him and his family, and peace). **7** And its lord[117] is in the fifth with Mercury (and he is retrograde), neither one being received,[118] in the trine of Saturn: that indicates there will be disease in the people from epidemic at the beginning of this year.[119]

8 And[120] because Venus pushed her management to Saturn (and he and Jupiter are in Scorpio, retrograde), it indicates powerful wars with much killing in the east, and the impairment of the people and their corruption, and the going away of their piety.

---

begin a profection from Aries at conjunction #0, then indeed the profection reaches Cancer in 749 AD. (2) The position of conjunction #0 was in Taurus, which reaches Leo this year.

[114] KP prfer "the *lord of* the fourth year," but this is not astrologically meaningful.

[115] Again, the distribution moves 1°/year (see Ch. 7, **10**). It was at 20° Pisces in 570 AD. There are 179 years between 570 and 749 AD, or 179°, thus yielding 19° Virgo.

[116] The opposition of Mars is exactly on the position of the small division (see previous footnote), and Mercury is opposing it by sign.

[117] That is, Mars. KP take "it" to mean "the year." But this is not grammatically possible, as the pronoun is masculine (as is "sign"), while "year" is feminine in Arabic. So Māshā'allāh is referring to Mars as the lord of the sign in which the mean conjunction takes place, Scorpio. He might be the lord of the year as well, but Māshā'allāh does not state this.

[118] Jupiter is retrograding in the early degrees of Scorpio. So, Mars is not applying and will not complete a connection with him, and Mercury is perhaps too far away by degree for reception to be considered effective.

[119] Perhaps what Māshā'allāh means is this. Mars is the lord of the Ascendant (the people) and of the sign of the conjunction (Scorpio). He is with Mercury, which makes Mercury more malefic. Neither is being received, and the closest aspect they make is to the malefic Saturn, also in the Ascendant, and retrograde. KP's interpretation of this passage is incorrect because they believe Saturn is related to Mars by a *square*.

[120] Māshā'allāh might have chosen Venus because she signifies Islam and the Arabs; but she is also the other benefic in the chart. Thus, Jupiter (a benefic) is retrograde and not received, and Venus pushes her management to a malefic, retrograde Saturn. Jupiter and Saturn being in the Ascendant, signifies the east. "Piety" might refer to Venus as a natural signification of hers. See also *RYW* Chs. 36, **5** and 46, **21**.

9 And[121] because the lord of the Ascendant and the lord of the ninth and the lord of the fourth pushed their management to Saturn (and he is in the Ascendant), it indicates that the people will submit to the people of the east, and the dynasty will pass into their hands.

10 And because of the place of the conjunction in Scorpio (which is the sign of the Arabs), and the corruption of Venus (and she is their planet), it indicates their ruin by epidemic and wars.

11 And indeed I judged tribulation and violence from two reasons:[122] (1) because Mars, the lord of the house, is in a sign having two bodies. **12** And there will also be war and the spilling of blood in the fifth year in the area of the west,[123] and many will be killed in it by people of the east because of the place of Mars (who is the lord of the Ascendant), in the area of the west.[124] **13** And (2) the indicator of epidemic [is] Mercury, and his place is with Mars, and he is corrupted by his retrogression: it indicates epidemic and the ruin of the Two Cities[125] and castles: and that will be general in the community of the Arabs.

14 And all of the years of this conjunction will be harsh upon [the Arabs], because he[126] is in their sign, and it is a stake; and Venus (who is allotted to them) is unfortunate in another stake, opposed to Saturn (and he is retrograde). **15** And the lord of their Midheaven is Mercury, and he is retrograde, made unfortunate: it indicates harshness of many kinds, from death and killing, and from the injustice of the Sultan and his oppression.

16 Then, after this tenth conjunction, in which the dynasty and kingdom was shifted away from the Banī 'Umayyah to the Banī al-'Abbās[127] (and wars happened in it, and the shedding of blood, and the ruining of cities), was the eleventh conjunction and the twelfth conjunction (and it is the last of the

---

[121] This is puzzling. The lord of the Ascendant is Mars, who is pushing to Saturn. But the lords of the ninth (Moon) and the fourth or IC (Jupiter), while configured with Saturn, do not actually apply or push to him. But see *RYW* Ch. 37, **2-4**, which nicely sums up much of this situation.

[122] Māshā'allāh does not number his reasons, but I take them to be the situations of (1) Mars, and (2) Mercury with Mars: see below.

[123] Or, "the Maghrib." By profection, the Ascendant reaches Mars and Pisces in 5 years. KP suggest that this refers to a victory by Abu Muslim in November 754 (1971, p. 111).

[124] KP suggest that this is because Mars is in a watery sign, which typically indicates the west; but it could equally be because Mars is in the western hemisphere of the chart.

[125] مدائن, referring to the combined cities of Ctesiphon and Seleucia (just miles from Baghdad). Although this word is sometimes used for cities in general, Māshā'allāh uses the normal plural below.

[126] I take this to be Saturn.

[127] That is the 'Abbasids.

conjunctions of the triplicity of Scorpio). **17** All of the years of these three conjunctions[128] is 59 years, 7 months, and 3 days.[129] **18** The last of them will be at the completion of 177 years, 1 month, and twenty-[two] days of Yazdijird.[130]

[Chapter 11: Conjunction #332, the shift to fire & Caliph al-Ma'mūn (809 AD)]

1 And the conjunctions shifted to the fiery triplicity of Sagittarius at this time, and the revolution of the year of the world in which the first conjunction of it took place, was at seven and one-half hours of the twelfth day of Bahman, 177 years of Yazdijird.[131] **2** And the form of the celestial sphere is according to what I have revealed in this image.

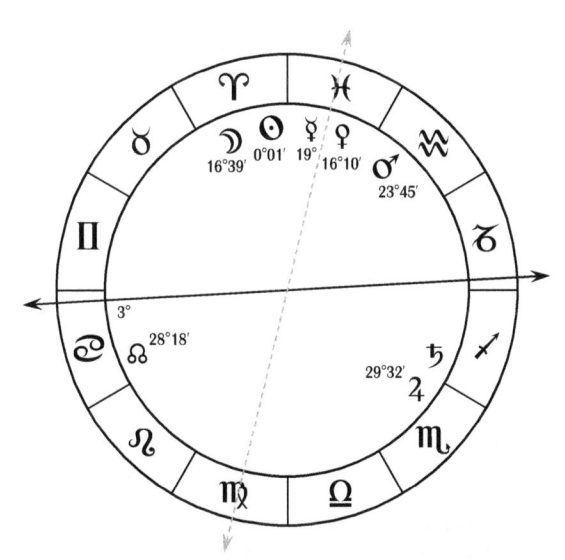

Figure 53: Ingress for #332, shift to fire & Caliph al-Ma'mun (809 AD)

---

[128] That is, conjunctions 10-12 of the series.
[129] Again, this is by multiplying 19y 10m 11d by 3, without regard for the 5 epagomenal days. The correct value is 21751.015 days, or 59y 6m 20.59d.
[130] A marginal note reads: "And that is in Sha'bān, 193 AH."
[131] This corresponds to March 20, 809.

[Comment by ibn Hibintā on chronology]

3 And this year had reached Cancer from the Ascendant of the conjunction[132] of the religion, and from the position of the conjunction in it to Leo,[133] and from the distribution, to 19° Scorpio.[134] **4** And this is the first conjunction of the fiery triplicity.

[Māshā'allāh's interpretation]

5 Māshā'allāh reported that when he looked in this image and contemplated its Ascendant and the positions of its planets, no planet in it was found to be better by position than Venus, because she is the lord of the triplicity of the Ascendant, in her own exaltation, in the degrees of the Midheaven,[135] received by the lord of the exaltation of the Ascendant and the lord of her house;[136] and the house in which she is, and the Ascendant, are of her nature.[137] **6** So, she indicates the excellence of the condition of the Arabs up to the sixth year from the conjunction.[138] **7** Then, a people of their own kingdom[139] will be strengthened over them, so they will be betrayed by them and they will excel[140] over them, and a people of the east and Isfahān will help them based on that, because the place of the conjunction is in Sagittari-

---

[132] Reading for "from the conjunction of the Ascendant." The Ascendant for the ingress of 571 was Libra (Ch. 7 above), so

[133] This seems to be incorrect. From the ingress of 571 to 809 AD is 238 years. By whole signs, the profection of the Ascendant in 571 would have reached Leo (and by 30° increments, to Leo-Virgo), and the profection of the conjunction of 570 in Scorpio would have reached Libra (and by 30° increments, Libra-Scorpio). On the other hand, #332 was supposed to have happened earlier in March (so technically, it pertained to 808): in that case, the profection from Libra in 571 would have reached Leo, and from Scorpio in 570 it would have reached Virgo.

[134] Incorrect: now ibn Hibintā has overestimated the time. By the direction of the Ascendant at 20° Pisces (in 571 AD), it would have reached 18° Scorpio in 809 AD.

[135] For the latitude of Baghdad, the MC is indeed at 16° Pisces (give or take a degree).

[136] She is applying (widely) to a trine of Jupiter, who is her domicile lord.

[137] Perhaps because she was widely considered to be cold and moist in the Arabic period, and both Pisces and Cancer are watery signs.

[138] If we count 809 AD as the first year, then this could be a profection from the Ascendant to Saturn (and the place of the conjunction in Sagittarius), or of Mars to the Ascendant. The latter seems more likely, as it is used in Ch. 8, **11**. Note also that the Ascendant of this shift is a movable sign, which according to Māshā'allāh (Ch. 2) means that the events will take place during the period of *this* conjunction.

[139] As KP point out, this may be because Mars will have profected to Cancer, which indicates Iraq.

[140] Reading يبارعنوهم.

us.[141] **8** And the rulership will be shifted from house to house in the fourth year from the conjunction,[142] and death will be increased in the tenth [year] from it,[143] and the dynasty will be shifted to a people of the east because of the shift of the conjunction to Sagittarius. **9** And the lifespans of the kings of this triplicity will be lengthened. **10** And the sword will be unsheathed in the causing of bloodshed, because Mars (and he is the lord of the eleventh)[144] was in the eighth, in the sign of that [same] thing,[145] and the planets are made unfortunate by him.[146] **11** And if there had not been reception,[147] the matter would have been hideous [and] terrible; however, the reception mitigated the evil.

[Comment by ibn Hibintā?][148]

Comment by Dykes. I have followed KP in separating the following from Māshā'allāh's account, but there are some ambiguities here. Māshā'allāh has apparently argued (**7-8**) that there will be a *complete* shift of rulership to the east and the Persians around 815 AD, which did not happen; therefore, KP argue (p. 113) that what follows is ibn Hibintā's attempt to explain *why* it did

---

[141] Sagittarius is fiery, so eastern; it also indicates Isfahān, according to Abū Ma'shar and ibn Labbān (see *AW1*, Part IV).
[142] KP take the Sun to be the indicator of the king and thus the "rulership" in this sentence; he will profect to the Ascendant in 4 years. This is likely, though a profection of the conjunction in Sagittarius would reach Venus as well.
[143] KP take this to mean that Saturn (who is also the lord of the eighth) will transit from his current position (in early Sagittarius, according to Māshā'allāh) to the Sun: Saturn's average annual motion is 12°, so 10 years or 120° puts him in early Aries.
[144] This seems to be ibn Hibintā's comment. Mars is the lord of the eleventh by quadrant division (Aries), but he is in the eighth *sign* or by counting. This is an unnecessary complication, and his rulership over the eleventh quadrant division does not contribute anything: it is enough to point out that he is in the eighth sign, indicating bloodshed and death.
[145] Namely, death.
[146] Perhaps this means that *because* he is a malefic in the eighth, any aspect from him will be harmful, even the sextiles to other planets. He is not configured in a bad way to any planet except Jupiter.
[147] KP take this to mean Mars's reception by Saturn, by a whole-sign sextile. But it is more likely Venus's reception by Jupiter, mentioned in **5** above.
[148] KP reasonably take the following to be by ibn Hibintā. In **6-8**, Māshā'allāh has argued that there will be a shift in rulership to the east due to collusion between Iraqis and Persians, around 815 AD, without terrible bloodshed (**11**). He had two primary arguments: first, the profection of Mars to the Ascendant (**6**); second, the profection of the Sun to the Ascendant (**8**); to this he added the transit of Saturn to the Sun (**8**). But this does not seem to have happened, since in 815 al-Ma'mun acceded to the throne, and he was the brother of the his predecessor.

not happen. And, being uncertain about what events are meant, KP suggest that because the shifting of the caliphate to al-Ma'mun in 813 came from his brother al-Amīn, it is "doubtful" that there was bloodshed involved. But in point of fact, a succession dispute between these brothers did lead to a bloody civil war, the "fourth uprising" or *fitna*. First, the Caliph and father of both brothers (Harun al-Rashid) died in the year of this shift (809 AD), leaving the rulership to al-Amīn, with his brother al-Ma'mun being designated the next successor. Al-Ma'mun himself was half-Persian and had much Persian support. But al-Amīn, along with his ministers, instigated conflict and betrayals against al-Ma'mun while the latter was in the east. Al-Ma'mun then defeated an army sent against him by his brother, and caused further groups sent against him to turn on each other. In the end, al-Amīn was killed in 813 and the rule passed to al-Ma'mun, who remained in the east and presided over widespread civil unrest and rebellions for several years.

So Māshā'allāh is correct on several points: there were uprisings and betrayals among the ʿAbbasids and within the population of Iraq in particular (**7**); the caliphate went to someone in the east and to Persians (**7**), especially considering that al-Ma'mun's Persian support was resented by the Arabs; and the rulership passed from "house to house" in the fourth year or 813, when al-Amīn was killed and al-Ma'mun succeeded (**7**). The good condition of the Arabs for 6 years (**6**) could refer to the fact that a particularly important uprising by the Zaydi Alids led to widespread vendettas and score-settling across Iraq and elsewhere. But Māshā'allāh does get one important point wrong: when al-Ma'mun returned to Baghdad in 819, violence *subsided* rather than increasing (**6**). This could be explained by Māshā'allāh's perhaps dying shortly beforehand, and assuming that his transit of Saturn to the Sun would be disastrous (**8**). But the symbolism of Saturn's trine to the Sun could easily be seen as the peaceful arrival of the new king (Saturn) to the rulership (Sun). At any rate, these points are a good argument that Māshā'allāh died in 813-14, and did not live through the end of 815.

If the following sentences (**12-19**) are by ibn Hibintā, then he is explaining why Māshā'allāh was wrong about a complete shift of power to the east. But if they are by Māshā'allāh himself, then he is explaining why a *temporary* shift to the east may have resulted in the survival of the ʿAbbasids in the west when al-Ma'mun returned in 819. At any rate, the argument is as follows. The previous shift into water (571 AD) indicated the rise of the Arabs. The Ascendant of *this* shift is not only of the same quadruplicity, but was the tenth house; moreover, the Moon (the lord of Cancer) is in the tenth of both charts, in a good condition. Therefore, something of the previous dynasty remains in this one—viz., the continuation of Arab rule, particularly in Iraq. (Note: Māshā'allāh's text only said that the rule would go from house to house, not "tribe to tribe," as sentence **13** has it.) This will continue through the entire fiery triplicity, but there will be a change at the earthy triplicity (in 1047 AD) because *its* angles will not have similar overlaps with the fiery ones (see end of **15** below). KP helpfully note that there was indeed a major political change in 1055 AD, when Turks entered Baghdad and ended the Buwayhid dynasty.

ಬಿ ಬಿ ಬ

12 And because the Ascendant of this conjunction at the beginning of the shift takes place in Cancer—and it is one of the stakes of the Ascendant of the first transit, which was in Scorpio and its triplicity, and indicated [1] the birth of the Prophet (the prayers of God be upon him, and peace) and [2] the dynasty of the Arabs and the shift of the rulership to them (and the house of the Sultan is from him)—and the house of the Moon, and the Moon in this conjunction was in the Midheaven, firmly established from the stake, received in her own place by the lord of her house,[149] increasing in light, it indicates the endurance of this dynasty in the hands of its people, and the survival of their authority[150] in it, because Cancer is the Ascendant of this shift, [and] is the house of the authority, from the elapsed conjunction and the establishment of the dynasty in the hands of the Arabs. **13** So the shift from one triplicity to the next did not shift from tribe[151] to tribe, and from one people to others.

14 And because [the conjunction] is in an eastern sign, the dynasty and the victory and the shift belonged to an eastern king. **15** And because the conjunctions rotate in Sagittarius and Leo and Aries, the triumph belonged to the easterners, of the people of Khurāsān and the Turks and what assists

---

[149] The Moon is applying to a sextile of Mars, her domicile lord.
[150] Or perhaps simply, their "Sultan," here and later in the sentence.
[151] بطن. I follow KP (p. 58), who must be following Lane (p. 221): this word normally refers to something interior and hidden (and anatomically, the belly), and in this case refers to some kind of kinship or other group which is smaller than the broader sense of class, type, and tribe. But the MS seems to indicate يطن .

those countries over the Arabs—without the rulership departing from them, because of the connection which was already mentioned by us with respect to the two conjunctions, and we explained their condition—and it will not cease to be like that until the conjunction shifts from the triplicity of Sagittarius to the next triplicity, and there is no mixture nor connection between its Ascendant and the stakes of this triplicity.

16 And the conjunction of Saturn and Jupiter also continues along in it according to what happened in the days of Persia, with the shift of the conjunctions from the triplicity of Gemini to the triplicity of Scorpio—and there is no kinship and no mixing between the transits.[152] **17** So [the lack of similarity] indicates the departure of the dynasty of Persia and the appearance of the dynasty of the Arabs, and the shifting of the rulership to them; and the matter does not cease to be [based] on disorder and what is fearful until the conjunctions continued in the triplicity and returned to Scorpio in the fourth conjunction.[153] **18** And [then] the king of Persia departed and the rulership of the Arabs became supreme, when there was not a kinship nor connection between [their] transits. **19** And as for *this* connected shift, it is like the one we described which was before it.[154]

[Māshā'allāh's interpretation continued]

20 And indeed Māshā'allāh reported that the lifespans of its kings will be lengthened in the triplicity of Sagittarius, due to the strength of the indication of the triplicity[155] of Sagittarius over the king.

[Comment by ibn Hibintā on the transition to the Buwayhids][156]

21 And the kingdom and dynasty will be in disarray in the last years of the seventh conjunction, when Mars and Saturn are united in Cancer and the

---

[152] Māshā'allāh or ibn Hibintā is saying that there was no great similarity between the shift into air in 333 AD (#308, indicating the Sassanians) and into water in 571 (#320, indicating Islam and the Arabs). Therefore, a more complete shift of power was likely.
[153] See Ch. 8 above. Māshā'allāh or ibn Hibintā means that the Arabs did not take power immediately upon the transfer into water and the conjunction in Scorpio, but only later, when the conjunction *returned* to Scorpio.
[154] That is, this shift into fire (809 AD) is like the shift into water (571 AD).
[155] Reading the singular for ibn Hibintā's plural.
[156] What follows is a remark by ibn Hibintā, somewhat hidden within the flow of Māshā'allāh's text, about the bloody transition from the 'Abbasids to the Buwayhids in Iraq. This occurred from 928-945 AD (see also Chs. 17-18 below).

rotation returns to Sagittarius.[157] **22** For at that [time] it is feared [because] it changes the king who will come at this time, [after] 15 years,[158] and he will unsheathe the sword among the people at the end of his command and his rule. **23** And in the eighteenth year of the seventh conjunction, the people will raid[159] each other and there will be wars until the eighth conjunction.[160]

[Chapter 12: Conjunction #333, the 2nd fiery conjunction (828 AD)]

1 And after the first conjunction of this transit, there transpired the second conjunction, and the beginning of it was in the year 197 of Yazdijird, and its period of time was 19 solar years, 10 months, and 11 days.[161] **2** And the form of the celestial sphere at the Sun's entrance into Aries for the year in which it happened, was according to this image.

3 And Māshā'allāh reported that when he looked in this image, he found the Ascendant to be Leo, at the end of its degrees, and Mars and Saturn in the sign, withdrawing from the stake, and the Moon in the Ascendant, [pushing] her management to Mercury,[162] and the Sun in the ninth, pushing to

---

[157] The seventh fiery conjunction (#338, Chs. 17-18 below) lasted from 928-48 AD. The mean conjunction returned to Sagittarius, Saturn and Mars were conjoined in Cancer in 945, and in that same year the profection of the Ascendant from Libra (in 571) did indeed reach Sagittarius as well. In this year the Buwayhid dynasty began. Astrologically, what this means is the following: normally, a shift indicates a change of dynasty; but because of the similarity between the shift to water and fire (discussed above), the change was not that dramatic. However, just as in the shift to water the change happened when the mean conjunction *returned* to the sign of the watery shift (Scorpio), so the changes during the fiery period happened when the conjunction returned to the sign of the fiery shift (Sagittarius).

[158] In the seventh conjunction (#338, in Ch. 17 below), Mars is in the tenth sign; his profection to the Ascendant takes place at 15 years (943 AD). KP connect this with al-Mustakfī's succession to the caliphate in 944 AD. This would be more accurate if Māshā'allāh or ibn Hibintā meant "the *fifteenth* year." This was also a time of warfare which led to the Buwayhid dynasty in 945 AD, so ibn Hibintā might be referring to the violence of the first Buwayhid Caliph in establishing his rule just before that time.

[159] Reading as يغير with KP for يغز.

[160] The eighteenth year of the seventh conjunction was 945 AD, the year of the Saturn-Mars conjunction in Cancer and the return of the Ascendant of the religion to Sagittarius (see above). In that year, the Persian Buwayhids took control of Baghdad and much of central Iraq, ending the 'Abbasid rule.

[161] In this case, the ingress is set for a date *after* the mean conjunction: the conjunction occurred either on 1/6/829 (KP) or 12/31/828 (Dykes).

[162] She is void in course in her own sign, but after crossing into Virgo her first connection will be with Mercury.

Saturn,[163] and Jupiter in his exaltation, falling away from the twelfth house, and Mercury in the eighth, entering into the opposite,[164] and Venus in the Midheaven, pushing her management and retrogradation to Mars[165] (who is opposite her in the celestial sphere and [by] house),[166] and she is not received, and Mercury was in his[167] stake, and in his own fall.

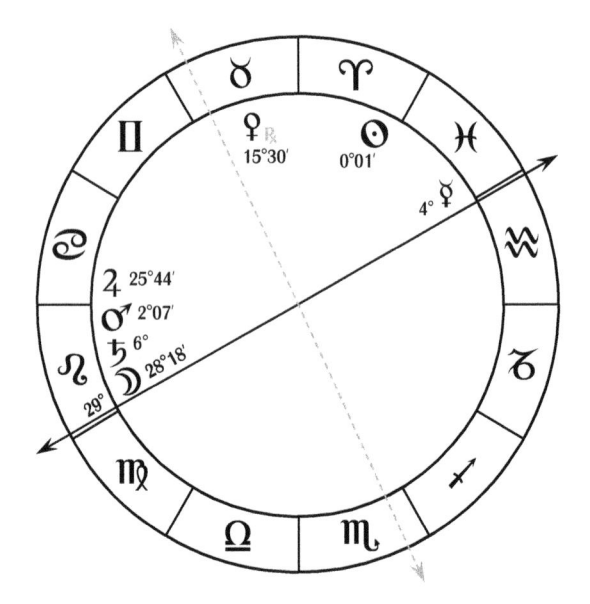

Figure 54: Ingress for #333, the 2nd fiery conjunction (829 AD)

4 What[168] he described indicated killing and great death in the area of the east,[169] and a militant will appear in the first year of the conjunction because

---

[163] But he is pushing to Mars first.
[164] النظير. This word comes from the same word as "look at, aspect," and can also mean "corresponding, equivalent, parallel." Māshā'allāh seems to mean that Mercury is entering the Descendant (which is opposite to, and the counterpart of, the Ascendant) by diurnal rotation. KP take this to mean that he is in the opposition of the Moon, but Māshā'allāh has already mentioned this, and besides it is the Moon who is entering into the opposition, not Mercury.
[165] This does not make sense to me: her next connection will be with Mercury, not Mars.
[166] This must refer to the fact that her domiciles are opposite his (as Taurus is opposed to Scorpio, and Libra to Aries).
[167] Or perhaps, "its." By whole signs he is in angles from his two domiciles (Gemini and Virgo), and he is also dynamically in or close to the axial degree of the Descendant.
[168] KP do not connect this chart to any particular events, and it is worth noting that by this time, Māshā'allāh was dead. Although Māshā'allāh does not identify a lord of the year

of the Sultan in these areas, and he will enter upon the first Sultan and be in charge of him, and he will call the people to a religion that is not their own religion, and they will be ruined and their loyalty[170] will depart, and they will seek what is false.[171] **5** And the citizens will go mad,[172] and respect for the Sultan and kings will disappear from their hearts, and evil people will be powerful and good ones weak (and the majority of them will die), and women will be raised up over men, and adultery will be widespread, and mercy will pass away. **6** And evil will arrive from the direction of the east and be strengthened by it, and there will be an appearance of the one bringing it at the beginning of this year, and he will falsely claim knowledge because of prophethood, and the result of his command will be corruption.[173] **7** And all of that will be in the first year of the conjunction.[174] **8** And in the second, there will be fighting and the shedding of blood, and in the third one death and extinction through pestilence and the corruption of the crops,[175] and in the eighth year there will even be killing.[176] **9** And in the ninth, locusts will be multiplied and the crops and plants will be corrupted, and all of the climes will be corrupt.[177]

[Chapter 13: Conjunction #334, the 3rd fiery conjunction (848 AD)]

1 And the third conjunction is in the year 219 of Yazdijird, and its period of time 19 years, 10 months, and 11 days. **2** And this is the form of the celestial sphere at the revolution of the year of the world in which it took place.

---

or indicator of the king, KP argue that the Sun is the lord of the year and Venus the indicator of the king.
[169] Probably because both of the malefics, and the sign of the conjunction are in the Ascendant; Leo is also a fiery, eastern sign.
[170] Or, "trustworthiness, faithfulness" (امانتهم).
[171] Perhaps because Mars rules Aries, which is in the ninth.
[172] Or perhaps, "covet greedily," as KP have it (تكلب).
[173] Again, this seems to be due to the malefics being in Leo, and Mars ruling the ninth.
[174] Probably because the Ascendant indicates the first year.
[175] This may be because Mercury in the eighth is an indicator of pestilence, and he is in a common sign (indicating two years). KP believe that the 3-year period is due to the profection of Venus to the Ascendant, but Venus is a benefic.
[176] Perhaps because the Ascendant (or Mars) will profect to Mercury in the eighth, after 8 years.
[177] KP are probably correct that this refers to Mars profecting to the Sun.

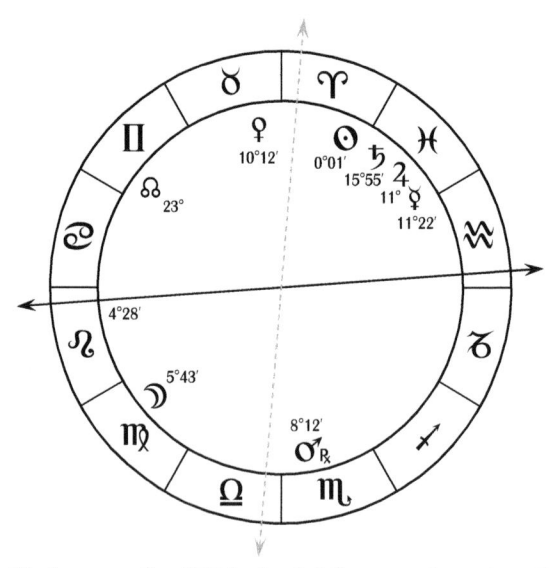

Figure 55: Ingress for #334, the 3rd fiery conjunction (848 AD)

3 Māshā'allāh related that in the revolution of this conjunction no star was found more suitable than the Sun, because he is the lord of the Ascendant, and the revolution is diurnal, and he is free of[178] the infortunes: he indicates the security of that fourth clime, and the length of its duration and the excellence of its condition.

4 And in the area of the east there will be death and war,[179] and the death of many people in the cities[180] from famine,[181] and the corruption of produce in this [and] the second, third, and fourth years of this conjunction.[182] 5 And in the first and fifth [years] there will be death and war among the Arabs.[183] 6 And in the first and second there will be locusts, and the cold will corrupt the plants, and death will spread in the land of Persia and al-Andalus.[184] 7 And in

---

[178] Lit., "untouched, pure" (نزيه).
[179] Perhaps because Mars squares the Ascendant.
[180] بلاد, which also refers generally to communities and towns.
[181] Perhaps because Mars is in the fourth (land, cities, towns).
[182] I am not sure why all of these years would be affected.
[183] Mars opposes Venus (the planet of the Arabs) in this first year, but I am not sure why the fifth year would have this effect; KP suggest that it is the profection interval between Mars and Saturn.
[184] KP connect this with the opposition of Mars to Taurus (as well as Saturn's and Mercury's sextiles to it). But normally Aries rules Persia, and Spain's (or al-Andalus's) significator varies. Perhaps it is because the conjunction itself is in Aries?

the eighth year the people of Tabaristān will encounter harshness.[185] **8** Then they will have victory over their enemies, and their land will be fertile, and their livestock in a good condition. **9** And God, be He exalted and glorified, is more knowledgeable and wiser.

[Chapter 14: Conjunction #335, the 4th fiery conjunction (868 AD)]

1 And the fourth conjunction: its period of time is 19 years, 10 months, and 11 days, and its beginning is in the year 237 of Yazdijird. **2** And the form of the celestial sphere at the revolution of the year of the world in which it happened,[186] follows this image (God willing, be He honored and revered).

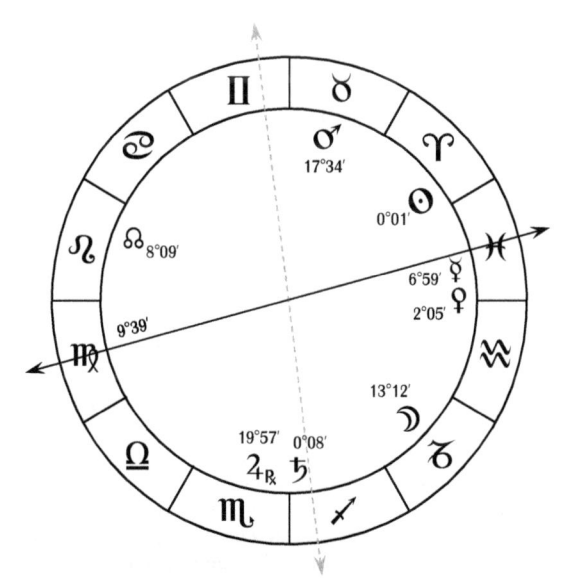

Figure 56: Ingress for #335, the 4th fiery conjunction (868 AD)

---

[185] This must be the profection of the Ascendant to the eighth (and Mercury and Saturn), as Pisces rules Tabaristān. But as Jupiter is there, and Venus sextiles it, the problems will be overcome (see **8**).

[186] The manuscript suggests that a partial word which follows was in error, as the rest of the sentence is written below it.

3 Māshā'allāh reported that the conjunction took place in Sagittarius, and the stakes of the Ascendant were upright,[187] and the stars withdrawing [from them] except for the Sun (and he is in the eighth,[188] and between him and the center of the seventh are 2°),[189] pushing his management to Saturn. **4** And Mars is in the ninth, and the Moon in the fifth, pushing her management to Jupiter, [she] not being received.[190] **5** So that indicates that the king of the fourth clime will perish in the fourth year from this conjunction,[191] and the rulership will shift from the people of his house,[192] and there will be harsh butchery in Isfahān and its areas,[193] and the king of the fourth clime will travel,[194] and a contention will take place in the land of the Arabs,[195] and diminishment and the spilling of blood.

6 And in the sixteenth year there will be a powerful, general plague,[196] and in the second clime there will be fighting and contention in religion, and the spilling of much blood in that.[197] **7** And the victory and result will belong to the nobility after the violence and plague in the fourth year, and the majority of the dying and plague will be in the sixteenth year in the areas of the west, until it reaches the areas of Mūsul.[198] **8** And several kings will die in this conjunction, and it will intensify their conditions, and livestock will die in the

---

[187] That is, the MC-IC axis falls in the tenth and fourth signs, rather than being displaced into the adjacent signs.
[188] الثامن, not "seventh" (as KP have it).
[189] KP say that the "center of the seventh place by division" is at 1° 48', making Māshā'allāh correct, but I do not understand it.
[190] But according to Māshā'allāh's values in the diagram she will apply next to Mars, and is received by him from his exaltation (although Māshā'allāh might not recognize such a reception in this work).
[191] The four years are probably the years of the profection of Mars to the Ascendant, but they could also be the profection of Saturn to the Sun (who indicates the fourth clime). KP claim the Sun is the lord of the year and Mercury the significator of the king; if so, we could reasonably assume that the Sun in the eighth, and Mercury in his fall and detriment, overcome by Saturn, indicate his death.
[192] The reason for this is unclear.
[193] Isfahān is ruled by Sagittarius, the sign of the conjunction.
[194] See *RYW* Ch. 42, but I do not see a clear indication of it unless one considers Mars to be in the ninth.
[195] Probably because Mars opposes Scorpio; KP suggest that the retrogradation of Jupiter in it supports the same interpretation.
[196] Mars will profect to the Ascendant after 16 years (not the sixteenth year itself).
[197] Perhaps the opposition of Mars to the retrograde Jupiter (who indicates the second clime).
[198] The profection of Saturn after 16 years will reach the Descendant and Mercury in fall, which is the west; al-Rijāl has Mūsul ruled by Aries (see below in Part IV.2, Ch. VIII.35). If Māshā'allāh follows this latter rule, then because Pisces borders on Aries, it might indicate the areas around Mūsul.

first year of it: the majority of that will be in riding animals and cattle,[199] but goats will be safe.

9 The first clime and seventh clime will be safe.[200] **10** And in the second clime a contention will take place with its people; then they will conquer. **11** And in the fifth and sixth [climes] there will be death, and the worst clime by [its] condition will be the third, because tribulation will enter upon it. **12** And it indicates the people of the fourth clime, and their obedience will be improved.[201]

[Chapter 15: Conjunction #336, the 5th fiery conjunction (888 AD)]

1 And the fifth conjunction was in the year 257 of Yazdijird, and its period of time 19 years, 10 months, and 11 days, and the form of the celestial sphere at the Sun's entrance into Aries in that year in which it took place, [is according to this image].

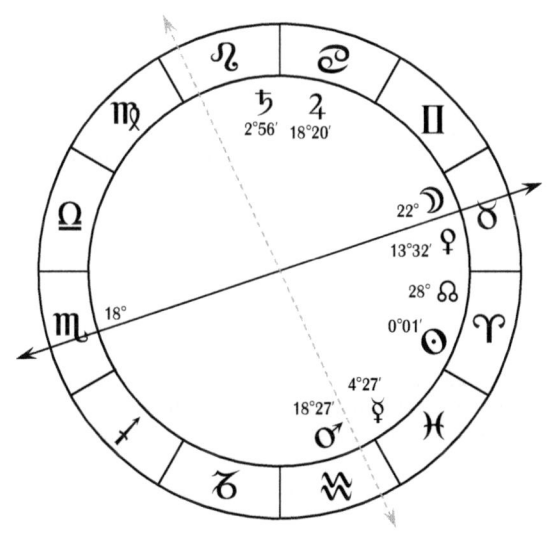

Figure 57: Ingress for #336, the 5th fiery conjunction (888 AD)

---

[199] These are ruled by Taurus, in which Mars is.
[200] Again, the first clime is ruled by Saturn, the second by Jupiter, etc., until the Moon indicates the seventh.
[201] Or more naturally, "it indicates *that* the obedience of the people of the fourth clime will be improved."

2 Māshā'allāh reported that when he looked in the revolution of the year of this conjunction, he found Mars to be the greatest of the planets in testimony in it,[202] and Venus the strongest by position.[203] **3** And she is pushing her strength to Jupiter, and he is not received.[204] **4** And the Moon (the light of the night) is pushing her strength to Saturn, and he receives it from her.[205] **5** The place of the Sun and Moon from Saturn indicates misfortunes which strike the kings in this conjunction (from illnesses and wars and a multitude of enemies), and a powerful war and killing will be in the area of Khurāsān.[206] **6** Then it will be prevalent [among] the people in the seventh clime.[207]

7 And the enemy will appear in the fourth clime, and the rabble will be elevated over kings.[208] **8** And these wars and events and misfortunes will be in the tenth year,[209] and what befalls the kings of the fourth clime will be in the fourth year.[210] **9** And the condition of the people of the fifth clime and sixth clime and second will be excellent,[211] and they will be blessed [by] calm and security from wars, and the condition of their leaders and those having their esteem will be good—except that the tenth year will be a difficult and intense year: the evil of it will be widespread [among][212] the people, because the rabble and the lower class will rise up against the nobility and kings in it.

---

[202] Mars is configured by sign to four planets, and is the lord of the Ascendant.

[203] This does not make sense to me. She is in her own domicile and an angular sign, but withdrawing (i.e., dynamically cadent) from the Descendant. The exalted Moon in the seventh seems stronger to me.

[204] Perhaps because the Moon (his domicile lord) is separating from him.

[205] She is currently void in course, but after crossing into Gemini she will apply to him. But she completes a sextile with the Sun first, so I am not sure why Māshā'allāh is saying this.

[206] Both the Sun and Moon (whom Saturn aspects by square, and it is a nocturnal chart) are royal planets. But I find different attributions for Khurāsān, Abū Ma'shar attributing eastern Khurāsān to Cancer (*AW1*, IV.5), and al-Rijāl attributing it to the Sun (see IV.2 below, Ch. VIII.36).

[207] The Moon (the seventh clime) is squared by both malefics and will soon connect with Saturn.

[208] Perhaps because the Sun (an indicator of the fourth clime and kings) is in the sixth, the house of slaves and the underclass.

[209] Saturn will profect to the Moon, and Mars to the Ascendant, in 10 years.

[210] Perhaps the profection of Saturn to the Ascendant (KP); but because the fourth clime is involved, it might be the profection of the Sun (the fourth clime) to Saturn.

[211] Mercury (sixth clime) and Jupiter (second clime) are in aversion to both malefics. Venus rules the fifth clime and is in a square to both malefics, but maybe being in her own sign is helpful.

[212] Reading بـ with KP, even though the manuscript seems to read فـي, which could be read as "the evil of it will distress the people."

[Chapter 16: Conjunction #337, the 6th fiery conjunction (908 AD)]

1 And the sixth conjunction was after there transpired 17 days of the third month of the year 277 of Yazdijird, and its period of time was 19 years, 10 months, 11 days.[213] **2** And the form of the celestial sphere at the revolution of the year of the world in which it took place, was thus.

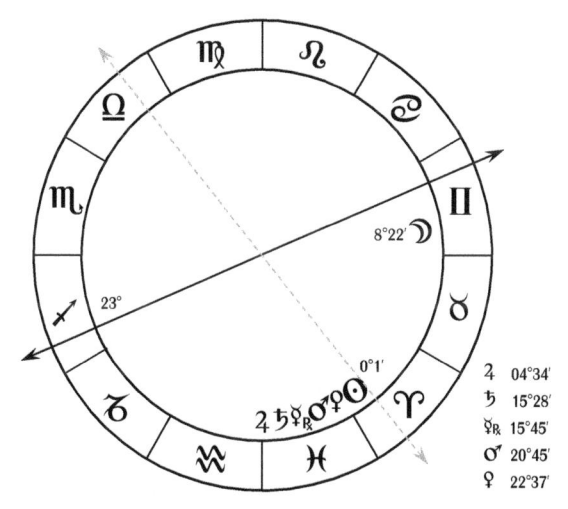

Figure 58: Ingress for #337, the 6th fiery conjunction (907 AD)[214]

Comment by Dykes. In the next paragraph, ibn Hibintā points out some errors in Māshā'allāh's calculations, enlisting the help of an otherwise unknown contemporary astrologer. The mistakes are as follows. (1) Instead of adding the equation for Venus (that is, a value that would convert her mean motion into the one), Māshā'allāh has subtracted it. According to KP (p. 121), the correct position of Venus using Māshā'allāh's parameters would have been 3° 07' 34", almost where the unknown astrologer puts her. Then, (2) Māshā'allāh has erred in calculating the Ascendant for the ingress, even by his own standards. Conjunction #336 had 18° Scorpio arising, and the custom for generating the next year's Ascendant was to add the excess of revolution in ascensional times or oblique ascensions (see Section II.1). The

---

[213] Conjunction #337 occurred on 5/27/908 AD.
[214] Note that this chart itself is in error, as it is cast over one year before the mean conjunction. The mean conjunction occurred on May 27, 908 AD, so Māshā'allāh should have cast the chart for 1 year later, at the ingress of March 908.

chart is dated to 907 AD, 19 years later (although it should have been cast for 908 AD). 19 multiplied by Māshā'allāh's excess of revolution (93° 15') is 1771° 45'. Reducing multiples of 360° yields 331° 45', so even in Māshā'allāh's incorrect method of adding degrees zodiacally, his Ascendant should have been 19° 45' Libra instead of 23° Sagittarius.

The correct method using ascensions would have been as follows. In the Babylonian system of ascensions, 18° Scorpio has an oblique ascension of 240° 36' or 241° 36'. The sum of that and the excess (331° 45') yields an oblique ascension of 213° 21' or 212° 21', which corresponds to about 24° 54' Libra. So Māshā'allāh not only got the wrong year, but did not even calculate his Ascendant correctly within his own erroneous method.

3 And one mathematician (and he was 'Abd Allah b. Muhammad b. Bishr, the astrologer),[215] remarked that he examined Venus and found her to be in Taurus, in 5° 22' 30", and that Māshā'allāh was neglectful in the section on her: because he ought to have added her equation (and it is 30° 22' 30") to the position of the Sun, but he subtracted it from it. **4** And he examined the Ascendant by adding on top of the Ascendant of the past conjunction what Māshā'allāh had added to it in degrees for every year (and that is 93° 15'), for 19 years: and the Ascendant of this conjunction came out to be 25° Libra.[216] **5** And our concern in what we have explained in this comment, is explaining how the Ascendants of the conjunctions are worked out, based on the path of Māshā'allāh in it, and what it is that he adds on top of the Ascendant of the past conjunction for every year, until the Ascendant of the next conjunction comes out. **6** And this calculation is by the [*Zīj al-*] *Shāh*, because it is the *zīj* which Māshā'allāh used to work with.

7 Māshā'allāh said that he looked in the revolution of this conjunction, and found the five planets in the fourth (and it is Pisces),[217] and the Moon in the seventh, withdrawing, pushing her power to Saturn, and the Sun in the fifth (he is in the fourth by division), and he is withdrawing, not received. **8** And [Venus] and Mars are under the rays, and Jupiter is eastern in his own house (and he is the lord of the Ascendant of the conjunction).[218] **9** So[219]

---

[215] Unknown at this time.
[216] This is the correct value using ascensions (see above), but since the Scorpio Ascendant for #336 was calculated improperly anyway, it does not really matter.
[217] Again, all of this assumes that the chart is correctly calculated.
[218] KP argue that Jupiter is the lord of the year, and Mercury the indicator of the king (p. 122).

that indicated that creation will encounter harshness [even] until that enters upon animals of the water;[220] blindness will take place through [various] types of tribulation, and mishaps will be prevalent in creation, and some people will move away from others. **10** And the beginning of that will be from the area of the south, and it will be repeated in it; then it will go towards the area of the west,[221] and it will be prevalent in the two lands.[222] **11** And the people will encounter submersion due to the abundance of waters, [and] violence[223] will corrupt all of the climes. **12** And the beginning of the corruption will be in the fifth clime and the third,[224] and it will ruin kings in the fourth year from this conjunction,[225] and there will be contention and the shedding of much blood in that year until not one of the lords of the wars remains long.[226] **13** And the people of the house of prophecy and knowledge will be strong, and the good will be distinguished from evil just as white is distinguished from black, and appropriate development will emerge in the people.[227] **14** And in the area of the west in the seventh and sixteenth year, people will die until not one will remain long, and kings will continue without soldiers, and the people will be diminished, and some of them will join forces with others.[228]

---

[219] KP read: "…which indicates that the people [الخلق] will encounter violence to the extent that it affects aquatic animals, causing blindness and misfortunes among them." The word الخلق really refers to created beings in general and can be used to mean "humankind," but because of the content of this sentence I am interpreting it in its broader sense.
[220] All of the references to water in this paragraph come from Pisces being a watery sign.
[221] KP connect this with Mercury ruling signs in the south (Virgo) and west (Gemini); but people in authority have not been specifically mentioned. The repetition could be due to those signs (and indeed, Pisces) being common signs.
[222] ارضين. This probably refers to Egypt, which since antiquity was known as "the two lands" (i.e., Upper and Lower Egypt).
[223] Or perhaps, "tension" (شدة).
[224] Venus and Mars (rulers of the fifth and third climes) are under the rays of the Sun.
[225] This is probably the profection of the Ascendant to Mars and Mercury (who rules the tenth and may be the significator of the king).
[226] كثير ("many, long"), though this does not seem quite right; there may be some idiomatic use of كثير احد here and in **14**.
[227] The Sun, lord of the ninth, is in the fifth (the house of Good Fortune), exalted, and in aversion to both malefics.
[228] The Ascendant will profect to the seventh house in the seventh year; in the seventeenth year, Mars will profect to Gemini as well.

[Chapter 17: Conjunction #338, the 7th fiery conjunction (rise of the Buwayhids, 928 AD)][229]

1 The seventh conjunction was at the beginning of the first month of the year 279 of Yazdijird,[230] and the form of the celestial sphere at the revolution of the year of the world in which it took place, was thus.

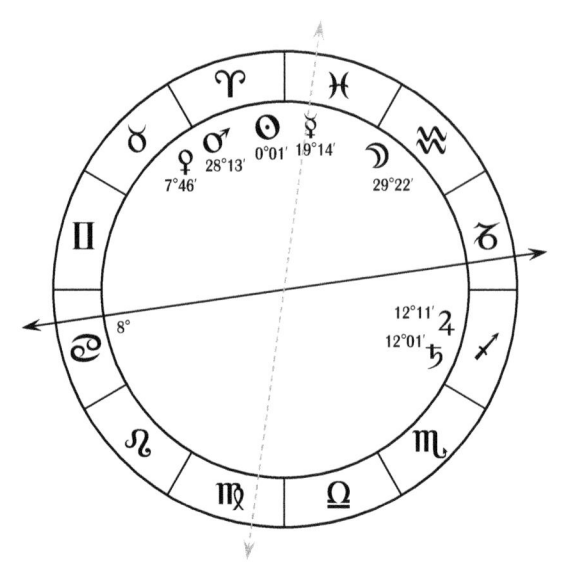

Figure 59: Ingress for #338, the 7th fiery conjunction (928 AD)[231]

2 And Māshā'allāh reported that he looked in the revolution of this year, and found the Sun to be the lord of the shift,[232] in the Midheaven (by division he was in the eleventh), and he was pushing his management to Jupiter. **3** And Jupiter was rendering the light to Saturn in the sixth place, and he is received.[233] **4** And the Moon, the lord of the Ascendant, is falling away from it in the eighth,[234] empty in course, and pushing her management into the next sign, to Jupiter (and he receives her).[235] **5** And Mars is in the tenth, and

---

[229] For more on this chart, see Ch. 11, **21-23**. The Buwayhid dynasty began in 945 AD.
[230] That is, 4/3/928 (Kennedy) or 4/2/928 (Dykes).
[231] I have changed the position of Venus in the chart. The Arabic diagram has her in Pisces, but the text clearly says she is in the eleventh, in her own domicile.
[232] *Nawbah*. That is, the sect: it is a diurnal chart.
[233] This must mean that *Saturn* is received.
[234] That is, she is in aversion to the Ascendant by being in the eighth sign.
[235] That is, she is entering into the ninth sign, where she will apply to Jupiter by sextile. He will receive her once this happens.

Venus in the eleventh, in her own house, free of the infortunes,[236] and Mercury is in his own fall, in the ninth (by equalization[237] he is in the tenth).[238] **6** So all of that indicates diseases will be in the clime of Babylon, and misery will enter upon its king in the sixth year of it.[239] **7** And because of the place of Venus and the Moon, it indicates the security of the citizens and the excellence of their condition.[240] **8** And the place of Mercury indicates repute and rank attained by the people of knowledge and scribes.[241] **9** And [for] those of the first conjunction who lived, it is unavoidable that in the people of this conjunction as well, there will be illnesses and smallpox in the sixth year, and the eighteenth.[242]

[Comment by ibn Hibintā]

(**10** And this judgment is rather dubious, because the rest of what he reports in the sixth conjunction, we saw in the seventh conjunction; I believe [its was] the copyist of Māshā'allāh's papers switching around what there was between the two judgments, making the judgment of the seventh [year] that of the sixth—or, Māshā'allāh did it on purpose, for he often makes what is in his books cryptic. **11** But we have expounded it just as we have found it.)[243]

---

[236] Venus is in aversion to the malefics.

[237] التسوية (or "arrangement"), referring to quadrant divisions, since the MC at Baghdad is within about a degree of Mercury's position. KP read this incorrectly as السوية, "equality," derived from the same verb.

[238] The MC at Baghdad is within about a degree of Mercury's position.

[239] KP argue that the Sun is the lord of the year, and the indicator of the king Mars. Since the Sun rules the fourth clime (Babylon), harm comes from his assembly with Mars in the same sign. They suggest that the trine to Saturn also adds to the problems, but note that the sign of the conjunction is in the sixth house (illness) anyway. What makes more sense is that Mars (the malefic contrary to the sect of the chart) is making an overcoming square to Cancer, the Ascendant and sign of Iraq.

[240] The Moon (lord of the Ascendant and indicator of the citizens) is in the eighth, but Māshā'allāh is counting on her being received in due time by Jupiter once she enters Pisces.

[241] Mercury is in the ninth and on the MC; Māshā'allāh ignores his being in detriment and fall, which he'd already mentioned.

[242] By "the people of the first conjunction," Māshā'allāh is referring to the first fiery conjunction, which was also in Sagittarius—of course, such people would have been at least 100 years old by now. The sixth and eighteenth years are the profection of the Ascendant to Saturn and the sign of the conjunction, in consecutive cycles.

[243] Ibn Hibintā's complaint is that the widespread violence which Māshā'allāh had predicted earlier in #337 (the sixth conjunction), actually appeared here in #338 (the seventh)—the seventh is very mild compared to the sixth. But KP rightly point out that this criticism is unjustified, "since each set of predictions can be justified from the horoscope" (p. 124).

[Chapter 18: Ibn Hibintā's true conjunction in Sagittarius (928 AD)]

Comment by Dykes. In this chapter, ibn Hibintā describes what he believes Māshā'allāh should have said about the rise of the Buwayhids, using his own first-hand knowledge of the events. In his presentation he makes three changes. First, he provides his own (incomplete) chart of the *true* conjunction of 928 AD. This differs from Māshā'allāh's and others' practice, but as I mentioned in my Introduction, al-Battānī had done the same thing (albeit paired with eclipses; there were no such eclipses paired with the true conjunction here). Second, ibn Hibintā uses a tropical zodiac, instead of Māshā'allāh's adjusted sidereal one. Third, he uses a different book of tables: the *Mumtaḥan Zīj*[244] instead of Māshā'allāh's version of the *Zīj al-Shāh*. Unfortunately, ibn Hibintā mentions only a few planetary positions and no Ascendant, so I have made Aries rise in my diagram. The chart information is too scanty to tell how it relates to the detailed account of events ibn Hibintā provides.

1 And after that, we state what he observed of the condition of the seventh conjunction:[245] and indeed the beginning of the year of the world in which it took place is at the beginning of Year 297 of Yazdijird. **2** And the time of the uniting of the two planets according to the *Mumtaḥan [Zīj]* was at 16° 41' Sagittarius, after 6 months and 9 days of the revolution of the year.[246]

But it is true that Māshā'allāh's predictions are so loose and general that one could indeed also predict terrible things for #338, too. In the next chapter, ibn Hibintā will substitute his own chart, for the *true* conjunction of 928.
[244] Kennedy (1956, p. 132) lists this *zīj* as his #51, composed around 810 AD.
[245] That is, what ibn Hibintā graciously assumes Māshā'allāh foresaw and mistakenly (or deliberately) assigned to the *sixth* conjunction.
[246] This corresponds to October 8, 928 AD (Julian Calendar).

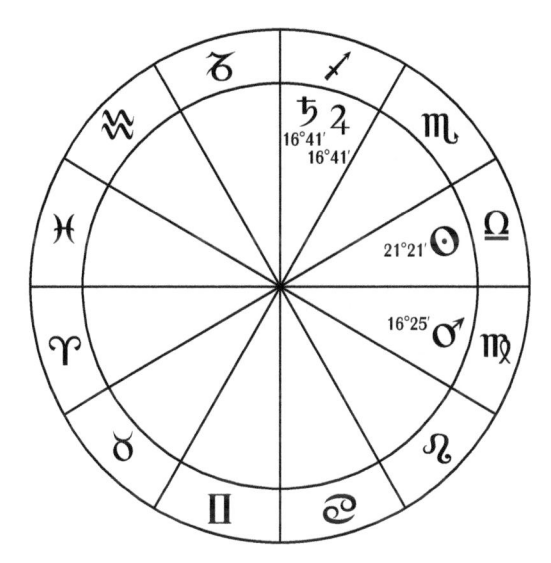

Figure 60: Ibn Hibintā's true conjunction for #338 (October 8, 928)

3 And Mars at the time was in 16° 25' Virgo, and he was in the tenth from those two [planets].[247] **4** And the Sun is in Libra 21° 21'. **5** And Mars is elevated over those two [planets] and in his own sector,[248] the rising one of the circle of his apogee and of the circle of his epicycle, east,[249] rising in his latitude in the north as well. **6** And Saturn was transiting in the circle of his apogee above Jupiter.

7 And whereas it was on the first of the eleventh month of this year,[250] the soldiers provoked discord against[251] [Caliph] Muqtadir b'Illah, and deposed him. **8** And Nāzūk and Abū al-Hayjā were killed, and that crowd was dispersed, and Muqtadir returned to his position. **9** And after that by one year, the men killed, in their territories[252] at one time, several ten-thousands of people.

---

[247] In other words, he was overcoming (or decimating) them. See the Glossary.
[248] Reading with KP for بطاق.
[249] I believe this means he is coming out of the rays (مشرق).
[250] KP say that this refers to December 928.
[251] Reading as شغف...على for سعب...على, though this should probably be Form 4, اشغب ("rebel...against").
[252] Reading tentatively as بابتوضهم for بابتوصهم. , which suggests "their territories" and invasion (Lane p. 282). But for the possible root بيص, Lane points to حيص, which would suggest killing "during their flight."

10 And the civil unrest and discord continued until the eighth month of the fifth year from the conjunction: for in it Muqtadir b'Illah was killed,[253] and al-Qāhir succeeded in his place.

11 And when it was in the second month of the seventh year of the conjunction,[254] al-Qāhir was deposed and his eyes put out, and al-Rādī succeeded to the Caliphate in his place.[255] **12** In his days there were wars and civil strife, and the killing of the leadership of the Hajariyyah and the Sājiyyah; and the remaining ones dispersed (and they were roughly 4,000 young men), and the vizierate was discontinued.

13 And the lords of swords took command until it was the beginning of the tenth month of the thirteenth year of it:[256] [Caliph] al-Rādī b'Illah died, and al-Muttaqī succeeded him in this place, and in his days there occurred civil unrest and misfortunes until the end of the seventh month.[257]

---

[253] In August-September 932.
[254] In January-February 934.
[255] On April 24, 934.
[256] In 940.
[257] Following this, in 945 the Buwayhid dynasty began.

SECTION II.5:
ABŪ MA'SHAR, *SCITO HORAM INTROITUS*

Comment by Dykes. This Latin work (hereafter designated by its incipit, *Scito*), attributed to Abū Ma'shar, is a pastiche of different views and texts taken largely from Māshā'allāh's *RYW*, but with generous helpings from Sahl's Arabic work on mundane revolutions (forthcoming), as well as other things. Its Arabic identity seems to be unknown and its Latin translations have perhaps caused confusion, since the explicit refers to it as "The Book of Tested Things" (*liber experimentorum*)—the title of the work in Section II.6 below. Sezgin does not seem to list it. But since it definitely draws on the Arabic original of *RYW*, it helps correct readings in the latter and even shows where *RYW* has apparently truncated certain discussions. My primary sources were as follows:

- Paris BNF 16204 (13th Cent.), pp. 302-333 (but the page numbering is jumbled around 329).
- Erfurt UFB, Amplon. Q 365 (12th Cent.), 1r-18v.
- London BL, Harley 1 (13th-14th Cent.), 31r-40v.

Obviously for sourcing and often correcting the material, *RYW* was valuable, not to mention Sahl's own Arabic work on mundane revolutions (Vat. Ar. 935, Beatty Ar. 5467): indeed it was a surprise to see that the lengthy example chart (Ch. 95), along with at least some of the other examples in Ch. 96, come directly from Sahl. Since Bonatti quotes liberally from *Scito* in his *Book of Astronomy* (*BOA*), his work also helped clarify some passages.

Nevertheless, *Scito* is confusing at certain points. Its division into chapters sometimes seems arbitrary, and I have inserted chapter divisions when they have seemed necessary (I have also numbered all of them). Although it often matches *RYW* sentence-by-sentence, it often jumps around within *RYW*, pulling a sentence from here, then there, to form a text that is surprisingly consistent within each chapter. To help make sense of it and its sources, I have inserted numerous footnotes directing the reader to *RYW* and other works. Following are a few notable features of *Scito*:

Lords of the year in the signs. In Chs. 90-93, Abū Ma'shar begins a series of cookbook delineations of four planets (Saturn, Jupiter, Mars, Mercury) in the signs. Although one might expect these lists to be copied from elsewhere, they do not match lists in *Flowers/Report*, BRD, or even Sahl. I am sure that future translations will reveal the source.

Sahl's example chart. In Ch. 95, Abū Ma'shar begins a lengthy analysis of an Aries ingress from 656 AD, which is in fact taken practically verbatim from Sahl (see my *Comment* to that chapter). What is interesting about this is that, directly after the analysis of the houses, *Scito* departs from Sahl's text in order to apply some timing techniques to the chart. These techniques would seem to be Abū Ma'shar's own work, which give us a nice example of how he might have approached charts in practice. Unfortunately, the Latin version of Sahl's example is so confused in spots as to be almost unreadable, so I have decided to omit the Latin altogether and substitute a translation of Sahl's Arabic (with sentence numbers beginning with **A**).

"Rules" drawn from actual examples. In Ch. 96, Abū Ma'shar presents what appear to be rules for interpreting mundane ingresses, but which seem to have no connecting or ordering principle to them. Again, most of this material is taken directly from Sahl's examples—in other words, presenting individual statements from Sahl's chart examples as though they were abstract rules. I have been able to find the source of most of these sentences, which come from consecutive examples in Sahl's text. I supply translations from the Arabic of the actual examples in Appendix C.

Finally, a note about terminology. *Scito* often shows traces of its Arabic source, particularly in its use of "fall" to speak of where planets are located: for example, "If Mercury *fell* in the fourth," or "If the Sun's falling was in the sixth." This translates a common Arabic verb whose concrete meaning is indeed "to fall," but metaphorically means "to occur, take place," and from that simply "to be" somewhere. Because there is already so much vocabulary and uncertainty about different ways to "fall" in these texts (declining, falling away from, being in one's own fall), I have tried to avoid using "fall" in these instances, using "occur" instead.

ဢ ဢ ᜒ

Chapter 1. 1 Abū Ma'shar said: Know the hour of the Sun's entrance into the first minute of Aries, and establish the Ascendant and its angles, and the three Lots,[1] and the places of the planets in longitude (that is, from the beginning of Aries) and latitude (that is, from the path of the Sun), and the projection of their lights into the angles.

2 And know the rulers of the Ascendant by nature (that is, by house and bound and exaltation and triplicity), and the lord of the hour and revolution,[2] and the sign of the profection and its lord. **3** And identify the testimonies and aspects and occurrence of the planets in their own places, and what they own in terms of climes and cities, and what of this belongs to their signs by division,[3] according to what I will tell you in its own chapter.[4] **4** And [calculate] three Lots, which are:[5] the Lot of the kingdom, and the Lot of Fortune, and the Lot of rain (which in the day is from the Moon to Venus, and conversely in the night, and it is projected from the degree of the Sun).[6]

Chapter 2: On the knowledge of the lord of the year. 1 And[7] when you have done this, and you knew it well, know the eight places which are established for this,[8] which are: [1] the Ascendant and [2] the tenth and [3-4] their opposites, also [5] the eleventh and [6] the ninth and [7-8] their opposites, of which the ascending angle is more worthy, after [that] the tenth angle, then the seventh, afterwards the fourth angle, then the degree of the eleventh, after that the degree of the ninth, finally the degree of the fifth. **2** But in the end, the degree of the third.

3 And once you knew this, look at four testimonies in these, through which you will know the significator in these places: from the lord of the Ascendant and the lord of the exaltation of the Ascendant, and the luminary whose authority it is (that is, from the Sun in the day and from the Moon in

---

[1] See **4** below.
[2] I assume this is the same planet (the lord of the hour) and that the "and" here is an error; see Ch. 2, **5**, which seems to support my interpretation.
[3] *Divisione*. This probably refers to one of the ways in which the signs are organized and divided over regions of the world: see *AW1* Part IV.
[4] Again, see *AW1* Part IV for this type of information.
[5] Paris has a Lot of the rustics instead of the Lot of Fortune, but I am following Erfurt and London.
[6] For Lots of rain, see *AW1*, Section I.1.
[7] For **1-2**, see *RYW* Ch. 6, **2-3**.
[8] That is, the various lords of the Ascendant should be judged according to whether they fall into these places.

the night), and from a strong planet in a conquering place (namely, which has strength of testimony in the Ascendant, according to the nature of the circle at the hour of the revolution, after the situation of the lord of the Ascendant and the lord of its exaltation and the luminary).[9] **4** Therefore, the first testimony is that of the lord of the Ascendant, and the second one that of the lord of the exaltation of the Ascendant, but the third the luminary whose authority it was, and the fourth the conquering planet.

5 And[10] even know lords of the [lesser][11] testimonies, which are three: namely the lord of the triplicity, and the lord of the bound, and the lord of the hour of the revolution. **6** And the lord of the triplicity, if it were in the Ascendant, [has] one-third of the signification of the lord of the Ascendant, and one-fifth for the lord of the bound, and one-seventh for the lord of the hour. **7** And the places of [full strength for] these three are only[12] the Ascendant and the angle of the Midheaven. **8** But in the other remaining eight places,[13] they take away testimony.[14]

9 And once you knew this, know the testimony of the lord of the houses of the luminaries (in which they were),[15] and of the lord of the sign in which the lord of the house of the luminary (whose authority it is) was, because these have dignity in the revolution.

10 And[16] begin first from the Ascendant and its lord: if the lord of the Ascendant was in the degree of the Ascendant, in front of or below it (namely, in front or behind) by 3°, it will be the lord of the year, and the significator of the condition of the rustics.

---

[9] Meaning unclear. In **4**, this is clearly stated to be a victor (*planetae vincentis*).
[10] For this paragraph, see *RYW* Ch. 6, **6-10**.
[11] Added by Dykes for clarification. In *RYW*, the following three planets are intrinsically less valuable than the lord of the Ascendant or the lord of its exaltation.
[12] Reading *tantummodo* with London for *tammodo*. Also omitting "the third," in line with *RYW*.
[13] Or rather, "for the remaining ones of the eight places," which is more accurate and probably how the Arabic read.
[14] That is, different types of planets count for more or less by themselves, and this value can be intensified or diminished based on the type of house they are in. So, the lord of the hour in the third will have as little value as possible, while the lord of the Ascendant in the Ascendant will have the most.
[15] That is, in which the luminaries are. London has, "in which direction/part [*parte*] it was."
[16] For **10-11**, see *RYW* Ch. 6, **4-5**.

11 Which if fell from these cusps,[17] and in the sign of the Ascendant there was the exaltation of some planet, and the lord of the exaltation of the Ascendant is exalted in the degree of the Ascendant or below it by 3°, it will be the significator and the lord of the year.

12 If however these fell, and the luminary whose authority it was on the cusp of any of the angles, and there was any dignity in it, the luminary whose condition was such will be the lord of the year and the significator of the condition of the rustics.

13 Which if it fell from this and the house of the Ascendant was *its* house, or the sign of its own exaltation, and the luminary was in any of the trine or sextile aspects [to it], or in the second from the Ascendant, it will be the lord of the year.

14 If however it fell from this, revert to the lord of the Ascendant and the lord of the exaltation of the Ascendant. **15** Which if any of them were the lord of the house of the luminary whose authority it was, and the luminary looked at it, and how it occurred from it and from the Ascendant was optimal, and it was even strong in its own place, without a doubt the planet whose condition was such will be the lord of the year.

16 But if these three fell from these cusps and these figures, seek the signification from that one of the planets which was more in authority in the Ascendant or in the Midheaven, and more in allies[18] and testimony, and which was of a stronger condition: make that one the significator.

17 If however any of the lords of the dignities of the Ascendant were weakened by retrogradation and fall and burning and peregrination and the rest of the evils, see the signification from the better one of the planets by place, and with more aid through the handing over of management to it, and which was of a better condition than the rest, and stronger in light and body: make this one the significator.

18 Which if there were a convergence of these three significators (namely the lord of the house, and exaltation, and the luminary[19] whose authority it is), that is, if two of them assembled in the Ascendant, the one which was

---

[17] This and the next sentence suggest that while being so close to the Ascendant is preferred, other angular cusps would be acceptable as well.
[18] Erfurt reads "authorities." But aspecting planets can be viewed as allies, as suggested below.
[19] Reading *luminare* with Erfurt. Paris and London have *luminaris*, which would mean "the lord of the luminary whose authority it is."

stronger than the rest and better in condition, and greater in testimony and dignity in the cusp of the Ascendant (or in the tenth angle or in the house of the luminary whose authority it was), or closer to the cusp of the Ascendant, will be more worthy in the signification.

19 If however each of the significators were retrograde or under the rays, the luminary whose authority it was will be more worthy, and it should be begun with it: because retrogradation and burning is no strength in the signification.

Chapter 3. 1 If[20] the lord of the Ascendant was the lord of the house of the luminaries (or of one of them), without a doubt it is the lord of the year,[21] and it is said then [that] one does not look at another apart from it.

2 And[22] if the luminaries were in the angles, they will be ruling over the year, unless the one which was in the angle was impeded: because it signifies impediment and weakness in that same clime—and better than that if the Sun were in an angle by day, and the Moon in an angle by night.

3 And[23] he said that perhaps the significator will not be needy, on account of its own strength and management.[24] **4** And perhaps on account of its own weakness, it *will* need a planet which reflects its light upon the Midheaven, and will strengthen it in terms of[25] the management. **5** This is like if it is falling [away] from the Ascendant, in a place not looking at the Ascendant: and the lord is weakened by the receding of its place, and it will need a planet which looks at it from out of the Midheaven, and [which] will strengthen it in terms of the management. **6** Because if a planet had more[26] testimony and it was the lord of the year and was in the eighth, [it would need a planet which sees it from the Midheaven].[27] **7** And every planet falling [away] from the Ascendant looks at the Midheaven); except for one which was in the third from the tenth (that is, the twelfth): because this one is weakened and does not look.

8 And if a planet were weak through this condition, and needy on account of its own receding, and it was the lord of the year on account of its own

---

[20] For this sentence, cf. *RYW* Ch. 10, **2**.
[21] But **15** above has additional conditions.
[22] For this sentence, see *RYW* Ch. 7, **2-3**.
[23] For **3-7**, see *RYW* Ch. 11, **8-9** – Ch. 12, **2-5**.
[24] Or perhaps, "arrangement" (*dispositionem*).
[25] *Super*, evidently a translation of the Ar. ʿalā.
[26] Reading *pluris* with London, for *planetis*.
[27] Completing the sentence with *RYW* Ch. 12, **3**.

testimony, and a planet looked at it from out of the Midheaven and reflected its light, it is stated [that it is the lord of the year].[28] **9** And if its aspect were from the fourth, it will signify it in accordance with its essence and its place. And if it were from the eighth, it will signify it according to what there was with respect to its condition and weakness.

10 However,[29] once you knew the significator which is the lord of the year, look in its place: which if it were in the house of a planet, and it was joined to that same planet, and the planet in an optimal place from the Ascendant, it will be the lord of the year, and the significator of the condition of the rustics will be the planet which was in this manner: because the lord of the year is joined to it from its own house, and hands the management and strength to it, and the planet received it.[30] **11** For if a planet had such a condition, it would be in charge of the signification through the handing over of the lord of the year to it. **12** And [if] the luminaries (or one of them) looked at it, or the lord of their house [did so], it will be more worthy and stronger: because this increases the testimony and strength, so that it would push its own management to the lord of the house in which it was. **13** See therefore whether it has strength over the management in its own place: this is like if it was direct and strong, looking at the Ascendant, receiving and collecting the lights of the planets, or received in an optimal place of the planets from the Ascendant and from the luminary whose authority it was.

14 And[31] if the nocturnal planets in a revolution of the night were under the rays of the Sun, the Sun will be more worthy in the signification of the king, because he is the body receiving the strengths of the planets. **15** And if the lord of the house of the Ascendant were under his rays, he will be more worthy in the year.

Chapter 4.[32] **1** Know that every planet changing its own figure in a revolution of the years of the world—through its change from a sign into a sign, or through [its] exit from the east into the west, or equally to the degree of

---

[28] Adding the bracketed phrase very speculatively.
[29] For **9-12**, see *RYW* Ch. 8, **2-4**.
[30] That is (following *RYW*), if the putative lord of the year is in a sign ruled by some other planet which is in a good place, and they are connected by a degree-based aspect (especially or perhaps only applying), then that other planet will be the lord of the year.
[31] For **13-14**, see *RYW* Ch. 17, **4-5**.
[32] Oddly, this paragraph is found in ʿUmar al-Tabarī's *natal* work, *Three Books of Nativities* III.1.2 (in *PN2*), and attributed to Hermes.

the Moon or to the degrees of the Ascendant apart from the Moon—changes the signification and is made the lord of the year and its significator.

Chapter 5. 1 If[33] the revolution were in the day, and the Sun was joined to the lord of the Ascendant, [the Sun] hands the matter over to it. **2** And if the revolution were in the night, and the Moon was joined to the lord of the Ascendant, she hands the matter over to it. **3** And if the luminary whose authority it is, was in the Midheaven, and a planet [is] with it, it takes its strength and will be in charge of the matter (namely, the Sun in the day, and the Moon in the night).[34]

Chapter 6. 1 The[35] lord of the year is the lord of the Ascendant, and the condition of the king is known from Saturn and the Sun, and from the Midheaven and its lord. **2** But that of the soldiers and allies of the king [are known] from the eleventh, and the allies of the masses from the second. **3** Also, the condition of each [kind of] people [is known] from the nature of their houses in the circle, and the essences of the seven planets.[36]

Chapter 7: Through what the significator of the king is known. 1 Look[37] at it from the Midheaven and its lord, and from the Sun, and the lord of the exaltation of the Midheaven, and from the planets happening to be in it. **2** And for the place of the king it is looked for from the place of the Sun, and the Midheaven, and the aspect of the fortunes or bad ones to this, and you will gather the lord of the Lot along with these.

3 Which if the Midheaven were the house of the Sun, and the Sun in its cusp, not remote nor falling, he himself will be the significator of the king. **4** And likewise if he was in the Midheaven, received by Mars, and Leo in the Midheaven (because the Ascendant will then be Scorpio).[38] **5** And if the Midheaven were the sign of the exaltation of the Sun (which is Aries), and

---

[33] For **1-2**, see *RYW* Ch. 1, **3-5**.
[34] This is ambiguous: is the luminary taking over, or the other planet? The parenthetical remark about the Sun in the day (etc.) could modify "the luminary whose authority it is," not the planet which is taking over the matter.
[35] London makes this sentence continue from the previous one, and begins it with "because."
[36] See Ch. 12 below.
[37] For **1-2**, cf. *RYW* Ch. 11, **3-4**.
[38] By "receive," Abū Ma'shar or his source here must mean "receiving his application." Mars cannot receive the Sun by domicile when the Sun is in Leo.

the Sun in its cusp according to what I told you, and Mars falling from him,[39] [the Sun] will be the significator of the king. **6** Which if he looked at Mars, [Mars] will be his partner in the signification. **7** If however Mars was strong in his own place, and his condition was good, and if the Sun was joined to him, Mars will be the significator of the king, and more worthily so if he was in Capricorn and the Sun was joined to him from out of the Midheaven.

8 Which if his[40] position happened to be in the Midheaven (that is, if it happened that he is in the Midheaven) or in an angle from the Ascendant, and he projected his own rays, the Sun will be more worthy in the signification. **9** And likewise if the Sun were in the angle of the Midheaven or in the rest of the places looking at the Midheaven; and if he were in the Midheaven, he will be more worthy in the signification of the king.

10 If[41] however the Midheaven was a sign [belonging to] the lord of the year, or the sign of its exaltation, and the lord of the year looked at it, [the lord of the year] will be the significator of the king.

11 If[42] however the lord of the Midheaven or the lord of its exaltation handed over its management and strength to the lord of the year, or the lord of the Midheaven was in the house of the lord of the year, received by it, if it were so, [the lord of the Midheaven] will be the significator of the rustics, because the lord of the year is the significator of the king.

12 And if the Sun were the lord of the year, and he had testimony[43] in the Midheaven, or the lord of the Midheaven were under his rays, or it had already passed over the burning but had not yet appeared, the Sun will be more worthy in the signification over the condition of the king in that clime.

13 And if the Sun handed over management to the lord of the Ascendant, and the lord of the Ascendant had any testimony in the Midheaven, the lord of the Ascendant will be the significator of the king. **14** Which if the Mid-

---

[39] That is, in aversion.
[40] I believe this is Mars, but I do not understand how it connects with the previous sentences.
[41] For **10-12**, cf. *RYW* Ch. 19, **4-9**.
[42] For **11-12**, cf. *RYW* Ch. 19, **3-7**. Reading this sentence with London, which contains extra phrases missing in Paris in Erfurt. The latter read: "Likewise if the lord of the Midheaven handed over in the house of the lord of the year, received by it, if it were so, it will be the significator of the rustics, because the lord of the year is the significator of the king."
[43] This probably translates the Ar. *shahādah*, which means both "testimony" and "witnessing": this suggests an aspect.

heaven were any of the houses of Saturn or the sign of his exaltation, and he was in its cusp, free from burning, Saturn will be the significator of the king.

15 And if the Sun did not have testimony in the Midheaven, look at the lord of the Midheaven and the lord of its exaltation: which of them is stronger and with more testimony, and of a better condition, and with more collecting and receiving of the lights of the planets, and has a better position from the Midheaven: that one will be the significator of the king.

16 Which if the lord of the Midheaven, and the lord of its exaltation, and the Sun, fell away from the aspects, and their condition was bad, and in the Midheaven there was a planet which had any testimony (by triplicity or by bound or by face), and one of these three significators was joined to it, that planet happening to be in the Midheaven will be the significator of the king.

17 If[44] however this were not [so], and the significators fell away, the significator[45] will already be in need of a planet looking at it from the Midheaven, that would reflect its light to the Midheaven (and it will strengthen it with regards to the management), or a planet which is in the Ascendant who would render its light by its own aspect to the Ascendant.

Chapter 8. 1 If it happened that the lord of the year is the significator of the king, [*missing*]; but if not, look at the lord of the Midheaven and the Sun, because they are the significators.[46]

Chapter 9.[47] **1** If the Sun were the lord of the Ascendant, the Midheaven will be Taurus: which if Venus were under his rays, she will not be worthy in the signification, and the Sun will be the significator of the king because the lord of the Midheaven is under his rays. **2** If however Venus had gone out from under the rays, in her own light, she will be more worthy in the signification, because she will be in the Ascendant or in a house from which she

---

[44] This sentence seems to be adapted by Abū Ma'shar from *RYW* Chs. 11-12.
[45] That is, the putative significator from among the various choices.
[46] Bonatti (*BOA* Tr. 8.1, Ch. 2) makes this sentence continue directly after Ch. 7, **16**, and fills it out: "If however you found none of these, then revert to the lord of the year, and to the lord of the tenth, and to the Sun: and the one of them you find stronger, or less weak, or better disposed, or less bad, or in a better place from the tenth, or [a place] less bad, make this the significator of the king."
[47] For this chapter, see my notes to *RYW* Ch. 41, **2** and **7**.

would look at the Ascendant;[48] and better than that if she were in her own house or in her own exaltation.

Chapter 10.[49] **1** If Venus were at the end of an angle and she pushed strength to the Sun, then if Venus were the lord of the Midheaven, she will already have pushed her own strength to the Sun, and the Sun will be the significator of the king. **2** But the angles of the planets are the aggregate of their equation [and] truth: and this is taken from the diameters of their short circles.[50]

Chapter 11.[51] **1** The[52] lord of the year will not be the significator of the king unless the lord of the Midheaven hands over the management to it: and [then] the lord of the year will be the significator of the king.

2 If a planet were at the end of its binding,[53] and it ran up to the degree of its exaltation, it will be in a place of strength and testimony.

3 And from [its] impediment is known its place (if it were competing in that same place), and it is sought through its own essence.

4 If the Sun were subject to it, the diurnal planets will be subjected to it; and if the Moon were subject to it, the nocturnal planets will be subjected to it.

5 And look for the citizens of his kingdom from the lord of the house and the lord of the year, in [their] complexion with each other.

Chapter 12. 1 You will look for merchants from the lord of the year and the Ascendant and its lord, and the Moon; and for magnates from the lord of the year and the manager; and for the wealthy ones of them from the signifi-

---

[48] Abū Ma'shar must mean that Venus is not also retrograde. If the Ascendant of the ingress is Leo and the Sun in Aries, then if she went out of the rays by retrogradation, she would be in Pisces, which does not aspect Leo.

[49] Again, cf. *RYW* Ch. 41, **7** and my commentary.

[50] This seems to refer to getting the planets' true positions in the epicycle, but I do not understand how it helps explain the situation of Venus in the previous sentence.

[51] This chapter seems to lack any principle of organization, and in **3** and **5** I have been somewhat lax in interpreting the somewhat unusual Latin syntax. If the original Arabic can be identified, I will update it for a second edition.

[52] For this sentence, see Sahl (Beatty Ar. 5467, f. 157), who makes it a continuation of Chs. 9-10 above.

[53] *Alligationis*, meaning unclear.

cator, in every clime. **2** Once you knew the lord of the year in your clime, grant the seven climes according to the ascensions of the lords of the circle.

Chapter 13. 1 And this is what there is among us in the viewing of all climes from the significator of the climes and its ascensions, and [from] the lord of its Ascendant, and the lord of the hour, and the lord of the year: because it is possible that the significator of one clime is the significator of two climes. **2** And there must be a revolution of every year by means of the ascensions of that region,[54] the condition of whose king or rustics you wanted to know. **3** And so, know the condition just as I have told you.

4 And if there were a revolution of the year which you revolved, [and] the significator of the king will be stronger than [the other], and with more testimony, in the Midheaven, not impeded, the king of that region will be exalted above kings and the wealthy, and his condition will be good.

Chapter 14. 1 Look at the Ascendant: if it were a fixed sign, the signification of the lord of the year will be general[55] from the beginning [of the year] until its end—and better if the lord of the Ascendant were in a fixed sign, so that in this you will be excused from the revolution of the quarters. **2** If however the sign were common, its signification will be up to the first half of the year, and it is necessary for you to revolve the other half, from the Sun's entrance into the first minute of Libra—and it will be more strong for this that the lord of the Ascendant is in a common sign. **3** And if the sign were movable, the signification of the lord of the year will be for the first quarter of the year, and it is necessary for you to revolve the quarter for the Sun's entrance into the beginnings of [all four] movable signs—and it will be more powerful for the revolution of the quarters that the lord of the year be in a movable signs.

4 After this, seek the significator in every revolution just as I have told you, and look with respect to this, just in the way that you look at the signification of the lord of the year. **5** And make the significator the partner of the lord of the year, in [every] quarter or at the middle.

---

[54] At a minimum, this simply means that one must calculate the ingress chart for a particular location.
[55] Reading *vleris* as *universalis*.

Chapter 15. 1 And[56] once you have done this wisely,[57] know the strength of the lord of the hour, and the Lot of Fortune and its lord, and the prosperity of their condition: because the Lot of Fortune and its lord aid the lord of the year and the significator of the king.

2 Therefore,[58] know the conjunction of the planets with the lord of the year and the significator of the king, and their conjunctions with the planets, and their separations from them, and their arrival at each other in the houses and by aspects, and fix the memory of their essences, and understand their works through [where] they are positioned, and commingle with these the essences of their signs, and what conquers from the receiver by nature, and understand the condition of the significators, and know [where] they are positioned from one another in terms of disagreement and concord, and binding and hurrying off[59] and reflection.

Chapter 16. 1 After this, look at the condition of the rustics in their bodies from the lord of the year and the lord of the Ascendant, and what is in the Ascendant (of the lights of the fortunes and the bad ones) in the way that you look in nativities. **2** Likewise, [look at] the condition of the king in his body from the Sun and the lord of the Midheaven, and the conjunction of the planets with them, and their conjunction with the planets.

3 And put down the fitness of the Lot of Fortune and the strength of its lord with them, and the increase in that which it signifies (of the good and the restraint from evil), and put down their impediment, the weakness for them,[60] and the significator of the rustics and the increase in evil.

Chapter 17.[61] **1** Look for magnates and nobles from Jupiter, and for soldiers and the king's allies and masters of armies from Mars, and the religious and those serving God from Saturn, and for women from Venus, and for merchants and scribes and eunuchs from Mercury, and the generality of the masses from the Moon. **2** And make the lord of the year and its lord a partner according to this, and make the best commixture [of them]. **3** Which if

---

[56] For the portion of this sentence dealing with the Lot of Fortune, see *RYW* Ch. 18, **3**.
[57] Reading *sapienter* for *sapientis*.
[58] For this sentence, cf. *RYW* Ch. 11, **7**.
[59] *Correptionem*, which I take to mean separation.
[60] There is clearly something wrong about this phrase, "their impediment, the weakness for them" (*impedimentum eorum debilitatem eis*).
[61] For this chapter, see *RYW* Ch. 30, **4-11**.

one of these were impeded, and it had a role in the year, it would signify severity and impediment and evil in it, in proportion to the conjunction and complexion—and more harsh than that if the Ascendant or Midheaven were its sign. **4** Except for Venus and the Moon: if their impediment and [where] they occurred was in the west or in the angle of the earth, they will signify severity, because these two places are feminine (and [this also applies to] Mars, but he is less than them).[62] **5** But the Sun and Saturn and Jupiter, their condition will then be more harsh if their houses were in the Ascendant or the Midheaven.[63]

Chapter 18. 1 If the condition of the significator of the year and the significator of the king was fit, and they were free from the bad ones,[64] and their places from the Ascendant and Midheaven were good, and they received planets and were received by them, and the luminary whose authority it was looked at them and the Ascendant and its lord, and they were free from the bad ones, in an optimal and praiseworthy place, this signifies acquisition and strength and the prosperity of the condition of the citizens of that same clime. **2** And[65] [it would be] more worthy than that if the luminary whose rulership or authority it was, handed over management to the lord of the Ascendant, and it received [the luminary] in its own place: because if it were so, the wealthy of the [various] parts of that same clime will be humble to their king, and rest and prosperity will be bestowed upon all.

3 And[66] if the planets handed over their management to the lord of the year, and it received [the management] from them, and they were joined to it, joy and happiness will enter upon the citizens of that same clime from every direction, according to the disposition of[67] the essences of the signs in which the planets are.

---

[62] What Abū Ma'shar (or rather, Māshā'allāh) means to say is that these three planets, along with the west and the angle of the earth, are *nocturnal*. It so happens that Mars is a nocturnal planet even though he is masculine. This blurring of sect and gender (which is most evident when speaking of Mars) was common in traditional texts.

[63] That is, if the planet's nature by sect (e.g., diurnal), its position (e.g., above the earth), and the location of its domicile (e.g., in the Ascendant or Midheaven) all harmonize, then the impediment will be more direct, powerful, and pure.

[64] Or, "evils" (*malis*), which could include combustion or burning, retrogradation, etc.

[65] For this sentence, see *RYW* Ch. 10, 2; also cf. Ch. 1, **3-5**.

[66] For this sentence, see *RYW* Ch. 9, 2.

[67] *Dispositionem ex.* Or perhaps, "according to the management [coming from] the essences...".

4 Also,[68] if the lords of the houses of the luminaries (or one of them) were looking at the luminaries from a strong place, and it received them, and they received it, there will be good health and rest and security in the clime, and justice and benefit will be bestowed upon it, and there will not be disobedience nor detriment in faith.

Chapter 19.[69] **1** The sign in which the place of the lord of the year is, and the lord of the year, if they were of a strong and good condition, in the trine of a receiving fortune and one received, it signifies the strength of the master of the portion [of the earth] which belongs to that same sign, and the prosperity of the citizens of that very city which is in the division of the sign of the lord of the year. **2** If the condition were such, [then] the master of that same clime will be of a better condition and more acquisition than the rest of the climes.

Chapter 20.[70] **1** For every clime, establish the planet from which the condition of its king is taken, until you know what will happen for the wealthy people of the climes, by the command of God.

Chapter 21.[71] **1** The stronger one of the wealthy or kings will be the one whose clime or cities belonged to the lord of the year; after that it follows by the succession of strength.

2 And every nativity which was under that same sign or under the sign of the lord of the year, will be more trustworthy for the good, and of a better dignity and rank among men, unless his nativity is impeded in [its] root.

Chapter 22. 1 If[72] the revolution was at the setting of the Sun and the receding of the day, and the Sun is handing over management to the Moon (because she is the luminary of the night), look therefore at her and where her place is from the Ascendant. **2** Which if she were fit so as to manage [the chart], look at the lord of her house and the aspect of the planets to her, and speak according to what you saw of the fortunes and bad ones. **3** And look at

---

[68] For this sentence, see *RYW* Ch. 1, **6**.
[69] For this chapter, see *RYW* Ch. 16, **2-5**, and Ch. 17, **5**.
[70] For this chapter, see *RYW* Ch. 17, **6**.
[71] For this chapter, see *RYW* Ch. 17, **7-8**.
[72] For **1-5**, see *RYW* Ch. 35, **2-7**.

her place from Saturn [and] what kind it is (namely whether she would receive management from him or would hand it over to him), and look at the increase and diminishment of her light.

4 See also whether an eclipse would happen to her in that same year. **5** And it is good that in an eclipse of the Moon, her place and the degree of the fullness be looked at, and in an eclipse of the Sun, his place and the degree of the conjunction. **6** And the victor over them, and the planets looking at them, should be looked at. **7** "Fullness" is the degree of the prevention (from which degree the Moon is opposite the Sun), and the "victor" is the one which is in charge over the degree of the conjunction or prevention.

Chapter 23. 1 Know what belongs to every sign and planet, in terms of cities and climes. **2** And once you found the lord of a city strong and received, of a good condition and free from the bad ones, or [if] the sign of that same sign were free from the bad ones, say [there is] joy and fitness and happiness in this. **3** And if you found the planet and sign impeded, say [there is] evil and detriment in it.

Chapter 24. 1 If[73] the lord of the Ascendant were impeded, it will send impediment upon men in that same year, according to the essence of the sign of the Ascendant, and especially in the land which belonged to that same sign from the perspective of the Ascendant. **2** Such as Libra: if Venus were impeded, the land of Libra will suffer impediment from winds and infirmity and blisters. **3** Therefore, look, for every sign, at the condition of its lord, and its place in the circle, and what quarter it is, and speak according to what belongs to it in terms of the signs.

4 And once you knew this, begin from the Ascendant and know its condition and the condition of its lord, and their fitness and detriment, and speak in this according to what you saw. **5** After this, look at the second and its lord, until you run through all the houses and their lords. **6** But the angles[74] have work and strength above the rest of the signs.

---

[73] For this chapter, see *RYW* Ch. 35, **8-12**.
[74] Reading "But the angles" for "because they," to match the meaning of *RYW* Ch. 35, **12**.

Chapter 25: What is completed by the planets in a revolution of the world. **1** The Sun and Midheaven and the lord of the bound of the Midheaven, signify the matters of the wealthy. **2** Which if they were safe from the aspect of the bad ones from out of the angles, the wealthy will be saved; and if these places were impeded from out of the angles, the condition of the wealthy will be made worse, and this signifies evil.

3 And the eleventh belongs to the king's soldiers: if it were safe (that is, fit), the king's soldiers will be made fit; and if it were impeded, they will suffer impediment.

4 And Mercury signifies scribes and businessmen and astrologers, and teachers and sages: if this one were fit and strong, they will be made fit. **5** And likewise Jupiter signifies consuls and leaders [of society]: if he were fit and safe, they will be saved. **6** And likewise, Venus signifies women.

Chapter 26. **1** In matters, the Ascendant and the Moon signify the matters of the masses and low things[75] in the cycle[76] of the year of the world. **2** Which if they were impeded, it signifies many infirmities and pains, and more harshly in the sixth and eighth. **3** Which if the impediment was from Mars, there will be a hot fever and sudden death; and if the impediment was from Saturn, there will be fever from black choler, and gnawing pain.[77]

Chapter 27. **1** The Sun and Saturn signify the wealthy and kings. **2** Therefore, however you found the planet to be impeded from out of the four angles, say evil in its essence; and however you found the planet made thusly fortunate, say good in its essence.

Chapter 28: On wars. **1** Mars manages wars, and signifies the masters of armies and the leaders of soldiers. **2** Which if he were in strong in an angle, it signifies war; and if he fell away, it does not signify it.

3 But the Moon is the key of these:[78] which if she were fit, they will be fit; and if she were impeded, they will be impeded.

---

[75] This probably means "the lower classes."
[76] This probably means, "revolution."
[77] *Morsus.* Or, a "bite." But London reads *mors*, "death."
[78] I believe Abū Ma'shar is referring to *all* types of people now: that is, the Moon is a general significator for everyone.

Chapter 29: In which direction the severity will be, and for what reason. 1 A[79] bad one, if it impeded the lord of the Ascendant,[80] and it impeded it from out of the Midheaven, and [the bad one] itself was retrograde, and [so] was the lord of the year, severity will enter upon all men. **2** Which if it were in the east, the evil will be from the direction of the east; and if it were in the west, from the direction of the west; and likewise in the direction of the south and north. **3** And the condition of the citizens of the land or city which were in the division of the sign in which the bad one was retrograde, will be more harsh, and their impediment will be more harsh if it[81] were in an angle.

4 Which[82] if the aspect of the bad one to the lord of the year or the significator of assets[83] were from the Ascendant, the severity will be in the body; and from the second, in assets, and from the third, in brothers; but from the fourth, in connection with parents and older relatives. **5** From the fifth, from a child and minors, and from those who are under [the power] of his hand; the sixth, from infirmity; the seventh, from war and contention and women. **6** The eighth, from what is left behind by the dead, and contention. **7** Which if the sign were movable or common, death will be feared for the king if it was the significator of the king which the bad ones were looking at. **8** And in the same way, [if the bad ones looked] from the eighth at the significator of the rustics, it will be feared for the rustics. **9** And if their significator were one,[84] it will be feared for all, for death will invade them. **10** And if it were from the ninth, in connection with foreign travel and from all religious men who seek justice. **11** And if it were from the tenth, in connection with the king and his rulership; and if it were from the eleventh, in connection with friends; and if it were from the twelfth, in connection with enemies. **12** And speak likewise for the good if the aspect was from a strong fortune, and [each] bad one fell away.[85]

13 And speak likewise in a revolution of the years of nativities.

---

[79] For **1-3**, see *RYW* Ch. 14, **7-9**.
[80] Māshā'allāh has the lord of the year.
[81] The malefic planet, according to *RYW*.
[82] For **4-13**, see *RYW* Ch. 15, **2-7**.
[83] *RYW* has the significator of the king, which makes more sense.
[84] That is, if the significator of the king and of the rustics were the same planet.
[85] This seems to mean, "in aversion," and not simply being cadent from the angles.

Chapter 30. 1 If[86] the lord of the Ascendant is inimical to the Ascendant (this is if it fell into a place of enmity), it signifies impediment in accordance with its enmity. **2** That is, if [where] it occurred was in the sixth, there will be infirmity in men; in the eighth, death; and in the twelfth, enmity—according to the essence of the sign in which it was. **3** And likewise, if the lord of the exaltation of the Ascendant was impeded in [a place] like these places, there will be impediment, [but] less so than what the place of the lord of the Ascendant signified; and the lord of the bound and triplicity, if they were imimpeded [or] are inimical to the Ascendant in what is like[87] these places, their impediment will be less than that which I said before.

4 And all of this will be in accordance with the aspect of the fortunes and bad ones, and according to the complexion which existed between the significators, and the places in which they occurred. **5** And the fortunes repel evils by their aspect, and they are profitable unless they are retrograde or burned up; but the bad ones impede unless they are direct, receiving, and of a good complexion.

Chapter 31.[88] **1** The work of the planets in the climes will be according to their places. **2** If a planet were under the rays, the citizens of its clime will be weakened, and their condition destroyed, and they will acknowledge their own dejection and subjection; and more harshly than that if the lord of the revolution was in an angle, or a bad one looked at it. **3** Because if it was under the rays and a bad one looked at it, [and] after this it was at the end of the sign in which it was,[89] and a bad one looked at it in front and behind (this is, that there is a bad one or its rays in front of it, and the other bad one or its rays after it), the citizens of that clime will find evil[90] according to the greatness of the evils. **4** If it was a conjunction (that is, if it were with it in one sign), they will take away the generality of them; and if it was an opposition (that is, if it were from the opposition), they will take away a [one-half] portion of them; and if it was from the square aspect, they will take one-fourth of them. **5** And if Saturn came first, they will be captured and they will not be

---

[86] For **1-3**, see *RYW* Prologue, **6-8**.
[87] Reading in a more Arabic style for "in the likeness of."
[88] For this chapter, see *RYW* Ch. 28 (all).
[89] This sounds like being void in course, *in addition* to the besieging which follows.
[90] Reading *invenient...malum* for *inveniet...ex malo*.

killed (unless it is [only] a few); and if instead of Saturn it was Mars, all will be killed.

Chapter 32. 1 If the lord of the Ascendant or the Moon were impeded in the sixth or eighth, it signifies infirmities and death, because the Ascendant and its lord and the Moon signify the generality of the masses.

Chapter 33. 1 If[91] the bad ones looked at the significator [of the year][92] from the opposition, and they were impeded, there will be impediment from enemies (because this aspect is one of injustice). **2** And if they looked from out of the square aspect, the impediment will be from all those who are not known to be enemies—that is, whose enmity was concealed at first (because this aspect is in the middle, [and] signifies enmity).[93] **3** And if they looked from out of the sextile or trine aspect, the impediment will be in connection with friends.

4 Which if the aspect of the bad ones in such a figure was from their own places to the significator of the rustics, impediment will enter upon the rustics. **5** And if it was to the significator of the king, it will enter upon the king. **6** It is good that this be looked at: whether the rustics would aid the king, or the king would aid the rustics. **7** And this is known by the complexion which was between each of the significators and the bad ones that are looking.

8 Which[94] if the house in which the bad one was, was impeding the house of the significator of the king or of the significator of the rustics, and it signified impediment from enemies, the enemy will be from his own clime, in accordance with its testimony in that same house. **9** And if the significator of the year were in charge and the significator of the king was not in charge,[95] the enemy will be from the same clime, and the king will be weak in repelling and blocking him. **10** And if the significator were in charge and the significator of the rustics was not in charge, the enemy will be not be from that same clime, nor from his rulership.

---

[91] For **1-7**, see *RYW* Ch. 13 (all).
[92] Adding with *RYW*: this is the lord of the year.
[93] London reads, *non publicat inimicitiam*, which suggests "does not make the enmity public," but *publico* does not quite properly have this meaning.
[94] For **8-10**, see *RYW* Ch. 14, **2-4**.
[95] Māshā'allāh might be saying that we must choose the more authoritative and stronger between the two.

11 The[96] significator is the lord of the year, and the Moon is the significator of the rustics and the generality of the common people. **12** Now, every one which is in charge will be a significator, however not every significator will be in charge.

Chapter 34. 1 If Mars at the revolution of the year were in any of the angles of the Ascendant, wherever he was, he will stir up wars in accordance with his strength. **2** And therefore[97] he stirs up war if he were in the square aspect of Saturn and Jupiter.

Chapter 35: [On] the enemy. 1 See[98] the bad one looking at the significator of the king. **2** If the aspect were out of a sign in which [the significator of the king] had testimony, the enemy will be from his own land in accordance with the testimony. **3** And if the aspect was out of the sign of the significator [of the king],[99] the enemy will be from the household members of the king. **4** And if its aspect was out of the sign of the exaltation, he will be from the nobles, of those who are of his rank and just like him. **5** And the triplicity and bound signify the citizens of his rulership.

6 Also, the opposition signifies enemies. **7** And the first square aspect signifies the children of concubines, but the second square aspect signifies well-born people, of those who are fit for a kingdom. **8** And the trine and sextile aspects signify relatives. **9** And even the conjunction (that is, if they were in one sign): if they had testimony in it, he will be of the relatives of those who are just like him in name or dignity, or those more lofty than him. **10** And if [the two planets in the same sign] did not have dignity in it, their blood-relation will be one [and the same].[100]

---

[96] The following two sentences are difficult and inconsistent in the MSS. But this seems to be a comment by Abū Ma'shar. In **11**, he is clarifying that the "significator" mentioned in **1** is the lord of the year, as I have indicated above; then he again repeats the general significations of the Moon. In **12**, he is clarifying **9-10** but also making a general point: in any chart, there will be multiple significators (e.g., of the year, the rustics, the king, and so on). Of these, one of them can be taken as the more authoritative or preeminent (the one "in charge"), so while the one in charge will be a significator, not every significator can be the one in charge.

[97] *Ob hoc.* This statement is not the conclusion of any argument, and seems unconnected to the previous sentence. But see Ch. 38 below.

[98] For **1-10**, see *RYW* Ch. 29, **2-10**.

[99] According to *RYW*, this is the house ruled by the significator of the king.

[100] This seems to mean they will be of the same lineage, but not the same household.

11 And[101] it is good in addition to look at the luminaries and their condition, and their conjunctions and separations from the planets. **12** And the signification will be in accordance with the conjunction and aspects: because the square aspect is strong, and the sextile weak, and the conjunction harsh.

Chapter 36.[102] **1** Look at war from the part[103] in which Mars was. **2** If he were direct, the war will be from excellent men who do not want to flee; and if he was retrograde, the war will be from men rising up who are like robbers, who do not rest in one place and are not stable in war. **3** And then the war will be stronger if Mars was standing still (that is, if he was in his own station).

4 Now Saturn signifies the severity of the condition of the citizens in the part in which he is, in accordance with the essence of the sign in which he is, and with regard to the bound of his place, afterwards following it in succession (like the Ascendant, and the house of assets, and brothers), up to the end of the twelve signs, and if Saturn pushed[104] in just the way I told you about Mars—but this is more harsh.

Chapter 37. 1 And[105] if the bad ones were conjoined to the lord of the year, that is, if they were with it in one sign, this will be severe upon the rustics. **2** And if the significator of the king were joined with them, the severity will be upon the king from the land of the sign in which the bad ones are.

3 And for victory one looks at loftiness and at the bad one [which is] stronger in its journey. **4** And in this, one should look at the testimony of Saturn and Jupiter, according to what I revealed to you in the chapter on conjunctions.[106]

Chapter 38: On wars. 1 If the year were revolved, and you saw a thing from which you feared war, establish the Ascendant and the planets, and see from whom Mars would be separated: because that is the one who sends it and who stirs up the war. **2** Which if Jupiter sent it, [a member of the king's

---

[101] For **11-12**, see *RYW* Ch. 30, **2**.
[102] For this chapter, see *RYW* Ch. 21, **2-4**.
[103] Normally this means the "direction" in which he is: for example, if in an earthy sign or near the Midheaven, the south. But here it seems to mean, the "part of his cycle," namely being direct, etc.
[104] *RYW* reads, "if he were retrograde."
[105] For this chapter, see *RYW* Ch. 21, **5-7**.
[106] This refers to *RYW*, Ch. 22.

household] will be its provoker;[107] and if Saturn sent it, the king will stir up war.

3 And there will be war if Mars handed the management over to Saturn and he was joined to him, and Saturn did not receive him.

4 And[108] if you saw Mars separated from Jupiter and joined to Saturn without reception, know the one who is its provoker and provokes it for justice, will be of the household members of the king. **5** If however he was not separated from Jupiter and you saw him being joined to Saturn, the insurgents will be those who are not fit for a kingdom.

6 And if you saw him separated from Saturn and joined to Jupiter, this will not enter upon the citizens of the kingdom and province.[109]

7 And if you saw the insurgents and did not see reception, the hour of this will be the conjunction in one latitude or the conjunction of Mars or Saturn.

8 After this, see which of them is stronger in its own place and in its own domain, and which of them is going over its partner:[110] because you will know the weakness of the war if Mars passed under Saturn or there was reception between them. **9** And we have already revealed to you the knowledge of this matter—that is, how a planet goes above its own partner—in the first book, of which this is the second. **10** But what it is good for you to know in this chapter, is the strength of the kingdom in them[111] and what it is.

11 Then, you should know the time of the kingdom's duration. **12** And once you knew what there would be for the kingdom, and what the time of its duration would be, look at the hour of the destruction of the insurgents from the impediment of Saturn, Jupiter, and Mars, or that one of them which sent them. **13** And know his destruction from the destruction of these three planets: because it is that which stirred up the war.

---

[107] Reading *Iupiter* with Paris, and adding the material in brackets based on **4** and *Skilled* VIII.22, **12**.

[108] For this sentence, see *Skilled* VIII.22, **12** and *BRD* II.4, **9**.

[109] This does not really make sense; cf. *Skilled* VIII.22, **14**. If this sentence is valid, it may simply mean that because Mars is applying to Jupiter, the war directly affects the wealthy (Jupiter), not the people as a whole.

[110] This probably refers to a medieval Arabic theory of transits, in which one compares two conjoined planets to see which of them is proportionately closer to its apogee than the other: this planet will be "above" the other, and is considered more powerful. See Kennedy 1958.

[111] Reading *in eis* with Paris and Erfurt; London has "of the beginning" (*initii*). Nevertheless, I do not quite understand its meaning.

14 And[112] if a war was stirred up, and Mars was retrograde, as well as the two Lots,[113] the hour of their fitness will be when they were direct. **15** But if a war was stirred up, and Mars was falling from the Ascendant of the year or peregrine, [the war] will be weak.

16 And if you saw a Lot received by the enemies of the first one, and it was opposite the first Lot or in its square aspect, this will be the strength of the sword.

17 If however the first Lot received the [second] Lot, there will not be war. **18** But if the [second] Lot was not received and you did see war, and the first Lot was received, the insurgents will not have strength, and there will be a stability of men with the first king,[114] and their inclination toward him.

19 And likewise, look for the second Lot, because reception is aid and esteem and mercy and strength for the received. **20** If therefore it is not received, he will be a foreigner and there will not be trust in him nor will there be strength.

21 The first Lot in the condition of kings, and their custom and intention, the degree of Saturn and the Sun;[115] the second one, the degree of Mars; the third,[116] the degree of Jupiter.

22 And we have already revealed this to you from the *Book of Conjunctions*,[117] through which you will work if God wills.

Chapter 39: [On] the elections of wars from the first significator.[118] 1 If war appeared, look at Saturn and Jupiter and Mars at the hour of the revolution of the year. **2** Which if they were retrograde and war had already

---

[112] The next few paragraphs refer to the three superior planets, and particularly describe Saturn and Jupiter as the first and second Lots. If we think of it this way, the passages are mostly understandable (although it seems clear that some background information is missing). However, **21** is particularly puzzling and garbled in the MSS. For my interpretation of this sentence have relied a bit on Bonatti's version in *BOA* Tr. 8, Part 1, Ch. 33.
[113] I.e., Saturn and Jupiter.
[114] This seems to mean, "the original" king, not the would-be conquerors.
[115] Bonatti omits the Sun.
[116] Reading *tertia* for *in marte*. In Bonatti, the first Lot is simply the degree of Saturn, and the second is the degree of Mars. So either there is a mixing of doctrines here, or these manuscripts of *Scito* are particularly confused at this point.
[117] Reading *hoc ex libro coniunctionum*, for *ex hoc libro coniunctionum* ("from this book of conjunctions"). At present I cannot be sure of what the title of this work was, so I am reluctant to say that this is a *Book of Conjunctions*.
[118] I do not understand what Abū Ma'shar means by "the first significator." This chapter appears simply to speak of what changes of figure will mark the changes in war, but the title suggests that it is an electional text. (Indeed, it may be originally from Theophilus.)

appeared, [go to war when they go direct]. **3** And if they were direct, [it will continue] up until they returned backwards, or were burned up or would arise [out of the rays] (if they were sinking [under the rays]), or if they were changed from the sign where they were while they showed war: because then they will change their figures and their essences will be corrupted. **4** And[119] [as] for reception, if Mars is received he extinguishes war and they will make peace.

Chapter 40. 1 In the circle are customs which are not likened to other customs. **2** For in rulership there is a certain custom which is not like the custom of the household members of the king,[120] and in the household members is a custom which is not likened to the custom of the wealthy, and in the wealthy is a custom which is not like the custom of nativities, and in nativities is a custom which is not like the custom of interrogations.

Chapter 41. 1 Know the category of the one committing the assault. **2** If he were of the Arabs,[121] know his category through Venus; and if he were of the soldiers, through Mars; and if he were of kings or the wealthy, through the Sun and Saturn; and if he were of consuls and magnates, through Jupiter; and if he were of scribes, through Mercury; and if he were of merchants, through the Moon.

Chapter 42. 1 After this, know the place which they go out of[122] or which they are in charge of. **2** And if the bad ones met with or were opposite the sign of the city in which it is, or the planet of the attacking man, they will take the victory from him, or distress and difficulty and tribulation and grief will enter upon him. **3** And likewise if his planet were burned up. **4** And likewise, in retrogradation it signifies flight and falling. **5** And its change from a strong place from the Ascendant to a weak place, signifies his weakness.

---

[119] See below, Ch. 67, **1**.
[120] *Regni* ("kingdom, rulership"), but reading as *regis*.
[121] Reading *arabibus* with Paris and Erfurt (London is illegible). But note that this clashes with the other significations. It is true that Arabs and Muslims are normally associated with Venus, but the other planets identify parts of society, not ethnic and religious groups. Perhaps to be consistent, we should think of this as "women" (*mulieribus*), although one might not standardly expect the threat of war to come from women—especially since women are not a professional class (like "the wealthy," "merchants"), but a gender class.
[122] *Exeunt*. This probably translates the Ar. *kharaja*, which is the root both for "going out," "rising up," and "rebelling."

Chapter 43. 1 If the Moon were in the seventh, increased in light, and the lord of her house looked at her, and she was joined to a planet receiving her, or to a fortune, the king will be revered, and the rustics will acknowledge him, and they will hear him and obey him, and none will be contrary to him, nor will they raise an army against him, nor will they initiate any attack against him, and the king will see what he esteems. **2** But if the Moon were impeded and diminished in light, and no planet received her, it signifies that the king will be in wars and battles, and he will be unable to retain his rustics and make peace with them. **3** And likewise if she were in [her] descension or she was falling, in any of her own impediments.[123]

Chapter 44. 1 A retrograde planet signifies a confusion in matters, and turning back, and disagreement, also war and fear upon the master of that same clime which belongs to that planet. **2** And a standing planet (that is, which was in its own station)[124] signifies a desire for evil and a repetition of what had already ceased and gone inactive. **3** And [if it is] looking,[125] it signifies evil and a fight, and seductions, and cunning.

Chapter 45. 1 If Mars were in charge of the signification of the year, and he was strong, there will be war; afterwards [it will be] with ingenuity[126] and worries, and with plundering and powerful killing.

2 And if Saturn were in charge of the year or quarter, there will be war through seductions, cunning, and through instruction[127] and ingenuity (that is, images).[128]

3 And if one of the bad ones were in charge of the year, and the other bad one was the lord of the quarter, there will be no doubt about wars in that same quarter.

4 If it[129] looked at the lord of the year from the opposition or square aspect, or the lord of the quarter were in the seventh or retrograde, and if it is

---

[123] Or, "if she occurred in any of her own impediments."
[124] This must mean a planet which *was* direct but is now stationing toward retrogradation.
[125] Reading *aspiciens* (along with Bonatti); an alternate reading would be *accipiens* ("taking"). But it does not fit well with the discussion of stations and direction in **1-2**.
[126] *Ingeniis*. That is, craftiness and cleverness.
[127] *Disciplinam*. I am not sure what Abū Ma'shar or the Latin translator (probably John of Spain/Sevile) means by this.
[128] This parenthetical comment in Paris suggests that Saturn involves deception and subterfuge, while Mars is more straightforwardly hostile.
[129] That is, the malefic in charge of the quarter.

inimical to the lord of the year,[130] it will be in that same quarter. **5** And likewise, if it is inimical to the lord of the month, it will be in that same month.

Chapter 46. 1 If the significator were made peaceful with the lord of the year, there will be good in that same year. **2** And if it were made peaceful with the lord of the quarter, there will be good in that same quarter. **3** And if it were made peaceful with the lord of the month, there will be good in that same month. **4** And if it were made peaceful with the lord of the profection,[131] there will be good at the end of the month. **5** And if it were made peaceful with the lord of the day or hour, it will be on that same day and in that same hour. **5** Which if it were at the beginning of the sign, it will be in the first hour; and if it were at the end of the sign, it will be in the last hour.

Chapter 47. 1 If[132] one of the bad ones were in a sign of the human signs (that is, in signs which are formed in the images of men), slow, and each bad one was joined to it[133] (and it was direct or retrograde) from the conjunction or square aspect or opposition, the end will exist in men (that is, mortality). **2** And if it were retrograde, it will be more quick and cunning. **3** Also, if the conjunction were in this manner from an angle, it will be more cunning and harsh.

4 Which if the planet [which was] looking was in the Ascendant, and the retrograde one which is joined to it [was] in the Midheaven, it will be a powerful[134] evil for men, and the root of it will be from the direction of the east,[135] and there will be serious mortality in men. **5** And if the bad one was looking out of the Midheaven, and the retrograde one which is joined to it

---

[130] Reading *anni* for *quartae* ("quarter"), else the text would have the lord of the quarter harming itself. But the division of sentences is a bit unclear here. The point is that the lords of the year, quarter, and month, should be in a poor condition and harming each other.
[131] Probably the lord of the mundane profection (of which there could be several profections).
[132] For **1-12**, see *RYW* Ch. 22, **4-14**.
[133] Reading in the plural with the MSS, but clearly this does not quite make sense. *RYW* has both of the malefics in the same signs, but *Scito* might mean that *one* malefic is in these signs, and the *other* is looking at it.
[134] Reading as *valide*.
[135] Omitting Erfurt's *et nigrum* ("and black"). London also has *et nigrorum* ("and of the blacks") when speaking of the direction of the west in **5**. This probably refers to the Zanj. See *RYW* Ch. 26, **12**.

[was] in the fourth,[136] the root of it will be from the direction of the west, and the thing will be made greater in that same [place], and [the evil] will be abundant and made severe, and it[137] will be destroyed.

6 And if the bad one [which was] looking was in the west, and the retrograde one which is even joined to it was in the fourth, the beginning of the matter (from which it will be) will be when it reaches the west; and the manner in which the beginning will be, will be in connection with the quicker one which is joined to it.[138] **7** Know therefore that the evil will arrive from the place of the slow and heavy one.

8 And if the retrograde one or the one which is joined to it by aspect, was in a common sign, the end will be from death or killing. **9** And if it was in a movable or fixed sign, it signifies what the stronger bad one signifies in its own place. **10** If Mars were stronger, there will be killing or every hot infirmity; and if Saturn were stronger, there will be death and every cold infirmity. **11** Which if it were of the category of Saturn, and the strength of Mars will be commingled with it, [it will be both].[139]

12 If however what I said were outside an angle, this will be moderate, [and] afterwards it will be dissolved, by the command of God.

13 But[140] the evil and destruction will be in the direction in which the impeding bad one was. **14** Know therefore what belongs to the sign (of cities and provinces) in which the bad one was, if God wills.

Chapter 48.[141] **1** The age of the enemies' leader is known from the bad one and from the place of the Sun. **2** Because if the bad one were eastern of the Sun, he will be a youth; and if it were western, he will be an old man. **3** And between each, see what agrees with the bad one from its exit from under the rays up to its burning.

4 Which if the bad one were in the Midheaven, and the lord of the year was the lord of the Ascendant, destruction will enter upon all men.

---

[136] This should perhaps be "seventh," with *RYW* Ch. 22, **8**.
[137] This may refer to the king of the region.
[138] From "will be in connection," reading very loosely. Paris has *ex parte velocis erit in malo ex duobus et qui iungitur ei*. Erfurt reads: *ex parte velocius erit in malo ex duobus qui iungitur ei*. London has: *ex parte velocius erit in malo ex duobus et qui iungitur ei*. Each speaks of a "faster one," and *in malo ex duobus* suggests one malefic of the two. But if both malefics are involved, then obviously Mars is always the faster one.
[139] Tentatively adding the material in brackets, as the sentence is incomplete.
[140] For **13-14**, see *RYW* Ch. 14, **5**.
[141] For this Chapter, see *RYW* Ch. 14, **6-7**. This material is based on the age of a thief, which can be found in Dorotheus and Hephaistion (*Apotel. III*). See diagram below.

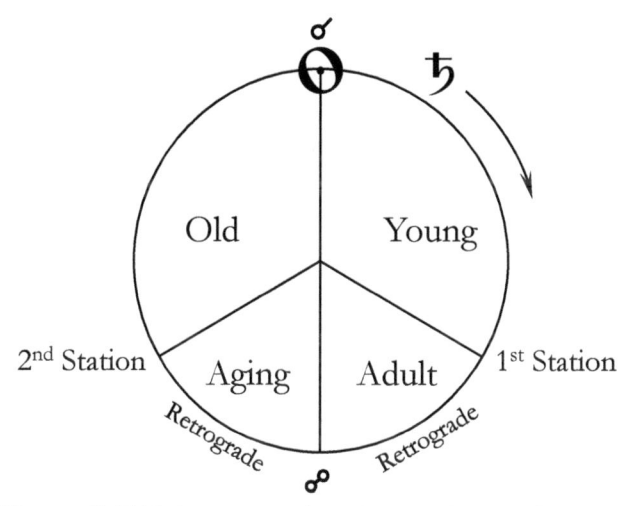

Figure 61: Thief age, superior planets (Heph. III.45, 13)

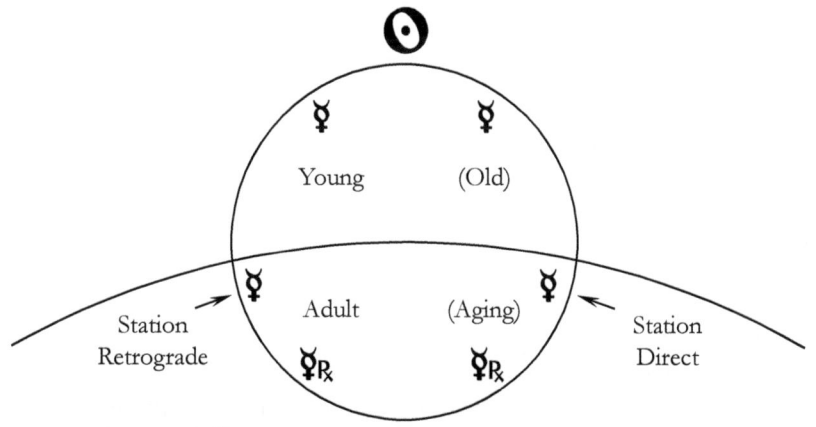

Figure 62: Thief age, inferior planets (Heph. III.45, 15)

Chapter 49. 1 But[142] if the significator of the year or the significator of the king were one of these two planets—namely, the Moon and Mercury—and one of the bad ones looked [at it] and impeded it, the condition will be weakened and made severe, and [the evil] would not be able to be blocked

---

[142] For this sentence, see *Skilled* VIII.16, **19** (in Section IV.2 of this book).

because of this, [nor could there be] a repelling of the impediment, on account of the weakness of the planet.

2 Then,[143] the Lot of Fortune and its lord, if they were in the place of a fortune, it signifies good and fitness and [good] fortune and the respectability of the condition. **3** But if they were impeded under the rays, they will signify impediment and evil according to the essence of the place they were in (namely, of the signs), and they will be inimical to the significator.

4 Look[144] therefore and know whether [the significator of the king] hands over his own matter to his own rustics,[145] and if it is separated from the lord of the year and is being joined to a bad one or to a planet which is inimical to the Ascendant.[146]

Chapter 50: On the king. **1** If[147] the lord of the Midheaven were in charge of the signification, and Saturn were under the rays, in [his] burning, it signifies the ruin of the king. **2** If however at the hour of the revolution he were going out from burning, it will take away from the evil, and it will [go] towards the good.

3 And[148] if the significator of the king was joined to the lord of the year, and the lord of the year to a planet in the eighth (or the fifth)[149] from the opposition or square aspect, death will be feared for the king in [that] year. **4** Likewise if it was conjoined to the lords of [these places] somewhere outside these places; and more severely so if the lord of the place was a bad one, and it was joined to a planet in the third or sixth: infirmity will be feared for him. **5** And likewise if the lord of these places was joined outside of these places: and this is these two places, if the lord of the Midheaven handed over its own management to the lord of the year. **6** But if it did not hand [it] over, it will be of greater signification in what was stated. **7** Therefore, it is good that one look for him in the twelve places, in difficulty and bounty, and likewise for all wealthy people of the climes and parts [of the earth].

---

[143] For **2-3**, see *RYW* Ch. 18, **3-5**.
[144] For this sentence, see *RYW* Ch. 19, **10-11**.
[145] According to *RYW*, this will be if the significator of the king is being joined to the lord of the year.
[146] *RYW* combines these two, and says that it will be bad for the rustics if this is so.
[147] This first paragraph reads as though it begins in the middle of another discussion.
[148] For this paragraph, *cf. Skilled* VIII.18-19.
[149] The fifth is the eighth from the tenth, hence the death of the king.

Chapter 51: Even [more] on the king.[150] **1** If the significator of the king were entering into burning, the king will perish unless God averts [it]. **2** And if it was at the extremity of the rays, enter and sorrow and fear will enter upon him. **3** If however a fortune looked at it, this will be dissolved and will go down, by the command of God. **4** And if it were so, and it had already crossed over burning, anger and contention[151] will enter upon him; afterwards, this will be released from him and his condition will be improved unless a bad one looks at it: then what it signifies by its aspect (according to what I said in terms of difficulty) will be feared for him, in accordance with the essence of the sign in which the bad one was. **5** If it were in the sixth, it will be infirmity; and if it were in the eighth, it will be death; and likewise with the rest of the signs.

6 And for the time of this matter, look to the conjunction of the significator of the king with that same bad one, and likewise when the bad one looks at the significator of the king from the opposition or conjunction or from the square aspect: it will be feared concerning the king. **7** If however this was from an angle, the hour of this will be the burning of the significator or the arrival of that same bad one to the place of the significator or to the Midheaven or Ascendant—unless a fortune would participate with it [by body or] by aspect, and if that bad one were a helper in the essence.

Chapter 52. 1 If[152] the significator of the king were one of the bad ones, and it impeded the place of the Midheaven or Ascendant from the opposition or square aspect or conjunction, it will send in difficulty upon men in connection with their king; and more harshly if it were in an angle.

2 Which if it were in the Midheaven, the difficulty of the time will find them because of this,[153] and this will be according to [where] the bad one occurred. **3** If it were in the east, in the east; and if it were in the west, in the west. **4** And in the Midheaven, it will be worthless for all,[154] and more so in

---

[150] For this chapter, see *RYW* Ch. 26, **2-7**.
[151] Reading with Paris, for *combustio* ("burning").
[152] For this chapter, see *RYW* Ch. 26, **8-14**; also *Skilled* VIII.4, **176-77** and VIII.7, **137**.
[153] Reading this clause somewhat uncertainly, as none of the MSS is quite grammatical.
[154] Reading as *omnibus vile*.

the parts of the north, and in the cities of the Yemen[155] (that is, in the land of the blacks).[156]

5 And likewise if a fortune were in charge, it will send joy upon the citizens of the part in which it was,[157] unless it is retrograde or in its own descension, or in the opposition of its own house: because it is weakened and made inimical.

Chapter 53.[158] **1** If the lord of the house of the lord of the year looked at [the lord of the year], and it received it, men will be in security and peace, in joy and happiness. **2** But if it did not look at nor receive it, there will be sorrow and severity in them, and fear, in accordance with the complexion and essence of the sign in which the significator was.

Chapter 54: The condition of the king with his rustics.[159] **1** Also, the condition of [the rustics] with him will be in accordance with the handing-over of the significator of the king, and its reception, by [its] communication and light. **2** And his condition is known every day from its signification and its perfection, from its conjunction and also separation, and [where] it is positioned throughout the days.

Chapter 55.[160] **1** If the lord of the year handed over the management to the significator of the king from a square aspect or the opposition, the king will pressure them in the seeking of assets, and for this reason anxiety will enter upon them. **2** And if it was from a trine or sextile aspect, it will render revenue without the entering of difficulty upon the rustics. **3** Which if it handed over the management without an aspect, this will be without the work of the king, or the king will think that he did not instruct it.

4 And if the significator of the king handed over the management to the lord of the year, the king will withdraw assets in that same year. **5** If however

---

[155] Reading for *Alioman* (Erfurt), *aliamam* (Paris), and *Aleemani* (London).
[156] *Nigrorum*. In Arabic, black southeastern Africa in the east was known as the land of the *Zanj* (hence, Zanzibar). This is not the same as the Yemen in the south of the Arabian peninsula, but the black slave population of southern Iraq was also called the Zanj because of their origin.
[157] That is, the area of the earth ruled by the sign in which it is.
[158] For this chapter, see *RYW* Ch. 19, **19**.
[159] For this chapter, see *RYW* Ch. 26, **15-16**. The version from the Arabic is in *Skilled* VIII.16, **15-16**.
[160] For this chapter, see *RYW* Ch. 19, **21-23** (but **23** reads differently).

the lord of the eleventh looked at the significator of the king, this will be with his good [state of] mind.

Chapter 56.[161] **1** And look at the condition of the king. **2** If the significator of the king was the lord of the Midheaven, look therefore for his assets from the eleventh. **3** If however the lord of the year was the significator of the king, look for it from the second. **4** And [look] for the soldiers from the lords of the triplicity of the sign in which it was (and [the lords] of the bound and face).

5 And [look] for a helper in all of this through the Lot of Fortune and its lord: because if the significator of the king looked at [the Lot] or was with it, it will signify the [good] fortune of the king. **6** And the work of the rustics will likewise be from the lord of the year and [the lord] of the Lot of Fortune.[162]

Chapter 57.[163] **1** If each of the significators were retrograde,[164] they signify the weakness of the king and the rustics, and the destruction of the kingdom. **2** If however one of them was retrograde, look in the bound of the planet which is retrograde, and use it in your work: because if the retrograde significator was in the bound of a bad one and in the house of a bad one, its condition will be worse; and if its retrogradation was in the bound of a fortune and the house of a fortune, its condition will be better. **3** And the retrogradation of the significator of the king signifies the weakness of the king, but the retrogradation of the lord of the year signifies the weakness of the citizens of his kingdom.

Chapter 58. 1 If the significator of the king were in the angle of the Midheaven, it signifies the king's battle. **2** But if it was in the Ascendant, the condition of men will be fit. **3** If however it was in the west, his rustics will be destroyed; and likewise if it was in the angle of the earth.

---

[161] For this chapter, see *RYW* Ch. 19, **24-27**. For **5-6**, see also *Skilled* VIII.5, **67**.
[162] Reading with Paris and Erfurt. London has "and the Lot of Fortune," not its lord.
[163] For this chapter, see *RYW* Ch. 20 (all).
[164] That is, the lord of the year and the significator of the king.

Chapter 59. 1 If Mars stood still and Saturn reached him,[165] it signifies loss and the cutting off of piety, and the slave will not be inclined towards his own master, nor will he be subject to the service of a greater person. **2** And Saturn will be more cunning if the revolution was toward the setting of the Sun, and Saturn was retrograde in the opposition of the Sun, in his own exaltation (that is, in Libra), and the Sun is being joined to him, and Mars (in his own station) is looking at the Sun.[166] **3** Look therefore at Mars: if he is being joined to Saturn and he was peregrine in a house, then since[167] Saturn is strong he takes up his weapon and a fight and war will occur between the citizens of the east and west, and there will be battles in diverse places. **4** If therefore the year were revolved in this condition, look well.

Chapter 60. 1 If[168] a significator of evil were in an angle, it signifies a multitude of evil, and its slowness. **2** And if it was before an angle, it will be moderate and short. **3** And help [yourself] in this through the dignity of the figure, because this signifies the time, and it is helpful for good and evil.

Chapter 61.[169] **1** If in a revolution of the year you saw a thing about which you had fear, see if this coincides with a conjunction of Saturn and Jupiter in that same year: it will be more harsh and worse. **2** And if it did not coincide [with one], it will be easier.

Chapter 62.[170] **1** If the lord of the year or the significator of the king went[171] to a bad planet or to the light of a slow and bad planet in an angle, then destruction or death will be feared for him whose significator it was.

Chapter 63. 1 And[172] the bad ones, if one of them was joined to the other (in whatever sign it was, of the signs of men), from a square aspect or the opposition or from the conjunction, and one of them was diurnal or noctur-

---

[165] That is, if Saturn perfected an aspect with a stationary Mars.
[166] Mars would then probably be in Capricorn.
[167] From here through "he takes up his weapon," reading with Sahl (حيث يقوى زحل ياخذ سلاحه) for an incomprehensible Latin phrase.
[168] For **1-2**, cf. *RYW* Ch. 22, **13-14**.
[169] For this chapter, see *RYW* Ch. 23, **2**.
[170] For this chapter, see *RYW* Ch. 23, **3**.
[171] Reading *venerit* in the sense of *RYW*, for *abierit* or *habuerit*.
[172] For this chapter, see *RYW* Ch. 23, **4-8**.

nal or masculine or feminine,[173] and they were received, their impediment will be less; and one who will become infirm in that same year, safety will be hoped for him without medical doctors. **2** Which if they signified killing, and it was with such a figure, there will be blisters,[174] and the death and killing will be less, and [men] will sympathize with one another.[175]

Chapter 64. 1 And[176] if there were a conjunction of Saturn and the Head, it signifies the impediment of the essence of the sign in which they are joined, just as it signifies in an eclipse of the Sun and Moon. **2** If there were a conjunction of the Head and Saturn in Aries and its triplicity, there will be impediment in animals and wolves and in all four-footed things, according to the essence of the sign in which they are joined. **3** And if it was in Taurus and its triplicity, it will be in fields and fruits and trees and herbs, in sheep and cows, and the rain and yield will be moderate. **4** And if it was in Gemini and its triplicity, it will be in men and birds, and harmful winds will blow. **5** And if it was in Cancer and its triplicity, rain and water will be multiplied, also seed and milk and locusts, and creeping things of the earth.

6 Also, if Mars were conjoined to the Tail, it signifies destruction and evil, killing, famine, and a multitude of evil. **7** And the conjunction of Saturn and the Tail signifies famine and a scarcity of good, harsh difficulties, and cold, and the greatest fears, and the destruction of the harvests, and this will be in that direction in which he is.

Chapter 65. 1 Look at the conjunction of the rays[177] of Saturn and Mars,[178] to see whether they meet with a planet in the degree of its own exaltation. **2** Which if it were this, and Saturn looked at it, it signifies evil and the destruction in the direction of that same planet. **3** And[179] if his aspect was from a fixed sign, the evil will be prolonged; and if it was from a movable sign, it will be moderate and short; and if it was from a common sign, it will be mediocre. **4** If however he did not see [it], but some star reflected their

---

[173] This way of expressing it is unhelpful; see *RYW*.
[174] Or perhaps, "wounds."
[175] Reading *invicem* with London for *vincere* ("conquer").
[176] For **1-5**, see *RYW* Ch. 24, **2-7** and *Skilled* VIII.5, **26-30**.
[177] Reading *radiorum* with London, for *malorum* ("of the bad ones"), although Bonatti reads *malorum*.
[178] Omitting "the Sun," following Bonatti (*BOA* Tr. 8.1, Ch. 18).
[179] Cf. *RYW* Ch. 39.

light to the planet which was in the degree of its own exaltation, it signifies the entrance of foulness and detriment upon the citizens of the clime from some [other people], and difficulty will find them, and they will be forced to this by those same people, or it will be by reason of certain people who are not of the citizens of their region. **5** But if a planet did not reflect their light to that planet which was in the degree of its own exaltation, fear will enter upon them, [but] afterwards it will be dissolved by the command of God, and nothing of this will reach them.[180]

Chapter 66: [On] battle.[181] **1** A slow planet signifies war, a retrograde one signifies flight, but a direct one peace (especially if a fortune looked at it from the Midheaven). **2** And if any of the lords of its own dignities looked at a planet, his allies and subordinates will be multiplied through this, and he whose condition it signified will be helped by[182] many allies and subordinates or soldiers from his own relatives, and so on.

Chapter 67. 1 If[183] Mars were conjoined to the lord of his own house or to the lord of his own exaltation at the hour of the revolution, or the lord of his house or exaltation were joined to him, it extinguishes war in that same year, and signifies peace.

Chapter 68: On enemies and warriors.[184] **1** If the significator of the warrior was in its own house, he will be noted and of the household members of the nobility. **2** And if it was in its own exaltation, he will be noble and is suitable for a kingdom. **3** And if it was in its own triplicity it will be less than this, and in the bound less than this (and he will be noted), and in the face it will be less than all of this. **4** If however it was not in any of these dignities (that is, if it was not in the house nor in the sign of the exaltation, nor in the triplicity nor in the bound nor in the face),[185] he will not be noted nor be of good stock, and it is said that he is the child of fornication.

---

[180] Bonatti adds that Mars will be similar, except that he signifies iron, fire, and the shedding of blood.
[181] For this chapter, see *RYW* Ch. 25, **2-4**.
[182] Reading for *quaerit/quaeritur* ("seeks, is sought"), which does not make sense here.
[183] See *Skilled* VIII.13, **3**.
[184] For this chapter, see *RYW* Ch. 25, **5-7**. Sahl evidently adapted **1-3** for his horary material in *On Questions* §25 (see *WSM*).
[185] In other words, if it is peregrine.

Chapter 69. 1 After[186] this, look from the lord of the house of foreign travel, and its place in the circle. **2** And if you saw his foreign travel, look at the condition of the lord of the house of foreign travel. **3** Which if it were direct and received in its own place, going toward its own sign, look at the hour of his turning back and his entrance from its place and the condition of its[187] significator. **4** If it was retrograde, it signifies the quickness of his turning back. **5** And if it was not received and it was retrograde, he will go out with difficulty, and detriment will be multiplied on his foreign journey.

6 And if it was just as I said, and it had a slow course, it signifies the great extent of [his] stay, and being detained in [those] regions if the planet were in its first slowness.[188] **7** If however it were in the second [station], he will return when the planet is direct, and he will not complete his foreign journey.

8 After[189] this, look at how the condition of the lord of foreign travel is: which if it was retrograde and it looked at it[190] from the square aspect or the opposition, he will go on a foreign journey for war with an enemy, and he will go out from his own clime. **9** And if it was from the trine or sextile aspect, he will go out to certain rustics of his, for detriment will have reached him from them, and he wants to make them fit.[191] **10** And if they were joined to each other [by bodily conjunction], it signifies that he will take part in a contention.

11 After this, look at how the condition of the lord of the house of foreign travel is, in relation to the lord of its own house. **12** Which if the lord of the house of foreign travel were retrograde, and it looked at it from a square aspect or the opposition, he will travel to do war with an enemy, and he will go out from his own clime.

13 After[192] this, look for his safety and the condition of his body on his foreign journey, and in his turning back, at his significator. **14** Which if it were free of the bad ones and from its enemies from among the planets, and the lord of foreign travel [is] in an optimal and praiseworthy place from the

---

[186] For **1-5**, see *RYW* Ch. 42, **3-4**.
[187] Or, "his." *RYW* seems to make this the lord of the ninth.
[188] That is, "station."
[189] For **8-9**, see *RYW* Ch. 42, **5-7**.
[190] In *RYW*, this means the ninth. But I could also see this being the significator of the king.
[191] Reading *aptare eos* for *aptare eum*. *RYW* does not connect this with rustics but rather with making peace with enemies.
[192] For **13-16**, see *RYW* Ch. 42, **8-11**.

Ascendant, not falling into the eighth and sixth and twelfth, he will be saved, by the command of God. **15** And if the significator were free from the bad ones which I said, and the lord of the house of foreign travel was impeded, what he despises (of difficulty and grief) will befall him on his foreign journey, and [also from] what is different from[193] his infirmities, according to the essence of the sign in which the lord of the house of foreign travel is. **16** If however the lord of the house of his foreign travel were free, and his significator impeded, what he feared (of difficulty) will befall him, and from which he became infirm at every hour.

17 And this is the explanation of those things which are looked at for the king, if he went on a foreign journey.

Chapter 70: On foreign travel.[194] **1** Look at the lord of the house of foreign travel. **2** Which if it were in the Ascendant, it signifies that he will travel to a land in which he will build when he decamps there. **3** And if it were in the second, it signifies that he will go out to seek assets and collect them. **4** And look at the lord of its house in the chapter which I stated.[195] **5** Which if it were in the third, it signifies that he will go out for a contention and war. **6** And if it were in the fourth angle, it signifies that he will be full of labor and evil, and it will be feared for him on that same journey, and more cunning if it looked at a bad one from the conjunction or opposition or square aspect, with it pushing management to the bad one: because then it will signify his loss on that same foreign journey, unless God averts [it]. **7** And if it were in the fifth, he will build a building on that same journey, and he will think to stay there, but he will not last there. **8** And if it were in the sixth, death will be feared for him in that same year, and the strength of [his] enemies over him. **9** And if it were in the ninth, it signifies prosperity and a good condition in that same journey, and his departure will be in the acquisition of the other world—that is, on account of the love of God—unless a bad one looks at it from the opposition or square aspect, because then it signifies that grief or sorrow will enter upon him in connection with his own household members. **10** And from the first square aspect, what I said will be from enemies; and in

---

[193] That is, "something other than." This is an Arabic idiom.
[194] For **1-6**, see *RYW* Ch. 42, **12-16**. But Bonatti contains (and expands upon) all the houses (*BOA* Tr. 8.1, Ch. 15).
[195] See Chapter 69.

the second square aspect, from the place of slaves and ignoble people.[196] **11** After this, look at the sign of the second aspect from the place of foreign travel: if there were a bad one in that same place, what is its essence? **12** Because if it were in the image of men, it will be feared for him from beasts.[197] **13** And if it were in the tenth, it signifies that the foreign journey will be prolonged, or he will go out to strengthen his kingdom, and see in it what makes it fit.[198] **14** And if it were in the eleventh, it signifies that he will go out for leisure[199] and will come to a place which agrees with him and he will be delighted. **15** And if it were in the twelfth, see how the lord of that same house looks at it. **16** If it looked from the trine or sextile aspect, it signifies that he will go out to enemies whom he fears, who at first did not show him enmity. **17** And if it was from the opposition, they will already have prepared enmity for him. **18** And from the square aspect it will be less than this. **19** I have already made this chapter clear to you: therefore test it with all chapters.[200]

20 Afterwards, look for his nuptials just as you looked for his foreign travel. **21** Because perhaps there will be a marriage-union on account of seeking assets: look then at the lord of the eighth and the second. **22** If the lord of the eighth handed over the management to the lord of the second, he will find assets from her. **23** But if the lord of the second handed over the management to the lord of the eighth, she will find assets from him. **24** And if the lord of the house of marriage were in the eleventh, he will be betrothed to her on account of love, and more seriously so if the significator of the king and the lord of each other were looking at each other. [**25** And if it were in the tenth, his kingdom will be increased from this.][201] **26** And if it were in the fifth,[202] he will seek a child from her.

27 After this, look at the significator of the king and the lord of the seventh,[203] and judge according to what I told you before in the chapter on foreign travel, and look at the aspect of the bad ones to them in their places.

---

[196] That is, the sinister ("first") square to the twelfth indicates enemies; but the dexter ("second") square to the sixth indicates slaves.
[197] This does not make sense: the sentence should probably read: "if it were in the image of men, it will be feared for him from men; but if in the image of beasts, from beasts."
[198] Reading somewhat broadly (and with Bonatti, *BOA* Tr. 8.1, Ch. 15) for what seems to be *aspiciendum in eo quod aptet eum.*
[199] *Spacium.*
[200] *Capitula.* Or perhaps, "topics."
[201] Adding with Bonatti (*BOA* Tr. 8.1, Ch. 15).
[202] Reading with Paris and London, for "fourth" (Erfurt).
[203] Reading with Paris and Erfurt, for "second" (London).

28 Also, look at this in nativities according to what I told you with respect to children: what kind of condition they will have, also their friendship and enmity, and their condition with one another.

Chapter 71. 1 If[204] the lord of the fourth were in the place of foreign travel—and that is in a place which signifies foreign travel for those who are in prisons in that same land and in that same clime—they will go out without the will of the king, unless the significator of the king would look from an agreeable aspect (because then the king will lead them out). **2** If however it were from a contrary aspect, they will go out apart from the will of the king.

3 If however the significator of the king was in the place which signifies foreign travel, and the lord of the fourth pushed its own management to the significator of the king, it signifies that the king will lead the fettered people out of the prisons.

4 And if the lord of the ninth received[205] the management from the lord of the fourth, [and] in the place of the ninth, an enemy of the king will lead the aforesaid fettered people out.

5 And mix together with this the conjunction of the planets with each other and their commixture. **6** Which if the significator of the king handed over its management to Mercury, scribes and merchants and consuls[206] of the king will find good from the king in that same year, and donations, and he will draw them near to himself. **7** And if it handed it over to Venus, women and all those whose significator is Venus will find good from the king, and he will hear them and draw them near to himself. **8** And if it handed it over to Mars, soldiers and bearers of arms, and the heads of armies and frontier regions[207] will find good from the king, and they will win the greatest seat from the king, and he will hear them and draw [them] near [to himself]. **9** And if it handed it over to Jupiter, the more respectable people will attain good from the king. **10** And if it handed it over to Saturn, religious people and old men of good sects will find good from the king, and he will pay out [money] for buildings. **11** And if the management [which is handed over] to Saturn was above the earth,[208] he will build a building. **12** But if it was under the earth,

---

[204] For **1-4**, cf. *Skilled* VIII.3, **28** and *BRD* VIII.1, **18**.
[205] Bonatti reads, "did *not* receive" (*BOA* Tr. 8.1, Ch. 53).
[206] Or perhaps, "counselors."
[207] *Extremorum*, lit. what is far away, foreign, the outer edges.
[208] I am not sure if this refers to the location of Saturn, or the location of the significator of the king (who is handing it over).

he will dig channels and wells and will make courses of waters and will plant[209] lands (and especially if it were near the Ascendant or falling,[210] because this signifies planting). **13** And if it handed it over to the Sun, his citizens and relatives, and those who are fit for a kingdom will find good from him. **14** But if it was the Moon, look at the one which bears the management away to her,[211] because it signifies the essence of the one who bears the management to her.

Chapter 72. 1 The lord of the ninth in the third signifies king's foreign travel in the seeking of the future world from God, because this place is the lower opposite[212] of the ninth and signifies what the ninth does.

2 And[213] if you looked in any of these twelve houses, you should look[214] at its aspect from the places. **3** And the significations of the opposites will be stronger (so that its signification and the signification of the sign of the opposite[215] belongs to one planet, or it was its house or exaltation): because then it will be what I said.

Chapter 73. 1 If[216] the significator of the king were in the Ascendant, the king will seek rest and he will not travel abroad. **2** Which if it was remote from the Ascendant,[217] and there was another planet with it in the Ascendant, not remote, see which planet this is.[218] **3** Which if it was an enemy of the significator, he will go out with regard to one who would contend with him in the kingdom, and he will seek him. **4** And if it was a friend and suitable, the significator will hand over the kingdom to the man to which that planet belongs, and he will be watching [matters] in his kingdom, and he will be practically the defender of his kingdom.

---

[209] Reading *plantabit* with London for *populabit* ("settle, colonize").
[210] *Cadens.* I have translated this as-is, but based on this text's use of *cado*, this probably simply means that it "falls" or "is" near the Ascendant.
[211] Reading *eam* for *eum* ("him, it"), here and later in the sentence.
[212] Reading *nadir* with Paris and Erfurt, for London's *radix* ("root, foundation").
[213] The meaning of this sentence is unclear to me.
[214] Omitting the *non/nisi* ("not"/"unless") which appears in each MS.
[215] *Nadir.*
[216] For this chapter, see *RYW* Ch. 42, **17-39**.
[217] That is, in the rising sign but in an earlier degree than the degree of the Ascendant, so as to be cadent in strength.
[218] This is a nice example of using whole sign houses for topics, and the axial degrees as regions of power.

5 And if the significator of the king were in the second, it will distract him with revenues[219] in that same year, and he will seek assets. **6** And if it were in the third, it will multiply riding and he will desire foreign travel. **7** And if the lord of the house of foreign travel looked at it, he will travel abroad. **8** And [also] if the lord of the house of foreign travel handed over its own management to a planet in the place of foreign travel. **9** And if it were in the fourth, he will not travel abroad and he will desire delight.[220] **10** And if it were in the fifth, he will find a son and will long for him. **11** And if it were in the sixth, infirmity will be feared for him. **12** And if it were in the seventh, he will find a marriage-union and his sexual intercourse will be multiplied. **13** And if it were in the eighth, death will be feared for him. **14** And if it were in the ninth, he will travel abroad. **15** And if it were in the tenth, he will be strengthened in his kingdom, and he will follow his own will and his desire. **16** And his will is going to be known from the direct motion or retrogradation or slowness[221] of his significator. **17** For direct motion signifies fitness, and retrogradation signifies destruction; and the first slowness signifies destruction, and the second one fitness.[222] **18** And if it were in the eleventh, it signifies fitness and piety and trust, and the fulfillment of desire. **19** And if it were in the twelfth, it signifies seeking enemies, and his safety in this. **20** If however the lord of its own house looked at it,[223] he will get them.

21 And speak likewise if the significator of the king handed over its own management to the lords of these houses which I said, because they are more worthy as to what[224] their houses signify.

22 If the significator of the king were conjoined to a planet in the ninth or in the third, it signifies the king's foreign travel.

23 And if the significator of the king is being separated from the significator of his ruin, it signifies good.[225] **24** And likewise a conjunction with the

---

[219] Reading a little loosely as *distringet in censum*. The MSS read: *distringet esse suum* [sic] (Paris), *distinguet in censu* (Erfurt), and *distinguet in censum* (London).
[220] This should probably be "rest" or "quiet," as in *RYW*.
[221] That is, "station."
[222] Nevertheless this does not tell us what the content of his will actually is.
[223] *RYW* has the significator of the king doing the aspect, and it is probably to the lord of the twelfth.
[224] *Quemadmodum*. *RYW* is clearer: if the significator of the king hands management to the lords of the houses, it is the same as if it were actually in those houses.
[225] Reading more with Erfurt. Paris reads: "And if it is being separated it signifies ruin and his infirmity." Erfurt reads: "And if the one which signifies ruin and his infirmity is being separated from the significator of the king, it will be good." London reads, "And if the

lord [of the house of infirmity or death indicates that] he will be infirm [or die].[226]

25 If the significator of the king entered under the rays and wanted to appear towards the east or west, and in the revolution of the year it was less than 12°, it will be feared for the king because then he will be prepared for his own burning, and this will be at the time of its burning,[227] one month for every degree between it and the Sun.

26 And likewise, if [the lord of the ninth][228] were impeded and was positioned in a bad place, it will be feared for the king on his foreign journey.

Chapter 74. 1 If[229] the lord of the Ascendant were burned up in one of the angles of the Ascendant, it will send tribulation upon men. **2** And if it were burned up in the Midheaven, the difficulty will be because of the king. **3** Which if the Sun was the lord of the Midheaven, difficulty and sorrow will reach men from the king. **4** And if it was burned up in the angle of the earth, it signifies death in that same year.

5 If however the Ascendant of the year was a feminine sign, this will be more in women; but if it were masculine, it will be more in men. **6** After this, see if the lord of the house of the Ascendant was Mercury: it will be more in boys.[230] **7** And if it was Venus and the Moon, it will be more in women. **8** And the age is known from [the planet's] condition from the Sun.

9 Which if Venus were in her exit from the [rays of the] Sun, it signifies youth and childhood if she were eastern. **10** And the Moon likewise [signifies youth and childhood] if she were between the conjunction and prevention (which is the fullness, when it is namely the fourteenth [day]). **11** And the fullness [of the Moon] signifies completion, that is, an age of 30 years or less. **12** And from fullness up to her burning, it signifies old age.

13 And if its[231] burning was in the seventh, they will suffer detriment and plundering and a multitude of contentions will enter upon them. **14** If how-

---

significator of the king is being separated from the significator of his ruin, it signifies his infirmity.

[226] Adding the missing phrases from *RYW*.
[227] The rest of this sentence is very muddled in the Latin, but this seems to be its meaning.
[228] Inserting with *RYW*.
[229] For **1-8**, see *RYW* Ch. 43 (all).
[230] *Pueris*. Or more likely, "children."
[231] That is, the lord of the Ascendant.

ever it was in the Ascendant, it will be of less impediment and easier, and the condition of men will be less than this.[232]

15 After[233] this, look at the essence of the Ascendant for this [topic]. **16** Which if it were of the essence of seed, seed will be destroyed; and likewise the other essences.

17 Look for the lord of the Midheaven in the way you looked for the lord of the Ascendant. **18** If however the lord of the Midheaven were burned up in the Ascendant, and the lord of the Ascendant was the Sun, killing [by] the rustics will be feared for the king, and that they will engineer his ruin, and then it is important that the king not entrust himself to them.

19 If[234] however the revolution were in this way, and you wanted to know in what way one must fear for [the king], see which one looks at the Sun in the hour of the revolution. **20** Which if Mars looked at him or was conjoined to him, killing will be feared for the king; but if [the Sun] was joined to Saturn, infirmity will be feared for him. **21** And if the Sun burned up the lord of the Ascendant in the Midheaven, as well as the lord of the year,[235] what I said will be feared for him in the way that I described it. **22** But what there will be because of this will be in his own region in which he is: for [the difficulty] will come to him from another land. **23** But if the burning of the lord of the Midheaven was in the angle of the earth or the opposite [of the Ascendant],[236] it will be what I said about this: that it will come from another land outside the one in which he is, and the condition will be just as I said.

24 And for the bad one,[237] do it according to what I said in the chapter on the Sun for the king and his rustics, in addition to what [I said] in the chapter on the bad ones in this for[238] the revolution of the year.[239]

25 Which[240] if the lord of the Ascendant or the lord of the Midheaven were joined to a bad one in an angle, [it is] just as I told you in the first chap-

---

[232] Namely, if the lord of the Ascendant were burned up and in the Ascendant, it would at least be in its own sign; but in the seventh, it would also be in its detriment.
[233] This sentence is based on Sahl.
[234] For **19-23**, see *RYW* Ch. 44, **2-5**.
[235] This might mean that the rule works for the lord of the year too, and not just the lord of the Ascendant.
[236] Adding based on *RYW*.
[237] Reading *malo* (which could be read as "for the evil") with Erfurt for London's *in alio* ("for another"). Paris omits an equivalent word, saying "And do according to what I said…".
[238] *Ad*.
[239] I am not sure which chapter Māshā'allāh or Abū Ma'shar means; likewise in the next sentence.

ter; and the [square]²⁴¹ aspect of the bad ones in this place is more serious than the conjunction.

26 And²⁴² if the Sun were the significator of the king, and in the revolution he looked at Jupiter from the opposition, [the king] will be inimical to his own household members, and he will be suspicious of them and will do evil to them. **27** Look therefore with respect to the condition of the stars just as I said in the chapter on the Sun, because every planet which was the significator of the king, if it looked at a planet from the opposition in the revolution, the king will be inimical to the essence of that planet and will destroy it, just like Jupiter. **28** Know this, if God wills.

29 If²⁴³ Mars was in Gemini at the revolution of the year, and he was in the Midheaven, it signifies that in that year many men will be crucified. **30** Which if he were in the Ascendant, the hands of men will be cut off. **31** And if he were in the angle of the earth, it signifies the cutting off of hands and feet.

32 And speak likewise about the entrance of²⁴⁴ warriors and magnates and kings into his kingdom.²⁴⁵

Chapter 75. 1 If the Sun impeded through his burning, it signifies burning and exile from the regions. **2** If Saturn impeded, it signifies long-lasting pains and death; if Mars impeded, there will be killing [while] in flight.

Chapter 76. 1 And²⁴⁶ know that the condition of the year will be made severe if the bad ones were in the upper part of the circle, that is, in the

---

²⁴⁰ For this sentence, see *RYW* Ch. 44, **6**.
²⁴¹ Adding with *RYW*.
²⁴² For this sentence, see *RYW* Ch. 44, **7**.
²⁴³ For **29-31**, see *RYW* Ch. 36, **2-4**.
²⁴⁴ Omitting Erfurt's *Solis* ("of the Sun").
²⁴⁵ I do not understand this sentence.
²⁴⁶ For **1-6** and **8** see *RYW* Ch. 37, **2-5**. This passage presents problems both in terms of whether it correctly identifies when a planet is "upper" or "lower," but also which circle we are speaking of. I suspect that what is really being described is a malefic that is (a) near the apogee of its deferent, and (b) in either northern declinations or northern ecliptical latitudes. For example, at the time of Abū Ma'shar Saturn's apogee was in Sagittarius, and Mars's was in Gemini: this means that in **2**, Mars near his own apogee would be squaring Saturn (who is still roughly in the lower part of his apogee circle). This might require that in **5**, we follow London by saying that the Moon in Sagittarius is in [Saturn's] *upper* circle. Now, all of this could simply refer to signs of northern ("upper") and southern ("lower") declination; but if so, then the example of **2** does not involve a planet in the lower circle at all, since both Gemini and Virgo are signs of northern declination—but it would also be

north (where the axis in their images is), because when they go out to the end of the circle, they will return and signify destruction and killing with slowness and prolonging, and destruction in every ensouled thing, and tribulation and desolation[247] will appear in men. **2** And [it will be] harsher than that if one of them were in the lower circle and the other in its square aspect, like Saturn in the middle of Virgo and Mars in Gemini, and Mars pushed management to Saturn, and Saturn received it[248] and he was retrograde. **3** And[249] it signifies[250] harsh, widespread things and plundering among men, also insurgents who seek destruction in the land, and the condition of the king will be weakened, and he will seek the rustics and merchants, and faith and religion will be removed in men, and piety and compassion will be taken away from them, and this will be prolonged. **4** And this will be if one of these bad ones were in the Midheaven. **5** Which[251] if the Moon handed over her own management (along with Mars) to Saturn [but] from Sagittarius,[252] from the lower circle,[253] it signifies destructions and various tribulations, and the destruction of the wealthy up to the point that the kingdom is corrupted and is changed from certain people to others. **6** Moreover, if the Moon handed over her own management to Saturn, and it was at its perfection [by conjunction] with him (or in his square aspect or opposition), and the lord of the perfected [connection][254] was impeded, it signifies much impediment in many ways. **7** And if the Lot of Fortune was even impeded similar to this impediment when the

---

correct to read **5** as the "lower" circle. Until we can find a good Arabic source, the precise meaning of this passage an in *RYW* will remain unclear.

[247] Reading with London for "dissolution" (*dissolutio*).

[248] Reading *eam* (to match the gender of *dispositionem*, "management"), rather than *eum* ("it, him," suggesting Mars).

[249] For now, omitting the puzzling *fluxe corde contrario huic*. Bonatti reads, "But Saturn has greater harm, wherefore then it will signify..." (*BOA* Tr. 8.1, Ch. 114).

[250] Up to this point it is not clear whether we have begun a new sentence or not, and frankly the Latin does not make much sense. Paris has *et fluxe corde [or cordis or conditionis] contrario huic significat*; Erfurt has *et fluxe cordis et contrario huic significat*; London has *et fluxe conditionis et contrario huic significatores*.

[251] For **5-6**, see *RYW* Ch. 37, **3-4**.

[252] *RYW* reads this as *sub terra* (instead of *Sagittario*), but Abū Ma'shar seems to be imagining what we would call a T-square: Mars in Gemini and the Moon in Sagittarius, each applying to Saturn in Virgo.

[253] Reading with Paris; London reads "in the upper."

[254] Reading *perfectionis [coniunctionis]* with the sense of Bonatti (*ibid.*), for "profection" (*profectionis*). In other words, if the lord of the Lot is impeded as well, just as the lord of the sign of the Moon's conjunction was in **6**.

perfected [connection of the Moon] was impeded,[255] it signifies an increase of destruction and a multitude of it in diverse ways.

8 Likewise,[256] look at the Sun and [his] condition, and his aspects to an impeding bad one, and the lord of the bad one, just as I told you about the Moon and [her] perfection and the lord of the perfection.

9 And make the Lot of Fortune and its lord partners with them and aid the dignities[257] of the seven [planets], because they are helpful and signify the time.

10 And if the significator were in an angle, the evil will be prolonged, and the rest [of the houses] it is shortened. **11** And the lord of the course and profection[258] signifies according to what the significator signified, in terms of good or evil, and likewise the lord of the Ascendant and the lord of the house of the distribution.[259]

12 If the Moon received [management] from Saturn in an optimal place of the circle, in a strong place, it signifies the repelling of the evil (by the command of God) and the blocking of the evil of destruction through [her good] fortune. **13** And likewise in nativities: if the Moon were thus in a place, testifying to the Ascendant and aiding it, and the lord of the Ascendant had strength and a good complexion, it signifies a long length of life and of the kingdom, and a native will be wise and fortunate. **14** And the fortunes dissolve the evil of the one pushing,[260] if they were strong, in an optimal place, and they had testimony and were direct. **15** But if they were to the contrary, they will be weakened and will not be successful.

16 If the stars were united[261] under the rays, that is, with the Sun in one degree (and Mercury especially), it will have strength and a kingdom, unless [the Sun] was with Saturn (whose nature is contrary to the nature of the Sun).

---

[255] Again, reading with the sense of Bonatti for *similis [or similiter] huic impedimento qua impedita fuerit profectio*, which is barely grammatical.

[256] For this sentence, cf. *RYW* Ch. 37, **5**.

[257] Reading *dignitatibus* for *dignitates*, though I do not really understand the sentence.

[258] Reading *profectionis* instead of *perfectionis*. In this sentence, I believe Abū Ma'shar is discussing mundane profections and distributions (see the end of the sentence), though I am not sure what he means here by "course."

[259] I take *divisionis* here to refer to mundane distributions, rather than the bland and uninformative "division."

[260] Reading *pulsantis* for *pulsanti*.

[261] Reading *unitae* with Bonatti (*ibid.*), for an illegible word. This clearly refers to being in the heart of the Sun or "cazimi" (see *ITA* II.9).

17 And if there were 15° between Mercury and the Sun, he will be in a praiseworthy place and if he was received.

18 And if the Moon were strong, increased in light and number in a revolution of the night, it signifies exaltation and the repelling[262] of a strong matter [of impediment]—and likewise the Sun in the day—if she was free of the bad ones.

19 Beware[263] lest the significator (or any planet) has gone out from burning and a bad one is looking at it: because then [the planet] will be like a delicate boy, and if a bad one looks at it, it will ruin and finish him. **20** And likewise when it entered into burning or was joined with [the Sun], it will be like a decrepit old man who suffers some disease.

21 Consider[264] the condition of the four superior planets[265] in the degrees of their own exaltations, especially Saturn: because if he received [management while] in the degree of his own exaltation, in addition to what he has from testimony and strength, he will have the management and will signify the greatest matter about the kingdom and strength and command, in accordance with his nature and the essence of that place. **22** And likewise Jupiter. **23** [As for] the rest of the planets, however, one sees in a revolution of years if any of them happened to be in the degree of its own exaltation: and if that planet were received in that same place, it signifies a great matter and strength in its essence, and it will be in the manner of Saturn in strength and management. **24** But Mercury is looked at[266] in the revolution, [to see] if there was any planet in his exaltation which received him and received management from him: it will be of the condition of his signification which I said, by the command of God, because it will happen in the revolution of the years and quarters of his exaltation.[267] **25** If however the planet which received him was in its own exaltation, it will be like that.

26 After[268] this, look in the conjunction of the bad ones and their aspects: what planet is in the degree of its own exaltation, according to what was revealed to you.

---

[262] *Pulsationem*, but reading with the sense of Ch. 79, **17**.
[263] For **19-20**, see *RYW* Ch. 38, **2-3**.
[264] For **21-23**, see *RYW* Ch. 39, **2-4**.
[265] Omitting *super annos* ("over the years"); this is perhaps a truncated form of "in a revolution of years."
[266] Reading the passive, as this is probably what it was in the Arabic.
[267] This does not make much sense, but perhaps Abū Ma'shar is suggesting something about the Libra ingress, when Mercury can indeed be in his exaltation in Virgo.
[268] For this sentences, cf. Ch. 65, **1**.

27 The Sun:[269] if the Moon were made peaceful with him, and she[270] was strong in her own place in a revolution of the night, he will hand over his own rulership and kingdom to the Moon.

Chapter 77: On an eclipse. 1 If[271] an eclipse happened in that same year, look at the sign of the eclipse and at its lord. **2** And[272] know its condition from the lord of the Ascendant of the eclipse, and its condition from the lord of the year and the significator of the king, and the aspects of the planets to it. **3** And if some impeded planet looked at the obscured [luminary], and afterwards the bad ones looked at it, what it signifies will be made severe and multiplied, and more harshly than that if the lord of the house of the eclipse was the significator of the king. **4** And if it were so, and the bad ones looked at it, it will be feared for the king when the Sun reached the Midheaven of the eclipse. **5** And if the lord of the house of the eclipse was the significator of the year, it will be feared for the common people when the Sun met with the Ascendant of the eclipse, in accordance with the essence of the Ascendant. **6** If it was in the image of men, the evil will be in men; and if it was in the image of animals, the evil will be in animals; and if it was of the essence of seed, in seed; and if it was of the essence of waters, in those things which are in the waters—according to the essence of the sign. **7** And for every hour of an eclipse of the Moon, there will be a month of destruction; and for an eclipse of the Sun, a year.

8 After this,[273] look at the portion [of things] about which you have fear, from the place of the eclipse and the place of the lord of its house, according to the essence of each sign.

9 And look at the flying stars which are sparks of fire, because they always appear in the place of Mercury. **10** And if Mercury were in the east, they will appear in the east; and if he was in the west, they will appear in the west. **11** And their receding will be [at] the burning of Mercury.

---

[269] Cf. *RYW* Ch. 35, **2**.
[270] Reading as masculine; the Latin does not specify whether this is the Sun or Moon.
[271] For **1-7**, see *RYW* Ch. 40, **2-8**.
[272] Reading this sentence with Erfurt and London. Paris reads from **1** more simply, "If an eclipse came in that same year, look at the sign of the eclipse, and its condition from the lord of the year and the significator of the king, and the aspect of the planets to it."
[273] For **8-21**, see Sahl's treatment of eclipses and comets in *AW1*. But for **12-13**, see *RYW* Ch. 40, **9-11**.

12 Look at the part in which they were. **13** If they were in the lower journey, the evil will be in the part of Mars and Venus; and if it was in the upper journey, the evil will be in the part of Saturn and the Moon and the Sun. **14** After this, see in what kind of sign they appear, and what kind of condition that same sign has in its place, and how the aspects of the bad ones and the fortunes are to the lord of the sign and of the mansion. **15** And if they were seen in a sign of the wealthy, and the lord of the sign looked from a strong place, it signifies that from that same part will enter one who contends in the kingdom, [and who is] of the household members of the king, and he will be famous. **16** And if it was in a sign of the wealthy in the way that I said, and the lord of the sign did not look, he will be of the sons of the nobles and will be fit for a kingdom. **17** And judge likewise about all of the signs.

18 And know that the signs of the Sun and Jupiter and Mars signify the children of the wealthy, and the signs of Saturn signify famous and ancient people. **19** And the house of the Moon is less than[274] the house of Saturn, and the house of Mercury less than that of Jupiter, and the house of Venus less than the house of Mars, and the house of Mars less than the house of Jupiter, and the house of Jupiter below the house of Saturn—because their circles are below the circles of those which I said. **20** However, Saturn in Aquarius is famous and refers to wisdom; but in Capricorn he is bad. **21** The mansions, in their rising, do not signify except for the condition of the common people, and [only] generally that of the wealthy and magnates.

Chapter 78: On the time of the signification of the eclipse.[275] **1** Once you took the signification over evil, the time in an eclipse of the Sun will be one year for every hour [of the eclipse], and in an eclipse of the Moon a month for every hour. **2** And the hour in which [the event] will appear, is that you should count from the Ascendant[276] of the eclipse [to the eclipse] or from the place of the eclipse to the Ascendant of the middle of the eclipse, a month for every sign. **3** And when you reached that sign in which [the eclipse] was, or the Ascendant of the middle of the eclipse, it will be this without a doubt (whether it was good or bad). **4** Or perhaps the matter will appear (if it was faster) at the Moon's entrance into the Ascendant, especially

---

[274] *Infra*, which can also be translated as "below." But the text is relating the physical relation of the circles, to the social level of the persons indicated: thus I have translated the social level as "less than."

[275] This chapter is taken from Sahl, which I have used to correct and clarify the text.

[276] Reading "Ascendant" for "ascension," here and later in the sentence.

if it was at an eclipse in the days of a battle: namely, some corruption and adversity in the weather.[277]

Chapter 79: On the significations of the planets in the year. 1 If[278] Mercury were the lord of the year and the lord of the Ascendant, and he was free from the bad ones, and the fortunes looked at him,[279] that same year will be fit for boys and the wise, and those doing business. **2** And better than that if the lord of his own house received[280] him: they will find a seat of honor from the king[281] and he will hear them, and they will gain good for this reason. **3** And if it were otherwise, speak to the contrary; and more harshly than that if the lord of his own house did not receive[282] him: because it signifies that difficulty will find them from the king, and their seats will be impeded in his presence. **4** If however in addition to what I said, a bad one looked at him, his condition will be destroyed in relation to what I said. **5** And if in addition the Moon were free from the bad ones, rains and cold will be multiplied, and legates will rejoice and find good, and better and more worthy than that if she were received, because then they will find a place of dignity from the wealthy and kings, and it is seen in its own time when it was necessary.[283]

6 And if Mars were in charge, and he was not impeded, there will be fertility in that same year, and the year will be rainy, and there will be pestilences and earthquakes, and this will be moderate, and there will be joy and happiness in the same [year], and warriors and bearers of arms will become

---

[277] This latter is not in Sahl and may represent a corruption by Abū Ma'shar. Here, Sahl has three main methods of predicting the beginning of the events: (1) by counting from the Ascendant (taken at the time of the center or middle of the eclipse) to the eclipse, or from the place of the eclipse to the Ascendant; (2) when the Sun enters the sign of the eclipse or the Ascendant, a method not mentioned in *Scito*; (3) when the Sun is in the sign of the eclipse, it will be either at the Moon's entrance to it or her entrance into the Ascendant. But *Scito* seems to make the Moon's ingress a matter of the general time predicted by the eclipse: for instance, if events are moving quickly or the time period itself is small, her transit in the Ascendant will mark the time.
[278] For **1-13**, see *RYW* Ch. 36, **5-13**.
[279] Reading with Paris and Erfurt for London's redundant, "nor did they look at him."
[280] Reading *receperit* with Paris and Erfurt for London's "regarded" (*respexerit*).
[281] Reading with *sedem* with London for the ungrammatical *eiusdem*.
[282] Again, reading with Paris and Erfurt for London's *perciperit*. Thus, Paris and Erfurt understand this as "receiving," while London understands this as looking and aspecting.
[283] *Aspicitur in tempore suo cum necesse fuerit*. I am not sure what this means.

wealthy and will find good, and there will be war and contention near[284] the king.

7 And if Jupiter were in charge, and he was free of impediment and the bad ones, it will be a year of security and rest, and all things will be fit, and good and things wished for will abound in men—that is, good work and justice, also peace and rectitude, and the wealthy will be made fit. **8** Which if he was received, the common people will find good from the wealthy, and they will esteem their king, and the condition of the nobles and the respectable and magnates will be good. **9** And if he were impeded, speak to the contrary.

10 And if Venus were in charge and she was free from the bad ones and impediment, the year will be just as we said before, and nuptials will be multiplied, and there will be joy in men (and especially in women). **11** But if she were impeded in the way that I said before, it will be a year of little good, and there will be earthquake in diverse lands or places, and walls will fall down, and there will be moderate war, and the king will be saddened, and this will be in his own clime and in his own land.

12 And if Saturn were in charge in the way that I said, it will be a year of harsh cold, many rains, and robberies will be multiplied, and losses in the world, and there will be severe and harmful rains, and discord will fall in men, and lying, and blasphemy, and the rain will be fitting.

13 And if the Sun was the lord of the year and he was free of the bad ones, the wealthy will rejoice and will have happiness and security, and the annual yields will be multiplied, also sheep and animals, and birds, and every thing in which they have rulership. **14** But if he was impeded, it signifies impediment in everything which I said.

15 And if Mercury were with Saturn, and[285] he looked at him, and was a partner to him and received management from him, it signifies what came before [but] in diverse climes, and the harvests will suffer detriment, and robbers will be multiplied, and fear will enter upon men, and especially in those which were of the nature of Mercury, or whose significator he was, and animals will die in the land of the west. **16** And if he was in a sign of four-footed things, it will be according to the essence of the sign.

17 And look in addition at the luminary whose authority it was: because if the luminary were strengthened, and its light and number was increased, and

---

[284] *Prope*, but it would sound better to have *propter* ("because of").
[285] This should probably read, "or."

it was not impeded, it will repel[286] the great impediment and will be prohibited from evil.

18 If[287] the Ascendant was a movable sign, the time of those things which the authority[288] signified (of good or evil) will be in the first quarter. **19** And when the Sun will have entered Cancer, Libra, and Capricorn, revolve these quarters and establish the Ascendant over them, and know the significator, and speak in that just as I said for the first quarter. **20** And if the Ascendant was a common sign, the time of those things which the authority signified will be the first half of the year: and when the Sun will have entered Libra, revolve the last half and establish the Ascendant for it, and know the significator, and describe in just the way you described in what preceded. **21** And if the Ascendant was a fixed sign, the time of those things which the authority signified will be at the end of the year: because the revolution will be in charge of all the quarters.

[Chapter 80: Infortunes in the triplicities] 1 And[289] if one of the bad ones were in an angle at the hour of the revolution of the year, it signifies contention and war.

2 Which[290] if [the infortune] was direct, the time of these things will be when it turns backwards; and if it was retrograde, the time of these will be when it goes direct. **3** But if the light was commingled with the light of the significator of the king, and in its commixture with the significator of the rustics, it signifies a multitude of robbers and injuries. **4** And if it were in a place where it looks at the Ascendant, and not in an angle, and it was retrograde, it will impede the land in which the bad one was, and this will not be general among men unless it is commingled with the light of the lord of the Ascendant or the light of the lord of the Midheaven. **5** And if the significator of the king was one of the bad ones, and it was falling from the Ascendant,[291] it will not impede the year unless it is [also] the lord of the year or the lord of the Ascendant.

---

[286] Reading *repellit* for *pulsabit*.
[287] For this paragraph, cf. *RYW* Ch. 4, **2-5**.
[288] *Auctor*. This must refer to the lord of the year.
[289] For **1-5**, see *RYW* Ch. 45, **2**.
[290] For this paragraph, see *Skilled* VIII.4, **177-80**, and *BRD* VIII.1, **18**. However, *BRD* cuts off the last part of **2** (the planet turning direct) and blends it with **3**. The text is probably from Sahl.
[291] That is, in aversion to it.

6 If[292] Mars were the lord of the year and he was in one of the angles, it will impede men and will send battles and wars and the shedding of blood upon them. **7** And [it is] more harsh than that if he was in Gemini and its triplicity, because then he will impede in the signs of men. **8** And if he was direct, this will be in the seeking of truth; and if he was retrograde, it will be in injuries and enmities. **9** And if he was in Gemini and its triplicity, outside an angle, and he was in a place where he would look at the Ascendant, it signifies infirmities and winds and mortalities, and more harshly in every land in whose sign the light of his body was, or the opposition or square aspect. **10** If however he was retrograde and he was the significator, it will signify pestilence which[293] God averts. **11** And if he were in these signs and its triplicity, and he was falling, not looking at the Ascendant, and he was direct, it will impede men and it will make the occurrence of fires, and every hot infirmity from blood, and winds will destroy seeds. **12** If however he was retrograde, many men in what I said will die from winds and infirmities and fires.

13 And[294] if Mars was the lord of the year and he was in Aries and its triplicity, and in an angle, and he was direct, there will be a hot and dry infirmity in men, and princes will contend with each other in the climes. **14** And if he were retrograde in this triplicity, Kurds[295] (that is, the people) and robbers will be strengthened, and there will be contention in the clime of Babylon, and impediment in animals, and harshness upon every hairy thing, and wolves will be weakened, and the heat will be made severe until he would go out from these places. **15** And if he was in these signs and their triplicity, outside an angle, and he looked at the Ascendant, men will afflict each other, and there will be impediment in the land of the sign in which he was, and his square aspect and opposition, according to what I said in the first chapter.[296] **16** Which if he were retrograde, it will be harsher. **17** And if he were in this triplicity, and he was falling from the Ascendant and was direct, there will not be anything of what I said, but the heat will become severe, and it will impede the land and clime which he looks at, according to the essence of the sign and its nature.

---

[292] For **6-12**, see *RYW* Ch. 45, **7-11**; also *BRD* II.8, **27**.

[293] *Quam*. But this should probably read *nisi*, "unless" (in line with similar statements throughout, and *RYW*).

[294] For **13-17**, see *RYW* Ch. 45, **12-17**; also *BRD* II.8, **23**.

[295] *Alaclad/alardad*. Reading with the proper spelling from *BRD* II.8, **23**.

[296] Or rather, in the material above.

18 If[297] however Saturn was in this triplicity, remote, [but][298] looking at the Ascendant, and he was direct, difficulty will enter upon the nobles. **19** And if he was retrograde, it will destroy the houses of assets and their secret places,[299] and more serious than that if he received the management of Mars, because it signifies severe cold and the death of animals in addition to what I said about battles and wars. **20** And if he was in this triplicity, falling from the Ascendant, not looking at it, and he was direct and did not look at Mars, the cold of that winter will be severe and strong, and many animals will die in it. **21** But if he were retrograde, there will be contention between those doing business, and plundering and evil, if he looked at Mars from an angle. **22** And if he looked at Mars from a falling place, there will not be anything of what I said.

Chapter 81. **1** If[300] Saturn were in charge, and he was in Taurus and its triplicity, direct, in an angle, it will signify contention and war, and the death of sheep and cows, in the land in which he is, and particularly in his own sign. **2** And if he was retrograde, the harvest will be destroyed (and little growth of plants),[301] and there will be war in every place, and many boys and youths will die, and it will be harsher and more general if he was in the Mid-heaven. **3** Which if he was in these signs, remote from the angle, and he looked at the Ascendant and he was direct, what I said in this chapter will be less. **4** Which if the Moon[302] was in the third from him, it signifies the death of the king through the testimony of the matter of the years.[303] **5** And if he were retrograde, it will destroy seeds and the harvest will be modest, and youths will die. **6** And if Saturn was in this triplicity, falling, not looking at the Ascendant, and he was direct, and Mars not looking at him, he will be of little evil, for he would not be able to seek evil. **7** Which if he were retrograde and impeded by Mars, it signifies the destruction of the harvests, and death in the lands in whose sign he was (or in the square aspect of that same sign, or the opposition).

---

[297] For **18-22**, see *RYW* Ch. 46, **4-6**; also *BRD* II.8, **22**.
[298] Omitting "not," in line with *RYW* Ch. 46, **4**.
[299] Reading *archanas* with London for *areas* ("open spaces, courtyards").
[300] For **1-6**, see *RYW* Ch. 46, **7-11**.
[301] Reading with *BRD* II.8, **24**, for "if there were not a change for the seed."
[302] Reading with *BRD* II.8, **24**, for "Saturn."
[303] That is, through a primary direction (following *BRD*).

Chapter 82. 1 If[304] Saturn were in charge of the year, and he was in Gemini and its triplicity, and he was direct, in an angle, the winds and cold and storms will be made severe, and there will be fewer birds, and every infirmity which was of the essence of Saturn will befall men, and there will be lying and contention in men, and the shedding of blood. **2** Which if he were retrograde, it signifies the contention of the wealthy, and death and earthquake will be feared for them. **3** And if he was remote, the winds of the east and west will be multiplied, and the cold of winter will be made harsh, and there will be earthquake among men. **3** And if he was retrograde, it will be just as I said about earthquake, and there will be infirmities from the winds and dew. **4** But if he were falling, not looking at the Ascendant, and he was direct, it will be harsh for this in the region whose sign it was. **5** And if he was retrograde, the winds of the south will be multiplied, and storms, and much more if he was direct and not weakened, and infirmity and dissolution and plundering will find the citizens of the land whose sign it was, and this will be general in the ignoble. **6** If however he were in the angle of the earth in this triplicity, and he was the lord of the year (and if he was not the lord of the year and received the management of the lord of the Ascendant, and he was in the same place), many men will die in an earthquake. **7** But if he received the management of the Midheaven, it signifies contentions and battles in the seeking of a kingdom.

Chapter 83. 1 If[305] Saturn were in charge of the year and he was in Cancer and its triplicity, in an angle, direct, and Mars did not look at him, the cold will be made severe and heat will be diminished, and one who was in the land of that same sign will be infirm (and one who was in the land of his square aspect). **2** And if he were retrograde, death will be feared for the king of that same part.[306] **3** Which if Saturn did look at Mars, and the fortunes were absent from him, there will be the greatest battle and powerful death in the land which it signifies, by the command of God, and evil and destruction will be multiplied. **4** And if Saturn was in Cancer and its triplicity, remote, not looking at the Ascendant, rains and dew and cold will be multiplied. **5** If however he was direct and the fortunes were joined to him, his evil will be diminished unless the Moon is in the Ascendant in this topic. **6** If she were in the elev-

---

[304] For **1-5**, see *RYW* Ch. 46, **12-19**; also *BRD* II.8, **26**.
[305] For this chapter, see *RYW* Ch. 46, **20-26**.
[306] Reading *partis* with Paris for *temporis* ("season, time").

enth from him,[307] it will be feared for the wealthy. **7** But if Saturn were retrograde and looked at Mars, it signifies destruction and the ruin of the land in whose sign he was (and the square aspect and opposition of that same sign); it even signifies locusts. **8** And if he were falling, not looking at the Ascendant, and he was direct, and Mars did not look at him, men will be secure—and better than that if he had already crossed over one-half of the sign—and there will wholly be infirmity in the land in whose sign he was. **9** Which if he were retrograde and Mars looked at him, also the fortunes were absent from him, evil and tribulation will attack men and the ignoble, and cold will be made severe, and waters and locusts will be multiplied.

[Chapter 84] 1 If the Moon were impeded in a sign, then that portion [of the world] which belonged to that same sign in which she is, will find evil and tribulation according to what that bad one signifies through its own aspect and nature.

2 Look, at the revolution of the year, at the Ascendant and its angles, also the position of the planets in their own places, and their commixtures with each other, and their significations in the categories[308] of the signs and animals and their natures, and the alighting[309] of the Sun at the beginning of the signs.

Chapter 85: On heat and cold. **1** Aries and its triplicity are hot and dry. **2** And if Mars alighted in them, it will increase the nature of heat; and if Saturn alighted in them, it will take away the nature of heat.

3 Taurus and its triplicity are cold and dry. **4** If Saturn alighted in any of them, it will increase the nature of cold; and if Mars alighted in them, it will take away the nature of cold.

5 Gemini and its triplicity are hot and moist. **6** And if Mars alighted in them, it will increase the nature of heat; and if Saturn alighted in them, it will take away the nature of heat.

7 Cancer and its triplicity are cold and moist. **8** If Saturn alighted in them, it will increase the nature of cold; and if Mars alighted in them, it will take away from the nature of cold.

---

[307] Reading somewhat uncertainly. The text could perhaps read, "if he were in the eleventh from *her*."
[308] *Generibus*. But perhaps this should read, "peoples" (*gentibus*).
[309] *Descensionem*. That is, his ingresses.

Chapter 86: On the figures of the signs from the four seasons. 1 Summer is hot and dry, the likeness of which is Aries and its triplicity. **2** Autumn is cold and dry, and its likeness is Taurus and its triplicity. **3** Winter is cold and moist, whose likeness is Cancer and its triplicity. **4** Spring is hot and moist, whose likeness is Gemini and its triplicity.

Chapter 87. 1 If the fortunes alighted in any sign, there will be fertility and good in the essence of that sign. **2** And if a bad one landed in any sign, there will be tribulation and destruction in the essence of that same sign.

3 Consider the fortune and the bad ones: because if Jupiter[310] alighted in Aries, the condition of sheep will be good, and the price of all meats (namely, of four-footed things) will be inexpensive.[311] **4** And if he alighted in Taurus, there will be an abundance of harvests and the price of the annual yield will be inexpensive, and the condition of cows will be good, and [there will be] an increase of the harvests.

5 But if the bad ones alighted in these signs, speak to the contrary and let your description be in accordance with the essence of the signs, if God wills.

6 If however the lord of Aries was in his own exaltation, the fertility or fear will be in the wealthy and the nobles; and if he was in his own descension, it will be in sheep and in all four-footed things, and likewise all signs according to their essences.

Chapter 88. 1 If you found the bad ones in the triplicity of the Sun,[312] and the Sun was in the Ascendant of the year of the world, it signifies war and burnings and battles and mortalities and endings, also grief and many sorrows, and plundering in men and a multitude of burning in villages, and destruction in cities and regions, the dejection of women and the destruction of men in the land of the sign which the bad one is looking at, or in which it was, or in the land in which that bad one had power.[313]

---

[310] Reading with Paris and Erfurt, but London more generically has *fortuna* ("a fortune").
[311] *Leve.* That is, "cheap," here and below.
[312] This is probably the fiery signs.
[313] *Valitudinem.* This seems to mean "dignity."

Chapter 89. 1 If at the revolution Saturn pushed to the Sun upon the sign of the region,[314] and the fortunes were absent from him, it signifies ruin and impediment from water, and fear also, and infirmity and death in the land of that same sign.

2 And if Mars was commingled with him,[315] there will be war and the shedding of blood, and snows, and a multitude of fevers in the direction of the east, even quartan fevers and pestilences, and magnates will fall and kill each other with swords, and the annual yield and wine will be made difficult, and wine will be destroyed, and butter will be multiplied.

3 Which if Mars[316] was near the Ascendant of the year, there will be many battles happening, and pains of the eyes and inseparable [illnesses],[317] and thunders will be multiplied, and the detriment[318] of the earth of every kind. **4** If however Jupiter and Venus were commixed with him, they will repel the evil and will render it mild, and will make the matter easy in all of this, and will block the impediment of Saturn and Mars (and Jupiter especially [does this]), by the command of God.

Chapter 90.[319] **1** If Saturn were the lord of the year and he was in Aries, it signifies a multitude of winds and creeping things, and the death of women, even plundering in the parts of Khurāsān,[320] and fights, also a scarcity of the annual yield and wine and butter and ointments. **2** If the Sun was also impeded, it signifies a multitude of robbers and the cutters of roads, and tribulations.

3 And if Saturn was in Taurus, and an eclipse of the Moon took place, it signifies killing in the direction of the east and west, also snows and many rains, and the multitude of the harvests and creeping things, also the death of cows, and wine and butter will be diminished in the direction of the east.

---

[314] This does not really make sense, and I have not found another reading or source for it.
[315] In Bonatti, this is Saturn (*BOA* Tr. 8.1, Ch. 57).
[316] Reading Mars for Venus, with Bonatti (*ibid*.).
[317] That is, "chronic" illnesses.
[318] Reading *detrimentum* with Bonatti for *incrementum*.
[319] For this entire chapter, cf. *BRD* V.1.
[320] *Carocane*, here and below.

4 And if he was in Gemini, it signifies a multitude of waters and the flooding of rivers, and submersions and a multitude of snows, and detriment in the annual yield, also[321] many winds and death in men.

5 And if he was in Cancer, it signifies a scarcity of waters and rains, and winds, also coughing and pain of the chest, and the foreign travel of men from their own habitations, and a multitude of commotion in men. **6** If however Mercury and Venus were looking at the Ascendant of the year, there will be pains in the eyes.

7 And if he was in Leo, it signifies wars and quartan fevers and the death of women, also labor and exhaustion in men and a multitude of the cutters of roads, and loss in the direction of Khurāsān; men will even find difficulties, and it signifies hot and dry winds which are likened to the dryness of Leo. **8** Which if Mars and Venus were looking, there will be the greatest killing in Khurāsān. **9** However, Jupiter and the Moon will repel this, by the command of God. **10** But if Mercury was with Saturn, pestilence will be multiplied in magnates, and the color of the Sun will be changed to blackness, because Leo is his house.

11 If however Saturn was in Virgo, it signifies pestilence in men, and especially in young women, and a scarcity of rains and a multitude of infirmities and fevers. **12** Which if the Sun looked at him or was commingled with him, there will not be pestilences, and killing will be multiplied in the regions which are in the middle of the western region, and signs from the stars will appear in the heavens.

13 On the other hand, if he was in Libra, it signifies a multitude of winds and detriment in trees, also sultriness and heat, and the scarcity of the annual yield and wine and butter, and a multitude of battle, the adversity of women from their men, too, and a pain of the belly and the heart in men. **14** And if Mars was commingled with him, killing and commotions will be multiplied. **15** If however the Moon and Jupiter were commingled with him, they will repel wars but there will be pestilences and powerful death.

16 And if Saturn was in Scorpio, it signifies blood and destruction, also impediment in youths, and the abortion[322] of pregnant women. **17** If however the Moon and Mars were commingled with him, birth will be with severe fear, and perhaps the one born will go out [while] having been cut out. **18**

---

[321] Omitting *aerem* ("air, atmosphere"), which is in the accusative but does not exactly fit—at any rate, we know that the weather will be affected.
[322] Or, "miscarriage" (*abortiva*).

And there will be back pains and crying in men, and severe labor, and there will be submersion and a multitude of waters and snows, also severe cold, and the destruction of the harvests and of the rest of the seeds. **19** And if Jupiter was commingled with him, war will be modest, more of those born will be male. **20** And if Venus was commingled with him, much blood will be shed and there will be pains of the eyes.

21 But if Saturn was in Sagittarius, it signifies pestilence in magnates and nobles, and war in the west. **22** Which if Mars looked at him, there will be pestilences and pains of the eyes, and severe fevers, and the vexations of demons will be multiplied in men. **23** If however the Sun looked [at him], these things will be foul, and the annual yield will be modest, and locusts will be multiplied, and birds will die.

24 And if Saturn was in Capricorn, it signifies bad dews and detriment in the harvests, and a multitude of rains and harsh winds in the regions and in men, and impediment. **25** If[323] however Jupiter looked [at him], the modest harvest will be made fit, and wine and butter will be multiplied, [and it will be good for wine and watering trees, and it signifies][324] the good condition of flock-animals.

26 And if Saturn was in Aquarius, it signifies a multitude of waters and the flooding of streams, and the impediment of the regions from these; it even signifies a multitude of dews and winds. **27** [And the people will be][325] without piety, and there will be difficulty in men and the regions, and men will travel abroad from their habitations. **28** And the yield[326] of trees and harvests will be diminished, and locusts will be multiplied, [and] impediment in wine, and butter and ointment will be diminished, and death and roaming[327] will be multiplied in men. **29** If however Jupiter looked at the Ascendant of the year or he was commingled with it,[328] it alleviates the pestilence and infirmities, and there will be thunders and many lightning flashes.

30 And if Saturn was in Pisces, it signifies severe cold and the diversity of the atmosphere. **31** Which if the Sun and Venus were looking, and the Moon was far from Saturn, there will be infirmities and pains of the eyes, and the

---

[323] *BRD* V.1, 15 has a parallel sentence to this, but the content is totally different.
[324] Reading rather uncertainly for *vinum namque hoc conversionem aquarum in arboribus dic*.
[325] Adding along with the sense of the sentence and *BRD* V.1.
[326] *Redditus*.
[327] *Vagatio*.
[328] But London adds *domini anni*, suggesting that perhaps Jupiter could be commingled with the lord of the year instead.

annual yield will be modest, also butter and ointments will be multiplied, and the condition of men will be made harsh, and plagues or inseparable accidents[329] will be multiplied. **32** If however Mercury looked at him, it will be more severe for the infirmity.

[Chapter 91][330] **1** If Jupiter were the lord of the year and he was in Aries, it signifies a multitude of winds from the direction of the places[331] and from the direction of Khurāsān and the moisture of the winter and its cold, also a multitude of rains and the flooding of streams, and vineyards and trees will be made fit, and rain will be diminished, and vegetables will be good.

2 And if Jupiter was in Taurus, it signifies a good balance[332] [in the atmosphere] in the winter, and a multitude of rains in it, and a multitude of snows in the last half of the year, and severe cold at the end of winter, and the annual yield and produce will be multiplied (except for grapes), and birds will be diminished, and difficulty will happen on the sea, and there will be diverse winds, and earthquakes will happen.

3 And if he was in Gemini, it signifies winds and the severity of the winter, and in the other half the air will clear up, and water will be diminished. **4** And summer will be balanced, and the southern wind will blow, and the annual yield will be abundant. **5** And the fruits of the trees will be diminished at the end of autumn, and the waters of springs will be multiplied.

6 And if he was in Cancer, it signifies the moisture of the winter and a multitude of snows in the mountains and the fertility of the year, and pains of the mouth in the days of autumn.

7 And if he was in Leo, it signifies the cold of the winter and a multitude of waters, and powerful winds eradicating trees, and it signifies the balance of the atmosphere and the brightness of it in the second half of winter, and a multitude of rains in the spring, and the balance of the summer, and the scarcity of waters in springs and the scarcity of the pasture[333] in winter, and a multitude of infirmities from coughing, and the fertility of the year.

---

[329] That is, chronic ailments.
[330] For this entire chapter, cf. *BRD* V.2.
[331] This probably means, "from the direction in which Aries is, in the chart of the revolution."
[332] *Temperamentum*. Really, this refers to a balanced *mixture* of elements and qualities. I will continue to translate it as "balance" or "balanced" below.
[333] *Pastus*. This can refer both to the action of feeding animals or putting them out to pasture, and the feed or fodder itself.

8 And if he was in Virgo, it signifies a multitude of rains from the beginning of winter up to its end, and a pain of the head in the second half of winter, also snows and cold, and the balance of the spring,[334] and a pain of the head and a scarcity of the flooding of waters and a scarcity of dew in the autumn.

9 And if he was in Libra, it signifies cold at the beginning of the winter, and a multitude of snows and dew, and waters in the springs, also a multitude of rains and thunders and lightning.

10 And if he was in Scorpio, it signifies cold at the beginning of winter, and the severity of cold at the end of winter, and a multitude of rains and snows, and the flooding of streams, and rains impeding trees in the days of spring, and dews in the summer.

11 And if he was in Sagittarius, it signifies the balance of the beginning of winter, and the coldness of the middle of winter, severe winds at its end, also snows and frost in the spring, and southern winds, and a multitude of pasture on the plains, and the destruction of vineyards by snow and cold, and the scarcity of the produce [of the fields], and the fertility[335] of the trees.

12 And if he was in Capricorn, it signifies the balance of the winter and a multitude of filling up [with moisture] and the flooding of rivers on account of snows, also severe cold at the end of winter, and a multitude of rains in the spring, and the balance of the summer and moisture of the atmosphere, and the fruits of vineyards will be made severe, and the fruit of seeds will be good.

13 And if he was in Aquarius, it signifies many[336] winds at the beginning of winter, and its moisture, and the fruits of trees will be destroyed, and the spring will be cold and have many rains, and it signifies a multitude of snows. **14** And summer will be fit, and the southern wind will blow in it, and the annual yield will be destroyed. **15** And there will be wind and dew in autumn and the fruit of trees will be destroyed, and there will be pains and infirmities in boys on account of dew [and] the moisture of the atmosphere, and dew will be multiplied at the time of the vintage, and grapes will be diminished, and the harvests will be good in many places, and there will be detriment in birds and wolves, and ships will suffer shipwreck on the sea.

---

[334] Reading *veris* with Paris and Erfurt, for *aeris* (London).
[335] *Pregnationem*.
[336] Reading *plurimos* with Erfurt and London for *pluviosos* ("windy").

16 And if he was in Pisces, it signifies a multitude of rains at the beginning of the year and a multitude of winds in its middle, also a multitude of cold and snow and powerful winds at its end, even severe heat in the summer, and the winds will destroy seeds, and the fruits of vineyards will be destroyed.

[Chapter 92][337] **1** If Mars were the lord of the year and he was in Aries, it signifies many and powerful winds, also heat and pains of the eyes, and a scarcity of rains, and war in the direction of the east, and the multitude of the annual yield.

2 And if he was in Taurus, it signifies a multitude of clouds and thunder and lightning, also rains and mists, and women and cows will die very much in that same year, and there will be war between the citizens of the east and the citizens of the west, and pain in the eyes will abound (and especially the left eye), and water will be abundant, nor will the cultivation of the earth be multiplied, and if he is not optimal in his own place[338] there will be scarcity in the annual yield, and there will be modest abundance[339] in the annual yield.[340]

3 And if he was in Gemini, it signifies impediment in men. **4** Also, impediment will find them from rivers and thunders and lightning, and ointment[341] will be modest, and there will be war in the north, and robbers will be multiplied, and their king will be exalted in that same year and will be successful; also, pains of the ears and blisters will be multiplied.

5 And if he was in Cancer, it signifies a quarrel in the west, and war will appear upon them and they will render tribute, and an infirmity of fevers and the chest will abound, and pains of the throat, and rain will be modest and the heat will be made severe, and it will be a dangerous year, and ointment will be modest, and death will abound in horses and in every four-footed thing.

6 And if he was in Leo, it signifies that death will occur in beasts, and the annual yield will be modest in the direction of the east, and the rains will be few, and death will be abundant, and pain of the belly and the death of boys will be multiplied.

---

[337] For this entire chapter, cf. *BRD* V.3.
[338] Reading somewhat tentatively. Paris reads, "and if he were optimal in his own place"; Erfurt and London read, "and he will not be optimal in his own place." This should mean that he is in his own domicile or exaltation, and in a house that aspects the Ascendant.
[339] Reading *habundatio* with Paris, for *benedictio* ("blessing").
[340] There may be something wrong in the MSS, as these two statements about the annual yield (*annona*) are redundant.
[341] Or more probably, "oil," here and below.

7 And if he was in Virgo, it signifies pains of the eyes and the effecting of battles and shedding of blood in the direction of the north, and the annual yield will be multiplied, and wine, and ointment, and death will be abundant in women.

8 And if he was in Libra and Saturn was in it, it signifies that rains will be abundant, and gloominess and winds and mists, and there will be pestilences and mortality[342] in the direction of the south, and the wine and ointment will be modest, and robbers and the cutters of roads will be multiplied, also fears and trembling, and quarrels and evil will be abundant in men.

9 And if he was in Scorpio, it signifies that rains and cloudiness will be abundant, and the severity of the cold in the winter, and heat in the summer, and this will impede the annual yield and trees, and pains of the eyes will be abundant, and robbers and wars will be multiplied, and the wine and ointment will be modest, and pains will be abundant in the kidneys of men, and the majority of these things will be in the direction of the north.

10 And if he was in Sagittarius, it signifies that there will be war in the west, and the wine will be modest, and spring will be bad and impeded, and death will occur in the citizens of the west and in those doing business, and infirmity and severe coughing and worms[343] and pains of the eyes will be abundant, and the rains will be modest, and cold will be made severe up until trees and the annual yield are destroyed by it, and death will be abundant, and impediment in bees.[344]

11 And if he was in Capricorn, it signifies death and tribulation is going to be in the direction of the east, and rains and wars and the annual yield will be multiplied, and wine and ointment will be modest, and death will be abundant in youths, and there will be wars and plundering between the citizens of the east and the south.

12 And if he was in Aquarius, it signifies that there will be an ending[345] and severity and tribulation in men, and snows and rains will be abundant, also the annual yield and wine, and the good will be modest in connection

---

[342] Omitting London's extra "and trembling" (see below).
[343] *Lumbrice* (Paris, Erfurt), *lubrici* (London). The adjective *lubricus* (from London) suggests slipperiness or sliminess, which makes sense in the context of coughing and phlegm; but an adjective does not make sense here. *Lumbrice* or *lumbricae* is a possible word, but should be *lumbrici*, and earthworms do not quite match the illnesses here. Perhaps the author is thinking of parasites in general.
[344] Reading *apibus* with Erfurt and London, for Paris's *avibus* ("birds").
[345] That is, "death."

with those doing business, and the king will change [residence] in that same year, and will die. **13** Which if then Venus looked at the Ascendant, and she was northern, the wine will be modest and spring will be good.

14 And if he was in Pisces, it signifies a multitude of snows and rains, and death will be abundant in the direction of the south, and the hauls of fish will be abundant, and the reign of many men will disappear, and killing will abound in magnates and the wealthy, and the annual yield will be modest, and the majority of wine will be destroyed, and flies will be destroyed. **15** Which if Venus looked at the Ascendant of the year, death will be abundant in men, and pains of the eye, and thunders and lightning will be multiplied, and the seed of the earth will be fruitful and multiplied.

Chapter 93.[346] **1** If Mercury were the lord of the year and he was in Aries, it signifies powerful winds and a multitude of waters, and a scarcity of rain, and the death of boys, and the scarcity of the annual yield in the direction of the west, and much destruction of wind. **2** If however the Moon was commingled with him, fish will be multiplied; and if the Sun were commingled with him, women will be freed,[347] and wine will be multiplied. **3** If however Mars was there, and the Sun and Venus, women will not perish. **4** And if Saturn was there with Mars, the flooding of waters will be multiplied. **5** And if Mars was in that same place, wars will be multiplied in the east and west, and pains of the eyes.

6 And if Mercury was in Taurus, it signifies a multitude of waters and the destruction of the harvests, and a diverse atmosphere, and detriment in wine, and a scarcity of butter and ointment, and war in the citizens of the east and west, and pains of the eyes in the direction of the east, and death in princes and magnates. **7** If however Jupiter and Venus looked at the Ascendant of the year, they will repel pestilence, by the command of God. **8** But if Mars looked at the Ascendant and Venus was commingled with him, there will be a severe war and death in cows.

9 And if he was in Gemini, it signifies [war][348] in connection with the Latins from the citizens of Khurāsān,[349] and death in magnates, and a multitude of snows, and detriment in the harvests and ointments, and butter, and a

---

[346] For this entire chapter, cf. *BRD* V.5.
[347] The rest of **2** and all of **3** appear only in London.
[348] Tentatively adding "war," as there is no object mentioned.
[349] *Curacem* (and variants), here and below.

multitude of wine, also pestilence and death in women[350] and a multitude of blisters and inflammation, dew, and moisture. **10** Which if the Sun and Jupiter looked at the Ascendant of the year, pestilences and death will be diminished, and men will be stronger and richer in the direction of the east.

11 And if Mercury was in Cancer, killing will be multiplied in the direction of *Ammarot*,[351] and the annual yield and ointment will be modest, and seed and trees and wine will suffer detriment, and infirmity of the neck will be multiplied in men. **12** Which if he was commingled with Venus and Mars, nobles and magnates from the direction of the west will be killed; however, the aspects of the Moon and Venus will repel [the evil].

13 And if he was in Leo, the heat of wind will be made harsh. **14** Which if he was in the west, there will be impediment, and the annual yield and wine and ointment and rains will be modest, and the harvests and dates will be successful and improved, and there will be death in wolves, and pains of the eyes will be multiplied, and the condition of the nobles in Khurāsān will be made worse. **15** And the aspect of the bad ones will increase the evil, but the aspect of the fortunes will show mercy and restrain [it], by the command of God.

16 And if Mercury was in Virgo, the rains and harvests will be multiplied, and pains of the eyes will be abundant, and death, in the direction of *Ammarot*.

17 And if he was in Libra, it signifies severe and powerful winds, and a scarcity of the wine and the annual yield. **18** Which if Saturn approached him, it signifies pains of the head and belly; and the aspect of the Sun repels [it].

19 And if he was in Scorpio, rains and snows will be multiplied, and war in the regions of the west and *Abaghir*.[352] **20** Which if Mars was looking, the citizens of *Abaghir* will be stronger, and robbers and cutters of roads and pestilences will be multiplied in *Abaghir*, and fevers which make men tremble,[353] and a pain of the eyes with redness and burning [in the eyes].

---

[350] Reading *mulieribus* with London for *militibus* ("soldiers").
[351] Unknown at this time, but a transliteration for something like *al-Marot*.
[352] Unknown at this time, but it must be closely related to Khurāsān, since in **23** these two lands are said to be at war.
[353] Erfurt has "quartan fevers."

21 And if he was in Sagittarius, snows and rains will be multiplied, and the atmosphere will be diverse, and waters and the annual yields and produce will be modest,³⁵⁴ and war and battles will be multiplied in the west.

22 And if he was in Capricorn, tribulation and battles will be multiplied in the land of Khurāsān. **23** If however he was conjoined to Venus and Mars, there will be war in Khurāsān from the men of *Abaghir*.

24 And if he was in Aquarius, it signifies the diversity of the atmosphere, and a scarcity of rains, also itching and blisters, and locusts will be multiplied. **25** And if Venus was commingled with him, there will be earthquake and pestilences and robbers will be multiplied. **26** And if Saturn was commingled with him, rains will be abundant.

27 And if he was in Pisces, winds and the upper waters will be multiplied, and it will be night in the direction of *Ammarot*, and creeping things and fish will be multiplied; and all of this will be in accordance with the aspect of the planets, and their strength.

Chapter 94. 1 If you knew the significator over the condition of the rustics, and you understood [it], the significator of the king will be revealed³⁵⁵ to you and it will be evident to you what will happen in his kingdom in that same year. **2** Know [this] from the reception of the planets (that is, through their rays),³⁵⁶ and [where] they are positioned in the twelve houses of the circle, and what belongs to those signs (of climes and cities), so that their destruction and fitness will be evident to you through the rays of the bad ones and inimical and contrary ones, and the rays of the friendly bad ones, and likewise through the rays of friendly and inimical fortunes: speak according to their friendship and enmity towards the houses.

3 For if the fortunes were made peaceful,³⁵⁷ they signify a multitude of goods; and if they were inimical, they signify a scarcity of good. **4** And likewise, if the bad ones were inimical to the houses, they signify a multitude of evil; and if they were made peaceful, they signify a scarcity of evil.

---

³⁵⁴ London adds that wine will be abundant.
³⁵⁵ This should probably read something like, "*let* the significator of the king *be revealed* to you."
³⁵⁶ That is, which planet applies to which planet; the author does not mean classical "reception" proper.
³⁵⁷ This probably means "if they were in a good condition and making important sextiles and trines."

5 Then,[358] see what belongs to each sign (of lands) in the east and west. **6** And if a sign were impeded in the west, it signifies impediment in the west (of the lands). **7** And if it were impeded in the Midheaven, it signifies impediment in the lands in the east and west, and especially in the lands which were towards the north and south (namely in the part of Mars and Venus), and[359] in the land of the Ethiopians.

ଓ   ଓ   ଓ

Comment by Dykes. In the remainder of *Scito* (including probably the passages at the very end), Abū Ma'shar draws on chart examples taken directly from Sahl b. Bishr's mundane work, which I will translate for my future Arabic series. Since the Latin of Chapter 95 in particular is rather mangled and full of bad transliterations, I have inserted my own provisional translation of Sahl's Arabic, following the Latin description of the chart (sentences prefixed with **A**).[360] The Latin description (probably by John of Spain) refers to the Toledan tables (late 11th Century) and recalculates the chart with an Ascendant slightly different from the two Arabic versions I consulted.

In Chapter 95, Abū Ma'shar uses Sahl's example #1 from the Aries ingress of 656 AD, the year of the famous Battle of the Camel (December 656), part of the first Islamic *fitna*, or civil uprising, or civil war. After Muhammad's death in 632, the leadership of the Muslims passed to four Caliphs ("successors") who had been closely associated with him. The most important issue in the early Caliphates was that of power: not only who should be Caliph, but who should have governorships, financial privileges, and so on. There were two main poles of thought. On the one hand, many thought that Muhammad's own tribe, the Qurayshis of Mecca, should be the source of political authority. But even here there was a difference: first, not all Qurayshis had supported Muhammad in the first place, being rather latecomers to the cause; second, there were smaller clans and family units within the larger tribe, the foremost being the 'Umayyads, so-called because they descended from a relative of Muhammad's named 'Umayya. (This branch formed the first dynasty in 661.) On the other hand, some argued that people should be favored based on their allegiance and activity in support of Mu-

---

[358] For this paragraph, cf. *BRD* VIII.1, **22**, and *Skilled* VIII.7, **136-37**.
[359] London omits "and."
[360] Sources: Vat. Ar. 955, f. 170L; Beatty Ar. 5467, p. 259.

hammad, particularly those Medinans who had helped Muhammad after his flight from Mecca (the Hijrah). (Again, even here there were debates about who counted the most.) The first four Caliphs prior to the formal 'Umayyad dynasty all had good Islamic credentials but their elections were fraught with these tensions over authority and finances, as they did not all hold the same views. These struggles play a role in Examples #2 and #3, so must be understood at least in broad outlines.

The third Caliph, 'Uthmān b. 'Affān (r. 644-656), belonged to the 'Umayyad branch of the Qurayshis, but he was also one of the first (probably within the first 20) converts to Islam—so his credentials were based both on the length and depth of his allegiance, and his family ties. However, he himself insisted on favoring not just Qurayshis in positions of power, but the 'Umayyad branch especially. Over time, this dominance by the Meccan elite created more tensions and enemies, including al-Zubayr b. al-'Awwām (of whose son, more in Example #3), who was a well-known and respected Qurayshi, but not an 'Umayyad.

In 656, 'Uthmān was murdered while at home (**A18** and **A61**), by persons unknown (although Medina and his home were surrounded by various rebels): thus Sahl says that it was without an explicit quarrel (**A18-19**). The political situation was very tense, and was made worse by the election of the fourth Caliph, 'Alī b. Abī Tālib, who in fact had been 'Uthmān's rival in 644. 'Alī recognized that centralizing power among the Qurayshis (not to mention a single branch, the 'Umayyads) was creating many problems, and he wanted other groups to be able to enjoy the recognition and benefits as well. But this was doubly resented by people like al-Zubayr b. al-'Awwam. For others there was also the question of how devoted 'Ali was to finding the murderers of their kinsman (**A20** and **A24**).

In the end, certain embittered Qurayshis went to Basra (in southern modern Iraq) to drum up support against 'Alī, while 'Alī himself went to Kūfa to do the same (**A42-43**). 'Alī got more supporters, and the two sides clashed around Basra in December of that year (656), in the Battle of the Camel—so called because 'A'isha, Muhammad's widow and partisan of the Qurayshis, led or supervised the battle from a howdah atop a camel. 'Alī used his troops to protect the endangered treasury during the conflict (**A23**), and with less funding and support, the Qurayshi side (and 'A'isha) lost the battle. Sahl's view is that the Caliphate of 'Ali was just and good (**A22**), but as in any situation arising out of a civil war, that assessment would be contested by others.

SECTION II.5: ABŪ MA'SHAR, SCITO HORAM INTROITUS

Turning to the chart, it is cast for the Aries ingress of 656 AD: according to the Latin version of the dating, it was the 18th of Ramadan, which equates to March 20. However, based on the position of the Moon in Scorpio, and that of the Sun in the seventh, it must have been March 19, 656 AD. Moreover, the Ascendant and planetary positions given in the Latin are not those found in the Arabic texts. I have inserted two versions of the chart: (1) a construction of my own using my best reading of the Arabic manuscripts (which do not always agree), (2) a modern tropical chart. From the example here and in Appendix C, we can see that his planetary values are about 2-3° *earlier* than the tropical, and about 4° *later* than the Fagan-Bradley sidereal. If we calculate the Julian Day for each tropical chart (via a computer program), it is easy to see that Sahl is working with a sidereal year of about 365.259 days (typical for his time). However, he has cast chart #1 a little too early, and chart #2 a little too late, even within the logic of his own tables. Following are the JDs for the four examples, timed from the Ascendants of the manuscript charts at their appropriate locations:[361]

#1 (656 AD): 1960740.184630 (but see below)
#2 (657 AD): 1961105.488148 (but see below)
#3 (692 AD): 1973889.538009
#4 (719 AD): 1983751.544306

By counting the days between charts, and dividing by the number of years between them, we can deduce the length of Sahl's year. All combinations except those involving #2 (such as 1-2, 2-3, 2-4) give us a year of 365.259 and some fraction, which is clearly a sidereal year, and one commonly used in medieval sidereal tables (see my Introduction). But the period between 1-2 is much too long (365.303518), and 2-3 and 2-4 have a year that is too short (365.258 and a fraction), so Sahl has miscalculated the chart times for both, even based on his (incorrect) sidereal year. Let us try to correct them a bit by subtracting multiples of 365.259 from the later charts (#3 and #4). For example, there are 62 years between #2 and #4, so multiplying 365.259 by 62

---

[361] My conclusions here, from the exact length of Sahl's year to the exact date of his tables, are based solely on the four charts discussed here (which I have also corrected slightly, see below). For my edition of Sahl I will also analyze the rest of his charts to get a better picture of the tables he used.

and subtracting the resulting days from #4, should get us a better Julian Date.

For #2, subtracting multiples of 365.259 from the later charts give us a JD of 1961105.473009 (from #3) or 1961105.486306 (from #4). Each of these is only minutes earlier than the JD based on the manuscript. If we average them, then we can provisionally assign chart #2 JD 1961105.4796578, only 12' 13" earlier than the JD of the chart in Appendix C.

For #1, subtracting multiples gives us a JD of 1960740.214009 (from #3) or 1960740.227306 (from #4), again only minutes apart from each other. The average would be JD 1960740.220658, which is 51' 52" *later* than the chart below. This difference of almost an hour would put the Ascendant into Scorpio and change the whole chart; fortunately perhaps for us, Sahl's parameters are incorrect anyway.

In what follows, the chart description is divided into two parts. First, Sahl runs through each sign of the chart, treating the houses both in terms of whole signs and quadrant divisions (**A6-69**). Then Abū Ma'shar (or some other author) applies some predictive techniques to the chart (resuming at Latin **67-87**). I will discuss these techniques below.

Chapter 95: [Example #1 from Sahl]. 1 And this is an admirable example through which you will contemplate a revolution, namely which was made with 12 days remaining of the month of Ramadan (which is the ninth[362] lunar month). **2** And the year had reached Scorpio.[363]

[Later/European recalculation of chart]

3 And the Ascendant was Libra 15°, the bound of Jupiter,[364] and the planets and their rays according to what they are in this figure, if God wills. **4** And the revolution was the second of Benesaphar,[365] at[366] one equal hour

---

[362] Reading *nonus* more correctly for *octavus* ("eighth").
[363] Sahl follows the tradition that the Ascendant of the 571 ingress (heralding Islam) was Libra: the annual profection from Libra to 656 AD would have reached Scorpio. I'm sure that Sahl would have thought this was important for the Islamic community as a whole (as it indeed was), since Scorpio was the sign of the Saturn-Jupiter conjunction for Islam.
[364] Reading with London, although Paris and Erfurt correctly read "21." For 15° does fall in the Egyptian bound of Jupiter, but 21° (which does not mention the bound of Jupiter) does not. This comment about Jupiter must have come from the Latin manuscript tradition.
[365] *Secundum benesaphar.* Safar is a month in the Islamic calendar, but I am not sure what the *bene-* prefix means.

and 20[367] minutes from the beginning of the night of the Sabbath, which began to shine[368] on the 18th[369] day of the aforesaid month of Ramadan, in the 35th year of the Arabs. **5** And the Ascendant by the ascensions of Toledo was 15° Libra, and the planets according to what I will describe to you. **6** For Saturn was in Virgo, 27° 39',[370] and Jupiter in Capricorn, 8° 16', and Mars in Leo, and Venus in Aries, 27° 58',[371] and Mercury in Aries, 6° 35',[372] and the Moon in Scorpio, and the Sun in Aries, and the Head in Libra, 15° 30'.[373]

[Sahl's Arabic][374]

A6 And the year had reached Scorpio,[375] and it was the 35th year of the Hijrah, toward the twelfth night remaining of the month of Ramadan.

A7 I looked in the revolution of this year at the Ascendant, and at the stakes, and the positions of the stars in their transit, and the pushing of their management, and the projection of their rays.

A8 And the stakes are upright.[376]

A9 And the Sun is in the opposition of the Ascendant, withdrawing.

A10 And the revolution is at night, and the Moon is in her fall, absent from the fortunes,[377] connected to the infortunes, and she is the lord of the stake of heaven.

---

[366] *Super*, reading this as a translation of the Arabia ʿalā.
[367] Reading arbitrarily with Paris. Erfurt: "12," London "11."
[368] *Lucescet*, meaning uncertain here.
[369] Reading with Paris and London, for Erfurt's "8." Since there were 12 days left in Ramadan, it must have happened on the 18th day.
[370] Reading with Paris. Erfurt has 28° 39', London 27° 59'.
[371] Reading with Paris. Erfurt and London have 59'.
[372] Reading with Paris (and London). Erfurt has 17° 37'.
[373] Reading with Paris. Erfurt and London have 15° 33'.
[374] The circular chart I have created below is based on the square chart in Beatty. Vatican's numbers were sometimes unreadable and diverged more from the modern tropical versions than Beatty did. Also, Vatican includes intermediate cusp values and an MC (19° 49' Cancer), which are close to a Baghdad location and something like Porphyry cusps. I believe this is due to a later recalculation, and that the original chart was cast for Basra (the location of the battle). Baghdad was not the capital of the Caliphate until ʿAbbasid times (founded in 762 AD), and as I point out in Appendix C, casting the charts for the locations of the events solves some problems in the chart images in Sahl's other examples.
[375] From the alleged Libra Ascendant of the Aries ingress of 571, the annual profection of it would have reached Scorpio in 656.
[376] That is, the axis of the Midheaven is in the appropriate whole signs, the tenth and fourth.

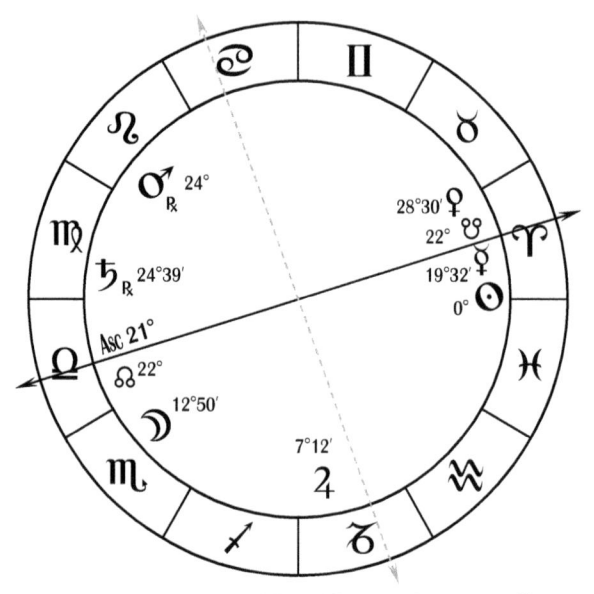

Figure 63: Version (from MS) of Sahl's Example #1, 656 AD

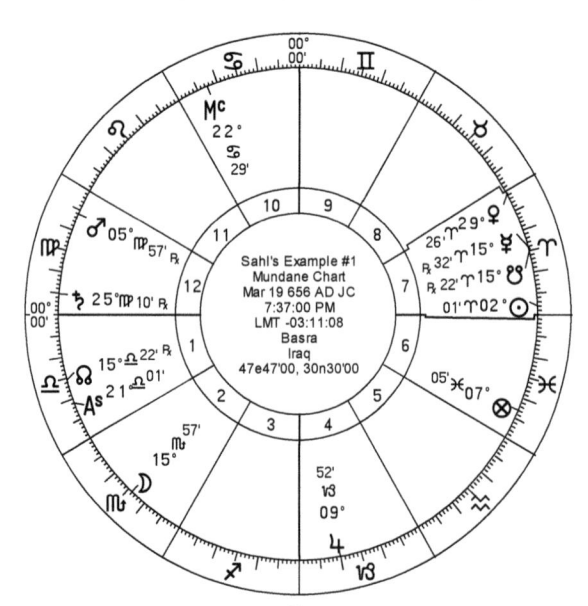

Figure 64: Sahl's Example #1, 656 AD (modern tropical)

---

[377] She is not actually in aversion from both infortunes, but she is in aversion from the nocturnal fortune, Venus.

A11 And Venus and Mercury are in Aries, in the opposition of the Ascendant.

A12 And Mars (their lord, looking at the Ascendant) is in the house of the Sun, in the eleventh,[378] not received because Jupiter is cutting off the light of the Sun from him.

A13 And Saturn is declining[379] in Virgo, in the twelfth, not received.

A14 And Jupiter is in the fourth, in his fall.

A15 And Venus was the indicator of the citizens, because she is greater in testimony and she was in a stake, in the contrary of her own house, coming from easternness, reaching her westernness, not received.[380]

A16 And the indicator of the king is the Moon, because the revolution is at night, and she is the lord of the stake of heaven. **A17** And she is connecting with Saturn, and he is falling away from Mars, and [Mars] is retrograde in the eleventh. **A18** What I described of her position and condition signifies that the king of this clime was killed by his citizens, because Mars signifies his killing: for he is the lord of the house of the luminaries and the lord of the house of the lord of the Ascendant. **A19** And because of the declining of the Moon from the stake, it signifies that this is without a [violent] contention,[381] and the king will[382] struggle with the citizens.

A20 And because of the position of Venus in the contrary of her own house, it signifies that after this the citizens will fall into civil unrest and disorder, and [there will be] fighting and contention in the kingdom.

A21 Because of the place of the Moon from Saturn, and for that reason the light of Saturn's sextile, that was in the first quarter [of the year].

A22 And because of the place of the Sun (who is the lord of the eleventh) in the square of Jupiter, it indicates that he who accedes [to the throne] after him intends the good, and the citizens will thrive in his time.[383]

---

[378] According to Sahl's incorrect tables, Mars is in Leo.

[379] Or, "falling" (ساقط). In this case, he is both in a declining or cadent sign (the twelfth sign, Virgo) as well as "falling away from" or in aversion to, the rising sign itself.

[380] By "not received," Sahl seems to mean that she and her lord (Mars) cannot complete an exact aspect because she is separating from him. Here at least, Sahl seems to have a strict view of classical reception.

[381] The Arabic root of this word has to do specifically with trying to take something away from someone. Etymologically then, it suggests that the king had not done anything wrong or tried to take something away from them.

[382] The Latin adds "not," which makes more sense.

[383] This refers to 'Alī, who indeed was considered a righteous man, but his reign was tumultuous because of the opposition from powerful 'Umayyads.

A23 And because of the place of Mars in[384] the eleventh from the Ascendant, retrograde, it necessitates the dispersion of the assets which belong to kings; and after the killing of this king, there is a powerful fighting and the shedding of blood.[385] A24 And because of his place in the house of the Sun, there is there is contention among the nobility of the people and their kings.

A25 Then I looked in the twelve places and what is in them, of the lights of the planets:

A26 And the Ascendant was Libra, and in it the light of the opposition of the Sun and Mercury and Venus, and the light of the second square of Jupiter, and the first sextile of Mars.[386] A27 That indicates a contention in the clime of the Romans and the shedding of blood, and it is also in the direction of Kirmān and Sijistān and China and Kashmīr. A28 And their livestock will flourish, and their land will be fertile, and in those lands there will be illnesses in youths, and their commerce will be improved.

A29 The second sign is Scorpio, and in it the Moon, unfortunate, and the second sextile of Jupiter, and the first square of Mars, and the first sextile of Saturn. A30 That necessitates the shedding of blood and civil unrest in the clime of the Arabs, and it shifts from there because the Moon is unfortunate in what is not [her] sign, the one she is in.[387] A31 Then that becomes powerful and in it there will be a shedding of blood, and the condition of the clime of the Arabs intensifies, and in it their livestock will die. A32 And because of the position of Venus and her being in a stake, a foreign enemy will[388] enter upon them. A33 And in Rayy and its direction there will be great death (and that will be greater in women), and produce will be corrupted, and it will be likewise in Basrah.

A34 The third sign is Sagittarius: in it is the light of the second trine of Mercury, and the first trine of Mars, and the second trine of Venus, and the first square of Saturn.[389] A35 And its lord is in his own fall: it signifies the weakness of the people of Isfahān, and distresses, and an abundance of thieves, and the death of riding animals. A36 And that will also be in the

---

[384] Reading "in" for "from."
[385] That is, after the killing of 'Uthmān there will be fighting—especially, at the Battle of the Camel.
[386] As with Māshā'allāh's *RYW*, the "first" aspect is one cast later in the zodiac, and the "second" one is cast earlier.
[387] I do not see why this means that the unrest will spread. The phrase literally reads, "because she is unfortunate in what is not the sign in which she is."
[388] Omitting ‏لا‎ ("not").
[389] There is also the second trine of the Sun.

middle of the sea of Upper Armenia, and more who will die in this year will be youths.

A37 The fourth sign is Capricorn, and Jupiter is in it, and the second square of the Sun, and the [second] square of Mercury, and the second square of Venus, and the first trine of Saturn, and the first sextile of the Moon. **A38** That necessitates the safety and excellence of the condition of the people of the clime of India, and the goodness of their planting and their livestock, and their Sultan will be righteous, and their land will be fertile. **A39** And they will be victorious over those of their enemies who contend with them, and the revenues of their commerce will increase. **A40** And the people of the Ahwāz will be fertile, and the Cities,[390] and their conditions will be fine, in safety and leisure, and in the propriety of their Sultan.

A41 The fifth sign is Aquarius, and in it the second sextile of the Sun, and the second sextile of Mercury, and the first square of the Moon, and the opposition of Mars, and the [second] sextile of Venus. **A42** The falling of Saturn [away from Aquarius],[391] and the light of the opposition of Mars, and the light of the sextile of Venus, indicates contention and fighting in the region of Kūfa and its agricultural areas,[392] and civil unrest, and fanaticism, and social confusion;[393] and that is also in Egypt,[394] and blood will be shed for this reason. **A43** And they will meet in that direction and the great countries in the west.[395]

A44 The sixth sign is Pisces, and there is not a planet in it, and in it is light of the opposition of Saturn, and the first sextile of Jupiter (the lord of the house), and the first trine of the Moon. **A45** The light of Saturn necessitates the intensity of the cold in Tabaristān and its areas, and the intensity of the tribulation of its Sultan (because of the weakness of Jupiter). **A46** And the condition of its people will be made unfortunate, and they will be strengthened in relation to their Sultan, and the will demand justice from him, and their rains will multiply, and their waters, and their animals will flourish. **A47**

---

[390] The combination of ancient Seleucia and Ctesiphon, near modern Baghdad.
[391] That is, his aversion from it (as he is in Virgo).
[392] سوادها.
[393] Or more simply, "mixing" (اختلاط) but I take it that Sahl wants the negative connotation.
[394] The Latin text adds Jurjān.
[395] البلدان غرباً كثير .

And the sea of India will increase,³⁹⁶ and the region of Armenia, and what borders on Rome.³⁹⁷

A48 The seventh sign is Aries, and the Sun [is in it], withdrawing, and Mercury and Venus in the stake, and the first square of Jupiter, and the light of the second trine of Mars. **A49** So Venus was in the stake, and the light of Mars (who is the lord of the house, and he is retrograde in Leo, in the eleventh from the Ascendant): and what it indicated for this or the years³⁹⁸ [is] the ruin of the king of Babylon, and that there is war in the clime of Babylon, and contention, and much blood, and the corruption of their Sultan; and the beginning of that is from outside this clime. **A50** Because of the position of Mars and the place of Mercury (who is the lord of the third), it indicates that in addition to what I described of wars, there is piety, and many people will be destroyed on account of this war. **A51** And the condition of youths will be flourishing, and camels, and every [animal, and heat will be made harsh for them],³⁹⁹ and what I said will also be in Babylon and Azerbaijān.

A52 The eighth sign is Taurus, and no planet is in it, and its lord not falling,⁴⁰⁰ and in it is the light of the first trine of Jupiter, and the second square of Mars, and the second trine of Saturn, and the opposition of the Moon. **A53** The⁴⁰¹ second square of Mars (who is an enemy of this house),⁴⁰² and the light of the opposition of the Moon (who is the lord of the exaltation of this house) necessitates that the Sultan of Harah⁴⁰³ (a city in Khurāsān, and Sind is said to belong to it, and where it is, and it is of the country of Kābul from [*unreadable*] and Sijistān and Cyprus (and especially that because it is in the area of the west)....and will rise up against them.⁴⁰⁴ **A54** Enemies will be in their hands, and they will encounter violence from them, and robbers will

---

³⁹⁶ يزيد. Meaning unclear: what does it mean for the sea to increase?
³⁹⁷ That is, the Byzantine region.
³⁹⁸ ما دلت عليه ام السنين.
³⁹⁹ Reading with the Latin, as Vatican and Beatty have wildly different (and uncertain) readings.
⁴⁰⁰ This must mean "declining," namely cadent by quadrant divisions or by whole signs. My preferred reading would be to omit the "not," so that it read "and its lord is falling," namely, in aversion to Taurus, just as in **A42** above.
⁴⁰¹ The middle of this sentence is unreadable and confused at points in both MSS.
⁴⁰² Probably because he rules Scorpio, which is opposed to Taurus.
⁴⁰³ هراه, but this is probably Herat (هرات), which was indeed an important city in Khurāsān.
⁴⁰⁴ I have inserted this ellipse because Sahl or the original scribe seems to have forgotten that the subject of the sentence was the Sultan of Herat and the other places: thus there is no verb to complete the sentence.

be multiplied in it, and their fear will be intensified, and the rabble will abandon their Sultan, and their livestock will be ruined, and the rabble will be safe from the Sultan, and they will be affected well by their Sultan.[405]

A55 The ninth sign from Libra, which is the Ascendant of the year in which 'Uthmān b. 'Affān was killed (may God be pleased by him!), in the 35th year from the Hijrah, is the sign Gemini; and no planet is in it, and in it is the light of the first sextile of Mercury, and the second sextile of Mars, and the second square of Saturn. **A56** And the place of the second square of Saturn and the contrariety involving the light of Mars and Mercury (who is the lord of this house), signifies that Daylam and Sind and their areas, and Kābul, will triumph over all of their contenders from among their enemies, because of the strength of the position of Mercury and his reception. **A57** And the mixture of Mars and Saturn indicates illnesses in the areas of those countries, and great death in youths.[406] **A58** And because of the second square of Saturn in more degrees, they will submit to their Sultan and obey him. **A59** And what I said will be in Jurjān also, and al-Zān[407] and Lower Māah, and the Alans, and Mūsul.

A60 The tenth sign is Cancer, and in it the second trine of the Moon (who is its lord, and she is unfortunate, in her fall), and the second sextile of Saturn, and the first square of the Sun, and the first square of Mercury, and the first square of Venus. **A61** And because of the place which I described to you of the corruption of the lord of the house and what they indicated for that or the years, it necessitates that the king of the clime of Iraq will be overcome, and his authority will be corrupted, and his command will be confused, and there will be a contention among their leaders, and illnesses in the people from cold and moisture, and produce will be corrupted, and the condition of the people will be made severe, and their profit will be diminished. **A62** And likewise [this will be in] Hajar and Bahrain and Egypt and the Cities, and Dabīl.

A63 The eleventh sign is Leo, and in it Mars, retrograde, and the light of the first trine of the Sun, and Mercury and Venus by the first trine, and the

---
[405] At this point Sahl begins a long digression on weather and other things; I follow *Scito* here in moving directly to the ninth sign, and continue the numbering uninterrupted.
[406] Reading الصبيان with the sense of the Latin, for الاحداث ("the events"); this is more appropriate also because Gemini and Mercury signify youths.
[407] Reading as best I can from Beatty (والزان وماه ه السفل واللان والموصل), with some places unknown. Vatican has: اللاه وماه السعلي واللات العليت والموصل.

second square of the Moon, too. **A64** The retrogradation of Mars[408] indicates, [for] the Sultan in the clime of the Turks and Abrashar[409] (and it is Nishapūr) and Makrān (and it is of the countries of Sind), that there are wars and the shedding of blood, and corruption from thieves, and that is in Basrah also. **A65** And a great man[410] is destroyed in that year, and there is contention among the authorities on account of the light of the second square of the Moon.

A66 The twelfth sign is Virgo, and Saturn retrograde in it, and the light of the second trine of Jupiter, and the second sextile of the Moon. **A67** There are illnesses in the area of al-Andalus from the land of the west and what overlooks[411] the Nile and Fars, and there will be illnesses in them from cold and dryness. **A68** And because of the place of Mercury they will be paralyzed by death, and their planting will be corrupted, and their trees, and their coldness will intensify, and the heat of their summer will not have strength.

A69 Then I looked in the management of the days [at] the condition of the king from the direction[412] of the Moon, who was the indicator of the king (because she is the lord of the Midheaven).

[Abū Ma'shar's [?] interpretation of the management over the year]

Comment by Dykes. At this point we return to the Latin sentences, and what I presume is Abū Ma'shar's own attempt to perform the operation in **A69** above, which Sahl notably omits.[413] Based on Sahl's straightforward statement, I expect we should direct the body of the Moon itself by ascensions for the condition of the king, *because* she is the lord of the Midheaven and the significator of the king (**A10**, **A16**). However, the author (hereafter, Abū Ma'shar) instead directs the trine ray which she casts *into* the Midheaven, and not even by ascensional times. His procedure is simply this: divide the 360° of the circle by 365.25 days, yielding 1 day for every 59' 08". Then, we simply

---

[408] Beatty and the Latin each add some version of "and the square of the Moon."
[409] See also *Skilled* VIII.35.
[410] Reading with the sense of the Latin for what seems to be خلق ("moral character," "creation"). But Vatican could also be read as حلف ("treaty," "confederation"), which makes more sense.
[411] Or, "is in charge of," "has control over" (اشرف).
[412] That is, by directing the Moon through the zodiac. This should be done by ascensions or primary directions, but it seems that Abū Ma'shar himself (below) follows 'Umar al-Tabarī's method of simply dividing the circle into 365 days of 59' 08" apiece.
[413] This is reinforced by the fact that the degree values below do not match those of the later European calculation—although they do not match Sahl's either.

count forward from her trine until we encounter the body or ray of some other planet, whose signification will then be activated: the degrees between these successive points, divided by 59' 08", will tell us how many days each planet's body or ray assumes the "management" of the year. Thus in **69-70**, Abū Ma'shar counts from her trine in Cancer (which he takes to be in 18°) up to the square of Mercury (which he takes to be in 19°: the difference is a little more than 1°, so that a little more than 1 day passes before the Mercurial significations take effect. The next manager is Saturn, through his sextile (**75**), and so on.

Note however that the author accidentally switches the order of the planets, and his reference to the position of Saturn means he is not following the chart data. In terms of planetary order, the trine of the Moon should be followed by the square of Mercury, sextile of Saturn, square of Venus, trine of Sun, and square of Moon—and then after more steps, the body of Saturn. But the text switches the order of Venus and the Sun, while still referring to her square. The diagram below represents the proper order based on the chart data. Also, the time frame mentioned in sentence **83** means that something is wrong either with the chart data or the author's understanding of the position of Saturn (see footnote).

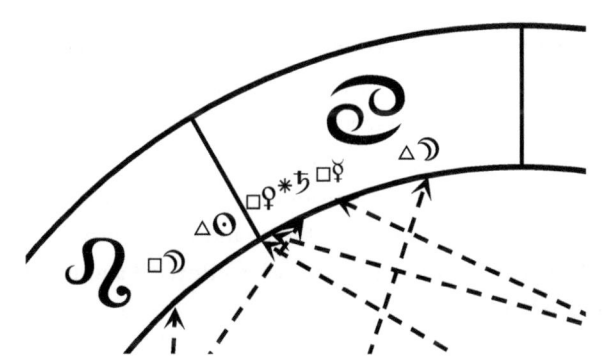

Figure 65: Zodiacal direction for Sahl's Example #1

67 The significator of the king was the Moon, and she was falling[414] in her place. **68** Therefore we looked at whether she had light in the Midheaven, which is her place (that is, her house) or in the Ascendant. **69** The light of her trine aspect was [in the Midheaven], in the 18th degree and 12th minute.[415]

---

[414] That is, in her own fall.
[415] Reading with Paris for Erfurt's *7th*.

70 Therefore we saw to whom she handed over her own management in this place, and closer to that (more so than the other lights) was the light of the first square aspect of Mercury, and it was in the 19th degree[416] and a fraction. **71** And we subtracted the light of the Moon from this, and there remained one degree and a fraction; also we divided this by 59' 08", and there was one day and a fraction (that is, part of one day).

72 And through her light the Moon managed one day and a fraction from the Midheaven; and because the management was handed over to Mercury, who was the lord of the house of enemies and the house of foreign travel and faith, this signifies the sorrow of the king in this management, from the ruin of religious people and the faith of people in sects, and their statements and enmities. **73** After this, Mercury will receive the management from the Moon through his first square aspect. **74** And he is the lord of the ninth and twelfth house, and his light (that is, his rays) are from them in the ninth house:[417] all of this signifies a work for which a measure of good work is hoped, namely from penance and prayer and fasting, and he will find sexual intercourse in that management.[418]

75 Then, Saturn receives the management through the light of his second sextile aspect, from the light of Mercury's first square aspect. **76** And he will manage the remainder of the sign in which his light was, and of the next sign from that same place.[419] **77** And he is the lord of the exaltation of the Ascendant, and the lord of the fourth and fifth (which is the eighth from the management):[420] in this management therefore, because he receives this light from the square of Mercury, it signifies that little papers (that is, letters and rumors) will find him in these days from the direction of the west, which will sadden him, and he will be sad over them, and he will have a clever mind, and there will appear,[421] in the citizens of his efforts[422] and in their children, what will sadden him.[423]

---

[416] Reading with Erfurt for Paris's *18th*.
[417] I do not understand this.
[418] This is perhaps because Mercury is in the seventh, the house of marriage.
[419] That is, until the distribution or direction reaches the aspect or body of the next planet. This should be the first square of Venus (cast from Aries), but for some reason Abū Ma'shar skips this and treats the Sun's trine into 0° Leo as the next aspect.
[420] The fifth is the eighth from the tenth (where the management currently is).
[421] Reading *videbitur* with Paris for *videbit* ("he will see," which has no object in the sentence).
[422] *Civibus operis*, which should probably read *civitabitus* ("cities") or *civitabitus operis* ("cities of his efforts/works"), which would connect the signification to the fourth house. Unless

78 After this, the Sun will receive the management from Saturn through the light of his first trine aspect, and he is the lord of the eleventh house from the Ascendant ([which] is also the second from the house of the king). **79** This signifies the extraction of assets, and expenses because of women: and this happens on account of the place of the Sun, and because he hands the management over to Venus.

80 And Venus receives [the management] through the light of her first square[424] aspect, from the light of the Sun's first trine aspect, and she is the lord of the Ascendant and is in its opposition. **81** Therefore, she receives the management from the Sun and gives it over to the Moon: and this signifies the entrance[425] of assets in this management, and contention with the rustics because of the king, and the nuptials of his son in connection with [some] woman, and the consolation of them.[426]

82 Then, the Moon receives the management through the light of her second square aspect, from the square[427] aspect of Venus. **83** And she manages [it], and she herself is the lord of the Midheaven, in the second from the Ascendant: it signifies the ruin of the king in that same year and in that same management, and all of these things [will be] in the management of the planets from the Midheaven up to the place of cutting through their rays, 73 days and one-half and one-sixth.[428]

84 Consider therefore by means of this, and convert in it what is necessary for you in the revolution of the years of the world, if you worked it out in the management of days through the projection of rays according to what I described about the houses and their lords, and the receiving of light and

---

it is a mistake, I am unsure of the role of *operis* ("work, effort") here. The phrase should probably read, "citizens of his cities."

[423] Abū Ma'shar seems to mean this: because of the management of Mercury (who indicates communication), Mercury's handing over to Saturn means letters will come to him. Then, because of Saturn's nature, and his being in the twelfth and ruling the fourth and fifth, the king will be sad (Saturn, twelfth) about his cities or citizens (fourth) and their children (fifth).

[424] This is an indication that the author has made a mistake, as the square of Venus should have come earlier; see my *Comment* above.

[425] This should perhaps be "extraction," as in **79**.

[426] Reading with the sense of Bonatti, for *ad locutionem earum* ("to their speech").

[427] See **82** above, and my *Comment*.

[428] This is equivalent to 73.66 days. At the rate Abū Ma'shar is moving the disposition (59' 08" per day), 73.66 days is 74° 44' 47". Abū Ma'shar seems to mean that there are almost 75° between the Moon's trine in Cancer, and the body of Saturn in Virgo. Currently, there are 71° 49' between them. So if the Moon's position is correct, Saturn should be at 27° 34' Virgo; but if Saturn's position is correct, then the Moon should be at 9° 54' Cancer.

the sending of it to the receiver in the seven ways (that is, the seven aspects: from the sextile and trine, or square aspect and the opposition).

85 After[429] this, know the light of the receiving and sending, and work with the lights of the contrary and inimical bad ones, and the lights of the friendly and agreeable or peaceful bad ones. **86** And speak likewise about the inimical fortunes: if they were inimical to the houses, [they signify] a scarcity of good, [but] if they were made peaceful [they signify] a multitude of good. **87** [And for the] lights of the bad ones, if they were inimical to the houses [it signifies] a multitude of evil, and if they were made peaceful, a scarcity of good.

Chapter 96: On the revolution of the years of the world, about which I did not make mention in my greater book on the revolution of years (that is, in the present one).

[Sahl's Example #2: 657 AD][430]

1 [A13-14] The falling of the significator[431] into the opposition of Mars signifies the shedding of blood, and [the falling] of the significator of the king and of the Sun likewise.

2 [A15] The remoteness of the bad ones from the angle, in the third and ninth, signifies the scarcity of men's fear, and battle, and[432] the scarcity of the king's fear.[433]

3 [A17] The impediment of the Sun signifies the detriment of Babylon.

4 [A20] The opposition of the bad ones to each other, namely when one of them is opposed to the other, signifies the occurrence of a great matter.

5 [A8, 15-16, 19] The falling of Mars under the rays of the Sun, if he[434] was the lord of the Midheaven, remote, signifies the end[435] through the sword and the going out of someone who seeks the kingdom.

---

[429] Now follows a version of the instructions from Ch. 94, **1-3**.
[430] Now the Latin text summarizes key points of Sahl's Example #2, from 657 AD. For a discussion of this example with charts, see Appendix C. In brackets I have inserted the Arabic sentence numbers which correspond to the Latin.
[431] In this case, Saturn.
[432] Reading the rest of this sentence with London.
[433] This is not quite right; see the Arabic.
[434] That is, Mars.
[435] That is, death.

[Sahl's example #3: 692 AD][436]

6 [A7-9, 12] And if the Sun handed over management to Saturn, and Saturn was in charge of the matter of the common people (namely so that the Ascendant is one of his signs, and he himself was in an optimal place from the Ascendant);[437] and if he handed over his management to the Moon from the Ascendant,[438] and she had the authority,[439] it will be feared for the king from the common people.

7 [A6, 13] And if Saturn were in charge of the matter in the year, and the lord of the Midheaven was impeded after the conjunction of Saturn (who does not receive it), it [will be] according to the standard of the preceding.[440]

8 [A3-4] If Venus and the Moon did not have testimony in the condition of the common people, and the lord of the Ascendant (it being Saturn) was in the eleventh, and with him the lord of the Midheaven, and the Moon (whose authority it is) in the Ascendant, and Saturn is made to have testimony in the condition of the common people. **9 [A6]** And Mars does not look at his place,[441] and is not received. **10 [A7]** Nor is the Moon received.

11 [A7-8] Saturn even signifies, from the place of the Moon (who is the luminary of the night) [from him], what the matter of the Sun[442] signifies. **12 [A8-9]** And through the handing over of the management and strength of the Sun[443] to Saturn, [it indicates] that the king will perish in that same year: for the common people (namely, his own) will kill him.

13 [A10] And in men there will be poverty and tribulation, and war, and severity. **14 [A12]** And this will arise in the eleventh year from the conjunction.[444] **15 [A13]** And this will be in the sixth month on account of the

---

[436] The following is a summary of Sahl's Example #3 (692 AD). For the full Arabic translation, with charts and discussion, see Appendix C.

[437] In the example, the Ascendant is Aquarius and Saturn is in the eleventh sign.

[438] This could mean that his ray falls into the Ascendant, but may refer to Sahl's monthly profection from the Moon in the Ascendant, to Saturn in the eleventh.

[439] The example is a nocturnal chart, so she is the sect light.

[440] In the example, Mars and Saturn are conjoined, which Sahl uses to time the civil unrest.

[441] Mars is in Sagittarius, so does not see his sign, Scorpio.

[442] The Ar. reads "year," but "Sun" is interesting because the next sentence (here and in Arabic) immediately points out the Sun's relation to Saturn. So perhaps the Latin text is correct.

[443] Reading with the Ar. for "Jupiter."

[444] Abū Ma'shar or the Latin translator has gotten this wrong; Sahl is pointing out that because Saturn is in the eleventh from the *Ascendant*, the indications will not be as harsh as

degrees of Saturn and Mars, and because there are 6° and [some] minutes between them.

16 [A14] And flock-animals will be successful in that same year, and the cold of their winter modest.[445]

[Sahl's Example #4: 719 AD][446]

17 [A3, 5, 9-10] Moreover (I have said), the occurrence of the fortunes in the Ascendant, and Mars falling from them, signifies the fitness of the matters of the common people, and better than that if Saturn were in an angle so that he would receive the fortune from the Ascendant, and he would be in charge of the signification, and Mars would fall away from him.

18 [A11] Moreover, (I have said), the moist and watery planets in the Ascendant[447] signify the coldness of the year in that same city, [and an abundance of] locusts.

19 [A12] And flock-animals [will flourish].[448]

20 [A13] And likewise if the fortunes landed in Aries with the Sun.

21 [A13] Moreover, the presence of the occurrence of the lord of the Midheaven in the third with Jupiter signifies the ease of the king and his orders[449] and rulership.

22 [A16] If Saturn were in Scorpio in the Midheaven, and the Ascendant [was] Aquarius, and he himself was the lord of the year and retrograde, it signifies the shedding of blood and pestilences.

23 [A17] If however the fortunes were conjoined to him, and especially from the Ascendant, they will extinguish these things and block them, and they will block that malignity or impediment, by the command of God.

24 [A17] And when the management reached the bound[450] of Saturn, it will stir up evil.

---

his example #2 (see above). On the other hand, in **A15**, Sahl suggests that there will be problems in the eleventh *month* of the year, due to a monthly profection to Saturn from the Ascendant. See Appendix C.

[445] The Ar. reads, "intense."
[446] See Appendix C for the full Arabic translation of this example, with charts and discussion.
[447] Namely, Venus and the Moon.
[448] Adding based on the Ar.
[449] *Missiones.*
[450] Or, his body (Ar.).

25 [A18] And if Mars looked at Saturn in this condition, it will destroy and will signify evil.[451]

[Rules from unknown source][452]

26 Moreover, the falling of Mars in Cancer signifies that the citizens of the clime of Iraq[453] will encounter severity from the authority, and likewise because this sign[454] belongs to their clime, and Mars is the significator of the authority.

27 The falling of the planets into the seventh from the Ascendant (which is its nadir, and the place of its enmity) signifies that the king will fight, if the planet had signification in its place over the kingdom or over the year.[455]

28 And if the first Lot[456] were in the Midheaven, not in its own dignity, and the second Lot [was in the fourth],[457] war will abound in the land generally.

29 And if a bad planet in the eleventh was pushing, and it impeded the lord of its own house from the square aspect or the opposition, it signifies the pillaging of assets and the spending of them.[458]

30 And the impediment of the lord of the Ascendant in a malign place in the Midheaven,[459] signifies the severity which will encounter the rustics (that is, from their rulers).

31 And the detriment of the Sun in the seventh or sixth or twelfth, or in whatever aspect it was with a bad one, [signifies the harm] of the king of Babylon. **32** And the impediment of the Moon signifies the bad condition of the king of the Romans or Greeks, and the strength of their enemies.

---

[451] The Arabic actually says that *even if* Mars aspected Saturn, "it would not corrupt what Venus and the Moon had indicated about the soundness of the condition."

[452] I cannot seem to locate the rest of this chapter in any of Sahl's remaining examples. Unfortunately, the text is often unclear, and I rely on Bonatti's version for certain readings (*BOA* Tr. 8, Part 1, Ch. 116).

[453] Lat. *Abrach*.

[454] Reading in the singular with Erfurt.

[455] This simply seems to mean, "if the planet in the seventh was the significator of the king or of the year."

[456] The first and second "Lots" are Saturn and Jupiter, respectively.

[457] Adding with Bonatti (*ibid*.).

[458] That is, the assets of the treasury: the eleventh is the second (assets) from the tenth (the king).

[459] Here, "place" must mean a counter-dignity like detriment or fall, as the Midheaven is not a malign place.

33 And the fitness of Venus in Pisces or any of her own houses, signifies the fertility of the regions of the Arabs, and their security. **34** And if a planet which receives her from the Midheaven, would hand over its own management to her from a similar place, and she is in an angle, not remote, and receiving [the management], and the Moon were in the sign of their profection from Scorpio,[460] the Arabs will contend in the kingdom, and will seek it from their own citizens, because she is conjoined to a planet in the Midheaven and fell into a good place, and better than that if the sign of the Midheaven matched [her] nature. **35** Therefore, Venus and the rest [of the planets], if they did not have testimony in the Midheaven, they are weakened and become impossible.[461]

36 The fitness of Venus signifies the fitness of the Arabs in their bodies and the fitness of their provisions. **37** If however she fell into the enmity of the Ascendant,[462] it signifies wars and diminishments in the middle of the year, with ignoble people and robbers.

38 If you found the Lots to be distinguished,[463] those whose significator they were, will prevail: this is that the Lot would be joined to its own lord in the watery triplicity. **39** And it agrees with[464] their presence in the revolution before the conjunction in any of the signs of the water triplicity is a minor conjunction (such as Gemini and its triplicity). **40** And it agrees with [their] presence before the conjunction, in the circle of the conjunction or in the two circles outside that triplicity (that is,[465] in Aquarius). **41** With this therefore, the citizens of the kingdom of this triplicity are strengthened.

42 And if Saturn were in charge, and the conjunction was in Scorpio, it will strengthen Scorpio. **43** If however he received the management of Mars, it signifies battles and the shedding of much blood. **44** And if he received the management of Mars from Scorpio, and he was in the Midheaven and he was in the charge of the year, and Mars was in the Ascendant, and he was in charge in the handing over of his management to Saturn in the Midheaven in

---

[460] This probably means the mundane profection from Scorpio itself (where the 570 conjunction took place), *not* the profection of the luminaries themselves.
[461] *Impossibiles.* This could mean that they have no *power* (from the verb *posse*), which is exactly what *impossibilis* means.
[462] In **27**, this was said to be the seventh. But see Māshā'allāh's *RYW*, Prologue **5-6**.
[463] Reading *insignes* for *in signis* and *in signo* ("in the signs," "in a/the sign"). The "Lots" here must be Saturn and Jupiter.
[464] *Congruet.* I am very uncertain about the meaning and even the sentence division of this paragraph.
[465] Adding "that is" with Erfurt. Paris and London simply say, "in Aquarius."

Scorpio, it signifies that the king will perish in the direction of the east, and he will leave his kingdom.[466]

45 And if in addition it happened that Venus was in her own exaltation or she was strong, and the conjunction was in Scorpio, it signifies the strength of the Arabs and [their] seeking in the kingdom, if God wills.

46 *The Book of Tested Things* by Abū Ma'shar is completed, with the praise of God, and ends happily with His support.

---

[466] Adding this last clause with Erfurt and London.

SECTION II.6:
"ABŪ MA'SHAR," *BOOK OF TESTED THINGS* (*LIBER EXPERIMENTORUM*)

Comment by Dykes. The identity of this book, and its history, seems to be a little vexed. According to Sezgin (pp. 142-43), Abū Ma'shar's Arabic *Book of the Revolutions of the Years of the World* had been translated into two forms: first, a work of the same name or going under the title of *Liber Experimentorum* (such as the present work), or possibly as *Flowers* (see Part III of this book). There also seem to have been various excerpts of the Arabic work floating around, or else this work is allegedly part of a larger one, etc. Adding to the confusion is the fact that both this work and the end of *Flowers* III (**9-12**) assert that Abū Ma'shar "has tested" (*expertus sum*) the rules in them, and the end of *Scito* (Section II.5 above) also ends with the appellation *Liber experimentorum*. So even the origin of the title is confusing.

But this first modern translation (from Paris BNF lat. 7282 [s. XV], 38va-39va) shows conclusively that Sezgin was wrong on both counts, at least so far as the present work goes. This *Book of Tested Things* is nothing other than a pastiche of two Latin translations, by John of Seville, of other works which appear in this book: (1) the prologue and first 6 chapters of Māshā'allāh's *RYW*, and (2) some of the significations of Mars in the signs, from *Flowers* VI.3. I include it here because its title occasionally crops up in secondary literature, and readers may find it interesting to know its actual contents.

However, there is one unusual feature to this work: sentence **26** includes the Hebrew names of the planets right along with the Arabic and Latin ones. This suggests a later, Jewish arranger, since neither Abū Ma'shar nor John of Seville does this, nor would they need to. And since it was compiled from two other sources already in Latin, why would a Latin-speaking reader need to be reminded of the Hebrew names of the planets, whether he was Jewish or not?

I will not add many footnotes here; the reader should consult the original texts elsewhere in this book, since they are dealt with in more depth there.

ಙ ಙ ಚ

Abū Ma'shar's *Book of Tested Things*, begins:

[RYW's Prologue]

2 May sublime God reveal to you the revolution of the years of the world, the knowledge and arrangement of which is that you should know when the Sun enters the first minute of the sign of Aries. **3** Know this, and [*illegible word*] you will establish the Ascendant and the four angles and the places by degrees and minutes, [and] you will establish the places of the planets by their degrees, and their being according to the order of the circle: namely, their direct motion, and retrogradation, and slowness, and elevation, and magnitude, and latitude, and the projection of their rays. **4** And know that a retrograde planet has no strength over good, until it goes direct.

5 After this, look at the Ascendant and the lord of the exaltation of the Ascendant, that is, the planet which is exalted in that sign[1] (if that sign was the exaltation of any planet), and the lord of the bound and the lord of the triplicity, and the place of the lord of the hour from the Ascendant, and of what kind are their places from each other, and how they are in a place inimical to the Ascendant or in a place of friendship. **6** Because if the lord of the Ascendant is inimical to the Ascendant, it signifies the detriment of that same clime, in accordance with the enmity. **7** If it were in the sixth it will be infirmity; and if it were in the eighth it will be death; and if it were in the twelfth, enmity according to the lord of the sign in which it is. **8** Likewise if it was the lord of the bound, exaltation, and triplicity—but [that] will be below what I have told you of the lord of the Ascendant.

[RYW's Ch. 1]

9 After this, look at the places of the luminaries from the Ascendant, and [from] the lord of the Ascendant. **10** Because if the revolution were in the day, and the Sun looked at the Ascendant or its lord, and the Sun was free from the bad ones, it signifies the strength and attainment or victory of the citizens of that same clime—and better than that if the Sun pushed to the

---

[1] Omitting "of the house in which the lord of the Ascendant is," as it does not quite fit grammatically and *RYW* omits it.

managing lord of the Ascendant,[2] and he himself was received in the place in which he was. **11** Because if it was just as we have said, the wealthy and powerful of that same clime will be humbled by and subjected to the master of that clime, and prosperity and peace and health will be bestowed upon him, with a good condition, by the will of God. **12** And likewise the Moon just as we said about the Sun, if the revolution were in the night. **13** And if the lords of the luminaries (or one of them) were looking at them from a strong place and received them, there will not be detriment in men, nor any disturbance, but they will be secure and calm, and seeking justice, and judging by means of it.

14 [But] if it were the contrary, say the contrary: that is, turn the good things which we said, into bad. **15** And after this look at the reception of the planets by each other, and their enmity in [their] portions, and pronounce according to what you saw of the lands and regions in which they were.

[RYW's Ch. 2]

16 And know that the signs signify parts of the world through their own natures, not through their own places. **17** Which if a part [of the world] agreed with the nature of a sign, it will be stronger for that. **18** Aries and its triplicity ([being] of the signs of the east), if it agreed [with the Ascendant], this will be stronger for their signification. **19** Taurus and its triplicity ([being] of the signs of the south), if it agreed with the sign[3] of the Midheaven, it will be stronger for their signification. **20** Gemini and its triplicity ([being] of the signs of the west), if it agreed with the sign of the angle of the west, it will be stronger for their signification. **21** Cancer and its triplicity ([being] of the signs of the north), if it agreed with the angle of the earth, it will be stronger for their signification. **22** Now,[4] we say these things (in that which we have said) if there were a planet in these places.

---

[2] *Disponenti domino ascendentis* (reading *disponenti* for *disponente*). This suggests that he could be pushing or applying to a victor over the Ascendant which is other than its domicile lord. But the equivalent sentence in *RYW* (Ch. **1, 3**) clearly has the Sun pushing his *own* management to the domicile lord.
[3] Reading the singular here and in the next few sentences.
[4] Reading as *nam*.

[RYW's Ch. 3]

23 And know that there are two divisions of the earth: the east and south is one, because they agree in heat; the other is the west and the north, because they agree in cold.

24 After these, the earth is divided by the seven divisions of the seven planets [in the climes],[5] according to the order of the circles. **25** From the circle therefore are known the planets according to the order [of the circles],[6] as [are] the lords of the hours. **26** Therefore, the first clime belongs to Saturn, and he is called *Zuhal* and *Shabbatai*;[7] the second clime [is] for Jupiter, and he is called *Tzedek*; the third clime [is] for Mars, and he is called *Madim*; the fourth clime [is] for the Sun, and he is called *Hammāh*; the fifth clime [is] for Venus, and she is called *Nogah*; the sixth clime [is] for Mercury, and he is called *Kôkab* or "the Secretary"; the seventh clime [is] for the Moon, and she is called *Lebanah*. **27** But the climes are according to the nature of the circle.

28 Finally, there is a well-known thing for every sign, of lands and cities, and likewise [there is] a bound: for perhaps there will be the city belonging to some sign, and the bound of some planet will conquer in [the city] in that same sign. **29** For example, Iraq—which is said to belong to Cancer, and its planet [is] Jupiter, who is said to be its planet because the place of Iraq is from the nineteenth degree of Cancer up to the twenty-sixth, which is the bound of Jupiter.[8] **30** And the alighting [or] presence of the fortunes in this place signifies the fitness of the citizens of Iraq in particular, and likewise the alighting of the bad ones signifies evil. **31** Likewise you will know this from the alighting of the fortunes and the bad ones in the rest of the bounds, as I have already put together for you. **32** And know all of this in the manner I have told you, because if you did this, it will not be concealed from you which sign or which bound a city belongs to.

---

[5] Adding with *RYW*.
[6] Adding with *RYW*.
[7] Lat. *Zoal et Sabtay*. These are the Arabic and Hebrew names for Saturn, respectively. The rest of the planets are only given in their Hebrew form.
[8] The bound of Jupiter in Cancer runs from 19°—25° 59' (i.e., up to 26°).

[RYW's Ch. 4]

33 After this, look at whether the ascending sign is either fixed or movable or common, and look likewise at the lord of the year. **34** Because if the Ascendant of the year was movable, revolutions of the quarters in the year will be necessary, and more than that if the lord of the year [was also in a movable sign]. **35** If it was a common sign, there will however be two revolutions necessary (that is, at the beginning of Aries and Libra), and more than that if the lord of the year [was in a common sign]: therefore, do [it] at the entrance [of the Sun] into the first bound[9] of the sign of Libra [as well], and do [it] at the movable [signs] through all quarters of the year. **36** But if the Ascendant was a fixed sign, the revolution of the year [in Aries] will be the one prevailing over all the quarters of the year, and it will be more strongly than that if the lord of the year was in a fixed sign. **37** If however the lord of the year were in a movable sign, the abundance or want which it signified will be only in the first quarter of the year, unless [such a] distinction is even in the second and third and fourth quarter: then it will be according to what that same quarter signified, in terms of abundance and want.

[RYW's Ch. 5]

38 Therefore, if you wished to know the lord of the year, look in the hour of the revolution (namely, when the Sun enters the first minute of Aries, and this is in March), at the planet which was stronger than the rest of the planets in its own place, and with more testimony, and make that one the lord in the clime in which you were; afterwards, with the seven climes.[10] **39** And I will explain to you the planets and their testimony, so that you may know the lord of the year.

[RYW's Ch. 6, 2]

40 Know that the stronger of the planets is the one which was in the Ascendant of the revolution, not remote nor falling.

---

[9] This should be "minute" (*minutum*) as with *RYW*, but the Latin reads *terminum*.
[10] *RYW* has the seven "planets" (see **26** above), but Paris 16204 has *plagis*, "regions."

[*Flowers* VI.3, *37-77*]

41 And if Mars were in Libra and his latitude were northern, it signifies [the darkness of the air and the severity of the winds. **42** And if it were southern, it signifies][11] a multitude of thunders and lightning. **43** And if he were eastern, it signifies a battle among the wealthy. **44** And if he were western, it signifies the occupation of the wealthy with scribes.[12] **45** And if he were retrograde, it signifies the severity of the things which I told you. **46** If he were direct, it signifies a multitude of wars among the wealthy.

47 And[13] if Mars were in Scorpio and his latitude northern, it signifies a scarcity of the waters. **48** If it were northern, it signifies the multitude of the waters of springs. **49** But if he were eastern, it signifies a multitude of infirmities in men, in the lower parts of their bellies. **50** If he were western, it signifies a scarcity of men's piety toward one another. **51** If he were retrograde, it signifies a multitude [of good][14] in that same season, and terror in the hearts of those doing business, and the multitude of their profit. **52** If he were direct, it signifies the multitude of the taking of [state] revenue, and the devastation of the houses of assets of the wealthy.

53 If Mars were in Sagittarius and his latitude northern, it signifies the beauty of the complexion of the air, and its goodness. **54** And if his latitude were southern, it signifies the profit of those doing business, and their acquisition. **55** And if he were eastern, it signifies peace and rest and security and a scarcity of wars. **56** And if he were western, it signifies the salvation of the trees and a multitude of field produce. **57** If he were retrograde, it signifies [a multitude of coughing and chest pains. **58** If he were direct, it signifies][15] the greatest pestilence falling upon the land and in animals of the coast.

59 If Mars were in Capricorn and his latitude northern, it signifies a multitude of snow and cold. **60** But if it were southern, it signifies heat in the air and its obscurity. **61** And if he were eastern, it signifies the killing of the Emperor of the Romans. **62** And if he were western, it signifies a multitude of pustules in men. **63** If he were retrograde, it signifies the severity of the yield

---

[11] Adding from *Flowers* VI.3, **37-38**.
[12] *Flowers* VI.3, **40** adds: "the wrath of the king."
[13] The next couple of sentences are different in *Flowers* VI.3, **43-44**.
[14] Adding with *Flowers* VI.3, **47**.
[15] Adding with *Flowers* VI.3, **53-54**.

(that is, that it will be sparse). **64** And if he were direct, it signifies the multitude of the vintage and olive oil.

65 If Mars were in Aquarius and his latitude northern, it signifies a multitude of cold and snows, and a multitude of locusts in its season. **66** And if his latitude were southern, it signifies obscurity and the severity of the heat. **67** And if he were eastern it signifies the joy of the wealthy. **68** If he were western, it signifies a multitude of tremors. **69** And if he were retrograde, it signi-signifies a multitude of hot wind and its impediment in trees. **70** If he were direct, it signifies the ruin of trees and a case of [vermin][16] in them.

71 And if Mars were in Pisces and his latitude [northern, it signifies the goodness of the air and its complexion. **72** If it were][17] southern, it signifies a multitude of locusts and a scarcity of their impediment. **73** And if he were eastern, it signifies the killing of the wealthy among each other. **74** And if he were retrograde, it signifies the salvation of men and the multitude of the profit of those doing business. **75** And if he were western, it signifies a multitude of infirmities in male and female slaves, and in low-class men. **76** And if he were direct, it signifies the salvation of sheep.

77 And know that I have already diligently tested the latitudes of the [superior][18] planets and their portions in the equinoctial circle, and the inferior planets. **78** And I have seen [the expected effects of the inferiors] sometimes come about, but sometimes go astray, and therefore I have not put them in this my book. **79** And I have already diligently tested everything which I have put in it. **80** Know this, and you should not overlook anything of these things which are written in it. **81** And test (concerning this) everything which you want of the judgments, because you will not go astray, if God wills. **82** *[The book] ends.*

---

[16] Adding with *Flowers* VI.3, **66**.
[17] Adding with *Flowers* VI.3, **67-68**.
[18] Adding with *Flowers* VI.3, **73-74**, here and in the next sentence.

PART III: ABŪ MA'SHAR'S *FLOWERS*

Comment by Dykes. Abū Ma'shar wrote at least three major mundane works in the 9th Century, apart from *Scito* (in II.5 above, if it was assembled by him). In no particular order, the first was (1) the *Report*, which was known in its Latin translation as the *Flowers of Abū Ma'shar* or the *Flowers of Astrology*; the second was (2) the *Indications*, which was never translated into Latin (so far as we know); and finally there was (3) the *Book of Religions and Dynasties* (BRD), known in its Latin form as *On the Great Conjunctions*. I have followed Yamamoto and Burnett in using the abbreviated titles *Report* and *Indications*, based on their discussion in their edition in *BRD*.

The full Arabic title of *Report* (the Arabic original of *Flowers*) was: *On the report of what the upper things (of what is heavenly) indicate for the effects in lower things, and what there is in the revolutions of the years and months and days and hours.* It was a popular work, being found in numerous manuscripts and printed editions. Part of its popularity was no doubt due to its clarity and brevity, unlike the sometimes sprawling *BRD*. The Latin translations of both *Flowers* and *BRD* were attributed to John of Seville. In my English version, I have primarily used the following manuscripts and editions:

- Augsburg, Erhard Ratdolt 1488 (printed edition).
- Venice, Johannes Baptista Sessa 1488 / 1506 (printed edition).
- Paris BNF 16208 (12th Cent.), ff. 53vb-59ra.

The Latin *Flowers* as we have received it, is missing some parts found in the Arabic, particularly in Book IV and four unnumbered chapters at the end of Book VII (which I will later translate in another book). I have chosen not to fill in these gaps, apart from making some corrections here and there where the Latin was unusual or seemed wrong: in those cases, I consulted Paris BNF Ar. 2588, ff. 4b-29b, a complete version of the Arabic. (In it, we may find that some interpretations in *Flowers* are rather different in the original Arabic.) Also, as the use of Book and chapter section titles is intermittent and incomplete in the Latin, I have added the Arabic ones (or my own, when missing): where they replace Latin titles, they have received sentence numbers; otherwise I have put them in brackets without numbers.

Flowers is a fine, general work in seven short Books, on the basics of interpreting annual Aries (and other seasonal) ingresses—it makes only fleeting references to conjunctional theory. It covers the following:

> Book I: Finding and interpreting the lord of the year, based on its natural significations, triplicity, and aspects.
> Book II: Natural significations of the planets.
> Book III: Prices, weather, disasters.
> Book IV: Malefics in the triplicities and in the twelve places.
> Book V: Fixed stars.
> Book VI: Superior planets in the signs, and in different solar phases and motions.
> Book VII: Nodes and comets.

There are numerous items of interest in *Flowers*, but I will point out three things here. First, Book I's method of finding and interpreting the lord of the year is clear and straightforward; its interpretation seems to depend particularly upon its closest aspect, which will show who is doing what to whom.

Next, Book V on the fixed stars provides both rare and puzzling material. In the first place, Abū Ma'shar discusses two ways in which to use the fixed stars: when a fixed star is on the lord of a house or the cusp of that house; or, what it means if someone is born that year with an Ascendant precisely on that star-cusp combination. For example, if some malefic fixed star is on the degree of the fourth of the ingress, then it connects the meaning of that star with fourth-house matters for that region during that year. Then, if that star also happens to be on the Ascendant of someone born that year, the native's life will be affected in accordance with those malefic, fourth- house indications.

On the other hand, Abū Ma'shar's list of stars is puzzling, because they do not all seem to exist, or at least their identities are not all known. Let us take Aldebaran as an example of a known star. Ptolemy lists Aldebaran as being at 12° 40' Taurus, and Abū Ma'shar gives it as 19° 15' Taurus, a difference of 6° 35'. Now, Ptolemy's value for precession (widely accepted for many centuries) was 1°/100 years, which means that the 6° 35' difference (or 6.58°) equates to 658 years: added to Ptolemy's dates for recording the stars around 137 AD, yields 795 AD. By the same token, Abū Ma'shar's values for Sheratan and Mesarthim (in the horns) are 6° 45' greater than Ptolemy's, a difference of 675 years (or 812 AD). So, we can assume that if Abū Ma'shar's source was following Ptolemy's rate of precession, its star positions were calculated for about 800 AD, only a few decades before *Flowers* was written.

So far, so good. But the list of stars in *Flowers*—all malefic—is a subset of a longer list of malefic *and* benefic stars in Bonatti,[1] also attributed to Abū Ma'shar. In that list, for virtually every star of a given nature, Abū Ma'shar says there is a star exactly opposite it in the zodiac, of the contrary nature! Again, Abū Ma'shar has Aldebaran at 19° 15' Taurus, being of the nature of Mars; but Bonatti's Abū Ma'shar also claims that at 19° 15' Scorpio is another star, *benefic*, of the nature of Jupiter! It is possible that this star is meant to be Antares, which (like Aldebaran) is one of the four classical "royal" stars. But not only is Antares not exactly opposite Aldebaran, the pattern of contraries continues throughout the list, with unknown (and unlikely) pairs of stars even being given contrary names, such as "Evil-doer" being paired with "Good-doer."

Another puzzling thing about Abū Ma'shar's list is that it is very different from another well-established star list used in nativities, originally in Persian and used by Rhetorius, "Hermes," Zarādusht, Māshā'allāh, and Abū Ma'shar himself.[2] This list is notable for including all or mostly first- and second-magnitude stars, the brightest. Why would Abū Ma'shar have generated a different list, perhaps based on Ptolemy, when he already had an existing one complete with delineations—for note that the list here (and the more complete one in Bonatti) lacks any concrete interpretive information apart from the stars' planetary complexions. For these reasons, most of the stars on the list are suspicious, but I have identified the ones I am certain of and offered suggestions for others.

Finally, Book VI lists numerous indications for politics and weather for each of the superior planets in the signs, under various conditions (being retrograde, direct, and so on). Although the structure of this list, and many of its contents, match those in *BRD* V, many of the sentences in the *Flowers/Report* give different information. I cannot account for these differences, but the reader should use caution in applying these significations to astrological weather theory.

ඃ ඃ ඃ

---

[1] *Book of Astronomy*, Tr. 8, Part 1, Ch. 109.
[2] See Burnett and Pingree 1997, pp. 146-51; also Lucentini *et al.* (2001). This list appears in my translation of Māshā'allāh's so-called *Book of Aristotle*, in *PN1*.

Here begins the treatise of Abū Ma'shar,
on the Flowers of Astrology:

[BOOK I: THE LORD OF THE YEAR]

[Chapter I.1: Introduction]

1 Abū Ma'shar said: It is good for you first to know the lord of the year. **2** And the knowledge of this matter is known at the hour of the Sun's entrance into the first minute of the sign of Aries. **3** And so, know the Ascendant at this same hour, as exactly as you can. **4** Verify the cusps of the twelve houses of heaven, because error falls in this if it is neglected.

5 And when you have done this, look at the lord of the Ascendant, along with the rest of the planets, [to see] which one then has more strength from the testimony of an angle of the circle.[3] **6** And [look at] whatever planet you found in the ascending, tenth, seventh, or fourth angle; afterwards, the eleventh, the ninth, [and] lastly the fifth. **7** And you should not prefer the Midheaven to the Ascendant, nor the fifth house to the ninth, but let it come to be according to the aforesaid account.

8 And if you found a planet in the Ascendant, you should not look for another (of those planets which were in the other places). **9** Likewise, if there were not a planet in the Ascendant, and there was one in the Midheaven, you would not look at the rest of the places of the planets. **10** Likewise if there were not a planet in the Midheaven, but [there was one] in the seventh, you would not look at the rest of the places. **11** Likewise if [there were] not one in the seventh, but [there was one] in the fourth, you would not care about the other places of the planets.

12 And the one which you found in these places will be the manager of the year if it had some dignity (namely either a house, or exaltation, triplicity, bound, or face).[4] **13** If however there were a planet in the Ascendant which had no dignity in it, and there was a planet in the Midheaven having a bound and face, since it doubled the dignity it is the one which is sought, and you would not seek another. **14** And if after these[5] there were a planet in the sev-

---

[3] This seems to mean simply that it is *in* an angle.
[4] This seems to mean, having a dignity *in the Ascendant*.
[5] That is, if there were nothing in the Ascendant or Midheaven which fit the criteria.

enth, to which is joined[6] a house, exaltation, bound, triplicity, or face, it is the one sought.

[Chapter I.2: Saturn as the lord of the year]

1 And so, Saturn being found to be the lord of the year, if he were in Aries or its triplicity, [the effect] will appear in the cities which the sign will be in charge of (of those which are in the division of the east), from the wealthy, the powerful, and those ruling, who do things through subtle skills and beautiful arrangements, and the display of amazing[7] things; and [there will be] prophetic signs without any haste, but rather with silence and a beautiful appearance in them. **2** Which if Saturn was of a good condition in [his] place, it will signify the things I have said: namely patience, sweetness, and inquiry into the matters of the whole of the common people and the rustics, and their obedience toward the king, with their humbleness toward him; and the extending of his voice (namely, his rule), and his loftiness. **3** And if he was of a bad condition, it signifies the death of the wealthy, and envy and hatred of them;[8] accusations and lack of concern, with the rustics' hatred toward them.

[Chapter I.3: If Jupiter looks at Saturn]

1 And if Jupiter were with him [by conjunction], their work in this which I have said will be with silence and religion and a show of faith, with justice and the observing of their instructions.[9] **2** If however Jupiter looked at him from esteem,[10] donations and services[11] will come upon the wealthy who are staying in the regions which are in the division of Aries or its triplicity, from those wealthy people who are in the division of the region of that sign in

---

[6] That is, it is in or has these dignities where it is—but perhaps in the Ascendant?

[7] Paris 16208 reads, "changeable" (*mutabilium*).

[8] This might also be translated as "their envy and hatred," i.e., wealthy people's *own* envy and hatred. But based on the following clause I think it refers to envy and hatred of others toward them.

[9] *Praeceptorum*. That is to say, they behave as they should. Nevertheless, the phrase about silence does not make sense to me. The Arabic reads, "And if Jupiter looked at Saturn from an assembly, it indicates (of the situations of Saturn) justice and fairness and religions, and the manifestation of the king and the laws."

[10] That is, from a good aspect (a sextile or trine).

[11] *Servitia*. "Service" was the medieval term for the feudal obligations a vassal had toward his lord. So the author means that tribute, obligations, and service will be offered up by representatives of one region toward another.

which Jupiter was; and every good thing in which they rejoice, will assist them from those same directions. **3** But if the aspect of Jupiter to Saturn were from the opposition, instead of donations and services there will be fear and contention from those cities of the region which are in the division of Saturn, towards the wealthy of those cities which are in the division of Jupiter; or contrariwise, towards those wealthy people who are in the division of Saturn, seeking war with them and their surrender; and this will be according to the amount[12] of the degrees of aspect which there are between Saturn and Jupiter, up to the hour in which the war and contrariety would be.[13] **4** And if the aspect of Saturn to Jupiter were from a square aspect, instead of wars there will be disagreement in matters between those who are in the districts of Saturn and Jupiter.

[Chapter I.4: If Mars looks at Saturn]

1 If, however, it were Mars instead of Jupiter, join to him the condition which I laid out for you concerning the condition of Saturn, with haste in the deeds of the wealthy who are in these regions, with a multitude of quickness and consideration, and a scarcity of piety, compassion, and lightness. **2** Which if his aspect were from a trine or sextile aspect, donations and services, joy, and happiness, will come upon the wealthy who are in the division of the sign of Aries and its triplicity, from the wealthy who are from the division of the sign in which Mars is. **3** Likewise, there will be good in all of their rustics, and their cities, and there will be sustenance[14] for them from those cities which are in the division of the sign in which Mars is, and things will be conveyed from[15] those cities, of the nature of things that are proper to those cities. **4** And I have already disclosed this to you in the greater book which I published on the natures of the climes and cities,[16] and what things are applied to them in terms of estates and the natures of their cities. **5** Which if Mars looked at Saturn from the opposition, instead of donations and services there will be evil (such as quarrels and enmities and contrarieties) between the wealthy of the regions of the sign in which Mars is, [and those of the

---

[12] This is from an Arabic phrase which can also simply mean "in accordance with."
[13] This suggests a symbolic timing system based on the number of degrees from exactitude.
[14] Or, "support" (*sustentatio*).
[15] Probably for reasons of commerce.
[16] For more on chorography, see *AW1*.

region of the sign in which Saturn is]; and those wealthy will go to them in order to defeat them, so they might be defeated and expelled. **6** And likewise, the things which were carried away from those regions will be cut off and destroyed,[17] and its citizens will be evil to the citizens of these regions. **7** Wherefore, if the aspect of Mars were from a square, instead of fear there will be disagreement and the cutting off of revenues[18] from those parts, and [the cutting off] of things sought; and there will not be a war appearing with this.

[Chapter I.5: If the Sun looks at Saturn]

1 And if it were the Sun instead of Mars, in addition to what I said about the condition of Saturn in the matter of the wealthy, [there will be] the claiming[19] of a kingdom and of splendid things; and the pursuit of heavenly[20] matters. **2** But if he looked at Saturn from a trine or sextile aspect, donations and services will come[21] upon the wealthy people who are in the division of Saturn, from the wealthy who are in the division of the sign in which the Sun was, and something good and things for sale will be conveyed from these parts, and rumors will come upon the rustics from those parts, making them glad; and what is brought [to market] in that year will be of the essence of the Sun. **3** And I have already expounded this in the *Book of Great Natures*.[22] **4** If however he looked at Saturn from the opposition, instead of donations and services there will be a fight and war in the seeking of those things which the Sun signified (of splendid things and a kingdom), in those cities; and what (of the good) was conveyed from them to these cities, will be cut off and destroyed, and what was coming in terms of rumors making [them] glad, will be converted into rumors terrible to hear. **5** And if the Sun looked at Saturn from a square aspect, there will not be an open war, but among the wealthy there will be strife and a disagreement of opinion between them.

---

[17] This must refer to breaking off trade.
[18] *Censuum.* The Latin *census* refers primarily to national revenues, particularly through taxes. The Arabic simply has "assets, funds, monies" (*amwāl*).
[19] *Petitio.* This might also be read as "seeking."
[20] Or, "celestial," which might imply astrological matters.
[21] Reading *venient* for *veniet*.
[22] *In libro naturarum maiori*, but reading with the Arabic here and below. Possibly his *Book of Natures* (Sezgin p. 149, #28).

[Chapter I.6: If Venus looks at Saturn]

1 And if it were Venus instead of the Sun, in addition to what I told you about the matter of Saturn (with respect to princes'[23] pursuits), there will be the pursuit of games, and rest and delight and singing, and the appearance of all games; and the appearance and manifestation of them for the citizens of those cities, among the wealthy and the rustics. **2** If however she looked at Saturn from a place of friendship, donations and services will come upon the wealthy who are in the division of the sign in which Saturn is, from the wealthy who are in the cities which are in the division of Venus: for every good thing will come from them, and what will be conveyed will be in the same season; and all will be inclined towards Venereal things. **3** On the other hand, if she looked at him from a place of enmity,[24] instead of donations and services there will be wars and contrarieties, and the wealthy themselves will march to their war [against] the wealthy,[25] and that of the good which was being conveyed from those cities will be cut off, and the assets of those parts will be decreased; and the revenues will be broken; and evil and foul rumors will come; and all good will be turned into evil, and all delight into sorrow;[26] and women and Venereal matters will be the root of all these things. **4** Which if she looked at Saturn from a square aspect, war will not be appearing, but there will be disagreement in matters between the wealthy themselves and the rustics and with the citizens of that same part, indeed so that if there had been a father in the cities which are in the division of Saturn, and a son in the cities which are in the division of Venus, disagreement will fall between them in everything that they will write down between them, and in business matters and other reasons; and likewise what I told you about the matter of the planets and their aspects in this book will be in all men and [their] relatives.[27]

---

[23] Reading *principum* with Paris 16208, for *principium*.
[24] I.e., from the square or opposition.
[25] *Pergent ipsi divites ad bellum eorum divitum*. It is possible this is a mistranslation for something like "the wealthy will march off to a war *because of their wealth*." But sentence **3** in the next chapter supports my translation here.
[26] Reading "sorrow" with Bonatti, instead of "thought" (*cogitatio*).
[27] *Propinquis*, which can refer to neighbors and generally people who are close.

[Chapter I.7: If Mercury looks at Saturn]

1 If however it were Mercury instead of Venus, [in addition to] what I said about the matters of Saturn (in the pursuits of the wealthy) there will be the seeking of grammatical pursuits, and of an abundance of speaking and philosophy and astronomy and medicine and dialectic: and their appearance at this time [will be] among the wealthy and the citizens of the regions which are in the division of Saturn. **2** And if Mercury looked at Saturn from a trine or sextile aspect, donations[28] and gifts[29] will come upon the wealthy who are in the division of Aries and its triplicity, from the kings who are in the cities which are in the parts of Mercury,[30] and things for sale and assets will be conveyed from thence, and the assets of revenues will be multiplied from them, and this will be praised in the cities which are in the division of Saturn; and more of these things will be Mercurial things. **3** But if he looked at Saturn from the opposition, instead of donations and services there will be contrariety and war; and these wealthy people will to go to war with those wealthy people; and whatever of the good was being conveyed will be cut off, and assets from those same parts will be decreased, and revenues will be decreased; and evil and foul rumors will come; and every good thing will flee away, and every evil thing will appear from out of those cities: this will be if Mercury is clothed with the bad ones (that is, if he had some complexion with them).[31] **4** And if he were clothed with the fortunes in the hour of his conjunction[32] [with Saturn], he will be of less evil and less impediment, but it will not block the action of the aspect of opposition [or] his impediment. **5** Know these things and understand it. **6** And if Mercury looked at Saturn from a square aspect, war will not appear; and there will be disagreement among the wealthy; and even disagreement between the rustics and the soldiers: and Mercurial things will be the cause of these matters. **7** And all of this is made clear in the *Book of Great Natures*.

---

[28] Reading *donationes* for *dona*.
[29] *Exenia*, which specifically means gifts to guests.
[30] Omitting *omne bonum*, "every good thing," attached awkwardly at the end of the sentence and a redundant emphasis of the good things that will happen.
[31] That is, by aspect or conjunction. Arabic writers occasionally refer to these mixtures as being "clothed" by another planet.
[32] Or simply, "connection," by whatever type of aspect or conjunction it happens.

[Chapter I.8: If the Moon looks at Saturn]

1 If it were the Moon instead of Mercury, then in addition to what I said of the matter of Saturn (concerning the pursuits of the wealthy), there will be an appearance of legates and explorers,[33] and the establishment of things for sale: this will be[34] in abundance among the wealthy and the rustics in that same time. **2** Which if the aspect of the Moon to Saturn were from the trine or sextile aspect, donations and services will come upon the wealthy who are in the division of Saturn, from those in the division of the Moon. **3** And things for sale will be conveyed from those cities, and assets and revenue (of those things which are of the nature of the Moon) will be multiplied and will be brought away to the cities in which Saturn is, and more of these will be Lunar things. **4** And if the Moon looked at Saturn from the opposition, instead of donations and services there will be war and contrariety, and the wealthy themselves will go to make war with those wealthy people; and whatever was being conveyed out of those parts will be cut off, and the revenues will be broken; and they will find evil and terrible rumors; and every good thing will disappoint, and be turned around, and become evil. **5** And if the aspect of the Moon to Saturn were from a square aspect, war will not appear, and there will be disagreement between the wealthy and the rustics, and contrariety between relatives because of Lunar things.

[Chapter I.9: On Saturn as the lord of the year in the triplicities]

1 If Saturn were the lord of the year and was in Taurus or its triplicity, all that I said before about the matter of Saturn will be in the wealthy and the rustics. **2** And the good or bad which was in the direction of the east [in the case of the fiery triplicity] will be in the direction of the south, in the cities which are in the division of the sign in which Saturn was, according to what I laid out for you. **3** If Saturn was [the lord of the year and] in Gemini or its triplicity, all that I said of good and evil will be in the direction of the west.[35] **4** If Saturn was [the lord of the year and] in Cancer or its triplicity, all that I said of good and evil will be in the direction of the north.

---

[33] *Exploratorum.* This can refer to examiners, those who search things out, or even spies.
[34] Reading *habundaverit* as a simple future statement.
[35] Reading *occidentalis* for *septentrionis*.

Figure 66: The fiery, eastern triplicity

Figure 67: The earthy, southern triplicity

Figure 68: The airy, western triplicity

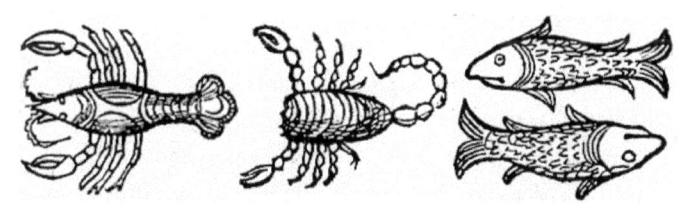

Figure 69: The watery, northern triplicity

[Chapter I.10: On Jupiter as the lord of the year in the triplicities]

1 If Jupiter were in charge of the year and was its lord, and he alighted[36] in Aries or its triplicity, there will appear, in the cities which he rules toward the east, religion, and rest, and the appearance of sects, and the observance of precepts, with justice and good works. **2** Which if Jupiter were then of a

---

[36] This simply means he is "in" Aries; this word translates the Ar. *nāzil*.

good condition, he signifies a multitude of assets for the wealthy and the goodness of their minds, and their joy, and the obedience of the rustics, and their esteem toward them in that same place. **3** Which if he were of a bad condition, it signifies the contrariety of those things. **4** And know that the workings for Jupiter in the planets' aspects to him comes to be just like the workings in the matter of Saturn, and equally the aspects of the planets to him.

5 Which if Jupiter were in Taurus or its triplicity, the appearance of the events will be in the direction of the south. **6** And if he were in Gemini or its triplicity, the appearance of those things which I said (of events), will be in the direction of the west. **7** But if Jupiter were in Cancer or its triplicity, the appearance of those things which I said (of events), will be in the direction of the north.

8 And know that this which I told you concerning the workings in the matter of Jupiter [are] as I have tested it; and that which I told you about the matter of Saturn, is of the secrets of the wisdom of the stars in the revolution of years.

[Chapter I.11: On Mars as the lord of the year in the triplicities]

1 If Mars were the lord of the year and was in charge of it, and he was in Aries or its triplicity, there will appear in the cities (over which he rules, toward the east), evil and injury and rapine and anger, and victory in war,[37] and flight, and[38] the use of the instruments of war. **2** And men will instruct their sons toward war and struggles and Martial things. **3** Which if Mars were then of a good condition in his own place, it will signify the victory of the king over his enemies, and those who contend with him, and the greatness of his heart and [his] quickness, and in addition the esteem of the rustics, and their obedience towards him. **4** And if he were of a bad condition, it will signify a scarcity of victory over them, and that they will conquer him, and a scarcity of stability concerning useful and just things, and his dejection[39] in everything in which he is engaged. **5** And the workings in the matter of Mars, and the aspects of the planets to him, is just like the workings in the matter of Saturn, and equally the aspects of the planets to him.

---

[37] Reading with Paris 16208 (*ira et victoria in bello*) for "and pretention to wars" (*imitatio ad bella*).
[38] Reading *et* with Paris 16208, for "in" (*in*).
[39] Or, "being thrown down."

6 If Mars were in Taurus or its triplicity, there will be an appearance of those things which I told you (of events), in the direction of the south. **7** If Mars were in Gemini or its triplicity, there will be an appearance of those things which I said (of events), in the direction of the west. **8** And if he were in Cancer or its triplicity, there will be an appearance of those things which I told you (of events), in the direction of the north.

[Chapter I.12: On the Sun as the lord of the year in the triplicities]

1 If the Sun were the lord of the year, it signifies the glory and loftiness of the king and the seeking [of] the height of kings,[40] and of all loftiness, and exhibiting advantage; and the advancement of love and affection in divine things, and a multitude of them in the rest of the men who are in the cities which are in the division of the sign in which the Sun is, each man according to the greatness of his nature. **2** Which if the Sun was in Aries or its triplicity, it will be in the direction of the east. **3** And if the Sun was of a good condition in his own place, it signifies the rectitude of the soldiers, and their justice, and their fitness, and victory over their enemies and over those who contend with them. **4** But if he was of a bad condition in [that] place, it signifies the scarce appearance of the wealthy[41] in those cities, over their enemies; and the fall[42] of their honor.

5 And if he were in Taurus or its triplicity, the appearance of these things which I said will be in the direction of the south. **6** And if he was in Gemini or its triplicity, the things which I said will be in the direction of the west. **7** If in Cancer or its triplicity, the appearance of those things which I said (of events) will be in the direction of the north.

[Chapter I.13: On Venus as the lord of the year in the triplicities]

1 If Venus were the lord of the year and she alighted in Aries or its triplicity, there will appear (in the cities which she is in charge of, [in the east]) a seeking of games and singing, and the works of instruments, and the teaching[43] of men in that very time, and the lust of the wealthy and rustics in this.

---

[40] This seems to mean that kings themselves will seek greater loftiness.
[41] Reading *divitum* with Paris 16208, for "riches" (*divitiarum*).
[42] Reading *casum* with Paris 16208, for *causam*.
[43] *Doctrina*. This accurately translates the Arabic, but it does not seem like a Venusian signification.

2 And if Venus was then of a good condition, it signifies the fertility of the year,[44] and joy, and the happiness of the wealthy and the rustics, and the achievement of the king,[45] and his victory over the enemies who contend with him. **3** If however she was of a bad condition, it signifies the contraries of all these.

4 If she were in Taurus or its triplicity, the appearance of these things which I said will be in the direction of the south. **5** If in Gemini or its triplicity, these will be in the direction of the west. **6** If in Cancer or its triplicity, these will be in the direction of the north.

[Chapter I.14: On Mercury as the lord of the year in the triplicities]

1 If Mercury were the lord of the year and was in Aries or its triplicity, there will appear, among the wealthy of the cities which those signs rule (in the direction of the east), the seeking of forms of wisdom, namely astronomy and medicine and philosophy; and subtlety in these things, and likewise among the rustics; and men will teach it to their sons. **2** Which if Mercury was of a good condition in that same place, it signifies excellence[46] and respectability among the wealthy, and their attainment and victory over their enemies; and the excellence and respectability of their judges, bishops, abbots, and the rest of such people; and [the excellence and honesty] of people doing business, children, and the concubines of the wealthy. **3** But if [he was] of a bad condition, it signifies the contraries of all these things. **4** And the workings in the matters of Mercury by means of the aspect of the planets to him, will be equally just as in the matter of Saturn.

5 And if he were in Taurus or its triplicity, these will be in the direction of the south. **6** If in Gemini, in the direction of the west. **7** If in Cancer, these things in the direction of the north.

[Chapter I.15: On the Moon as the lord of the year in the triplicities]

1 If the Moon were the lord of the year and was in Aries or its triplicity, there will appear, in the cities of which she is in charge (toward the east), a frequency of whisperings, with a multitude of legates and rumors, and the

---

[44] Reading *fertilitatem anni* with Paris 16208, for "loftiness of the mind" (*subtilitatem animi*).
[45] Reading *et rusticis, et adeptionem regis atque victoriam eius*, for *et rusticorum adeptionem regionis et victoriam eorum*.
[46] Lit., "beauty" (*puchritudinem*).

wealthy and the rustics will delight in these. **2** And if she was of a good condition it signifies the appearance of journeys and of roads, with the safety of those going on foreign travels, and the achievement of the wealthy with victory against their enemies. **3** If however she was of a bad condition, it signifies to the contrary for the whole [of the people]. **4** And the workings of the Moon, through the aspect of the planets to her,[47] will be just as in the matter of Saturn.

5 And if she were in Taurus or its triplicity, these things will be in the south. **6** If in Gemini [or its triplicity], in the west. **7** If in Cancer or its triplicity, these things will be in the direction of the north.

---

[47] Reading *eam* for *eum*.

[BOOK II: THE INDICATIONS OF THE PLANETS BY THEMSELVES]

[Chapter II.1: Significations of Saturn by himself]

Figure 70: Saturnus

1 Saturn is the significator of the wealthy, old things,[48] the religious, farmers, and old people. **2** Which if he were impeded at the hour of the revolution, then whatever belongs to him in his division[49] (in terms of things), will be destroyed. **3** If[50] he were in signs of men, it signifies that long-lasting infirmities will happen to [people], and the heating[51] of the body (namely from its drying out), and leanness, and quartan fevers, and flight, and confusion, and difficulties and fears, and death, the killing of the wealthy, and the destruction of provisions, and the wealthy will be made paupers, and paupers will die, and great men will be saddened. **4** Which if he was in an earthy sign, it signifies the destruction of those things which are in his division, like a scarcity of their seed, and detriment of trees from vermin befalling them (such as locusts). **5** And if he was in airy signs, it signifies a

---

[48] Or, "the ancients."
[49] Reading *in divisione* with Paris 16208, for *indictione*.
[50] Largely reading this sentence with Paris 16208, as the printed editions mix up and misspell some of the indications here.
[51] Reading *calefactio* for Paris 16208's *cabefactio* and the others' *tabefactio*, though it does not really make sense to me.

severity of cold with a multitude of clouds, strong frost, and the corruption of the complexion of the air, and thunders, and flashings of lightning-strikes, and impediment from a multitude of rains. **6** And if he was in a watery sign, it signifies impediments in rivers and seas [by] shipwreck; and animals of the waters will suffer. **7** But if he was fit and without some impediment they will be to the contrary of what I said. **8** Which if he was impeded at the hour of the revolution, judge destruction and impediment; and if he were made fortunate, judge fortune. **9** If however he was in a fiery sign, it was already stated what he has, above. **10** And if in earthy ones, it signifies tribulations and injuries from tremors and earthquakes and the destruction of cities, estates, and houses. **11** And if he was in an airy one, there will be a corruption of the air, and its darkness, with thunderings and lightning with fiery sparks and lightning bolts rushing through the air—and especially if he were made unfortunate in airy signs. **12** And if he was in watery ones, there will be impediment in waters, and shipwreck, and the overturning of boats on the sea, in which foreign travelers will be imperiled in the water; and animals of the waters will die. **13** If however it was a fortune instead of a bad one, turn your statement around and say good instead of evil; and instead of fear, say safety.

14 And look at the planet impeding him, which[52] is Mars and the Tail (namely, the Tail by conjunction, and Mars by aspect and conjunction), to see in which sign it is. **15** Because if it was in a fiery sign, the root of the impediment will be from fires and burning. **16** Which if it was in a sign of wolves,[53] the impediment will be from wolves. **17** If however the bad one was in an earthy sign, the root of the impediment will be from the direction of terrestrial things. **18** Your account will be likewise for the other signs.

19 If however a fortune looked at him in the hour of the revolution, judge strength and good. **20** If however a bad one looked at him [at the same time], judge according to the one which had more testimony, and you will not be disappointed, [nor] the work weak.[54] **21** In short,[55] know these things and operate through them, and you will not go astray, if God wills.

---

[52] From here to the end of the parentheses, adding from Paris 16208.
[53] Wolves are typically associated with Leo, but Abū Ma'shar might mean the bestial signs in general, which are: Aries, Taurus, Leo, Sagittarius, and Capricorn.
[54] Reading with Paris 16208 (which well matches the Arabic), and deleting the puzzling "because nature does her work unless she is absolutely, wholly weak" (*quare natura facit opus suum nisi sit prorsus omnino debilis*).
[55] Adding *prorsus* with Paris 16208.

[*Chapter II.2: Significations of Jupiter by himself*]

Figure 71: Jupiter

1 Jupiter is the significator of nobles and judges, bishops and consuls, the religious, good people, citizens, and sects.[56] **2** Which if he were impeded at the hour of the revolution, then all that is appropriate to him will suffer detriment. **3** Which if he was in human signs, it signifies the casting down of the nobles and the wealthy and the wickedness of their affairs, and the scarcity of their donations, and disappointment with their ranks, with anxiety towards their relatives; also the destruction of the kingdoms of Babylon and the Arabs; and a scarcity of assets with a multitude of curiosity;[57] and this will be upon the cities which are in the division of the sign in which Jupiter is; with the employing of falsehoods in the speech of men, with a displaying of evil and injuries; and the infirmities of bodies with the weakness of men's acquisition [of wealth]. **4** If however he was in an earthy sign, it signifies the destruction of lands and a scarcity of the fruits of trees, of wheat and barley; and a case of mold in the harvests. **5** If he were in an airy sign it signifies a scarcity of rains, and the corruption of the winds and the air. **6** If however he was in a watery sign, it signifies the destruction of those sailing the sea, with the scarcity of their acquisition, and the wasting of the waters, and a scarcity of fish. **7** And if he was in a bestial sign,[58] it signifies impediments in beasts

---

[56] This might refer to political parties in the modern sense, in addition to religious sects.
[57] *Curiositatis.* This seems wrong, but Paris 2588 is not quite legible at this word.
[58] Typically: Aries, Taurus, Leo, Sagittarius, Capricorn.

(especially in those which humans use, of those which pertain to that sign). **8** If however it was a fortune instead of a bad one, turn the statement around and say good instead of bad, justice instead of injury, loftiness [instead of] being cast down, honor [instead of] shame. **9** And look at the planet impeding him, to see in which sign it is, and commingle it, and speak according to what was expounded in the matters of Saturn. **10** And your description will be likewise for the assistance of Jupiter with a fortune or a bad one.[59]

[Chapter II.3: Significations of Mars by himself]

Figure 72: Mars

1 Mars [signifies] agents[60] of wars and the authors of battles, and those rising up against the king; also sudden death with a multitude of infirmities, severe fevers and the cutting of roads,[61] sheddings of blood, and attacks of fires, and the wasting of the river. **2** Which if he were in earthy [signs] he signifies the destruction of trees by the burning of heat, and strong, harmful winds, and the burning of new field crops in its own season. **3** Which if he was in an airy one, it signifies a scarcity of rains and the severity of the heat, and lightning bolts and harmful heat. **4** And if he was in a watery sign it signifies the dangerous, sudden shipwrecks of those sailing, with strongly-

---

[59] This seems to refer back to Saturn, in Ch. II.1, **19-20**.
[60] Or, "advisors" (*conciliatores*), which is closer to the Arabic.
[61] That is, highway robbery.

blowing winds. **5** And in a sign of four-footed things, he signifies impediment in four-footed [animals] which humans use, and of those which pertain to this sign itself. **6** Afterwards, look at the planet impeding him, to see in which sign it is, and commingle your statement about this according to what was said in the matters of Saturn. **7** And your description will be likewise[62] concerning the clothing of Mars with a bad one or a fortune.[63]

[Chapter II.4: Significations of the Sun by himself]

Figure 73: Sol

1 The Sun signifies great men, the wealthy, and honorable men. **2** Which if he were impeded at the hour of the revolution, everything which is his will suffer detriment, indeed so that they will be greatly impeded; and infirmities will happen to the common people as a whole. **3** Which if he was in human signs, the impediment will be in those things (of men) which pertain to him. **4** If in an earthy one, it will be in those things which are of the substance of the earth and metals. **5** If he was in an airy one, the impediment will be in the air. **6** If in a watery one, those things which are of animals of the water will suffer impediment. **7** And if it was a fortune instead of a bad one, then turn the statement around and say good instead of bad. **8** And look at the planet impeding him, as above.

---

[62] Reading *similiter* with 1488 for *simili*.
[63] Again, a reference to Ch. II.1, **19-20**.

[Chapter II.5: Significations of Venus by herself]

Figure 74: Venus

1 Venus[64] is the significator of women and eunuchs and the [marriage] engagements of girls. **2** Which if she were impeded at the hour of the revolution, everything which is hers will be impeded. **3** If in human signs, whatever is hers (among men) will suffer impediment. **4** If in earthy ones, those which are of the substance of the earth. **5** If in an airy one, those which are in the air. **6** And if in a watery one, those which are of the substance of water. **7** And if it was a fortune instead of a bad one, then turn the statement around and say good instead of bad. **8** And look at the planet impeding her,[65] as above.

---

[64] I have added to this sentence from Paris 16208.
[65] Reading *eam* for *eum*.

[Chapter II.6: Significations of Mercury by himself]

Figure 75: Mercurius

1 Mercury is the significator of writers, arithmeticians,[66] those doing business, children, and masters of works. **2** Which if he were impeded at the hour of the revolution, everything which is his suffers detriment. **3** And your description will be about those things which pertain to him, and about what he reveals in human, earthy, airy, watery, [and] bestial signs, also according to the aspect of the fortunes and bad ones to him, and according to his being clothed with them, just as was said for Saturn.

---

[66] A category that would include anyone using mathematics and calculation (including astrologers).

[Chapter II.7: Significations of the Moon by herself]

Figure 76: Luna

1 The Moon is the significator of legates and legations, and the whole of the common people, and their livelihood and matters day by day.[67] **2** Which if she were impeded at the hour of the revolution, everything which pertains to her will be destroyed. **3** And your description concerning her and concerning everything which is hers will be[68] according to her presence in the signs (human, airy, earthy, watery, bestial), according to the aspect of the bad ones and the fortunes to her, and their being clothed with her, [and] from which signs they look at her, just as was said about the others. **4** Know and understand this secret, and there is nothing which could be kept hidden from you, should you wish to investigate it (if God wills).

---

[67] Reading with the Arabic, as the Latin reads confusedly. For example: "...common people and their movement of self-control and relaxation every day" (1488). Paris 16208 seems to contain *vieret*, which could be a misspelling for *victus* ("livelihood").
[68] Omitting *sunt*.

[BOOK III: PRICES, WEATHER, WAR, DISASTERS]

Chapter III.1: On expensiveness and cheapness[69]

2 However, you will know these things from each of the superior planets, since every burden is of the work of Saturn, and all ease is of the work of Jupiter. **3** Therefore, however often you saw Saturn (in the revolution of the quarters[70] of years) in a sign in which there was a conjunction which signified a sect,[71] and Jupiter (or Venus, along with the Head), did not look at him, without a doubt this will be of the signals of severity. **4** Therefore, commingle your account of him [using these factors], and do not have fear. **5** And if it were so that the Tail was with [Saturn] in one [and the same] sign, judge the burden of the yield[72] and the terror of men, unless Jupiter aspects this place at the hour in which the Tail is being separated from him. **6** Moreover, the years that signify famine, are themselves those over which Saturn is in charge, in the conjunction or opposition in which the revolution was,[73] and more severely so if he was in the conjunction or opposition of Mercury—this is [in the revolutions] of years. **7** For the months, if you saw him in the ninth place or the third at the conjunction or opposition, this will be a signal of ease.

8 Therefore, know the Ascendant of the prevention or the conjunction. **9** After this, look at its lord: which if [the lord] were increased in light or course, then the yield will be increased in price in that same month; and likewise, if it was increased[74] in the Midheaven, the price of the yield will be increased in the same way. **10** And if it was decreased in course, the price of the yield will be decreased. **11** And if it was going to its own descension,[75] likewise the price of the yield will go down. **12** But if it was in the subterrane-

---

[69] The original title in the Latin was "On the severity and ease of the yield." For more in prices, including likely sources of this chapter, see *AW1*.

[70] Adding with Paris 16208.

[71] That is, a mean Saturn-Jupiter conjunction signifying a new religion, which typically happens at the conjunction of a triplicity shift.

[72] That is, the expensiveness of the agricultural yield.

[73] That is, the New/Full Moon preceding the annual (and perhaps seasonal) revolution. For more on prices, see *AW1*.

[74] Reading *auctus* for *aucta* as above, referring to the lord of the *syzygy*. *Aucta* would refer to the Moon (which the text does not specify), but one is usually only interested in the light and course of the Moon for this sort of thing.

[75] That is, its fall.

an angle, or in the seventh [angle], the price will be stable, [remaining] in its own condition.

13 However, in other matters besides wheat and barley, you should look at the manager of the year,[76] to see if it was made fortunate; look even to see in what kind of sign it is, and what the essence of that same sign is. **14** Which if it were of the essence of fire, this will be in silver and gold, and in everything which is worked through fire. **15** Which if it was in the earthy ones, this will be in earthy things. **16** If however it was in a sign of air, then this will be in animate things: look at the place of that same sign from the Ascendant, and speak about that.[77] **17** Look to see if it was in watery signs: this will be in animals of the water, and in everything which comes from out of it. **18** However, all of these [are] places in which there will be every burden of the yield. **19** If however [the lord of the year] were in Aries or its triplicity, it will be in the direction of the east; if in Taurus or its triplicity, in the direction of the south; if however in Gemini or its triplicity, it will be in the west; but if in Cancer or its triplicity, it will be in the north.

20 Consider the market value of the yield when the Sun has entered the first minute of Aries or the signs in which the exaltations of the planets are (which are the movable ones).[78] **21** Now, the alighting of the Sun onto the first minute of Aries is stronger and more lofty than all of his [other] alightings in the beginnings of the movable signs,[79] and more lofty than his alightings at the beginnings of each sign.[80] **22** Know[81] this secret in market value, and do not pass over it, and do not look at [anything] else. **23** And if you wanted to have the knowledge of some thing by [its] name, look at the planetary significator of that thing and the market value of that thing, [and] in what kind of sign it is; and look at what belongs[82] to that sign and to that planet. **24** And I have already made that clear[83] to you in the *Book on the Na-*

---

[76] The lord of the year.
[77] This seems to mean that the house will identify what kind of person it is, whether children (fifth), spouses (seventh), and so on.
[78] In other words, the seasonal ingresses.
[79] Reading the rest of this and the next sentence with Paris 16208, for "These are his alightings in the mobile signs."
[80] That is, monthly ingresses.
[81] Reading this sentence with Paris 16208.
[82] Reading with the Arabic for an illegible word in Paris 16208; 1488 is relatively complete but rather choppy.
[83] Reading with the Arabic for an illegible word in Paris 16208.

tures of the Signs. **25** Therefore, know and work through that, and you will discover [it], if God wills.

Chapter III.2: On the knowledge of rains

2 But the knowledge of this matter is from Mars. **3** If he was in some one of his own houses at the hour of the revolution, this will be an indication of a multitude of rains. **4** And if he was in a house of Saturn, this will be a judgment of a scarcity of rain. **5** But in the other houses of the other planets it signifies a middling amount of rain.[84]

Chapter III.3: On war and civil unrest[85]

2 The knowledge of battles and war is from the place of Mars, in his assemblies[86] with Saturn, from his opposition, or a square: for if it were thus, it signifies war. **3** And if was Jupiter instead of Mars, this will signify war provoked for justice, and those who say they were moved to war based on that.[87] **4** And likewise the coursing[88] of the rest of the planets ought to be mixed in, in accordance with their natures. **5** And the nature of the images in the signs should be looked at, according to what we said in the *Book of Images*.[89]

---

[84] Amusingly, ibn Ezra comments that he has tested this rule but was unsuccessful—nevertheless, he reports it "so that you will not trust [Abū Ma'shar's] book" (Sela, p. 93).
[85] The Latin title was, "On war and battles."
[86] *Comparationes* (lit., "comparisons"), a very literal translation of the Arabic *muqāranah* for a conjunction or assembly, although Paris 2588 uses a word for Mars being with Saturn by "body."
[87] Reading the end of this sentence somewhat loosely, so as to match the Arabic more closely.
[88] Reading with the Arabic, for "conjunctions."
[89] Exact identity of this book unclear.

Chapter III.4: On the frequency of death and disease[90]

2 And the multitude of death and pestilence is known from the Ascendant of the year, and[91] what was ascending in any of the beginnings (mention of which came before), such as the sign of the present conjunction or the sign of the conjunction which signified a sect: namely, if these and their lords were impeded, there will be a powerful pestilence, and death in proportion to [the impediment]. **3** Consider therefore, because you will find it, and you would be able to judge death in one-half of men, or one-third, or one-fourth, [and] you will not go astray, if God wills.

Chapter III.5: On earthquakes and sinkholes and flooding and submersions[92]

2 Earthquakes and floods are known from Saturn, if his rays were in signs of the first conjunctions and [in] their Ascendants: that is, in of those signs whose description has preceded [this], which are the beginnings, namely, the sign of the conjunction, that is, [or][93] the Ascendant of the year, and the sign of the conjunction of a sect, or its Ascendant.[94] **3** For if Saturn were in them, and projected his own rays to them[95] from the opposition or from a square aspect, and in addition he would be impeded, [then] look to him to see if he were in earthy signs: he makes sinkholes[96] and earthquakes and famine; in the airy signs, snows and cold, [and] darkness of the air, and its corruption, the blowing of winds eradicating trees and palms; if in watery ones, submersions and floods. **4** These happenings will be in proportion to his own strength and weakness.[97]

---

[90] The Latin title was, "On pestilence." In this paragraph, Abū Ma'shar seems to identify three charts whose Ascendants must be examined: (1) the Aries ingress, (2) the New/Full Moon which preceded the ingress, and (3) the most recent Saturn-Jupiter conjunction *or* the most recent triplicity shift. It is not obvious that he means (2), but his use of the word "beginning" is a typical phrase referring to the New/Full Moon.
[91] Reading with the Ar. for "that is."
[92] The Latin simply has, "On earthquakes."
[93] Adding "or" to match the next sentence.
[94] The Arabic is much briefer: "If his rays were in the aforementioned signs (I mean, the beginnings)."
[95] *Ea*, indicating whole-sign aspects.
[96] Reading with the Ar. for "darkness of the air."
[97] The printed editions make this sentence continue with statements about fiery signs, as though still speaking of Saturn, but Paris and the Arabic continue with the fiery signs in the next section.

[Chapter III.6: On the knowledge of fires in the air and horrible signs][98]

1 However, the knowledge of fire in the air, and terrible prophetic signs, and horrible things which are in the air—these are known from Mars if he were in charge of[99] any of the years mentioned before. **2** Then,[100] it will have happened [if], in that same year in which he was in charge, he would be in charge in the same sign which he was in charge of in the aforesaid beginnings. **3** In proportion to his strength in that same year, [so] will be the strength of those things which will happen, in terms of the aforesaid sparks and prophetic signs.

[Chapter III.7: How many ingress charts to use][101]

1 And know that [in] a year, if its Ascendant were in its own strength in that same year (that is, if the Ascendant were a fixed sign), at the hour of the Sun's alighting upon the first minute of Aries, you should not revolve the quarters in that same year. **2** For the Ascendant of that year would be able to suffice for you, since the trust[102] in this matter is a fixed sign. **3** For it will not require a revolution of the quarters and months except for [the purposes of discovering] market value especially. **4** For that reason,[103] know this. **5** On the other hand, if it were a common sign, it is always necessary that you revolve the year for the hour of the Sun's alighting upon the first minute of Libra. **6** But if the Ascendant of the year were a movable sign, it is necessary for you to calculate the Sun's entrance in every quarter of the revolution. **7** And you will operate through these figures[104] just as you have operated in the beginning of the year: that is, at the time of [the Sun's] alighting upon the first minute of Cancer, and the first minute of Libra, and the first [minute of] Capricorn. **8** Know this, and operate by it, because you will find [what you

---

[98] This chapter should be compared to BRD VIII.2, **7**, and al-Rijāl's Ch. VIII.1, **15** (which has the same information).

[99] That is, if he was lord of the year. The Arabic refers to his "governorship." I have simplified the end of this sentence somewhat, as the Latin makes unusual sentence breaks that do not really help one understand what Abū Ma'shar means.

[100] This sentence makes more sense than the Arabic, which is barely comprehensible.

[101] This section had no Latin or Arabic title, but it is different enough that I have given it one.

[102] *Fiducia*.

[103] Reading *propterea* with Paris for *praeter cetera*.

[104] That is, "charts."

want] in every one, since you have operated in the Ascendants of these quarters equally just as you did in the revolution of the beginning of the year.

[Comment by John of Seville][105]

9 And you should not turn against this, because I have zealously tested what the ancient sages said, and I have found a portion that comes out [successfully], [and] a portion that goes astray; and this is on account of the diversity of aspects which is variable in every month. **10** For they said you should not do for the Ascendant of the quarter and for the Ascendant of its month just as you do for the Ascendant of the year: because you do it for the Ascendant of the year through the planet which had more testimony and [was] strong in [its own] place. **11** For they said it is not necessary that you do likewise in the Ascendants of the quarters, but you should look at a planet strong in its own place—not by the multitude of the testimony, but, however, by the goodness of the place.[106] **12** Others said you should do it through the lord of the conjunction or prevention which was before this.[107]

---

[105] At this point in Paris 2588, Abū Ma'shar adds a few summary sentences which bear little to no relation to **9-12**: so what follows must be a comment by John.

[106] In other words, the ancient sages (or one group of them) said that for the lord of the year we ought to look at the planet that (a) has more testimonies by dignity and rulership and (b) is strong in his own place; but that for the quarters and months, we should look at (b) alone. John does not clarify what he finds right or wrong as the result of his testing, but Abū Ma'shar himself does seem to follow (a) in Ch. I.1 above.

[107] Ptolemy would be an example of this, as explained in *AW1*.

[BOOK IV: THE MALEFICS IN THE SIGNS & PLACES]

[Chapters IV.1-4: Saturn in the triplicities][108]

[Chapter IV.5: Mars in the fiery triplicity][109]

[Chapter IV.6: Mars in the earthy triplicity][110]

1 And if he did not look at the Ascendant, the tribulation will be particularly in the cities which are in its[111] division. **2** And do with the aspect of the planets to him, just as you did in the workings of the planets to him in Aries and its triplicity. **3** And speak about the direction in which the impediment will be, [that it is] because of those things in the essences of the signs in which the planets looking at the lord of the quarter, are—just as I have demonstrated in the chapter on Saturn.

[Chapter IV.7: Mars in the airy triplicity]

1 If however Mars were in Gemini or its triplicity, and Mars himself was the lord of the year, and direct in an angle, he signifies war and the shedding of blood, and contention (because that triplicity is of a human likeness). **2** If retrograde, [it signifies] its[112] strength and severity. **3** But if he was not in the angles and he is direct, and he looked at the Ascendant, it signifies infirmity coming from winds and blood. **4** And [it will be] more severe in the region which was of the division of the sign in which he alights, within the triplicity.[113] **5** If retrograde, [it signifies] pestilences. **6** And if he did not look at the

---

[108] The Latin versions make a sudden break here, and jump immediately to the middle of Mars in the earthy triplicity. An examination of Paris 2588 shows that this whole discussion of the malefics in the triplicities is virtually identical to *BRD* II.8, **21-29,** rather than the shortened form appearing in John's translation. (I should also point out that John makes it seem as though Abū Ma'shar deals fully with Saturn first, then with Mars; but in the Arabic, he deals with each triplicity in turn, describing Saturn in it first and then Mars.) So, I will only supply the missing chapter headings and continue with the Latin translation. To see very similar versions of what would have appeared here in the Arabic, see *RYW* Chs. 45-46, *Scito* Chs. 80-83, and *BRD* II.8, **21-29.**
[109] See footnote above.
[110] See footnote above.
[111] Or perhaps, "his."
[112] I.e., the war's.
[113] Reading *infra triplicitate* with Paris 16208, for *extra triplicitates*.

Ascendant, and was direct, [it signifies] a multitude of burnings, and impediments by fires, and malign infirmities for men.

[Chapter IV.8: Mars in the watery triplicity]

1 If Mars were in Cancer or its triplicity, and he himself was the lord of the year and direct, battles and contention will happen in the land of the Arabs, and blood and pestilence, and overflowing death; and regarding the king, a change from region to region will be feared. **2** If however he is not in an angle, and he looked at the Ascendant, and he is direct, in this case one must beware of speaking about it.[114] **3** If retrograde, it signifies the severity of the matter. **4** But if he did not look at the Ascendant, this will be particularly in one place.[115]

5 Regarding the aspect of the planets to him, it is just like in the chapter which preceded, regarding Saturn and equally the aspect of the planets to him.

[Chapter IV.9:] The conjunction of Saturn and Mars[116]

1 If they were conjoined in the Ascendant of the revolution of some year, they signify a general evil in the rustics. **2** And if they were conjoined in the second from the Ascendant of the year, it is a sign of the destruction of their assets and their houses,[117] and the memory of the wealthy will be given over to forgetfulness,[118] and their slaves and soldiers will be haughty, and will observe [only] middling faithfulness [with] them. **3** And if they are conjoined in the third, they signify the destruction of the houses of religion and the descent of horrible things upon those worshipping God. **4** But if they were conjoined in the fourth, the destruction of buildings and mansions and farms and estates. **5** If in the fifth, a multitude of destruction in children and changes in the hearts of friends. **6** In the sixth it signifies impediment per-

---

[114] *In hoc cavendum est loqui in eo.* This does not parallel the Arabic in any way.
[115] I end the sentence here, as the next one mirrors similar closing sentences above.
[116] The Latin originally added, "in the twelve signs." It is unclear to me whether this refers to mean or true conjunctions.
[117] This probably refers to "treasuries," as "house of assets/money" is an Arabic idiom for a treasury.
[118] The Arabic is a bit clearer: "the obscurity of the mention of the wealthy": in other words, they will not be highly esteemed or cared about.

taining to animals and all four-footed [animals] which men use, and to their male and female slaves. **7** In the seventh, the falling of evil and quarrels between partners and spouses, and those contending amongst themselves, and those seeking the departure of their enemies. **8** In the eighth, a multitude of those wandering, and their death and poor health, and being occupied;[119] and in the petitions for those things which are sought on account of what is left over from the dead; and death will fall upon those who go astray in that year. **9** In the ninth, roads will be destroyed, and journeys to distant places (and more in these), by which one reaches the greater and famous[120] houses of prayer. **10** In the tenth,[121] the destruction of the condition of kings and the wealthy, and the death of a great king. **11** In the eleventh, destruction falling between friends; and everyone having a friend will be changed concerning his own associate. **12** In the twelfth, impediment descending upon all four-footed things, and tribulation will fall upon all sellers of beasts.

13 And everything that I have told you about this, will be in the regions which are in the division of the sign in which they are conjoined. **14** Even should they be joined in signs and in the bound of some planet, then the tribulations will be in the cities of the division of that same planet whose bound it is.

---

[119] This has connotations both of being busy, and being preoccupied or distracted (or worried).
[120] *Nominatas*, lit. "named." This refers to destinations with special names, like the Church of St. Mark in Venice (an example from Bonatti).
[121] Paris 16208 (and the Arabic) reads, "Midheaven."

[BOOK V: ON THE FIXED STARS]

[Chapter V.1: On the knowledge of the fixed stars][122]

2 I will reveal the knowledge of the fixed stars and their workings to you.[123]

3 Know therefore that in the head of Aries are two stars: one of 13° 25',[124] and the other 14° 25',[125] and their latitude in the north, and their complexion of the complexion of Saturn and Mars.

4 The Pleiades, of the complexion of Mars and the Moon, and they are in Taurus between 9° 55' up to 13°; their latitude in the north, 6°.[126] **5** Aldebaran, whose nature is of the nature of Mars, is in Taurus, 19° 15'.

6 In Gemini is a star, 18° 55' (in another book, 16°),[127] whose latitude [is] southern, and its complexion is of the complexion of the Sun.

7 In Cancer are two stars, of which one is 12° 55', of the complexion of Mars; and the other 2° 55', of the complexion of Saturn.[128]

8 In Leo [are] two, of which one is 15° 55', the other 7° 22'.[129] And their latitude [is] northern, of the complexion of Saturn.

9 In Virgo is a star of the complexion of Mars, 7° 01' (in another [book] 4°),[130] and another of the complexion of Saturn, 25°.

10 In Libra is a star of the complexion of Saturn, 26°.[131]

11 In Scorpio [are] three stars, of which the first is in 1° 03',[132] another 9°; another 8° 07', and their complexion [is] of Mars.[133]

---

[122] The Latin reads, "On the fixed stars which operate in revolutions and nativities."
[123] See my introduction above for comments on this section.
[124] Mesarthim.
[125] Sheratan.
[126] This seems to be a mistake for the word "and": in Arabic *abjad* numerals, the letter *waw* ("and") means "6."
[127] Perhaps Alhena.
[128] These are most likely Castor and Pollux. Paris 2588 has it that the first star is in 15' of Cancer, and the second in 4° 15', which equate to 23° 50' and 27° 50' Gemini, very close to Ptolemy's values. Paris then adds another star of the temperament of Saturn, at 15° 55'.
[129] Perhaps Adhafera. But Paris 2588 has only one star, at 1° 15' (which would be 24° 50' Cancer in Ptolemy's time).
[130] This is probably Vindemiatrix: Paris 2588 has it at 20° 15' Virgo, or 13° 50' in Ptolemy's time (the *Almagest* has 12° 10' for Vindemiatrix).
[131] Perhaps Zuben Elgenubi.
[132] Perhaps Zuben Eschemali.
[133] Paris 2588 lists these stars as: 1° 02', 8° 09', and 28° 04'.

12 In Sagittarius [are] two small ones, of which one [is] 19° 02', another 21° 01', another, 25° 08';[134] and they are of the nature of Saturn.

13 In Capricorn [are] two, of which one [is] bad,[135] 27° 02',[136] another 29° 05', of the complexion of Saturn.

14 In Aquarius [is] one, 9° 04', of the complexion of Saturn.[137]

15 In Pisces [is] one, of 4° 07' (in another [book], 4°).[138]

[Chapter V.2: On the lord of the Ascendant with one of the stars][139]

2 If therefore you saw the lord of the year joined to any of these stars which I stated (that is, if you saw it in a like [degree] to these degrees which I have distinguished), know that impediment will fall upon kings and the wealthy and the nobles, and there will be grief and malign thoughts in them, and infirmities from headache and maniacal behavior.

3 Which if one of these fell onto the degree of the Ascendant, [then] if someone were born in that same year and his Ascendant were in those degrees of that sign, he will be a bad boy and be made unfortunate, [and] have many illnesses (of which more will be in the head).

[Chapter V.3: On the lord of the second with one of the stars]

1 And if the lord of the second from the Ascendant of the revolution of the year fell with these stars which I told you, know that impediment will fall upon the houses of assets, and the assets of the wealthy and the nobles will be destroyed, and complications and disturbances of the mind will fall upon them, and they will judge themselves to be paupers, with grief; and malign infirmities will happen to them in the neck and ears, like catarrh and deafness. **2** And [likewise] if any of these [stars] fell onto the degrees of the second from the Ascendant of the revolution of the year. **3** And [if] a boy were born in that year, and [this] sign of the revolution would be the As-

---

[134] Perhaps Rukbat. Paris has 24° 08'.
[135] But "The Evil One" (*mala*) could also be its name. Bonatti lists a good star directly opposite this one (in Cancer), which he said is called *bona*, ("The Good One."). This designation is missing in Paris 2588.
[136] Perhaps Achernar. Paris 2588 has 25° 40' (19° 15' in Ptolemy's time).
[137] Paris 2588 adds another star at 29°.
[138] Paris 2588 reads either 14° 04' or 17° 04 (unclear).
[139] The Latin title reads, "On the lord of the year: how it is made unfortunate by the stars."

cendant of that native, and that star itself is in the degrees of his Ascendant, he will be a pauper and of a bad condition, and of scarce acquisition, and of little skill among his relatives; and if he has assets, he will lose it. **4** And [he will have] many infirmities of the throat and ears.

[Chapter V.4: On the lord of the third with one of the stars]

1 If however the lord of the third from the Ascendant of the revolution of the year were joined to some one of these stars I stated, know that impediment and destruction will fall upon the houses of prayer,[140] and especially upon a man who went on a foreign journey. **2** And a quarrel will fall between siblings, and everyone will be saddened on account of[141] his brother, without cause. **3** And there will be many severe and long-lasting infirmities among men from the shoulder blades and the collarbone and the arms at that time. **4** And [likewise] if any of these stars fell in the degrees of the third of the revolution. **5** And [if] a boy were born in that same year whose Ascendant is this third sign, and the star is in the degrees of his own Ascendant, the native will be a bad man toward his siblings and friends, and [toward] him who considers him a friend; he will decide [he is] of an evil will, of evil thoughts, of no good designs.[142] **6** And if he would go on a foreign journey, he will have no good in it, and if he has assets, they will perish. **7** And there will be many infirmities in his shoulder blades and collarbone and his arms.

[Chapter V.5: On the lord of the fourth with one of the stars]

1 If the lord of the fourth from the Ascendant of the revolution of the year were with any of these stars which I stated, know that impediment and evil will fall upon lands and harvests and farmers; and war will fall upon cities and rural estates, and a quarrel between parents and children, with much jealousy; and they will be saddened with regard to one another; and the most recent things (of those which will come in that same year) [will come] to eve-

---

[140] *Orationum.* This word also means "pleading," which could mean place where people plead their cases and seek help—perhaps a courtroom?
[141] Lit., "with" (*cum*).
[142] *Et eum qui habet constituet amicum sibi malae voluntatis, malae cogitationis, nullius boni propositi.* The role of *qui habet* ("who considers/has") is ambiguous. If it is omitted, the clause would run: "and he who makes him a friend will be of an evil will, of evil thoughts, of no good designs."

ry evil.[143] **2** And if someone bought real estate or rural estates, he will not see what he values in them. **3** And likewise if one of these stars fell onto the degree of the fourth house from the Ascendant of the revolution. **4** And if a boy were born in that same year, [and his Ascendant were the fourth of the revolution, and the degree of his Ascendant is on the same degree as that of the star],[144] he will be born wholly evil toward his parents, having hatred for them. **5** And the most recent of things will be for the bad. **6** And if it is someone's work, he will not be praised on account of it; and his infirmities [will be] many, and these infirmities which will happen in that same time will be in the chest and lungs, and in these parts of the body.

[Chapter V.6: On the lord of the fifth with one of the stars]

1 And if the lord of the fifth from the Ascendant of the revolution of the year were with any of these stars, infirmity, destruction, and impediment will fall between those who are loved,[145] and those gave will not be repaid, and men will hate their children and the seeking of children. **2** And sexual intercourse will be decreased, and infirmities will happen to him in the belly and the stomach, preventing them from [having] sexual intercourse. **3** And likewise if any of these stars fell onto the degrees of the fifth from the Ascendant of the revolution. **4** And if a boy were born in that same year, whose Ascendant is those degrees themselves of that sign, he will be disagreeable to his parents, of little reverence towards those who mix with him, he will not persevere in the esteem of someone, nor will he repay someone for something good;[146] and his infirmities will be more in the belly and the stomach.

[Chapter V.7: On the lord of the sixth with one of the stars]

1 But if the lord of the sixth from the Ascendant of the revolution of the year were with any of these stars, infirmity and destruction and impediment will fall upon all four-footed things, and upon those serving the king, and his slaves, and likewise upon the rest of slaves, and he will be made a pauper. **2** And impediment will fall upon [him] whose job is the selling of male slaves,

---

[143] *Et novissima horum quae evenient in eidem anno ad omne malum.*
[144] Adding based on the other paragraphs of this section.
[145] *Dilectos.*
[146] *Ex bono.*

especially if the lord of the sign is in a masculine sign (or on female slaves and women, if [the lord] is in a feminine sign); and fugitives suffer in that year, and certain ones of them will not return. **3** And there will be many infirmities in men, and more of them in the intestines, from overflowing heat.[147] **4** And likewise, if some one of these stars fell onto the degrees of the sixth of the Ascendant of the revolution. **5** And if a boy were born in that same year, and these very degrees of [his] Ascendant are of that sign,[148] he will have little passionate desire[149] for slaves, and if he had slaves he will not see good from them. **6** And from childhood he will love to run away from his parents. **7** If he should wish to make use of four-footed animals, he will not see good from them, but they will die [while they are] with him. **8** And his and men's infirmities in that same time will be in the lower part of the belly.

[Chapter V.8: On the lord of the seventh with one of the stars]

1 And if the lord of the seventh from the Ascendant of the revolution of the year were with any of these stars, litigants and those making war against the king will be multiplied, and will kill each other, and evil and quarrels will fall between men, and society will be torn apart by much discord; and the king will be angry with his household intimates, and husbands will forsake their wives, and piety and compassion will be reduced, and their hearts will be made hard, and few weddings will take place, and assets will not be rendered to the seller, and inquisitions will be weakened,[150] and capital will decrease, and there will be illnesses of men in the bladder and the kidneys, and the hips and hind parts. **2** And likewise if some one of these stars fell onto the degree of the seventh of the Ascendant of the revolution of the year. **3** And if a boy were born in the same year under the degrees themselves,[151] he will not see good from his own wife, nor will anyone who partners with him. **4** And if he gave capital,[152] he will not see what he loves in

---

[147] Reading *ex calore superflua* with Paris for *et collica*.
[148] Or rather, they are on the degrees where the star fell.
[149] *Cupiditatis*, which normally has an erotic overtone. But this might simply mean he does not want to own them.
[150] Reading *debilitabuntur* with Paris, for "delayed" (*dilatabuntur*).
[151] I.e., if his Ascendant is the same degree as that of the fixed star.
[152] That is, in investments or as a loan.

it. **5** [Someone] contending with someone, will be conquered, and his infirmities will be in the bladder, kidneys, hips, and hind parts, as was said above.

[Chapter V.9: On the lord of the eighth with one of the stars]

1 But if the lord of the eighth from the Ascendant of the revolution of the year were with any of these stars, infirmities, destruction, and impediment will fall upon those wandering; nor will someone steal something in that time which he will return,[153] and the king will miss something of his treasure, nor will it be found. **2** And impediment and many quarrels will fall between those inheriting the assets of the dead, and much death in low-class and dejected people, and much impediment [will fall] upon the assets of those contending with a greater king of that clime, and they will need the help of the greater king (of the kings of Babylon and the king of the Romans and of the Indians), and there will be more infirmities of men in the penis and the groin and the testicles. **3** And if any of these stars fell onto the degrees of the eighth from the Ascendant of the revolution, it will happen in the same way as was said before about the lord of the eighth, if it fell with any of them. **4** And if a boy were born in that same year under these degrees, he will be a vagabond, and neither will he enter under a roof, and he will join hands with his enemies, and he will try to be with demons; nor will good be seen in him for his own labor and for his foreign travels; and he will most often be in places of the dead and cadavers and stinking things. **5** And his infirmities (and men's)[154] in that time will be more in the testicles and private parts.

[Chapter V.10: On the lord of the ninth with one of the stars]

1 And if the lord of the ninth from the Ascendant of the revolution is with any of these stars, impediment, destruction, and infirmity will fall on those worshipping God, and on the greater houses of prayer, and in the journeys of those making foreign travels to faraway places; and the sects of men will be destroyed, and confusion and astonishment of the mind will befall them, and thoughts[155] about celestial [or heavenly] things, and doubt, and denial[156] of the lord God most high; he who went on a foreign journey will

---

[153] Omitting an extra "not," with the Arabic.
[154] Omitting *sed* as redundant.
[155] Or better, "hesitation," which is closer to the Arabic.
[156] Reading *negatio* with the Arabic for *negociatio* ("business").

not see good in his journey; and the customs[157] of men will be destroyed, and their judgments will be malignant. **2** And rebels will go forth and they will seek the death of the king of Babylon, and this will be prolonged by them: that is, it will last until the year has run out. **3** And in that year there will be a scarcity of war and killing and battles.[158] **4** And in the same way, if any of these stars fell on the degrees of the ninth from the Ascendant of the revolution. **5** And if someone were born in that year under these degrees, he will be stupefied in his affairs and in the cultivation of his faith, nor will foreign travel or changing [from one place to another] be suitable for him. **6** And more of his infirmities (and of men at that time) will be in the thighs and because of blows to the thighs.

[Chapter V.11: On the lord of the tenth with one of the stars]

1 And if the lord of the tenth from the Ascendant of the revolution is with any of these stars, evil and destruction will fall upon kings, nobles, and the wealthy, and upon those who are in charge; and jealousy and contention will come between them, and weakness in their affairs, and little money, [and] accusations against them, and their respect and kingdom[159] will vanish,[160] and even low-class people will be extended over them, and their rustics will revile them, giving them derisive names to the extent that if their chief went through the forum, he would be mocked by [even] the low[est] of merchants. **2** And this will last until the year runs out. **3** [And likewise if the degree of the tenth fell on any of these stars.][161] **4** And if a boy were born under the same degree of the Ascendant,[162] he will be low-class and looked down upon by those around him [or his kin] and among those who are conjoined to him; and he will be of little reverence,[163] and he will have much dejection and a laborious life, and of little acquisition [of wealth] concerning these things which remain to him, and his infirmities will be more in the knees.

---

[157] Or, "morals."
[158] How could this be, if rebels are seeking the death of the king throughout the year? Perhaps the rebellion only pertains to the king (or the king of Babylon), while there will be little fighting in other areas.
[159] Or perhaps, "rulership."
[160] Reading *abibit* for *abbibit* ("he drinks, listens eagerly").
[161] Adding a sentence to match the other paragraphs, and omitting "And their infirmities will be more in the genitals."
[162] I.e., if the degree of his Ascendant were the same as this star.
[163] That is, *other* people will revere him little.

[Chapter V.12: On the lord of the eleventh with one of the stars]

1 And if the lord of the eleventh were with any of these [stars], anxiety will strike in the hearts of friends,[164] and there will be discord between them, more than usual; and one will be suspicious of another, and there will be little trust in any of those things which one thinks about; and the house of the king's assets will be destroyed, and his assets will be lost, and he will have few ministers, and his allies will be unfaithful (and if war came to him, they will abandon him). **2** And the infirmities of men will be in the legs. [**3** And likewise if one of these stars fell on the degree of the eleventh.][165] **4** And if a boy were born under these degrees, he will be of little trust, and little good, and distasteful to all people; he will not avoid evil, nor will he think about what is good, and he will be of little praise and atonement; and his infirmities will be from the legs.

[Chapter V.13: On the lord of the twelfth with one of the stars]

1 And if the lord of the twelfth were with any of these stars, then robbers and the cutters of roads will be multiplied, and slaves will be useless to their masters, and the ignoble and the low-class[166] will be diminished and looked down upon, and nobles and magnates, the wise, and the rational, will be elevated. [**2** And it will be likewise if one of these stars fell on the degree of the twelfth.] **3** And if a boy were born in the degrees of that same Ascendant, he will be laborious, clever, and bad, [and will have] many enemies hating him, everyone who saw him will hate him from his childhood until old age, and his infirmities will be in the feet.

[Chapter V.14: On the aspects of the planets with the fixed stars, except for Saturn]

1 And if Jupiter or Venus looked at these places[167] from friendship,[168] and they projected rays to those very degrees, and it[169] was in its own place or own houses, it will break the malice of these stars. **2** And if they were weak in their own place, they will not work anything of their own operations which

---

[164] Reading *amicorum* for *inimicorum* ("enemies").
[165] Adding based on the previous paragraphs.
[166] Adding with Paris 16208.
[167] The Arabic reads, "degree," suggesting quadrant-based houses.
[168] That is, a sextile or trine.
[169] I.e., either Jupiter or Venus.

would have [any] force, and the quantity of the evil will be in proportion to the strength or weakness of the planet. **3** And if it looked from a place of enmity, it will not repel the evil, especially if it was weak in its own place, but it will strive to expel [it] and will not be able to [do so].

4 If however Mars[170] looked from a place of friendship,[171] the evil will be what I said, with quickness;[172] and another [evil] will follow this evil. **5** And if the bad one[173] looked from a place of enmity and contrariety,[174] all that I said will be from the beginning of the appearance [of the evil] until the end.[175] **6** If however the Sun looked at the place, it will not conceal the evil but it will make it open, and everyone who strives to conceal it will not be able to, but this will belong to the population as a whole, and cities. **7** And if Saturn looked, one tribulation after another will come down. **8** And if Mercury looked, his working will be just like the working of the Sun, but it will be less and somewhat faster, on account of the quickness of his course.

9 And know that the general things which were said will be in the cities which are of that same sign. **10** Therefore consider this diligently, and you will not go astray, if God wills.

---

[170] Reading with the Ar. for *malus* ("bad one"), a mistake for what must have been John's *Mars*.
[171] Reading with the Ar. for *directionis* and *deiectionis* ("direction," "dejection"), mistakes for what must have been John's *dilectionis* or *delectionis* ("esteem," "delight").
[172] This seems to mean it will be quick and easy, as compared with negative aspects below.
[173] Again, Mars; the Arabic simply has "he."
[174] That is, from a square or opposition.
[175] I take this to mean the end of the year.

[BOOK VI: ON THE DIRECTION OF THE SUPERIOR PLANETS IN THE SIGNS][176]

[Chapter VI.1: On Saturn in the twelve signs]

2 You ought to consider the planets in the hour of the revolution and reckon their latitudes in their directions, in the north, south, west, and east. **3** If Saturn were in Aries and his latitude northern, it signifies the corruption of the air and its density and obscurity in its season. **4** And if his latitude were southern, it signifies the severity of the cold with a multitude of frost. **5** And if he were eastern it signifies the death of the wealthy, and their thoughts with sadness, and frost. **6** If western, it signifies an earthquake and famine and the darkness of the air. **7** And if he were direct [there will be] less evil for him. **8** If retrograde, greater evil.

9 If Saturn were in Taurus and his latitude northern, it signifies the goodness of the air and the excellence of its complexion, and there will be useful rains without impediment, and things bought and sold publicly will be mediocre. **10** And if his latitude were southern, it signifies frights and the comminglings of storms, and mortalities and corruptions of the air and its destruction, with a scarcity of good. **11** If eastern, it signifies a multitude of rains, and men will be made infirm by this. **12** If western, it signifies fear in rich men on account of the rustics, and a commingling of their affairs with one another. **13** And if he were direct it signifies infirmities happening to men in the upper parts of the body, and long-lasting ones. **14** If retrograde, it signifies the death of great and noble men, with a multitude of fear and difficulties between men.

15 If Saturn [were] in Gemini [and] his latitude northern, it signifies the blowing of harmful winds and the darkness of the air, and an earthquake and corruption. **16** If southern, it signifies the heat of the season with a scarcity of rain, and a multitude of deadly pestilence. **17** If eastern, it signifies the infirmity of kings and magnates. **18** If western, it signifies the dryness of the air with a scarcity of water from springs and rains. **19** If direct, stronger. **20** If retrograde, he will perform them more weakly.

---

[176] "Direction" here (Ar. *jihāt*) does not refer to primary directions, but more to the solar phase, latitude, and motion of the planets. The Latin title read, "On the latitude, arising, and setting of the planets in the signs." Many of these significations are the same or similar to *BRD*, but some contrast greatly.

21 If Saturn [were] in Cancer and his latitude northern, it signifies a scarcity of the waters in rivers, and of rain. **22** If southern, it signifies the occupation of men with their deeds and the scarcity of their acquisition [of wealth]. **23** If eastern, the corruption of the air and its darkness, and a multitude of cold in its season. **24** If western, it signifies a multitude of rains, and corruption and impediment in things bought. **25** If retrograde, it signifies their strength and the disgrace of the king and his impediment, [and] death will be better than what happens to him. **26** And if direct, the clarity of the air and the goodness of its complexion.

27 If Saturn [were] in Leo and his latitude were northern, it signifies a multitude of rains, and the wealthy and an occupation with the matters of the wealthy and the rustics, and the acquisition of those doing business will be destroyed. [**28** If southern, it signifies a scarcity of rain, and it confuses the matter of the king and the citizens, and it attacks the profit of businessmen.][177] **29** If eastern, it signifies infirmity falling upon low-class and ignoble people. **30** If western, it signifies pestilence befalling the earth, and powerful death. **31** If retrograde, the severity of those things which we stated, and the long length of their endurance. **32** If direct, it signifies something more abated.

33 If Saturn [were] in Virgo and his latitude northern, it signifies the goodness of the winds and their sweetness, [and] growth in harvests and seeds. **34** If he were southern, it signifies the scarcity of the waters of springs. **35** If eastern, the abortion of pregnant women and other animals. **36** If western, it signifies deaths and terrible fevers. **37** If retrograde, it signifies the king's fear of his enemies, [and] he will fear their increase over him. **38** If direct, it signifies the king's attaining victory over his own enemies, and his strength.

39 If Saturn [were] in Libra and his latitude northern, it signifies the dryness of the air, and its heat, and a scarcity of rains, and the wasting [or consumption] of the waters from springs. **40** If southern, it signifies the goodness of the winds and the sweetness of the air's complexion. **41** If eastern, it signifies the commingling of men and the pursuit of lewdness and crimes. **42** If western, the dejection of fornicators, and their fall, and horrible things. **43** If retrograde, it signifies the infirmity of female slaves and low-

---

[177] Adding from the Ar.

class people. **44** If direct, the mediocrity of the yield and of barley, and the breaking of the revenue of kings.

45 If Saturn [were] in Scorpio and [his] latitude northern, it signifies a multitude of rains and an abundance of river waters and their corruption. **46** If southern, famine for men and the burden of market goods. **47** If eastern, a multitude of wars among the wealthy. **48** If western, the destruction of the abundance in the sea, and the occurrence of evil in it. **49** If retrograde, pestilence in that land. **50** If direct, the salvation of the climes of Babylon.

51 If Saturn were in Sagittarius and his latitude northern, [it indicates the heat of the atmosphere and a scarcity of winds and rain. **52** If his latitude was southern,][178] it signifies a multitude of waters from springs, and great cold in winter. **53** If eastern, the nearness of the wealthy to their own regions. **54** If western, a battle between the wealthy, the magnates, and nobles. **55** If retrograde, the severity of men's affairs, and a battle among them. **56** If direct, the prosperity of those making foreign journeys on the seas and waters.

57 If Saturn [were] in Capricorn and [his] latitude northern, it signifies the goodness of the air's complexion, and a middling amount of rains. **58** If southern, darkness of the air in the season of winter, with a multitude of cold. **59** If eastern, the bad disposition of the wealthy, and [their] error, and their evil partnership with the rustics. **60** If western, a multitude of locusts and the impediment of the harvest on account of excessive heat. **61** If retrograde, a multitude of confusion[179] among the rustics. **62** If direct, it signifies the justice of the wealthy and kings, and their humbleness and rectitude.

63 If Saturn [were] in Aquarius and [his] latitude northern, it signifies a multitude of rains, [and] the severity of the cold, with frost. **64** If southern, a scarcity of waters from springs and rivers. **65** If eastern, scarce acquisition from real estate, with the scarcity of the assets of the rustics. **66** If western, a multitude of burning, and its strength. **67** If retrograde, the severity of the same thing. **68** If direct, the death of animals which men use.

69 If Saturn [were] in Pisces [and his latitude] northern, [it signifies] much blowing of the northern winds and the severity of the winter. **70** If southern, the destruction of ships at sea, and the occurrence of impediment in those things which likewise operate in the waters. **71** If eastern, back-and-forth killing among the wealthy. **72** If western, the dejection of the nobles and the

---

[178] Adding from the Ar.
[179] Reading with the Ar. for "commingling," although the Arabic is misspelled. The Arabic suggests a range from being confused to meddling.

exaltation of the ignoble. **73** If retrograde, the death of the religious and those worshipping God.[180] **74** If direct, the populating of the houses of religion and of the care of what is divine.[181]

[Chapter VI.2: On Jupiter in the twelve signs]

1 If Jupiter were in Aries and his latitude northern, it signifies the goodness of the air's complexion and a scarcity of rains. **2** If southern, the corruption of the winds and their severity. **3** If eastern, it signifies the joy and happiness of rich men and their inclination towards games. **4** If western, the loftiness of the wise and the nobles. **5** If retrograde, the impediment of voyages at sea. **6** If direct, a multitude of fishes, animals of the waters, and the health of the same.

7 If Jupiter [were] in Taurus and his latitude northern, it signifies the immobility of the air, and its heat. **8** If southern, an abundance of rains and much waters from springs. **9** If eastern, the hatred of the rustics toward their king. [**10** If he was western, it indicates the security of the people and the scarcity of their fear.][182] **11** If direct, the lust of men for treasure and the hoarding of assets. [**12** If he were retrograde, it indicates the fear of the Sultan and his dissatisfaction].[183]

13 If Jupiter [were] in Gemini, it signifies the goodness of the winds and a middling amount of rains if his latitude [were] northern. **14** If southern, a multitude of thunder and lightning strikes. **15** Eastern, much speaking in sects and about faith. **16** Western, a multitude of battles and contentions and commingling. **17** Retrograde, difficulty in acquisitions. **18** Direct, the contrary of all these things.

19 If Jupiter [were] in Cancer and [his] latitude northern, [it signifies] the goodness of the air and an abundance of waters and a multitude of thunder and lightning strikes. **20** Southern, the excellence of the air and its complexion. **21** Eastern, a multitude of wars and of the contention of regions toward one another. **22** Western, a multitude of contention in sects. **23** Retrograde,

---

[180] Abū Ma'shar probably says this because Pisces is ruled by Jupiter, who rules religious people (and Christians especially).
[181] *Divinae culturae.*
[182] Adding from the Ar. But this does not quite make sense to me, and Paris 2588 is missing Jupiter being direct—perhaps this is what it should read for that?
[183] Adding from the Ar.

the severity of all of those things which were said. **24** Direct, salvation in the mountains and their harvests.

25 If Jupiter [were] in Leo and [his] latitude northern, it signifies the severity of thunder and lightning strikes. **26** If southern, the dryness of the air and a scarcity of waters.[184] **27** If eastern, the disagreement of the wealthy with one another. **28** If western, it signifies that the rustics will overthrow their king. **29** If retrograde, the taking away of the hands of the soldiers from [their] obedience to their king.[185] **30** Direct, the profit of sheep and cows and camels.

31 If Jupiter [were] in Virgo and [his] latitude northern, [it signifies] a scarcity of lightning strikes and thunder, and a multitude of rains. **32** Southern, the excellence of the air and its complexion. **33** Eastern, a multitude of battles and wars between the wealthy. **34** Western, the contrariety of the soldiers and of those bearing arms, against the wealthy. **35** Retrograde, the severity of those things which I said about this. **36** Direct, the religion of kings and their fitness.

[**37** And if Jupiter was in Libra, and his latitude was northern, it indicates an abundance of the blowing of the west wind. **38** And if his latitude was southern, it indicates the scarcity of the rains. **39** And if he was eastern, it indicates predatory beasts {attacking} the people.[186] **40** And if he was western, it indicated the dissatisfaction of kings with their citizens. **41** And if he was retrograde, it indicates the bad management of kings. **42** And if he was direct, it indicates the integrity of the king, and his good condition.][187]

43 If Jupiter [were] in Scorpio and [his] latitude northern, [it signifies] the goodness of the winds. **44** Southern, a multitude of thunders. **45** Eastern, the coming of impediment in the nobles. **46** Western, a multitude of deadly pestilence. **47** Retrograde, the severity of all these things. **48** Direct, the obscurity of the air and the coming of impediment from that.

49 If Jupiter [were] in Sagittarius and [his] latitude northern, [it signifies] the temperateness of the air and its goodness. **50** If southern, a scarcity of rains. **51** If eastern, disagreements of the rustics toward one another. [**52** And

---

[184] Or rather, "rains" (Ar.).
[185] *Ablationem manuum militum ab obedientia regis eorum.* I am reading *ab obedientia* along with the delineation for the Head in Pisces (see below), instead of *ad obedientiam* ("toward/for [their] obedience").
[186] BRD V.2, **10** reads "pains occurring to" the people, which makes more sense.
[187] Adding from the Arabic.

if he was western, it indicates denial.[188] **53** And if he was retrograde, [*missing*]. **54** [And if he was direct,] it indicates the good condition of kings with one another.][189]

55 If Jupiter [were] in Capricorn and [his] latitude northern, it signifies [an abundance of snow and the cold of winter in its time. **56** And if it was southern, it indicates][190] an abundance of thunder and lightning strikes and [a scarcity of][191] rains. **57** If eastern, the loftiness of the sects.[192] **58** If western, the honor[193] of the wise and doctors of the law. **59** If retrograde, the impediments of consuls and scribes. **60** If direct, the suitableness of them and of the rest of men.

61 If Jupiter [were] in Aquarius [and] northern, [it signifies] the darkness of the air and a scarcity of rains. **62** If southern, a multitude of thunder and lightning. **63** If eastern, the cutting off of hands and feet in that season.[194] **64** If western, a multitude of commingling [or confusion] among the rustics. **65** If retrograde, the severity of all these things which I mentioned. **66** If direct, the suitableness of the nobles and their loftiness.

67 If Jupiter [were] in Pisces [and] northern, it signifies a multitude of the waters of rivers and springs. **68** If southern, a multitude of rains and a scarcity of thunder. **69** If eastern, wars. **70** If western, pestilence. **71** If retrograde, infirmities happening to men in the lower parts of the body. **72** If direct, the commingling[195] of men with each other.

[Chapter VI.3: On Mars in the twelve signs]

1 [If] Mars [were] in Aries and [his] latitude northern, it signifies the heat of the air and a scarcity of rain. **2** If southern, the severity of thunder and lightning. **3** If eastern, the severity of the wars among the wealthy. **4** If west-

---

[188] This general word for rejection can also refer to denying or shirking one's obligations.
[189] Adding from the Arabic. Note that, as written, retrogradation would have had an entirely positive meaning. So, I have taken the retrograde sentence **53** as being incomplete, while the positive meanings are assigned to the missing beginning of **54**.
[190] Adding with the Ar.; 1485 connected the beginning of **54** to the end of **55**.
[191] Adding with the Ar.
[192] Reading with Paris (and the Arabic) for "of the stars, and their goodness."
[193] The Ar. has it that they will have a middling position, or perhaps be mediators.
[194] The Arabic has "it indicates moisture and dew and muddiness."
[195] Again, this should refer to great confusion (Ar.).

ern, the multitude of men's terror. **5** If retrograde, infirmities in the eyes and head. **6** If direct, a multitude of illumination in faith and trials.[196]

7 If Mars [were] in Taurus and [his] latitude northern, it signifies a multitude of rains with the goodness of the vegetation. **8** If southern, a multitude of northern winds. **9** If eastern, it signifies a multitude of peace and security in the east.[197] **10** If western, it signifies a multitude of infirmities and much infirmity and death. **11** If retrograde, infirmities happening in children. **12** If direct, the hatred of women.[198]

13 If Mars [were] in Gemini and [his] latitude northern, it signifies a multitude of rains. **14** If southern, a scarcity of waters from rivers and springs. **15** If eastern, a multitude of blisters in men. **16** If western, the hiding[199] of consuls and scribes, and their flight. **17** If retrograde, disagreements in sects. **18** If direct, a multitude of poverty in men.

19 If Mars [were] in Cancer and his latitude northern, it signifies the scarcity of waters from springs, with a multitude of cold in its season. **20** If southern, the blowing of winds and the destruction of trees. **21** If eastern, a pestilence that is going to fall on animals that travel on the plains.[200] **22** If western, the whispering of the common people, with betrayal. **23** If retrograde, the appearance of fornication and lewdness. **24** If direct, the goodness of the air and the excellence of its complexion.

25 If Mars were in Leo and his latitude northern, it signifies the scarcity of waters from springs and rivers. **26** If he were southern, it signifies a multitude of waters from springs and rivers.[201] **27** If eastern, impediment in animals which men use. **28** If western, the scarcity of fish and the death of aquatic animals. **29** Retrograde, the sorrow of the nobles and the wealthy. **30** Direct, the joy of judges and of those who know the laws.

31 If Mars were in Virgo and his latitude northern, it signifies the impediment of men in the harvests and seeds. **32** If southern, the salvation of men in the harvests and seeds. **33** If eastern, much death for old people. **34** If

---

[196] The Arabic more sensibly reads, "disputes in religions, and intimidation." Actually, the Arabic seems to choose the wrong form for "intimidation" (*al-'irhāb*), using instead *al-rāhib* ("monk"). But perhaps it should read *al-ruhbān* ("the monks").
[197] The Arabic reads, "an abundance of diseases in the people of Babylon and the desert of the west."
[198] The Arabic reads, "wounds occurring in women."
[199] Or, "disappearance" (Ar.).
[200] Or rather, "which seek shelter in the deserts" (Ar.).
[201] The Arabic has, "the safety of plants and plantings."

western, dryness and famine in Spain and its parts.[202] **35** Retrograde, the multitude of men's battles. **36** Direct, the honest habits and interactions of the wealthy.

37 If Mars were in Libra and his latitude northern, it signifies the darkness of the air and the severity of the winds. **38** If southern, a multitude of thunder and lightning. **39** If eastern, a battle among the wealthy. **40** If western, the wrath of the king and the occupation of the wealthy with scribes. **41** Retrograde, the severity of the things which I told you. **42** Direct, a multitude of wars among the wealthy.

43 If Mars were in Scorpio and his latitude northern, it signifies a multitude of clouds, rains, thunder and lightning. **44** If southern, much water from springs.[203] **45** If eastern, a multitude of infirmities among men in the lower parts of the belly. **46** If western, a scarcity of men's piety toward one another. **47** Retrograde, a multitude of good in that season and the fear of those doing business, and the multitude of their profit.[204] **48** Direct, much taking of [state] revenue, and the devastation of homes and of the assets of the wealthy.

49 If Mars were in Sagittarius and his latitude northern, it signifies the excellence of the air's complexion and its goodness. **50** If southern, the profit of those doing business and the goodness of their profit. **51** If eastern, peace and rest. **52** If western, the salvation of the trees and a multitude of field produce. **53** Retrograde, much coughing and chest pains. **54** Direct, a multitude of contagious disease in the [vermin of the][205] earth and in animals of the coast.[206]

55 If Mars were in Capricorn and his latitude northern, it signifies a multitude of snow and cold. **56** If southern, the heat of the air and its obscurity. **57** If eastern, the killing of the Emperor of the Romans, and the safety of the

---

[202] Paris 2588 lacks most of Mars in Virgo, but this is probably Isfahān, not Spain.
[203] Sentences **43-44** read very differently in the Arabic: **43** And if Mars was in Scorpio and his latitude was northern, it indicates an abundance of the water of springs. **44** And if it was southern, it indicates the cloudiness of the atmosphere.
[204] The Arabic reads: **47** And if he was western, it indicates the scarcity of the people's compassion with each other.
[205] Adding with the Ar.
[206] Or who live along banks and shores of any kind (*animalibus litoris*). The Arabic reads: "wild animals."

islands.[207] **58** If western, a multitude of pestilences among men. **59** Retrograde, the severity [or burden] of the yield. **60** Direct, the multitude of the vintage and olive oil.

61 If Mars were in Aquarius and his latitude northern, it signifies a multitude of snow and cold, and of locusts in its season. **62** If southern, obscurity and the severity of the heat. **63** If eastern, the peace and joy of the soldiers. **64** If western, much trembling among men. **65** Retrograde, a multitude of hot wind and impediments in trees. **66** Direct, the ruin of trees and a case of vermin in them.

67 If Mars were in Pisces and his latitude northern, it signifies the goodness of the air and its complexion. **68** If southern, a multitude of locusts and the scarcity of their impediment. **69** If eastern, the wealthy killing one another. **70** If western, a multitude of infirmities in male and female slaves and low-class men. **71** Retrograde, the salvation of men and much profit for those doing business. **72** Direct, the salvation of sheep and cows.

73 And know that I have already diligently tested the latitudes of the superior planets, and their directions and condition in the circle of signs. **74** However, I have seen [the predicted effects of the] inferior planets sometimes come about, [and] sometimes go astray, and therefore I did not put [them] in my book.[208] **75** And I have diligently tested everything which I have put in it. **76** Know this and do not neglect anything of these things which are written in it. **77** And concerning this, test what you wish of [these] judgments, and you will not go astray, if God wills.

---

[207] Reading "islands" (*al-juzur*) as the Arabic seems to, for the printed editions' *alkahizhir*, which sounds like an Arabic transliteration for *Caesar* (pronounced like the German *Kaiser*).

[208] This is an unusual statement, since in *BRD* Abū Ma'shar does indeed include the inferior planets.

[BOOK VII: ON THE NODES & COMETS]

[Chapter VII.1: On the Head, the Tail, & the comets in the twelve signs]

1 Know that the Head, if it were in Aries, signifies the loftiness of great and noble men, and the dejection of low-class and ignoble people. **2** If the Tail was in the same place it signifies the bad disposition of kings and their injuries against[209] the rustics. **3** And if any of the stars which is called a comet appeared in that place, it signifies the detriment of the wealthy of the east and of Babylon, and a bad condition, and much sorrow among the rustics. **4** And if its appearance were in the east,[210] its work[211] will be faster. **5** If the direction of the west, it will be slower.

6 If the Head were in Taurus, it signifies the killing of the wealthy in the direction of the north, and a multitude of disagreement between the wealthy of the west and the rustics. **7** And if the Tail [was] in the same place, it signifies a scarcity of piety in the hearts of men, and a multitude of foreign travel in the direction of the north, and the scarcity of their profit. **8** And if any of the stars which is called a comet appeared in in a straight line with it,[212] it signifies the evil of men, and the scarcity of their good, and the injuries of rebels against them. **9** While if it appeared in the direction of the east, its work will be faster. **10** If in the direction of the west, slower.

11 If the Head were in Gemini, it signifies the infirmities of men from winds, and an earthquake, and wars taking place between the rustics and the wealthy. **12** If the Tail was in the same place, it signifies the pouncing[213] of the rustics upon the king and nobles, and [the rustics] will mock [or deceive] them; his soldiers will rise up against them, and dukes against kings. **13** Which if any of the stars which is called a comet appeared in a straight line with it, it signifies the appearance of lewdness and fornication, and the dejec-

---

[209] Reading with the Ar. for "among."
[210] This must mean eastern or western of the Sun (namely, rising before or setting after him), otherwise the comet's signification would depend on who saw it first, in what part of the sky, which would not make sense.
[211] Reading *opus* for *opera*.
[212] *In directo eius.* Or more informally, "in" it. Many comets will not actually appear in or right next to the ecliptic, so Abū Ma'shar is speaking of the geometric relationship with the signs. This phrase does not appear here in the Arabic, but does so in BRD.
[213] *Saltum*, which is one meaning of the Arabic, but not as accurate as "pounce" or "jump" or "rush."

tion of those serving and praying to God the Most Holy. **14** While if it appeared in the east, its work will be faster; and if in the west, slower.

15 If the Head were in Cancer, it signifies the goodness of the king towards the rustics, and his largesse toward them, and that he will gather assets, and that he will distribute more than he will collect in his policies.[214] **16** And if the Tail was in the same place, it signifies a multitude of pestilence and sudden deaths, and lying confusion,[215] and the appearance of luxury and a scarcity of justice, and the breaking of the [state] revenues, and the destruction of the houses of assets; and the foreign travel of the wealthy, and their changing from place to place, and the impediment of scribes and for the masters of professions (namely those who work with their hands). **17** And if a comet appeared there, it signifies a multitude of locusts and the detriment of the harvests from them, and a case of vermin in wheat and trees, and the scarcity of field produce, and a multitude of vermin in them. **18** Which if it appeared in the east its work will be faster; if in the west, slower.

19 If the Head were in Leo, it signifies a multitude of lightning strikes and fires in the air, and the greatest killing, and great evil and injuries. **20** And if the Tail was in the same place, it signifies a multitude of sinkholes[216] in the earth, and an earthquake and the increase of waters, and the decrease [or destruction] of trees, and the destruction of harvests. **21** And if a comet were in the same place, it signifies an infestation of wolves and the impediment of men from them, and a case of vermin in the wheat, and the destruction of the houses of assets. **22** And if it appeared in the east its work will be faster; and if in the west, slower.

23 If the Head were in Virgo, it signifies the destruction of the harvest and of the rest of the field produce, and a scarcity of reaping, and a case of vermin in the trees; and the destruction, by burning, of what remains of them at the end of the time.[217] **24** And if the Tail would be in the same place, it signifies hatred falling between the wealthy, and they will go to war against each other, and captivities will multiply, and the depredations of the Church and of the greater houses of prayer, and the occurrence of disagreement between men in speech and faith. **25** Which if a comet were in the same place, it signifies the carrying away of certain goods from the households of the

---

[214] Reading with the Arabic for "in his own places."
[215] Or, "confusions, liars" (*stupores mendaces*).
[216] Reading with the Arabic for "obscurities."
[217] Reading with the Arabic for "burning of what remains in them in the season of its watch."

wealthy, and their moving to other regions out of the area of captivity and evil, and their goods will never be returned to them again. **26** And if it appeared in the east its work will be faster; and if in the west, slower.

27 If the Head were in Libra, it signifies the injustices of the king and of all the wealthy among their rustics, and deceptions and inquisitions into what is not among them nor in their hands;[218] and on account of this, depredation will take place upon certain people, and poverty upon others; and the affliction of certain people, and deceiving and suffering. **28** Which if the Tail was in the same place, it signifies the coming of death upon flock animals, and that year will be dry with a severity of cold in its season, and [the severity of] the heat in its season, destroying harvests and vegetation and seed and trees; and little collecting of the produce. **29** If however a comet were in the same place, it signifies the wide extent of robbers and cutters [of roads] in [those] parts, and the breaking of the [state] revenue, and the appearance of poverty in the hearts of men in diverse ways, that is, at one time by cold, at another time by heat; and this will be prolonged in men. **30** And if it would be in the direction of the east, its work will be quicker; if in the west, slower.

31 If the Head were in Scorpio, it signifies a multitude of abscesses in men and blisters in the great men among them, and a multitude[219] of battles, wars, and a multitude of fornication in women with dejection and their falling into the hands of kings, with their grief and sorrow. **32** And if the Tail was in the same place, it signifies a case of pleurisy[220] in men, and infirmities occurring in the chest, and a multitude of catarrhs in the throat; the joy and delight of the wealthy in that same season; and the collection of assets and the population[221] of their homes. **33** Which if a comet appeared in the same place, it signifies a multitude of battles and wars, and of rebels against kings; and the change of soldiers with regard to them; and searching by them with the impossibility [of their desired results]. **34** And if it were in the east, its work will be faster; if in the west, slower.

35 If the Head were in Sagittarius, it signifies the affliction of the rustics by the king of Babylon, and the severity of his injury [to them], and impediment in sheep and cows and horses particularly, and in every animal which

---

[218] Reading "into what" for "by what." This seems to mean they will meddle in things which are not their business.
[219] Reading *multitudinem* for *multae*.
[220] An inflammation of the lung.
[221] Or, "building" (Ar.).

those making war use. **36** And burning will fall upon the instruments of war, and the air will be corrupted and made obscure, and heat will be burdensome in its season. **37** Which if the Tail was in the same place, it signifies the dejection of great and noble men, and the exaltation of low-class and ignoble people; and doctors of the law, the wise, scribes, and counsellors will be made sad; and hidden impediments will come to them. **38** And if a comet appeared in the same place, it signifies the bad disposition of scribes and doctors of the law, and [their] annihilation;[222] and the taking of their assets, and their being hidden with a multitude of tribulation which will descend upon them. **39** Which if it were in the direction of the east, its work will be faster; if in the west, slower.

40 If the Head were in Capricorn, it signifies the joy of the wealthy and the nobles, and the loftiness of great men with the elevation of the same; and the occurrence of mockery[223] and their impediment with the dejection of ignoble men, and their ruin. **41** If the Tail [was in] the same place, it signifies an earthquake and plagues that kill. **42** If a comet [appeared in the same place] it signifies the extensiveness of fornication in men at that time. [**43** And if its appearance was in the area of the east it hastens in its action, and in the area of the west it slows its action down.][224]

44 If the Head were in Aquarius, it signifies the death of doctors of the law in that season, and [the death of] judges and sectarians of faith. **45** And if the Tail was in the same place, it signifies the king's investigation against the owners of real estate in that which he ought not to have, and their being misleading by means of unassessed [property], and injuries and afflictions with their capture. **46** While if a comet were in the same place, it signifies a multitude of battles and killing, and of much affliction in that season. **47** And if it appeared in the east, its work will be faster; if in the west, slower.

48 If the Head were in Pisces, it signifies the loftiness of the nobles and the advancement[225] of any man in his own rank, more so than he would have reached according to the greatness of his own nature; and the collection of

---

[222] Reading *annihilationem* with Bonatti for *ante lationem*. Paris reads, *annullationem*, which is close enough to *annihilationem*. The Arabic reads, "idleness."

[223] *Caudarum*. A *cauda* is not only a tail (as with the southern node of the Moon), but is also used in the context of mockery ("having a tail" or *caudam trahere* being equivalent to looking like a fool). A remnant of this concept is probably seen in the children's party game, "pin the tail on the donkey." At any rate, the Arabic has "the falling of the despicable/low."

[224] Adding with the Ar.

[225] Reading *provectionem* for *praeventionem*.

assets in the houses of assets. **49** And if the Tail was in the same place, it signifies the extension of the soldiers over the king, and likewise that of dukes; and the moving of the majority of the wealthy from their own homes, with much speaking in the sect;[226] and the appearance of false new things. **50** If a comet were in the same place, there will be the greatest war upon the kin of the king, and they will kill each other, and those who will be elevated above them will be killed by others, and the taking away of their hand from obedience.[227] **51** If its appearance were in the east, its work will be faster; if in the west, slower.

52 However, if you wished to know the direction in which what the comet signifies will come, look at the [tip] of its tail, to see in what direction it is: and in that same direction will be what it signifies in terms of tribulation. **53** But for the remaining works [of the comet], the hour (which I told you in this book) in which everything which was said, will be, will be when [the Sun][228] has arrived at the sign which was of the essence of those things which I told you, or [at his arrival] at the planet whose nature is in [that] work, just like the nature of the event (which would appear to you) would be in that same year. **54** This is of the secrets of astronomy which is worth the trouble to be hidden.[229]

---

[226] Or, "discussion/philosophical discussion in the religion."
[227] Again (as with Jupiter in Leo in Ch. VI.2), this means that they go back on their promise of obedience.
[228] Adding with the Arabic.
[229] *Quod occultari opere precium est.*

PART IV:
AL-RIJĀL, *THE BOOK OF THE SKILLED*

SECTION IV.1: INTRODUCTION

Comment by Dykes. In this Part, I translate the complete[1] Book VIII of al-Rijāl's *Book of the Skilled in the Judgments of the Stars* (or *Skilled*), from Arabic. Portions of this already appeared in *AW*1.

Abū al-Hasan ʿAlī b. Abī al-Rijāl (fl. first half of 11th Century) is best known for his huge compilation, the *Book of the Skilled in the Judgments of the Stars*, which was written in Arabic in Muslim Spain and contained the views of most of the central authorities in Perso-Arabic astrology (along with numerous minor authorities). It was translated into Old Castilian by Alvaro de Oviedo (or Aegidius de Thebaldis) in the 13th Century at the court of Alfonso X the Wise, and thence into Latin, becoming a popular resource. Unfortunately, not much is known about al-Rijāl's life. He was a respected personage at the court of al-Muʿizz bin Bādīs, a ruler of the Tunisian Zirid dynasty in the 11th Century.

As in many other parts of *Skilled*, al-Rijāl rarely names his sources, and sometimes interjects his own opinions. Nevertheless it is not difficult to see that Book VIII contains many passages from ʿUmar al-Tabarī's *Book of Questions* and Abū Maʿshar's *BRD* (or perhaps, their common source or some other version of Abū Maʿshar). And al-Rijāl is not entirely committed to any particular approach in mundane astrology. Chapter VIII.1 begins by pointing out that mundane astrology contains numerous perspectives and methods, that one should use both ingresses and the lunations prior to the ingress (as Ptolemy does)—and then spends the next few pages cribbing from *BRD* VIII. Much of the rest contains long sections taken from other authors (such as Hermes, al-Kindī, ʿUmar, Abū Maʿshar) with little overall organization except that most of ʿUmar's material is grouped in the middle (Chs. VIII.18-22, 26-30, 32-33), with most of the chorographic material near the end (VIII.34-37), followed by a short review of some Lots and time lords (VIII.38-40) and a concluding chapter on falling stars (VIII.41).

---

[1] Complete, apart from long lists of city and village names, with their latitudes and longitudes, in Chs. VIII.36-37.

My Arabic sources were the following:

- British Library Add. 23399.
- Nuruousmaniye 2766.

In addition, I relied on my own translation of the 1485 Latin edition, *De Iudiciis Astrorum* (Venice: Erhard Ratdolt, 1485).

SECTION IV.2:
THE BOOK OF THE SKILLED VIII

[Chapter VIII.0: Invocation *& Prologue*]

1 'Alī ibn Abī al-Rijāl said: God be praised, Possessor of power and splendor and protection and favor, Maker[1] of creatures and Knower of what is hidden, Hearer of what is secret and confidential, and Remover of harm and affliction, Organizer of affairs through His own power and Sender of rains[2] through His compassion, Governor of governors and Supplier of what is begged of Him, King whom kings serve through His own power, Almighty who subdues the mighty through His own mightiness, and He does not revise His judgment, and He is the Kindly, the Aware One.

2 In this book I have gathered, from the statements of the scholars on the revolutions of the years of the world, what I have deemed right, and what was nearer to the truth than what was not; and what I have tested of them, their indication is correct. **3** And God is the master of the outcome, and upon Him be all trust.[3]

Chapter VIII.1: On[4] mentioning the introductory things, from [which] the knowledgeable person will seek aid

2 Know (may God guide you) that the knowledge of the revolution of the years of the world is discovered from many and numerous perspectives. **3** And of them, one discovers it from the conjunctions, and from the Ascendant of the year, and the place of its terminal point, and the terminal point of the sign of the turn, and from the terminal point of the degree of the distribution, and the place of the Ascendant of the year from the Ascendant of the recent conjunction, and the sign of the conjunction.[5] **4** And the subject is based on these principles.

---

[1] Several of the following titles belong to the traditional 99 Arabic names of God, but I have capitalized all of them.
[2] Following what 1485 seems to read as منزل المطر, for منزل القطر.
[3] Reading for التكلان.
[4] Chapter title from Nur.
[5] This probably means the profection of the sign of the conjunction itself to the present year.

5 And in general, and among the generality of the astrologers, one knows it from the Ascendant of the revolution of the year of the world (which is necessary [for] the knowledge of its conditions), and from the place of the meeting and the fullness[6] coming before the alighting of the Sun into Aries, and its Ascendant, and the governor over it and over the place of the meeting and fullness. **6** And for one who wanted an accurate description[7] in the knowledge of events, it is not sufficient [without] all of that.

[Abū Ma'shar: BRD VIII.1, 5-10]

7 And the events are divided into four divisions. **8** The first of them is [1] the lowest, which includes classes [of things] like disease, and fertility and drought, and differences in the atmosphere and rain, and what is like that. **9** And the second division of lower events are those which are [2] universal and concern [things] such as earthquakes and sinkholes, and floods.[8] **10** And the third is [3] things which concern one class [of people], such as wars and what is like those. **11** And the fourth is [4] events which happen in the atmosphere, such as fires [in the sky], and shooting stars, comets,[9] and what is like that.

(**12** And among the ancients, one makes the inference from the occurrence of eclipses which are presented in the year of conjunctions and revolutions of the world—for example Ptolemy: for his greatest reliance was on this conjunction. **13** And [also] based on [that] is the view of Muhammad b. Jābir al-Battānī[10] and others besides him of those who follow the method of Ptolemy.)[11]

14 And the indicator (from among the planets) for these categories is what resembles every type of them,[12] and that is shown with the reaching of the

---

[6] That is, the New or Full Moon.
[7] Reading التقفي (BL) or النقص (Nur.) somewhat uncertainly as though it comes from نقصّ.
[8] Reading الطوفان for الطوفات.
[9] Here and in **15**, I omit a word (ذوائب) which has connotations of melting away or flowing, which does not appear in *BRD*. But if it is authentic, it may be an adjective describing how the tails of comets trail off or their entire form disappears over time.
[10] Reading along with the hint in Kennedy et al. 2009-10, p. 14. BL reads, "al-Mutānī," while 1485 and Nur. read, "al-Shibānī."
[11] This parenthetical remark is al-Rijāl's own; Abū Ma'shar's account continues in the next paragraph.
[12] I am not quite sure what al-Rijāl means by this, or how exactly it relates to the list of predictive techniques which follow.

terminal points, and the Turns, and the directions, and the distribution, and the rays, and the Ascendants of the times, [in addition] to their assemblies and to their oppositions and squares, and victorship over the bounds[13] of their Ascendants.

15 And as for the knowledge of the manner of the occurrence of the lights [in the sky] and shooting stars and comets, that is known from the governorship of Mars over the conjunctional years and in others besides them, and especially if his rays were in the airy signs and the Moon is made unfortunate by him in such airy signs—and especially if [she is][14] the king of the tenth sign and is victorious over it.

16 And as for the knowledge of [2] the occurrence of earthquakes and sinkholes and flooding, indeed that is known from the indication[15] of Saturn, and especially if his rays were in the earthy and watery signs, and he had the role [of governorship], and [his] rays or [he] were in the earthy signs with the Moon, and the Moon was made unfortunate by him: for indeed if it was like that, sinkholes happen. **17** And if it was in the watery ones, it causes floods; and in the airy ones, snow and deadly cold and ice takes place, and the darkness of the air, and a multitude of the winds of destructive tempests.

18 And[16] as for the knowledge of [1] general things of belonging to all types, like epidemics and disease, and fertility and sterility and rains, it is known from: the Ascendants of the beginnings[17] before the alighting of the Sun [in] Aries, the time of the alighting [in Aries],[18] and from the place of the Moon at the revolution and the beginning[19] which is before it, and from the portion[20] of the meeting and the fullness existing before these places (I mean, the revolution and the years of the conjunctions). **19** And if everything were placed safe from the infortunes, it indicates safety; and if it was not like that, it indicates disease.

---

[13] Abū Ma'shar has "one" of their Ascendants.
[14] I take this to be the Moon, but grammatically it could also be Mars.
[15] Reading دلالة for دلائل ("indicators").
[16] From here through **26**, the text matches BRD closely, but also al-Rijāl's VIII.31.1, **2-9**, which is drawn from al-Kindī's *Forty Chapters* Ch. 39.
[17] That is, the New and Full Moons.
[18] Reading نزول for زوال ("disappearance").
[19] Reading بادئة for بادية ("desert," "appearance").
[20] That is, the degree, but probably indicating the bound.

20 And if the lord of the two Ascendants (or one of them) and the Moon are together unfortunate, connected to the lord of its[21] eighth, it indicates a multitude of death from that disease. **21** And if it is the contrary, the disease is without excessive death, and [even] if the diseases are abundant: for this illness, it does not include the [mortal] kind.

22 And if [all of] these indicators, or more of them, were connected to the lords of their eighths, that indicates sudden death by what is other than diseases. **23** And if [they were] connected to the lords of their sixths, the diseases follow in succession and the diseases multiply, and their duration is long-lasting; and if they were short, the illnesses multiply and are not lengthened.

24 And if the one making [them] unfortunate was Mars, and he was in a hot sign, and especially if he was eastern [and] strong, it indicates hot diseases, and pleurisy,[22] and what is like that. **25** And if the one making [them] unfortunate was Saturn, the diseases are Saturnian, enduring, and especially if he was slow [and] strong in the dry signs: for example, melancholy[23] and insanity, and paralysis, and leprosy, and plague, and consumption of the body, and melancholic diseases.

26 And as for the years indicating plague, they are those in which the distribution terminates at the bounds of Mercury, especially if Mercury was mixed with Saturn, and likewise if the turn[24] terminated at the houses of Mercury, and Mercury was mixed with Saturn.

Chapter VIII.2: On years indicating fertility & sterility

*[Abū Ma'shar: BRD VIII.1, **11-13**][25]*

2 And as for the years indicating [1] fertility and sterility, it is that you look at the Ascendants of the[26] beginnings in the meeting and fullness, and their

---

[21] This could mean the eighth from either Ascendant (namely, the eighth house itself), or else the eighth from the Moon, or perhaps all of these.
[22] Inflammation of the lung.
[23] Or: anxiety, etc.
[24] 1485 reads as though this is the revolution itself, in which case it may refer to the mundane profection of the Ascendant of the earlier Jupiter-Saturn conjunction. BRD does not include this phrase.
[25] For **2-10**, compare with VIII.31.2 below.
[26] Reading "of the" for "and the," with BRD.

portions.[27] **3** So if the portion of the meeting and the fullness is connected with Jupiter, and especially if he had a claim[28] in it, and the lord of the Ascendant was made fortunate, with the safety of the lord of the fourth, and the terminal point from the Ascendant of the religion[29] or the shift of the triplicity has reached the place of Jupiter or Venus by body or ray: fertility will occur in that year, and especially if the lord of the second was favorable to the lord of the Ascendant and connected with it or looking at it from a praiseworthy place, and especially [with] the witnessing of the Lot of Fortune: for it indicates the increase in fertility.

4 And as for years of sterility and the things in that, [they are]: Saturn being the governor over the meeting or fullness by rulership or by connection, and especially if he was the lord of the Ascendant or the victor over it, or he brought misfortune[30] to it, or Saturn was in the chief[31] posts (and they are the stakes), and the corruption of the lord of the fourth by the infortunes (and especially Saturn); and that is more powerful if he was parallel to[32] Mercury.

5 And if Saturn was in the stakes of the beginnings (mention of which I presented [before]), or in the posts [of the Moon],[33] indeed that is indicative of expensiveness. **6** And likewise, if the Moon reached him[34] at the time of her emergence from the knot,[35] and Saturn was rising,[36] it indicates severe expensiveness. **7** And whichever of the two infortunes the misfortune belonged to, that is more difficult if there was a mixing of Mercury with them.

---

[27] That is, their degree (but probably their bound).
[28] That is, a dignity.
[29] Reading الملة with Nur. for المسلة. Another option (but not as neat) is المسألة, "issue, matter."
[30] Reading as ناحسا for ناصبا.
[31] Reading الرئيسية for الريسة.
[32] Ar. *muwāziyān* (adverb). In *BRD* V, Abū Maʿshar uses this to mean that a planet is "in" a sign, that is, tracing a circle parallel with the zodiac. So al-Rijāl's source might mean that Saturn and Mercury are conjoined or that their epicycles are moving together.
[33] Or, the "centers" of the Moon, her phases which are used for weather prediction. See *AW1*.
[34] Or more literally, "fell towards him," suggesting an application. *BRD* reads "pushes," which is spelled similarly and is probably correct.
[35] This at least refers to the conjunction at the New Moon, but probably also to the Full Moon.
[36] According to the Latin version of *BRD* and its commentator, this means rising to the top of his epicycle. But it seems to me it could also be moving towards the apogee of his deferent.

8 And if misfortune befell the second [house] and the Lot of Fortune and the Ascendant, from the lord of the Lot of Fortune,[37] there would be an increase in the sterility. **9** And what there was in it of the misfortune of Saturn in this topic, is more difficult than the misfortune of Mars. **10** And likewise, the good fortune of Jupiter in the topic of fertility is stronger than the good fortune of Venus.

11 And[38] as for rains, indeed if Mars (in a revolution of the year in which acceder acceded)[39] was in the houses of Saturn, it indicates a scarcity of rains. **12** And if he was in his own houses, it signifies an abundance of them. **13** And if he was in the remaining houses, it indicates a middling [amount].

Chapter VIII.3: On years signifying unrest & wars

*[Abū Ma'shar: BRD VIII.1, **14-15, 19**]*

2 Indeed you discover the knowledge of this from the time of the conjunction of Jupiter with Saturn, and his square and opposition, and from the stakes of the Ascendant of the year. **3** And as for the clarification of that from the years, it is with the parallel of[40] the more powerful luminary[41] to the degree of Saturn by assembly or by looking (and that he attains it), and with the termination of the Ascendant by direction at the places of the infortunes, a month or year for every sign, and likewise when the year and the conjunction of the [current] condition reaches the places of the infortunes. **4** For indeed the emerging events that are the reasons for the wars will be in those times.

5 And[42] the years in which there is unrest and rebels and deniers, are recognized when the two heavy ones are in square or opposition at the time of the revolution of the year. **6** And if that was from the stakes, the matter will happen with the equality of Jupiter with Saturn by degree, from the square and opposition. **7** And if it was not that, it begins with the entrance of Jupiter into his exaltation or one of the stakes of the Ascendant.

---

[37] Omitting an extra "lord of," with *BRD* and al-Rijāl's VIII.31.2, **18**.
[38] For this paragraph, see *Flowers* III.2.
[39] *BRD* omits this parenthetical remark.
[40] That is, when their positions are equivalent in the zodiac.
[41] The Sun, but perhaps Abū Ma'shar would include the Moon in a nocturnal revolution?
[42] This paragraph is drawn from part of *BRD* VIII.1, **19**.

8 And[43] the indicator of their victory is recognized from the transit of the two heavy ones in their travels around, and it is known which of the two was moving above its partner and the one being elevated above it.[44] **9** And if Jupiter was rising over Saturn, the rebel will win; and to the contrary with the elevation of Saturn.

10 And if Mars was also in one of the stakes of the Ascendant of the year or [a stake] of the Sun, [the war] is in the direction of the world in which the sign of that planet is, which he is looking at from the square or the opposition. **11** And especially, if [the other planet] was in the fiery triplicity, then the emerging war will be in the east. **12** And the statement on the remainder of the triplicities is based on this viewpoint. **13** And it is said to be on the right of the places and their left, based on the calculation of the positions of the signs: because every sign arises before a sign (and it is [on] its left), and every sign rises after a sign (and it is [on] its right).[45]

14 And the arrival of the infortunes in the eighth already indicates an example of that.[46]

[Abū Ma'shar: BRD VIII.1, 17]

15 And one looks at the Lot of peace-making,[47] taken from the degree of the Sun to the degree of the west, and it is projected from the Ascendant, and where [the counting] terminates, there is the Lot of peace-making.

16 And [one looks] from the Lot of fighting, taken from Mars to the Moon, projected from the position of the Sun:[48] and where it terminates, there is the Lot of fighting.

---

[43] I have been unable to find the source of this paragraph.

[44] The one which is elevated or moving above, could be the one having a greater latitude, but it might refer to which of the planets is proportionately closer to the apogee of its epicycle. For a difficult but thorough discussion, see Kennedy 1958. I hope to publish a volume which explains traditional astronomy, which will include these points.

[45] This statement only refers to the northern hemisphere. So, Gemini rises after Taurus, which is on Gemini's right (if one faces the east); and Gemini rises before Cancer, which is on Gemini's left.

[46] This is drawn from the last sentence of *BRD* VIII.1, **16**.

[47] Reading صلح with al-Rijāl; it can also mean "reconciliation." Burnett reads فلح in *BRD*, but this means "cultivation"; he evidently mistook it for فلاح, "prosperity." But since peace and war are at stake here, "peace" is more appropriate.

[48] This may be an error, as there is already a Mars-Moon Lot of rulership and/or authority that is cast from the *Ascendant*.

17 When Mars is with one of these two in the revolution, and especially if they were the fiery signs, then that indicates the occurrence of war in that year. **18** If the Lot of peace-making[49] was strong, not corrupted, it indicates that the victory belongs to the people of the truth (from one of the two sides, the corresponding one between them); and if it was weak, it indicates that the victory will belong to the people of what is false (of the two [sides]).

*[The time of the conflict: Abū Ma'shar, BRD VIII.1, **18**]*

19 And[50] you may discover the times in which the wars come to be, from the distance which is between Mars and Saturn, and the stake and the infortunes, indeed a month for every two-and-a-half degrees between them. **20** And the time in this is recognized from the direction of its motion, as well: for if [the infortune] was direct, it indicates the events at its retrogradation; and if it was retrograde, then it is [when it is direct].[51]

21 When its light is mixed with the light of the indicator of the king, and in the mixture of its light with the light of the indicator of the public, it indicates an abundance of thieves and injustice. **22** And if it was not in a stake and it was retrograde, it causes damage in the land of the sign in which [the infortune] is, and it will not be universal [for] the people unless its light is mixed with the light of the lord of the Ascendant or the light of the lord of the Midheaven (if it is the indicator of the king). **23** And if it is not looking at the Ascendant, it does not have an indication [for harm] in that year unless the infortune is the lord of the year or the indicator of the king.

24 And if Mars was in the stakes, and the distribution reached his bound, and the turn[52] reached his place in[53] the recent conjunction or in the shift of the transit, the wars will be in the direction which belongs to that sign in which the direction terminated, or in the country whose Ascendant is that sign. **25** And likewise if Mars was opposed to Saturn or square to him, and is received, it indicates wars; and if Mars is not received, and Saturn is received, that is an indication of a scarcity of wars.

---

[49] Reading الصلح for الفلح: see footnote above.
[50] For **19-23**, see also *Scito* Ch. 80.
[51] Both this passage and *BRD* truncate this sentence (i.e., omitting the part about going direct) and attach it to the next sentence. But *Scito* Ch. 80, **2-3** more sensibly shows that the sentences are separate.
[52] This could be a mundane profection.
[53] Reading "in" with *BRD* for "of."

26 And if Mars was under the rays, it indicates wars in that year, and that is more severe if he is in one of the movable signs; and if he was in signs having [two] bodies,[54] it does not indicate that; and if he was in the fixed signs, it indicates that there will be wars because of what is false.[55]

27 And if he was in the Midheaven, and especially in Gemini, it indicates crucifixion in that year.

28 And[56] if the lord of the fourth was in the ninth, it indicates the opening of prisons and the freedom of the majority of the imprisoned from [their] confinement.

[General examination of the revolution]

29 And this is the sum of what is needed when you establish the Ascendant from the signs and degrees and minutes, and the correction of the places of the planets in longitude and latitude, and ascent in the north and south (and descent in it), and quickness and slowness (I mean the first and second station), and easternness and westernness, and [their] apportionment [of dignities].[57] **30** And you judge all of it in this, and preserve it, and establish the four stakes of the twelve houses in their places. **31** And do not neglect anything I have explained, with the entrance of the Sun into the first second of Aries.

32 And if that Ascendant was in a movable sign, you revolve all four quarters [of the year]: for indeed at those times the affairs of the world are changed over and modified from condition to condition, and from nature to nature. **33** And if it was a fixed one, then the power of [all] the quarters[58] belongs to the entrance of the Sun into the first second of Aries. **34** And if it was a double-bodied one, the power of the autumnal and winter quarters[59] belongs to the Sun's entrance into the sign of Libra.

35 And likewise, you carry out the meetings and fullnesses [of the Moon] which come to be before the revolution of the quarters, and assign their Ascendants and the places of the planets among their stakes, and see in which

---

[54] That is, the common signs.
[55] Or, "empty": in other words, for false or empty reasons.
[56] This sentence is from *BRD* VIII.1, **19**.
[57] Reading التحصيص for التصحيح ("correction").
[58] Reading more naturally (and more astrologically correctly) for "the power of the first season" (N) or "the power of the first seasons" (BL, which is ungrammatical in the Arabic).
[59] Reading more correctly for "spring and autumnal quarters."

region the infortunes are located (in the east, west, north, and south), and how is the position of the fortunes with respect to these. **36** And you inspect these sections, for they are introductory [and] supportive in the knowledge of the conditions and the revolution of the year of the world.

[Miscellaneous rules]

37 Antiochus[60] said, the two heavy [planets] cause conflicts and overthrowings, and that is from their shifts from triplicity to triplicity, and from [one] essence[61] to its contrary, and from *ḥalb* to *ḥalb*.[62]

38 What is more intense and more fixed is the indication of the planets is if [a planet] was the lord of the bound of the meeting and opposition, especially if the Moon pushed to it, and it[63] is the lord of the year of the world.

39 The indication of the Ascendants of the year of the world is a general indication, and the indication of the Ascendants of the quarters are particular.[64]

40 If the lord of the bound of the meeting or opposition happening before the Sun's alighting in the beginning of Aries happened to be harmful to the lord of the bound of the meeting or opposition happening before the Sun's alighting in Cancer or any of the quarters, it stirs up rebels and hypocrites[65] against the king.

41 If Saturn was ascending[66] to the summit[67] of his rotating circle or his apogee,[68] and the Moon is separating from the Sun and connecting to [Saturn], it[69] signifies that things of the nature of that sign will be expensive.

---

[60] Reading with BL, but Nur. has "Ptolemy." Ptolemy did not discuss this, but al-Rijāl might be getting this from some variant of pseudo-Ptolemy's *Centiloquium*.
[61] This probably refers to the essence of each sign, and the kinds of things it typically indicates.
[62] *ʿalb* (exact translation unknown) is a sect-related concept (see *ITA* III.2) in which planets are in the same hemisphere (upper or lower) as the Sun if they are diurnal planets, or in the opposite one if they are nocturnal planets. But I am not sure how to apply that notion here.
[63] The Arabic does not make clear whether this is the Moon or the other planet.
[64] Or, "partial."
[65] Or perhaps, "liars, dissemblers" (المنافقون).
[66] صعد.
[67] Reading ذروة with 1485 for دور \ دورة ("turning," "rotation").
[68] That is, the apogee of his epicycle and the apogee of his deferent circle.
[69] Reading the rest of this sentence with 1485. The other MSS are garbled and seem to introduce a benefic into the equation. But this reading from 1485 is completely in line with the instructions for finding high prices (see *AW1*).

42 If[70] a planet was in charge of one of the years of the world, and it is in the degree of its exaltation, its indication appears, and the king moves to its cities and its climes, and its army [and] its residences.

43 And know that [in] any year of the world, if it began and Jupiter is unfortunate, then injuries will happen in the nobility and great men, at the beginning of the month of the year. **44** And likewise, if all of the fiery triplicities were made unfortunate at the revolution of the year of the world, plagues will be powerful in the chiefs [of society] and the authorities; and to the contrary in the opposite [situation]. **45** If the eleventh sign and its opposite were fortunate, and in the *ḥayyiz* of both,[71] powerful good and high rank befalls the nobility of the people and their leaders.

46 If[72] the two infortunes were conjoined in the Ascendant of the year, general harm will befall the people. **47** And if it was in the Midheaven, it is ruin for the king of that clime. **48** And if it was in the setting [place], power will incline to the rebels, and it strengthens their command.[73] **49** And if it was in the fourth, the destruction is huge and structures will collapse. **50** And if they were not like that, then pursue it according to your opinion.

51 Kings whose commands will be implemented quickly, and they will be quickly assisted, and what they want is completed quickly, are those for whom the ascending sign was fiery at the beginning of their rule, and likewise the sign of their Midheaven, or one of them is fiery and the other airy, or both of them are airy.

52 From the conjunction of the two heavy ones in the movable signs is known the alteration of the conditions of the world, and from their conjunction in the fixed signs is recognized the persistence of things, and from the double-bodied ones are recognized the kings over particular peoples[74] (and the kingdom is divided into [more than] one [part]).

53 If the two heavy ones were in the Midheaven or in the second from the Ascendant of the world in the year of their union, one will appear who

---

[70] For this sentence, see *BRD* II.2, **4**.

[71] Reading uncertainly with 1485. BL has غيل ("thicket," which makes no sense), and Nur. has جنس ("type/kind"). *Ḥayyiz* is a sect-related concept (see *ITA* III.2). This might mean that both the eleventh and fifth are masculine or diurnal signs, or perhaps that the eleventh or fifth is a fiery sign (since both the eleventh and fiery signs can indicate noble people, and the fifth is a house of good fortune generally).

[72] For this paragraph, cf. *Flowers* IV.9.

[73] Or simply, "matter, affair."

[74] الطوايف or الطوائف, which can also refer to sects and factions of various types.

communicates by means of supernatural[75] communications, and he performs astonishing works in accordance with the essence of the sign and the lord of the bound of the two [heavy ones].

54 If the two infortunes meet, and the Moon was conjoined with Saturn by latitude, then famine and plague will occur; and if Mars, a shift of leaders and the spilling of much blood, and fighting, and the passing away of what that sign indicates by its essence.

55 If the two fortunes would be united or[76] the Moon would be conjoining with Jupiter by latitude, justice and gentleness and fertility will occur; and if it was Venus, joy and pleasure and the health of bodies will occur, and safety.

56 If a planet were at the edge of the [Sun's] rays, its resemblance is of one who is opposed [and] is contending; and if it was entering under the rays, it indicates exhaustion and it loses its power;[77] and if was going out of the rays, it indicates piety and amiability and obedience.

57 The harm of a comet is greater for the people if it manifests in a sign [formed] in the image of [a human].

58 If the Moon conjoined with a planet by longitude and latitude, then the indication and nature of that sign and planet, and their mixture,[78] cannot avoid manifesting in the world.

59 From the abundance of the indicator's strength, and its loftiness and elevation,[79] is known [its] effects, or from the planets which collect all of its strengths.

60 [For] every thing [that] takes place, its abiding lasts long, and its rejection is stimulated; its remaining [as it is] takes place, and it undergoes alteration and disappears and is corrupted. **61** The long-lasting of its abiding is from the indication of Saturn,[80] and [for] everything [which] happens quickly and reverts quickly and is corrupted is from the indication of Mars. **62** And every thing happens quickly and is corrupted quickly, and [whose]

---

[75] Or more simply, "hidden"; 1485 makes this more specific by using "prophesy."
[76] This should probably be "and."
[77] Combining BL ("exhaustion") and Nur. ("loses its power").
[78] That is, the mixture of the sign and planet, not of the Moon and the planet.
[79] This undoubtedly refers to its elevation in its celestial circles, not elevation in the chart (i.e., being near the Midheaven).
[80] The text uses the Persian names for Saturn and Mars in this paragraph, which could be one clue to it being from a much older source.

durability lasts long in [its] corruption, that is of the nature of Saturn and Mars.

63 And also, for the body of the Sultan when he accedes, or one in charge when he takes control [of his] job, one looks from the Ascendant; likewise one looks for his authority and profit from the Midheaven.

Chapter VIII.4: On the knowledge of the lord of the year

2 And as for Hermes, he said if you wanted to know the lord of the year, then see which planet you found in the four stakes: for that one is the lord of the year. **3** And judge in accordance with its position and its strength and its weakness, and the aspects to it.

4 And if you did not find a planet in the four stakes, and there was a planet in the eleventh or fifth, then it is the lord of the year. **5** If there wasn't one, and there was a planet in the ninth or third, then it is the lord of the year. **6** And if there was no planet among these places, then see which of the planets (except for the Moon) was more hurried in course and departed from the sign in which it was, into the next one: for that one is the lord of the year. **7** And if two or three planets of the sign met [together], then that one of them greater in degrees and closer to [the end] of the sign, departing [from it], that one is the lord of the year—if the lord of its house or its bound or its exaltation was looking at it.

8 And if many planets happened to be in many stakes of the circle at the revolution of the year, and all of them deserve to be the lord of it, then look from the lord of the day or the lord of the hour in which the year was being revolved,[81] and prefer it over all of them, and take it as the indicator. **9** And if the lord of its own bound is looking at it, or the Sun by day or the Moon by night is looking at it, then it is preferred.

10 And if the lord of the day in which the year is revolved is not among the planets in the stakes, nor is [the lord] of the hour, then look from the one stronger in indication and greater in testimony, and prefer it over the remaining ones of them. **11** And the lord of the hour has a share with the lord of the year: you should not reject looking at who is a partner with it among the planets, and grant it a portion, and blend its indication with [the other's] indi-

---

[81] That is, if any of the possible lords of the year *also* happened to be the lord of the day or hour.

cation. **12** And if it was the lord of the hour, and these indications or the majority of them were present with it, then it rules [the year] and manages it from its beginning to its end, and the [other] planets are subordinate to it.

13 And I say[82] that the lord of the year is the planet uniting the testimonies of the lords of the divisions[83] of the Ascendant. **14** And the Sun by day or the Moon by night in one of the stakes, is the lord of the year.

15 And[84] if the lord of the Ascendant is the lord of the house of one of the luminaries, then it is most certainly the lord of the year: with that one does not look for another, and it is the indicator over the condition of the citizens, too. **16** And know the condition of the planet in its strength and weakness, and firmness and withdrawing, and its advancement and retreat,[85] and good fortune and misfortune.

17 And if the planet was strong, fortunate, firm, elevated or approaching [its] elevation,[86] then that year is a safe year, and the conditions of the people in it are excellent [and] praiseworthy. **18** And if it was predominately falling[87] and weak and unfortunate, then that year is a ruinous year, and the condition of the people in it is loathsome and reprehensible, and especially if the Moon experienced such things: for she is the indicator of the lower world in the root, and in the births of years[88] she has a great share and a strong indication.

19 And know that the indicator of the year is indeed indicative for the condition of countries and climes which are in the classification of the sign or its quarter of the circle, in its east and west and north and south: and indeed good fortune and bad fortune will occur according to the place in which the indicator is. **20** And if it was made unfortunate in the Ascendant, the harm and distresses are in their bodies; and if it was in the second, in

---

[82] This seems to be al-Rijāl's own view.
[83] That is, the dignities.
[84] For this sentence, see *RYW* Ch. 2, **2** and *Scito* Ch. 3, **1**.
[85] The pairs of words used here are: *thabāt* (ثبات, firmness) and *zawāl* (زوال, withdrawing), and *ʾiqbāl* (إقبال, advancement) and *ʾidbār* (إدبار, retreat). Each of these pairs refers to angularity and cadency, but are the two angular terms synonymous (and likewise with the cadent terms), perhaps from separate translation streams? Or do they denote something different? "Withdrawing" always refers to dynamic cadency (i.e., declining from the axes), so my tentative thought is that firmness and withdrawing refer to *dynamic* angularity and cadency (i.e., a relationship to the axes), while advancement and retreat refer to *whole sign* angularity and cadency.
[86] الاستعلاء. This probably means being near or approaching its deferent apogee or epicyclic apogee.
[87] This probably means being cadent dynamically or in whole signs.
[88] That is, in revolutions of the year of the world.

their livelihood; and if it was in the third, they disagree and scatter and interrupt [their] kinship and curse amongst themselves; and if it was in the fourth, there are distresses in their lands and immovable property; and if it was in the fifth, it is in their children; and if it was in the sixth, in their grazing livestock and animals and slaves; and in the seventh, wars and hatreds[89] take place in what is between them; and in the eighth, it hastens death and general distresses[90] in them; and if it was in the ninth, it corrupts their religions and journeys; and in the tenth it brings oppression and injustice to them from their rulers; and if it was in the house of hope, they will despair and their opinions will become bad; and if it was in the house of enemies, their enemies will appear.

21 And know that the Sun and Moon participate with all of the planets, and the planets do not participate with the Sun and the Moon—and the meaning of my statement "the Sun participates with a planet" is that the Sun participates with the planets by day, and the Moon by night: so the condition of the luminaries is looked at in the revolution, and their good situation and their corruption. **22** And the Moon by day is stronger than the Sun is by night.

23 And it is necessary for you to know the lords of the foundations (and they are the four quarters).[91] **24** The first belongs to the Sun's alighting in Aries: what is the condition of the Sun? **25** And the second is his alighting in Cancer: what is the condition of Jupiter? **26** And with his alighting in Libra, what is the condition of Saturn? **27** With his alighting in Capricorn, what is the condition of Mars? **28** Because they are the lords of the exaltation of these signs, and you see how these planets look at the places of their own exaltation. **29** After that comes your examination for kings from the Sun's entrance into the sign of Aries, and for the powerful from his entrance into the sign of Sagittarius. **30** So, preserve their Ascendants and the aspect of the planets to them, and their conditions.

31 And you look at the Lot of Fortune and the Lot of the Hidden:[92] where is the place of the lords of their houses and their bounds, and the lords of their triplicities? **32** And if they were in good places and the fortunes looked at them with an aspect of friendship, then say there is every good in

---

[89] This especially means secret hatreds or grudges (ضغائن).
[90] Or, "plagues" (الآفات).
[91] That is, the exalted lords of the signs of the quarterly ingresses or movable signs: see below.
[92] The Lot of Spirit.

it, and surplus, and it grows [and] increases.[93] **33** And if the infortunes looked at them and they were in places of hostility and falling, then say every evil and tribulation and corruption is upon that place and that clime. **34** And if the one looking was Mars, in a place of enmity and position of destruction, then it is made difficult by death and killing, and nosebleeds, and the agitation of the blood, and smallpox, and epidemics, and an abundance of lightning, and wars, and what the nature of Mars desires. **35** And if Saturn was looking, and Mars was not looking, then it is made difficult by disaster and annihilation from aches of the belly and waist, and colic.

36 And it is necessary for you to know that the lord of the house of the Sun is the indicator over the matters of the king in every clime, and that it is the lord of the condition. **37** So look from the aspect to him from the fortunes and infortunes: from the place from which the fortunes are looking, in that clime is fertility and the good and surplus in accordance with the aspect of the fortunes; and the infortunes indicate the contrary of that.

38 Every[94] planet which squares the Sun comes with its essence: for it if was a fortune, it indicates victory for the kingdom, and delight, and rest, and a good condition, and what its nature resembles; and if it was an infortune, it indicates adversities and fear, and accidents, and what the essence of the planets resembles. **39** If the revolution was diurnal, and Mars was in the square of the Sun or opposed to him, and he was barring[95] from a movable sign, it indicates the attack of a foreigner against the king, and he will remove his hand from obedience. **40** And in a revolution of the year, always look at Mars: for if he was in fiery signs, what injures the king will arrive from the eastern area; and if he was in airy signs, the mishap will arrive from the western direction; and if he was in the earthy signs, what he detests will reach him from the southern direction; and in the watery ones, from the northern direction. **41** And if it was Saturn in the square of the Sun,[96] sadness and distress will afflict the king in his assets. **42** And if the Moon was placed[97] with Saturn, disease will afflict his house and his relatives. **43** And if Venus came close to Saturn, distress will afflict the king's women. **44** And if Jupiter was

---

[93] Lit., "it grows in increase."
[94] See **181ff** below, where this is attributed to Abū Ma'shar.
[95] حال. This is not the usual technical term for the configuration called "barring" or "blocking" (*ITA* III.14).
[96] Perhaps we should add "or the opposition," to parallel the situation with Mars (see below, **181ff**). Likewise, this should be in a nocturnal chart.
[97] Lit., that she "occurs" with Saturn.

approaching Saturn, it indicates harm in the[98] nobility and the powerful and the ministers, and those having a sense of honor. **45** And if the Head was with Saturn, it indicates harm in the leaders and the powerful.

46 And know that when it chances to be that the Ascendant is Aries, and the Sun is in the Ascendant of [the revolution],[99] and Jupiter is in his exaltation or Saturn in his exaltation, then that indicates a conflict of kings and leaders in the search for victory and rulership and leadership. **47** And if Mars, too, was in his own exaltation, it indicates fighting and wars and the shedding of blood in Babylon and the rest of the climes, and the corruption of the all the people is universal, and [in] youths and livestock and birds; and powerful civil unrest will arise until it reaches the quarter in which Jupiter was.[100] **48** And if the Moon was also in her exaltation, the conflict and killing will be increased until the end of the year. **49** And if these planets were in the stakes, the conflict is among the kings; and in what follows the stakes, it is among the ministers and leaders; and in the ones declining from the stakes, it is among the general public and the citizens. **50** And if Jupiter was not in his exaltation, but Saturn is in his own exaltation, and the Sun is in his own exaltation, it indicates the wars of two kings, one of them from the east and the other from the west; and the intensity of the war and killing is between them, and there is also tribulation in Babylon.

51 And if Venus was the lord of the year, then look at her place: is it good or bad? **52** And likewise look at the Sun: If he was in a bad place and the lord of the year in a good place, then the citizens will improve their condition, and the condition of the kings will be corrupted. **53** And if both [places] were corrupting and the lord of the year and the Sun were all corrupted, the corruption will include the citizens and the king. **54** And if they were all in a good situation, the safety [of their condition] will include them all. **55** And if they were all with the Tail, then it will be bad for the king and the citizens, so speak according to that.

56 And if Saturn was in the Ascendant, the tribulations and distresses will afflict the king especially. **57** And if he was in the second, that is in his assets. **58** And [it is] in accordance with the houses: in the eighth it is from death in his army; and in the ninth it confers the corruption of his messengers and

---

[98] Reading the rest of this sentence with Nur., as BL blends it with **45**.
[99] This phrase is slightly garbled in the MSS. What al-Rijāl means is that (1) Aries is the exaltation of the Sun, and (2) he is in it, and so exalted, at (3) the Aries ingress.
[100] This probably means the Sun's ingress into Cancer, if we are still maintaining the conditions of **46**.

replies; and the tenth the ones in charge of his works; and in the twelfth, his enemies and his riding animals.

59 And if Mars was in the second place from the Sun, it indicates powerful killing and diseases, and a scarcity of the people's loyalty, one to the other, in these places which are governed by the sign in which Mars is and which it has authority over. **60** And look at the Moon and the second place from her: for if Mars was in it, it indicates diseases in the people; and if that sign was masculine it is in males, and if it is feminine it is in females.

61 And if Saturn was in the eighth from the Ascendant, it indicates diseases of the generality of the people. **62** And likewise look at the rest of the planets: if Jupiter was with the Tail in a bad place, it indicates the death of the powerful, and killing, and diseases of the generality of the people. **63** And likewise if he was burned up, it indicates the ruin of the ministers and judges and the pious, and the powerful, and the ruination of the houses of religious practice.

64 And look at the praiseworthy places in which the fortunes are: for indeed they indicate good according to those places, and their natures, and what strength they have in them.

65 And if you wanted knowledge of the time in which that will happen,[101] then look at the Moon and Mars. **66** For if they were in movable signs, then what they indicate is days; and if it was in [double]-bodied signs, then what they indicate is six months; and if they were in fixed ones, it lasts from the beginning of the year to its end. **67** And look also at the place of the lord of the Ascendant: how much has it traveled in its sign? **68** Assign a month or day or hour to each degree?

69 And the planet which you find to be strong, it is one which you find in a stake or in what follows a stake, except that the strength in the year which is greater than that belongs to the lord of the Ascendant. **70** And if the lord of the Ascendant was good in [its] condition, it indicates the king's escape from the distresses. **71** And if it was in the second, he profits from his assets; and if it was in the third, he profits by means of his brothers; and if it was in the fourth, he profits by means of the villages and residences and the ancient people of his house; and [so on] based on the course of the houses.

72 And if the Sun and the lord of his house were in the house of travel, it indicates a general migration and general travel, and the king will go on a

---

[101] See **59-60**.

journey, and his army and commanders will go along. **73** And if Mars was in a stake and he was looking at the Sun or the Moon [with] an aspect of friendship and strength, then the reason for the travel and the migration is for the combatting of enemies.

74 If at the revolution of the year the Moon was connected with a fortune, it indicates the good health of the bodies of the people, and the moderateness of the air and its mixture, and an abundance of the Sun's glowing, and the proper condition of produce. **75** And if it was the connection of the infortunes, then say the contrary of that. **76** And if her connection was with Saturn, it indicates the difficulty of the king's assets and his works, and the occurrence of harms in every area, and in the water and the earth, and the poor, and it confers evil and loss upon those traveling by land and sea, and those residing in the mountains.

77 And when the lord of the tenth was made unfortunate and its condition becomes evil by falling, and the infortunes were looking at it, [government] workers will encounter evil. **78** And if Mars was looking at it or at Mercury, they will be dismissed and some of them ruined. **79** And if the lord of the tenth was made fortunate, it indicates the prestige of the king's works and his affairs, and the strength of his governors in the regions.

80 If the lord of the second was in a bad condition, his coffers and his assets will come to an end. **81** And if it was declining from the stakes and Mars was looking at it, there is an abundance of expenditures because of wars and what is like that (of the nature of Mars). **82** And if the one looking at it was Saturn, it indicates the breaking of the command of the land tax and an abundance of the remainders.[102] **83** And if the Lot of Fortune were in the second, and Mars and Saturn were looking at it, it indicates the expenses of the houses of assets in wars; and [if] Jupiter and Venus were looking at it, to the contrary of that.

84 And if the lord of the twelfth and sixth were both declining from the stakes, the king will pounce upon his enemies and those rebellious to his command until they are humbled before him.

85 If the lord of the ninth was declining from the stakes, the king will go on a journey. **86** Now if you wanted to know the reason for his journey, then know the direction [in which the lord of the ninth is], and the one looking at it, and mix them together.

---

[102] Reading البقايا with Nur. for البغايا ("whores"). That is, the government will not be able to collect land taxes properly.

87 If you found the Tail in any of the houses and the lord of that house corrupt, then it makes what that sign indicates be rough with corruption in that year.

88 And look at the Lot of Fortune, [for it indicates] the assets[103] of kings. **89** And also look at the condition of the Lot of the Hidden, for it indicates the ambitions of the kings, and their way of life.[104] **90** And if you found the Lot of Fortune made unfortunate, it indicates the king's giving away of his treasures[105] and the destruction of his coffers. **91** And if the Lot of the Hidden was made unfortunate, the ambitions are wicked and his associations are reprehensible—and speak in accordance with the misfortune. **92** If it was made unfortunate by Mars, it is the killing of the pious and God-fearing and judges, especially if it was in a sign in the image of people. **93** And if it was made unfortunate by Saturn, the ominous events and corruption will be in seas and rivers, and one who boards ships and vessels is doomed.

94 And if Mercury was eastern at the entrance of the year or of the quarter, that is indicative of extreme strength for the king and his scribes. **95** And if he was made unfortunate, that is indicative of extreme corruption for the king and his scribes. **96** And if the misfortune and his corruption was by means of Mars, it dismisses the workers, and the king's anger at writers intensifies, and his minister over that deceives him in his matters.

97 The indicator of the king: if there was a planet with it in its sign, participating with it in it,[106] then the indication of good or evil which is attached to the king pervades him and the people of his house. **98** And if Jupiter was stronger in the place, that is in their leaders (and the opposite to that).[107] **99** So judge for the powerful and the general public based on this method.

100 If the Moon was in the house of travel (or one of the planets other than her), and she was strong, it indicates travel and the departure of the people to the area which is attributed to the sign indicating the travel.

---

[103] Reading مال in the spirit of 1485 for امر ("matter, command"). I have had to reconstruct this and **89**, which are truncated and mixed together in the MSS.
[104] سير. This can also refer to their "conduct," or their "movement," both literally and in the sense of putting plans into motion, pursuing something, and how one's actions are progressing.
[105] Or, "supplies."
[106] This might mean that it has some rulership in that place (which is how 1485 reads it).
[107] Reading uncertainly والضد لذلك. I believe al-Rijāl means that if Jupiter is in a good condition, it means something good for such people; but in the opposite situation, the opposite.

101 The contemplation of the Lot of war, and courage, and conquering, and victory.[108] **102** If these Lots were located with the Sun or Moon, in something of their shares and appropriation,[109] they indicate conquering and victory [for the king]. **103** And if they were located with the lord of the year, the citizens of the king will profit with him, and goodness from the region reaches them.

104 If the condition of Mars was excellent at the revolution of the year, it indicates the fidelity and obedience of the king's slaves towards him. **105** And if in addition [Mars] was the lord of the year, his good will be multiplied and the obedience of the slaves towards the king is improved. **106** If the condition of Mars was bad and corrupt and unfortunate, it indicates an attack upon the king from among the rebellious ones of the people. **107** And likewise this should be your examination in war or civil unrest.

108 If you saw Mars in one of the four stakes, then determine the reason for the war from the nature of the sign in which Mars is staying. **109** And always look at Mars in the revolution: for when he is suitable by condition, it improves the servants[110] and army of the king; and if he was unfortunate, it indicates the commotion of the lower class and [their] falling upon the powerful and the leaders. **110** And if it was like that and he was falling away from[111] Jupiter, it indicates the agitation of the wars and an attack of the enemies upon the king. **111** And the knowledge of its condition is from the nature of the sign in which he is staying.

112 And if Mars was under the rays, the wars will last long, and they will be carried out by trickery and deception and silence, until he is eastern; and when he arises [out of the rays], [the trickery] will be cut off. **113** And likewise, if Mercury was under the rays, it slows down the commands of the king and the generality of his writers and his servants, and it brings difficulty until he is eastern: then his commands will be released and go smoothly.[112]

114 When Jupiter is implicated in three or two misfortunes, it indicates the bad condition of the powerful and kings, and ministers, and judges. **115** And

---

[108] Although I am not sure they are the same, the Lot of courage is taken by day from Mars to the Lot of Fortune (and the reverse by night), and projected from the Ascendant (see *ITA* VI.1.6). The Lot of Victory is taken by day from the Lot of Spirit to Jupiter (and the reverse by night), and projected from the Ascendant (see *ITA* VI.1.7). I am not sure if the Lot of war and Lot of conquering are synonyms for these.
[109] That is, in some *dignity* of the Sun or Moon.
[110] Or perhaps better "the vassals," as 1485 has it.
[111] That is, "in aversion to."
[112] Reading somewhat loosely from تستوی.

if he was retrograde or under the rays, it indicates victory for the Turks[113] and their wars, over the king.

116 If Mars was in a movable sign, it indicates the difficulty of the war; and in those having two bodies, [the war happens] at one time, [then] another; and if he was in a fixed sign, it indicates the harshness of the war between the kings and rebels.

117 And look from the places of the king and his allies, and the places of the enemies and the rebellious:[114] for if Mercury was looking at the [last] two, and is strong, they conclude the war by means of ruses and deception.

118 Look at the eighth from the Sun: for if Mars was in it, there will be powerful slaughter, and it will fall upon the king, and especially the people of the area of the sign in which Mars is. **119** And if Mars was in the eighth of the Moon, it indicates great killing and powerful diseases in the people.

120 And if Saturn was in these places from the Ascendant, it indicates a general infirmity. **121** And if the sign was masculine, it is in the men of the kingdom; and in the contrary [gender], in women. **122** And the second is in the likeness of the eighth. **123** And if he made the luminaries unfortunate, killing will take place in the army[115] of the king and his allies. **124** And if Saturn was unfortunate, the corruption will take place in his essence.[116]

125 The Sun indicates the soul[117] of the world: so when he is corrupted, it corrupts the atmosphere. **126** And if the Moon is corrupted, it corrupts the earth.

127 Every planet which is not looking at the Midheaven, is hostile to the king.

128 The places in which the fortunes are, and those which they look at, indicate good; and the places in which the infortunes are or are looking at, indicate corruption. **129** And if the Ascendant and its lord are corrupt, it indicates harm in the kings and the powerful. **130** And if [the corruption] was in the Midheaven and its lord, the harm will be in actions and state reve-

---

[113] 1485 reads this as "low men," which seems appropriate here: for if Jupiter is unable to act well and visibly, then people other than the powerful should be more prominent.

[114] Reading العصاة for القضاة.

[115] Reading جند for خير. But perhaps it would be read as خيرات, "resources, treasures": this would make sense if the affliction of the luminaries is connected to Saturn being in the second (which indicates both resources and allies).

[116] Reading جوهره for جوهرة ("jewel"). I am not sure if this refers to the king, or to Saturn.

[117] The word used for "soul" (روح) is also a word which is etymologically related to wind and the atmosphere, much as the Latin *spiritus* means "spirit," "breathing," and "air."

nue.[118] **140** And if the corruption was in the seventh and its lord, it indicates that the harm which reaches the people is from diseases and illnesses. **141** And[119] if the corruption was by means of the fourth and its lord, the corruption is from an abundance of troops and the chain. **142** If the lord of the tenth was corrupted, it indicates that what attaches to the king (of corruption) is from the direction of the people of his house and his own people. **143** And if the sign and its lord were all corrupted, it indicates a scarcity of respect for the king, and his land tax will be disrupted. **144** And if the lord of the exaltation of the tenth was corrupt, it indicates that the king's acquisition from assets is little.

145 If[120] the Moon is conjoining with Mercury, writers will increase in strength. **146** And if she is conjoining with Jupiter, it indicates fighting and wars.[121] **147** And if she is conjoining with Mars, it indicates earthquakes and burning, and evils and war multiply. **148** And if she is conjoining with Saturn, it indicates the corruption of produce. **149** And if she is conjoining with the Head, it indicates that waters and flooding will increase. **150** And if she is conjoining with the Tail, there are harms in four-footed animals.

151 If[122] Mercury is conjoining with the Moon, indicates the strength of writers and merchants. **152** And if he is conjoining with Venus, it indicates the great pall [of sorrow in] the people and women.

153 If Mars was conjoining with Saturn, it indicates the death of chieftains and withered men, and wars, and civil unrest. **154** And if he was conjoining with Venus, there is ice and cold. **155** And if he is conjoining with the Moon, it indicates earthquakes. **156** And if he is conjoining with Jupiter, it indicates killing and wars.

157 If Mercury is conjoining with Saturn, it indicates an abundance of fleas, bedbugs, and mosquitoes. **158** And if he is conjoining with Venus, it indicates the sorrow of women, and their conflict.

159 If Jupiter is conjoining with Saturn, it indicates the stopping of the disease.[123]

---

[118] Reading المالية for Nur.'s النال (omitted in BL).
[119] Reading **141-42** in parallel with 1485, as they are missing in both MSS.
[120] I believe the following conjunctions all have to do with the planets being unfortunate.
[121] This does not seem right (unless either she or Jupiter is unfortunate). There may be a sentence missing which has dropped out of the manuscript tradition.
[122] See also **157-58** below for Mercury.
[123] Reading الداء in line with 1485's "evil" for Nur.'s الآلاء.

160 If Saturn is conjoining with the Head, it indicates the falling of the powerful. **161** And if he was conjoining with the Tail, it indicates the shedding of blood, and drought, and tribulation, and poverty, and corruption. **162** If the Sun was with the Head, it indicates the death of the powerful and the emergence of diverse kings: and they will seek the leadership. **163** And if the Moon was conjoining with the Head, it indicates the death of those who are socially prominent, and corruption in produce. **164** And if Jupiter was conjoining with the Head, the powerful will increase in power. **165** And if Mars was conjoining with [the Head], he puts on the apparel of weapons, and wars will multiply.

166 If the Tail was conjoining with the Sun, it indicates a scarcity of grasses and vegetation, and the ruin of wild beasts and riding animals. **167** If the Tail was conjoining with Venus, it indicates the ruin of women.

168 If Jupiter was conjoining with Saturn, it afflicts the people; and if the sign was Sagittarius, it indicates the death of kings. **169** And if he was conjoining with Mars, it harms leaders and men of importance. **170** And if it was Venus, women will grieve because of men. **171** And if he was conjoining with the Head, the people will crave religion and will increase in their assets. **172** And if he was conjoining with the Tail, it is contrary to that. **173** And if he was conjoining with Mercury, it indicates the falling of writers and merchants. **174** And if he was conjoining with the Moon, it indicates the departure of the good from the people, and sorrow and worry will increase in the common people, and an abundance of crying and mourning. **175** If the Tail was conjoining with Mars, it indicates tempestuous winds.

176 And[124] you ought to see what belongs to every sign, of lands: for if Mars was unfortunate in the east, it indicates harm taking place in those lands which are in the east; and if he was unfortunate in the west, the harms are in those lands which are in the west; and if he was in the Midheaven, it confers the harms upon those lands which belong to it in the east and west; and if it was in the stake of the earth, it confers it on the lands which are in the area of Canopus[125] and the south.[126]

---

[124] For this paragraph see also VIII.7, **137**, *RYW* Ch. 26, **9-12**, and *Scito* Ch. 52.

[125] سهيل. That is, the fixed star α Argo, whose longitude corresponds to Cancer and so indicates the north (as Cancer is a watery, northern sign).

[126] Reading القبلي for القبلة.

177 And[127] if one of the two infortunes was in one of the stakes at the revolution of the year, it indicates contention and fighting. **178** If[128] it was direct, then it makes that necessary when it goes retrograde; and if it was retrograde, then it is when it [goes direct. **179** And if there were a commixture of] the rays of the indicator of the king [with the indicator of the citizens, it signifies a multitude of robbers and injuries.] **180** And if it was in a place looking at the Ascendant and it was not in a stake, and it is retrograde, the corruption of the people is not general unless the light of the lord of the Midheaven is mixed [with it].

181 And Abū Ma'shar said, look at the square of the Sun at the time of the revolution. **182** For if there was a fortune in it, it indicates the victory of the king and the increase of his assets; and if there was an infortune in it, it indicates the contrary of that—in proportion to the power of the fortune and the infortune. **183** And if Mars was in his square by day, or in his opposition, it indicates civil unrest and conflict, and it will reach some of the kings, and that will be in the area [belonging to the sign] in which Mars is. **184** And if Saturn was in the square of the Sun or his opposition [by night],[129] it indicates the illness of kings and corruption enters upon him in his assets. **185** And if the Moon was with Saturn, it indicates emaciation and chronic illness. **186** And if Venus was with Saturn, it indicates illnesses in the children of kings and ministers. **187** If Jupiter was assembled with Saturn, it indicates insanity and unrest. [**188** And if the Head were joined with Saturn, it signifies pains and complications.][130]

189 And if the Sun and the lord of the hour[131] were together in a bad place, it indicates the destruction of the year for the king and the general populace.

190 And if Saturn was the lord of the year and the Tail assembled with him, it indicates illnesses in the king's women.

191 And if Mars was in the eighth, it indicates powerful slaughter conferred upon the people, and especially in kings and his enemies. **192** And if he was in a masculine sign, the death is in men.

---

[127] For this paragraph, see *Scito* Ch. 80, **2-4** and *BRD* VIII.1, **18**.
[128] For **178-79**, I have divided the sentences according to the statements in *Scito*.
[129] I have added this to match the statement about Mars, so that each infortune is contrary to the sect of the chart.
[130] Adding with 1485, and in accordance with **45** above.
[131] I do wonder if this should be the lord of the *Ascendant*, as it is often referred to as the lord of the "hour" (viz., *Hour-Marker* or Ascendant) in Greek texts.

193 And if the lord of the Ascendant was purified of the infortunes and in a strong place, it indicates the strength of the king, and his joy, and his authority. **194** And if he was in the second in this condition, it indicates an abundance of assets. **195** Then, see in which houses he is, and judge that the good is provided in connection with the lord of that house: if it was the house of children or brothers or slaves or travel or women or authority, so the good and benefit in all things is in accordance with the essence of that sign.

196 And when you found Jupiter to be eastern at the revolution of the year, or looking at the Sun, then it gives victory and prosperity[132] to the king.

197 And when Mars was the lord of the year and is retrograding [in] that year in a corrupt place or in an alien[133] position, and none of the fortunes is looking at him or approaching him, it stirs up enemies against the kings, and provokes wars.

198 The meeting of Jupiter and Mars[134] indicates the ruin of a powerful man of stature, and especially if the sign was fixed; and the time is taken from the lord of the house in which they meet, a day for every degree. **199** And the meeting of Saturn and Venus destroys a powerful woman of stature; and if Mercury was with them, it destroys her child with her.

200 And if Venus and Mercury were both unfortunate in the revolution, then they indicate the corruption of the king with the citizens, and the corruption of the matter of the citizens by the king (and especially if the Moon was unfortunate), and the shedding of blood, and revenge, and perhaps they both corrupt everyone (I mean, the king and the citizens, by the matter of the powerful): the corruption appears and the civil unrest increases, and that is multiplied in the division of the sign in which they both are.

---

[132] Reading الفلاح for الفلح.
[133] That is, "peregrine."
[134] The Persian name for Mars.

Chapter VIII.5: On the conjunction [of the planets], by Hermes

2 And Hermes said on the conjunction:[135]

3 *Aries*: If [the Moon][136] was united with Jupiter, Venus, and Mercury in Aries, it indicates the excellence of the situation in all of the provinces and an abundance of cold and rains, and the benefit of women and writers in connection with kings. **4** And if it was only the Moon and Jupiter, it indicates justice and fairness.

5 *Taurus*: If Venus and Mars are united in it, it indicates the violence of women against men, and an abundance of disease and death in riding animals, and fighting[137] increases, and the raging of winds, and the corruption of the produce and trees. **6** And if Jupiter, Venus, Mars, and the Moon met in Taurus, they indicate an abundance of lying and betrayal in the people, and earthquakes, and an abundance of waters, and the ruin of the princes and the nobility, and it indicates the lower classes and an attack of rebels[138] from the area of the mountains, against the king. **7** And if Saturn, Jupiter, and Mars were united in this sign, it indicates the death of livestock and the departure of kings from their homelands to another place, and an abundance of illnesses from a disturbance of the bile, and an abundance of death in livestock and the people.

8 *Gemini*: If the Sun, Venus, and Mercury were united in it, they indicate the corruption of the condition of writers and accounting, and the masters of offices, and the army's associating with the king, and the cheapness of prices, and the sabotaging of highways and paths.[139]

9 *Cancer*: If Saturn, Jupiter, Mars, the Sun, the Moon, and Venus were united in it, it indicates a scarcity of the good, and the fear of the people from the injustice of the authorities, and the injustice of some against the others, and the appearance of wonders in the air, and an abundance of earthquakes, and the corruption of the seas and waters.

10 *Leo*: If Saturn, Jupiter, Mars, and the Moon were united in it, it indicates the fighting of some kings against others, and the intensity of the war, and the corruption of the people.

---

[135] This is undoubtedly the Arabic source that inspired the Latin work attributed to al-Qabīsī, in Section I.6.
[136] Adding the Moon with 1485, especially as she is mentioned in the next sentence.
[137] Reading القتال with Nur. for العمال ("workers").
[138] This should probably read as an attack by *both* lower classes *and* rebels.
[139] That is, through highway robbery.

11 *Virgo*: If Saturn, Mars, and Mercury were united in it, it indicates the corruption of women and the arrogance of kings. **12** And if the Sun was eclipsed in it at the Tail, and Mars was assembled with him, wars and great fighting will take place between the nobility and the lower classes. **13** And if Saturn and Venus were united in it, it indicates the increase of waters.

14 *Libra*: If Mars and Jupiter were united in it, it indicates the badness of the condition of the people of honor,[140] and the appearance of redness in the air of that year. **15** And if Jupiter, the Sun, and the Moon were united in it, it indicates death falling in women and people of a good condition, and an abundance of rains and fog, and the corruption of the atmosphere.

16 *Scorpio*: If Saturn, Mars, and Venus were united in it, it indicates that the king chases something, and it will be feared for him from it;[141] and kings will leave their homelands, and the transgression of some against others, and it breaks up the happiness between them. **17** And if the Moon was united with them, it indicates an abundance of rains and an increase of the waters. **18** And[142] if Scorpio was the Ascendant of the year, and Saturn is in it and Mars also with him (or far from him [but] in the division of the Ascendant), and Venus burned up, and Jupiter retrograde, then judge every evil and civil unrest, and the ruin of cities and earthquakes and trembling, and fighting, and plague and defects, because Scorpio is the most unfortunate of the signs just as its lord is the most unfortunate of the planets. **19** And also judge the attack of kings (one against the other), and the death of powerful people, and tribulations in the world. [**20** And if both fortunes were joined at the same time in this sign, it signifies that men will be betrayed, or an enemy who will invite men to disobedience to God.][143]

21 *Sagittarius*: If Saturn, Jupiter, and the Moon were united in it, it indicates an abundance of waters and submersions, and the coercion of kings, and the elevation of [government] ministers and the masters of the stars,[144] and sorcerers, and fortune-tellers.[145]

---

[140] Or rather, the nobles.
[141] This seems to refer to hunting.
[142] This sentence describes many of the conditions of one of Sahl's mundane charts, the Libra ingress of 778 AD. I will translate Sahl's mundane work in a future volume.
[143] Adding with 1485.
[144] That is, astrologers.
[145] Or, "priests" (الكهنة).

22 *Capricorn*: If the Sun, Mars, and Mercury were united in it, it indicates the ruin of kings by hot[146] diseases, and an abundance of fires and burning, and the blowing of the winds, and a scarcity of the plants of the earth, and an abundance of thieves.

23 *Aquarius*: If Saturn, Mars, and the Moon were united in it, it indicates a scarcity of rains and an abundance of the water of springs, and the corruption of the roads and paths, and an abundance of snakes.

24 *Pisces*: If Saturn, Jupiter, and Mars were united in it, it indicates the death of the powerful and the nobility, and an abundance of harm,[147] and the killing of kings. **25** If it was the Sun and Mars, it indicates scarce rains and an abundance of the fishing of the sea.

26 And[148] know that if the Head and Saturn met in a sign, then indeed they indicate harm and evil, in accordance with the sign in which they are meeting. **27** For if they were in the fiery signs, it is in riding animals and everything having fur. **28** And if it was in the earthy ones, it is in the trees and produce and grasses, from[149] the scarcity of rain and its benefit. **29** And if it was in the airy ones, disease and fear and injustice and dread strike the people. **30** And if it was in the watery ones, it indicates the corruption of the waters and the death of their animals, and an abundance of locusts and vermin, and pains, and phlegm.

31 Abū Ma'shar said,[150] always look for the vizier of the king from Jupiter, if he was in a stake of the year, [whether in] a [bad] condition or good condition—his condition is recognized from the condition of Jupiter. **32** And if he was burned up, or retrograde going towards the opposition of the Ascendant, or made unfortunate by Saturn, then the king will punish his minister in that year, and perhaps he will kill him. **33** And if Jupiter was eastern, in his own triplicity, strong in it, it indicates the strength of the command of the minister and the goodness of his condition.

34 And Mars is indicative of the king's deputy and the master of his troops: so if he was in the opposition of Saturn, then the king will be angry with the master of his troops, and his rank will fall in [the king's] opinion,

---

[146] Or, "quartan" (الحارة), referring to fevers and symptoms that recur in cycles of about four days.
[147] Nur. has "diseases" or "illnesses."
[148] For this paragraph, see *RYW* Ch. 24, **2-7** and *Scito* Ch. 64, **1-5**.
[149] Reading with Nur. for "and."
[150] I am not sure how much of the following is from Abū Ma'shar.

and the army will encounter what it hates. **35** And[151] if Mars was in the square of Saturn and Jupiter (both of them),[152] then there are wars in that quarter,[153] and a [military] delegation [which is] sent out will strike the army, and they will find attacking to be troublesome, and some of them will run away for that reason, and they will escape to the enemies of the king. **36** And if Mars was the lord of the Midheaven, the king will go out personally. **37** And if Mars was retrograde in that year or that quarter, then the army will flee and be defeated. **38** And if Mars was in a human sign and he was made unfortunate, then they spread the killing in the army of the king. **39** And if the tenth sign was purified of the infortunes, then it is improved; and if it was made unfortunate, then they are angered.

40 And if Venus were corrupted by retrogradation and burning at the revolution of the year and quarter, then death circulates in the king's women and his servants.

41 And if Mercury were corrupt, it indicates the badness of the condition of writers; and if he was corrupted by Mars, then indeed they will engage in fraud against the king and his seal. **42** And if the Moon was bodily with Mercury, and the Moon was increased in light, quick in motion, made fortunate, and the revolution was at night, then it indicates the safety of the king, and his duration and respect; and if he had a child who was heir [to the throne], he will promote and increase him in his condition. **43** And if the Moon was in the contrary of that, it indicates the badness of the king's condition and the corruption of the condition of his heir. **44** And if the misfortune of the Moon increased, and the revolution was nocturnal, the heir of the king will die in that year.

[Abū Ma'shar / Hermes / Abū 'Abd Allāh bin Masrūr][154]

45 And I say that if Saturn was the indicator of the year and he was made unfortunate, there will be plague in chieftains and slaves and the Berbers. **46** And if it was Jupiter, it will be in middle-aged people; and if it was Mars, it will be in youths; and if it was the Sun, it will be in the powerful; and if it was

---

[151] Cf. Ch. VIII.13, **16**.
[152] Nur. and 1485 have, "in the square of Saturn or Jupiter, or both of them."
[153] Reading بر with BL, but Nur. reads that Mars is "retrograde" (راجع). Grammatically, "quarter" makes more sense, but retrogradation makes astrological sense, too.
[154] See **62** below.

Venus, it will be in women; and if it was Mercury, it will be in young boys; and if it was the Moon, it will be universal in all the people.

47 And if the lord of the year looked at the Ascendant from the square or opposite, then that year is a year of violence and tribulation, and restriction and plagues, and great tribulations, and especially the opposition.[155] **48** And if the lord of the year was standing opposite [the Ascendant], it is hostile to the year; and that will be more intense and harmful than the misfortune of the unjust,[156] destructive infortunes.

49 And I also say that if the lord of the year is connected with a falling planet, and [the lord of the year] is in a stake or in what follows a stake, then that year is excellent [except that] at its end there is severity and weakness and harmful matters. **50** And if the lord of the year was falling and it is connected with a planet that is received, strong, then it raises it up and returns its condition and strength to it: and the beginning of that year is bad, and at its end there is a good condition and good, and benefit, and strength, and good fortune.

51 If at the change-over of years the sign of any city was corrupt, or its lord harmed by retrogradation or burning or being in [its] downfall[157] or falling, or an enemy from among the planets would be looking at it, it indicates corruption in accordance with that infortune, in accordance with the harm and damage belonging to that sign and planet. **52** And the strength in good and evil belongs to the country whose sign is that of the Ascendant of the year.

53 And know that the indicative planet over the year, if it was in one of the signs, it indicates by means of its own essence and the essence of that sign, and the place of the sign from the Ascendant, in accordance with the condition of the planet in misfortune and good fortune. **54** [And] by the permission of God it provides the good and usefulness and joy in [a good] indication, and its misfortunes indicate evil and damages and unforeseen mishaps.

55 And if Saturn were the one in charge [of the year], and he was strong, it indicates leisure and a scarcity of travels, and ease of life,[158] and mildness.

---

[155] This sentence contains an extra "especially" with an awkward transition to **48**. I have a feeling the sentence should read, "and especially the opposition, *particularly if it is [also] the lord of the Ascendant.*"
[156] Reading الجائزة for الجائزة ("prize, reward").
[157] That is, its fall or descension.
[158] الخفض.

56 And Jupiter indicates the goodness of income and fertility and capacity and comfort. **57** And Mars[159] indicates triumph over enemies and conquering and subjugating [them], and victory. **58** And the Sun indicates the justice of the king, and his compassion, and good deeds, and mercy. **59** And Venus indicates delight, and joy, and comfort. **60** And Mercury [indicates] ease in the land tax, and benefit, and revenues in commerce and buying and selling, and what is like that. **61** And the Moon indicates good and benefit for the people generally.

62 These sections which I have presented are based on the view of one who appoints the Ascendant as the indicator of the king:[160] and that is Abū Ma'shar and Hermes, based on the account of Abū Ma'shar and based on the view of 'Abū[161] 'Abd Allāh bin Masrūr: it is equivalent to the first page,[162] and that is the excerpt which begins "I say, if Saturn was the indicator."[163] **63** And as for the view of Ptolemy and the majority of the sages, and the view of al-Tabarī and the eminent people of this craft, indeed they assign the Ascendant of the revolution and the Moon to the citizens, and the tenth and its lord and the Sun (the one of them which was the victor) to the king, and [they take] the assets of the citizens from the second, and the assets of the king from the eleventh, and based on this the similarities [between them] end:[164] and I advocate this view and work according to it.

64 And know that the lord of the year indicates the citizens, and the lord of the exaltation of its house or the exaltation of the sign of the Ascendant indicates the powerful. **65** And the lord of the triplicity indicates distinguished people,[165] and the lord of the bound and the face indicate those of the people who are beneath them. **66** And inspect Jupiter with the indication of the nobility.

67 And[166] turn for help from the Lot of Fortune and its lord, for if it[167] looked at the indicator of the king, it indicates his good fortune; and likewise if it looked at the indicator of the citizens.

---

[159] The Persian name for Mars (بهرام).
[160] This does not seem right, and al-Rijāl probably means to say "indicator of the *year*."
[161] Adding "Abu" with Nur.
[162] This does not quite make sense to me, but the point is that al-Rijāl is identifying where his quotation begins.
[163] See **45** above. Nevertheless, al-Rijāl does not tell us precisely who he is quoting.
[164] Reading "the similarities…end" very broadly and uncertainly for فقس سائر الاشكال.
[165] الشرفة.
[166] For this sentence, see *Scito* Ch. 56, **5-6**, and *RYW* Ch. 19, **26-27**.

Chapter VIII.6: The matter of the populace & the citizens

[Al-Kindī: Forty Chapters Ch. 40]

2 Establish the Ascendant for the meeting and the fullness which was before the Sun's alighting in in Aries, and the places of the planets, and the stakes. **3** Then, look at the one with whom the Moon is connecting when she separates from the meeting or fullness: is it a fortune or infortune, is it strong or weak? **4** So, speak about the condition of the general public based on that.

5 And if the Moon was advancing,[168] in her own shares, and connecting with a strong fortune, advancing, in its own shares, the condition of the general public is excellent in that year, and they will be moved from abundance to abundance, and good to good. **6** And if Jupiter was the one connecting with her, they will be in justice, and safety, and good health, and an abundance of offspring, and purity, and high-minded ethics. **7** And if Venus was the one connected with her, they will be in abundance and pleasure and the occurrence of copulating and marrying off, and rejoicing.

8 And if the matter was the opposite of that, such that the Moon is declining[169] or in what is not her own shares, it will also be according to what we described of good fortune, except that they will move from restriction and inactivity to abundance and good fortune, and from weakness to strength. **9** And if the Moon was advancing and it was according to what we described of the strength of [her] condition and being situated in her own shares, and her connection was with a fortune [that was] falling [but] in its own shares, they will be moved from abundance and strength to an abundance of condition [that is] weaker than that, and to inactivity. **10** And if the fortune, along with its falling, was weak [and] alien, there are symptoms of good fortune and good luck [but] what it needs [to fully manifest] is incomplete; but they personally will be in good health and security from diseases.

11 And if the Moon was weak, in exile,[170] and connected with the infortunes, and the infortunes were advancing, that indicates the bad condition of the general populace and their falling, and the weakness of their conditions, and the restriction of their income, and the abundance of their diseases, and

---

[167] This probably means the lord of the Lot, but it would be good for the Lot itself to be configured to these significators.
[168] That is, "angular" and probably also "succeedent."
[169] Cadent (lit., "falling"), probably by quadrant divisions.
[170] That is, peregrine.

the calamity[171] of the situation in that. **12** And if the infortune to which the Moon is connecting was the lord of the eighth of the Moon, or it had a strong share in the eighth [from] the Moon (so that it is not its lord), there is an abundance of death in them. **13** And if the infortune was not like that, and the lord of the eighth [from] the Moon was looking at the Moon, it indicates that death increases. **14** And if Saturn was the infortune to which the Moon was connected, the diseases will be Saturnian, and they will be the reason for the death in that. **15** And if it was Mars instead of Saturn, the diseases will be hot and bloody. **16** And if he was in one of the human signs, there will be killing in addition, and a great shedding of blood, and especially if the year had reached the place of Mars at the beginning of the matter[172] or to his place in the shift of the transit,[173] or to his place at the conjunction which was prior to the revolution: for indeed these years indicate wars and the shedding of blood. **17** And the wars will be in the portions of the earth which the sign in which Mars is, resembles, in the revolved year and the [places listed above].[174] **18** And the conclusion of the war will be in that year (by the permission of God) [in which there is] the burning of Mars and his downfall or the burning of Jupiter.

19 Then, look at the place of Mars: for if he was eastern or western, or southern or northern, then the victory belongs to those in whose direction Mars was. **20** And if Mars was mixed with Mercury, it increases epidemics in that year; and if Mercury was like that with Saturn, and he is in the earthy signs in the revolution of the year, they will immediately suffer[175] earthquakes in extreme[176] places for that, and they are the places near coasts and islands, what is barren, rugged, and the mountains.

---

[171] Reading الداهية for الدوية ("medications")

[172] المسئلة, precise role unclear here. The Latin al-Kindī reads "the beginning of that people." I take the next two options to be: (2) a mundane profection to his place at the time of the triplicity shift; (3) a mundane profection to his place at the time of the most recent Saturn-Jupiter conjunction.

[173] Reading with Nur. BL has "center," which I take to be the "centers" of the epicycles of Saturn and Jupiter: namely, the triplicity shift of their mean conjunctions.

[174] Reading with the Latin al-Kindī for conflicting phrases in BL and Nur. I cannot decipher.

[175] Reading as ام توّ (MS: لم تو). But "immediately" seems like an extreme statement. Hugo's Latin al-Kindī does not state this, but indirectly supports my use of "suffer," saying that earthquakes will "shatter" the following places.

[176] Reading tentatively for what seems to be المنتهية. But "appropriate" seems like a better term.

21 And if the conditions of the Moon and the infortunes is like what we have described in the advancing of some of them and the retreating of some of them, it is a shift from evil to the good, and from the good to evil, based on what we described in the situation of the fortunes.

[The Lot of Fortune]

22 And if the Lot of Fortune was eastern, and Jupiter and the lord of its[177] house were both looking at it, it indicates there is goodness in the country in which the Lot of Fortune is, and security, and a scarcity of fear. **23** And if it and its lord (I mean, the Lot of Fortune) were in a good place, it indicates good and usefulness. **24** And if it was in a reprehensible place, it indicates harms and loss based on the essence of the sign in which they both were.

[Planets as the victors of the year]

25 And from that, if Saturn is strong in the revolution of the year, and he had the role of victor in the places of strength, it indicates building and gentleness and the increase of the condition [of the people] and the proper condition of [one's] livelihood. **25** And if he was unfortunate and weak, it indicates demolition, and flooding and cold, and injustice and disgrace, and earthquakes.

26 And if Mars was strong and he had the role [of victor] in the year, it indicates the victory and strength and conspicuousness of the people of that clime over those who are close to them (among the people of the seven climes). **27** And if he was retrograde or weak, it indicates burning and the shedding of blood, and epidemics, and hot pains.

28 And if Jupiter was strong and more suitable in the revolution of the year, and he had the victorship, the people will manifest the good, and abstinence, and piety, and [their] creed, and religious practice. **29** And if he was to the contrary to this, they will break off relations with one another, turn away from one another, and remain aloof,[178] and the well-to-do will refrain from

---

[177] The Arabic does not specify whether this is the lord of Jupiter or of the Lot, but probably the latter: see **23**.

[178] تعافوا, which means to "recover" or "recuperate" (from عفا), but may rather be Form 6 of عفّ, which means to abstain from something forbidden or shrink away from something. 1485 understands it as similar the latter, saying they will not "hold tight to the law nor will they obey it."

charity and what properly goes to[179] the people, and the giving of counsel,[180] and [there will be] poverty and need, and hunger and harm and submissiveness will appear in the people. **30** And if Jupiter was in the opposite of the Ascendant in the revolution of the year, good fortunes will be diverted away from the citizens, and will be at odds with them, and they will not have good fortunes.

31 And if the Sun was strong, safe, the king[181] will be strong, and [also] the powerful and the nobility, and the leadership and important positions[182] will be increased in the people, and the ranks of many peoples will be raised up, and they will reach the heights and [high] rank and nobility. **32** And it is necessary that you establish the Sun as the king, [and] the place of the Ascendant, and the houses are arranged from him just as you manage the indications of the twelve houses from the Ascendant:[183] and you look at the places of the fortunes and infortunes from that, and they have influence over what every house from him indicates. **33** And do likewise for the general public by means of the lord of the year. **34** And if [the Sun] was degraded [and] humbled, it humbles the kings and degrades their ranks, and injustice will overwhelm the people due to their governors, and powerful, loathsome things will enter upon them from their kings.

35 And if Venus was strong, made fortunate, good fortune and delight will appear in the people, and comfort and luxury, and [their] livelihood will be in a good condition, and the populace will expand, and it increases their delight in women and children and the [other] indications of Venus. **36** And if she was bad in condition, corrupted, it corrupts their condition and their delights will be spoiled, and increases their sadness and their worries, and their livelihoods will be constricted, and evil and injustice will appear in them.

37 And if Mercury was strong [and] safe, revenues will appear, and winds will rise, and literature will spread in the majority of the world and the populace, and the people will love one another and live harmoniously, and they will be connected with one another, and speeches and poetry will appear in them, and every [kind of] elegant, admirable speech. **38** And if he was cor-

---

[179] العائدة إلى.
[180] الإفتاء.
[181] Reading as the singular to match the verb.
[182] الاخطار.
[183] In other words, look at the derived houses from the Sun's place.

rupted, made unfortunate, it makes the condition of the people more severe, and their governors will oppress them in the land tax and their land, and literature will decrease, and the winds will be tempestuous, and revenues will decrease, and false rumors and lying will increase.

39 And if the Moon was fortunate, the general populace will be safe, and it decreases distresses and illness in them, and the waters will be moderate, and the rains will be useful, suitable, fortunate, fertile. **40** And if she was corrupted, harms will enter upon the general public from their leadership, and diseases will multiply, and perhaps rain in the time which is not wanted for that, and withheld from the people [when] it is wanted.

[General significations of the planets]

41 And look from the Moon for the general public, and from the Sun for kings and the powerful and the nobility, and from Mercury for writers and commerce and the seeking of knowledge and youths, and from Jupiter for judges and legal knowledge and the nobility, and from Mars for commanders and soldiers and the masters of the hinterland[184] and the leadership of wars, and from Saturn for household managers and farmers and unpleasant things, and from Venus for women and singers and amusements and the friends[185] of delight.

[Saturn as lord of the year]

42 And after that, when Saturn is the lord of the year and he is retrograde in Libra, it indicates wars between the kings of the land of the west and the north. **43** And if he was retrograde in Scorpio, it indicates wars and civil unrest and epidemics and disease and corruption in the people and waters and the lords of the islands.[186]

44 And see in whose bound (of the planets) [he is] in, and where the lord of his bound is, and upon which (of the planets) Saturn casts his rays, and decree that the events will be in the allotment of the earth and the country belonging to those planets; and that will be [more] evil if his aspect was from enmity.

---

[184] That is, distant borders being held by military outposts.
[185] That is, people who get involved with, or are associated with, delight and music.
[186] Or, "Algeria" (الجزائر).

45 And if Jupiter was transiting above [Saturn] in the sector,[187] a man who commands justice will rise up against the king. **46** And if the planets were looking at [Jupiter], it multiplies his assistants and followers and victory. **47** And if they were looking at Saturn without [Jupiter], the king will have victory over him.[188]

[Each planet as lord of the year]

48 And if Saturn was the lord of the year and he had strength, then that year will be one of many buildings and structures, and [new] rivers will come to be in the earth [which] were not [there], and prices will be cheap, and the land fertile, and the good of the populace will be increased, and especially servants and the lower class and [those who suffer] coercion. **49** And if he was bad in condition, it makes the cold severe, and diseases multiply, and attacks become widespread in the people, and the winds become tempestuous, and rains become scarce, and the harms will enter upon servants and the people of war, and death will be speedy for the sheikhs and old men, and the earth will tremble in diverse places, and injustice and oppression will appear from the leadership against their household managers and those who are above that. **50** And the majority of that is in the countries attributed to Saturn. **51** And know that the opposition of Saturn to Mars is more severe than his conjunction, and worse in [its] indication.

52 And if Jupiter was the lord of the year, and he was strong, good in place, then in that year the commands of judges and their jurisprudence will be proper, and the God-fearing and pious, and they will acquire good and power, and the joy of the people will be powerful, and it improves the condition of the nobility, and the [political] authority is just, and he commands what is accepted as being good, and he is restrained from what is detestable, and renunciation and piety appear in the populace. **53** And if he was received,[189] the populace will have profit from the king and benefits will accrue to them from him, and advantage and what is useful. **54** And if he was made

---

[187] This refers to a medieval theory of transits (see Kennedy 1958), which I hope to describe in a later book on astronomy. Given two planets, the one which is proportionately closer to its apogee (of the deferent or the epicycle) is transiting "above" the other.

[188] In other words, the aspecting planets indicate allies. Therefore, if more (or all) are aspecting Saturn but not Jupiter, then the king (Jupiter) will be victorious.

[189] Reading لا مقبول with 1485 and Nur. for مقبلا ("advancing," or angular by quadrant divisions).

unfortunate, it debases the decrees and jurisprudence, and tribulation will enter upon them, and great detestable things, and the people of Babylon will get harm and corruption, and it strengthens[190] the powerful ones of the people and their rank and nobility, and the majority of mosques are destroyed, and poverty and need and humiliation will spread in the people, and it makes the condition of the general populace bad, and good people will abstain from the good, and corruption and injustice increase in the land. **55** And if Jupiter was the lord of the year and Mars was transiting in the sector above him, a powerful foreigner will rise up against the king, doing outrages against what is just, a shedder of blood; and the king will be good [and] honorable. **56** And indeed that one of the two which [more] planets were looking at will have more assistance and victory, and the analogy with the rest of the planets is based on this.

57 And know that Saturn is the indicator of kings by nature, because he is the highest of the planets, and gathers their connections to himself,[191] and he does not [himself] connect with [any] planet. **58** And Jupiter is the indicator of the rebels, because he succeeds him [in order],[192] and only one who is like [the king] and is close to him, rises up against him.[193]

59 And if Mars was the lord of the year, and he was strong, fortunate, then that year will be one of a good condition for commanders and the army, and they will be distinguished and accepted and it strengthens their confirmation, and the people of the hinterlands and what borders on that will be conquered, and it increases the rains in days [appropriate] for it, and the people will be happy with the rain and the victory and conquering. **60** And if he was made unfortunate, harms will enter into the communications and the people of the hinterlands and the lords of the sheikhs and the manufacturers of arms, and fear and disunity and dissent will spread—and that will be mostly in the lands and climes attributed to him.

61 And if the Sun was the lord of the year, and he was safe from the infortunes, then the king of that clime will be victorious over all kings of the climes, and it will strengthen the kings and nobility and the powerful, and

---

[190] 1485 says that *harms* will appear in the powerful and the nobles. But I take this to mean that law and morality will decrease, while raw power (i.e., among the powerful) will increase.
[191] That is, all planets apply to him, but he does not apply to others.
[192] This verb also has the connotation of "approaching": in other words, rebels are usually people close to the king but not quite at his level—they are "approaching" his rank.
[193] Nevertheless some of our texts say that Mars indicates rebels.

they will think [about] what is good, and [there will be] safety and security, and it increases the food and profit and animals and birds: everything which belongs to [the Sun] based on his authority and indication will be in a good condition. **62** And if he was made unfortunate, it weakens the [political] authority, and [indicates] the humiliation of the nobility, and slaves and servants and the lower class will prevail over kings. **63** And if at the revolution of the year the Sun was in the tenth, [and] Mars in the Ascendant, it indicates disease at the beginning of the year, and civil unrest in its middle, and evil between kings. **64** And if Mars was in his own fall, it indicates that the warriors of the king will not be faithful to him, and not thoughtful. **65** And if the Tail was with Mars, it indicates civil unrest and fighting. **66** And if the lord of the year and the Sun were both made unfortunate, it indicates the corruption of the king's matter.[194] **67** And if the Ascendant and its lord were corrupt and unfortunate along with them, it indicates the corruption of the matter of the citizens along with their [political] authority.

68 And if Venus was the lord of the year and she was in what we mentioned about good fortune and strength, that is a good condition for women, and they will be safe from distresses and diseases, and pregnant women will give birth, and their delight with husbands and children will take place, and she strengthens amusements and singers, and they will gain in rank from kings, and entertainment and intoxication and music will be increased in the people. **69** And if she was weak, corrupt, then that year will be one of a scarcity of good, and the people will be disturbed in their pleasures, and disturbed in their livelihoods, and diseases will take place in women, and pregnant women will die, and there will be earthquakes in diverse lands, and buildings will be demolished, and there will be little fighting, and concerns and sadness will enter upon the king. **70** And that is greater in her lands and her climes.

71 And if Mercury was the lord of the year and he was safe from the infortunes and the fortunes looked at him and joined with him, then that year is one of a good condition for youths and the people of knowledge and literature, and merchants. **71** And that is good if the lord of his house was receiving him: and if he was received, [the people of his] party will get a [good] position from the [political] authority, and they will achieve leadership and honor. **72** And if he was falling or burned up or corrupted by the infor-

---

[194] Or perhaps specifically, his commands and orders (امر).

tunes, and he was in a bad place of the circle, it indicates restriction in livelihoods, and severity in the land tax and lands, and it increases worry and false rumors, and harm will be prevalent in writers and merchants. **73** And the majority of that is in the area of the west and the places attributed to Mercury.

74 And if the Moon was the lord of the year, and she was safe from the infortunes, rains will multiply and diseases will be scarce,[195] the people become rich, and reports are useful, and that is better if she was received: for then they will have a [better] rank from kings, and there are rains in the days [appropriate to] it. **75** And if she was corrupt or made unfortunate, harms and corruption will be widespread in all of the world, and that is more severe and appears [more] in the countries which belong to that sign in which the misfortune of the Moon is.[196]

Chapter VIII.7: The indications of the planets in their arrival in the Ascendant & the remaining houses[197]

[Saturn]

2 If Saturn was in the Ascendant of the year and the revolution was diurnal, and the lord of his house was looking at him from the signs of friendship and love,[198] and the lord of the Midheaven was like that in terms of looking and reception, that indicates that the people of the clime will have restraint, and it decreases their journeys, and improves their condition, and they see great good and courtesy from their kings and important people, and they will acknowledge their higher rank and comfort in their livelihood. **3** And if he was in that position and if he was made unfortunate, harmed, there is intense harm in the bodies of the people (with other distressing, Saturnian things),

---

[195] Reading with Nur., as BL reads "diseases multiply and rains become scarce."
[196] نحس. But I could also see this as the active participle (ناحس), which would mean the countries belonging to the sign in which the one *making her unfortunate* is.
[197] In what follows, the descriptions are of the planets when they are the lords of the year (see **26, 54, 101, 119**). See also VIII.11, which does seem to describe every planet in every house regardless of any special role in the chart.
[198] This probably means from signs whose *aspects/configurations* are those of friendship (i.e., trines and sextiles).

especially if he was western in the signs[199] or falling,[200] the fortunes not looking at him.

4 And if he was in the second from the Ascendant, and the lord of the second is connecting with him, it indicates the excellence[201] of craftsmen and menial servants and forced laborers in their earnings and livelihoods, and that is better in what is of the essence of the signs in which Saturn is. **5** And if he was in that place, made unfortunate, it indicates the scarcity of assets and the restriction of the general public, and the idleness of the craftsmen, and an economic slump in Saturnian commerce.

6 And if he was in the third from the Ascendant, and he was strong, made fortunate, it indicates the delights of the people with one another in that year, and their friendliness, and their trials and sympathy [with one another], and the disappearance of grudges and tribalism between them, and [the removal] of calamities from them. **7** And if he was in the third from the Ascendant, made unfortunate, the roads will be cut off and it diminishes journeys, and it increases bad dreams in the people, and the lying of the masters of reports in their reports, and it causes the people to retaliate, and it severs the kindliness and friendship between them.

8 And if he was in the fourth from the Ascendant, and he was received, strong, it indicates building and structures, [and that men will esteem this and get involved very much with it. **9** And if he were harmed there, it signifies that things and buildings will fall, settlements will be diminished],[202] and waters will be cut off, and the general populace will be constricted, and a blockade will afflict the people of that clime, or they will refrain from departing from their own countries due to fear of their enemies—and that will be more severe if the fourth sign was fixed (for indeed it indicates, in addition, the [long] duration of that evil and severity).

10 And if he was in the fifth sign and he was made fortunate, it indicates the delights of the people in their children, and sheikhs and adults will get benefit from them, and conveniences in their means of subsistence. **11** And if

---

[199] This probably means that he is either western of the Sun, or under the rays—not "in western signs," as 1485 seems to have it.
[200] This word normally refers to planets in cadent signs or in aversion from something: since the next clause explicitly says that the fortunes are not looking at him (i.e., they are in aversion to him), I believe this simply means that he is in aversion *from the fortunes*.
[201] Reading حسن in the spirit of 1485 ("good state") for حبس, "confinement."
[202] Adding with 1485.

it was the contrary of that, it indicates the harm of unforeseen events from what is like those [types of fifth-house things].

12 And if he was in the sixth, and that sign was one of the human ones, it indicates Saturnian and melancholic pains from wicked disturbances and madness and servants, and every pain which is of coldness and dryness. **13** And if it was a four-footed sign, that indicates the occurrence of distresses in animals and predatory beasts and livestock.

14 And if he was in the seventh, it indicates the pleasures of men in women, and the marrying of women in that year (with old people, if it was of the signs of people). **15** And if it was of the signs of earth, it indicates the seeking of what is of the essence of that sign, of living things and vegetation.

16 And if he was in the eighth, it indicates that death and extinction will enter upon the essence of that sign: and if he was in the signs of people, sheikhs and old people will die; and if it was of the signs of animals, animals will perish.

17 And if he was in the ninth, it indicates an abundance of journeys [if] that sign was movable, and people will remain on the journey. **18** And if it was fixed, it indicates the seeking of faith by the people, and their desire for the good and piety. **19** And if he was in the ninth and made unfortunate, it multiplies fear on journeys and drowns passengers on the sea.

20 And if he was in the tenth and was received, made fortunate, it indicates the goodness of the condition of the general populace in connection with the kings, and their kindness towards them, and their approval. **21** And if he was made unfortunate, harmed, then since his place operates and rises above all of the [other] planets, his cold and misfortune and evil pervades the land and atmosphere, and it indicates that the [political] authority will move the government,[203] and his injustice intensifies, and his evil is made manifest, and he will tower over the people[204] in his oppression and cheating.

22 And if he was in the eleventh, then since he is in a sign of the good and good fortune, and if he was made fortunate, it improves the suppositions of the people and confirms their assets, and they come to know properness and goodness in their travels and their changes. **23** And if it was to the contrary of that, their tribulation will become powerful and their assets disturbed, and

---

[203] That is, from one place to another.
[204] Notice the connection between his place high in the chart, and the king "towering over" the people.

[the fulfillment of] their demands will depend on them, and they will see hardship and restriction in their own livelihoods.

24 And if he was in the twelfth, [and] was strong, safe, the people will be reserved [with one another], and they will be equal [to each other],[205] and hatred and malice will depart from them. **25** And if he was made unfortunate, harmed, they will wage war and be hostile to one another, and that clime will get evil or tribulation from their heretics[206] and their boldness, and their godlessness.[207]

[Jupiter]

26 The indications of Jupiter, if he was the victor in the revolution of the year, and he was in the houses of the circle.

27 If he was in the Ascendant, and he was strong, made fortunate, looking at the lord of his house, the people of the clime in that year will get beneficence and surplus and good fortune in every area, and their bodies will be healthy, and their delights multiplied, and a sound condition and good and piety will pervade the people, and mosques will be prevalent, and the people's charitable giving in the faith. **28** And if that was to the contrary, assets diminish and livelihoods become constricted, and the people abstain from what is good, and the desires of people wanting [to be] beneficent and giving alms will diminish, and the thoughts of the king are about his own country and authority and rulership and child.[208]

29 And if he was in the second, and he was received, the revenues of the general populace become great, and their livelihoods suitable, and that is even better for what is of the essence of the sign he is in. **30** And if the lord of the second was connecting with him, profit and benefit will reach them from wherever they do not [even] request it and do not [even] consider it. **31** And if Jupiter[209] was the pushing one, they take hold of assets, and crimes

---

[205] تكافوا, apparently a rare example of Form 6 (Lane, p. 2618). 1485 says that people will "esteem" each other, but the verbs here have a more neutral, cautious sense (which befits Saturn).

[206] Or, "defectors" (مرّاق).

[207] Or more generally, those who violate customary views about sin and morality (فسقة).

[208] That is (as 1485 elaborates), he will think about his own matters and not those of the people.

[209] Reading المشتري for المتصل ("the connecting"). The point is that the roles are reversed.

are attributed to them,[210] and they provide what has not come to their hands,[211] and[212] their tribulation will be powerful because of the assets [taken] from them; and the thoughts of the king will be about assets and the coffers and gifts, and what he seeks in this from other rulerships and their assets.

32 And if he was in the third, that is where his indication in faith and the good and piety is strong, because the third indicates creeds and religious worship, and where the people desire explanations and harmony and continuity, and the desire of the people of affluence for piety and alms; and the thoughts of the king are about brothers and kin and sisters, and prophecy and the stars, and faith, and travel, and people of distinction, and [even] those who are not of the nobility of his own kingdom.

33 And if he was in the fourth, the people will work their land, and people's use of[213] real estate and villages will be powerful, in their villages and real estate.[214] 34 And if he was made unfortunate, it indicates gloom reaching them, and restriction at the end of their year, and the thoughts of the king will be on protection and forts, and his desire for protection and concealment, and working on what is secret, and delight in carrying that out in secret and silence, and sorcerers and talismans.

35 And if he was in the fifth, the people will be secure in their children, and pregnant women will conclude their pregnancy [successfully], and offspring and sons will be multiplied among them, and the thoughts of the king will be about what is gentle[215] and the building of cities.

36 And if he was in the sixth and he was made fortunate, that is suitable for slaves if it was of the signs of people. 37 And if it was of the signs of animals, animals will be secure, and illnesses few [and] safe. 38 And if he was

---

[210] Reading الجنايات with BL ("crimes"), although Nur. has الجبايات ("taxes"). In either event, the verb وصف is not supposed to take على as its preposition, so I am reading somewhat improperly. The point is that when Jupiter does the applying or pushing, the people have to find their own assets with some effort, and even then some are taken away from them. 1485 has what might be a key to a better reading, that they must pay "double": this would be the case if we could read وصفت as some form of صنو, which has connotations of doubling and being a twin, but does not seem to have been an actual verb.

[211] That is, "what they do not have" (1485).

[212] Reading somewhat loosely with 1485 up to the semicolon, as the Arabic does not seem to be properly constructed but has all the elements of the thought.

[213] Or, "benefit from" (انتفاع).

[214] This last clause is redundant and awkward.

[215] الرقيق. Or, "tender."

made unfortunate, the people will fall ill from swelling and winds and what is like that. **39** And the thoughts of the king will be about court rulings[216] and slaves and medications.

40 And if he was in the seventh, women will be pleased with men, and *vice versa*. **41** And if he was made unfortunate, they will be angry, and evil between them will increase. **42** And the thoughts of the king will be about his enemies and those of the people of his own authority who are envious of his kingdom, and what is indicated by the seventh.

43 And if he was in the eighth, made fortunate, it diminishes death, and the people will comply with treaties, and they will preserve the rights of the dead. **44** And if he was made unfortunate, it increases death and distress in the category [of things belonging to] the sign in which he is. **45** And the thoughts of the king will be about inheritance and [*uncertain*].[217]

46 And if he was in the ninth, good will befall men from journeys, and they will profit from their move and relocation, and passengers by sea will be safe (if the sign was fixed), and people will act in a trustworthy way[218] and desire the good and abstinence and religious practice. **47** And the thoughts of the king will be about travel and relocation, and the stars, and visions, and the auguries[219] of birds.

48 And if he was in the tenth [and made fortunate],[220] then he is where justice will pervade the people in that clime, and they will see well-being,[221] and compassion, and friendliness, and charity from their kings and their governors, and benefit and good deeds will reach them from their direction. **49** And if it was to the contrary of that, their governors will renounce them and good and evil will be balanced in them, and the thoughts of the king will be about what he is in charge of and is released from,[222] and on gifts and [political] relationships.

---

[216] القضاة or القضاء. This also has the connotation of passing judgment and sentencing people, including condemnation and killing.

[217] 1485 has: "ditches, enclosures, and revenues." BL and Nur. have an unknown word (الصوافي), followed in BL by "gazelles" (غزلان). The former word could possibly (with some contortions) relate to a word referring to calm and mental clarity (صفو \ صفاء). These are astrologically possible, if Jupiter taken to bonify the 8th and make his worries disappear.

[218] ادى الناس الامانة.

[219] Reading with 1485 for زجر, "suppression, rebuke."

[220] Adding with 1485.

[221] Reading الرفه for الرافة.

[222] يعزل.

50 And if he was in the eleventh, good fortune is multiplied and [people's] livelihood is improved, and the people of that clime will see [good things] they did not request and did not wish for, and the thoughts of the king will be about what he is required to [do] and what he hopes for, and they request of him.

51 And if he was in the twelfth, made fortunate, the people of that clime will get benefit from enemies, and they will take much booty, and they will have a good condition and good fortune because of fighting and combat. **52** And the thoughts of the king will be about what has already transpired, and regret about that, and on the matters of the enemies.

The arrival of Mars in every house

54 If Mars was the lord of the year and he was in the Ascendant, made fortunate, received, that will be useful for the people of the clime in that year, through fighting: and they will triumph over [a people] who borders on them, and they will wander about the countries adjacent to them. **55** And if he was made unfortunate, civil unrest will take place in them, and wounds and blood will be increased in them, and from that, powerful evil will reach the world.

56 And if he was in the second, thefts will multiply in men, and thieves and gangs will become widespread in the land, and people promising protection will betray their own assurances of it,[223] and livelihoods become restricted, and injustice and oppression will be general in the people.

57 And if he was in the third, [people] will separate from one another and be opposed to one another, and fanaticism and hostilities[224] will be brought about in them.

58 And if he was in the fourth, it is where his heat and the injustice of his temperament rises towards all of the planets.[225] **59** And if he was in one of the signs of fire, many lands and cities will be burned, and epidemics will take place, and the damage of the fire is increased in the world. **60** And if he was in one of the signs of people, blood will be shed and casualties will be multi-

---

223 خان اهل الامانات اماناتهم (reading the first word with Nur.), lit. "the people of assurances/protection will betray their assurances/protection." Linguistically and astrologically, this could include personal protection (the 2nd as allies), or the protection of wealth deposited in trust (the 2nd as assets).

224 معادات, which I take to be from عدو.

225 Reading فهو حيث برتفع الى الطواطب كلها حرّة for فهو حيث يرتفع الى الكواكب كلها حرّه وجور طبيعه وجور طليعة. Nevertheless, I do not quite understand what al-Rijāl's source means.

plied, and there will be civil unrest and wars at the end of the year; and that will be widespread in the people of the clime which belongs to that sign.

61 And if he was in the fifth, miscarried fetuses increase, and accidents and hardship will reach pregnant women.

62 And[226] if he was in the sixth and the sign was a dry one, there will be hot and dry pains; and if the sign was moist, the pains will be from heat and moisture; and if that sign was Aquarius, epidemic and wind will take place in men, and what is like that of bloody pains. **63** And if it was one of the signs of animals, death and extinction will take place in animals and predatory beasts.

64 And if he was in the seventh, then he is malignant in contrarieties and hostilities, and there will be theft and fighting and lawsuits in that year, and a great event will happen to the people of that clime, and the evil and tribulation will be oppressive for their souls.

65 And if he was in the eighth, there will be much rapid death in the type [of thing belonging to] that sign in which he is.

66 And if he was in the ninth, roads will be cut off, and thieves will multiply, and force and thieves and vagabonds will afflict the roads. **67** And if the sign was watery, passengers on the sea will be drowned.

68 And if he was in the tenth, the rudeness and brutality [of the leaders][227] intensifies, and they shed each other's blood, and they extend their hands toward the citizens by means of killing and oppression and injustice.

69 And if he was in the eleventh, the people will cut themselves off from one another and be opposed to each other, and friendship and kindness will depart from them.

70 And if he was in the twelfth, fear of their enemies will descend upon the people of that clime, and there will be [the shedding of] blood in what is between them.

The arrival of the Sun in all of the houses

72 If the Sun was in the Ascendant, received, made fortunate,[228] the year is suitable for the leadership and the nobility and the powerful. **73** And if he

---

[226] For the first half of this sentence, reading the order of clauses with 1485; the Ar. has matched dry signs with moist infirmities, etc.
[227] Adding based on 1485.
[228] 1485 adds that he is also the lord of the year itself.

was unfortunate, it indicates the falling of honor, and the powerful are humbled, and harm will reach the bodies of kings, and great houses will be hum-humbled and decline.

74 And if he was in the second, assets will be scattered and [*uncertain*],[229] and cash and paper will diminish in the hands of the general public, and kings will love to hoard, and revenues will be diminished, and the condition of the people restricted.

75 And if he was in the third, the people will desire faith and prefer the good, and will be seeking[230] in religious observance and piety.

76 And if he was in the fourth, structures will be demolished and vegetation corrupted (if it was of the signs of vegetation), and people of honor will be [brought] low. **77** And if it was of the signs of water, waters will be diminished[231] and the grass of the earth will be burned.

78 And if he was in the fifth, it corrupts the fetuses of pregnant women and diminishes offspring, and one [should] not hope for any pregnancy without it being abolished or[232] corrupted.

79 If he were in the sixth, there will be a multitude of pains and illnesses, and that is more intense in the eyes; [and it indicates] the death of animals if it were of the signs of four-footed animals.

80 And if the Sun was in the seventh, it indicates the seclusion of the king.[233]

81 And if [he was in the eighth, it indicates death[234]] if the lord of the eighth looked at him.

82 And if he was in the ninth, and he had strong testimonies in it, and he was made fortunate, his indications [are] for faith and religious observance and the desire of the people for faith[235] and piety, and it strengthens the faith and its people.

83 And if he was in the tenth, it distinguishes kings (and especially the king of that clime), and his command will be manifest, and he will be raised

---

[229] اصطلحت (BL) or اصطلتها (Nur.).
[230] The primary meaning of this is to "compete" (تنافسوا), but that does not harmonize with the spirit of the sentence.
[231] Adding with 1485 and Nur.
[232] Reading "or" for "and."
[233] Omitting "the roughness of" (خشونة). For the next few sentences, I am organizing the text along with 1485, as both BL and Nur. break up their sentences in the wrong place, or have switched clauses around, or are missing words.
[234] Adding with 1485.
[235] Reading with 1485 for "gold," which was part of 1485's translation of **74** above.

up above the people of his kingdom, and they will submit to him and humble themselves before them, and they will be under his foot.

84 And if he was in the eleventh, that indeed is suitable for the delight of that clime, and some will benefit from others, and [it indicates] the friendship of their kings and powerful people and nobility, to [the people], and sympathy towards them.

85 And if he was in the twelfth, the people of that clime will be hostile to their king, and tribulation and mishaps will enter upon them from the powerful ones of them and their nobility.

The arrival of Venus in all of the houses of the revolution, if she was the lord of the year

87 If Venus was in the Ascendant, the bodies of the people will be secure, and it multiplies their delight and joy.

88 And if she was in the second, she improves the condition of the populace, and their produce is protected and secure, and their livelihood is expanded.

89 And if she was in the third, they will have conflicts and be hostile.[236]

90 And if she was in the fourth, warning[237] will be increased in them, and men will restrict women; and the end of the year is more praiseworthy than its beginning.

91 And if she was in the fifth, the people and children and the young will rejoice, and pregnant women will be safe, and more of those born in that [year] will be females, and fondness and love for women will increase, and singers and amusements, and joy and delight, and music, and putting on garlands and [what] smells good, and putting on embroidered and silk garments, and there is an increase in women having splendor and beauty.

92 And if she was in the sixth, and it was a sign in the image of people, slave-traders will have profit in slaves, and singing will increase, and the desire of the people for singers. **93** And if it was of the signs having four feet, animals will be dear, and they will be safe from infirmities[238] and distresses, and pain and illnesses will take place in women from eating and drinking and indigestion.

---

[236] To me this seems like a strange signification, but see Ch. VIII.11, **76**.

[237] العبرة, exact meaning and role here uncertain. Perhaps it means that men will warn women, *and also* restrict them.

[238] Reading with 1485 for النفاق ("trade"), since trade is already assumed by their being expensive.

94 And if she was in the seventh from the Ascendant, [and] she was strong, made fortunate, received, the people will desire women in that year, and weddings and wedding-contracts will increase, and they will see delight in that. **95** And if she was made unfortunate, harmed, women will quarrel[239] with men and leave their own homes, and people will hasten [to] divorce and disunity.

96 And if she was in the eighth, death will take place in women if she was harmed in that place.

97 And if she was in the ninth, travels in that year will be suitable, and men will abstain from women, and the people will promote faith and piety, [and] pleasure and comfort.

98 And if she was in the tenth, kings will raise women up and ennoble their destinies, and [women] will have command and reason in [the kingdom's] authority, and the condition of the citizens and the general populace will be suitable, and good and good fortune will reach [the people] from kings and authorities, and those who are of the good and religion will govern the matters of the people, and kings will promote those who are amusing, and in addition singers [and] what is Venusian.

99 And if she was in the eleventh, the corruption of what is forbidden increases in the people, and men and women will befriend each other, and fornication and wedlock increases, and it will be a year of delight and joy, and affection, and immorality.

100 And if she was in the twelfth, men will criticize women, and they will fall into enmity with them, and many [men] will not have esteem for them, and no value in the opinion of their husbands.

The arrival of Mercury in all of the houses of the revolution, if he was the lord of the year

102 And if Mercury was in the Ascendant, it strengthens children and they will be safe from distresses and ominous events, and the year will be joyful for them, and they will be well-behaved and receive knowledge from their teachers and educators.

103 And if he was in the second, made fortunate, merchants are more profitable, and trade crafts are useful, and the people will be beneficial (one to another), and they will take care of what is entrusted to them, in what [there is] between them. **104** And if he was made unfortunate, it indicates

---

[239] Reading with 1485 for an illegible or nonsensical word.

restriction in livelihoods and strain in what is forbidden, and the sheikhs and merchants will be undermined, and the poverty of the people of literature and knowledge will be powerful.

105 And if he was in the third, the people will seek knowledge of the faith, and they will study jurisprudence, and debate and quarrel in their sects.

106 And if he was in the fourth, many people [who are] writers[240] will be captured in that year, and rulers of the treasury account books and the land tax. **107** And if the sign was fixed, the captivity or detention will last [a long time]; and if it was movable, it hastens their deliverance and release from it. **108** And if Mars[241] is looking at that place, it indicates severe blows and painful punishments and the like, and killing.

109 And if he was in the fifth, made fortunate, it will be a year of pregnancy, and the children from pregnancy in that year will be people of intelligence and cleverness.[242] **110** And if he was made unfortunate, it indicates an abundance of travels, and pregnant women will not complete their term.[243]

111 And if he was in the sixth, there will be defects and illnesses in youths, according to his good fortune and misfortune in that sign.

112 And if he was in the seventh, men will avoid women and will make use of slaves and eunuchs, and homosexuality will spread, and whoredom in them.

113 And if he was in the eighth, death will take place in youths.

114 And if he was in the ninth, travels and transfers [from one place to another] will multiply, and the people will be eager to seek faith and knowledge.

115 And if he was in the tenth, it strengthens writers and the people of literature, and they will be the leaders and managers of the commands of the [political] authority. **116** And if a fortune looked at that place, they will be forgiving and just; and if an infortune was looking, they will be treacherous, and harm and powerful tribulation will enter upon [and] between the people.

---

[240] This could also be understood as "people of the book" (referring to Jews, Christians, and Sabians), but the word for "people" here is قوم rather than the idiomatic اهل.
[241] The Persian name for Mars.
[242] This word can also mean "boldness, energy, the noble-minded, decent" (الشهامة).
[243] Lit., "[what they] bear will not be completed for pregnant women."

117 And if he was in the eleventh, men will live harmoniously and love one another, and will be beneficial to one another in [both] their clashes and friendships, and their reunions and letter-writing.

118 And if he was in the twelfth,[244] because of the harms [perpetrated] upon the people, their children, and their youths [by enemies], [the people] will reduce the status of the enemies and those hostile to them.

The arrival of the Moon in the houses of the revolution, if she was the lord of the year

120 If the Moon was in the Ascendant, made fortunate, it will be a suitable year for the people in their bodies and livelihood. **121** And if it was the contrary of that, then reverse [your] statement about that.

122 And if she was in the second, the revenues of the people will increase, and they will be fortunate in assets and the [agricultural] yield. **123** And if she was made unfortunate, the situation in them is restricted, and terrible poverty will take place in them, and need, and famine.

124 And if she was in the third, they will delight in journeys and kinship and relations.[245]

125 And if she was in the fourth and that sign was made unfortunate, [the people] will fall into a powerful siege, and there will be prisons and severity and restriction upon the people.

126 And if she was in the fifth from the Ascendant, the people will be fortunate in children and will delight in the increase of prices.

127 And if she was in the sixth from the Ascendant, it indicates an abundance of abstention[246] in the people.

128 And if she was in the seventh from the Ascendant, men will be fortunate with women.

129 And if she was in the eighth from the Ascendant, death will take place in the people. **130** And if she was made unfortunate, it will be worse than

---

[244] What follows is my best reconstruction of the conflicting Arabic MSS. BL reads, "for/because of the evils upon the people or their children and youths, and they reduce the status of the enemies and those hostile to them." Nur. reads, "by means of the evil upon the people and upon their children and their youths, and they descend upon the rank of [those who are] enemies to them." On the other hand, 1485 reads very differently (and perhaps astrologically more correct): "children and those serving will quarrel with men, and will treat them in the manner of enemies."

[245] This word (اهل) also has connotations of group membership and adherents or followers, which might be pertinent to the religious meaning of this house.

[246] Or, "renunciation" (زهد).

what I mentioned. **131** And if a house of Mars[247] was in the eighth, it indicates war.

132 And if she was in the ninth, it will be a year of journeys and emigration and transferring [from one place to another] in accordance with the sign in which she is (by land or by sea).[248]

133 And if she was in the tenth, the condition of the general public will be suitable, and their standing with their [political] authority is strengthened, and they will profit from their rulers, and [especially] if she was received by the lord of the Midheaven.

134 And if she was in the eleventh, it will be a sound year in goodness and good fortune.

135 And if she was in the twelfth, the people of the clime in which she is by her sign, will receive evil and enmity and combat.

[Further rules on the lord of the year]

136 Know[249] that if Saturn corrupted the lord of the year, the evil is upon the countries attributed to its sign. **137** And if that planet was in the Ascendant, it indicates what belongs to it (of lands) in the east; and if it was in the west, it indicates what belongs to it in the west; and if it was in the Midheaven or the stake of the earth, it indicates what belongs to it (of countries) in the east and west.[250]

138 And if it was Mars, the distress and damage, and its root, is [attributed] to that clime, from fires and heat, and hot and dry pains, [and likewise if the corrupted planet was in a hot sign].[251] **139** And if it was a cold one, it is from drowning and thirst and cold infirmities. **140** And if it was of the signs of air, it indicates that it is from winds and darkness, and dust, and windy pains. **141** And if it was of the signs of earth, it makes an indication of earthquakes and ruins and demolition and the discontinuing of building. **142** And likewise the mishaps and evil will enter upon what belongs to that sign, of

---

[247] The Persian name for Mars.
[248] This must mean that dry signs (especially earthy ones) indicate travel by land, while moist signs (especially watery ones) are by sea.
[249] For this paragraph, cf. VIII.4, **176**; also *RYW* Ch. 26, **9-12** and *Scito* Ch. 52.
[250] 1485 has the southern and northern lands (corresponding to the Midheaven and IC), which makes more sense.
[251] Adding with 1485.

[its] division of living things and vegetation, and other things of what belongs to [its] allotment and division.

143 And know that if the infortunes were in the signs, corruption or evil will be brought forth in accordance with the essence of that sign and its type. **144** If it was of the signs of people, the distresses will be in them; or, [if of the signs of animals], in animals; or, [if] it is a sign of vegetation, they are in vegetation; or, [if] it is a sign of waters, they are in the waters and animals of the water—based on what belongs to that sign in terms of [its] allotment and indication, of the essence which belongs to it.

145 And if it was in the earthy signs, it indicates vegetation. **146** And if the infortune was in Taurus, it indicates the corruption of the trees and aromatic plants and fruits and flowers,[252] and other things of the vegetation of beautiful shrubs. **147** And if it was in Virgo, it indicates the disaster of wheat and grain,[253] such as green beans and lentils and Indian peas. **148** And[254] likewise [for watery signs], Pisces indicates sweet water and powerful rivers, and Cancer indicates swampy waters and reeds and diving places,[255] and Scorpio indicates salty waters and everything powerful of the seas; and God knows [more].

Chapter VIII.8: On knowing the place of the earth in which the event happens

Comment by Dykes. This chapter involves al-Rijāl's (or his source's) adoption of, and astrological overlay onto, Ptolemy's geography. As I discussed in *AW1* (Section IV.2), at the time Ptolemy wrote the *Geography*, he believed that the world was somewhat larger than it actually is, but that only 180° of it was inhabitable, from the Canary Islands in the Atlantic in the west, to somewhere between India and China in the east (**2**). The first diagram below shows this model as viewed from the North Pole. Suppose we assign the Canary Islands 0°, much as we do Greenwich, England today. Every day, the Sun will pass from China in the east (at 180° E) westward over all of the inhabitable land on the earth, reaching the Canary Islands after 12 hours.

---

[252] Adding "flowers" with Nur.
[253] Or, "seeds" (اللوبيا).
[254] The attributions for Scorpio and Pisces are incorrect: Scorpio should have swamps, and Cancer saltwater and seas.
[255] Reading المغائص for المعايص, though I cannot confirm that this is the correct plural.

Therefore, at any given moment during that time he will be directly above some region whose longitude corresponds to that portion of his journey (**3**): so after 3 hours he will have passed ¼ of the inhabitable earth, which corresponds to 135° E, after 6 hours to 90° E, after 9 hours to 45° E, and so on.

According to this model (now in its Arabic version), there is a place on the equator called Tārah,[256] which is at exactly 90° E and serves as the center of the world (**4**). To the west of that by 1 1/3 hours, or 20°, is Baghdad (**4**):[257] Baghdad is therefore 110° westwards from the eastern limit in China, and 70° east of the Canary Islands. (Some of the confusion in al-Rijāl's discussion is because he tends to measure longitudes *from* the east, in imitation of the Sun's motion.)

The purpose of all of this is to determine the terrestrial longitudes at which there will be good fortune or misfortune. To put it simply, since only ½ of the earth is inhabitable, al-Rijāl needs a way to condense a complete 360° circle into 180° of the earth: the answer is to divide longitudes in half (**5-6**). So, suppose we cast our mundane ingress chart for the geographical center of the earth (at Tārah), on the equator, 3° Aries is rising, and 10° Capricorn is being harmed somehow (**7**)—in my diagram, I have made it suffer a superior square from Mars. So whatever city or land corresponds to those degrees, will suffer misfortune. Now, there are 83° between the horizon or Ascendant, and the degree in Capricorn (**8**); but because we must fit the entire zodiac onto the inhabitable earth, we must condense the angle by ½. So the longitude of the misfortune will not be 83° west of China, but 41° 30" west of it, or 138° 30" east of the Canary Islands.

But as al-Rijāl points out (**10-12**), one must also remember that each sign and each bound is also assigned to directions in space and countries. Notably, certain bounds are assigned to specific regions (as the bound of Jupiter in Cancer is famously assigned to Iraq), and both Hermes (**16-17**) and others (**19**) had ways of assigning them. Maddeningly, I have never seen an author actually describe how it was done—even including the bound of Jupiter in Cancer. Al-Rijāl concludes with some puzzling comments about anatomy

---

[256] But see below for some spelling variants. It is possible that this is 'Ujjain or at least plays the same role: 'Ujjain, in India (23°10'N, 75°46' E), was thought to be a city in the middle of the inhabited world, and was used for certain astrological purposes. See Pingree 1977, p. 12, n. 14.

[257] If the Sun moves 180° in 12 hours, then he moves 20° in 1 1/3 hours.

and cryptic instructions about timing, which suggests that he may be quoting from some other source and may not understand the meaning himself.

ಹ ಹ ಛ

2 Know that when Ptolemy wanted to know the longitude of the tract of the earth, he took from the well-known Canary Islands[258] in the Roman sea (it is not known what comes after them except that the Sun sets there), to the remotest city of China in the east—and it is not known what is beyond that place as well, except the Sun rises from it. **3** And he found the journey of the Sun in twelve hours and knew that the amount of its longitude was 180°, and each degree of it was above [some place] of the countries, which is its longitude from the east, in the likeness of its number from 180°.[259]

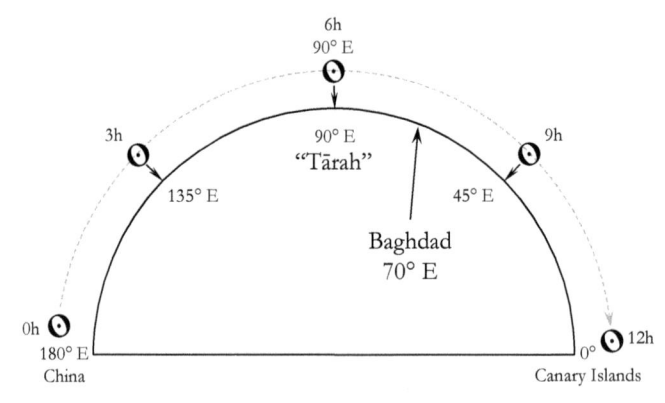

Figure 77: Motion of Sun over longitudes in 12h (al-Rijāl VIII.8, 2-3)

4 So when you wanted to know the country which is opposite the bound in which there is good or bad fortune, then come to know the Ascendant of the year of the world in the middle of the land called Tārah,[260] and after it from the east is 90°, and likewise from the west, and it does not have latitude; and it is always with a decrease of 1 1/3 hours from Baghdad, because [Baghdad's] longitude from the east is 110°.

---

[258] Lit., "the Immortal Islands."
[259] Thus, if 45° of this distance in the heavens is above some city, then the longitude of the city will be 45° from the east (or China) on the earth: the two distances are "like" each other.
[260] Nur. reads, "Yārīn," and 1485 "Catha."

5 Then, take from [the Ascendant at Tārah] up to[261] the degree of the body or rays of the planet which you wanted to know:[262] what is between the indication (in degrees of equality according to the path of the Midheaven[263]) and its share, and see how much it is of 360°, and take by its proportion[264] from 180° (and indeed it is one-half). **6** And he has also said: take the degrees arrived at ([which] he mentioned), by assigning them from what is not a ratio, and do not go beyond one-half of them, and distribute them by the longitude of the countries: and for every country, its longitude from the east is the amount of that degree, and it is the zenith [of the place], and in it takes place the indication of good and evil.

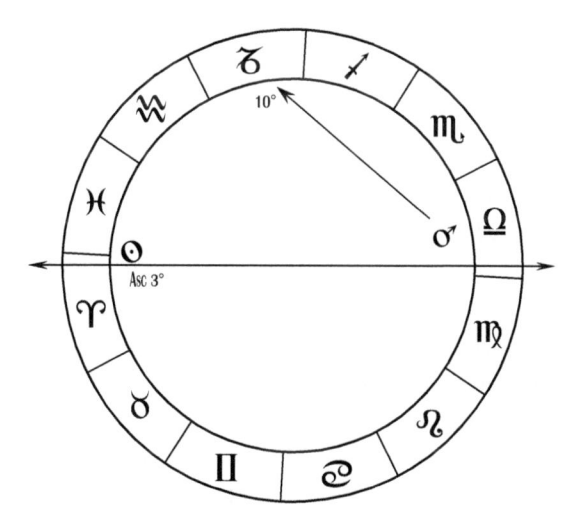

Figure 78: Finding terrestrial longitude of the misfortune (VIII.8, 7-9)

7 An example of this: that the Ascendant is 3° of Aries, and the planet indicating the good and evil is in 10° of Capricorn. **8** So, we take 3° from Aries,

---

[261] Omitting "ten degrees of," with 1485 and Nur.
[262] Reading the rest of this sentence with Nur., as it is more coherent; BL seems to contain spelling or transcription mistakes that only make sense in Nur. 1485 reads: "And after this, take from the degree of the Ascendant up to the body or rays of the planet whose signification you wanted to know, by equal degrees, going by means of the Midheaven: and you should know how many they are, and the proportion of it which they have relative to 360°, and take that proportion of 180°, and it will be the double of that."
[263] This phrase makes it seem as though we are to measure by right ascensions rather than zodiacal degrees, but the example uses only zodiacal ones.
[264] Reading قسط with 1485 as "proportion."

and 60° [from] Pisces, and Aquarius, and 20° from Capricorn: and the total is 83°. **9** We take one-half of it, by the proportion of 180° to 360°, and it is 41° 30": and every country whose longitude from the east is this amount, has its zenith on this degree, and the indication takes place based on that.

10 Then you look at the bound of the sign: [of] which triplicity is [the sign]: of the eastern, or of the western, or of the northern, or the southern? **11** And is it on the center of the area, or on its right or left—for the event is brought about on that side. **12** And you consider what belongs to the sign (of countries), and their locations by direction [in space], and their longitudes, so that you may know the place of the event and what is close to it (by the permission of God).

13 Then, you look at the bound and to whom it belongs, and where is the place of its lord from the perspective of the planet which is in [the bound]? **14** For if they were both fortunes, you ascertain an indication of good; and if they were [both] infortunes, you ascertain an indication of evil. **15** And if they differed with respect to the condition between them,[265] [the indication goes] to the one of them which is stronger.

16 And as for Hermes, he used to take the bounds of the planet[266] from the beginning of Aries (which is the triplicity of the east), and proceed bound by bound, and he assigned a country to every degree by its zenith until he reached the degree in which the planetary fortune or infortune was, whose effect he wanted to know. **17** So you see which of the countries it is opposite to, for the effect will take place in it. **18** And this is general for eclipses [of the Sun] and other things of the rest of the effects which Hermes mentioned.

19 And apart from him [were others] in their books, where they said: look at the bound in which the misfortune is: to which of the countries does the one it is in belong, since all of the effects are apparent [and] found from these signs and the planets; the provinces and quarters are divided by them. **20** And he divided the body of man between [the signs] as well, and between the planets. **21** So if you wanted the indicator of disease in a man, you specify the limb[267] which that sign governs (of the body), and you judge its greater or

---

[265] For the rest of this sentence, reading roughly with 1485 because it makes more astrological sense (although 1485 continues with "and the one which was the significator." BL seems to refer both to the planet in the bound and to the main city of the region; the first part does not quite make sense, because then the planet in the bound would always be the indicator. Nur. seems to say that the emphasis is on the planet which is the "sole" one in the indication (الفرد).

[266] Reading in the singular with BL, which significantly narrows its meaning.

[267] Reading with 1485 for "harm" (الضرّ).

lesser extent based on that, and the time of the recovery [from] it [is] based on the amount of the elevation of the fortunes or infortunes over it, and the years and months which are decreed.[268]

22 And if you wanted the periods of time and what they indicate[269] (of misfortune and good fortune), it is just like granting [time] to a planet from years and months of the *firdārīyyāt*. **23** And the planets also [indicate] limbs, as was said their place [above].[270]

24 And if the Sun was in the square of Saturn, and Mars was assembled with [Saturn] or square to [the Sun] from the other side,[271] indeed that misfortune is the greatest for [the Sun], and [especially] if that corresponded to his entrance into his own exaltation, or [it was] the entrance of [any] planet into its exaltation, and those two were looking at [the Sun] and at [the other planet], and the Lot of Fortune or its lord were absent from[272] [the other planet's] aspect—that is a bad sign and detestable indication for the people of the countries which that planet governs: their king will oppress them and they will get tribulation and injustice from him, and corruption and evil will multiply in them. **25** And if the aspect from the infortunes was from the fixed signs, the tribulation will be long; and if it was from the movable ones, it will be short; and if it was from the [double]-bodied ones, it will be repeated.

Chapter VIII.9: On the indications of the planets

2 If Saturn was the lord of any of the quarters of the year, and you found him to be in a stake of Mars, then it indicates powerful fighting, [and] the victory will go to Saturn and to his place of the countries of the signs which

---

[268] This sentence is ambiguous as to exactly which planet is doing what. First of all, we should expect the disease to be greater or lesser based on the benefic/malefic quality of the planet in the sign, and its condition. Second, the "time" of the recovery should be based on some attribution of years to some planet, but here we have some ambiguity as to what the "elevation" or "superiority" (على قدر استعلاء) means. 1485 suggests that it is the most powerful planet ruling the place (which is a reasonable astrological view). But we would also expect the planet in the sign itself to give the year.

[269] Reading ازيدت مدد الماء ويدل عليه, for إن ارادت مدد وما تدل عليه.
[270] Reading somewhat loosely for ما مضى القول عليه في موضعه.
[271] In other words, being besieged by the malefics from a square on each side.
[272] That is, "in aversion to."

belong to Saturn, because he is the lord of the year[273] and lord of that quarter.

3 And if Jupiter was the lord of the quarter, it indicates the peace of that clime, and there will not be fighting nor a mishap in it. **4** And Saturn is of assistance to Jupiter in the place which he collaborates in.[274]

5 And if Mars was the lord of that quarter, and he was in the place which we said about Saturn,[275] falling away from[276] Jupiter and connecting with Saturn, then in that quarter damages will happen, and powerful false rumors, and everything which is ugly, and falsehoods will happen in that clime whose authority belongs to the sign in which Mars is—unless you find Jupiter in any of the stakes of Mars: for if it was that, there will not be false rumors (however there will be everything which we said besides the false rumors).

6 And if the lord of that quarter was the Sun, and he had a powerful share[277] in it, then it indicates calm and tranquility and friendship and good. **7** And if the Sun was made unfortunate by Mars, then grief from wars enters upon the nobility and the powerful and the sages of the clime, and pains occur in them—unless Jupiter is found in a place [which] destroys the calamity of Mars.[278]

8 And if Venus was the lord of the quarter, and Mars was falling away from[279] her view, she indicates joy and delight and a scarcity of evil in that quarter.

9 If Mercury was the lord of that quarter, it indicates rumors occurring in the people, and discussions and books and messengers, and they indicate the coming of one of the kings to the land which Mercury has authority over.

10 And if that quarter belonged to the Moon, and you found her to be strong, then there is no killing and damages [in] that [quarter]. **11** If the Moon was made unfortunate by Mars, then it indicates illnesses in that quarter, and

---

[273] 1485 says, "the lord of the [sc. that] season of the year," which makes more sense because none of the planets in this chapter is required to *also* be the lord of the year.
[274] Or, "has partnership with, cooperates in," (اِشترك), etc. The meaning of this is unclear to me.
[275] Probably in **2**.
[276] That is, "in aversion to."
[277] That is, "dignity."
[278] Reading with the sense of 1485, otherwise something seems to be missing or wrong. At any rate the ambiguity stems in part from the use of "a place": what kind of place would destroy the calamity of Mars? Also, the spelling of the verb itself (برد) could mean "want, return, perish," and several other things. At any rate, the sense seems to be that Jupiter's involvement will mitigate the problems.
[279] That is, "in aversion to."

pains afflict the youths, and the events will be in proportion to what you see of the strength of Mars over the Moon.

12 And if at the time of the Sun's entrance into Aries no planet is found [so that] you [could] assign it as the lord of that quarter, then give Mars a role and partnership at the time of the Sun's entrance,[280] in accordance with what you see of his place.[281] [**13** And do likewise with the Moon at the Sun's entrance] into Cancer, and do likewise with Venus at the quarter of Libra, and Saturn at the quarter of Capricorn.

Chapter VIII.10: On knowing the places of the things which happen[282]

2 And if you wanted to know the places of the accidents, then look at the lord of the sign of the Ascendant: which one is it of the planets?

3 If Saturn was the king of the year[283] or the king of the quarter, then good strikes the land of Rome, and they will triumph over their enemy, and their king will die, and death will fall upon some of them. **4** And it will strike the land of Daylam well; and Jīlān and Tabaristān belong to the place of Saturn. **5** And if you found Jupiter or Venus clothed by[284] Saturn, then take away from the evil we described about the land of Rome, and it elevates their king above death, [and] then they escape. **6** And what Saturn is, is worse if the Sun entered Aries and [Saturn] was in [the Sun's] opposition, going retrograde, or [the Sun] was connected with him and [Saturn] was in an alien[285] sign: for it indicates evil and fighting between the people of the east and the west,[286] and wars in diverse places.

7 And if you found Jupiter to be the king of the year or the king of the quarter, then men will be fertile, and severity strikes the land of the Persians, and the wheat and barley increases, and a good condition increases in men. **8** And if Mars was clothed by Jupiter, and Mars had strength, then food be-

---

[280] Rewriting the last part of this sentence and the first part of **13** with 1485, as it is partly missing and partly blended together in the MSS.
[281] This is probably because Mars rules Aries, which is the solar ingress we are examining: see the next sentence.
[282] Title missing in the Ar.; I have used 1485.
[283] I.e., "lord" of the year or quarter.
[284] That is, "looking at" or aspecting.
[285] That is, "peregrine."
[286] Or, "the Levant and the Maghrib."

comes expensive at the end of that [quarter] and the end of the year, and depravity[287] will happen in the land in which you found Mars, according to his sign.

9 And if you found Mars to be[288] the king of the year or the king of the quarter, then look at the sign in which he was: for indeed he indicates an increase of rains in those countries, and the people of the lands around which Mars falls, will flourish. **10** And[289] an enemy will be located in the places of the land of Iraq. **11** And death will take place in the people, and more frequently in its occurrences, and especially in youths. **12** Mars, if he was standstanding [still] and moving the motion of Saturn,[290] indicates disaster and the breaking of kinship, and slaves will not submit to their masters, nor will the young do so to adults. **13** And if you found Jupiter to be clothed by Mars, then take away from the evil based on the extent which you believe [there is] of the [good] condition of Jupiter.

14 And if you found the Sun to be the king of the year or of the quarter, then good will befall the land of Iraq, and some of the severity will strike the powerful ones of them, and death is increased in them. **15** And if Mars was clothed by the Sun, it indicates this.[291] **16** And if you found [it was] Saturn instead of Mars, it indicates an increase of diseases. **17** And if Jupiter and Venus were falling away from[292] the Sun, then indeed [there will be] death in the land of Iraq, and [judge][293] the nobility and the kings based on the level of strength which you believed the Sun [had].

18 And if you found Venus to be the queen of the year or of the quarter, then she indicates joy and delight, and fighting and plague strikes the people of Persia to the shore of the sea, toward India, or plague from the fighting [strikes] the youth. **19** And if you found Mars clothed by Venus, then famine and severity strikes the land of the Arabs,[294] and death increases in them. **20** And they will be changed from their own land to another land, [and] they will seek food from it, unless Jupiter and Venus are found to be looking, with power [being] from Jupiter: for then it takes away from that.

---

[287] Nur. reads, "earthquake."
[288] Omitting "Mars by the sign of it."
[289] BL omits this sentence, which I have translated from Nur.
[290] That is, moving very slowly (or perhaps even stationary).
[291] 1485 has "it signifies burning," which makes sense.
[292] That is, "in aversion to."
[293] Reading with 1485 for the uncertain فاعط.
[294] Reading al-ʿarab with 1485 for "the west" (al-gharb).

21 And if you found Mercury to be the king of the year or of the quarter, then good and joy strike the people of Isfahān, and severity and starvation and earthquake strike Azerbaijān, and good and benefit strike the people of Daylam and Hablān. **22** And if you found Mars clothed by Mercury, then fighting and forcefulness takes place in those countries whose sign Mars is in, from their nobility; and unrest will strike them, but their prices will decrease.

23 And if you found the Moon to be the queen of the year or of the quarter, and she was clothed by Jupiter or Venus, then the rains and snow will increase in that year, and severity and earthquake will strike Rome, and tribulation will strike the people of India, and death in the nobility will strike the people of China up to the side of Sijistān.

Chapter VIII.11: Likewise on the revolution of the year of the world

2 When you wanted to know the revolution of the year of the world, look during the Sun's entrance into the first minute of Aries, and establish the Ascendant in the country in which you are, [and] then the Ascendant of the world,[295] and the Ascendant of every clime and every country, and establish the planets for them, for every country an Ascendant differing from the next one.[296] **3** And when you knew that, you would know the Ascendant of every clime and town: so establish the planets for them as well. **4** Then see where the Ascendant of every clime is located, and indeed you will know the matter of the world through this procedure. **5** For perhaps the king of one clime will die, [and the king of another will have prosperity and good],[297] and perhaps [one] clime is barren, and another clime is fertile: and knowledge of this is not possible for you except through this procedure.

---

[295] This is unusual, because it suggests that the Ascendant should be cast for a separate place. This could be the equator, or perhaps 'Ūjjaīn (a location in India sometimes taken to be the middle of the world: see Pingree 1977, p. 12 n. 14).

[296] The text actually has "town" (بلدة) at the end of the sentence, which does not properly contrast with "country." For this reason I have left the end of the sentence neutral; the point is that different cities and countries (depending on how they are politically situated) will have different Ascendants.

[297] Adding with 1485.

[Superior planets in the Ascendant]

6 And if the Ascendant of the year was Aries, and Mars was in the Ascendant or looking at it,[298] and he was safe, it indicates safety in that year unless he was in Libra: for if he was in Libra, it indicates war in that year (because the lord of the year is in the contrary of the Ascendant). **7** And if he was retrograde, it indicates [sorrows and anxieties in men of the land whose Ascendant it was.

8 And if Saturn was in the Ascendant,[299] it signifies][300] the entrance of miseries upon the people by means of the [political] authority in that year. **9** And if Mars[301] was looking from the opposition or square, from a fiery sign, it indicates the killing of some [people] of that clime in that year. **10** And [you will know] the time by the amount of what is between them, of degree[s].

11 And if Jupiter was in the Ascendant, except that Jupiter is not looking at the lord of the Midheaven and the lord of the Lot of Fortune, then if Jupiter were retrograde, their conditions are worse.

12 And if the Sun was in the Ascendant, it indicates an abundance of the children of kings. **13** And if he was connecting with Saturn (he being the lord of the Midheaven),[302] the people and the nobility will aid the [political] authority—unless the lord of the Midheaven was in the eighth, and the Sun in the second: for if it was in that condition, it indicates the death of the king and the disappearance of his assets.

[The planets in the houses]

14 And know that the Sun in the Ascendant or in the Midheaven indicates the justness of the king, and his gentleness. **15** And if the Sun was in the stake of the west, it indicates the intensification of the king's concealment[303] [from the people]. **16** The Sun in the stake of the earth indicates the con-

---

[298] In this first section (through **13**), the planet in the Ascendant also seems to rule it by domicile or exaltation: Mars in an Aries Ascendant, Saturn in a Capricorn Ascendant, and so on.

[299] This now seems to be Saturn also *ruling* the Ascendant, since **9** has Mars squaring or opposing from a fiery sign: this would be the case if Saturn was in a Capricorn Ascendant (with Mars squaring from Aries) or an Aquarius Ascendant (with Mars opposing from Leo).

[300] Adding the material in brackets from 1485.

[301] The Persian name for Mars.

[302] This could be the case if Aries was rising at the Aries ingress.

[303] Lit. "veil" (حجاب), but reading as احتجاب.

finement of the king,[304] away from the people. **17** The Sun in the ninth indicates the king's traveling. **18** The Sun in the eleventh indicates an abundance of the king's conventionally good behavior[305] in that year. **19** The Sun in the fifth indicates the king's entertainment. **20** The Sun in the third indicates the diligence of the king towards the troops. **21** The Sun in the second indicates the king's gathering of assets in that year. **22** The Sun in the sixth indicates the king's gloom, and [especially] when the lord of the eighth would be looking at him. **23** The Sun in the twelfth indicates the king's concern in that year about an abundance of those rising up against him.

24 The Moon in the Ascendant signifies the properness of the condition of the citizens in all of their bodies. **25** The Moon in the second indicates that good[306] will affect[307] the people in that year. **26** The Moon in the third indicates the abundance of the people's traveling so that they have good. **27** The Moon in the fourth indicates the abundance of the people's gloom in that year. **28** The Moon in the fifth indicates the delight of the people in the cheapness of prices. **29** The Moon in the sixth indicates an abundance of inflammation of the eyes in the people. **30** The Moon in the seventh increases marrying in that year. **31** The Moon in the eighth indicates death; and if the eighth was a house of Mars, it indicates war and killing. **32** The Moon in the ninth indicates the beauty of the faith if it was a house of Jupiter; and if it was a house of Mercury, it indicates the corruption of the faith. **33** The Moon in the tenth indicates the abundance of the people's actions by means of their hands. **34** The Moon in the eleventh indicates an abundance of aggression towards adulterers.[308] **35** The Moon in the twelfth indicates an abundance of enemies in that clime.

36 If Saturn was in the Ascendant, it indicates that the corruption of the nobility increases. **37** Saturn in the second indicates an abundance of revenues. **38** Saturn in the third indicates death taking place on journeys. **39** Saturn in the fourth indicates gloom entering upon the people in prisons. **40** Saturn in the fifth indicates the death of the young [children] of the people. **41** Saturn in the sixth indicates harm being conferred upon beasts. **42** Saturn

---

[304] I am not sure if this means the king will literally be imprisoned, or that his life will be conducted as though he is confined.
[305] معروف. That is, acts which are generally agreed upon as being beneficial.
[306] That is, conventional financial benefits or an improvement in their livelihoods.
[307] Reading as the verb اصاب for the noun اصابة ("affliction").
[308] Or more broadly, "immorality" (فساق).

in the seventh indicates the divorce of old people. **43** Saturn in the eighth indicates the death of camels. **44** Saturn in the ninth indicates an abundance of the work of bees.[309] **45** Saturn in the tenth indicates the elevation of what is evil. **46** Saturn in the eleventh indicates the fairness of the [political] authority. **47** Saturn in the twelfth indicates the death of the people of the Sūwād.[310] **48** And if Saturn was retrograde, it corrupts the good and increases in evil.

49 Jupiter in the Ascendant indicates the safety of that year. **50** And in the second he indicates the revenues of merchants and the people. **51** And in the third he indicates good fortune. **52** And in the fourth he indicates the expensiveness of food at the end of the year if that sign was earthy. **53** And in the fifth he indicates the safety of children in that year. **54** And in the sixth he indicates fever and its heat. **55** And in the seventh he indicates an abundance of good in the middle of the year, and the condition of produce is excellent. **56** And in the eighth he indicates sudden death. **57** Jupiter in the ninth indicates an abundance of pilgrimages. **58** And in the tenth he indicates the expensiveness of food. **59** Jupiter in the eleventh indicates the profit of commerce. **60** Jupiter in the twelfth indicates the dryness of trees and their fruit. **61** If Jupiter was retrograde, it corrupts the good and increases in evil.

62 Mars[311] in the Ascendant indicates an abundance of the pouring out of blood in that year. **63** Mars in the second indicates spending on animals and everything having claws. **64** Mars in the third indicates an abundance of evil between brothers and sisters and people of the household. **65** Mars in the fourth indicates an abundance of war at the end of the year, from captives. **66** Mars in the fifth indicates the miscarriage of women carrying [children]. **67** Mars in the sixth indicates wounds, and smallpox, and stones, and headaches. **68** Mars in the seventh indicates an abundance of fornication in that year and a scarcity of marrying. **69** Mars in the eighth indicates death from a hot,[312] bloody disease. **70** Mars in the ninth indicates an abundance of thieves and the cutting-off of roads. **71** Mars in the tenth indicates joy bestowed [upon] the masters of wars and fetters.[313] **72** Mars in the eleventh indicates an

---

[309] Or, "the people of bees," suggesting beekeepers.
[310] This is the rich agricultural region in Iraq, between and around the Tigris and Euphrates rivers.
[311] The Persian name of Mars, here and throughout the paragraph.
[312] Omitting رطب ("moist"), as Mars is agreed to be a heating and *drying* planet.
[313] اسوارة, which 1485 and John (in his Latin translation of *BRD*) translate as "soldiers." But this word seems to come from the verb meaning "to shackle, fetter, bind," and has other connotations of force and confinement.

abundance of the army's donations of assets in that year.[314] **73** Mars in the twelfth indicates an abundance of killing by iron[315] in that year.

74 Venus in the Ascendant indicates an abundance of the people's joy and an abundance of their journeys in that year.[316] **75** Venus in the second indicates the expensiveness of produce (along with their abundance), and the improvement in the condition [of trees].[317] **76** Venus in the third indicates the travels of the people based on a false matter not resembling the truth. **77** Venus in the fourth indicates the worship of their lord [by the people] in that year. **78** Venus in the fifth indicates the beauty of the condition of youths and every juvenile. **79** Venus in the sixth indicates the pains of the people in their noses and what is like that. **80** Venus in the seventh indicates the excellence of the condition of women and every effeminate person of the people. **81** Venus in the eighth indicates an abundance of death in juveniles. **82** Venus in the ninth indicates the corruption of the faith of the Arabs in that year. **83** Venus in the tenth indicates the expensiveness of perfume in that year, and its scarcity. **84** Venus in the eleventh indicates the expensiveness of grains and what is like them. **85** Venus in the twelfth indicates the decline[318] of precious gems and an economic slump in them in that year. **86** And if Venus was retrograde, she indicates the corruption of that and an increase in evil; and her good condition indicates a good condition.

87 If Mercury was in the Ascendant, he indicates the excellence of the condition of merchants and writers. **88** Mercury in the second indicates the strength of knowledge in that year. **89** Mercury in the third indicates the traveling of the people for commerce. **90** Mercury in the fourth indicates the gloom of writers and merchants. **91** Mercury in the fifth indicates an abundance of the people's children. **92** Mercury in the sixth indicates a scarcity of youths. **93** Mercury in the seventh indicates the spreading of homosexuality and what is sinful. **94** Mercury in the eighth indicates the death of youths and donkeys. **95** Mercury in the ninth indicates the spread of knowledge and [the judgments] of the stars. **96** Mercury in the tenth indicates the conspicuousness of the knowledge of the stars in that year. **97** Mercury in the eleventh

---

[314] This probably means donations *to* the army.
[315] That is, the sword.
[316] Nur. adds that there will be a reduction of prices in commerce.
[317] Adding with 1485.
[318] It is interesting that al-Rijāl's source applies exactly the same verb to describe an economic situation ("decline"), within the context of a declining or cadent place (سقوط).

indicates the nearness of the people of knowledge to the king. **98** Mercury in the twelfth indicates the decline of people of knowledge and of merchants. **99** And if Mercury was retrograde, it indicates the corruption of the good and the increase of evil.

Chapter VIII.12: On the judgments of the Lots in the houses

2 And as for the Lot of Fortune, if it was in the Ascendant, it indicates the good and esteem, and its increase. **3** And in the second, it indicates an abundance of assets. **4** And Ptolemy said[319] if it was in a fiery sign [in the second], it indicates the strength of fire and fiery matters; and if it was in an earthy sign, it indicates an abundance of vegetation; and if it was in an airy sign, it indicates an abundance of winds.

5 And likewise, the Lots of good indicate good, and the Lots of evil indicate evil. **6** And he relies on these rules in all roots.

Chapter VIII.13: On the indications of war

2 If you wanted to know the indications of wars, then look at Mars. **3** If he was received in the year of a conjunction, it extinguishes wars in all of that conjunction. **4** And if he was the lord of war in that year,[320] it extinguishes it.

5 If the conjunction was in the Ascendant or the year had reached it[321] in the revolution, it decreases the king's assets, and increases distresses and illnesses, and harms will enter upon the people in their bodies (and that is in the first year); and it also indicates the ruining of lands [which fall under] the indication of that sign. **5** And in the second it indicates the death of the nobility and the spreading of ignorance. **6** And in the third, the destruction of the houses of assets[322] and the destruction of the houses of worship. **7** And in the fourth, moving and the destruction of countries and cities. **8** And in the fifth, the bad condition of children and vegetation. **9** And in the sixth, an abundance of illnesses and captives. **10** And in the seventh, the severity of

---

[319] Certainly a pseudo-Ptolemy.
[320] I am not sure what this means.
[321] This must mean a mundane profection from a previous Saturn-Jupiter conjunction.
[322] This probably belongs in the second house, indirectly confirmed by its omission in 1485.

the condition of the people from [their] kings, and the injustice of the authority. **11** And in the eighth, death and killing, and [also] when the terminal point reaches that place in the revolution. **12** And in the ninth, harm in the people of the faith, and the places of sorrow.[323] **13** And in the tenth, the strain of kings' assets and that area which belongs to the sign in which the testimony is.[324] **14** And in the eleventh, the accumulation of kings' assets, and [their] treasures increase. **15** And in the twelfth, malicious acts [by] the authority [against] the people, and the cavalry.

16 If Mars was in the stakes of the year, it stirs up war in accordance with his strength; and likewise if he was in the square of Saturn and Jupiter.

17 The Ascendant, the Moon, and their lords belong to the general public: and if the lord of the Ascendant and the Moon were in the sixth or eighth, made unfortunate, it indicates disease and death.

18 Know that Mars[325] is the indicator of fighting and wars which are in the world. **19** So when he entered into one of the stakes (and the stake under the earth intensifies that), then at that time it increases civil unrest and the shedding of blood, and wars and fighting take place among the people of the earth—and that is more intense if he was in Gemini or its triplicity.

[Mars as lord of the year in the triplicities]

20 And if he was in [Gemini] or in its triplicity, and he is direct in course, those wars will be in the seeking of justice. **21** And if he was retrograde, it is with unfairness and arms and injustice. **22** And if he was in one of these signs and not in the stakes, but he is in a place looking at the Ascendant, it indicates powerful illnesses from the air and blood; and that is more intense in every land[326] which belongs to the signs which he squares or the light of his opposition is. **23** And if he was retrograde, it is like what I described: it indicates epidemic and illnesses coming from the blood.

24 And if Mars was the lord of the year and he was in Aries and [its] triplicity, and he is direct in that, in the people is every hot, dry illness, and some of the kings will contend with others. **25** And if he was retrograde, there is a contention in the clime of Babylon, and harm will come to live-

---

[323] Meaning of this last phrase unclear. 1485 includes harm on journeys and in the law.
[324] That is, the area of the earth ruled by that sign (1485).
[325] The Persian name for Mars.
[326] Reading ارض with 1485 for مرض ("illness").

stock, and especially to what has a cloven hoof and is hairy; and it weakens predatory beasts and intensifies the heat. **26** And if he was in these signs and not in a stake but was looking at the Ascendant, some of the people will oppress the others. **27** And the harms and evil which I described will be in [the places and people belonging to] where he is by sign or his light from the opposition or square.

28 And if Mars[327] was the lord of the year and he was in Taurus and its triplicity, in a stake, direct, it indicates the corruption of produce, and the death of livestock, and there is contention and fighting among the people. **29** And if Mars was in this triplicity, and not in an angle but he was looking at the Ascendant, it indicates that the land [belonging to where] he is by sign [will have] harm.

30 And if Mars was the lord of the year and he is in Cancer and its triplicity, in a stake, direct in course, and he is not pushing his management to Saturn in this triplicity, there will be civil unrest in the clime of the west and the Arabs, and a bloody infirmity and wars and epidemic and great death, and injustice against their king (by death) or tribulation will take place in it. **31** And if he was retrograde, it is more intense and powerful.

[More on Mars in general][328]

32 And know that the matter of Mars, if he was in one of the stakes of the year (and it is worse under the earth), provokes civil unrest and wars, and fighting and blood among the people. **32** And if he was in a fixed sign, it indicates the fixity of that evil and its duration. **33** And if he was in a movable sign, it indicates its shifting and going away. **34** And if he was in a sign having two bodies, it indicates the repetition of the maliciousness in the wars.

35 And likewise if Mars[329] was direct, it indicates [its] length and intensity. **36** And if he was made unfortunate, it indicates decline and safety. **37** And if Mars was established[330] [in place] and was partnering with Saturn, it indicates disaster and killing: and that is in the area in which Mars[331] is, of the east of the clime and its west, and its north, and its south. **38** And indeed that is

---

[327] The Persian name for Mars, here and through **30**.
[328] This continues the discussion from **19** above.
[329] The Persian name for Mars.
[330] That is, stationary.
[331] The Persian name for Mars.

worse if it was the entrance of the Sun into Aries at the time of his falling,[332] and Saturn was retrograde, returning [Mars's] light and management upon him: for in this condition that indicates the persistence of killing, and capture and extortion and unfairness and injustice and violence in the countries, and especially if at the revolution of the year he was in Gemini or in the Midheaven, for then in that year there will be killing an squandering, and many people will be crucified. **39** And if he was in the Ascendant or the west, it indicates the cutting off of hands, and shortcomings[333] in the people.

40 And look in the separation of Mars: for if he separated from Jupiter, those wars will be because of seeking faith and justice and truth. **41** And if he was separating from an infortune, it was because of seeking injustice and extortion and oppression.

42 And[334] if Mars was direct in course, it indicates the good and reliability and patience.[335] **43** And if he was retrograde, then the war is short, and those seeking it are a disreputable people in the likeness of thieves and riffraff of the leaders of the civil unrest, and their command will end in fleeing and dispersion and defeat.

44 And the fighting will be more intense if Mars was slow and in a fixed sign, for that indicates the calamity of the people of the area in which he is in, according to that sign and his place in the circle. **45** If he was in the Ascendant, [there is] a shedding of their blood and it multiplies wounds and cuts in it. **46** And if he was in the second, it extorts their assets. **47** And if he was in the third, it cuts off their kinships and brings about hatred and evil and wars between them. **48** And if he was in the fourth, it intensifies their sieges and cuts off their supplies and provisions. **49** And if he was in the fifth, the years of their offspring and children [will be shortened].[336] **50** And if he was in the sixth, they will be thin and enslaved. **51** And if he was in the seventh, they will violate their harems and women, and marry [them]. **52** And if he was in the eighth, then [there will be widespread death, and][337] few of

---

[332] That is to say, Mars is cadent—but whether this is simply from the stakes, or being in aversion to the Ascendant or even to the Sun, I am not sure.

[333] Tentatively reading مثلبة for مثلثة ("triplicity"), although this seems rather weak when compared to amputations.

[334] For this paragraph, see *RYW* Ch. 21, **2** and *Scito* Ch. 36, **2**.

[335] This does not mean there is no war, but rather that it is carried out by honest men who will continue in it. See the next sentence.

[336] 1485 says that "children and their assets will be robbed."

[337] Adding based on 1485.

them will escape. **53** And if he was in the ninth, they will flee from their country and homeland, and depart from their homes. **54** And if he was in the tenth, enemies and the [political] authorities will prevail over them, and they will be under their obedience and their kings. **55** And if he was in the eleventh, they will quarrel and lose courage.[338] **56** And if he was in the twelfth, the enemies will get what they want from [the people].

Chapter VIII.14: On the survival of kings & their conditions[339]

2 For[340] the survival of kings, look from two perspectives: from the revolution of the year of the world, and from the [actual] time of their accession.[341] **3** And they both should lead to one [and the same] time; [but] if they are in conflict, then he will go beyond [the stated times].

4 And[342] as for looking in the revolution of the year, it is that you should begin from the First Lot up to the Second Lot. **5** In a superior house,[343] [whether there is] an aspect [between them] or he is not looking, then take one year for every 30°. **6** And if they were in an inferior house[344] and [there is] an aspect, then take a year for every 30°. **7** And if it was not looking, then split off one-half of the degrees which are between them, and take a year for every 30° from the remaining half. **8** And[345] the beginning is from the weaker of the two in the places, up to the stronger of them. **9** And if they were equivalent in strength in the places, then see the one which is in its own *ḥalb*,[346] and lead up to that one.

10 And when the distribution in which it is feared from him is completed, then consider the sign at which the year terminates:[347] for if it is corrupted at

---

[338] 1485 adds, "and they will be conquered for that reason." This is a fair interpretation of Form VI of this verb, which does have a basic meaning of failure as well.
[339] This chapter (with its very confusing second half) is similar to 'Umar's *Book of Questions*, Ch. 94 (see VIII.20 below), but also has similarities with *BRD* II.5, **4**.
[340] For this sentence, see *BRD* II.5, **2**.
[341] The rest of this chapter deals with revolutions, while Ch. 15, **3ff** discusses accession charts.
[342] For this paragraph, cf. VIII.15, **14-16**, and VIII.20, **8-10**. Cf. also *BRD* II.5, **4**.
[343] That is, if Saturn is in one of the domiciles of the superior planets.
[344] That is, a domicile of the inferior planets.
[345] This sentence probably continues the instructions from **7**.
[346] Reading with Nur. for خلفه.
[347] This suggests a profection from the Ascendant, for as many years as the calculation yields. But see **11** below.

the revolution of the year, and the Sun is in the square of Mars or Saturn,[348] then decree disaster for him; and if not,[349] it bestows another turn.[350] **11** And see if the turning reaches the square of the infortunes, and judge based on what it presents; and you do not decree based on that unless it is with the corruption of the sign which the year terminates at from the mightiest direction,[351] *and* the Sun.[352] **12** And if it corrupted one of them and the other one was in a good condition, then decree corruption for him from an illness and what is like that. **13** And the misfortune is from the square of Mars or Saturn in the revolution of the year, and the reaching[353] of their square in the root of the religion or the conjunction,[354] or to the square of the conjunction itself. **14** And if the First Lot is in his own houses, then it is understood[355] from its place just as you turn the foundation, if God (be he exalted) wills.

Chapter VIII.15: On the knowledge of the [king's] accession & its period

2 If you wanted knowledge of that, you take from the lord of the exaltation of the Lot of Fortune up to [the Lot], and take what there was between them, a day or month or year for every sign.[356]

[Abū Ma'shar: BRD II.5, 19]

3 And as for looking at it from the time of the accession,[357] then you look for him from the Ascendant and the Midheaven, then you extract for him the releaser and the house-master just as you do equally in nativities. **4** Then, you direct for him the degree of the Ascendant for his body, and you direct the degree of the Midheaven for his authority, and you arrange the turnings

---

[348] This must mean he is besieged by them.
[349] That is, if no disaster happens.
[350] That is, one more year or revolution.
[351] For the "mighty" direction, see the time lord techniques in the Introduction.
[352] Namely, the corruption of both the Sun and the sign.
[353] This word suggests a mundane profection.
[354] I am not sure if the root of the religion is the same as the conjunction itself.
[355] Reading somewhat uncertainly for فادركه. Nur. reads اذل or اذك (ادل, "indicate for it from…"?).
[356] This is probably performed at the Aries ingress for the year of the accession, since al-Rijāl distinguishes this from the event chart of the accession in **9**.
[357] That is, as opposed to the mundane revolution as described in VIII.14 above.

of them together for him until an infortune meets it: and judge ruin for him. **5** And if it was the corruption of one of [the releasing points] but not another, then decree something of corruption for that. **6** If the misfortune was powerful where you directed the terminal point of the Ascendant to the infortunes, then decree disaster for him; and if [the misfortune] was below that, then decree an illness for him (this is if the direction from the degree of the Midheaven was in a good condition). **7** And if the corruption was from the degree of the Midheaven but not the Ascendant, then decree corruption for him in his rulership. **8** And if [the corruption] was of them both together, then you do not doubt his ruin.

9 And it is necessary for you to direct what comes out for you from this procedure [along with] the first procedure:[358] for they should not conflict unless the time he took [for the accession] was not determined accurately.

10 And it is necessary for you to cite the Ascendant of the religion[359] and the Ascendant of the conjunction and the terminal point of the direction and the turnings,[360] to the square of the infortunes in those places. **11** And the time of the incident which the year indicates is when the direction from the sign of the terminal point or from the Ascendant reaches the square of that indicator and the place of the indicator, and the amount of what is between them in degrees.

12 And if you are working on the knowledge of the durability of the king it is necessary that you look in the year in which he acceded, to see which sign the year reaches, and in which degree the distribution is, and which bound and which Quarter,[361] and is there in that [degree or bound] the ray of the planet in the root or conjunction [which occurred] in the year in which the dynasty began, and is it in conformity with one of the quarters or not in conformity. **13** And one looks at the degree of the terminal point in that year, and at the lord of the distribution, and one looks at the degree of the direction: how much is between them and the rays of the infortunes?

---

[358] This probably refers to the methods in Ch. VIII.14 above.
[359] This is probably Libra, the commonly-accepted Ascendant for the ingress of 571 AD.
[360] Burnett prefers "periods," but this may refer to profections.
[361] For the Quarters, see the Introduction to *BRD*.

[Cf. 'Umar's Book of Questions Ch. 94 / BRD II.5, 4]

14 Then,[362] one looks at the [First] Lot in the house of a planet: how much is between it and the Second Lot? **15** For if the First Lot is in the house of a superior planet, you take a year for every sign; and if it was in the house of an inferior planet, you take a year for every sign, *if* they both were looking closely [at each other]. **16** [If they were not looking at each other], you discard half of that.[363]

17 Then,[364] in the year in which you judged for them, one looks (on the part of the Sun) at the lord of the foundation:[365] how is it? **18** And if it was unfortunate, then that time is a confirmation of it; and if it was other than that, then judge according to what you see.

[Abū Ma'shar: BRD II.7, 11]

19 And if you wanted to know the one who will come after him,[366] then look at the Sun [and] the one to whom he is pushing, at the revolution of the year in which he arrived [at the kingship]. **20** For if he was pushing to the lord of the fifth, then it is his son; and if it was the lord of the third, then it is his brother; and say likewise about the meaning of the house of the one pushed to, and its indication. **21** And if it was the lord of the house of children and you wanted to know which of them it was, then look at the lord of the triplicity of the house of children: the one which was greater by share[367] in the house of children, is the one whom he loves [more]. **22** And if it was the first one, then he is of the older ones; and if it was the second, he is from the middle ones; and if it was the third, he is from the younger ones.

23 And on the whole, [the reign will go] to the one having the lord of the house of children [in the father's chart], rising in his own nativity. **24** Speak likewise for the brothers, by the permission of God.

---

[362] Note the similarity between this and VIII.14, **4-9**, and VIII.20, **8-10**.
[363] Both BL and Nur. append **16** to **15**, as though one only takes half the years if they were indeed aspecting. But this goes against similar passages in Abū Ma'shar as well as 'Umar (and 1485), so I have separated the sentences.
[364] I do not understand the meaning of this paragraph.
[365] "Foundation" here should refer to some kind of root chart.
[366] That is, the new king's successor.
[367] That is, "dignities."

Chapter VIII.16: On the death of kings

2 If the lord of the Midheaven was in the sign in which the power[368] of the years[369] terminated, it indicates the death of kings. **3** And if Mars made it unfortunate, it indicates his killing. **4** And especially if the sign of the transit was unfortunate by the arrival of an infortune in it, it indicates the death of the king. **5** And if the lord of the sign of the transit was in a sign having two bodies, it indicates the death of two kings in that conjunction. **6** And if an infortune was in the sign of the Midheaven, it also indicates the death of the king.

7 And[370] if the lord of the Midheaven was burned up or was opposite the degrees of the Sun, it indicates the death of the king; and if had [already] exceeded [the Sun's] degree,[371] anger will enter upon him. **8** If the lord of the Midheaven was in a sign having two bodies, two kings will die in that conjunction.

9 And[372] if the indicator of the king is entering into burning at the revolution of the year, then the king of that clime dies; [but] if it was [at] the tip of the rays, envy and sorrow and worry will enter upon him. **10** But if a fortune was looking at it, it will subside. **11** And if it was at the tip of the rays and it had already passed by burning, it would be anger and contention, then it would go away unless it was an infortune: for then it indicates the power of that, and its intensity, and it will be feared for him according to the essence of the sign in which the infortune is: if it was [the house of][373] illness, then illness, and if it was [the house of] death, then death. **12** And[374] if the fortunes looked at it, it will subside. **13** And[375] also look for this from the assembly of the indicator with the infortune, and one speaks in accordance with this likewise: if an infortune was looking at the indicator of the king from the opposition or the square and the assembly, death will be feared. **14**

---

[368] امر, which I usually translate as "matter," but this seems more appropriate.
[369] Reading with Nur. (and suggested by 1485), for "direction." This would then be a profection.
[370] For this paragraph, see *RYW* Ch. 19, **8-9** and *BRD* II.7, **6**.
[371] 1485 understands this as passing by the exact opposition only.
[372] For this paragraph, see *RYW* Ch. 26, **2-7**. Abū Ma'shar's version is in *BRD* II.7, **6**, but has the lord of the Midheaven rather than the indicator of the king.
[373] Adding with Abū Ma'shar, here and in the next clause.
[374] Adding with Abū Ma'shar; 1485 contains the beginning of this sentence but blends it with the next.
[375] Reading more with Abū Ma'shar for the first part of this sentence (see previous footnote).

And if what I mentioned was from a stake, then the time of that is at the burning of [the king's] significator, and the agreement[376] of that infortune with the place of the indicator or the Midheaven or the Ascendant—unless a fortune participates with it in the aspect and that infortune is assisting it in the essence.[377]

15 And[378] look at the planet which is informative in [this] about the condition of the king, and relates what is and what happens to him day by day in terms of harshness and comfort, and good and evil.[379] **16** Then, look at his receiving of the lights and his pushing, for it indicates what befalls the citizens from him, and what befalls [him] from them.

17 And[380] if Mars was retrograde in Taurus or Scorpio at the arrival of the year of the world, ruin will be feared for the king in that year. **18** And if Mars was retrograde in one of those two after the entrance of the year; and the first [indication] is more sure.

19 And[381] if Mercury or the Moon was the indicator of the year or the indicator of the king, and one of the infortunes looked at it, it would be bad because he would not be able to ward off an enemy.

20 And[382] if an infortune corresponded to the Ascendant or the lord of the Midheaven, the occurrences of wars and impairment are feared for the king. **21** And likewise, if the harmful infortune was retrograde.

22 And[383] if an eclipse [of the Moon] took place in Aries, with Saturn in Cancer and Mars in Capricorn, then there is no doubt about the ruin of the king when the Sun enters Aries in that year. **23** And if the Sun was eclipsed in Libra, and Saturn in Capricorn and Mars in Cancer, then the king will be killed or poisoned or betrayed: and that will be when Saturn conjoins with

---

[376] This seems to mean that the infortune comes to these places by transit, sometime after the revolution.
[377] "Essence" normally refers to the essence of a sign, but I am not exactly sure what Abū Ma'shar means by this. 1485 says that the fortune will "diminish the harm" of the infortune, according to the *fortune's* own essence, which makes more sense.
[378] For this paragraph, see *RYW* Ch. 26, **15-16** and *BRD* II.7, **6**.
[379] That is, watch the ongoing transits of this planet.
[380] For this paragraph, see *BRD* II.7, **6**.
[381] For this sentence, see *Scito* Ch. 49, **1**.
[382] For this paragraph, cf. *BRD* II.7, **6**. In *BRD*, this is if the Ascendant or Midheaven or even the lord of the Midheaven comes to a malefic by primary direction.
[383] For this paragraph, see *BRD* II.7, **8**.

him[384] in Capricorn. **24** And[385] if it was Jupiter at the entrance of the Sun into the beginning of the degree of Cancer, then judge [good] for him.

25 If[386] Mars[387] was the lord of the Midheaven, entering into burning, it indicates the ruin of the king, and especially if he was connecting with a planet in the eighth or the fifth, from the opposition or square: for that is with the fear of ruin upon him in that year. **26** And likewise if he was connecting with the lords of those [places] outside of the places which I mentioned. **27** And that is more intense if it was the two infortunes.

And pertaining to that, on the lifespans of kings:

29 Also, the sign of the preceding conjunction belongs to the new occurrence[388] and the dynasty, and [it is] the indicator of the emergence of that matter and dynasty, and it is the root from which the period of their remaining is inferred.[389]

30 And the sign of the conjunction is what indicates their birth year: from the sign of their conjunction it is the indicator of what befalls them, of disasters and the badness of [their] condition in every year, with the return of the conjunction to their sign which indicated the beginning of their authority.[390]

31 And when the conjunction returned to Scorpio and[391] the power[392] of the years reached Scorpio (which is the sign of their conjunction), violence[393]

---

[384] Grammatically this is Mars, but Abū Ma'shar says "the Sun with Saturn in Capricorn or with Mars in Cancer."

[385] This does not appear in BRD or in 1485, and I am unsure of its meaning. The end of the sentence blends with the next, putting the Persian name for Mars in the place of whatever is indicated by Jupiter here—so I have inserted [good], since Jupiter should certain indicate something good. The meaning might be that if Jupiter is *also* in Cancer at the time of the Sun's entrance into it (so as to conjoin with Mars), then things will improve. The sentence could possibly be read as "If Jupiter was at the beginning of the degrees of Cancer at the Sun's entrance [into *Aries*]...".

[386] For this paragraph, cf. *RYW* Ch. 19, **8-12**.

[387] Al-Rijāl uses the Persian name for Mars here. But Māshā'allāh does not mention Mars. The Māshā'allāh version is probably correct.

[388] حدث. The text seems to mean "the new situation in regional and world politics."

[389] That is, the sign *describes* something important about them, it indicates *that* they arose, and *how long* they may remain.

[390] See for example Māshā'allāh's *Conjunctions* (Chs. 8 and 10), when the watery conjunction returned to Scorpio.

[391] Reading "and" with Nur. for "or." Nur.'s version matches 1485 more and makes more sense.

[392] Or, "matter" (امر). I believe this means that both (a) the mean conjunction and (b) the annual profection from some unnamed point, had returned to Scorpio in the same year. For example, the Scorpio mean conjunction of 570 AD (but taken to be in 571) returned

entered upon the Arabs and on the people of Tahāma[394] from enemies, and death from unhealthiness and epidemic, and killing in wars, and their intense affliction from chronic illness—unless the original indicators of their emergence were strong, in the angles and their shares, [and] they were safe from the misfortune of the infortunes: for they will be strong in their contention (and in addition there will be no avoiding violence).

32 And the indicators of the Arabs are Venus (the lord of the Ascendant of their conjunction),[395] and Mars (the lord of the sign of their conjunction), and the lord of the Ascendant of the year in which the conjunction in Scorpio was.[396]

33 And you do likewise for kings when you cite the First Lot and the lord of his house in the year in which he acceded.[397]

34 And know that the work in the lifespans of kings is like the work in the lifespans of prophets, so combine the work of them with the work of the prophets (the prayers of Allah be upon them!). **35** Infer[398] the matter from the work of the year in which the master of the religion ([that is], the one who accedes by means of his religion), died: for from the revolution of the year is made clear his survival and his condition with his citizens, and likewise is known the death of every king who accedes after him. **36** And his lifespan is from the revolution of the year in which the one who accedes acceded, and is known the condition [of the one] who accedes after him. **38** And you do not include kings [who accede out of] civil strife into your work.

39 And[399] if there was a kingdom or leadership, [and] you did not know the death of the lord of it and of its religion, then look [at] the nearest con-

---

to Scorpio in 630 AD. The profection of the assumed Libra Ascendant of 571 reached Scorpio in 632 AD, during the period of that conjunction. This happened to be the year of Muhammad's death and the subsequent accession of Abu Bakr as the first Caliph, after which Abu Bakr was driven to enforce militarily numerous agreements that various tribes had made under Muhammad.

[393] Or perhaps, "severity" or "stress" (شدة).
[394] A coastal plane on the southern and southwestern parts of the Arabian peninsula.
[395] That is, the Libra Ascendant of the 571 AD Aries ingress, shortly after the mean conjunction in 570 AD.
[396] This seems to be a reference to the Aries ingress of 570 AD itself. This could not refer to Mars, as it is impossible that a Libra Ascendant (571 AD) could have been preceded one year before by a Scorpio or Aries Ascendant. There might be some error in the text.
[397] This probably refers to the method in BRD II.5, **4**, and will be described in *AW3*.
[398] The sentence divisions in the rest of the paragraph are a little unclear; 1485 seems to have encountered the same problem.
[399] From here through **46**, cf. BRD II.5, **9**.

junction ([whether] it was [before his rule] or it is [at the time of it]):[400] look at the place of the conjunction from the Ascendant, and count from the Ascendant up to the sign of the conjunction, a year for [every sign]. **40** Except that if the Ascendant was a house of Saturn or his exaltation, or [it was] a house of the Moon or her exaltation, then it is likewise the amount from the place of the conjunction up to the Ascendant, a year for every sign. [**41** And you will begin from that year, and where the numbering ended, there will be the determination of the loss of that king—unless he escaped on account of other indications.][401]

42 And if the Ascendant of the revolution of the year of the conjunction[402] was (by sign) in the houses of the superior planets, it indicates the rising of a king in that year which the conjunction we introduced, indicated. **43** And if the Ascendant of the year of the conjunction was one of the houses of Saturn or his exaltation, or a house of Jupiter or his exaltation, the counting is from the sign in which the conjunction is, to the Ascendant (a year for every sign); except that if Saturn and the Ascendant of the conjunction was [in] the house of one of them or its exaltation, and Saturn and Jupiter in one of the stakes of the Ascendant by number or by equation,[403] then the direction is from the Ascendant to the sign in which the conjunction is, a year for every sign. **44** And[404] if the Ascendant was in something other than what we described, then the counting is from the sign in which the conjunction was, to the Ascendant, a year for every sign. **45** And if the Ascendant of the revolution of the year of the conjunction was, by sign, of the houses of the inferior planets, then if the conjunction was in the third or ninth it indicates just what the superior planets do. **46** And if the Ascendant of the year of the conjunction was of the houses of the superior planets, or the conjunction was in the third or ninth, and the conjunction was in Aquarius, then it is strongly established, and it should not be feared for kings when the year reaches it—I mean, when it was counted from the Ascendant to the

---

[400] Relying on 1485 for some of the sense of this choppy sentence.
[401] Adding with 1485. The only part of this sentence that seems to be represented in BL and N are the words "And the indication is from that sign."
[402] One important difference between this passage and *BRD* II.5, **9**, is that Abū Ma'shar makes this the sign of the conjunction itself, not the Ascendant.
[403] That is, by whole-signs or by a quadrant division. See also *BRD* I.3, **9** for a similar passage.
[404] This sentence (missing in 1485) originally read "from the Ascendant to the sign in which the conjunction was," which is redundant. *BRD* II.5, **9** more reasonably has it the other way around if they are in succeedent or cadent places, so I have switched them here.

sign of the conjunction or from the sign of the conjunction up to the Ascendant.

47 And[405] I have put [this] to the test in the conjunction which was at the time of Mutawakkil,[406] and he did not die at the time [when] the year arrived.

Chapter VIII.17: On the changing of kings[407]

2 See[408] when the Sun enters the first minute of Aries, and look at the Ascendant and the places of the planets. [**3** If the revolution is by day, look at the Sun and the Lot of highness and victory and flourishing[409] (which is taken by day from the degree of the Lot of the absent[410] to Jupiter, and by night the opposite, and cast out from the Ascendant) and at the lord of the bound of the Midheaven.][411] **4** And if the revolution was by night, then seek the indicator of the king[412] from the Moon and the Lot of highness and the lord of the bound of the Midheaven.[413] **5** And the one of them which was in a stake or in a good place, is more worthy in the indication, and it is the indicator of the king. **6** And if the indicator of the king was safe from the infortunes and harm in it, and[414] [safe] from the lord of its own seventh and eighth and twelfth and sixth and fourth, then the king will be safe in that year. **7** And if it was made unfortunate by some of them, and one of them was the lord of the fourth, and it was Mars,[415] it attacks the king in that year, and the king will be killed in custody. **8** And if the infortune which was mak-

---

[405] My sense is that this comment is al-Rijāl's own, and not Abū Ma'shar's (if indeed this passage does come from Abū Ma'shar). For *BRD* II.7, **5** speaks of Mutawakkil in the context of another technique, and so one might expect Abū Ma'shar to have said more; at any rate Abū Ma'shar does not seem to be in the habit of stating when techniques do not work, only confirming their validity.

[406] The 'Abbasid caliph from 847–861 AD. Mutawakkil took over from his brother, and was killed in December 861.

[407] Taking the title from 1485. BL and Nur. have دول or "countries" (actually, BL misspells this as الدلو, "Aquarius," drawing on the previous chapter). It could perhaps be better read as دور, "turn," i.e., when a new king takes his turn.

[408] For this paragraph, see *BRD* II.7, **9**.

[409] That is, the Hermetic Lot of victory.

[410] That is, the Lot of Spirit.

[411] Adding this from *BRD*.

[412] That is, of the new king (according to *BRD*).

[413] BL now adds a partial reflection of **3**, saying "And if it was by day, then from the Sun."

[414] *BRD* adds, "especially."

[415] *BRD* has, "and *especially if* it is Mars."

ing it unfortunate was the lord of the sixth, and it was Mars, his pain will be more intense.

9 And[416] if the year was revolved and you knew that the king was dead, and you wanted to know to whom his kingdom would pass, then look at the indicator of the king: to whom does it push it management? **10** For that will be the one to which the kingdom will pass. **11** For if the one to which the management of the kingdom was pushed, was of the essence of the sign of the indicator of the king,[417] he will be of the people of [the dead king's] own house. **12** And if the indicator of the king was of the planets which have two signs, then look at which of them it sees, and it is of its form, of the signs (for it is its sign).[418] **13** And if it was pushing to a planet in a sign not similar to its sign, then it is pushed to one who is not of his house, and it[419] leaves from one nation to another. **14** And if the indicator of the king was not pushing, then[420] after the king it passes to one in whose sign the Lot of rulership is located: if that sign is of the essence of the indicator of the king, then he is of the people of his own house; if not, it is to others.[421]

15 And[422] if you wanted to know how many kings will reign who are of the people of this house (of the king), and how many are their years, then look at the Lot of rulership.[423] **16** For if it was located in a stake, and its lord in a stake, they will rule for the greatest division, and that is 960 solar years. **17** And if it was withdrawing from the stake, and its lord was in a stake, they will rule for the middle division, and that is 240 solar years. **18** And if they

---

[416] For this paragraph, see *BRD* II.7, **11**.
[417] This is ambiguous Abū Ma'shar seems to mean that it is pushed to a planet which is like a sign *ruled by* the indicator of the king, not the essence of the sign which the indicator of the king happens to be in at the moment.
[418] This latter phrase is missing in *BRD*. 1485 reads, "which of them it looks at and was of its own form, and that will be his sign." Again this is ambiguous, especially the use of the word "form." *BRD* says to look at "which of them it looks at better, for that is the sign to be guided by." The issue of rulership seems to indicate whether the successor is of the same lineage, while I should think that the character of the successor is indicated by the planet receiving the application. But I do not understand exactly how the aspecting is supposed to work, nor exactly how Abū Ma'shar or his source understands the notion of the signs being related in essence.
[419] I take this to mean "the rulership."
[420] Reading the rest of this sentence more with *BRD*; BL and Nur. combine and truncate what follows.
[421] *BRD* text now continues above in VIII.15, **19**.
[422] For this paragraph, see *BRD* II.3, **2-3**.
[423] Abū Ma'shar clarifies that this is the position of the Lot at the triplicity shift indicating their dynasty. I take this to mean the *Aries ingress* of the year in which such a shift takes place.

were both falling [away], not looking at the Ascendant,[424] they will rule for 20 solar years.

19 And[425] the number of the kings who will reign is known by the amount of what is between the Lot of rulership and its lord, and the amount of that is the number of their kings.[426]

20 And[427] if you wanted to know when the kingdom will move to what is not that nation, [namely] to what nation of the world the rulership passes, then see to which planet the Lot of rulership passes, for it will be among the people of that planet.

21 And[428] when you wanted to know if the people of that kingdom would obey God or not, then see if the Lot of rulership[429] is in the ninth or tenth: then they will obey God in the truth. **22** And if it was in the eighth or twelfth,[430] they claim that and do not do it. **23** And if you wanted to know whom they obey, then if the Lot of rulership is in the houses of Venus, they obey silver idols; and a house of Jupiter [means] they obey golden idols; and a house of Mars [means] they obey fire; and a house of Mercury [means] they obey trees; and the house of the Moon [means] they obey cows;[431] and the house of the Sun [means] they obey wooden idols.

24 And[432] if you wanted to know from which direction they are (of the earth), then if the Lot of rulership[433] is in the east, they arise from the east; and if it is [in] the west, they arise from the west; and if it was in the stake of the earth, they arise from the furthest, non-Arab and non-Persian part of the earth; and if it was in the Midheaven then it arises with them from their own clime.

---

[424] This could mean that it is *both* dynamically cadent and in aversion to the Ascendant (so by definition in the 12th or 6th), or simply in aversion.

[425] For this paragraph, see *BRD* II.3, **6**.

[426] That is, the number of signs. Abū Ma'shar adds that a common or double-bodied sign will indicate two kings.

[427] For this paragraph, cf. *BRD* II.7, **11**; it seems to be an alternate version of **13** above.

[428] For this paragraph, see *BRD* I.4, **6**.

[429] In *BRD*, this is specifically the Mars-Moon Lot (reversed at night).

[430] The sources disagree on this. BL and Nur. have "eighth or eleventh," *BRD* has "eleventh or twelfth." But it does not make sense that the eleventh would indicate hypocrisy: so I have changed this to "eighth or twelfth."

[431] Or, "the Moon" (Nur.).

[432] For this paragraph, see *BRD* II.2, **3**.

[433] According to Burnett (in *BRD*), this is the same Lot as in **21**.

25 And[434] if you wanted to know what [the new people] will do with the nation which used to have the kingdom in their hand, see if the lord of the Lot of rulership looked at the indicator of the first king with friendship: they will not act evilly with them. 26 And if it looked at it with enmity, they will kill them by the sword, and especially if Mars[435] was in one of the stakes.

27 And if the lord of the Lot of rulership, or the Lot [itself], was in the house of one of the planets [whose] circles are above the circle of the Sun, they will have fear.

28 And[436] if you wanted to know whether the lord is just or unjust, then look: if the lord of the Lot of rulership is a fortune,[437] the lords will be just; and if it was an infortune, the lords will be unjust.

29 And[438] if you wanted to know in which direction is the city of their kings, then look at the lord of the Lot of rulership: where is it? 30 For if it was in the Midheaven (or rather, in [the middle of] the dome [of the heavens]), they will be in the middle of the clime. 31 And if it was withdrawing, [the city] will be remote. 32 And if it was a sign of water, they will be on the shore of the sea.

33 And[439] if you wanted to know whether good or evil would affect the people from them, then see if the lord of the Lot of rulership was separated from the lord of the house of assets: it indicates that the assets will be spent freely.[440] 34 And if it was connected [to it], they will have an accumulation [of assets]. 35 And if it was not looking [at all], then the king will not have an opinion about it. 36 And if it was looking at the ninth, journeys will be many.

37 And[441] if you wanted to know whether a nation not their own would come out [in order to] take the kingdom from them, then look at the Lot of rulership: for if it is located at the end of the sign, [a people which is] not theirs will rise against them, seeking the kingdom. 38 And if it is located at

---

[434] For this paragraph, see *BRD* II.3, **8**.
[435] The text uses the Persian name, whereas *BRD* does not; this is an indication of an older, Persian source.
[436] For this paragraph, see *BRD* II.4, **11**.
[437] Or perhaps, "fortunate" and "unfortunate" (later in the sentence). *BRD* speaks of the lord being in the *bound* of a malefic or benefic.
[438] For this paragraph, see *BRD* II.2, **4**.
[439] For this paragraph, see *BRD* II.4, **11**.
[440] *BRD* reads that it will be wasted. The verb here (بذل) has the connotation of being generous in spending, which suggests something good for the people—but it might also mean that the royal coffers will be empty. So perhaps what is good for the people will be bad for the state.
[441] For this paragraph, see *BRD* II.1, **7**.

the beginning of the sign, then some of that nation will fight others [of the same nation]. **39** And if it was in the middle of the sign, their kingdom will persevere.

40 And[442] if you wanted to know the first one of that nation to rule, (a boy or an old man), then look at the lord of the Lot of rulership: where is it from the Lot? **41** For if it was in its square, he was middle-aged; and if it was in its trine, he was a man advanced in years; and if it was in the opposition, he was a great old sheikh.[443]

42 The[444] Lot of rulership and authority is taken by day from the Sun to Saturn (and by night the converse), and it is projected from the Ascendant.

43 The[445] Lot of rulership as we have found it in another book on it, is taken from the Ascendant of the year of the conjunction up to the degree of the conjunction [itself], and it is projected from the Ascendant.[446]

44 And if, at the accession of the king, Saturn is in the seventh from the Ascendant of the year of his accession, then it indicates that his citizens will oppose him and fight him for six years, the number of what is between Saturn and the Ascendant. **45** And[447] if in addition Mars[448] was in a house of Saturn, it reduces the rain in the time of that rulership.

46 And from the *Book of Examples*:[449] if Saturn is the one in charge of the matters of the year, and he was falling down towards the earth in the stake or in the apogee, it indicates famine in the people, and restriction, and drought.

---

[442] For this paragraph, see *BRD* II.4, **6**.
[443] *BRD* adds that a conjunction shows youth.
[444] For this sentence, see the calculation in *ITA* VI.2.39, which is from Abū Ma'shar's *Great Introduction*.
[445] For this paragraph, see *BRD* I.4, **8**.
[446] This does not make sense, as the Lot would always be on the degree of the conjunction itself. *BRD* I.4, **8** has what is probably the correct reading: from the Ascendant of the time of the conjunction itself to the degree of the conjunction, and projected from the Ascendant of the *revolution* for that year. The "time of the conjunction" is probably the time of the *mean* conjunction.
[447] For this sentence, cf. *BRD* VIII.1, **13**.
[448] The Persian name for Mars.
[449] Abū Ma'shar is credited with a *Book of Examples*, subtitled *The Book of Anecdotes in the Revolutions of Years* (Sezgin, p. 149 #27), but so is the earlier Persian astrologer Buzurjmihr (Sezgin p. 138).

Chapter VIII.18: On kings & their lifespans

['Umar al-Tabarī: Book of Questions Ch. 91]

2 The knowledge of the lifespans of kings from the revolution of the year of the world, according to 'Umar b. Farrukhan [al-Tabarī]: assign the Ascendant of the revolution to the citizens, and the Sun to the king, and the seventh to the enemies of the citizens, and the fourth to the results of the matter of the citizens. **3** And as for the enemies of king, that is from the ninth from the Ascendant of the revolution of the year, and that is the house of the king's enemies.[450] **4** And appoint the second as the house of the citizens' assets, and the eleventh from the Ascendant as the house of the king's assets (and it is the second from the Midheaven). **5** And the lord [of the Midheaven], and the Sun, and the lord of each [are indicators of the king].[451]

6 Then, look at the lord of the eighth from the Ascendant belonging to the king (and that is the Midheaven):[452] how is it looked at and its connection with the lord of the Midheaven and the Sun? **7** For if there was not an aspect between them, and not a connection, then look: is there a collecting planet bringing their light together, or a transferring [planet]? **8** Then, look at the sign of the Midheaven: and if [the collecting or transferring planet] was looking [at it], it indicates death and he dies in battle with that.

9 A connection of the Moon with the fortunes indicates rescue, and her connection with the infortunes his destruction and ruin, unless those infortunes were receiving her: for there would be a fiasco and [then] he would be safe. **10** And this is if the Moon would have a share of the house or exaltation or triplicity or face in the sign of the Midheaven.

---

[450] The ninth is the twelfth (the house of enemies) from the tenth (the house of the king).
[451] Adding with 1485. Hugo evidently did not know quite what to do with this either, so he made these planets indicators for the king's money as well. Nur. adds a few comments about examining them, but is likewise unclear as to what they indicate.
[452] The eighth from the Midheaven is the fifth.

Chapter VIII.19: On the knowledge of the death of kings from the revolution of the year of the world

['Umar al-Tabarī: Book of Questions Ch. 92][453]

2 The time in this is from the assembly of the indicator of the king [and] the lord of the eighth of the Midheaven, or the Sun,[454] or the aspect to them from the square or the opposition, and the sign in which they are assemble or are squaring or opposing, has something of its[455] shares and its power, and it is not retrograding, and not burned up, and not alien,[456] and not in its own downfall: for with that is the time of the death.

Chapter VIII.20: On the amount of the king's longevity, from the year of his accession

['Umar al-Tabarī: Book of Questions Ch. 94][457]

2 See when the Sun entered Aries and he acceded [to the throne] in that year, and look at Saturn at the hour of the Sun's entrance into Aries. **3** If Saturn was in his own house or in one of the houses of the superior planets, it indicates the survival of the king who has acceded, for a complete conjunction,[458] and especially if he was in the tenth from the Sun or the eleventh from him: for we do not doubt in his survival for a complete conjunction if it was like that. **4** And if was not like that, subtract from his power[459] in accordance with what he subtracts from his power.

5 And know that Saturn is the First Lot: so if he was looking at the Second Lot (and that is Jupiter), it indicates the increase of the survival. **6** And if [Jupiter] was in a strong place, then it enumerates his lesser years in months;

---

[453] See also *Judges* §10.31.
[454] That is, between the lord of the eighth *from* the Midheaven (viz., the fifth) and either (1) the indicator of the king or (2) the Sun.
[455] I take this to mean the lord of the eighth from the Sun.
[456] Or really, "exiled." I take this to mean peregrination, though Hugo takes this to mean "western" (which comes from the same verb).
[457] See also *Judges* §10.29 and *BRD* II.5, **10**. Parts of this chapter are also reflected in Ch. VIII.14 above.
[458] According to *BRD* II.5, **10**, this means "until" the next mean conjunction of Saturn and Jupiter.
[459] Or perhaps, the king's *"survival,"* which is how 1485 understands it.

and that is when he was in something of his own shares. **7** If he was in what follows a stake, it increases by one-half of his lesser years.

8 And[460] if you found the First Lot in the houses of the inferior planets at the revolution of the year, and especially if he was not looking at the Sun (and especially in Virgo), then he receives what belongs to the [First] Lot in the sign in which he is, from 30 [degrees]: and what remains of the degrees, for every degree a year, is the amount of the duration of the accession.[461] **9** And if he exceeds that [time], direct for him from the place of the [First] Lot to the place of the first infortune he encounters. **10** And if the turning[462] reaches that sign in which the accession was, it indicates his ruin; [and for this], assign a year to every sign.

11 And[463] another way is that you take from the lord of the house of the [First] Lot up to the Lot, and for every sign you find between them, you equate it to a year: and that is the amount of the accession of the acceder.

Chapter VIII.21: On a question about the matters of kings

['Umar al-Tabarī: Book of Questions Ch. 95a][464]

2 If you were asked about something of the matters of kings, then look for them from the Sun, and the Midheaven and its lord: take as the indicator the greater one of them in testimony, and the better of them by place, and do for it just as you direct the Ascendant in degrees of ascensions. **3** And you direct for the general populace from the degree of the Ascendant, and the place of the Moon, and the degree of the lord of the year. **4** And the motion[465] of Mercury in the revolution of the year or question is for writers or ministers and the manager of the affair of kings. **5** And you direct Mars for the commanders and the leaders of soldiers. **6** And Saturn is directed for plowmen and the people of villages and rural communities, and castles. **7** And the motion of Venus is for the women of the king and his marriage.

---

[460] Cf. also VIII.14, **4-9**, and VIII.15, **14-16**. Cf. also *BRD* II.5, **4**.
[461] In other words, suppose Saturn is at 10° Virgo: since 20° are left in Virgo, he will last for 20 years.
[462] That is, the direction just mentioned ("direct" and "turn" here come from the same verb). On the other hand, it could refer to either a profection or mundane revolution.
[463] For this sentence, cf. also *BRD* II.5, **4**.
[464] See also *Judges* §10.30.
[465] That is, the direction.

8 Then, see how the condition of each one of them is, and in terms of its connection with the fortunes or infortunes, from the trine and sextile, and square and opposition, and assembly: and its meaning will be in that time in accordance with their nature and direction and place. **9** And the infortunes indicate evil, and the fortunes indicate the good.

10 And look at the fortunes and infortunes as to how their claims [in dignities] are in these places and signs. **11** For what there was of these signs in which the infortunes are, indicates good and joy and profit, in accordance with that sign, and that good will be from what is other than fear and death. **12** And as for the signs in which the infortunes are, they indicate harm and fear and the removal of the hand from obedience.

13 And if the question was confined to the political authority,[466] you will assign [the harm] to [the house] in which that infortune is. **14** If the Ascendant or its lord were corrupt, then it indicates harm in the king's livelihood and his soul and life, and he winds up with the weakness of illnesses, and fighting, and killing at the end of his life.[467] **15** And if the corruption was in the stake of the earth, it indicates that the result of his command winds up with evils and perhaps he will die because of that in his lifespan [in office]. **16** And if the bound[468] of the Ascendant was the corrupted one, it indicates that he acquires the mishap from the people of his own house. **17** And if the degree of the Sun was the corrupted one, then his [role as a] model will be small. **18** And if the lord of the sign [of the Sun] was corrupt, then it is like the lord of the Ascendant. **19** And if the face [of the Sun] was corrupt, it indicates that he acquires the mishap from the people of his own house and his people, and he does not have respect in his work, and he is mocked in it, and he will increase in weakness and his land tax [revenues] will be broken.

20 And as for the Lot of Fortune, if it is connected to the fortunes, it shows just governors, and they command what is good and act by it. **21** And if it is connected with the fortunes, it shows corruption and they do what is not allowed.

---

[466] Reading with 1485 for واذا كانت المسئلة الذي هو دون السلكان. The word دون normally refers to things which are inferior, "under," excluded, and so on—so a literal translation would be "the question was *under* the political authority," suggesting perhaps that the question was about something other than the king himself, or asked by someone other than him. But the reading by 1485 seems to make the most sense.
[467] Or perhaps, at the end of his term in office.
[468] 1485 has "the lord of" the bound.

[Another view][469]

22 And from the Moon is known the matter of the work from its beginning to its end, and from the connection is known what is,[470] and from her separation is known what has already been.

Chapter VIII.22: On considering the revolution of the year of the world for the accession of the acceder

['Umar al-Tabarī: Book of Questions Ch. 96][471]

2 Look in the revolution of the year of the world for the accession of the acceder, first from Saturn (for he is the First Lot) and from Jupiter (the Second Lot), and [see] how much is between them in degrees and minutes, and do not worry whether they look [at each other] or not, and preserve [that number]. **3** Then, look at the lord of the Midheaven (in which sign [he is]), and assign those degrees by the ascensions of that sign in which it is: and what that came to, is the amount of what follows, in years or months or days.[472] **4** And if those two[473] were in their own houses or exaltations, then it is their years; and if they were alien, in what follows a stake, then it is months or days, and like that.

5 If[474] the Sun was connected with Mars, and Mars empty in course, and not connecting with Saturn, the soldiers will be stirred up against the acceder, and it corrupts his soldiers, and rebels will rise up against him, and he will suffer grief from that, from the rebellion against him. **6** And if Mars was

---

[469] The following sentence is so general that it could be attributed to anyone; but it does not appear to be from the previous material of 'Umar's.
[470] Or perhaps better, what *will* be.
[471] See also *Judges* §10.33.
[472] At first glance, this means to add (1) the number of *zodiacal* degrees between Saturn and Jupiter, to (2) the position of the lord of the Midheaven, but using *ascensions* from its position. This suggests some kind of primary direction. For example, if there are 32° zodiacal degrees between Saturn and Jupiter, then we would have to add 32° in the (oblique) ascensions of the signs, to the position of the lord of the Midheaven, and figure out what the directional arc would be between the lord of the Midheaven and that point. But to me it does not make sense to start out with zodiacal degrees like this, only to add them as ascensions. It seems more sensible to project the zodiacal degrees from the lord of the Midheaven, and direct him (by ascensions or Ptolemaic methods) to that *zodiacal* position.
[473] Saturn and Jupiter.
[474] Sentences **5-16** appear in almost identical form in *BRD* II.4, **9**.

connected with Saturn, then their natures surrender to each other[475] and none will be stirred up against him.[476]

7 And if the Sun was connected with Jupiter and Jupiter is empty in course, and not connecting with Saturn, [one] of the citizens of the people of the house will rise up against him, and the acceder will suffer grief from that, from the rebellion against him. **8** And if Jupiter was connected with Saturn, their natures and the nature of the connection are a gift of submission,[477] and none of the people of the house will rise up against him, nor anyone apart from that—and if one did rise up, [the king] will be victorious over him.

9 And if the Sun is not connecting to Mars, nor to Jupiter, and he is connected to Saturn, the acceder will be safe and victorious, triumphing, strong, and especially if Saturn was in his own house, cleansed [of misfortune].

10 And if the Sun was separating from Jupiter and connected with Mars, [and] then connected with Saturn before he goes out of the sign in which he is, it indicates that a man of the people of the house of the acceder, or of his own rank, will rise up against him and he will suffer grief from that—then he will be victorious over him, and especially if Saturn was in his own house, cleansed [of misfortune]. **11** And if the Sun does not connect with Saturn before he goes out from the sign in which he is, then violence will be attached to the acceder until it is feared for his kingdom.

12 And if Mars was separating from Jupiter and connecting with Saturn, a propagandist from the people of the house will rise up against him.[478] **13** And if Jupiter was connected to Saturn, they will submit to [the king] and he will have victory over them.

14 And if Mars was separating from Saturn and connecting with Jupiter, the acceder himself will agitate against a man of the people of the house and will confront him until [the other man] rises up against him. **15** And if Jupiter was connecting with Saturn, they will submit to him and he will have victory over them, especially if Saturn was in his own house, cleansed of infortunes. **16** And if Jupiter was empty in course and he was in his own light and nature,

---

[475] اعطية طبيعتهما معا (BL), عطاء طبيعتهما جميعاً (Nur.).
[476] See also Ch. VIII.23, **65** for another example of the malefics' configurations to each other not being bad. Abū Ma'shar omits this odd phrasing about submission and surrender in *BRD* (see **8** below).
[477] See **6** above.
[478] *BRD* has "people of prophecy," and Burnett indicates that one manuscript also added "house." So it is likely that Jupiter represents either some noble lineage, or religious movement or personage.

strong, it strengthens the propagandist and intensifies his command, and he will do what he wants to [the king].

17 And as for the thing which was demanded,[479] [namely from] Saturn and Jupiter: if the former was in his own house, in the Midheaven or the eleventh or the Ascendant, or any of the stakes, then see what comes after him or is in front of him (if there were years before him): the number of the matter asked about is years or days, and one does not look at what he has [already] traversed in the sign, nor what is left [in it]. **18** And if you found Saturn at the end of the sign by one degree, wanting [his] departure [from the sign], then that degree is [still] one year even though he is bidding farewell to it:[480] then Saturn will grant [time] in accordance with his position in the circle and what follows after him between [him and] Jupiter.

['Umar's Book of Questions, Ch. 95b][481]

19 Valens said in this, if you wanted to know how much the king will reign or how long the one in charge will be in charge, then look at what is between the Sun and the degree of the Ascendant, for that is counted as being his reign in months or years or days.

20 And that is known from the Lot of work or authority, and it is that one takes from the degree of Jupiter up to the degree of the Midheaven, and it is projected from the degree of the Ascendant:[482] and where it terminates, there is the Lot. **21** So look at the bound: of which planet is it? **22** Then, look at the lord of that bound: where is it? **23** If it was in its own house or exaltation, then it distributes the complete lesser years [of that planet]. **24** And if that planet was under the rays or it was made unfortunate or in the signs of the infortunes, or in their bounds, or retrograde, then it distributes what is like those lesser years, [but] in months or days. **25** And look at the lord of the

---

[479] Namely, the length of time in office.
[480] Or, "until" he bids farewell (حتّى). In other words, every degree between Saturn and Jupiter counts, even if Saturn is at the end of his sign.
[481] See also *Judges* §10.13.
[482] Reading "Ascendant" with 1485 for "Jupiter." But variations on this Lot appear in several texts. Hugo's Latin version of this passage (*Judges* §10.13), like BL, uses Jupiter-Midheaven-Jupiter (obviously wrong). Nur. has Sun-Midheaven-Jupiter, which according to al-Qabīsī is a different Lot (*ITA* VI.2.43) but is repeated in Ch. VIII.38, **2** below. Then, al-Qabīsī specifically lists a *natal* Lot of work and authority according to Valens as being Sun-Midheaven-Ascendant (*ITA* VI.2.42), and another natal Lot showing whether someone will have authority as Sun-Midheaven-Jupiter (*ITA* VI.2.43). His mundane version of the latter (Sun-MC of the revolution-Jupiter) is in *ITA* VI.4.3.

house and the lord of its face: for if it was direct in course and is looking at that house and bound in which the Lot of authority is, then say that the lifespan of the authority is just like what we mentioned.

26 Also, if you wanted to know when he would govern and how much he governs for, then take from the stake of heaven[483] up to the lord of the stake of the earth, and see how many degrees are found between them: for the amount of that sign[484] is his position, in years or months or days. **27** And if it was a question as to when he would govern or until when, that is [the same amount] he will govern.

[Cf. Al-Kindī: Forty Chapters §408]

28 If Mars were from the tenth degree of Taurus to the one like it in Leo, then he is eastern; and from the tenth degree of Leo to the tenth degree of Scorpio, he is southern; and from the tenth degree of Scorpio to the tenth degree of Aquarius, western; and from those to the ones like them in Taurus, northern. **29** So where Mars is, to the lord of that area is the victory and triumph in the destruction of wars. **30** This is the statement of Hermes, and based on him is al-Kindī and others besides him.[485]

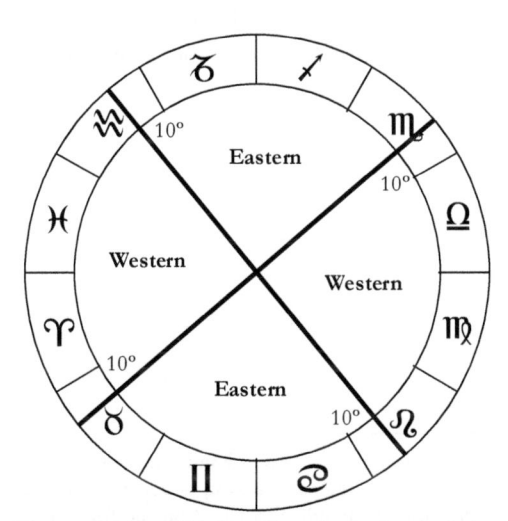

Figure 79: Al-Kindī's directions for fighting

---

[483] Hugo's 'Umar has it from the *lord of* the Midheaven, not from the Midheaven itself.
[484] 'Umar may mean that those *degrees*, converted into "signs" of 30° each, yields the number.
[485] For example, Sahl (*Fat.* p. 189).

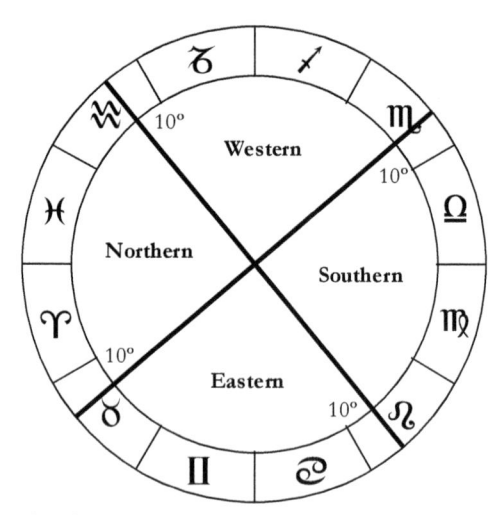

Figure 80: Al-Rijāl's proposed correction to al-Kindī[486]

[Unknown source]

31 The lord of the war of the east is Saturn, and the lord of war of the west is Mars. **32** So if there was fighting and Saturn is exalted,[487] then the victory and triumph belongs to the people of the east; and if Mars was exalted, then the triumph and victory belongs to the people of the west.

---

[486] In *Skilled* Ch. II.2, al-Rijāl points out that al-Kindī's division of the zodiac would only allow the armies to advance from the east or west, rather than from all directions. So he proposes a different division, apparently also based on the four royal stars and the seasons: the Sun is in Taurus at the middle of spring, a season associated with the east, and the constellation Taurus (with which the tropical sign Taurus used to correspond) contains the royal star Aldebaran; likewise for the other seasons and royal stars: summer and Regulus (Leo), autumn and Antares (Scorpio), and winter and Fomalhaut (really in Piscis Australis, but close to Aquarius).

[487] شرف. But al-Rijāl's source might simply mean that Saturn is in a more "distinguished" condition than Mars, not specifically that he is exalted.

Chapter VIII.23: On the overlooking[488] of the planets

2 From the *Book of Events*,[489] if any [planet] looks down upon another, and what it indicates for that.

3 If Venus looked down upon Mercury, flattery will take place in the people.[490] **4** And if she looked down upon the Moon, joy will happen to the people. **5** And[491] if she looked down upon Mars, women will be impregnated and harm will befall men in the stomach through an excess of eating. **6** And[492] if she looked down upon the Sun, expenses and blame will happen to the people. **7** And if she looked down upon the Tail, it will not be commendable. **8** And if she looked down upon Saturn, sorrow and weeping will happen to the people.

---

[488] اشراف. This chapter uses the verb اشرف (Form IV of شرف) which in its concrete form means to look down from above on someone, and metaphorically to superintend or manage (imagine an office manager looking over your shoulder). I use "overlooking" in the title, but will translate it as "looking down upon." It strongly suggests the astrological concept of "overcoming" (Gr. *kathuperterēsis*) and its specific form, "decimation" (*epidekateia*), in which one planet (the overcoming or decimating planet) is in the tenth sign from another (the overcome or decimated planet): see Schmidt 2009, pp. 47 and 178-80. So, any planet in Libra will overcome or decimate any planet in Capricorn, because Libra is the tenth sign from Capricorn. This is what I take the Arabic to be describing here, although the text adds some unusual examples, such as a planet overcoming a comet or Node (and sometimes distinguishing the Head itself and a Node), and even the Nodes looking down upon other things (highly unusual). Interpretations of overcoming in natal texts can be constructed from the following ideas: (1) these squares are almost always tense and difficult; (2) the specific combination of planets is important, as it composes a certain scenario or theme; (3) the overcome planet does not lose its meaning, but it is in some sense controlled by the themes of the overcoming planet. For example, Jupiter and Mars in combination are good for leadership; if Jupiter overcomes Mars, then while the native will have difficult Martial qualities and experiences, he will nevertheless be respected and successful (Jupiter); but if Mars overcomes Jupiter, then while he will still have some position and social standing (Jupiter), he will be erratic, scattered, and unlucky (Mars). In this Arabic text, we can see some of these elements, but the interpretations are too short to be sure how the author has derived them.

[489] This word (الاكوان) literally means, "things which come to be." I do not find it in Sezgin.

[490] 1485 simply has, "one will triumph over the other."

[491] Reading with 1485, since it seems to make more sense. BL seems to blend this with **6**: "expenses and blame will happen to the people." But Nur. reads that "arrogance and [*uncertain*] will happen to the people." In both **5** and **6**, the MSS and 1485 read very differently, and there seems to be a mixing of the sentences. Note also that the text does not have Venus rising above the Head, which may account for one of the missing or misplaced sentences.

[492] Reading with Nur.

9 If Jupiter looked down upon the Moon, it increases the nobility in good and honor. **10** And if he looked down upon Mercury, the actions[493] of kings are reinforced and increase in the good. **11** And if he looked down upon Venus, it improves the matters of young women. **12** And if he looked down upon Mars,[494] sorrow will enter upon the nobility. **13** And if he looked down upon Saturn, it indicates distress and sorrow. **14** And if he looked down upon the Head, it indicates surplus.[495] **15** And if he looked down upon the Tail, it indicates the ruining of structures. **16** And if he looked down upon a comet,[496] it indicates the killing of the nobility and those having social prestige.[497]

17 If Mars looked down upon Mercury, it provokes powerful fighting and discord. **18** And if he looked down upon the Moon, it indicates powerful earthquakes. **19** And if he looked down upon Jupiter, it indicates the use of arms and the killing of the nobility. **20** And if he looked down upon Saturn, there is a decrease of evil. **21** And if he looked down upon the Head, it indicates renown and victory. **22** And if he looked down upon the Tail, it provokes an intense fire. **23** And if he looked down upon a Node, it indicates the appearance of arms and powerful fighting.

24 And if the Sun looked down upon the planets, it indicates severe harms (except for Mercury).

25 If the Moon looked down upon Mercury, it indicates the appearance of good opinions and insight. **26** And if she looked down upon Venus, it indicates the power of kings and the nobility. **27** And if she looked down upon Mars,[498] it indicates the burning of buildings and houses, and there will be earthquakes and the shedding of blood. **28** And if she looked down upon Saturn, it indicates destruction and the badness of the people's daughters. **29** And if she looked down upon the Head, it indicates the corruption of the rivers and springs. **30** And if she looked down upon a Node, it indicates the corruption of assets. **31** And if she was located under the rays of the Sun, it indicates corruption.

---

[493] اعمال. 1485 reads "officials," which makes sense in light of Mercury; but that would be spelled عمال.
[494] The Persian name for Mars.
[495] Or perhaps, "distinction, superiority" (الفضل).
[496] Reading "comet" with 1485 (lit., "a tailed star"), here and below. In later sentences, BL reads "Node," which does not make sense given that the Head and Tail are already accounted for.
[497] وجوه.
[498] The Persian name for Mars.

32 If Mercury looked down upon the Moon, it indicates joy and the doing of admirable things. **33** And if he looked down upon Venus, it indicates ridicule[499] and amusement. **34** And if he looked down upon Jupiter, it increases kings and the nobility in power. **35** And if he looked down upon Mars,[500] it indicates fear and caution in the people. **36** And if he looked down upon Saturn, it indicates malice and deception. **37** And if he looked down upon the Head, it indicates thieves and the appearance of them. **38** And if he looked down upon the Tail, it indicates an abundance of joking. **39** And if he looked down upon a Node, it indicates the killing of the leaders of soldiers and those having social prestige.

40 If the Head of the Dragon looked down upon the Sun, it indicates corruption. **41** And if it looked down upon Venus, it indicates the goodness of the condition of young women, and pleasure. **42** And if it looked down upon Mercury, it indicates the building of cities and palaces. **43** And if it looked down upon the Moon, it indicates the corruption of assets. **44** And if it looked down upon Saturn, it indicates the union of arms and the commotion of war. **45** And if it looked down upon a comet, it indicates the strength of a great coldness.

46 If the Tail looked down upon the Sun, it indicates harms and the expensiveness of food. **47** And if it looked down upon Venus, it indicates the corruption of young women. **48** And if it looked down upon Mercury, it indicates the corruption of knowledgeable people and those endowed with intellects. **49** And if it looked down upon the Moon, it indicates the ruin of wealthy people and it tears apart their assets. **50** And if it looked down upon Saturn, it indicates the disaster of the sheikhs and weak people. **51** And if it looked down upon Jupiter, it indicates survival[501] and joy. **52** And if it looked down upon Mars,[502] it indicates distress. **53** And if it looked down upon a comet, it corrupts the conditions of women.

54 If a comet looked down upon Venus, it indicates the reduction of waters. **55** And if it looked down upon Mercury, it indicates a scarcity of youths, and their ruin. **56** And if it looked down upon the Moon, it indicates the ruin of all of their assets. **57** And if it looked down upon Saturn, it indicates powerful illnesses. **58** And if it looked down upon Jupiter, it indicates the killing

---

[499] Reading as سخر with BL. 1485 and Nur. read سحر, "magic, enchantment."
[500] The Persian name for Mars.
[501] Reading البقاء with Nur. for "building" (البناء).
[502] The Persian name for Mars, here and through the end of the chapter.

of the nobility and those with social prestige. **59** And if it looked down upon Mars, it indicates the union[503] of arms and powerful fighting. **60** And if it looked down upon the Head, it indicates the killing of the nobility and those with social prestige. **61** And if it looked down upon the Tail, it indicates the ruin of the fruits of trees. **62** And if it looked down upon Mercury, it provokes malice and evil.

63 And if Saturn looked down upon the Moon, it indicates a reprehensible death. **64** And if he looked down upon Jupiter, it indicates the killing of the nobility and those having social prestige. **65** And if he looked down upon Mars, it indicates a proper condition. **66** And if he looked down upon the Head, it indicates pleasures and joys for the nobility. **67** And if he looked down upon the Tail, it is commendable for the poor and the destitute. **68** And if he looked down upon a comet, poverty and hunger and powerful tribulation will appear. **69** And if he looked down upon Venus, it indicates the appearances of affectation and embellishment.

70 And this judgment is said about the planets when one of them looks down upon another, and when one of them conjoins with another, and when the lights of one of them fall upon another.

Chapter VIII.24: On the unions of the planets

2 If Venus was conjoined with Mars, there will be powerful misfortune in the Romans. **3** And if Mercury was united with Venus, there is severity. **4** And if Venus was united with Jupiter, she indicates expensiveness and severity in prices.

5 And[504] if Mercury was united with Saturn, it indicates a powerful conquest.

---

[503] "Union" here (الاتحاد) does not seem to mean "clash," but many people joining together to do battle.
[504] From **5** through **11**, the order of sentences and pairing of planets in Nur. is rather different. It reads: "**5** And if Mercury united with Mars, that is *not harmed* by Mars. **6** And if Jupiter united with Saturn it indicates the death of the king and the death of the powerful from an epidemic, and an abundance of locusts. **7** And if Mercury united with Jupiter, epidemic strikes the people, and there are locusts. **8** If the Moon eclipsed Saturn, a powerful king will die [and] the great affair in the west. **9** And if the Moon united with Venus and Jupiter, and Venus and Jupiter *had the rays and was absent in front of the Moon* [?], good and a proper condition will affect the people. **10** And if the Moon *was absent in front of her* [?] and [the Moon] did not have the rays, it indicates the ruin of the king of the east through pain or fighting. **11** And if what we mentioned belonged to Jupiter, the ruin will

6 And if Mars was united with Jupiter, it indicates the death of the king from epidemic, and an abundance of locusts.

7 And if Mercury and Mars were united, that is not harmed by Mars.[505]

8 And if Jupiter was united with Saturn, it indicates the death of a powerful king [and] an important affair in the west.

9 And if the Moon was united with Venus or Jupiter, and Venus had the rays and was absent in front of the Moon,[506] *good or a proper condition will affect the people.*

10 And if the Moon was absent in front of her and she did not have the rays,[507] it indicates the ruin of the king of the east through the pain of fighting. **11** And if what we mentioned was with Jupiter, there is the ruin of the king of the west.

12 And if Mars and Jupiter would be meeting in a sign, [it indicates] the people's fear for their king, until 75 nights are completed.

13 And if Venus united with Saturn, she indicates chaos which is in the region of the east.

14 And if what Mars was transiting was at the beginning of the two horns[508] of the Moon or in her middle, it indicates the fighting of kings in the direction in which Mars is. **15** And if what we mentioned belonged to Saturn, there will be expensiveness and tribulation. **16** And if Mars transited in the middle of *al-Jabha* and *al-Zubanayn*,[509] it indicates expensiveness and tribulation. **17** And if he transited in the middle of *al-Dabarān*, it indicates death.

---

belong to the king of the west." Note that Nur.'s marginalia in **5** would have it read "it indicates *that illness* by Mars." The phrases I have italicized here are either confusing in their meaning or are not properly grammatical.

[505] Meaning unclear, and this is probably in error.

[506] Meaning unclear, and the phrasing is ungrammatical in Arabic.

[507] Meaning unclear, and the phrasing is ungrammatical in Arabic.

[508] القرني. 1485 has a completely different reading (which seems very likely given the mansions listed in the following sentences): "the beginning of the mansion which is called *al-Tarf*, or in its middle." For the lunar mansions, see *AW1*.

[509] These are the 10th and 16th lunar mansions; the next sentence mentions Aldebaran, the 4th mansion. See my introduction to *AW1*.

Chapter VIII.25: On the connection of the planets[510]

[Planets connecting with Saturn]

2 The indication of the connection of Jupiter with Saturn: if Jupiter connected with Saturn from a trine or sextile, it indicates the appearance of guardians,[511] and kings, and the nobility, and revelation. **3** And if that was from a square and it was from the fourth, it indicates the concealment of the guardians and those seeking the rulership, and the modification of many matters among the affairs of the rulership and religion. **4** And if it was from the seventh, it indicates an abundance of disputes among the people and the nations, and an abundance of frights.[512] **5** And if that was from the tenth, it indicates an abundance of disputes and contentions and wars among the kings and authorities and judges.

6 The indication of the connection of Mars with Saturn: as for the indication of their union, [it is] the occurrence of smallpox and measles, and wounds, and surgeries, and deception and swindles and unheard-of things, and especially in the signs of the people,[513] and the king should beware a man from the land of that sign in which they are united. **7** And if the connection of Mars and Saturn is from a trine or sextile, it indicates difficulty in the matters of the people, and corruption for the situations of actions and kings, and confusions will occur among the people because of the affairs of faiths. **8** And if the connection was from a square and it was from the fourth, it indicates an abundance of robbers and theft, and the spreading[514] of the majority of that. **9** And if it was from the seventh, it indicates the contrariety of the people, one to another, and their estrangement and their enmity and their

---

[510] The following delineations are extremely close to (and sometimes verbatim with) *BRD* III.1-5, and are perhaps taken directly from Abū Ma'shar rather than from a source he and al-Rijāl share in common. Note that in each section, the author speaks of the connecting planet being in a certain angle *from* the planet in question. For example, the first section speaks of Jupiter in *Saturn's* fourth, his tenth, and so on—*not* from the fourth house or tenth house of the chart. Normally this would require a number of delineations that follow the rules for overcoming or decimation (i.e., one planet being in the tenth sign from the other), but in this case Abū Ma'shar or his source is only thinking in terms of (a) benefic/malefic aspects, and (b) derived houses from the planet in question.

[511] Or perhaps, "patrons" (الرعاة).

[512] Reading الاهوال with *BRD* for "desires" (الاهواء).

[513] Or rather, especially in the people *attributed to* those signs, as the rest of the sentence makes clear.

[514] *BRD* has "concealment."

conflict. **10** And if it was from the tenth, the people will get severity from the Sultan.

11 The indication of the connection of the Sun with Saturn: if the Sun conjoined with Saturn, it indicates the futility of theft and its departure, and the departure of falsehood and cheating. **12** And if he was connected with him from a trine or sextile, it indicates the kings' need for their citizens and desire for them. **13** And if it was from a square and it was from the fourth, it indicates the publicizing of kings, [namely] of many of their secrets and matters.[515] **14** And if it was from the seventh, it indicates the contention of kings with a group of their citizens, such as the monks, and the poor, and what is like them. **15** And if that was from the tenth, it indicates hardship and fear and alarm [which] kings will get from their own citizens, and the frequency of their use of prisons and their instruments such as handcuffs and shackles, and what is like that.

16 The indication of the connection of Venus with Saturn: if Venus conjoins with Saturn, it indicates the corruption of the conditions of the year, and an abundance of passionate love[516] in men, and an abundance of children, and false rumors among the people, and griefs, and that year will be severe for the people of the coasts and Egypt, and conflict[517] will increase in them, with the cheapness of watery gems (like pearls and what is like them), and poverty coming to the populace, and hardship. **17** And if she was connected to him from a trine or sextile, it indicates corruption occurring from children and pregnancy, and the difficulty of childbearing for women. **18** And if it was from a square and it was from the fourth, it indicates women falling into delirium from their relatives and husbands, and the corruption of their conditions for these reasons. **19** And if it was from the seventh, it indicates an abundance of the disputes of women against their husbands. **20** And if it was from the tenth, it indicates plague[518] befalling women, and disputes,[519]

---

[515] This is an awkward sentence, and I am not sure of whether kings are publicizing their own secrets (which is more accurate but does not make sense), or their secrets become publicized by some other means (which makes more sense).
[516] Reading with BL. *BRD* has "intense lewdness."
[517] Reading خلاف with BL for *BRD*'s "emigration" or "withdrawal" (جلاء).
[518] آفة, but this can also have general meanings of distress, harm, etc.
[519] Following BL and N. *BRD* reads "plague" as the particle أنّ, which does not seem right to me. If *BRD* is right, it means simply that women get involved in disputes or lawsuits.

and they will bring their case to the Sultan[520] for those reasons, and they will become known for that reason, and the weeping of women will increase, and garments will be corrupted, and the matters of Venus will be corrupted, such as perfume and what belongs to the categories of Venus.

21 The indication of the connection of Mercury with Saturn: if they were united, it indicates the people's use of sorcery and magic, and disasters befalling writers, and their being replaced, and distress befalling stewards, and death befalling the people, and starvation, and the occurrence of powerful matters. **22** And if the connection was from a trine or sextile, it indicates an abundance of looking in the books of religions[521] and what is like that. **23** And if it was from a square and it was from the fourth, it indicates the appearance of the secrets of knowledge and magic and sorcery. **24** And if it was from the seventh, it indicates the people's invention of outlandish things, and the forgery of books. **25** And if it was from the tenth, it indicates the announcements of books and the use of magic and sorcery.

26 The indication of the connection of the Moon with Saturn: if they were united, they indicate an abundance of difficulties in matters and their trouble, and harm coming to the people because of prison and bondage and distress and tribulations, and the destruction of villages and cities, and the emptying-out of people from them, and the scarcity of the water in springs and rivers. **27** And if they were connected from a trine or sextile, it indicates an abundance of false oaths, and falsehood, and bondage, and prison, and the striking of whips, and war,[522] and worry because of that, and the stirring up of yellow bile,[523] and an abundance of illnesses from that cause, and the appearance of demolition in most of the cities, and the miscarriage of pregnant women from an abundance of snow, and the disaster of the people because of that, and the use of plantings and building and the digging of wells and structures and tombs. **28** And if it was from the fourth, it indicates an abundance of dreams for the people, and their fear in their dreams, and an abundance of fantastic notions which are depressing to them. **29** And if it was from the seventh, it indicates disputes, and speculation and worry because of them, and some of the people falling into adversities. **30** And if it was from the tenth, it indicates the occurrence of disputes between kings and

---

[520] Following Burnett's translation of *BRD*, although ارتفع does not mean "appeal" or to bring one's case before someone—other Forms of the verb do, however.
[521] Reading with *BRD* for "books of the people/family of the king."
[522] *BRD* has "injustice" (جور).
[523] *BRD* has "black bile."

their citizens, and their oppression[524] towards them, and their confinement, and the abundance of their fear because of them.[525]

[Planets connecting with Jupiter]

31 The indication of the connection of Mars with Jupiter: if Mars conjoined with Jupiter, it indicates an abundance of division and wars and rebels and disputes, and the occurrence of epidemic in the clime of the sign[526] in which they are united, with the selling[527] of riding animals, and colors[528] will occur in the atmosphere, and fertility at the beginning of the time, and drought at the end of it, and [it signifies] the death of the king in that clime, in that revolution. **32** And if he connected with him from the trine or sextile, it multiplies the jihad and invasion because of religion. **33** And if it was from a square, it indicates an abundance of propagandists, and fighting, and overwhelming [the enemy], and robbers, and that is in secret and covertly. **34** And if it was from the seventh, it indicates the occurrence of lawsuits and accusations of robbery between some of the people and others. **35** [And if it was from the tenth],[529] there is tribulation and violence from the Sultan.

36 The indication of the connection of the Sun with Jupiter: if he was conjoined with him, it indicates the ruin of just people and judges, and the corruption of the religion. **37** And if he connected with him from the trine or sextile, it indicates the appearance of religion and knowledge and jurisprudence. **38** And if it was from a square and it was from the fourth, it indicates the strength of the judges and their use of power. **39** And if it was from the seventh, it indicates an abundance of lawsuits and oppression, and the conspicuousness of that. **40** And if it was from the tenth, it indicates the strength of arbitrators and the presentation of justice and impartiality.

41 The indication of the connection of Venus with Jupiter: if they were united, it indicates the modesty of women and the excellence of their condition, and the expensiveness of perfume and pearls, and that countries of the sign in which they are united will receive the good and fertility, and women

---

[524] Reading ظلم with BRD for "seeking" (طلب).
[525] Reading أسبابهم with BRD for "their names" (اسمائهم).
[526] Reading in the singular with Nur.
[527] نفاق, which can also refer to spending money *on* something. Burnett translates BRD's نفوق as "perishing," which seems to be an error.
[528] Reading تلوين for تلون.
[529] Adding with BRD.

will be devoted to their husbands, and modesty will appear in them in that clime belonging to the sign in which they are united, and luxury and fineness of living will be bestowed on them. **42** And if she was connected with him from the trine or sextile, it indicates the excellence of women's religion, and their abstinence in their daughters. **43** And if it was from the seventh, it indicates that women will multiply lawsuits because of faiths, and they will make that conspicuous, and that what is between them and their husbands will be of a proper condition. **44** And if it was from the tenth, it indicates that the king's women will be engaged in matters of charity and offerings.

45 The indication of the connection of Mercury with Jupiter: if they were united, they indicate people's search for knowledge and writing, and wisdom, and jurisprudence in religion, and secrets, and [there will be] plague (and especially if he was separated from Mars) with the intensity of the heat of the atmosphere. **46** And if he connected with him from the sextile or trine, it indicates an abundance of the people's lawsuits in faiths, and an abundance of debate. **47** And if it was from a square, and it was from the fourth, it indicates a quarrel among jurists, and their secrets coming to light. **48** And if it was from the seventh, it indicates an abundance of lawsuits concerning documents and the stipulations of contracts used by the people. **49** And if it was from the tenth, it indicates the abundance of kings' searching for knowledge and books and works and the arts, and the people's search for jurisprudence.[530]

50 The indication of the connection of the Moon and Jupiter: if they were united, it indicates an abundance of the people's employing righteousness and listening to sermons,[531] and the flourishing of the mosques, and the search for faiths and jurisprudence and peace, and the invoking of God.[532] **51** And if she was connecting with him from the trine or sextile, it indicates the conspicuousness of faiths and wisdom. **52** And if it was from a square and it was from the fourth, it indicates the concealment of the secrets of faiths. **53** And if it was from the seventh, it indicates a quarrel about faith and jurisprudence. **54** And if it was from the tenth, it indicates the elevation of judges and worshippers, and the building of mosques and houses of worship.

---

[530] الفقه. *BRD* reads, "advantage" or "profit" (منفعة).

[531] قصص, which normally means "stories" or "narratives," but in this context (and with a citation by Burnett and Yamamoto 2000, p. 171 n. 3), this can also be religious stories and narratives.

[532] الذكر, which more broadly means activities pertaining to recollection and memories: so I could see this indicating commemorative activities.

[Planets connecting with Mars]

55 The indication of Mars and the connections of the Sun with him: if the Sun was conjoined with Mars, it indicates an abundance of killing in the east. **56** And if he was connected to him from a square and that was from the fourth, it indicates a scarcity of lawsuits and debate, and the concealment of what comes to be from it. **57** And if it was [from] a sextile or trine, it indicates the [public] expressing of sacred laws and practices[533] [by] kings. **58** And if it was from the seventh, it indicates an abundance of wars and fighting. **59** And if it was from the tenth, it indicates an abundance of oppression and mistreatment [by] the authorities, and the appearance of fires.

60 The indication of the connection of Venus with Mars: if they were united, they indicate an abundance of fornication and immorality, and evil in women, and the ruin of the king of the Romans, and misfortunes affecting their[534] people, and tribulation. **61** And if she was connected from a sextile or trine, it indicates an abundance of children and the ease of childbirth in women. **62** And if it was from a square and it was from the fourth, it indicates an abundance of fornication and immorality, and friendship [between men and women],[535] and their being secretive [about] that. **63** And if it was from the seventh, it indicates violence coming [to] fornicators. **64** And if it was from the tenth, it indicates an abundance of women's public disgrace, and they will encounter tribulation and violence, and adversities will come to them from the authorities.

65 The indication of the connection of Mercury with Mars: if they were united, they indicate an abundance of [people minting][536] dirhāms and small coins and copper, and alchemy, and the occurrence of fear and alarm among merchants,[537] and an abundance of fugitives[538] and deceivers, and cultured people will find distresses, and their claims to the truth will be debased,[539] and alarm and fear will find them. **66** And if he connected to him from a

---

[533] Or more literally, "Sharias and sunnahs," but I am reading these in their broader senses.
[534] That is, the Romans (the Byzantines).
[535] المصادقات. Really, this word simply refers to sincere and friendly relationships, but it obviously is meant to carry a sense of disapproval here. Burnett and Yamamoto read, "fraternizing."
[536] Adding with BRD.
[537] Presumably because of the abundance of *false* coinage, as 1485 suggests.
[538] Reading somewhat uncertainly for الطرادين; 1485 reads, "false men."
[539] Reading more grammatically with Nur.

trine or sextile, it indicates the people's pursuit of alchemy and every work (among crafts) which is performed by means of fire. **67** And if it was from a square and it was from the fourth, then [it is works] of alchemy and weapons, and the concealment of them. **68** And if it was from the seventh, it indicates an abundance of lawsuits and deception and debate and extraordinary [violations] in medical treatments and works, and horrible things and killing and theft. **69** And if it was from the tenth, it indicates the authorities' use of crafts and jewels and weapons.

70 The indication of the connection of the Moon with Mars: if they were united, that indicates reports of what is untrue, and the shedding of blood, and an abundance of lying, and an abundance of dogs and wolves.[540] **71** And if she connected from a sextile or trine, it indicates a scarcity of faiths and an abundance of ignorance, with an abundance of animals for slaughter in feasts and banquets, and what is like that. **72** And if it was from a square and it was from the fourth, it indicates the injustice of the Sultan, and oppression. **73** And if it was from the seventh, it indicates an abundance of wars and fighting and contentions. **74** And if it was from the tenth, it indicates the oppression of the Sultan, and his injustice.

[Planets connecting with the Sun]

75 The indications of the connection of the Sun with Venus: it indicates harms coming to pregnant women.

76 And if Mercury conjoined with him, it indicates the suppression of matters and the concealment of knowledge and wisdom.

77 And if the Moon united with him, it indicates thefts and the concealment of them, and an abundance of fugitives [among] slaves, and the easiness of the work of alchemy by the people. **78** And if he connected with him from a sextile or trine, it indicates the conspicuousness of the nobility. **79** And if it was from the fourth, it indicates the difficulty of matters and works, and their slowness. **80** And if it was from the opposition, it multiplies contrarieties and lawsuits. **81** And if it was from the tenth, it indicates the appearance of the reports of kings.

---

[540] Reading ذناب with 1485 for ذبيب (Nur.) and ذيب (BL).

[Planets connecting with Venus]

82 And if Mercury conjoined with Venus, it indicates the appearance of secrets and reports, and books, and the people getting involved in ugly, repulsive matters, and the abundance of their delight in women, along with false rumors. **83** And if the connection with her was from a sextile, [it indicates] friendliness and correspondence [with] women, and what is like that.

84 And if the Moon conjoined with Venus, it indicates an abundance of the people's use of songs and sounds, and pleasure, and enjoyment in women, and perfume. **85** And if she connected with her from a sextile or trine, it indicates an abundance of the people's use of places of amusement, and songs, and outings, and gardens. **86** And if it was from a square, and it was from the fourth, it indicates coupling[541] for pleasure, and the concealment of that. **87** And if it was from the seventh, it indicates the lawsuits of women against their husbands. **88** And if it was from the tenth, it indicates immorality and fornication.

ঙ ৪০ ৫৭

89 And all of these unions and connections, if they were at the time of the revolution of the year, it necessitates that these things be present, clear, manifest in indication. **90** [And if they happen at the times of the quarters, they will appear but will not have as great a power as in the revolution.][542] **91** And as for [their taking place] at times other than the revolution of the year and quarter, then it is very weak: understand that and pursue [it] based on the roots, if God (may he be exalted!) wills—and God is more knowledgeable.

---

[541] Lit., "marrying off" (التزويج) for pleasure. This might be a form of temporary marriage for pleasure in Islamic culture, often using a different word (نكاح) but still adding "for pleasure."
[542] Adding with 1485.

Chapter VIII.26: On the consideration of the events of the weather & the variation of the atmosphere, the times, & their behavior with respect to heat & cold

['Umar al-Ṭabarī: Book of Questions Ch. 81]

2 That is known from the meeting and its degree, and the Ascendant of the meeting,[543] at the beginning of the Sun's arrival into Aries and his[544] degree, and the position of the luminaries in the signs of the celestial circle. **3** If you found Saturn in the stakes of the Ascendant or one of the stakes of the lord of the Ascendant, placed in any of his own shares,[545] and especially in the stake of the Midheaven, it indicates the changing of the atmosphere, and its corruption, and its darkness, and a changing of the weather; and [it indicates] the breaking of the heat of that time (if it was a time of heat), and the intensity of the cold and the increase of it (if it was a time of cold). **4** And if he was withdrawing from the stakes, the time will be in a condition of remaining [as it is]. **5** However, if Saturn was in the stake [of the lord of the Ascendant][546] as I mentioned, [his indication] will be diminished[547] or weakened.

6 And if it was Mars instead of Saturn, and it was according to what we described of Saturn, and especially in the Midheaven, his nature increases[548] the heat (if it was a time of heat) and his nature decreases the cold (if it was a time of cold), and the essence of the time is transformed. **7** And if it was a time of moderateness, then it tends towards heat.

8 And if it was Jupiter and Venus, or the Moon, instead of those two, the atmosphere will be balanced and its temperament pleasant, and everything of what was planted or cultivated in that time, will grow.

9 And he looks[549] at Mercury: for if he was in the Midheaven from the Ascendant of the meeting, and it was in one of the airy signs, and he is in a

---

[543] That is, the degree of the lunation (understood here to be a New Moon) and the degree of the Ascendant, prior to the Aries ingress. Reading with 'Umar for BL's Ascendant of the meeting and the portion of the meeting."
[544] The Sun's, though obviously it is the first degree of Aries.
[545] That is, "dignities."
[546] Adding with 1485. Bos and Burnett's edition has only the stake of the Ascendant, but 'Umar has already discussed that.
[547] Reading the root as نقص (with Bos and Burnett), for بعض.
[548] Reading زادت (with Bos and Burnett) for ذات.
[549] That is, 'Umar. The original Arabic (in Bos and Burnett) is in the imperative: "Look at…".

sign of air,[550] or one of the two infortunes was in one of his stakes, it indicates the trouble of the atmosphere and an abundance of destructive winds. **10** And speak thusly if you found the two infortunes in the stake of Mercury, and Mercury is in a stake of a fortune: it plays the role[551] of the two infortunes in the sign of the meeting.

11 So when you found [a planet] in one of the stakes of the Ascendant of the meeting, and in what succeeds the stake of the Ascendant of the meeting, you use it as the indicator.[552] **12** Then, you see Saturn and Mars: for if [the indicator-planet] mixes with Mars from a square or opposition or assembly, and Mars was in the fiery signs (which are Aries and Leo and Sagittarius), it increases in the nature of heat if it was a time of heat, and detracts from the nature of cold if it was a time of cold. **13** And if the aspect was from a trine and sextile, and Mars was in the fiery signs, it indicates what we mentioned but it will be less. **14** And if Saturn sees and mixes with the indicator-planet, and the planet mixes with him and is connected from a square or opposition or assembly, and Saturn was in the cold, dry signs, or the cold, wet ones, it increases in the nature of cold if it was a time of cold, and detracts from the nature of heat if it was a time of heat. **15** And if the indicator mixed with him from a trine or sextile, and it was according to what we mentioned[553] in these signs, it will be less.

16 And if Saturn was in the hot, moist signs (and they are Gemini and its triplicity) and the indicator was mixing with him from [an opposition or square or assembly, it moderates the atmosphere and the temperament is fine. **17** And if it was from][554] a trine or sextile in these signs, then it is better and finer.

18 And[555] likewise Mars, if he mixed with the indicator from [a square or opposition or assembly from the cold and dry or cold and moist signs, it

---

[550] This seems redundant; 'Umar's Arabic does not repeat this condition. But at certain latitudes the degree of the Midheaven might not be in the same quadruplicity as the tenth sign, so perhaps al-Rijāl is picking up on that here.
[551] Or, "has the [same] function" as (Bos and Burnett).
[552] In other words, an angular or succeedent planet. This is undoubtedly by quadrant divisions, to capture the intensity of those positions.
[553] Reading for "you mentioned."
[554] Adding based on Bos and Burnett.
[555] The bracketed material in this paragraph is based on 1485 and Bos and Burnett. It seems that the Arabic scribe got mixed up by the similarity of all of these sentences. The point is that Mars in the cold signs, when mixed with the significator, will temper the atmosphere away from excessive cold.

makes the air temperate and of a good mixture. **19** And if it was from] a trine or sextile, and he was mixing with it and he was in the cold, dry signs or cold, moist ones, and the mixture was from a square or opposition or assembly, it balances the atmosphere and makes its mixture fine, and every thing that is planted will grow and rise.

20 And the Lot of air and winds is consulted, and make it a partner with these indications. **21** For if Saturn or Mars was with the Lot or its lord, then speak just as we spoke before, if it was in a stake.[556] **22** Concerning the Lot, [it is] that you take it from the degree of Mercury (if he is not in his own house) to the degree of the lord of his house, and add on top of that the degree of the Ascendant, and it is projected from the Ascendant: where it terterminates, this Lot is found. **23** And if Mercury was in his own house, then take it from his degree and minute, and add on top of that the degrees of the Ascendant, and project it from the Ascendant: where it terminates, this Lot is found.[557] **24** And do likewise at the Sun's entrance into the quarters (and they are Cancer and Libra and Capricorn), and do thusly at the Sun's entrance into the twelve signs.

[Interpolation: Abū Ma'shar's Lot of days][558]

25 And Abū Ma'shar mentioned another Lot called the Lot of days: it is taken from the degree of the Sun to the degree of Saturn, and is projected from the degree of the Moon, at the rising of the Sun every day. **26** So if Mercury looked at this Lot, or he (he means Mercury)[559] was located with the Lot, then there will be wind on that day; and it is more powerful for that if the Moon was with it, and especially if Venus was participating with them.

27 Also, the days: let the Ascendant be established when the Moon enters the first minute of a sign, and see [it] from the one looking at her: for it is the indicator of what you want, if God (be he exalted!) wishes.

---

[556] I am not sure if 'Umar is simply referring to the interpretations above no matter where the Lot is, or if he is requiring that it be in a stake as well.
[557] Perhaps 'Umar means that we should count from Mercury *to* the Ascendant, and project that same amount *from* the Ascendant. Or, 'Umar could mean to take the degrees Mercury occupies *within* his own sign, and add that to the Ascendant. Either way, he could have been clearer. As I point out in *Judges*, 'Umar's Lots often do not make much sense.
[558] This interpolation is not al-Rijāl's own, but appears in the surviving 'Umar texts as well. 'Umar was long dead by the time Abū Ma'shar entered into astrology.
[559] This seems to be a clarification by al-Rijāl, though it is unnecessary.

Chapter VIII.27: On rains, thunders, lightning bolts, & winds

['Umar al-Tabari: Book of Questions Ch. 82]

2 Look for that from the Sun's entrance into 20° and one minute of Scorpio: establish the Ascendant for that time, and its stakes, and its planets. **3** Then, look at Venus and Jupiter and Mercury: for if the three of them were western or slow or retrograde, they indicate the abundance of the rains and moistures in that year. **4** And if they were eastern or moving direct or fast in course, they indicate a scarcity of the rains and moistures in that year.

5 Then, look at Mars: for if he was in one of the stakes (and especially in the Midheaven), in the airy signs, and Mercury was accompanying him, it indicates an abundance of thunders and lightning bolts, and powerful, damaging rains coming quickly and breaking off; and it indicates an abundance of locusts and the corruption of the atmosphere. **6** And if Mars was in the stake of the earth, in the earthy signs, and the fortunes fell away from him,[560] and Mercury was accompanying him, then it indicates an earthquake and the appearance of lights [from the earth],[561] and an abundance of tremors, and the corruption of minerals[562] and the sulphurs of the earth. **7** And if Mars was just as we described, in the fiery signs in the stake of the earth, it indicates the burning of the earth and the corruption of its gems and minerals, and the burning of the crops and their corruption. **8** And if Mars was according to what we described, in the watery signs in the stake of the earth, it indicates the diminishment of the waters and the corruption of everything of animals and other things dwelling in the water. **9** And if the fortunes were accompanying him and connected with him, it indicates an abundance of harm [which] is not from thunders and lightning in that year. **10** And if the fortunes were not accompanying him, the thunders and lightning bolts will be harmful and corrupting, and lightning bolts will increase.

11 And if it was Saturn instead of Mars, and especially [in] the Midheaven, and he was in the airy signs, and Mercury was accompanying him, and the fortunes were falling away from him, it indicates the damages[563] of the air and the corruption of the atmosphere, and lasting, harmful rain [which] cuts

---

[560] That is, are "in aversion to" him.
[561] Adding with Bos and Burnett.
[562] Or, "mines."
[563] 'Umar reads, "darkness" (Bos and Burnett).

off[564] slowly. **12** And if Saturn was in the earthy signs and he was in the stake of the earth, and Mercury was accompanying him, and the fortunes were falling away from him, an earthquake will take place, and tremors, and the appearance of black water from the earth, and what is like that. **13** And if he was in the watery signs, and he was under the earth in the stake of the earth, and the fortunes fell away from him, and Mercury was accompanying him, the waters from wells and canals will diminish and it corrupts every thing of animals and others dwelling in the water. **14** And if he was in the fiery[565] signs and the fortunes fell away from him, and Mercury was accompanying him, it indicates the corruption of the sulphurs of the earth and its gems and its minerals. **15** And if Mercury was not accompanying him, these will be the indications, but they will be lighter. **16** And if the fortunes were not[566] falling away from him, the matter of the year will be mixed, and they will balance it and decrease it from the indications of evil which we mentioned.

17 And know that for every superior planet is a bond, and its bond is another planet: an inferior one.[567] **18** And the superior one is the rank of the soul, and the inferior one the rank of the body, and in the world there is naught but the connection of the two and their mixture, by the will of God and His decree.

[More on rain, from an unknown source]

19 For rains, rely on looking at the Ascendant of the meeting and the opposition which was before the Sun's alighting in the movable signs, and the lord of the Ascendant, and the lord of the bound of the meeting and opposition. **20** So, the arrival of [either lord] into the moist places and the rainy signs indicates an abundance of rain, and its connecting with the moist and rainy planets indicates that [as well]. **21** And on the other hand, the westernness of the indicator and its retrogradation and its slowness indicates rains; and its burning also indicates that, unless it is Mars (for his burning diminishes it).

---

[564] Reading الانقطاع with Bos and Burnett, for "increasing" (الارتفاع).
[565] Reading with Bos and Burnett, for "earthy."
[566] Adding "not" with Bos and Burnett and the sense of 1485.
[567] Reading with Bos and Burnett for "…is a bond, or another bond for every inferior one."

22 And know that if the indicator was descending[568] or falling down,[569] it indicates an abundance of rain, and contrariwise.

23 And know that if the infortunes were rainy, that would be with corruption: Saturn by demolition and drowning, Mars by lightning bolts and burning.

Chapter VIII.28: On the opening of the door of rains, & other things

['Umar al-Tabarī: Book of Questions Ch. 83]

2 If you wanted the opening of the door for rain and wind and heat and cold based on one of these doors, then look at the Moon. **3** And if she was separating from Venus and connecting with Mars, or separating from Mars and connecting with Venus, then there is an opening of the door of rain. **4** If she was separating from Jupiter and connecting with Mercury, or separating from Mercury and connecting with Jupiter, then there is an opening of the door. **5** And if she is only connecting with Saturn, and she did not have a separation (or she did have a separation), then there is an opening of the door.

6 And look at the Moon: for if she was with what was mentioned [and also] in the place of a foundation,[570] it produced what was indicated of rain or wind or heat or cold.

7 And look at the Moon: if she was in a moist place, connected with a moist planet, and there was not an opening of the door, then have hope of rain.

---

[568] منحدر, meaning unclear.
[569] That is, in its fall or descension.
[570] One of the "centers" of the Moon: see the next chapter and *AW1*.

Chapter VIII.29: On the foundations[571]

['Umar al-Tabarī: Book of Questions Ch. 84]

2 If[572] the Moon was with the Sun in one minute, then it is a foundation; and if there were 12° between them, then it is a foundation. **3** And 45° is a foundation. **4** Then, if she came to 90° in front of [the Sun], that is a half-Moon;[573] then if she came from that to 135°, and if she came from that to 168°, and if she came from that to 180°, and if she passed from that to 192°, then that is a foundation. **5** And there is the loosening of the knot;[574] and if she came upon 225°, that is a foundation, and if she was on 270°, then that is the second half-Moon. **6** And if she was upon 315°, it is a foundation. **7** And if she was upon 348°, it is a basis; then the knot is knotted again.

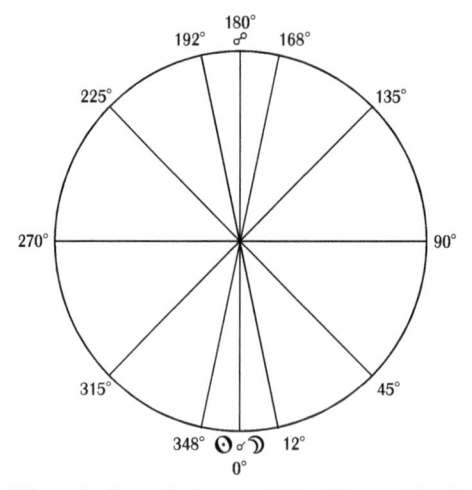

Figure 81: 'Umar's foundations of the Moon (*Skilled* VIII.29)

---

[571] According to Bos and Burnett (2000, p. 447 n. 50), this Arabic word (تأسيس) is a corruption of فاسيس, itself a transliteration of the Greek for "phase." These "foundations" are the so-called "centers" of the Moon, her relationships with the Sun which are used as timing devices for predicting rain. See *AW1*.

[572] From here through the rest of the chapter, reading with Bos and Burnett (2000, p. 440), as certain parts are missing in the MSS for the first paragraph, and their critical edition presents the more accurate 'Umar. I number the sentences with Bos and Burnett.

[573] النيمبرين (with Bos and Burnett's 'Umar), from a Persian phrase meaning "half full." This is also a foundation.

[574] 'Umar seems to mean that when the Moon is opposed to the Sun, she is as it were "tied" to him; thus when she moves 12° away from his opposition, the "knot" is undone. In **7**, she ties the knot again when she approaches him within 12°.

8 Then look at what you have established of the doors of the openings: if you establish the Ascendant of the meeting and the opposition, [then] look also at the lord of the seventh sign from them. **9** For if there was a connection between them (I mean, between the lord of the Ascendant of the meeting or opposition), or an aspect, or there was a reflection of light or a collection of light, or reception, or the Moon was upon what we mentioned of the openings or foundations, then indeed there is rain in that month during the time of rain, and heat in the time of heat, and cold in the time of cold, and wind in the time of wind. **10** And the rain will be good if Venus and Mercury were western or they were both retrograde or slow, or one or two of the superior planets were retrograde or slow. **11** For indeed there will most certainly be rain.

Chapter VIII.30: On the time in which rain is hoped for

['Umar al-Tabarī: Book of Questions Ch. 85]

2 Look at the indicator of rain:[575] if it was coming into one of the stakes of the Ascendant at the time which I prescribed for you for taking it for the knowledge of the matter of rains (and that is the entrance of the Sun into 20° of Scorpio and the first minute of it), **3** and it is looking at the planets[576] which indicate an abundance of rain in the year, and they were received by it, and especially if the Moon was joining with it or squaring it or receiving it, then rain will take place on that day. **4** And if it was not received, rain will arrive [but] it will not be strong. **5** And at the times which we mentioned that it was in a stake, [if there was] an assembly of the Moon with it, then there will be an earthquake and thunders and lightnings and other things besides that.

---

[575] 'Umar points out that this is the lord of the Ascendant of the year (Bos and Burnett p. 441).
[576] Adding "the planets" with 'Umar.

[Miscellaneous sources on rain][577]

6 And[578] you will know the situation of rain in the year: you look at the Moon and Venus and Mercury.

7 If[579] they would meet in Pisces, in a stake of the revolution of the year, then that indicates an abundance of rains and moisture and fog and humidity.

8 And if they were in Aries and Taurus, then that year will have a scarcity of rains, dry, barren.

9 And if the Moon was connected to Venus from a house of Mercury, it indicates an abundance of rain, and its persistence and reliability.

10 And[580] if the Moon was opposed to the Sun or Venus or Saturn, it indicates rain and fog and darkness.

11 If she met with Mercury and Venus in one bound, there is good rain (by the permission of God).

12 And if it was suitable that she would be [in] one of the signs of rain, and the Moon would look at those two from a trine, then that is what is stronger, and it would continue until one of the planets would shift from that bound.

13 And[581] what is greater for rain, and more intense and lasting in the winter of the year of the revolution, is when Mercury would connect with Jupiter, and the Moon with Saturn, and Venus with Mars:[582] because every planet of these emanates what enters into it from that planet opposing its house.

14 And if Venus was in front of the Sun, then that year is a year of fog and moisture and humidity, and there is a scarcity of rains.[583]

15 But[584] if she would be retrograde, and the Sun in Aries and Taurus, then the rains during that time will increase, and the spring of the year are fertile, and what is in it of rain will be intense [and] good.

---

[577] The rest of this chapter seems to be from a combination of sources, including three from *AW1*: Hermann of Carinthia's *Book of Heavy Rains*, Māshā'allāh's *Letter on Rains & Winds*, and Māshā'allāh's *Chapter on the Rains in the Year*.
[578] See Māshā'allāh's *Chapter*, **28**.
[579] Cf. Māshā'allāh's *Letter*, **56** and **58**.
[580] See Māshā'allāh's *Letter*, **59**.
[581] See Hermann Ch. 5, **7** and **9**.
[582] The Persian name for Mars.
[583] Stopping the sentence here with 1485; BL continues with "its coldness." But Nur. has simply "an abundance of rains."
[584] See Hermann Ch. 5, **10**.

16 And[585] if her retrogradation was in Capricorn and Aquarius and Pisces, it decreases the rain of the spring, and the middle of the winter[586] is moist, damp, rainy.

17 And when Mercury was stationary or direct (wherever he was, in the signs), then there occurs (by the permission of God, be he exalted!) humidity in the atmosphere, and in that time there are rains and clouds and dew.

18 And the more harmful thing there is of rains, and more intense, is when the planets of rains would meet in the signs of rains, and especially that Venus would be stationary: because Venus overcomes these planets [in this] and is more indicative of rains and humidity.

19 And if Mercury was in one of the dry signs, and the Moon and Venus were in the signs of rain, the rain is moderate [and] in the middle.

20 And if Saturn looked at those two from a cold sign, it mixes the rain with intense cold and darkness and ice and coldness.

Chapter VIII.31: On epidemics, health, drought, & fertility

[Chapter VIII.31.1: al-Kindī's Forty Chapters, Ch. 39][587]

2 Establish the Ascendant for the year, and the Ascendant of the meeting or fullness which was before the Sun's entrance into Aries. **3** And if the two Ascendants and the Moon were cleansed of the infortunes, and [so was] the lord of the portion[588] of the meeting, and its[589] connection was with a fortune, and the luminaries looked at it (or that one of the two which had the shift),[590] [the year] is safe from disease.

4 And if the lords of the Ascendants, and the Moon, and the lord of the portion of the meeting or fullness were made unfortunate (or the majority of them), it indicates disease in proportion to the misfortune and their difficulty, and the nature of the infortune, and the place in which the misfortune was.

5 And if you saw the lords of the Ascendants (or one of them) and the Moon (with [such] misfortune) connecting with the lord of their own eighth,

---

[585] See Hermann Ch. 5, **13-14**.
[586] Reading with 1485 and BL, for Nur.'s "year."
[587] This should also be compared with VIII.1, **18-26** above, and *BRD* VIII.1, **11-12**.
[588] This means at least its degree, but probably refers to the bound.
[589] I take this to be the lord of the "portion."
[590] That is, the "sect": the sect light.

that disease indicates an abundance of death. **6** And if it was contrary to that,[591] there is disease without excessive death; but if there was an abundance [of disease], death by this illness will be little. **7** And if these indications were by means of a planet among them connecting with the lord of its own eighth, there is great, sudden death by something other than illnesses.

8 And if the lord of the sixth of every one of them was connecting to them, [it is] with a disease, and [if it was] slow, the illnesses multiply [and last long; but if it was quick, the diseases multiply][592] and they do not last long.

9 And if the one making [them] unfortunate was Mars, the illnesses will be hot, and especially when Mars was fast [and] strong, in the hot, dry signs. **10** And if the one making [them] unfortunate was Saturn, the illnesses will be Saturnian, chronic, and especially if Saturn was slow [and] strong in the cold, dry signs.

[Chapter VIII.31.2: On drought & fertility][593]

11 And look, for drought and fertility, at the portion[594] of the meeting or fullness which was before the revolution of the year of the world: to whom of the fortunes or infortunes is [its lord] connecting? **12** For if the one to which it was connecting was Jupiter, and especially if he had a claim in the portion of the meeting or fullness, or he was the lord of the Ascendant, or he made the lord of the Ascendant fortunate, along with the safety of the lord of the fourth[595] from the two infortunes, and the year from the direction[596] of the religion or the turn of the middle[597] had reached the place of Jupiter or Venus, by aspect or rays, fertility will take place in that year—and especially if the lord of the second in the revolution of the year made the lord of the Ascendant fortunate or was connecting with it from friendship (whichever planet it was), and especially [if] it was making the lord of the Lot of Fortune fortunate, or making the lord of the Ascendant fortunate. **13** For that [indi-

---

[591] This seems to mean, "if the lords of their eights were applying to *them*."
[592] Adding based on Abū Ma'shar's version as well as the Latin *Forty Chapters*.
[593] Compare with VIII.2, **2-10**.
[594] Again, the degree (but probably especially the bound).
[595] Reading with 1485 and Abū Ma'shar for "Ascendant."
[596] Abū Ma'shar's version has "Ascendant," implying a mundane profection. The phrasing here implies some kind of primary direction.
[597] دور الاوسط. But BRD and VIII.2 have "shift of the triplicity." But the text above may be right, if we take the Saturn-Jupiter conjunction as the "greatest" conjunction, the triplicity shifts as the "middle" conjunction, and the conjunction every 19.8 years as the "smallest" conjunction.

cates] fertility [and] increases the assets of the general populace and even in commercial activities. **14** With the contrary[598] of that [situation], it decreases.

15 And as for the years of barrenness, that is with the contrary of these things, [and] equally with the governorship of Saturn over the meeting or fullness by connection, or by rulership[599] of the Ascendant, or the misfortune and corruption of the lord of the fourth by the infortunes (and especially Saturn). **16** And more intense than that is when he was mixed together with Mercury. **17** And whichever of the infortunes made the year unfortunate, the bad luck is more difficult if it mixed with Mercury. **18** And [it is also] if the second and the Lot of Fortune and the Ascendant, and the lord of the Lot of Fortune, exhibited the opposite of what I described as to their good fortune: that is an increase in drought.

19 And for the example which I described for Jupiter: if it was by means of Venus, the condition will be weaker than what Jupiter indicates for it. **20** And likewise for the unfortunate events I described for Saturn: if they were by means of Mars, the evil in them will be lower than what I described with Saturn—except that the distresses by means of Martial things are like dryness and burning and the severity of the lightning and hail. **21** And as for Saturn, his distresses are greater by means of thirst and submersion: and the indicator over which one of the situations it is, is: if he was in the increasing signs, it is by drowning; and if he was in the decreasing signs, it is by thirst.[600]

Chapter VIII.32: On the times of the occurrence of evil, civil unrest, fire, & submersion

['Umar al-Tabarī: Book of Questions Ch. 138][601]

2 Know that if the Moon was at the invisibility,[602] and was in the twelfth, in a hot sign, and they[603] were connecting with a planetary infortune under the earth, then it is most conclusive that tribulation will take place on that

---

[598] Reading بخلافها (with the sense of 1485) for BL's بالعهاء, and Nur.'s تلافها.
[599] Omitting a redundant "rulership."
[600] This suggests the signs of long ascension and short ascension (or straight and crooked signs), respectively. But 1485 has it that Saturn in dry signs indicates thirst, but in moist signs indicates drowning or submersion.
[601] For Hugo's Latin version, see *Judges* §Z.7.
[602] المحاق. That is, what we would call the New Moon, when she is still under the rays.
[603] That is, the Sun and the Moon.

day, in that country.⁶⁰⁴ **3** And likewise, if they were declining from⁶⁰⁵ the middle of the day, connecting with a declining infortune under the earth, then it is conclusive, and decree a submersion in that same time. **4** And likewise, if the Moon was at the invisibility and they were connected with a planetary infortune under the earth in a fiery sign,⁶⁰⁶ then decree that it will burn two places of the country and two persons in that time, when the luminaries are in the twelfth and the ninth—except that if it took place in the twelfth, then the misfortune will be at the beginning of the day, and if it took place in the ninth, then the misfortune will be at the end of the day. **5** And if she was at the invisibility in the evening, then judge that the affliction will take place after the evening.

6 If the Moon was with the invisibility, falling down in the south, falling down in the circle (I mean, that she is in Libra and Scorpio), and she is diminished in light and calculation, and especially if there were these misfortunes and the fortunes did not look at her, then judge that either fire or civil unrest or earthquake will take place at that time in that city (and it is not known whether it is in more cities).

7 And know that if the two infortunes met with the Tail in Aries, distress will take place in sheep and the nobility (and speak likewise according to the succession of the signs).⁶⁰⁷ **8** And in Virgo the misfortune takes place in food⁶⁰⁸ [and what is] of the image of men.

9 And be acquainted with the signs: for Aries is the beginning of the east, and Leo the middle, and Sagittarius belongs to its end: it causes what is of it.⁶⁰⁹ **10** Taurus is after the east, and its triplicity is like it.⁶¹⁰ **11** And⁶¹¹ Gemini is likewise the beginning of the west with its triplicity, in this manner. [**12** And Cancer and its triplicity indicate the north].⁶¹²

---

⁶⁰⁴ Omitting ليس له مثل ("he does not have an example") with 1485 and Hugo's 'Umar.
⁶⁰⁵ Reading عن for فعند.
⁶⁰⁶ This should probably read that the *lights* are in a fiery sign (as in **2**), but the infortune is in a *double-bodied* sign (for example, the luminaries in Leo in the twelfth, and the infortune in Sagittarius in the fourth.
⁶⁰⁷ That is, Aries signifies both small flock-animals like sheep, as well as nobility (since it is a fiery sign). In the same way, Taurus indicates cows, airy signs indicate humans, etc.
⁶⁰⁸ 1485 reads "bread-grains," which is appropriate for Virgo.
⁶⁰⁹ This last phrase is not in 1485 or Hugo's 'Umar.
⁶¹⁰ The earthy signs also indicate the south.
⁶¹¹ Adding this sentence with 1485.
⁶¹² Adding based on Hugo's 'Umar.

13 And know, at the Sun's entrance into Aries, which planet is eastern:[613] for that is the indicator of the year. **14** If Jupiter was arising, it is a proper condition and good; and Venus [indicates] fertility and good and cheapness [in price]; and Mercury is average. **15** If Saturn was eastern, [it indicates] the expensiveness of prices and intense cold. **16** And if Mars was eastern, [it indicates] disgrace, and destruction, and disturbance, and burning.

17 And see whenever the Sun enters one of the quarters: whichever planet was eastern is the indicator of the quarter. **18** And also look at the connection of the Moon with the Sun and the first one of them,[614] and decree it based on that.

[Teachings on comets][615]

19 And know that when a comet was arising at the time of the revolution of the year or quarter, in one of the signs, then indeed it[616] appears in the place of Mercury in the year: if he was eastern, it is seen in the east; and if he was western, in the west. **20** And it disappears when Mercury is burned.

21 And if it was in the belt of the sign,[617] the evil will be in the share of Jupiter and Mercury (in terms of countries and creatures). **22** And if it was in the upper belt (and that is what borders the north), it is in the share of Saturn and the Moon. **23** And if it was in the lower area (and that is what borders the south), it is in the share of [Mars and][618] Venus.

24 And see which one of the planets [the sign of the comet] belongs to, and is it a fortune or infortune, and how the infortunes are looking at it or are assembled with it, and judge evil for the people of the country which that sign is in charge of. **25** And if it was one of the signs of kings, a king will appear from the area in which the planet is, fighting and capturing and burning and destroying. **26** And if it was of the signs of the powerful, the fighting is between those who are below kings. **27** And based on the strength of the

---

[613] Or, "arising," suggesting that it is coming out of the rays.
[614] This seems to mean, "the first planet with which the Moon connects, after the New Moon."
[615] See *Scito* Ch. 77, **9-21.**
[616] 1485 takes this to mean "the disaster."
[617] That is, the middle (0° zodiacal latitude).
[618] Adding with 1485.

comet or the luminaries in their places, and the strength of the aspect of the infortunes to it, there will be an abundance of evil or[619] a diminution of it.

Chapter VIII.33: On prices

[Chapter VIII.33.1: Various views]

2 If the lord of the year was at the end of its direct motion,[620] wanting retrogradation, or it was descending (in its domination)[621] from the top of its apogee, or it was in the lowest [point] of the circle of its turning, then that indicates cheapness in the essence of the sign in which it is (so that it was of jewels, or fiery, or animal,[622] or vegetable).

3 And also the Moon, if she was diminished in light and calculation at the birth of the year or month, or she was connecting with a decreasing[623] or retrograde planet,[624] then that indicates the cheapness of the price and the loss of provisions.

4 Know the increase of the price from the variation of the condition of the significator at the beginning of the year and from the four Ascendants of the quarters (which are the movable signs), and from the meeting of the Sun and Moon in one degree every month, and from the entrance of Saturn or Jupiter into the signs of the climes of eastern and western countries. **5** And the misfortune of the planets in these places indicates decrease and cheapness and humbleness. **6** And their good fortune indicates an increase.

7 Every planet, through elevation or increase at the birth of the year, or exaltation, [whether] it had testimony in the Ascendant or not, indicates expensiveness of price and its increase in what belongs to that planet, from kinship[625] in the essence of the sign in which it is. **8** For example, if the Sun is in Aries, there belong to him red precious stones, and gold, and precious

---

[619] Reading "or" for "and."
[620] Reading with 1485 for "stake." But the Ar. might be correct in the sense that astrologers and astronomers often applied notions of houses to regions of the celestial circles. So "stake" might mean "the angular point in the epicycle at which a planet turns retrograde."
[621] في تملكه. This seems like an unnecessary addition, and should probably be omitted.
[622] Reading الحيوانية for الجنوبية ("southern").
[623] This probably means that its daily motion is slowing down and less than average.
[624] Reading with 1485 for مدبّر ("manager").
[625] Reading النسب for النصب ("the appointing, establishing").

gems. **9** Or [if] it is Venus, then there belong to her pearly stones,[626] pearls, and sea shells, and what is like that. **10** And every planet falling down[627] and descending indicates modesty and lowness for what belongs to that planet, of what is watery, and earthy, and airy, and fiery.

11 And for Abraham the Jew,[628] when Saturn is not in one of the stakes,[629] it indicates cheapness; and when he arrives [in] the stakes, it indicates expensiveness. **12** And if he was in one of the stakes and he was in one of his own shares, it indicates excessiveness in that.

[Chapter VIII.33.2: 'Umar al-Tabarī's Book of Questions Ch. 86]

2 On prices, according to al-Tabarī. **3** He said, in the knowledge of the expensiveness of prices and their cheapness, and the conditions of the people in their livelihoods, indeed it is shown from the course of the luminaries: so look in every month at the meeting[630] of the luminaries and establish the Ascendant for that hour. **3** And know that the Ascendant and what is in it are two indicators for what there is of the conditions of the people and the conditions of the atmosphere; and the lord of the house of the lord of the Ascendant assists those two. **4** And[631] an alien planet which was in the Ascendant, if it did not correspond to [the Ascendant], it indicates corruption in that month if it was an infortune, or corruption in proportion to its essence and its testimony. **5** And if you found a planet in a stake, and it was the lord of the exaltation of the Ascendant, then proceed with that one if you found the lord of the Ascendant withdrawing. **6** And every planet in a stake, having strength in it, also indicates what you want while the lord of the Ascendant is

---

[626] دُر. This sentence presents a problem because this word and the next can each mean "pearls." But the next word (لُؤْلُو) specifically refers to pearly and shiny colored objects, whereas this one comes from a verb meaning "to flow, be lavish," and so on—which to me suggests *strung* pearls or other sparkly, lavish gems or stones.

[627] This word normally refers to being in fall or descension, as a contrast to being exalted in **7**.

[628] I cannot find a reference to this paragraph in Sela's edition of ibn Ezra.

[629] 1485 adds, "at the revolution of the year or the quarter."

[630] Note that 'Umar only uses the New Moons (or, he takes them to be archetypal and so only mentions them). In Ptolemy's astrology (as I described in *AW1*), one takes whatever the lunation was (New or Full Moon) just before the seasonal ingresses, and *for that season* continue to use only that type of lunation.

[631] Reading "and" for "or."

absent from the stakes.⁶³² **7** And the alien planet [in a stake] provides the conclusions until it goes out from the stakes.

8 And if the lord of the Ascendant was in the Ascendant or in the remaining stakes, or in the eleventh, or in a good place, looking at the Ascendant, then it is foremost in the indication, and especially if it was eastern until it goes from the rays in its own light, quick in course: for then in addition to that it indicates the people seeking their livelihoods, and it increases in every respect in proportion to the increase of the planet, be it small or large, or especially on the day in which the Moon squares the Ascendant or is in the Ascendant, or looking at the lord of the Ascendant. **9** And as for when she was in the opposite,⁶³³ then [it is contrary to that].⁶³⁴

10 If [the indicator]⁶³⁵ was advancing,⁶³⁶ and⁶³⁷ it was a month in which food was wanted, and it reached the opposite of the Ascendant and is looking at the lord of the Ascendant, that is with an indication of a decrease [in prices]; and if it was decreasing,⁶³⁸ it indicates an increase: and that is the hostility of the opposite of the Ascendant.⁶³⁹

11 And look at the lord of the Ascendant: for if it was received and the one receiving it was advancing in a stake, then for all of that month the prices in it will be increasing. **12** And the lord of the house of the lord of the Ascendant is stronger after the fullness [of the Moon]. **13** And if you saw the lord of the Ascendant received, and it [and] the lord of the house of the lord of the Ascendant were all advancing, [the expensiveness will be more firm];⁶⁴⁰ and that is in proportion to their advancement. **14** And if the lord of the Ascendant or the planet which is found in the stake was connecting with

---

⁶³² That is, "not in." Normally this phrase is equivalent to "in aversion to," but no planet is in aversion from all the stakes.

⁶³³ Hugo adds, "that is, in the seventh," i.e., in the opposite of the Ascendant.

⁶³⁴ Adding based on 1485 and Hugo.

⁶³⁵ This might actually refer to the Moon: the Arabic does not specify.

⁶³⁶ زائد. Normally this word is used to mean "dynamically angular" or moving by primary motion towards the axes (as opposed to "withdrawing" or being dynamically cadent. But here it is opposed to نقصان, which is normally used for various kinds of decrease. My sense throughout the following sentences is that we should continue to understand this as "advancing," and so I will translate it that way.

⁶³⁷ Reading "and" for "or."

⁶³⁸ Again, I take this to be equivalent to "withdrawing," or being dynamically cadent, through **26**.

⁶³⁹ In other words, it indicates the opposite of what we would expect.

⁶⁴⁰ Adding with 1485, as BL has an unusual and (to me illegible) string of particles and probably undotted letters.

a falling[641] and decreasing planet, it brings down the price: and that is in proportion to its decrease. **15** And what is more intense for the abasement of it is if both were withdrawing,[642] for then it indicates the quickness of that [lowering of prices]. **16** And if they were all connecting with a withdrawing or decreasing planet, it is more intense for the lowness. **17** And if there were a planet in the Ascendant having testimony, then the increase and decrease is in proportion to the condition of that planet in its proper state and its corruption; [and in addition the lord of the Ascendant will be a partner with it. **18** And if the lord of the Ascendant was not received, you will not make it a partner with it, because it alone will be the indicator].[643]

19 And if the lord of the Ascendant and the luminaries were in that place from the Ascendant of the meeting, or in a stake from the place [of the conjunction itself], it indicates the fixity of the price. **20** And if the lord of the Ascendant was received, and those two were advancing in the eleventh or fifth, it is more intense for the increase. **21** And if the lord of the Ascendant was connecting with an advancing planet,[644] it indicates an increase on the day of connecting with it. **22** And it is more intense for the decrease if the luminaries were decreasing, and the lord of the Ascendant decreasing in the third or ninth or twelfth. **23** And as for the stakes, they indicate fixity. **24** And it indicates decrease if a decreasing planet connected with the lord of the Ascendant, or[645] [the lord of the Ascendant] connected with it. **25** And if the lord of the Ascendant was decreasing, [but the lord its house][646] increasing in calculation, there does not take place an increase [caused by] the lord of its house: because the root of the [whole] edifice is based on [the lord of the Ascendant], and it is the one which has the rulership and power—unless it is declining [and the other] planet is in a stake.[647]

26 And as for the Ascendant being one of the houses of the luminaries, look at their increase in calculation and their decreases, and [their place] from the Ascendant.

---

[641] Or perhaps, "declining" (ساقط).
[642] Now 'Umar uses the normal word for "withdrawing" or being dynamically cadent.
[643] Adding with 1485 for the partial sentence, "and it is the place [sc. partner?] of the lord of the Ascendant."
[644] Hugo and 1485 each have it the other way around: that if a planet "of the Ascendant" ("'in" the Ascendant") was connecting with the lord of the Ascendant.
[645] Omitting لم ("not"), with 1485 and Hugo.
[646] Adding a missing phrase with 1485.
[647] Reading with 1485 for "unless it is declining in an angle of a planet."

[Chapter VIII.33.3: Fīlīūs the Roman and "Dorotheus"][648]

27 And Fīlīūs the Roman said, when the Sun enters Aries, then look at the planet which was in the Midheaven or the planet to which the lord of the Midheaven is connecting: for that one indicates the price, by the permission of God. **28** And if that planet in the Midheaven was direct in course, then what is ascribed to that sign goes up and increases; and it is more than this and perseveres if that sign is fixed. **29** And if it was retrograde, or descending, or decreasing in light and calculation, it indicates the abasement of what belongs to that sign in which that planet is.

30 And Dorotheus said: look, in the expensiveness of prices and their cheapness, at the planet which is eastern in that year, for to that is ascribed what belongs to the planet in terms of things, and they are expensive. **31** And what belongs to the planet which is falling down[649] and corrupt is what becomes cheap and decreases. **32** And the corruptions are in its downfall, or burning, or being made unfortunate [by the infortunes], and retrograde, or withdrawing, or in one of the reprehensible places, and the fortunes are falling [away from it].[650] **33** And if it was good [and] bad, for example that it is in its own house [but] retrograde, or in its own exaltation [but] burned up, it is a little expensive and brought down,[651] and sells poorly, [but] afterwards it rises (God willing).

[Chapter VIII.33.4: 'Umar al-Tabarī's Book of Questions Ch. 89]

34 On the knowledge of increase and decrease: he reported what there is of increase and decrease according to what Māshā'allāh said.[652] **35** Look in this at the lord of the Ascendant and the Moon: for if the stronger of them was connecting with a planet in the stake of the Ascendant or Midheaven, then say that the value of its price increases and becomes expensive. **36** And if it was in the opposite [of the Ascendant] or the stake of the earth, it is suitable [in price] and sought.

---

[648] Fīlīūs is clearly a transliteration of the Lat. *filius*, which simply means "son," just as *ibn* or *bin* means "son" in Arabic. This author must be someone with Byzantine connections, perhaps a Greek writer such as Theophilus.
[649] I.e., in its fall.
[650] That is, they are in aversion to it.
[651] This seems to mean that it fluctuates.
[652] Cf. Māshā'allāh's *Book of Prices* **A53-54** (in *AW1*), where this material is attributed to an Abū Hawl.

37 And[653] look in addition at the planet which is in the square of those two unfortunate [places]:[654] for if it was received, or it received the lord of the Ascendant and the lord of its house and its bound,[655] [it signifies expensiveness].[656] **38** And if it was connecting with a falling planet and it did not receive it, then the commodities the commodities become cheap and demand for them decreases. **39** And what is a worse condition for sales is if the Moon and the lord of the Ascendant were connecting to a planet which was declining from the stakes[657] and one not received. **40** And if they would be connecting with a [declining][658] planet and it is received, and it is receiving the Moon or the lord of the Ascendant, then it guarantees demand for it; however, it will [not] be expensive.[659]

41 And he[660] said: in his book to his student, he reported that Ptolemy and a party of scientists in Egypt whom he came upon in his time, agreed that the work in that is from the luminaries. **42** And they used to begin in the knowledge of that from the Sun's entrance into Aries, and from the meeting which was in[661] every quarter, and from the meeting which was in every month—and from the opposition.[662] **43** Because Ptolemy used to sum it up that the primary revolution of the year of the world was the meeting or opposition which was before the Sun's entrance into Aries, because the matters of the world do indeed arise out of the meeting or opposition: the occurring of things is from the meeting, and their abatement is from the opposition. **44** Because the Moon is the smaller world, and she administers[663] the seven

---

[653] For this paragraph, see Māshā'allāh's **A55-57** (*ibid.*).
[654] Hugo's 'Umar has instead the planet which is *in* those two places (viz., the seventh and fourth).
[655] Probably not *all* of them: 'Umar must mean "any" of them.
[656] Adding with 1485.
[657] In Māshā'allāh, it is in aversion to ("falling away from") the Ascendant, not just declining from the angles.
[658] Adding with Māshā'allāh's **A57** (*ibid.*). Again, in Māshā'allāh it is in aversion to the Ascendant.
[659] Adding "not" with Māshā'allāh's **A57**.
[660] تادر (*Tādar*, unknown). 1485 reads simply "he," while Hugo has "Thābit" (probably Thābit ibn Qurra, the 9th Century astronomer).
[661] Or rather, which immediately preceded it.
[662] As I explained in *AW1*, Ptolemy's procedure was to take the New or Full Moon which immediately preceded the quarterly ingress, and to use only that *type* of lunation throughout the season. Then he would identify the type of lunation which immediately preceded the next season, and so on.
[663] اولي. Hugo may have read اعلى, which he understood to be "beyond." 1485 reads that our world is "closer" to the Moon. At any rate, my translation of the verb is a little awk-

through the lower world (and that is the world of generation and corruption): new occurrences and [their] extinction are from the current month, from her increase.

45 And so it is established among them that she is the foremost of the seven: in every completing or diminishing (I mean of trees and animals) and termination, it belongs to the Moon. **46** And the Sun partners with her, based on her conjunction[664] and opposition. **47** Then, Venus and Mercury partner with her because of their proximity to her circle and the abundance of their easternness and westernness, and the quickness of their movement.

48 And he puts the Moon and the Ascendant as being contraries.[665] [**49** And likewise, they made the property of coins and other things which are likewise sold, to be contraries (namely, one to the other), and when one is increased, the other is pressed down]:[666] like gold and silver, and food and clothing. **50** And[667] with a small amount of coin, there is a great amount of merchandise; and with a small amount of merchandise, there is a great amount of coin.

51 And he says that the more raised-up places in the circle are the stakes: and if the fortunes were in the stakes, it honors coin and merchandise is brought down; and if the infortunes in the stakes, coin is brought down and merchandise is honored. **52** And in the houses which are not in the stakes, if the fortunes were in them merchandise is honored and the prices are brought down; and when the infortunes were in them, it is the opposite of that. **53** And if [some of] the fortunes were in the stakes and [others in] the others than the stakes, the stronger of them is operative, except that the lowness of it through a planetary fortune[668] in exaltation, is in proportion to its allotment from the Moon.[669] **54** And each planetary fortune, [if] it was retrograde

---

ward, because while the basic verb ولي does mean to administer or govern, اولي means to have something committed to one as a responsibility, or to bring something closer or make it evident. So the text is saying she has been committed the responsibility of bringing forth the indications of all seven planets.

[664] Reading with 1485 for "her slowness" (مهله).
[665] I discuss this view in my Introduction to *Choices & Inceptions*.
[666] Adding with 1485, as much of this is missing in BL.
[667] This is a difficult sentence. 'Umar may be speaking of supply and demand: that when goods are scarce, prices (i.e., the amount of coin needed to buy them) go up, and vice versa. Neither 1485 nor Hugo are much clearer.
[668] For the rest of this sentence, 1485 and Hugo each say that the decrease through a fortune is "not large" or "not great."
[669] I am not sure what this means (حصّته من القمر).

and in a weak house, its strength is weaker. **55** And likewise for the infortunes, if one was in its exaltation.[670]

56 And if you considered the birth of the quarter or the birth of the half-year,[671] then look at the Moon. **57** If the first one of the planets which she encountered was a fortune, then merchandise becomes expensive; and if she encountered an infortune, merchandise becomes cheap (and an aspect is like an encounter [by body]). **58** And if the Moon was in a stake, the expensiveness of merchandise increases, and it is likewise if she were in her own exaltation, free of the infortunes.

59 And if the Sun was attached to a fortune or one is attached to him (such as Venus attaching to the Sun, or the Sun attaching to Jupiter), it honors coin, and especially if it was in a stake or he was in his exaltation. **60** And if he would attach to an infortune, it brings coin down low, and especially if [the Sun] was in his own weakness, withdrawing from the stakes.

61 And Mercury has a share in the two coins, which are gold and silver, and [so does Venus]. **62** As for the share of Venus, it is the beauty of their look and the lustre of their color; and as for the share of Mercury, it is what is in them of their images and inscription—except that Mercury is primary in gold because he experiences the Sun [more]. **63** So if he[672] was arising, coin is honored, and if he was brought low,[673] coin goes down—and especially if they were in their exaltation or weakness.[674] **64** If Mercury was with the Sun, [gold is venerated and other things go down; if Venus was with the Sun],[675] silver is venerated and kings love it. **65** And if they were not with the Sun, and they were turning [high][676] in their circles, it indicates the honoring of coin, and especially if they were wanting to go eastern and they were in their own exaltations or houses or shares. **66** And if [they were] being brought down in their circles and they wanted westernness,[677] or in the place of their

---

[670] What Māshā'allāh means is that its power to be a *malefic* is weakened, or rather that it is better than a problematic benefic: see Judgment 18 in his *Fifty Judgments* (in my *Works of Sahl & Māshā'allāh*, or the Appendix to *Nine Judges*).
[671] That is, the quarterly ingresses or the Libra ingress.
[672] This probably applies to Venus as well.
[673] This pairing of rising and being abased possibly refers to being high or low in his epicycle. See the following sentences.
[674] This must be a synonym for fall or descension.
[675] Adding with 1485.
[676] Adding based on 1485 and Hugo.
[677] التغريب. But this might refer to disappearing or sinking under the rays.

weakness or a place in which they do not have shares, coin is brought down and merchandise becomes expensive.[678]

67 And if the Ascendant of the year or quarter or month or half-month was established, and the stakes were proper,[679] and you came to know the degree of the house of assets,[680] then if the lord of the house of assets was in any of the stakes, and especially in a place in which it had a share, and especially if it was a fortune, there is an honoring of coin; and if it was an infortune in a stake,[681] strong in testimony, it indicates that honoring of coin, except that [it is not honored because][682] it passes into the hands of the lower class. **68** And as for the honoring of merchandise and its abasement, [that is] when there is a fortune and infortune [in the signs]: for if the fortune was in it, the merchandise in it is honored, [and if the infortune was in it, it is abased].[683] **69** For every sign has something of merchandise, just as to Aries belong sheep, and the rest of the signs what is appointed to them as well: so, get to know that.

70 And know that the Ascendant in animals is always attributed to the head, and the fourth the belly, and the seventh the body and tail and the rear, and the tenth the spine: so whichever one of them an infortune was in, or it was made unfortunate, sickness takes place [there]. **71** And for a human, the Ascendant [is attributed to] the head, and the second the neck, and the third the hands and shoulders, and then it follows the signs up to the twelfth according to this meaning, just as we have already indicated it at the beginning of this anthology.[684] **72** And as for vegetation, there is nothing but the front or back: so the Ascendant is for the front, and the seventh for the back.[685]

---

[678] Reading with 1485 and Hugo for "cheap."

[679] صلحت, which seems to be a synonym here for being "upright," meaning that the degrees of the MC-IC fall on the tenth and fourth signs.

[680] An indication that 'Umar uses quadrant-based houses.

[681] 1485 and Hugo read this as though the lord of the second is in a stake *and* there is also another planet (a fortune or infortune) in a stake. But BL reads that the lord of the second *is* a fortune, using an adverbial *alif* (لسعد). As for the infortune, the text does not use this adverbial mark: so it is possible that the lord of the second is in a stake (and possibly a fortune), but *also* there is an *infortune*, separately, in a stake as well.

[682] Adding with 1485 and Hugo. The Arabic scribe might have jumped from الا ان ("except that") to لان ("because") by mistake.

[683] Adding with 1485 and Hugo. The Arabic reads, "when the fortune or infortune was in it, if a fortune was in it, the merchandise in it (and the sign in which the Sun is), is honored."

[684] I am not sure whose comment this is.

[685] But see an alternative in *The Search of the Heart* II.3.1.

73 If there was vegetation and you were asked whether it would thrive or what its condition would be, then assign to it the Ascendant and its lord, and the Moon and its lord. **74** And if all of these were fortunate, then judge survival; and if they were corrupt, [judge] corruption. **75** And if two of them were corrupt and two fortunate, then judge in this according to what is middling (by the will of God, be he be exalted!).

Chapter VIII.34: On what belongs to the signs & the planets, of the regions & countries

2 Know that the world is divided into seven divisions; every division of them is a region, based on the number of the seven planets. **3** So, the first of them is Saturn, and the last of them is the Moon, in accordance with the succession of the planets in their circles.

4 The region of India belongs to Saturn, and the region of Babylon belongs to Jupiter, and the region of the Turks belongs to Mars, and the region of Rome[686] belongs to the Sun, and the region of the Hijāz belongs to Venus, and the region of Egypt belongs to Mercury, and the region of China belongs to the Moon.

5 And some of them[687] said that Aries and Jupiter belong to Babylon, and Capricorn and Mercury belong to India, and Leo and Mars belong to the Turks, and Libra and the Sun belong to Rome, and Scorpio and Venus belong to the Arabs.[688]

6 Look at each region according to its planet, if it entered its exaltation: is it entering it and is it advancing in its course, and rising in its sector,[689] appropriate in [its] condition, fortunate, or the contrary of that? **7** And indeed you know the news of the people of the clime from it, in the properness of their issues and their disturbance. **8** And when there is a contrast[690] between

---

[686] Or rather, the Byzantine empire.
[687] Ibn Ezra credits an Enoch the Egyptian (probably a Hermes), in *AW1* Part IV, Section IV.7.
[688] Reading ʿarab for gharb ("West").
[689] This is an astronomical consideration I hope to explain in a future book on traditional astronomy.
[690] Tentatively reading for what appears to be اعترضت. But what al-Rijāl means is that *different* planets *of the same type* rule the year and the quarter (as suggested in what follows). Thus if Saturn rules the year and Mars the quarter, the malefic features are magnified.

the indication of Saturn[691] [and] the indication of Mars, and the indication of Jupiter [and] the indication of Venus (and that is that one of them is the lord of the year, and the other the lord of the quarter), then what is good and what is evil in that year is stronger and greater.

9 And if the Sun was unfortunate in the year, one of the kings of the clime will die: and the knowledge of it is from the planet[692] which is bringing misfortune with the Sun, and the sign which it is in. **10** And so Jupiter and Aries, if they were both unfortunate, it destroys the king of Babylon; and Capricorn and Mercury [would destroy] the king of India, and Leo and Mars the king of the Turks, and Libra and the Sun the king of Rome, and Scorpio and Venus the king of the Arabs.

11 And the Indians and the Persians said that the first region belongs to Saturn, and the second one to Jupiter, and the third to Mars, and the fourth to the Sun, and the fifth to Venus, and the sixth to Mercury, and the seventh to the Moon. **12** Then they begin the allotment based on the signs:[693] so Aries and its triplicity belong to the east, and Taurus and its triplicity to the south, and Gemini and its triplicity to the west, and Cancer and its triplicity to the north.

13 And in every one of the regions of the planets are two powerful cities, by the reckoning of the houses of each planet. **14** In the region of the Sun there is one city, and likewise in the region of the Moon, because to each one of them belongs one house. **15** And in every one of them[694] there are (of the cities and forts) 21,600, a city and fort based on the amount of the minutes of the circle.[695]

16 And Hermes said that these minutes, if you [put it down as four],[696] it was the number of everyone who walks upon the earth: [and] if one of them died, another child is born.[697] **17** And [he said] that the first region which is at

---

[691] Omitting a repetition of "the indication of Saturn."
[692] Reading a singular for the plural, to match the verb here and below.
[693] What follows is the usual assignment of the triplicities to the quarters based on Aries being in the east (in the northern hemisphere): Aries (and so fire) in the east, Capricorn (and so earth) in the south, Libra (and so air) in the west, Cancer (and so water) in the north. This arrangement is commonly found in horary questions about travel and lost objects.
[694] That is, in all of them *taken together*: see below.
[695] That is, every circle has 21,600 minutes (60' x 360° = 21,600').
[696] Reading uncertainly for جعلت روابع. Al-Rijāl seems to mean that the population of earth will be some multiple of 4.
[697] Omitting what seems to be a redundant *jaylān*.

the ascending of the Sun[698] [has] 3,100 large cities and villages; and the second has, 2,713 large cities and villages; and the third has 3,970; and the fourth (and it is Babylon) has 2,974; and the fifth has 3,006 cities; and the sixth [has] 3,300 large cities and villages; [and the seventh has 2,537].[699] **18** Of all of them together, that is 400 cities in the Jazīrah.[700]

19 And if you gathered together the bounds of the planets from the course of the signs, what it conferred of the cities and villages with the amount of their degree and their minutes, [is] for every degree a city and for every minute a village.[701] **20** And its bound from every sign is a place of its management of the countries. **21** And the planets especially have authority over the countries of that sign, such what belongs to Jupiter: he rules over the countries of Babylon, [and] the place of his bound in Cancer is the indicator of Iraq. **22** And like Venus, since she is the indicator of the Arabs: the place of her bound in Scorpio (which is the sign of the Arabs)[702] is the indicator of their desert. **23** And likewise, [the] indicator of the whole matter[703] is distinguished by its bound in the sign of their[704] countries. **24** And if you saw misfortune[705] in the entire sign, then it is more confirmed and specified than that in the bound of the planet of the king from that sign, or the bound of the lord of its region.

---

[698] This could also be read as, "which is in/at the Ascendant of the Sun" (*fī ṭāliʿ al-shams*). But I am not sure what it means in any event.

[699] BL omits the seventh region, so I have added the number that would yield 21,600. 1485 has 3,100 for the sixth, and 2,810 for the seventh, but that would be too many.

[700] Reading for *al-jazāʾir*, "Algeria."

[701] I believe this means that since (for example) there are 76 degrees in Mercury's bounds, there are 76 Mercurial cities and 4,560 Mercurial villages (4,560 = 76 degrees of his bounds * 60' in each degree).

[702] Removing the *qāf* (in "Scorpio") to yield "Arab."

[703] Reading *āmr* for *'ummahi*.

[704] Al-Rijāl seems to mean that the primary planet in the chart (or any planet) will affect the peoples ruled by its bound throughout all of the signs.

[705] A tentative translation for the seemingly ungrammatical منحسة or منحسة. Still, what would al-Rijāl mean by the entire sign being unfortunate?

Chapter VIII.35: On the knowledge of what cities belong to the signs[706]

Aries has, of countries:[707] Babylon, and Persia, and Azerbaijān, and Palestine, and Jazīrah, and Cyprus,[708] and the coast of the sea of Asia Minor, and the land of the Slavs, and Akhlāt, and Mūsul.

Taurus has, of countries: Sūwād,[709] and Māhīn, and Hamadān, and the country of the Kurds, and Isfahān up to the boundary of the island of Cyprus, and the coast of the sea of Asia Minor, and Lesser Armenia.

Gemini has, of countries: Armenia, and Jurjān, and Azerbaijān, and Egypt, and Mūqān, and Daylam, and Jīlān, and Tabaristān, and Burjān, and the sides of Isfahān, and Kirmān.

Cancer has the land of Syria,[710] and Dūmah[711] and Halb, and Hamāh, and Hims, and Damascus, and Busrā and its territories.[712]

Leo has Antioch, and Tabaristān, and Nīshapūr, and Sicily, and the countries of the Yemen, and al-Kalwāniyyah.

Virgo [has] Babylon and the juncture of the two rivers[713] and their workings, and Eyvān, and Córdoba, and the Jazīrah of the Banī 'Umar.[714]

Libra has Khurāsān, and Bukhārā, and Tabaristān, and Kashmīr, and India, and Tibet, and some of the countries of Ethiopia, and Jurjān, and Tabaristān,[715] and the land of al-Sa'īd.[716]

---

[706] For the first part of this chapter, I have decided to follow Nur.; BL (which 1485 seems to follow) has longer lists of attributions apparently from different sources, but contains many misspellings and unusual phrases (which might be due to misspellings). Since the list from Nur. begins in the middle of a page as part of its Ch. VIII.34 (not VIII.35), I will simply translate it without sentence numbers, pending a future edition which will allow a comparison between both. I will resume with BL starting with sentence **32**, which is identical in both sources.

[707] Reading for "cities," which is more properly part of the chapter title.

[708] But see below, where al-Rijāl has the "island of" Cyprus, not "*Jazīrah and*" Cyprus.

[709] Reading with BL and Abū Ma'shar for اسويدا, a kind of misspelling for Sweden.

[710] Al-Shām.

[711] This seems to be a city in NW Saudi Arabia, but perhaps should be identified with some place in Syria, given cities like Hamāh mentioned later.

[712] BL adds, "And it is the Ascendant of Babylon."

[713] The Tigris and the Euphrates.

[714] This seems to have been a tribe living in the Hijāz, somewhere between Mecca and Medina.

[715] Note that Tabaristān has appeared twice here, another indication of how mixed-up some of these lists are—or that al-Rijāl is combining many sources together. BL includes Tukhāristān, which might be a better reading for one of these.

[716] BL adds, "And it is the sign of Persia and the sign of Alexandria the Great, and the Ascendant of Armenia, and the Ascendant of the Turks."

Scorpio has the land of al-Sa'id, and the desolate earth,[717] and the land of Qayrawān and that ground, and the beginning of Tūnis and what follows it.[718]

Sagittarius has, of countries: Qūs, and the Taurus mountains, and the land of the Maghrib,[719] and the Island of Spain,[720] and al-Batr.[721]

Capricorn has the land of India, and the sphere[722] of Sijistān, and the upper regions,[723] and Macedonia, and Granada, and Sūs al-Aqsā.

Aquarius has from the sides of al-Madā'in, and Mīsān, and greater Alexandria.

Pisces has Tabaristān and the northern side of the land of Jurjān; and it has a partnership in Rome, and it has from Rome to the north, and it has the Jazīrah and lesser Alexandria, and the sea of Yemen, and it has Nanūniyyah and Sahūniyyah, and Lamūrīts, and Harmah, and the land of China, and the land of Ethiopia, and the Green Sea which is the sea of the west,[724] and Samarqand. **32** And it is the Ascendant of Rome.

33 And Master Ibridaj[725] the Persian mentioned that he had found [by means of Kankah],[726] in a book of the assignment of the lower world,[727] that

---

[717] الارض المفقر, which may also refer to a particular desolate region.
[718] BL adds, "And it is the Ascendant of Persia."
[719] Or perhaps, the "land of the west."
[720] The Muslim lands in Spain, known as al-Andalus.
[721] BL adds, "And it is the Ascendant of Ahwāz, and the sign of Armenia, and the Ascendant of Babylonia, and the sign of Shāṭī al-Bahr."
[722] كرة, which must be used metaphorically here because it normally means an actual spherical object.
[723] راقية.
[724] Probably the Atlantic, but this term has also been used to describe the Arabian and Indian seas.
[725] This is my best guess at the name of this unknown Persian. In BL, his name is spelled twice without pointing and once with pointing (but without the letter that seems to be a *yaa'*): see slides 318L line 1, 319R line 7, and 375R line 5. In Nur., his name is spelled once in a shortened form (278R lines 4-5), and twice in full (278L lines 20-21, 324L line 15). But the difference in pointing between all of these instances, makes it difficult to know the exact spelling.
[726] Adding *b-Kankah* (بكنكة) with Nur., suggesting that perhaps what follows is also reported in the works of Kankah the Indian.
[727] كتاب عهد الدنيا. This could also be read as "a book of the age/epoch of the world," suggesting either an old book or one devoted to mundane epochs. Both readings are relevant here, since al-Rijāl proceeds to speak of a Persian *Thema Mundi* (chart of the beginning of the world), *and* the assignment of signs and planets to different countries.

the sign of the world is Aries, and its planet the Sun, and its Ascendant Cancer (and Jupiter in it).[728]

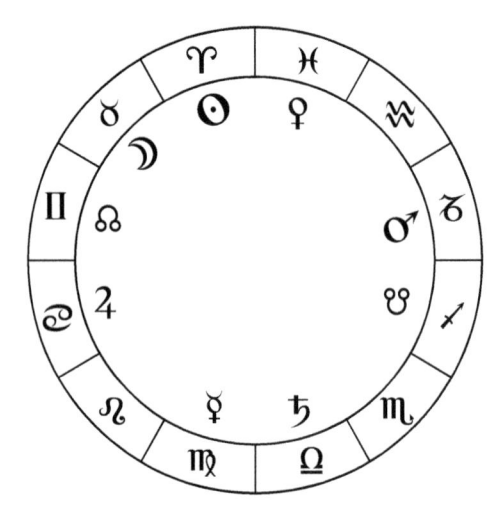

Figure 82: A Persian *Thema Mundi* (al-Rijāl Ch. VIII.35)

34 I distributed the regions among the seven planets and the twelve signs, and it came to be that Greater Irān[729] (which is Babylon) belongs to Jupiter and Aries; and Rome belongs to Libra and Saturn; and India and Sind and Makrān belong to Capricorn and Mercury, and the Hijāz and the land of the Arabs (all of it) belongs to Scorpio and Venus; and the Turks belong to Leo and Mars. **35** And as for what is beyond the Turks,[730] it belongs to the Moon and Virgo, and the land of Būdānjān[731] belongs to Aquarius and the Sun.

---

[728] This is a very short version of a Persian *Thema Mundi*, in which Cancer is rising (as in the Greek *Thema Mundi*), but the planets are placed in the signs of their exaltations. The Persians (perhaps drawing on the Indians, who emphasize the lunar Nodes) also gave exaltations to the Nodes. For this use in mundane astrology, see Pingree 1968, pp. 62-63.

[729] Reading as ایران شهر (Irānshahr) for what seems to be Abranshahr or Abransahr (ابران شهر). For the first word, BL has ابران ; Nur., ابرز or ابراز or ابران (below). Greater Iran refers to a large region of Iranian language speakers (and their culture), touching Syria, Irāq, and Azerbaijān in the west, to Pakistan and western China in the east, Uzbekhistān in the north, and to the Persian Gulf and Arabic Ocean in the south. Here, al-Rijāl's source (or perhaps al-Rijāl) identifies it broadly with Babylon, and distinguishes it from other cultures; then below, he divides it up and assigns signs and planets to various parts of it.

[730] Reading مرواء for موراء, from a Persian term that means "beyond." This term is also used in chorography to designate faraway places in Asia: see the entry for Marw al-Rūd in *AW1* IV.13.

[731] Nur. reads, "Azerbaijān."

36 And I distributed Greater Iran[732] among the planets and the signs, and it came to be that Sūwād belongs to Aquarius and the Moon, and Māhīn and Māsdān and Fahrjān Burq and Hamadān belong to Taurus and Saturn, and the Alāns and Mūqān and Azerbaijān belong to Aries and Venus, and Persia[733] belongs to Virgo and Mercury, and Khurāsān belongs to Sagittarius and the Sun, and Rayy and 'Amad belong to Scorpio and the Moon, and Daylam belongs to Gemini and Mars, and Ahwāz belongs to Capricorn and Venus, and Jurjān and Tabaristān and Rayhān and al-Sa'ad and Samarqand and Sarakhs and Bust belong to Pisces and Mercury, and Marw al-Rūd and the Two Risings[734] and Murghāb[735] belong to Cancer and Saturn, and Sijistān and Kirmān belong to Libra and Mercury, and Ayward[736] and Nīshapūr and Tūs and Abrashahr[737]—they [belong to][738] Leo and Venus.

Chapter VIII.36: What regions & also villages belong to the planets

2 Saturn has the first region, and it is India[739] and China and the Zanj and the Sūdān and the higher[740] of the seas, and Ethiopia. 3 Jupiter has, in the statements of the Romans, the fourth region: and it is Babylon and the land of Persia and Khurāsān, and Iraq; in the statement of the Persians [he has] Aswān, and it is the region of Ethiopia and the Nubians. 4 Mars has, in the statement of the Romans, the seventh region, and the land of the Turks, and Syria,[741] and Rome; and in the statement of the Indians, the region of Alexandria and Syria.[742] 5 The Sun has, in the statement of the Romans, their own region and the second region, and the east,[743] and the land of China and what follows that, and Khurāsān; in the statement of the Persians,[744] Babylon. 6

---

[732] Again, *Abrān shahr* and its variants.
[733] Or more likely the province of Fars.
[734] الطالعان, unknown at this time. But Nur. has الطالقان, al-Tālqān (unknown).
[735] Reading with Nur.; Br. Lib has مرعات, Mara'āt.
[736] Reading with BL; Nur. has either *Anburd* or *Abnurd*.
[737] Reading with BL; Nur. has Aīn Shahr.
[738] Reading فهي with Nur. for what seems to be بقي.
[739] Nur. has, "Sind."
[740] اعلا or اعلاء. This must refer to some region near the eastern coast of Africa.
[741] Al-Shām.
[742] Al-Shām.
[743] *Al-mushriq*, here probably meaning the Levant.
[744] Reading with Nur. for "al-Qūs."

Venus has, in [multiple] statements, the fifth region, and [it is] the Hijāz and the land of the Arabs, and Yemen. **7** And Mercury has, in the statement of the Romans, Alexandria and the land of the Greeks, and Syria;[745] and in the statement of the Persians, it is the sixth region and the third[746] region. **8** The Moon has, in the statement of the Romans, the sixth region and the land of the Maghrib[747] and the Franks, and Andalus and what follows it, up to the Turks and al-Jibāl; and in the statement of the Persians, it is the seventh region.

9 For[748] the cities of the signs which we said before, we named some cities of some of the signs, and the cities of other signs:[749] and this was in accordance with what we found in the statements of the scholars, and in the books—for example, the *Book of Regions and Countries*, and the book of Ptolemy, and the book of Abī Qimāsh and al-Muftī.[750]

10 And Kisrā[751] [ibn Abū Shīrwān][752] said, the[753] countries of the middle region [of the earth] are moved,[754] and the countries in the extremes remain firm, for no one rules those regions except their own people. **11** And he said[755] that for the hot side, Mars manages it; and for cold one, Saturn manages it; and the middle one, Jupiter manages it: and [therefore the people living in the middle should be secure][756] based on that, and he is of the temperate [sort] of mind,[757] [but] the two on his sides are harmful.

---

[745] Al-Shām.
[746] Nur. reads, "fifth."
[747] Or simply, the "west," especially when followed here by the Franks or Europeans.
[748] From the beginning of this sentence to the colon, I have translated from 1485, as it is clearer.
[749] The Arabic also specifies that he has listed only those which were "worthy of mentioning," implying a much longer list at his disposal.
[750] Unknown at this time.
[751] Nur. reads, "Kasbarī."
[752] Adding with Nur.. This is clearly an attribution to the Sassanian Persian king, Khusrau (or Kisrā) Anūshīrwān (but more likely, to someone in his court): if so, then these teachings probably go back to the 6th Century.
[753] Omitting a phrase in BL which begins with what might be an alternative name (البرز), and then says "he gathered together what is with the clans of the countries of the middle region…". Nur. has, "the beginning of the middle region," perhaps a misspelling for "countries" (دول, اول).
[754] That is, there are many changes of government, empires, conquests, etc.
[755] 1485 says that other people *disagreed* with him, "and *they* said that…". But note that Māshā'allāh himself endorses this view in Ch. 31 of *RYW*: see Section II.2.
[756] Reading with 1485. The Ar. reads, "for he [*unknown word*] what he supplies." 1485 further goes on in more detail about the malefics, saying that the extremes in their qualities moves the nations under them to war.
[757] Reading *al-sarb wa-* with Nur., for *al-sharīq*.

12 And Abū 'Aun[758] related from his father, Ibn Kisūn,[759] that he thought about this topic and he found the fixed stars to be spinning around the two [extreme] sides, the northern and the southern: and this was indicative of the constancy of the kingdom in them, and the moving, wavering planets spin around the area on the middle, and that was indicative of the movement in them.

[*Remainder of chapter omitted.*][760]

Chapter VIII.37: On the longitudes of countries *&* their latitudes, based on what Habs[761] mentioned in his *Zīj* (and they are from the extremity of the west), in addition to the position of every country[762]

2 It is mentioned by Ptolemy that the first clime begins from the east, from the extremity of the land of China, and it passes over it and over the coasts of the sea in the south of the land of India, then the country of Sind, then the mouth of the sea, over the island of al-Kūr[763] and cuts across the sea towards the Jazīrah of the Arabs and the land of Yemen, and cuts across the Red Sea, and passes through the country of Ethiopia, and cuts across the Nile of Egypt, and passes through the land of the Maghrib over the west of the land of the Berbers until it terminates at the [end of] the Maghrib. **3** And its greatest latitude is 16° 24', and the longest hour of its daylight 13 [hours] 29 [minutes], and its focus is on two cities, [and] they are behind the line of al-'Istiwayy, and they are affiliated with that. **4** The first of them is the city of al-Faqr: its longitude is 122°, and its latitude 3°. **5** And the other is the city of

---

[758] Nur. spells this as A'aun (اعون).
[759] Nur. reads, Kīsūn.
[760] The rest of this chapter attributes planets and signs to numerous cities, with the alleged authority of Ptolemy. But the lists in BL and Nur. differ wildly (including in their spelling, which affects the ability to locate them). Therefore I am omitting the remainder until I am better able to sort out and identify the cities.
[761] حبس. Nur. reads, "Khanash" (خنش). Unknown to me at this time.
[762] Throughout the rest of this chapter, al-Rijāl lists numerous cities (with their longitudes and latitudes) without interruption, in the form of a verbal table. Since these Ptolemy-based coordinates will not match modern geography and do not contain astrological information, I omit them here.
[763] Nur. reads, "al-Tawl." Unknown at this time.

Barūnā: its longitude is 135°, and its latitude 3°. **6** And of its [other] cities, the city of: [*list omitted*].

7 The second clime begins from the east and passes over the country of China and India and Sind[764] and the juncture of the Green Sea and the Sea of Basrah,[765] and cuts across the Jazīrah of the Arabs in the land of Najd and Tihāmah, and cuts across the Red Sea and passes through Upper Egypt and cuts through the Nile and passes through the land of the Maghrib on the middle of the country of Ifrīqiyyah, then passes over the country of the Berbers and terminates until about the Maghrib. **8** And its greatest latitude is 29° 12', and the hours of its greatest daylight are [13 hours 49 minutes].[766] **9** And of its cities: [*list omitted*].

10 The third clime begins from the east and passes over the northern land of the country of China, then over the Indian country and the north of the country of Sind, then over the country of Kābul and Makrān up to the coasts of the Sea of Basrah and passes over the villages of Ahwāz, then passes over the country of Syria[767] and cuts across Lower Egypt and passes over the country of Ifrīqiyyah and terminates towards the sea of the west. **11** And its greatest latitude is 33° 40', and the hours of its greatest daylight 14 [hours], [15 minutes].[768] **12** And of [its] cities: [*list omitted*].

13 The fourth clime begins from the east and passes over the country of Tibet, then passes over Khūrasān and its cities, then over the north of Syria[769] and in its sea, and over the island of Cyprus and Rhodes, then it passes into the country of the Maghrib, over Tangiers toward the country of the west. **14** And its greatest latitude is 39°,[770] and the longest hours of its daylight 14 [hours], 49 [minutes]. **15** And in it are (of cities): [*list omitted*].

16 The fifth clime begins from the east, from the country of Yājūj and Mājūj, then passes over the north of Khurāsān and its cities, then it passes over Khersheh and passes over it from the country of Rome, then it passes by the coasts of the Syrian Sea from what follows after the north, then it passes over the country of al-Andalus toward the country of the Maghrib. **17**

---

[764] Nur. reads, "the north of the country of Sind."
[765] This probably refers to the Persian Gulf and Arabian Gulf, on either side of the United Arab Emirates and 'Omān.
[766] Reading with 1485 (which is correctly calculated). Missing in BL, and 14h 21m in Nur.
[767] Al-Shām.
[768] Reading with 1485 (which is very closely calculated). Missing in BL, and listed as 12m in Nur.
[769] Al-Shām.
[770] Reading with Nur. (and 1485) for "40," as the former also gives the daylight hours.

And its greatest latitude is 43°,[771] and the hours of its longest daylight [15 hours, 10 minutes].[772] **18** And in it are (of cities): [*list omitted*].

19 The sixth clime begins from the east and passes over the country of the Romans and Burjān, and passes over the sea of the west. **20** And its greatest latitude is 47° 02', and the longest of its hours of daylight 15 [hours], 41 [minutes].[773] **21** And in it are (of cities): [*list omitted*].

22 The seventh clime begins from the east, from the land of Yājūj, and it passes over the country of the Turks, then over the coasts of the sea of Jurjān, from what follows the north, and cuts across the sea of the Romans and passes over the country of Burjān and the Slavs, and terminates toward the sea of the west. **23** And its greatest latitude is 50° 30',[774] and the longest hours of its daylight [16 hours, 13 minutes].[775] **24** And in it are (of cities): [*list omitted*].

Chapter VIII.38: On the knowledge of the procedure of the two Lots, [and] in it are two differing accounts[776]

[First view of "two Lots"][777]

2 Al-Mughīrah said (from al-Kindī):[778] as for the First Lot, it is taken from the Sun to Saturn, and projected from Jupiter; and as for the Second Lot, it is taken from the Sun to the degree of the Midheaven, and thrown out from Jupiter.

---

[771] Nur. reads either "42 [degrees] 33 [minutes]," or "42 [degrees] 38 [minutes]." 1485 has 43° 28'.
[772] Nur. has 15° 12', 1485 has 15° 15'.
[773] Reading the hours with Nur.
[774] Reading with 1485, as it is missing in BL and somewhat illegible in Nur. (but may be 53°).
[775] I have calculated this myself, but 1485 is very close (16° 16').
[776] Actually there are four different account, as I indicate below.
[777] It is unclear what exactly these Lots are supposed to measure, and at what kind of ingress they are used (i.e., for the year of anyone's accession, or the ingress of a Saturn-Jupiter conjunction, or the ingress of a triplicity shift).
[778] The sources of these quotes are currently unknown.

[Second view of "two Lots"][779]

3 And after that he said, the First Lot is taken from Saturn to Jupiter, and thrown out from the place of their connection at the beginning of the triplicity; and the Second Lot is from Jupiter to Saturn, and thrown out from the degree of their connection in the conjunction in which you [currently] are. **4** Then, you look from the place of the Lot to the lord of the Lot, or from the place of the lord of the Lot to the Lot [itself], and from the Lot to Mars, a year for every sign:[780] and that is the time which is sought.

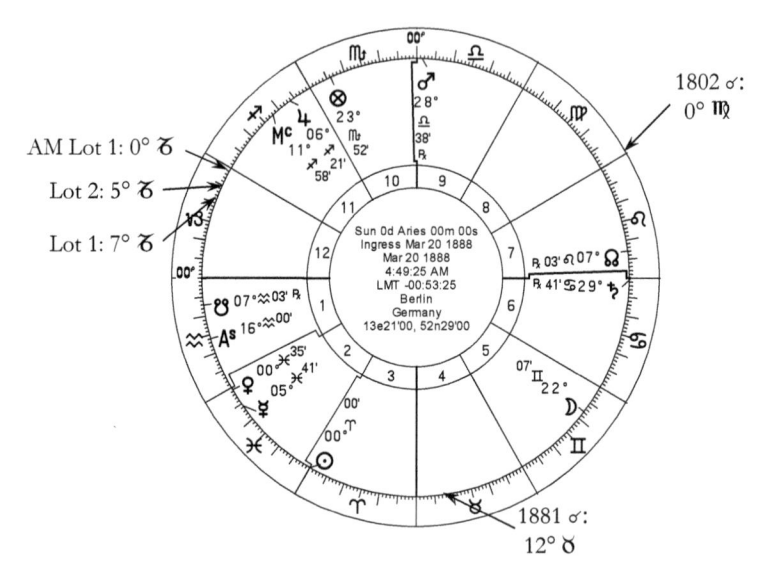

Figure 83: Illustration of "two Lots" version 2 (*Skilled* VIII.38, 3-4)[781]

---

[779] For these Lots and their use in kings' lifespans, cf. also BRD II.5, **16**. Note that Abū Ma'shar has the first Lot from the *Sun to Saturn*, while al-Rijāl has it from Saturn to Jupiter.

[780] Burnett and 1485 read "degree," but BL clearly has "sign." In BRD, this means that the degrees are grouped into "signs" of 30° apiece, rather than counting whole signs.

[781] This figure illustrates the Lots in **3-4** for Kaiser Wilhelm II, the German Emperor during WWI. He was born on January 27, 1859, and died June 4, 1941 (age 82). His reign was during the tropical earthy triplicity, whose shift occurred in 1802 at 0° 20' Virgo. The mean conjunction during which he acceded (1881) was at 12° 14' Taurus. He acceded in 1888, and abdicated in 1918 after 30 years of rule. He died 53 years after acceding. The first Lot is from Saturn to Jupiter, cast from the degree of the shift, yielding 7° Capricorn. The second is from Jupiter to Saturn and cast from the 1881 conjunction, yielding 5° Capricorn. Abū Ma'shar's (AM) version of the first Lot is from the Sun to Saturn, cast from the degree of the shift, yielding 0° Capricorn. Luckily, all versions of the Lot are so

[Third view of "two Lots"][782]

5 And al-Mughīrah said [that] al-Kindī said (from 'Abd Allāh b. Muhammad al-Hāshimī, [who took it] from Māshā'allāh): in the knowledge of the place of the two Lots, see where Saturn is (by sign and degree and minute); take from the beginning of Aries up to [that] minute by equality, and preserve it. **6** Then, see where Jupiter is, and do with him just like that. **7** Then, subtract what belongs to Saturn (of the degrees which you preserved) from what belongs to Jupiter. **8** (And if what belongs to Saturn is greater than what belongs to Jupiter, increase on top of that by a rotation,[783] and cast out[784] the degrees of Saturn from that.)[785] **9** And you preserve what remains,

---

close together we may treat them as a group. From the Lots to Saturn (their lord) is 7 signs/years, from Saturn to them is 5, from the Lots to Mars is 10, from Mars to the Lots 2, and from Mars to Saturn (if that is allowed), 9. Now, I take it that profections are allowed to go around the circle more than once, just as in nativities—so that if the leader does not die or leave office after so many years, we can go around for 12 more years (or even 24 more). If we take the 30-year period of Wilhelm's actual rule, this is close either to the Lots-Saturn or Saturn-Lots distances: for 5 years + 24 = 29, and 7 + 24 = 31. Wilhelm allegedly began to be marginalized and wielded less power in the last year or two of his reign, so 29 years seems like a slightly better choice. But if we are allowed to look at his actual lifespan after accession (53 years), this is the sum of 48 years (4 times around the circle) + the 5 years from Saturn to the Lots. (Finally, I do note that Saturn's lesser years are 30, which is the length of the reign—this is perhaps something that could be taken into account.)

[782] The source of these Lots is unknown at this time. Moreover, there is some confusion over just what kinds of degrees the calculation consists of, whether zodiacal or ascensional. [1] To begin with, we need both a recent conjunction and a triplicity shift to perform the operations. For each Lot, we add the absolute difference in longitude between Saturn and Jupiter, to one of the mean conjunctions. [2] So, for Lot 1, subtract (a) the absolute longitude of Saturn from (b) the absolute longitude of Jupiter: this difference is called the "secret." But if Saturn's longitude is larger than Jupiter's then it seems (due to a confusing sentence, 8) that we should add 360° to Jupiter and use that amount for the subtraction. Finally, we add "the secret" to (c) the absolute longitude of the degree of the triplicity shift (in this case, 4° 12' Scorpio for the conjunction of 570 AD). [3] For Lot 2, add the "secret" to the absolute longitude of the recent Saturn-Jupiter conjunction. [4] Finally, there is the question of what kinds of degrees are being used. The text in **5, 10,** and **13** refers to degrees of "equality" (السواء) which suggests zodiacal degrees, but in **10** speaks of "ascensions" (مطالع), which suggests either right or oblique ascensions. Unfortunately, the example in the text is a poor one, because 4° 12' Scorpio does not equate to 214° 12' in right *nor* oblique ascensions. And anyway, no other Lot is ever measured using ascensions, so I suggest we stick to zodiacal degrees.

[783] That is, add 360°.

[784] This should probably have read, "subtract."

[785] I believe this simply means, "subtract the absolute longitude of Saturn from the new amount of Jupiter + 360°."

and call it "the secret." **10** Then, take from the beginning of Aries up to the place of the conjunction of the religion—and the conjunction was in 4° 12' Scorpio, whose ascensions in equality are 214° 12'. **11** You add this on top of what "the secret" is, and what comes out you throw out from the beginning of Aries: and where it ends for you, is the place of the First Lot. **12** And if you had more than [one] rotation, then subtract a rotation from it;[786] then subtract what remains from the beginning of Aries, and this first one is the Lot of the religion.

13 Then, you take the conjunction in which you are, and you see how much is from the beginning of Aries up to it, in degrees of equality. **14** Add on top of that what is called "the secret," and if that was more than one rotation, you subtract a rotation from it, and cast what remains from Aries: and where the counting ends for you, that is the place of the second Lot.

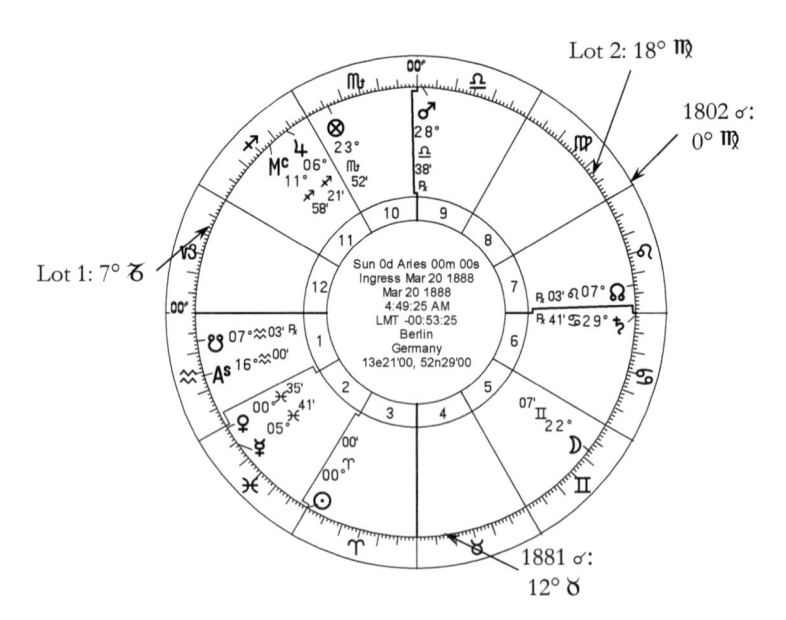

Figure 84: Illustration of "two Lots" version 3 (*Skilled* VIII.38, 5-14)[787]

---

[786] In other words, if the sum is over 360°, then subtract 360°.
[787] Again, this is the ingress chart for the accession of Kaiser Wilhelm II. For the first Lot, subtract the longitude of Saturn (119° 41') from that of Jupiter (246° 21') to yield a "secret" of 126° 40'. Add this to the longitude of the triplicity shift at 150° 20' (or 0° 20' Virgo) to yield Lot 1 at 7° 00' Capricorn. For the second Lot, add the "secret" to the longitude of the recent mean conjunction at 42° 14' (or 12° 14' Taurus) to yield a Lot at 18° 54' Virgo. Now, al-Rijāl does not tell us the purpose of this Lot (although it is must be related to length of reign or longevity), nor how to use it. If we profect from the Virgo

[Fourth view of "two Lots"][788]

15 And in this is another procedure: come to know the Ascendant of the year for the world in which the king acceded, and the places of the planets. **16** Then, take from the degree of the eastern planet (of Saturn and Jupiter) up to the portion of the Sun, and add on top of that the small years of the lord of the religion (and that of the Arabs is eight years), and cast what it comes to from the Ascendant; and where it arrives, is completed the first Lot.

17 And as for the second Lot, take from the degree of the Sun up to the degree of the western planet of them, and what it comes to, subtract from it what came out from the degrees of the first Lot before you added the small years of the lord of the religion to it; and cast out what was left from the Ascendant: and where it reached, is completed the second Lot.

Lot to Mercury and vice versa just as we did before, the years are 6: these, added to two complete profection cycles, yields the 30 years of reign. Profections using Mars (as before) do not give us much interesting. On the other hand, it seems odd to have two Lots and not to relate them together: if we count inclusively in whole signs from the Virgo Lot to the Capricorn Lot, we get 5 years. And of course, perhaps we are to use these Lots with other kinds of profections and transits.

[788] Burnett and Yamamoto (2000, vol. 1 p. 595) consider the following Lots to be those of *BRD* II.5, **15** (and al-Qabīsī's version in Section I.2 of this book), but al-Rijāl's version is totally different. For both Lots, one needs the ingress chart of the year of the accession. For Lot 1, measure from the more eastern planet (either Jupiter or Saturn) to the Sun, add the lesser years of the planet signifying that people, and project that number from the Ascendant of the ingress. For the second Lot, measure from the Sun to the more western of the two planets, add the lesser years as before, and project the total from that same Ascendant. Al-Rijāl does not tell us what to do next. Note also that, among the planets, only Saturn (for Judaism, 30 lesser years) and Venus (for Islam and Arabs, 8 lesser years) are generally agreed upon—so it is hard to know what planet to use for other cultures.

Chapter VIII.39: On the knowledge of the sign of the terminal point from the Ascendant of the shift of the transit indicating the religion [of the Arabs][789]

[Abū Ma'shar's mundane profection]

2 If you wanted to know that,[790] then add to the completed years of Yazdijird, 61 Persian years, and 2 months, and 12 days, and 16 hours: and that is the extent of what is between the dating of Yazdijird and the conjunction of the religion.[791] **3** And begin the projection from the sign of Libra, and where it ends, there is the terminal point from the Ascendant of the religion.[792]

4 And if you wanted the terminal point from the sign of the conjunction of the religion, then project from Scorpio.[793]

5 And if you wanted the [terminal sign of the] Turn,[794] then project from Gemini.

6 In[795] fact it is mentioned that [Gemini] is the Ascendant in the year of the conjunction of the religion, according to the way of the tables of Ptolemy).[796] **6** And as for [what is according to] the *Sindhind*, the Ascendant of the *qubba*[797] was 6° Aries. **7** And as for the *Mumtaḥan*,[798] it was Cancer.

8 And if you wanted the degree of the distribution, then your projection is from the degree of 20° Pisces, a year for every degree: where it ends is the

---

[789] For this chapter, see *BRD* VIII.2, **8-10** and al-Qabīsī in Section I.1 above.
[790] That is, Abū Ma'shar's profection from the Ascendant of 571 AD to the beginning of the era of Yazdijird (632 AD).
[791] For this math, see al-Qabīsī in Section I.1 above.
[792] Abū Ma'shar and others believed that the Ascendant of the Aries ingress of 571 AD was Libra. The profection of Libra in 571 AD would have reached Capricorn in 632 AD, but Abū Ma'shar does nothing with this.
[793] In other words, we may profect from the sign of the conjunction itself.
[794] Adding with *BRD* VIII.2, **9**. Abū Ma'shar seems to be suggesting we profect from Gemini, which is the sign of the Turn or mighty *fardar* of Gemini-Venus which began in 580 AD—see *The Universal Book* of 'Umar-Kankah, in Section I.5 of this book.
[795] Sentences **6-7** are by al-Rijāl.
[796] This is the view of al-Kindī, as mentioned in **10** below.
[797] According to Burnett (his *BRD* vol. 1, p. 559, n. 12), this is "an imaginary point on the equator between the east and west." It seems to be the city of 'Ūjjaīn, at 23° 10' N, 75° 46' E. See al-Bīrūnī's *Introduction*, §239.
[798] See Kennedy 1956, #51 on p. 132 (composed around 810 AD). This seems to be the same *zīj* referred to at length in Kennedy 2009-10.

degree of the distribution.⁷⁹⁹ **9** And if you were on the degree of the distribution at the entrance of the year, then add on top of it 10" for every degree which the Sun cuts off from the circle of the signs. **9** The amount of what the Sun cuts off is 5' for every sign.⁸⁰⁰

[Mundane profections according to al-Kindī]⁸⁰¹

10 And al-Kindī reported that what is between the year of the conjunction indicating the religion and the Hijrah, is 52 solar years, and the Ascendant of the conjunction of the religion was Gemini, and the year in which the Prophet of God fled (the prayers and peace of God be upon him!), reached Virgo.⁸⁰²

11 And between the Hijrah and Yazdijird is 3,624 days. **12** So if you wanted knowledge of that,⁸⁰³ then take the years of Yazdijird and expand them into days, and add on top of that what is between the Hijrah and Yazdijird, in days. **13** And divide what is summed up by 365 ¼ days: and what comes out is the solar years, and what remains of months and days is of an incomplete year. **14** And what is summed up (of the years) is the solar years from the Hijrah. **15** And for every year project a sign, and begin with Virgo: and where the counting of the signs ends for you, that is the sign which the year of the world reached from the Ascendant of the conjunction of the religion.⁸⁰⁴

[Interpretation of the mundane techniques]⁸⁰⁵

16 Know that the sign of the terminal point from the Ascendant of the religion indicates what occurs to the people of the religion.⁸⁰⁶ **17** And the

---

⁷⁹⁹ As *The Universal Book* points out, the year 570 AD corresponded to a mundane direction of the Ascendant to 20° Pisces.

⁸⁰⁰ This simply means that Abū Ma'shar wants to equate the Sun's motion throughout the year (starting at the Aries ingress) with the motion of the mundane direction of the Ascendant. The mundane direction of the Ascendant moves at a rate of 1° or 60' or 3600" in a year. Therefore, for every sign which the Sun transits through during year, the mundane Ascendant will move 5' (60' / 12 signs = 5'). And for every degree which the Sun transits through, the mundane Ascendant will move 10" (3600" / 360° = 10").

⁸⁰¹ Again, see al-Qabīsī in Section I.1 of this book.

⁸⁰² If the Ascendant of 571 was Gemini, then in 622 the Ascendant would have profected to Virgo.

⁸⁰³ That is, the profection from the Hijrah (in Virgo) to Yazdijird.

⁸⁰⁴ Al-Qabīsī does not give us the answer, but if the Ascendant reached Virgo in 622 it would have reached Cancer in the first year of Yazdijird (632).

⁸⁰⁵ For this section, cf. *BRD* I.1, 28.

terminal point from its tenth indicates the matter of the religion and its authority.

18 And the terminal point from the place of the conjunction of the religion indicates what befalls the faith in terms of increase and decrease, and a good condition and corruption.[807] **19** And its lord indicates what befalls the people of the house of the lord of the religion.[808]

20 The place of the distribution indicates the conditions of the sages in their communities.[809]

21 Understand this: the terminal point from the Ascendant of the conjunction of the shift, indicates what befalls the people of that dynasty and the general populace.[810] **22** And the terminal point from its tenth is for the authority of that shift.

23 The terminal point from the place of the conjunction of the shift[811] indicates what occurs in the rulership of the lord of the shift, in terms of increase and decrease. **24** And its lord indicates what befalls the people of the established houses in the administration of that shift.

---

[806] For example, the profection of the Libra Ascendant of 571 AD (if it were the correct Ascendant).
[807] That is, the profection of Scorpio (the sign of the conjunction of 570 AD).
[808] To me this suggests the lineage of Muhammad. But at any rate, this should mean the lord of the sign of the profected conjunction.
[809] This probably refers to the bound lord of the directed mundane Ascendant: in 580 AD, this would have been at 0° Aries, with Jupiter as the bound lord.
[810] For example, the profection of the Ascendant of the triplicity shift to fire in 809 AD.
[811] The triplicity shift to fire in 809 was in Sagittarius.

Chapter VIII.40: On the knowledge of the terminal points & the distribution[812]

[Abū Ma'shar's profection from the 570 conjunction or 571 ingress]

2 If you want that,[813] then take the years of Yazdijird (based on years of the Sun), and add on top of that 61 years, converted into years of the Sun. **3** Then, project what is summed up from Libra, a year for each sign: and where the sign ends, take the degree of it. **4** And indeed the terminal point has reached it, because the Ascendant of the conjunction was 18° of Libra.[814]

5 And if you wanted the terminal point from the place of the conjunction indicating the religion of Islam, then project from the sign of Scorpio, and where it ends, there is the terminal point from the sign of the conjunction.[815]

6 And if you wanted the distribution, then project it from 20° of Pisces, and where it ends, the distribution is completed.[816]

[Abū Ma'shar's profection from the 809 triplicity shift into fire]

7 And if you wanted the terminal point from the shift to Sagittarius,[817] then project the years of Yazdijird along with 61 years (converted to years of the Sun): [that is] 237 years, 239 days.[818] **8** And project the remainder from

---

[812] See another version of this material in al-Qabīsī (Section I.1 of this book) and Ch. VIII.39 immediately above. This chapter is a bit more jumbled and expressed in more difficult ways than the other versions. In it, al-Rijāl is expressing the views of Abū Ma'shar in *BRD* about identifying and profecting various Ascendants and signs between 570 AD and 809 AD. First, according to Abū Ma'shar the Ascendant of the 571 AD ingress was Libra (**3**), and the sign of the conjunction itself was Scorpio (**5**): both of these may be profected. The directed mundane Ascendant was at 20° Pisces in 570 AD, and may be increased by 1°/year after that (**6**). One may also profect the Ascendant of the 749 ingress, heralding the 'Abbāsids, which was Virgo (**10**). Finally, one may profect from the Ascendant of the 809 AD triplicity shift into fire, which was Leo (**8**), or from the sign of the conjunction itself in Sagittarius (**9**).

[813] That is, the profection from the 571 AD Aries ingress, to the first year of Yazdijird (632 AD). If the 571 Ascendant was Libra, it would profect to Capricorn in 632.

[814] Most Islamic astrologers agreed that the Ascendant of the 571 Aries ingress was Libra, but I am not sure who said it was 18°.

[815] This is the profection from the sign of the conjunction itself.

[816] In the theory promoted by 'Umar-Kankah and Abū Ma'shar, the direction of the mundane Ascendant had reached 20° Pisces in 570 AD.

[817] That is, the shift to the fiery triplicity in 809 AD, with the conjunction in Sagittarius.

[818] According to Burnett, this should be 238 solar years (of 365.25 days each), plus 2.5 days. This interval is simply the time between the 571 ingress and the 809 triplicity shift.

the sign of Leo,[819] a year for every sign: and where it ends, there is the terminal point from the Ascendant of the shift.

9 And if you wanted the terminal point from the conjunction of the shift, then project from Sagittarius:[820] and where it ends, there is the terminal point from the sign of the conjunction of the shift.

[Abū Ma'shar's profection from the 749 ingress, heralding the 'Abbasids]

10 And if you wanted it from the Ascendant of the dynasty,[821] then take the years of Yazdijird, along with 61 years (converted into years of the Sun), and project the remainder from Virgo:[822] and where it ended, there is the terminal point from the Ascendant of the dynasty. 11 And the terminal point from it also indicates what befalls the administration of the dynasty. 12 Understand that, and do not neglect it.

Chapter VIII.41: On falling stars

2 I appended this section in my book when it [seemed] correct to me, with the experience of the death of ibn Alī al-Hussein and Sa'īd b. Hardūn,[823] since[824] before he died I did not hold nor believe that it had a signification nor any efficacy.

3 If a star fell down from Aries, it splits the heavens and its effect remains; indeed the king dies, and in the land of the Romans and Babylon there is intense combat.

4 And if it fell down from Taurus, then many cities among the Romans are destroyed, and plague occurs in Babylon.

5 And if it fell down from Gemini, then evil afflicts the land of the Romans, and the king of Egypt dies in that year, and a good man will begin in his place, and there is plague and illness in the region of Persia.[825]

---

[819] The Ascendant of the 809 ingress (marking the shift into fire) according to Abū Ma'shar, was Leo.
[820] This is the sign of the conjunction in 809.
[821] That is, the 749 AD ingress and the 'Abbasid dynasty.
[822] According to Abū Ma'shar, the Ascendant of the 749 ingress was Virgo.
[823] Nur. reads this name as either Hazrūn or Hadhrūn. Both are unknown at this time.
[824] Reading the rest of the sentence with 1485, as the Arabic does not quite make sense to me and may involve idiomatic expressions.
[825] Or perhaps only the province of Fārs.

6 And if it fell down from Cancer, then there is evil in the Hijāz and the son of the king dies in battle, then a little later the king dies.

7 And if it fell down from Leo, then the king dies and his enemy is made happy, and there goes out in the region of Babylon one who contends in the kingdom, and predatory beasts are aroused.

8 And if it dropped down from Virgo, then the king kills his enemy in the land of Egypt, and he sows discord in it.

9 And if it fell down from Libra, the king encounters evil from [his] subjects in secret and [under] a veil.

10 And if it fell down from Scorpio, it increases fires in countries and decreases the water of rivers.

11 And if it fell down from Sagittarius, there is plague in the land of Babylon and Baghdad, and the king of them dies.

12 And if it fell down from Capricorn, there is great evil in the Hijāz from wars, and other things besides that.

13 And if it fell down from Aquarius, then a weak man goes out and takes the kingdom, and his survival in the kingdom is for a short time; then there is intense fighting after that.

14 And if it fell down in Pisces, then the king acts justly with respect to [his] subjects, and there is security and an abundance of rains.

APPENDIX A: TABLES OF MEAN CONJUNCTIONS

In this Appendix I provide accurate tables for both tropical and sidereal (Fagan-Bradley) mean conjunctions of Saturn and Jupiter. The conjunctions start in 185 BC, with the tropical shift to the watery triplicity. The numbers assigned to the conjunctions, and their Julian and Gregorian dates, are the same in both tables. But the positions of the conjunctions, and which ones count as triplicity shifts in their respective zodiacs, differ accordingly. Note that the position of the conjunctions coincide almost exactly at the triplicity shift to earth in 213 AD.

Table of Tropical Mean Conjunctions

This table was generated by using the following "epoch" date for a recent tropical mean conjunction, and thereafter projecting forwards and backwards using accurate contemporary tropical parameters (see my Introduction).

- Conjunction date: JD 2415585.836, or 8:03 AM, July 20, 1901.
- Tropical Position: 285.2043109°, or Capricorn 15° 12' 16".

☌	Julian Date	Date	Sign	Degree
Shift to watery triplicity				
1	1653973.471	May 1, 185 BC	♓	2.783888
2	1661226.922	March 11, 165 BC	♏	5.75932
3	1668480.373	January 19, 145 BC	♋	8.734753
4	1675733.824	November 29, 126 BC	♓	11.71019
5	1682987.276	October 8, 106 BC	♏	14.68562
6	1690240.727	August 18, 86 BC	♋	17.66105
7	1697494.178	June 27, 66 BC	♓	20.63648
8	1704747.629	May 7, 46 BC	♏	23.61192
9	1712001.08	March 16, 26 BC	♋	26.58735
10	1719254.531	January 24, 6 BC	♓	29.56278
Shift to fiery triplicity				
11	1726507.982	December 3, 14 AD	♐	2.538214
12	1733761.433	October 12, 34	♌	5.513646
13	1741014.884	August 22, 54	♈	8.489079
14	1748268.335	July 1, 74	♐	11.46451

APPENDIX A: TABLE OF SATURN-JUPITER CONJUNCTIONS

15	1755521.786	May 11, 94	♌	14.43994
16	1762775.238	March 20, 114	♈	17.41538
17	1770028.689	January 28, 134	♐	20.39081
18	1777282.14	December 7, 153	♌	23.36624
19	1784535.591	October 17, 173	♈	26.34167
20	1791789.042	August 26, 193	♐	29.31711
Shift to earthy triplicity				
21	1799042.493	July 5, 213	♍	2.29254
22	1806295.944	May 15, 233	♉	5.267972
23	1813549.395	March 24, 253	♑	8.243405
24	1820802.846	February 1, 273	♍	11.21884
25	1828056.297	December 11, 292	♉	14.19427
26	1835309.749	October 21, 312	♑	17.1697
27	1842563.2	August 30, 332	♍	20.14514
28	1849816.651	July 10, 352	♉	23.12057
29	1857070.102	May 19, 372	♑	26.096
30	1864323.553	March 29, 392	♍	29.07143
Shift to airy triplicity				
31	1871577.004	February 6, 412	♊	2.046866
32	1878830.455	December 16, 431	♒	5.022298
33	1886083.906	October 26, 451	♎	7.997731
34	1893337.357	September 4, 471	♊	10.97316
35	1900590.808	July 15, 491	♒	13.9486
36	1907844.259	May 24, 511	♎	16.92403
37	1915097.711	April 3, 531	♊	19.89946
38	1922351.162	February 10, 551	♒	22.87489
39	1929604.613	December 21, 570	♎	25.85033
40	1936858.064	October 30, 590	♊	28.82576
Shift to watery triplicity				
41	1944111.515	September 9, 610	♓	1.801192
42	1951364.966	July 19, 630	♏	4.776624
43	1958618.417	May 28, 650	♋	7.752057
44	1965871.868	April 7, 670	♓	10.72749
45	1973125.319	February 14, 690	♏	13.70292
46	1980378.77	December 25, 709	♋	16.67835

47	1987632.221	November 3, 729	♓	19.65379
48	1994885.673	September 13, 749	♏	22.62922
49	2002139.124	July 23, 769	♋	25.60465
50	2009392.575	June 2, 789	♓	28.58009
Shift to fiery triplicity				
51	2016646.026	April 11, 809	♐	1.555518
52	2023899.477	February 18, 829	♌	4.53095
53	2031152.928	December 29, 848	♈	7.506383
54	2038406.379	November 7, 868	♐	10.48182
55	2045659.83	September 17, 888	♌	13.45725
56	2052913.281	July 27, 908	♈	16.43268
57	2060166.732	June 6, 928	♐	19.40811
58	2067420.184	April 15, 948	♌	22.38355
59	2074673.635	February 24, 968	♈	25.35898
60	2081927.086	January 3, 988	♐	28.33441
Shift to earthy triplicity				
61	2089180.537	November 13, 1007	♍	1.309844
62	2096433.988	September 22, 1027	♉	4.285276
63	2103687.439	August 1, 1047	♑	7.260709
64	2110940.89	June 11, 1067	♍	10.23614
65	2118194.341	April 20, 1087	♉	13.21157
66	2125447.792	February 28, 1107	♑	16.18701
67	2132701.243	January 7, 1127	♍	19.16244
68	2139954.694	November 17, 1146	♉	22.13787
69	2147208.146	September 26, 1166	♑	25.1133
70	2154461.597	August 6, 1186	♍	28.08874
Shift to airy triplicity				
71	2161715.048	June 15, 1206	♊	1.06417
72	2168968.499	April 24, 1226	♒	4.039603
73	2176221.95	March 4, 1246	♎	7.015035
74	2183475.401	January 11, 1266	♊	9.990468
75	2190728.852	November 21, 1285	♒	12.9659
76	2197982.303	September 30, 1305	♎	15.94133
77	2205235.754	August 10, 1325	♊	18.91677
78	2212489.205	June 19, 1345	♒	21.8922
79	2219742.656	April 29, 1365	♎	24.86763

APPENDIX A: TABLE OF SATURN-JUPITER CONJUNCTIONS

80	2226996.108	March 8, 1385	♊	27.84306
Shift to watery triplicity				
81	2234249.559	January 16, 1405	♓	0.818496
82	2241503.01	November 25, 1424	♏	3.793929
83	2248756.461	October 4, 1444	♋	6.769361
84	2256009.912	August 14, 1464	♓	9.744794
85	2263263.363	June 23, 1484	♏	12.72023
86	2270516.814	May 3, 1504	♋	15.69566
87	2277770.265	March 12, 1524	♓	18.67109
88	2285023.716	January 21, 1544	♏	21.64652
89	2292277.167	November 30, 1563	♋	24.62196
90	2299530.619	October 20, 1583	♓	27.59739
Shift to fiery triplicity				
91	2306784.07	August 29, 1603	♐	0.572822
92	2314037.521	July 9, 1623	♌	3.548255
93	2321290.972	May 18, 1643	♈	6.523687
94	2328544.423	March 27, 1663	♐	9.49912
95	2335797.874	February 4, 1683	♌	12.47455
96	2343051.325	December 15, 1702	♈	15.44998
97	2350304.776	October 25, 1722	♐	18.42542
98	2357558.227	September 3, 1742	♌	21.40085
99	2364811.678	July 14, 1762	♈	24.37628
100	2372065.129	May 23, 1782	♐	27.35172
Shift to earthy triplicity				
101	2379318.581	April 3, 1802	♍	0.327148
102	2386572.032	February 10, 1822	♉	3.302581
103	2393825.483	December 20, 1841	♑	6.278013
104	2401078.934	October 30, 1861	♍	9.253446
105	2408332.385	September 8, 1881	♉	12.22888
106	2415585.836	July 20, 1901	♑	15.20431
107	2422839.287	May 29, 1921	♍	18.17974
108	2430092.738	April 8, 1941	♉	21.15518
109	2437346.189	February 15, 1961	♑	24.13061
110	2444599.64	December 26, 1980	♍	27.10604

Shift to airy triplicity				
111	2451853.091	November 4, 2000	♊	0.081474
112	2459106.543	September 14, 2020	♒	3.056907
113	2466359.994	July 24, 2040	♎	6.032339
114	2473613.445	June 2, 2060	♊	9.007772
115	2480866.896	April 12, 2080	♒	11.9832
116	2488120.347	February 20, 2100	♎	14.95864
117	2495373.798	January 1, 2120	♊	17.93407
118	2502627.249	November 10, 2139	♒	20.9095
119	2509880.7	September 20, 2159	♎	23.88493
120	2517134.151	July 30, 2179	♊	26.86037
121	2524387.602	June 9, 2199	♒	29.8358
Shift to watery triplicity				
122	2531641.053	April 19, 2219	♏	2.811233

Figure 85: Table of tropical mean Saturn-Jupiter conjunctions

Table of Sidereal Mean Conjunctions

This table was generated by determining the Fagan-Bradley difference between the tropical and sidereal Suns at the mean conjunction on July 20, 1901 (namely, 23° 22' 10"), which put the sidereal mean conjunction at Sagittarius 21° 50' 06". From there, I projected forwards and backwards using the parameters I described in my Introduction.

☌	Julian Date	Date	Sign	Degree
1	1653973.471	May 1, 185 BC	♓	8.519541
2	1661226.922	March 11, 165 BC	♏	11.21778
3	1668480.373	January 19, 145 BC	♋	13.91602
4	1675733.824	November 29, 126 BC	♓	16.61426
5	1682987.276	October 8, 106 BC	♏	19.31251
6	1690240.727	August 18, 86 BC	♋	22.01075
7	1697494.178	June 27, 66 BC	♓	24.70899
8	1704747.629	May 7, 46 BC	♏	27.40723

APPENDIX A: TABLE OF SATURN-JUPITER CONJUNCTIONS   515

		Shift to fiery triplicity		
9	1712001.08	March 16, 26 BC	♌	0.10547
10	1719254.531	January 24, 6 BC	♈	2.803711
11	1726507.982	December 3, 14 AD	♐	5.501953
12	1733761.433	October 12, 34	♌	8.200194
13	1741014.884	August 22, 54	♈	10.89844
14	1748268.335	July 1, 74	♐	13.59668
15	1755521.786	May 11, 94	♌	16.29492
16	1762775.238	March 20, 114	♈	18.99316
17	1770028.689	January 28, 134	♐	21.6914
18	1777282.14	December 7, 153	♌	24.38964
19	1784535.591	October 17, 173	♈	27.08788
20	1791789.042	August 26, 193	♐	29.78612
		Shift to earthy triplicity		
21	1799042.493	July 5, 213	♍	2.484365
22	1806295.944	May 15, 233	♉	5.182606
23	1813549.395	March 24, 253	♑	7.880847
24	1820802.846	February 1, 273	♍	10.57909
25	1828056.297	December 11, 292	♉	13.27733
26	1835309.749	October 21, 312	♑	15.97557
27	1842563.2	August 30, 332	♍	18.67381
28	1849816.651	July 10, 352	♉	21.37205
29	1857070.102	May 19, 372	♑	24.07029
30	1864323.553	March 29, 392	♍	26.76854
31	1871577.004	February 6, 412	♉	29.46678
		Shift to airy triplicity		
32	1878830.455	December 16, 431	♒	2.165018
33	1886083.906	October 26, 451	♎	4.863259
34	1893337.357	September 4, 471	♊	7.5615
35	1900590.808	July 15, 491	♒	10.25974
36	1907844.259	May 24, 511	♎	12.95798
37	1915097.711	April 3, 531	♊	15.65622
38	1922351.162	February 10, 551	♒	18.35447
39	1929604.613	December 21, 570	♎	21.05271
40	1936858.064	October 30, 590	♊	23.75095

41	1944111.515	September 9, 610	♒	26.44919
42	1951364.966	July 19, 630	♎	29.14743
Shift to watery triplicity				
43	1958618.417	May 28, 650	♋	1.845671
44	1965871.868	April 7, 670	♓	4.543912
45	1973125.319	February 14, 690	♏	7.242153
46	1980378.77	December 25, 709	♋	9.940395
47	1987632.221	November 3, 729	♓	12.63864
48	1994885.673	September 13, 749	♏	15.33688
49	2002139.124	July 23, 769	♋	18.03512
50	2009392.575	June 2, 789	♓	20.73336
51	2016646.026	April 11, 809	♏	23.4316
52	2023899.477	February 18, 829	♋	26.12984
53	2031152.928	December 29, 848	♓	28.82808
Shift to fiery triplicity				
54	2038406.379	November 7, 868	♐	1.526324
55	2045659.83	September 17, 888	♌	4.224565
56	2052913.281	July 27, 908	♈	6.922807
57	2060166.732	June 6, 928	♐	9.621048
58	2067420.184	April 15, 948	♌	12.31929
59	2074673.635	February 24, 968	♈	15.01753
60	2081927.086	January 3, 988	♐	17.71577
61	2089180.537	November 13, 1007	♌	20.41401
62	2096433.988	September 22, 1027	♈	23.11225
63	2103687.439	August 1, 1047	♐	25.8105
64	2110940.89	June 11, 1067	♌	28.50874
Shift to earthy triplicity				
65	2118194.341	April 20, 1087	♉	1.206977
66	2125447.792	February 28, 1107	♑	3.905219
67	2132701.243	January 7, 1127	♍	6.60346
68	2139954.694	November 17, 1146	♉	9.301701
69	2147208.146	September 26, 1166	♑	11.99994
70	2154461.597	August 6, 1186	♍	14.69818
71	2161715.048	June 15, 1206	♉	17.39642
72	2168968.499	April 24, 1226	♑	20.09467
73	2176221.95	March 4, 1246	♍	22.79291

APPENDIX A: TABLE OF SATURN-JUPITER CONJUNCTIONS

74	2183475.401	January 11, 1266	♉	25.49115
75	2190728.852	November 21, 1285	♑	28.18939
Shift to airy triplicity				
76	2197982.303	September 30, 1305	♎	0.887631
77	2205235.754	August 10, 1325	♊	3.585872
78	2212489.205	June 19, 1345	♒	6.284113
79	2219742.656	April 29, 1365	♎	8.982354
80	2226996.108	March 8, 1385	♊	11.6806
81	2234249.559	January 16, 1405	♒	14.37884
82	2241503.01	November 25, 1424	♎	17.07708
83	2248756.461	October 4, 1444	♊	19.77532
84	2256009.912	August 14, 1464	♒	22.47356
85	2263263.363	June 23, 1484	♎	25.1718
86	2270516.814	May 3, 1504	♊	27.87004
Shift to watery triplicity				
87	2277770.265	March 12, 1524	♓	0.568284
88	2285023.716	January 21, 1544	♏	3.266525
89	2292277.167	November 30, 1563	♋	5.964766
90	2299530.619	October 20, 1583	♓	8.663007
91	2306784.07	August 29, 1603	♏	11.36125
92	2314037.521	July 9, 1623	♋	14.05949
93	2321290.972	May 18, 1643	♓	16.75773
94	2328544.423	March 27, 1663	♏	19.45597
95	2335797.874	February 4, 1683	♋	22.15421
96	2343051.325	December 15, 1702	♓	24.85245
97	2350304.776	October 25, 1722	♏	27.5507
Shift to fiery triplicity				
98	2357558.227	September 3, 1742	♌	0.248937
99	2364811.678	July 14, 1762	♈	2.947178
100	2372065.129	May 23, 1782	♐	5.645419
101	2379318.581	April 3, 1802	♌	8.343661
102	2386572.032	February 10, 1822	♈	11.0419
103	2393825.483	December 20, 1841	♐	13.74014
104	2401078.934	October 30, 1861	♌	16.43838
105	2408332.385	September 8, 1881	♈	19.13663

106	2415585.836	July 20, 1901	♐	21.83487
107	2422839.287	May 29, 1921	♌	24.53311
108	2430092.738	April 8, 1941	♈	27.23135
109	2437346.189	February 15, 1961	♐	29.92959
Shift to earthy triplicity				
110	2444599.64	December 26, 1980	♍	2.627831
111	2451853.091	November 4, 2000	♉	5.326073
112	2459106.543	September 14, 2020	♑	8.024314
113	2466359.994	July 24, 2040	♍	10.72256
114	2473613.445	June 2, 2060	♉	13.4208
115	2480866.896	April 12, 2080	♑	16.11904
116	2488120.347	February 20, 2100	♍	18.81728
117	2495373.798	January 1, 2120	♉	21.51552
118	2502627.249	November 10, 2139	♑	24.21376
119	2509880.7	September 20, 2159	♍	26.912
120	2517134.151	July 30, 2179	♉	29.61024
Shift to airy triplicity				
121	2524387.602	June 9, 2199	♒	2.308485
122	2531641.053	April 19, 2219	♎	5.006726

Figure 86: Table of sidereal mean Saturn-Jupiter conjunctions

APPENDIX B: SATURN-MARS CONJUNCTIONS IN CANCER

As I mentioned in my Introduction, some astrologers paid attention to the conjunctions of Saturn and Mars in Cancer: in this sign, Saturn is in his detriment and Mars in his fall. Using basic astrological principles, one may surmise that these conjunctions indicate disaster and war, or at least important political changes or shifts of power which are often accompanied by war and social disruption. As opposed to the 20-year Saturn-Jupiter cycles, these conjunctions occur about every 30 years and are often followed by a second conjunction near the end of Cancer.

My parameters for these conjunctions are as follows:

	Tropical years	Sidereal years
Saturn period	29.4241473	29.45662578
Mars period	1.880752057	1.880815968
Frequency in early Cancer	30.13965366	30.13646336

The tables below provide the mean series for both tropical and sidereal (Fagan-Bradley) zodiacs, from 145 BC to 2211 AD. On the left is the date of the mean conjunction, in the middle is its position. To the right, I have listed all true conjunctions in Cancer: most are associated with a mean conjunction, but others stand alone. That is, sometimes there is a true conjunction but not an associated mean one (such as in 117 BC, tropical), because while their bodies may join in Cancer, the centers of their epicycles do not. This happens most often near the beginning of the sign. Likewise, sometimes there is a mean conjunction but not a true one (as in 63 AD, tropical); this most often happens near the end of Cancer.

Tropical Series of Saturn-Mars Conjunctions in Cancer:

Date of Mean ☌	In ♋	True Conjunctions
July 10, 145 BC	14.53°	July 15, 145 BC: 20.55°
August 30, 115 BC	23.26°	
		July 22, 117 BC: 4.17°

October 16, 87 BC	7.41°	August 25, 87 BC: 14.92°
December 4, 57 BC	16.14°	September 29, 57 BC: 25.08°
January 20, 28 BC	0.28°	April 1, 28 BC: 0.78°
January 24, 26 BC	24.86°	April 23, 26 BC: 27.85°
March 11, 3 AD	9.01°	May 11, 3 AD: 11.15°
April 30, 33	17.74°	June 13, 33: 21.80°
June 16, 61	1.89°	June 21, 61: 5.85°
June 19, 63	26.47°	
August 5, 91	10.62°	July 23, 91: 16.92°
		August 2, 119: 0.87°
September 24, 121	19.35°	August 24, 121: 27.88°
November 9, 149	3.50°	September 4, 149: 11.55°
November 13, 151	28.08°	
December 30, 179	12.22°	October 20, 179: 21.92° January 20, 180: 17.65° March 17, 180: 15.17°
February 17, 210	20.95°	May 10, 210: 24.82°
April 5, 238	5.10°	May 22, 238: 8.62°
April 8, 240	29.68°	
May 25, 268	13.83°	June 23, 268: 19.35°
		July 1, 296: 3.50°
July 14, 298	22.56°	
August 30, 326	6.71°	August 3, 326: 14.27°
October 18, 356	15.44°	September 4, 356: 25.25°
		September 19, 384: 8.00°
December 8, 386	24.17°	
January 24, 415	8.31°	April 13, 415: 11.10°
March 14, 445	17.04°	May 20, 445: 21.00°
April 30, 473	1.19°	May 30, 473: 4.50°
May 4, 475	25.77°	
June 19, 503	9.92°	July 1, 503: 15.03°
August 8, 533	18.65°	August 1, 533: 26.00°
September 24, 561	2.80°	August 9, 561: 9.10°
September 28, 563	27.38°	

APPENDIX B: TABLE OF SATURN-MARS CONJ. IN CANCER

November 13, 591	11.53°	September 12, 591: 19.68°
		October 12, 619: 1.47°
January 2, 622	20.26°	October 25, 621: 29.23°
		February 6, 622: 24.38°
		March 20, 622: 22.37°
February 17, 650	4.40°	April 22, 650: 4.72°
February 21, 652	28.99°	
April 8, 680	13.13°	May 26, 680: 14.90°
May 29, 710	21.86°	June 29, 710: 25.67°
July 14, 738	6.01°	July 6, 738: 8.93°
July 17, 740	30.59°	
September 2, 768	14.74°	August 6, 768: 19.93°
		August 15, 796: 2.98°
October 22, 798	23.47°	
December 8, 826	7.62°	September 21, 826: 13.40°
January 27, 857	16.35°	April 13, 857: 16.22°
March 14, 885	0.49°	
March 18, 887	25.08°	May 24, 887: 26.52°
May 4, 915	9.22°	June 3, 915: 9.87°
June 22, 945	17.95°	July 5, 945: 20.93°
August 8, 973	2.10°	July 13, 973: 4.78°
August 12, 975	26.68°	
September 28, 1003	10.83°	August 15, 1003: 15.78°
November 16, 1033	19.56°	September 18, 1033: 26.70°
January 2, 1062	3.71°	October 16, 1061: 9.23°
		December 22, 1061: 6.20°
		March 10, 1062: 2.36°
January 6, 1064	28.29°	
February 21, 1092	12.44°	April 29, 1092: 12.82°
April 12, 1122	21.17°	June 5, 1122: 23.42°
May 29, 1150	5.31°	June 14, 1150: 7.33°
May 31, 1152	29.90°	
July 17, 1180	14.04°	July 15, 1180: 18.35°
		July 24, 1208: 2.30°

September 6, 1210	22.77°	August 16, 1210: 29.72°
October 6, 1238	6.92°	August 26, 1238: 12.95°
December 11, 1268	15.65°	October 2, 1268: 23.70°
January 30, 1299	24.38°	April 25, 1299: 26.33°
March 18, 1327	8.53°	May 12, 1327: 9.37°
May 7, 1357	17.26°	June 13, 1357: 19.88°
June 22, 1385	1.40°	June 21, 1385: 3.52°
June 26, 1387	25.99°	
August 12, 1415	10.13°	July 24, 1415: 14.20°
September 30, 1445	18.86°	August 24, 1445: 25.23°
		September 4, 1473: 7.78°
November 20, 1475	27.59°	
January 6, 1504	11.74°	October 24, 1503: 17.78° January 3, 1504: 14.53° March 18, 1504: 10.93°
February 24, 1534	20.47°	May 7, 1534: 20.47°
April 12, 1562	4.62°	May 18, 1562: 3.40°
April 15, 1564	29.20°	
June 10, 1592	13.35°	June 18, 1592: 13.95°
July 31, 1622	22.07°	July 20, 1622: 25.02°
September 16, 1650	6.22°	July 28, 1650: 8.17°
November 4, 1680	14.95°	August 29, 1680: 18.93°
		September 17, 1708: 1.40°
December 26, 1710	23.68°	October 5, 1710: 29.10°
February 10, 1739	7.83°	April 6, 1739: 4.15°
April 1, 1769	16.56°	May 14, 1769: 14.57°
May 18, 1797	0.71°	
May 22, 1799	25.29°	June 16, 1799: 25.55°
July 8, 1827	9.44°	June 26, 1827: 8.97°
August 27, 1857	18.16°	July 27, 1857: 20.08°
October 13, 1885	2.31°	August 6, 1885: 3.80°
October 16, 1887	26.89°	
December 3, 1915	11.04°	September 10, 1915: 14.38°
January 22, 1946	19.77°	October 26, 1945: 24.77°

		January 20, 1946: 20.75°
		March 20, 1946: 17.95°
March 9, 1974	3.92°	April 20, 1974: 0.13°
March 12, 1976	28.50°	May 12, 1976: 27.87°
April 28, 2004	12.65°	May 24, 2004: 11.32°
June 17, 2034	21.38°	June 26, 2034: 22.28°
August 3, 2062	5.52°	July 6, 2062: 6.43°
September 22, 2092	14.25°	August 5, 2092: 17.35°
		August 19, 2120: 1.13°
November 12, 2122	22.98°	September 9, 2122: 28.58°
December 29, 2150	7.13°	September 27, 2150: 11.25°
February 16, 2181	15.86°	April 16, 2181: 14.40°
April 5, 2209	0.01°	
April 9, 2211	24.59°	May 25, 2211: 24.63

Figure 87: Table of tropical mean Saturn-Mars in Cancer conjunctions

Sidereal Series of Saturn-Mars Conjunctions in Cancer:

Date of Mean ☌	In ♋	True Conjunctions
July 10, 145 BC	19.70°	July 18, 145 BC: 25.62°
August 30, 115 BC	28.01°	July 25, 117 BC: 8.85°
October 16, 87 BC	11.76°	August 27, 87 BC: 19.18°
December 4, 57 BC	20.07°	September 111, 59 BC: 1.67°
		October 1, 57 BC: 28.92°
January 20, 28 BC	3.82°	April 3, 28 BC: 4.25°
January 24, 26 BC	28.38°	
March 11, 3 AD	12.13°	May 13, 3 BC: 14.17°
April 30, 33	20.44°	June 15, 33 AD: 24.40°
June 16, 61	4.20°	June 23, 61: 8.08°
June 19, 63	28.75°	
August 5, 91	12.50°	July 25, 91: 18.72°
September 24, 121	20.81°	August 3, 119: 2.28°
		August 25, 121: 29.27°

November 9, 149	4.57°	September 5, 149: 12.55°
November 13, 151	29.12°	
December 30, 179	12.88°	October 21, 179: 22.48° January 21, 180: 18.23° March 18, 180: 15.77°
February 17, 210	21.18°	May 10, 210: 25.00°
April 5, 238	4.94°	May 22, 238: 8.24°
April 8, 240	29.49°	
May 25, 268	13.25°	June 23, 268: 18.70°
July 14, 298	21.56°	July 1, 296: 2.47°
August 30, 326	5.31°	August 2, 326: 12.83°
October 18, 356	13.62°	September 3, 356: 23.38°
December 8, 386	21.93°	September 18, 384: 5.75°
January 24, 415	5.68°	April 12, 415: 8.42°
March 14, 445	13.99°	May 19, 445: 17.90°
May 4, 475	22.30°	May 29, 473: 1.02° June 22, 475: 28.12°
June 19, 503	6.05°	June 29, 503: 11.12°
August 8, 533	14.36°	July 30, 533: 21.67°
September 28, 563	22.67°	August 7, 561: 4.38°
November 13, 591	6.43°	September 10, 591: 14.57°
January 2, 622	14.73°	October 22, 621: 23.70° February 3, 622: 18.85° March 17, 622: 17.05°
February 21, 652	23.04°	May 12, 652: 26.12°
April 8, 680	6.80°	May 23, 680: 8.55°
May 29, 710	15.11°	June 25, 710: 18.88°
July 17, 740	23.41°	July 2, 738: 1.78° July 25, 740: 28.87°
September 2, 768	7.17°	August 2, 768: 12.35°
October 22, 798	15.48°	September 3, 798: 22.38°
December 11, 828	23.79°	September 17, 826: 5.02°
January 27, 857	7.54°	April 9, 857: 7.38°
March 18, 887	15.85°	May 20, 887: 17.28°
May 7, 917	24.16°	May 29, 915: 0.25°

Appendix B: Table of Saturn-Mars Conj. in Cancer

		June 21, 917: 27.33°
June 22, 945	7.91°	June 30, 945: 10.90°
August 12, 975	16.22°	August 1, 975: 21.57°
September 30, 1005	24.53°	August 9, 1003: 4.93°
November 16, 1033	8.28°	September 12, 1033: 15.43°
January 6, 1064	16.59°	October 25, 1063: 25.15° February 17, 1064: 19.72° March 14, 1064: 18.67°
February 21, 1092	0.35°	April 23, 1092: 0.73°
February 24, 1094	24.90°	May 16, 1094: 27.87°
April 12, 1122	8.66°	May 29, 1122: 10.92°
May 31, 1152	16.96°	June 30, 1152: 21.67°
July 17, 1180	0.72°	July 8, 1180: 5.03°
July 21, 1182	25.27°	
September 6, 1210	9.03°	August 9, 1210: 15.97°
October 25, 1240	17.34°	September 10, 1240: 26.07°
December 11, 1268	1.09°	September 25, 1268: 9.17°
December 15, 1270	25.64°	
January 30, 1299	9.40°	April 18, 1299: 11.35°
March 21, 1329	17.71°	May 27, 1329: 21.43°
May 7, 1357	1.46°	June 5, 1357: 4.10°
May 11, 1359	26.02°	July 7, 1387: 14.82°
June 26, 1387	9.77°	
August 15, 1417	18.08°	August 6, 1417: 24.85°
September 30, 1445	1.83°	August 15, 1445: 8.22°
October 4, 1447	26.39°	
November 20, 1475	10.14°	September 17, 1475: 17.93°
January 9, 1506	18.45°	October 29, 1505: 27.57° February 27, 1506: 21.87° March 15, 1506: 21.27°
February 24, 1534	2.21°	April 27, 1534: 02.23°
February 28, 1536	26.76°	May 19, 1536: 29.50°
April 15, 1564	10.51°	June 1, 1564: 12.40°
June 14, 1594	18.82°	July 13, 1594: 22.23°

July 31, 1622	2.58°	July 20, 1622: 5.53°
August 3, 1624	27.13°	
September 19, 1652	10.89°	August 19, 1652: 15.72°
November 8, 1682	19.19°	September 21, 1682: 25.97°
December 26, 1710	2.95°	October 5, 1710: 8.40°
December 29, 1712	27.50°	
February 13, 1741	11.26°	April 27, 1741: 10.88°
April 5, 1771	19.57°	June 7, 1771: 20.47°
May 22, 1799	3.32°	June 16, 1799: 3.45°
May 25, 1801	27.88°	
July 11, 1829	11.63°	July 19, 1829: 13.98°
August 31, 1859	19.94°	August 20, 1859: 24.53°
October 16, 1887	3.69°	August 28, 1887: 8.02°
October 19, 1889	28.25°	
December 6, 1917	12.00°	October 1, 1917: 18.25°
		October 26, 1945: 0.80°
January 25, 1948	20.31°	
March 12, 1976	4.06°	May 12, 1976: 3.45°
March 16, 1978	28.62°	
May 2, 2006	12.37°	June 18, 2006: 13.93°
June 20, 2036	20.68°	July 19, 2036: 24.25°
August 6, 2064	4.44°	July 28, 2064: 8.13°
August 10, 2066	28.99°	
September 25, 2094	12.74°	August 29, 2094: 18.57°
November 15, 2124	21.05°	September 9, 2122: 2.12° October 1, 2124: 29.25°
January 1, 2153	4.81°	October 14, 2152: 11.97°
January 4, 2155	29.36°	
February 20, 2183	13.12°	May 8, 2183: 14.77°
April 12, 2213	21.43°	June 17, 2213: 24.23°

Figure 88: Table of sidereal mean Saturn-Mars in Cancer conjunctions

APPENDIX C: CHART EXAMPLES FROM SAHL

In this Appendix I provide translations and some analysis of several of Sahl's own mundane charts, from his Arabic *Book on the Revolutions of the Years of the World* (full translation forthcoming). All of these were adopted virtually verbatim or in choppy summaries, in *Scito* Chs. 95-96, and in my translation of the Latin I provided Arabic sentence number references for easy cross-comparison. My Arabic sources for the charts and translation were:

- Vatican Ar. 935
- Beatty Ar. 5467

In my *Comment* at the beginning of *Scito* Ch. 95, I also discussed some of the dating and zodiac issued, which I will discuss at greater length in my complete translation of Sahl from Arabic.

Sahl's Example #1: The Battle of the Camel (Aries Ingress, 657 AD)

I have already discussed this chart and its dating at length in my *Comment* to *Scito* Ch. 95, and provided a translation of virtually all of the Arabic.

Sahl's Example #2: The Battle of Siffīn (Aries Ingress, 657 AD)

Comment by Dykes. This is Sahl's example of the Aries ingress of 657 AD, which was excerpted by Abū Ma'shar in *Scito* Ch. 96. The chart has numerous problems in its details.[1]

Vatican image. The square image below is largely based on Vatican, which (unlike Beatty) includes intermediate house cusps. Based on these cusps, the chart was cast for the equator or about 5° N latitude, using an unknown quadrant system. If the Ascendant were advanced to 19° Capricorn, then the intermediate cusps would align better with it and match something like Porphyry or Alchabitius Semi-Arc houses—but it would require that the chart be cast for a longitude in extreme east Asia or the Pacific Ocean, clearly not what Sahl used.

---

[1] Sources: Vat. ff. 173R, line 20 – 173L, line 10 (image on 173R); Beatty ff. 266, line 13 – 267, line 15 (image on 266).

Dykes's preferred image. On the other hand, there are good reasons to think that both Vatican and Beatty have incorrectly assigned the Midheaven to Libra, and that the Midheaven is really in Scorpio. First, Sahl says the axes or stakes are increasing or advancing (**7**), which only happens when the Midheaven is in the *eleventh* sign (Scorpio): if the Midheaven had been in the tenth sign, he would have said it was "upright." Second, in looking for the significator of the king, Sahl looks to the lord of the Midheaven (**6-7**), immediately pointing out that the stakes are increasing or advancing, which signals that the lord of the Midheaven will not be the lord of the tenth sign; he then argues that the significator of the king cannot be Mars, because Mars is under the rays: therefore the Sun is the significator (**8, 9**). But this would not make sense if the Midheaven were in Libra, because then Venus would be the presumed significator of the king, and she is *not* under the rays—in fact, there is no further discussion of her. (One would even expect that perhaps her exalted status in Pisces might be important, if she were the lord of the Midheaven.) Third, and perhaps most significantly, this change of the MC takes place automatically if we cast the chart for al-Raqqah (the rough location of the Battle of Siffin, the topic of the chart): a 15° Capricorn Ascendant requires a 7° Scorpio Midheaven, while 19° Capricorn puts the Midheaven at 10°-11° Scorpio.

Changing the Midheaven to Scorpio also helps us to understand sentence **8**, which has mismatches and oddities between Vatican and Beatty. (a) Vatican makes **8** say that Mars is the lord of the IC, and that he is withdrawing (i.e., cadent). That is true with the Libra Midheaven, since the IC would be in late Aries, and he would be withdrawing in early Aries. But it makes pointless Sahl's further statements about Mars not being the significator of the king: if he is only the lord of the IC and the fourth sign, he is not a candidate for being the significator of the king, anyway. (b) Beatty's version of **8** combines two types of statements about Mars *and Venus*, with one of them apparently being the lord of the *Midheaven* (not the IC), and entering into the beginning of the sign. Now, Venus is indeed entering into Pisces. And if the Midheaven were Libra, then she would be its lord—but in that case, the focus of the significator of the king would be precisely on her, not Mars. But discussion of Venus abruptly ceases.

Thus, I propose the following: (1) the Midheaven is in early Scorpio, and (2) the chart is cast for al-Raqqah. Then, (3) sentence **8** should run as follows: "And Mars is the lord of the Midheaven, withdrawing, entering under the rays, and Venus the lord of the stake of the earth, entering into the sign [of Pisces]." I have represented these changes in my own "preferred" chart below.

Planetary positions. The planetary positions are mostly about 2° lower than the tropical values, reflecting Sahl's sidereal zodiac established about 144 years before the chart was cast. Several of these positions require comment. Although Vatican *seems* to assign Venus a longitude of 2°, it is possible that she was understood to be just in the first degree, entering into Pisces (**8**). Next, Vatican omits Jupiter's position but Beatty gives it as 16° 61' (his tropical position was actually at 9°). This is perhaps a problem, since it would seem that Jupiter is meant to be in the second house, but since the cusp of the 2nd is at 19°, it puts him in the first house (albeit close to the cusp). I have put him in the second quadrant house anyway, in case there is a transcription error. Third, Saturn is listed by Vatican as being in 23° Libra, which is much too far (his tropical position was at 8°). However, this could have been a misunderstanding for the value of the Libra Midheaven, or even for the position of the Nodes, which were tropically at 25° Virgo/Pisces rather than Libra/Aries as the manuscript charts have them. So, I have put him at 3°, which is what the manuscripts assign to the Nodes.

Historically speaking, the text refers to the circumstances of the Battle of Siffīn (657 AD). In December 656, the fourth Caliph 'Alī had defeated the Qurayshi forces at the Battle of the Camel (Sahl's Example #1, see *Scito* Ch. 95), and turned to Kūfa for support and to establish a capital. However, others including the 'Umayyad governor of Syria, Mu'āwiyah, sought revenge for 'Uthmān's death (not to mention that 'Alī wanted to diminish the political power of the 'Umayyads), and so he refused to acknowledge 'Alī as the Caliph until various demands were met. 'Alī was in a precarious position because much of his Kūfan support derived from people implicated in 'Uthmān's death. So, from his base in Iraq 'Alī worked hard to drum up support for a military campaign in Syria, to make Mu'āwiyah recognize him. In the spring and summer of 657 'Alī's coalition half-heartedly clashed with Mu'āwiyah's near al-Raqqah, Syria, with fighting only becoming intense in July and August. After that, 'Alī's coalition and support began to disintegrate: he was forced to arbitrate with Mu'āwiyah as an equal, and the man arbitrating on his behalf cared more about the interests of Iraq and Kūfa than he did about 'Alī's. Certain parties were disgusted by the power politics involved (rather than a pure religious spirit), and rose up and left, going back to southern Iraq: these isolationists and puritans were the Kharijites, so-called because they "rose up" and "went out" of the coalition (Ar. *kharaja*). In the end, Mu'āwiyah declared himself Caliph (establishing the 'Umayyad Caliphate), and 'Alī was murdered by one of the Kharijites in a Kūfan mosque in 661.

Astrologically, a number of these elements are clearly present in the description below, but it is occasionally hard to know whether any particular planet indicates 'Alī or his opponents. Mars is the lord of the Midheaven and under the rays (**6-8**), so he gives up the signification of the king to the Sun (**8-9**). But the Sun is applying (or "pushing his management") to Saturn in the tenth sign (**4, 10**), so his affairs will be put into the hands of Saturn. Saturn indicates the people and is the lord of the year (**5**); he is both retrograde and is the malefic contrary to the sect (not mentioned by Sahl). This indicates that the people (Saturn) are causing trouble for the king (**13-14**), who must be 'Alī, and that they have lost their proper Islamic allegiance to him, drawing him to battle and violence (**14-15**). The exalted but weak and retrograde status of Saturn does not bode well for the prestige and strength of the Caliphate.

ଓ ଓ ଓ

1 A chapter on a revolution of a year. **2** The year was in the conjunction of the watery triplicity, and the year had reached Sagittarius from the Ascendant of the conjunction;[2] and this is its image.

3 I looked in the revolution of this year at the Ascendant and the stakes, and at the positions of the planets, and what they indicated for it.

4 And the Ascendant was Capricorn, and its lord was Saturn, and he is in the tenth sign, in his exaltation, receiving the management of the Sun and Jupiter; and he was with the Head. **5** And he was the lord of the year and the indicator of the citizens.

---

[2] Sahl takes the Ascendant of the triplicity shift into water (571 AD) to be Libra, which would make the profection to 657 AD reach Sagittarius.

APPENDIX C: CHART EXAMPLES FROM SAHL 531

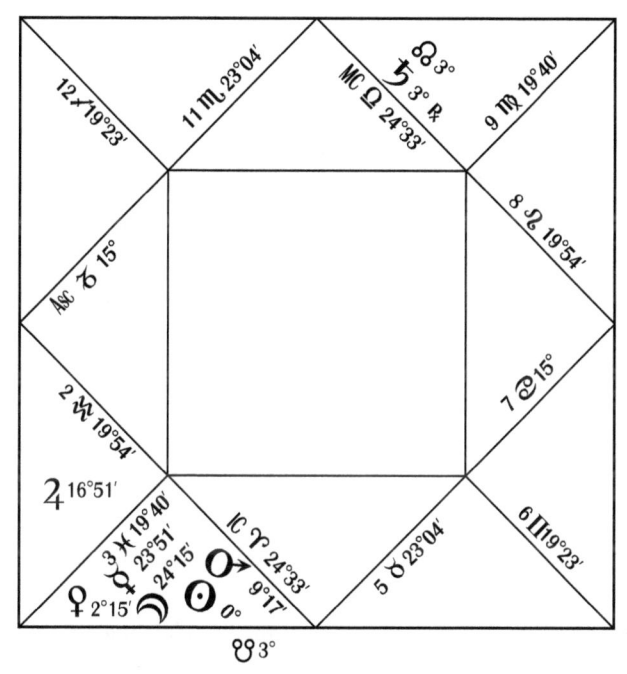

Figure 89: Version (adapted from Vat.) of Sahl's Example #2 (657 AD)

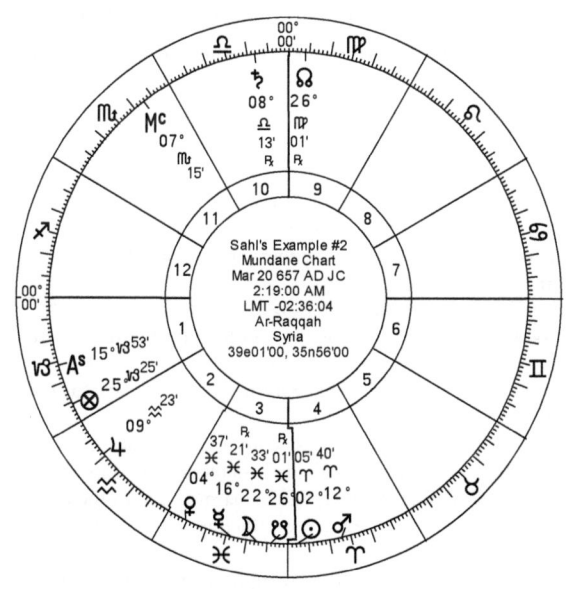

Figure 90: "Preferred" tropical version of Sahl's example #2

6 Then, for the indicator of the king I looked and the Midheaven and its lord. **7** And the stakes were advancing.[3] **8** And Mars is the lord of the Midheaven, withdrawing, entering under the rays, and Venus the lord of the stake of the earth, entering into the sign [of Pisces].[4] **9** So the Sun was leaving with the power of the king, and represented his indicator.[5] **10** And [the Sun] was in the opposition of Saturn, pushing his own management from his exaltation to Saturn in *his* exaltation; and [Saturn] is retrograde.

11 And the Moon, the luminary of the night, is with Mercury in the third from the Ascendant, in the sign of his fall. **12** And she[6] was the one with responsibility over the matter of the citizens in this year.[7]

13 And Saturn put the king to the test[8] since he is in the Midheaven, in the house of his exaltation (and the Ascendant is his house), and he is retrograde in his exaltation, opposed to the Sun and Mars. **14** It indicates the shedding of blood in this year, and the contention of the king, and the marching of some of the soldiers upon others, and the corruption of the condition of the people.[9]

15 And because the two infortunes are withdrawing in the third and ninth,[10] the piety of the people will disappear, and they will encounter violence from their Sultan while they bear responsibility for the killing. **16** And the king's coffers will be split up, and there will be fighting and the shedding of blood many times, and nation will be engaged with nation, and they will

---

[3] Reading زائدة for زائلة ("withdrawing, decreasing"), as the degree of the Midheaven is in the eleventh sign (Scorpio) rather than the ninth (Virgo). See my discussion above.

[4] See my discussion above for my formulation of this sentence. Vatican reads, "And Mars is the lord of the stake of the earth, withdrawing, entering under the rays." Beatty reads, "And Mars and Venus, the lord of the Midheaven, in a withdrawing position, entering in the sign under the rays."

[5] For this rule, see *RYW* Ch. 41, **2**.

[6] I take this to be the Moon since she is the sect light (rather than Mercury, who is in his fall).

[7] This does not make sense to me, since Saturn was already stated to be the lord of the year *and* the indicator of the citizens.

[8] Reading *balū* with Vat.; Beatty omits this word and says Saturn *is* the king, which does make astrological sense because Saturn is the exalted lord of Libra, and is in it. But Sahl seems to be saying (below) that the king will be harmed due to the disruption of the people's actions—so really the malefic Saturn is afflicting the king, who was already stated to be the Sun in **9**.

[9] Reading with Beatty. Vatican has "the corruption of the assets of the people," which may be relevant because Saturn rules the second house (assets).

[10] This is a clear indication that while Sahl respects whole-sign houses (e.g., Saturn is in the tenth sign), he also considers quadrant divisions: Mars is in the third quadrant division, and Saturn in the ninth.

seek the kingdom. **17** And that will be harsher in the clime of Babylon. **18** And merchants will be afflicted, and corruption will enter upon them and the generality of the people.

19 And because of the retrogradation of Saturn and the presence of Mars under the rays, they will be destroyed until nothing of them remains.[11] **20** And God knows and is wiser.

Sahl's Example #3: Defeat of 'Abd Allāh b. al-Zubayr (Aries Ingress, 692 AD)

Comment by Dykes. This example is the Aries ingress of 692 AD[12] (excerpted by Abū Ma'shar in *Scito* Ch. 96), cast for Mecca and illustrating the defeat of 'Abd Allāh b. al-Zubayr in that city in October 692. Most planetary positions are again about 2° earlier than the tropical ones. The tricky positions are those of Mars and Saturn, since Sahl requires them to be 6° apart (**13**). Their true positions are 5° apart, which was also my conclusion based on the conflicting manuscript information.[13]

Historically, this chart refers to the last year of the second Islamic civil war or *fitna*, which was still trying to settle the issues of religio-political succession not settled at the end of the first *fitna* (i.e., in 657 AD, Example #2 above). At the time, the 'Umayyad branch of the Quraysh tribe was still in control of the Caliphate but was experiencing threats to its authority from all directions. One source of challenges was 'Abd Allāh b. al-Zubayr, the son of the al-Zubayr b. al-Awwam who had been close to Muhammad and had died fighting against Caliph 'Alī at the Battle of the Camel in 656 (Example #1). Ibn al-Zubayr was a Qurayshi but not an 'Umayyad, and objected to the Caliphate being run by one branch (the Sufyanid) of one branch (the 'Umayyad) of the Qurayshi clan. He went to Mecca to garner support as the new Caliph, and remained there for some time. But the lands gained by him through his supporters were soon retaken by the 'Umayyads, until finally Caliph 'Abd al-

---

[11] Reading with Vat. Beatty reads: "until no great one of them remains."
[12] Sources: Vatican 173L, line 11 – 174R, line 2 (image on 173L); Beatty 268, line 1 – 269, line 3 (image on 268).
[13] Vatican has Saturn at either 19° 14' or 16' or maybe 17', while Beatty has him at what appears to be 16° 45'. Vatican has Mars at 26° 14' or 16', while Beatty has him at 14° 30' or 16° 30'.

Malik sent a general and troops to Mecca in 692, and Ibn al-Zubayr was killed in October 692. Thus ended the second—but not the last—*fitna*.

Astrologically, two things stand out about this chart. First, Sahl distinguishes this chart from Example #2 (**9-12**). In both cases, Saturn is the malefic contrary to the sect, and rules the Ascendant (signifying the people)—in fact, both charts show trouble for the king from the people. But in Example #2 (the Battle of Siffīn), he is exalted and retrograde in the tenth, while here he is in the eleventh, not retrograde, and is conjoined with the lord of the tenth (Mars). Sahl argues that, contrary to this chart, Example #2 shows the "power of the war and great killing," due to Saturn's exaltation and retrogradation. Against this we might point out that 'Alī was not killed at the Battle of Siffīn, whereas Ibn al-Zubayr was indeed killed at the siege of Mecca. So why was Example #2 worse? Sahl might think that exaltation magnifies the scope and significance of the events, and retrogradation draws things out over time: in that case, Example #2 could show a more protracted war, not to mention a result of greater significance: the death of 'Alī and transition to the 'Umayyads spelled the end of the "rightly guided" Caliphs who had been closely associated with Muhammad's own circle. By contrast, one might consider Ibn al-Zubayr as a pretender and rebel: by the time of the siege of Mecca, all of the areas he had claimed a few years earlier had been taken back by the 'Umayyads and he was virtually alone in his residence. In addition, we might observe that Saturn is withdrawing or dynamically cadent in Example #2, which suggests something that goes on for a while and peters out (as the conflicts at Siffīn were inconclusive and drawn out). But in Example #3, he is dynamically more angular or advancing (since his degree is later than that of the Midheaven), and so it might show a decisive blow and quick end. It is interesting that Sahl does *not* explicitly say that being in the eleventh sign makes Saturn any "better."

Second, Sahl introduces two symbolic and familiar timing techniques. He uses the 6° (or rather, 5°) in longitude between the two malefics to suggest that the unrest will culminate in so many months: from March to October is 6-7 months. Then, he profects from the Ascendant in Aquarius to Saturn in the eleventh sign: this means that at least certain things about the year will be stable until the eleventh month, or early 693 AD. I am not sure exactly what this refers to, but perhaps it is the invasions of northern Africa in 693 ordered by the Caliph 'Abd al-Malik as part of the "restoration" of complete 'Umayyad control.

♌   ♌   ♌

1 And this is another image. **2** I looked in the revolution of this year at the Ascendant, and the stakes, and the positions of the planets.

3 The Ascendant was Aquarius, and Venus and the Moon in it, and they did not have testimony [in it]. **4** And the lord of the Ascendant is Saturn, and he is in the eleventh from the Ascendant, and with him is Mars; and they are both in the eleventh from the position of the Moon. **5** And Saturn was the greater of the planets in testimony over the condition of the citizens.

6 And Mars is the lord of the Midheaven: he is not looking at his place, [and is] not received.[14]

7 And the Moon (who is the luminary of the night) is in the Ascendant, not received. **8** The position of the Moon from Saturn indicates what the matter of the years indicated.[15]

9 And the Sun pushed his strength to Saturn (and [Saturn] is the lord of the year, and the indicator of the citizens), indicating that a king is destroyed in this year: the citizens will kill him.[16] **10** And there will be rebellion and violence in the people, and tribulation, except that it is not an example of the year which I described before.[17] **11** Because the lord of *that* year is Saturn, and [there] he is in the tenth sign, in his exaltation, retrograde: [that] signifies the power of the war and great killing. **12** And in *this* year he is in the eleventh sign from the Ascendant.[18]

---

[14] Mars rules Scorpio and the Midheaven but is in aversion to it in Sagittarius, so cannot see it. He also is not applying to Jupiter nor any other slower planet.

[15] I am not sure exactly what this sentence is communicating. It could relate to a timing technique (such as 11 months: see **15** below), or could simply mean (as Sahl implies below) that being in the eleventh makes him less harmful. On the other hand, the Latin version has "Sun" instead of "year," which is suggestive because the next sentence immediately describes the Sun's relation to Saturn, too.

[16] Astrologically, this might mean that because Saturn indicates the people, but (a) is a malefic, and (b) the significator of the king (Mars) is in aversion and conjoined to him, harm will come to the king from the people. Sahl's mention of the Sun might be due to the fact that the Sun is a natural significator of kingship. Historically, ibn al-Zubayr suffered massive defections to the 'Umayyads, particularly during the final siege: so it is true that his former subjects turned against him. It might also be significant that Sahl says *a* king will be killed: could this indicate something about his political thoughts, namely that ibn al-Zubayr was not *the* proper Caliph?

[17] That is, Sahl's Example #2.

[18] Astrologically, the events should be different. In a historical sense, Sahl seems to say that the transition from the last "rightly guided" Caliph from the original period, to the 'Umayyads (i.e., devolving from the Battle of Siffin in Example #2) was more significant than the rebellion and death of ibn al-Zubayr.

536 APPENDICES

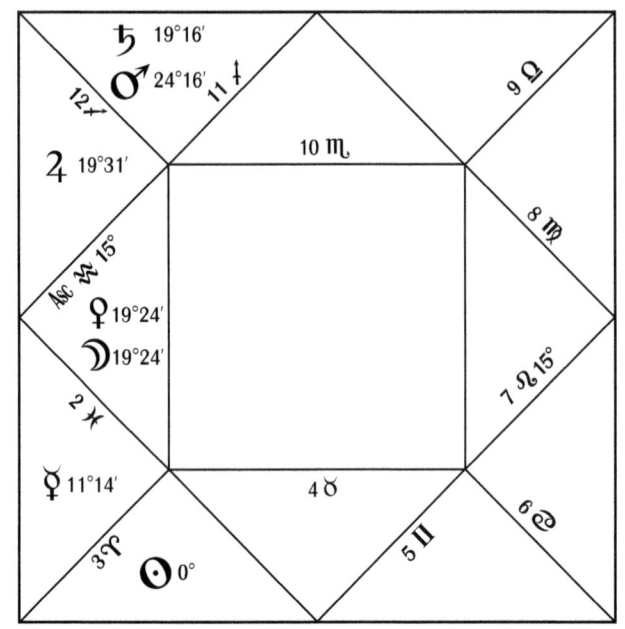

Figure 91: Version (adapted from MS) of Sahl's Example #3 (692 AD)

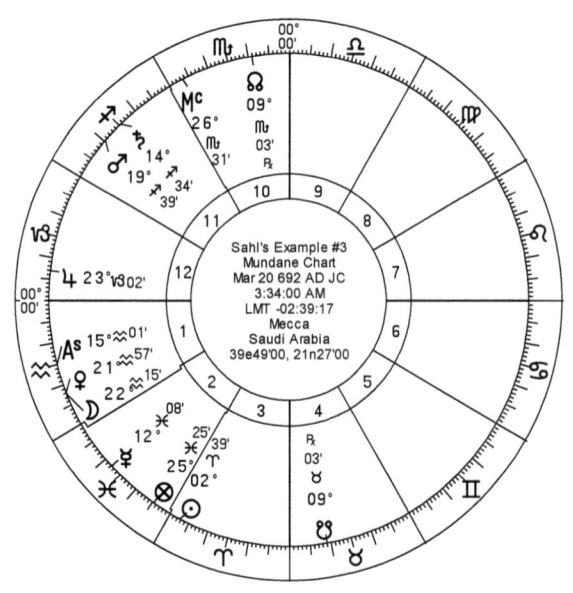

Figure 92: Sahl's Example #3 (692 AD), tropical zodiac

13 And that [civil unrest] will be in the sixth month because of the degrees of Saturn from Mars.[19] **14** And livestock will flourish, and the people will flourish, and the cold of their winter will be intense in addition to what I described.

15 And I also revolved the year, and its lord was Saturn: so it was safe until one month remained of it.[20] **16** So the king of the clime died, and the people were in confusion, and piety disappeared, and rebellion was stirred up.

Sahl's Example #4: Reign & death of 'Umar II (Aries Ingress, 719 AD)

Comment by Dykes. This is the Aries ingress for March 21, 719 AD,[21] excerpted by Abū Ma'shar in *Scito* Ch. 96. The planetary positions in Beatty are pretty reliably 2°-3° lower than the true tropical values, as we have seen before. The rising degree is missing in Vatican, and seems to be 8° in Beatty. It is cast for the 'Umayyad capital, Damascus.

Sahl's text describes a briefly positive period for the Muslim world, the reign of 'Umayyad Caliph 'Umar II (r. 717-720). He had been governor of the Hijāz (which included Medina) but had come to the Caliphate reluctantly, as his cousin, Caliph Sulaymān, died on the way to attack Constantinople. He was considered a very moral man (**13**), a reformer interested in education (**15**), which endeared him to the people (**12**): encouraging proper social behavior, public works, tax reform, institutions for the poor, allowing greater political participation for non-Arabs, and fighting state corruption. The first collection of the *hadith* (the sayings of Muhammad) was begun under him. However, military expansionists among the 'Umayyads were angry at his interests in arbitration or canceling certain military operations (such as the Constantinople siege), and other elites were upset by his cancellation or changing of their customary privileges, fiefdoms, and—to be succinct— financial handouts.

---

[19] There are about 6° (but actually 5°) between them, yielding 6 months. Ibn al-Zubayr was killed around October, 692 AD.

[20] By "revolve," Sahl seems to mean "rotate" by performing a monthly profection: that is, since the Ascendant (Aquarius) represents the first month, and Saturn is in the eleventh, the difficulties indicated by Saturn will not manifest until the monthly profection reaches him.

[21] Sources: Vatican 174R, lines 2-17 (image on 174R); Beatty 269, line 3 – 270, line 14 (image on 269).

In the end, he was poisoned by 'Umayyad elites in 720, near the end of this revolution (**14, 16-19**), which led to violent clashes as various political and military interests tried to reassert their power. This seems to be what Sahl alludes to in **14** and **17** when he speaks of the management of the chart coming to Saturn. I assume he is speaking of the profection or primary direction of the Ascendant to the body of Saturn, which would have corresponded to December 719 (but not in early 720, when the poisoning actually happened).

ის ის ის

1 And this year reached Aquarius from the root of the conjunction,[22] and the Ascendant and the places of the planets were based on what is established in this image.[23] **2** I looked in the revolution of this year at the Ascendant, and the stakes, and the places of the planets: and the Ascendant was Aquarius, and the stakes upright.

3 And in the Ascendant was the Moon and Venus, both alien,[24] not received, except for the Moon: she is pushing her power to Saturn, and he receives her. **4** And the year had reached the Ascendant.[25]

5 And Saturn is in the tenth sign, in the Midheaven, retrograde. **6** And Mars is under the rays, entering into burning and the third sign, in the place of religion.

7 And Venus and Jupiter are between his hands, mixing with him[26] in the east.[27] **8** And the revolution is in the night.

9 And Saturn is the lord of the year and the indicator of the citizens, and he is receiving the Moon (the luminary of the night). **10** And Mars is not looking at Saturn.

---

[22] From the alleged Libra Ascendant of 571, the annual profection would have reached Aquarius in 719.
[23] Omitting لم ينزلها in Beatty.
[24] That is, "peregrine."
[25] Again, the profection from the Libra Ascendant of 571, to the same sign as this Ascendant.
[26] This verb is in the masculine singular, so cannot refer to both Venus and Jupiter (i.e., Mars being between *their* hands).
[27] Or perhaps, "easternness" (المشرق). Nevertheless, I do not understand what Sahl means by this entire sentence.

APPENDIX C: CHART EXAMPLES FROM SAHL 539

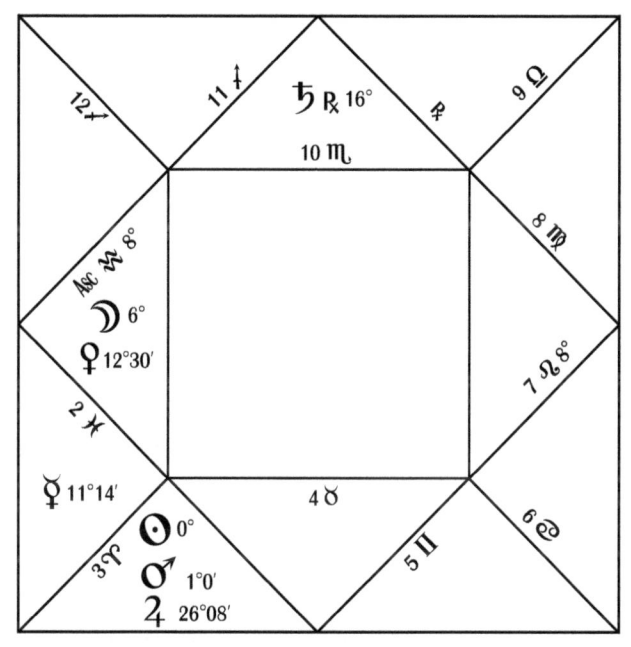

Figure 93: Version (adapted from MS) of Sahl's Example #4 (719 AD)

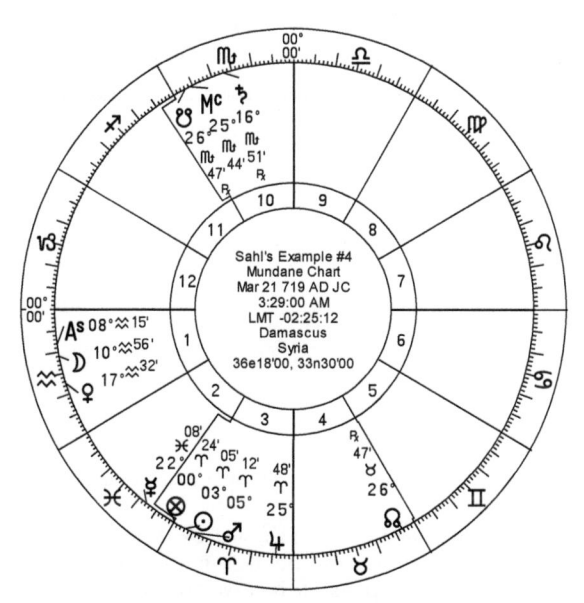

Figure 94: Sahl's Example #4 (modern tropical)

11 The place of Venus and the Moon from Saturn indicates the excellence of the condition of the citizens, and the harshness of the cold of winter, and the violent blowing of the winds, and an abundance of locusts. **12** And the thoughts of the people are good, and they are secure in good health, and the livestock flourishes.

13 And because of the place of Mars (the lord of the tenth) from the Sun (the indicator of the king), and because of the position of one from another, and their falling away from Saturn (the lord of the Ascendant, that is, the Ascendant of the year)—and he is in the position of the authority—it necessitates the gentleness of the king, and his piety, and the sincerity of his intention; and because of the place of Jupiter in the third.

14 And because of the place of Saturn and the degree of Mars in his position, it necessitates the ruin of the king and the confusion of the people's condition at the end of the month[28] of this year.

15 And because of the place of Mercury (the lord of the eighth) in the second from the Ascendant, it necessitates the excellence of the people's condition and the profit of their commerce, and the excellence of their learning, because Mercury [does not] suffer damage[29] by the infortunes.

16 And the lord of this year is Saturn, and he is retrograde in the Midheaven, in the place of [authority, and so he indicates][30] the shedding of blood, and plagues. **17** And whereas the Moon and Venus are connected to him,[31] the evil was extinguished until the management comes to be in the position of the body of Saturn (who is the lord of the year). **18** And even if Mars looked at Saturn, it would not corrupt what Venus and the Moon had indicated about the soundness of the condition. **19** And God is more knowledgeable.

---

[28] This should probably read "months" (plural), or perhaps even "last month," shortly after 'Umar II's assassination.

[29] Adding "not" and reading أذي for یری (Vat.) and دي (Beatty). As it stands, Vatican would read, "he *is* seen by the infortunes." But he is not seen by Mars, and the point is that he is not *damaged* by their bad aspects. He is in aversion to Mars, and trines Saturn.

[30] Added by Dykes, since the tenth by itself does not indicate the shedding of blood.

[31] But لها could also be read as a negative particle (لها), meaning they are *not* connected to him. The problem is that while Venus at least is connected to him, both Venus and the Moon are overcome by his superior square, which should damage them. But perhaps Sahl is thinking that because they are in his sign, he will not harm them.

APPENDIX D: TABLE OF TURNS (MIGHTY *FARDĀRS*)

In my Introduction I described the Turns, which are a form of mundane *fardār*. Each period is ruled by paired sign and planet, beginning with Aries-Saturn, and lasts for 360 sidereal years (of 365.259 days apiece). The question is: when do they begin? According to 'Umar-Kankah in Section I.5, Māshā'allāh's indicator conjunction in 3381 BC was the beginning of the Cancer-Saturn Turn (#64 below). Although the sidereal parameters of Abū Ma'shar and Māshā'allāh were incorrect, so that these dates did not actually correspond to the conjunctions and events they believed, I supply a table generated from Excel to show the length and order of the periods. Remember that the days listed here are in the (incorrect) medieval sidereal years; anyone wishing to use it should employ correct modern sidereal or tropical values for the length of the year.

			First Day	Last Day
1.	♈	♄	0.00	131,493.24
2.	♉	♃	131,493.24	262,986.48
3.	♊	♂	262,986.48	394,479.72
4.	♋	☉	394,479.72	525,972.96
5.	♌	♀	525,972.96	657,466.20
6.	♍	☿	657,466.20	788,959.44
7.	♎	☽	788,959.44	920,452.68
8.	♏	♄	920,452.68	1,051,945.92
9.	♐	♃	1,051,945.92	1,183,439.16
10.	♑	♂	1,183,439.16	1,314,932.40
11.	♒	☉	1,314,932.40	1,446,425.64
12.	♓	♀	1,446,425.64	1,577,918.88
13.	♈	☿	1,577,918.88	1,709,412.12
14.	♉	☽	1,709,412.12	1,840,905.36
15.	♊	♄	1,840,905.36	1,972,398.60
16.	♋	♃	1,972,398.60	2,103,891.84
17.	♌	♂	2,103,891.84	2,235,385.08
18.	♍	☉	2,235,385.08	2,366,878.32
19.	♎	♀	2,366,878.32	2,498,371.56
20.	♏	☿	2,498,371.56	2,629,864.80
21.	♐	☽	2,629,864.80	2,761,358.04
22.	♑	♄	2,761,358.04	2,892,851.28
23.	♒	♃	2,892,851.28	3,024,344.52
24.	♓	♂	3,024,344.52	3,155,837.76
25.	♈	☉	3,155,837.76	3,287,331.00
26.	♉	♀	3,287,331.00	3,418,824.24

27.	♊	☿	3,418,824.24	3,550,317.48
28.	♋	☽	3,550,317.48	3,681,810.72
29.	♌	♄	3,681,810.72	3,813,303.96
30.	♍	♃	3,813,303.96	3,944,797.20
31.	♎	♂	3,944,797.20	4,076,290.44
32.	♏	☉	4,076,290.44	4,207,783.68
33.	♐	♀	4,207,783.68	4,339,276.92
34.	♑	☿	4,339,276.92	4,470,770.16
35.	♒	☽	4,470,770.16	4,602,263.40
36.	♓	♄	4,602,263.40	4,733,756.64
37.	♈	♃	4,733,756.64	4,865,249.88
38.	♉	♂	4,865,249.88	4,996,743.12
39.	♊	☉	4,996,743.12	5,128,236.36
40.	♋	♀	5,128,236.36	5,259,729.60
41.	♌	☿	5,259,729.60	5,391,222.84
42.	♍	☽	5,391,222.84	5,522,716.08
43.	♎	♄	5,522,716.08	5,654,209.32
44.	♏	♃	5,654,209.32	5,785,702.56
45.	♐	♂	5,785,702.56	5,917,195.80
46.	♑	☉	5,917,195.80	6,048,689.04
47.	♒	♀	6,048,689.04	6,180,182.28
48.	♓	☿	6,180,182.28	6,311,675.52
49.	♈	☽	6,311,675.52	6,443,168.76
50.	♉	♄	6,443,168.76	6,574,662.00
51.	♊	♃	6,574,662.00	6,706,155.24
52.	♋	♂	6,706,155.24	6,837,648.48
53.	♌	☉	6,837,648.48	6,969,141.72
54.	♍	♀	6,969,141.72	7,100,634.96
55.	♎	☿	7,100,634.96	7,232,128.20
56.	♏	☽	7,232,128.20	7,363,621.44
57.	♐	♄	7,363,621.44	7,495,114.68
58.	♑	♃	7,495,114.68	7,626,607.92
59.	♒	♂	7,626,607.92	7,758,101.16
60.	♓	☉	7,758,101.16	7,889,594.40
61.	♈	♀	7,889,594.40	8,021,087.64
62.	♉	☿	8,021,087.64	8,152,580.88
63.	♊	☽	8,152,580.88	8,284,074.12
64.	♋	♄	8,284,074.12	8,415,567.36
65.	♌	♃	8,415,567.36	8,547,060.60
66.	♍	♂	8,547,060.60	8,678,553.84
67.	♎	☉	8,678,553.84	8,810,047.08
68.	♏	♀	8,810,047.08	8,941,540.32
69.	♐	☿	8,941,540.32	9,073,033.56
70.	♑	☽	9,073,033.56	9,204,526.80
71.	♒	♄	9,204,526.80	9,336,020.04

Appendix D: Table of Turns (Mighty Fardārs) 543

72.	♓	♃	9,336,020.04	9,467,513.28
73.	♈	♂	9,467,513.28	9,599,006.52
74.	♉	☉	9,599,006.52	9,730,499.76
75.	♊	♀	9,730,499.76	9,861,993.00
76.	♋	☿	9,861,993.00	9,993,486.24
77.	♌	☽	9,993,486.24	10,124,979.48
78.	♍	♄	10,124,979.48	10,256,472.72
79.	♎	♃	10,256,472.72	10,387,965.96
80.	♏	♂	10,387,965.96	10,519,459.20
81.	♐	☉	10,519,459.20	10,650,952.44
82.	♑	♀	10,650,952.44	10,782,445.68
83.	♒	☿	10,782,445.68	10,913,938.92
84.	♓	☽	10,913,938.92	11,045,432.16

Figure 95: Table of Turns (mighty *fardārs*)

GLOSSARY

This glossary is an expanded version of the one in my 2010 *Introductions to Traditional Astrology* (*ITA*), with the addition of other terms from my translations since then. After most definitions is a reference to sections and Appendices of *ITA* (including my introduction to it) for further reading—for the most part, they do *not* refer to passages in this book (and if so, are labeled as such).

- **Absent from** (Ar. *ghāʾib ʿan*). Equivalent to **aversion**.
- **Accident** (Lat. *accidens*, Ar. *ḥādith*). An event which "befalls" or "happens" to someone, though not necessarily something bad.
- **Adding in course.** See **Course**.
- **Advancing, advancement** (Ar. *'iqbāl, muqbil, zāʾid*; Lat. *accedens*). When a planet is in an **angle** or **succeedent** (sometimes ambiguous as to **whole sign** or **quadrant division**), preferably moving clockwise by diurnal motion towards one of the angular axes or **stakes**. The opposite of **retreating** and **withdrawing**. See III.3 and the Introduction §6.
- **Advantageous places.** One of two schemes of **houses** which indicate affairs/planets which are more busy or good in the context of the chart (III.4). The seven-place scheme according to Timaeus and reported in *Carmen* includes only certain signs which **aspect** the **Ascendant** by **whole-sign**, and suggests that these places are advantageous for the *native* because they aspect the Ascendant. The eight-place scheme according to Nechepso (III.4) lists all of the **angular** and **succeedent** places, suggesting places which are stimulating and advantageous for a planet *in itself*.
- **Ages of man.** Ptolemy's division of a typical human life span into periods ruled by planets as **time lords**. See VII.3.
- **Agreeing signs.** Groups of signs which share some kind of harmonious quality. See I.9.5-6.
- *Alcochoden*. Latin transliteration for **Kadukhudhāh**.
- **Alien** (Lat. *alienus*, Ar. *gharīb*). See **Peregrine**.
- *Almuten*. A Latin transliteration for ***mubtazz***: see **Victor**.
- **Angles, succeedents, cadents.** A division of houses into three groups which show how powerfully and directly a planet acts. The angles are the 1st, 10th, 7th and 4th houses; the succeedents are the 2nd, 11th, 8th and 5th; the cadents are the 12th, 9th, 6th and 3rd (but see **cadent** below). But the exact

regions in question will depend upon whether and how one uses **whole-sign** and **quadrant houses**, especially since traditional texts refer to an angle or pivot (Gr. *kentron*, Ar. *watad*) as either (1) equivalent to the **whole-sign** angles from the **Ascendant**, or (2) the degrees of the **Ascendant-Midheaven** axes themselves, or (3) **quadrant houses** (and their associated strengths) as measured from the degrees of the axes. See I.12-13 and III.3-4, and the Introduction §6.

- **Antiscia** (sing. *antiscion*), "throwing shadows." Refers to a degree mirrored across an axis drawn from 0° Capricorn to 0° Cancer. For example, 10° Cancer has 20° Gemini as its antiscion. See I.9.2.
- **Apogee.** Typically, the furthest point a planet can be from the earth on the circle of the **deferent**. See II.0-1.
- **Applying, application.** When a planet is in a state of **connection**, moving so as to make the connection exact. Planets **assembled** together or in **aspect** by sign and not yet connected by the relevant degrees, are only "wanting" to be connected.
- **Arisings.** See **Ascensions**.
- **Ascendant**. Usually the entire rising sign, but often specified as the exact rising degree. In **quadrant houses**, a space following the exact rising degree up to the cusp of the 2nd house.
- **Ascensions.** Degrees on the celestial equator, measured in terms of how many degrees pass the meridian as an entire sign or **bound** (or other spans of zodiacal degrees) passes across the horizon. They are often used in the predictive technique of ascensional times, as an approximation for **directions**. See Appendix E.
- **Aspect/regard**. One planet aspects or regards another if they are in signs which are configured to each other by a **sextile**, **square**, **trine**, or **opposition**. See III.6 and **Whole signs**. A connection by degrees or orbs is a much more intense of an aspect.
- **Assembly**. When two or more planets are in the same sign, and more intensely if within 15°. (It is occasionally used in Arabic to indicate the conjunction of the Sun and Moon at the New Moon, but the more common word for that is **meeting**). See III.5.
- **Aversion.** Being in the second, sixth, eighth, or twelfth sign from a place. For instance, a planet in Gemini is in the twelfth from, and therefore in aversion to, Cancer. Such places are in aversion because they cannot **aspect** it by the classical scheme of aspects. See III.6.1.

- *Azamene*. Equivalent to **Chronic illness**.
- **Bad ones.** See **Benefic/malefic**.
- **Barring.** See **Blocking**.
- **Bearing** (Lat. *habitude*). Hugo's term for any of the many possible planetary conditions and relationships. These may be found in III and IV.
- **Benefic/malefic.** A division of the planets into groups that cause or signify typically "good" things (Jupiter, Venus, usually the Sun and Moon) or "bad" things (Mars, Saturn). Mercury is considered variable. See V.9.
- **Benevolents.** See **Benefic/malefic**.
- **Besieging.** Equivalent to **Enclosure**.
- **Bicorporeal signs.** Equivalent to "common" signs. See **Quadruplicity**.
- **Blocking** (sometimes called "prohibition"). When a planet bars another planet from completing a **connection**, either through its own body or ray. See III.14.
- **Bodyguarding.** Planetary relationships in which some planet protects another, used in determining social eminence and prosperity. See III.28.
- **Bounds.** Unequal divisions of the zodiac in each sign, each bound being ruled by one of the five non-**luminaries**. Sometimes called "terms," they are one of the five classical **dignities**. See VII.4.
- **Bright, smoky, empty, dark degrees**. Certain degrees of the zodiac said to affect how conspicuous or obscure the significations of planets or the Ascendant are. See VII.7.
- **Burned up** (or "combust," Lat. *combustus*). Normally, when a planet is between about 1° and 7.5° away from the Sun. See II.9-10, and **In the heart**.
- **Burnt path** (Lat. *via combusta*). A span of degrees in Libra and Scorpio in which a planet (especially the Moon) is considered to be harmed or less able to effect its significations. Some astrologers identify it as between 15° Libra and 15° Scorpio; others between the exact degree of the **fall** of the Sun in 19° Libra and the exact degree of the fall of the Moon in 3° Scorpio. See IV.3.
- *Bust*. Certain hours measured from the New Moon, in which it is considered favorable or unfavorable to undertake an action or perform an **election**. See VIII.4.
- **Busy places.** Equivalent to the **Advantageous places**.
- **Cadent** (Lat. *cadens*, "falling"). This is used in two ways: a planet or place may be cadent from the **angles** (being in the 3rd, 6th, 9th, or 12th), or else

cadent from the **Ascendant** (namely, in **aversion** to it, being in the 12th, 8th, 6th, or 2nd). See I.12, III.4, and III.6.1.
- **Cardinal.** Equivalent to "movable" signs. See **Quadruplicity.**
- **Cazimi:** see **In the heart.**
- **Celestial equator.** The projection of earth's equator out into the universe, forming one of the three principal celestial coordinate systems.
- **Centers of the Moon.** Also called the "posts" or "foundations" of the Moon. Angular distances between the Sun and Moon throughout the lunar month, indicating possible times of weather changes and rain. See *AW1*.
- **Choleric.** See **Humor.**
- **Chronic illness (degrees of).** Degrees which are especially said to indicate chronic illness, due to their association with certain fixed stars. See VII.10.
- **Cleansed** (Ar. *naqiyy*, Lat. *mundus*). Ideally, when a planet in **aversion** to the **malefics** (but perhaps some would consider a **sextile** or **trine** acceptable?).
- **Clothed.** Equivalent to one planet being in an **assembly** or **aspect/regard** with another, and therefore partaking in (being "clothed in") the other planet's characteristics.
- **Collection.** When two planets **aspecting** each other but not in an applying **connection**, each apply to a third planet. See III.12.
- **Combust.** See **Burned up.**
- **Commanding/obeying.** A division of the signs into those which command or obey each other (used sometimes in **synastry**). See I.9.
- **Common signs.** See **Quadruplicity.**
- **Complexion.** Primarily, a mixture of elements and their qualities so as to indicate or produce some effect. Secondarily it refers to planetary combinations, following the naturalistic theory that planets have elemental qualities with causal power, which can interact with each other.
- **Confer.** See **Pushing.**
- **Configured.** To be in a whole-sign **aspect**, though not necessarily by degree.
- **Conjunction (of planets).** See **Assembly** and **Connection.**
- **Conjunction/prevention.** The position of the New (conjunction) or Full (prevention) Moon most immediately prior to a **nativity** or other chart. For the prevention, some astrologers use the degree of the Moon, others

the degree of the luminary which was above the earth at the time of the prevention. See VIII.1.2.
- **Connection.** When a planet applies to another planet (by body in the same sign, or by ray in **aspecting** signs), within a particular number of degrees up to exactness. See III.7.
- **Conquer** (Lat. *vinco*). Normally, the equivalent of being a **victor**, which comes from the same Latin verb.
- **Convertible.** Equivalent to the movable signs. See **Quadruplicity**. But sometimes planets (especially Mercury) are called convertible because their **gender** is affected by their placement in the chart.
- **Convey.** See **Pushing**.
- **Corruption.** Normally, the harming of a planet (see IV.3-4), such as being in a **square** with a **malefic** planet. But sometimes, equivalent to **Detriment**.
- **Counsel** (Lat. *consilium*). A term used by Hugo and other Latin translators of Arabic, for "management" (III.18). An **applying** planet **pushes** or gifts or grants its counsel or management to another planet, and that other planet **receives** or gathers it.
- **Course, increasing/decreasing in.** For practical purposes, this means a planet is quicker than average in motion. But in geometric astronomy, it refers to what **sector** of the **deferent** the center of a planet's **epicycle** is. (The planet's position within the four sectors of the epicycle itself will also affect its apparent speed.) In the two sectors that are closest to the planet's **perigee**, the planet will apparently be moving faster; in the two sectors closest to the **apogee**, it will apparently be moving slower. See II.0-1.
- **Crooked/straight.** A division of the signs into those which rise quickly and are more parallel to the horizon (crooked), and those which arise more slowly and closer to a right angle from the horizon (straight or direct). In the northern hemisphere, the signs from Capricorn to Gemini are crooked (but in the southern one, straight); those from Cancer to Sagittarius are straight (but in the southern one, crooked).
- **Crossing over.** When a planet begins to **separate** from an exact **connection**. See III.7-8.
- **Cutting of light.** Three ways in which a **connection** is prevented: either by **obstruction** from the following sign, **escape** within the same sign, or by **barring**. See III.23.
- *Darījān.* An alternative **face** system attributed to the Indians. See VII.6.

- **Decan**. Equivalent to **face**.
- **Declination**. The equivalent on the celestial **equator**, of geographical latitude. The signs of northern declination (Aries through Virgo) stretch northward of the **ecliptic**, while those of southern declination (Libra through Pisces) stretch southward.
- **Decline, declining** (Gr. *apoklima*, Ar. *saqaṭa*). Equivalent to **cadence** by whole sign, but perhaps in some Arabic texts referring rather to cadence by **quadrant house** divisions.
- **Deferent.** The circle on which a planet's **epicycle** travels. See II.0-1.
- **Descension**. Equivalent to **fall**.
- **Detriment** (or Ar. "corruption," "unhealthiness," "harm."). More broadly (as "corruption"), it refers to any way in which a planet is harmed or its operation thwarted (such as by being **burned up**). But it also (as "harm") refers specifically to the sign opposite a planet's **domicile**. Libra is the detriment of Mars. See I.6 and I.8.
- **Dexter**. "Right": see **Right/left**.
- **Diameter**. Equivalent to **Opposition**.
- **Dignity** (Lat. "worthiness"; Ar. *ḥaẓẓ*, "good fortune, allotment"). Any of five ways of assigning rulership or responsibility to a planet (or sometimes, to a **Node**) over some portion of the zodiac. They are often listed in the following order: **domicile, exaltation, triplicity, bound, face/decan**. Each dignity has its own meaning and effect and use, and two of them have opposites: the opposite of domicile is **detriment**, the opposite of exaltation is **fall**. See I.3, I.4, I.6-7, VII.4 for the assignments; I.8 for some descriptive analogies; VIII.2.1 and VIII.2.2*f* for some predictive uses of domiciles and bounds.
- **Directions**. A predictive technique which is more precise than using **ascensions**, and defined by Ptolemy in terms of proportional semi-arcs. There is some confusion in how directing works, because of the difference between the astronomical method of directions and how astrologers look at charts. Astronomically, a point in the chart (the significator) is considered as stationary, and other planets and their **aspects** by degree (or even the **bounds**) are sent forth (promittors) as though the heavens keep turning by **primary motion**, until they come to the significator. The degrees between the significator and promittor are converted into years of life. But when looking at the chart, it seems as though the significator is being **released** counterclockwise in the order of signs, so that it **distributes**

through the bounds or comes to the bodies or aspects of promittors. Direction by **ascensions** takes the latter perspective, though the result is the same. Some later astrologers allow the distance between a significator/releaser and the promittor to be measured in either direction, yielding "converse" directions in addition to the classical "direct" directions. See VIII.2.2, Appendix E, and Gansten.
- **Disregard**. Equivalent to **Separation**.
- **Distribution**. The **direction** of a **releaser** (often the degree of the **Ascendant**) through the **bounds**. The bound **lord** of the distribution is the "distributor," and any body or ray which the **releaser** encounters is the "**partner**." See VIII.2.2f, and *PN3*.
- **Distributor**. The **bound lord** of a **directed releaser**. See **Distribution**.
- **Diurnal**. See **Sect**.
- **Division** (Ar. *qismah*). In the context of **house** theory, it refers to any **quadrant house** system, as these are derived by dividing each of the the **quarters** by three. Synonymous with houses by **equation**, and opposed to houses by **number**.
- **Domain**. A **sect** and **gender**-based planetary condition. See III.2.
- **Domicile**. One of the five **dignities**. A sign of the zodiac, insofar as it is owned or managed by one of the planets. For example, Aries is the domicile of Mars, and so Mars is its domicile **lord**. See I.6.
- **Doryphory** (Gr. *doruphoria*). Equivalent to **Bodyguarding**.
- **Double-bodied**. Equivalent to the common signs. See **Quadruplicity**.
- **Dragon**: see **Node**.
- **Drawn back** (Lat. *reductus*). Equivalent to being **cadent** from an **angle**.
- **Dodecametorion**. Equivalent to **Twelfth-part**.
- *Duodecima*. Equivalent to **Twelfth-part**.
- *Dustūriyyah*. Equivalent to **Bodyguarding**.
- **East** (Lat. *oriens*). The Ascendant: normally the rising sign, but sometimes the degree of the Ascendant itself.
- **Eastern/western (by quadrant)**. When a planet is in one any of the **quadrants** as defined by the axial degrees. The eastern quadrants are between the degrees of the **Ascendant** and **Midheaven**, and between those of the **Descendant** and *Imum Caeli*. The western quadrants are between the degrees of the Midheaven and Descendant, and between those of the *Imum Caeli* and the Ascendant.

GLOSSARY 551

- **Eastern/western (of the Sun)**. A position relative to the Sun, often called "oriental" or "occidental," respectively. These terms are used in two major ways: (1) when a planet is in a position to rise before the Sun by being in an early degree (eastern) or is in a position to set after the Sun by being in a later degree (western). But in ancient languages, these words also refer mean "arising" or "setting/sinking," on an analogy with the Sun rising and setting: so sometimes they refer to (2) a planet arising out of, or sinking under, the **Sun's rays**, no matter what side of the Sun it is on (in some of my translations I call this "pertaining to arising" and "pertaining to sinking"). Astrological authors do not always clarify what sense is meant, and different astronomers and astrologers have different definitions for exactly what positions count as being eastern or western. See II.10.
- **Ecliptic.** The path defined by the Sun's motion through the zodiac, defined as having 0° ecliptical latitude. In tropical astrology, the ecliptic (and therefore the zodiacal signs) begins at the intersection of the ecliptic and the celestial equator.
- **Election** (lit. "choice"). The deliberate choosing of an appropriate time to undertake an action, or determining when to avoid an action; but astrologers normally refer to the chart of the time itself as an election.
- **Element.** One of the four basic qualities. fire, air, water, earth) describing how matter and energy operate, and used to describe the significations and operations of planets and signs. They are usually described by pairs of four other basic qualities (hot, cold, wet, dry). For example, Aries is a fiery sign, and hot and dry; Mercury is typically treated as cold and dry (earthy). See I.3, I.7, and Book V.
- **Emptiness of the course.** Medievally, when a planet does not complete a **connection** for as long as it is in its current sign. In Hellenistic astrology, when a planet does not complete a connection within the next 30°. See III.9.
- **Enclosure.** When a planet has the rays or bodies of the **malefics** (or alternatively, the **benefics**) on either side of it, by degree or sign. See IV.4.2.
- **Epicycle.** A circle on the **deferent**, on which a planet turns. See II.0-1.
- **Equant.** A circle used to measure the mean position of a planet. See II.0-1.
- **Equation.** (1) In astronomical theory, a value that is added to or subtracted from a mean or provisional value, in order to convert it to a true value. (2) In **house** theory, it refers to any **quadrant house** system, where house

divisions are derived by exact calculation or equation (Ar. *al-taswiyah*); synonymous with house division by **division**, and **whole-sign** houses by **number**.
- **Equator (celestial)**. The projection of the earth's equator into space, forming a great circle. Its equivalent of latitude is called **declination**, while its equivalent of longitude is called **right ascension** (and is measured from the beginning of Aries, from the intersection of it and the **ecliptic**).
- **Escape**. When a planet wants to **connect** with a second one, but the second one moves into the next sign before it is completed, and the first planet makes a **connection** with a different, unrelated one instead. See III.22.
- **Essence** (Lat. *substantia*). Deriving ultimately from Aristotelian philosophy, the fundamental nature or character of a planet or sign, which allows it to indicate or cause certain phenomena (such as the essence of Mars being responsible for indicating fire, iron, war, *etc*.). This word has often been translated as "substance," which is a less accurate term.
- **Essential/accidental**. A common way of distinguishing a planet's conditions, usually according to **dignity** (essential, I.2) and some other condition such as its **aspects** (accidental). See IV.1-5 for many accidental conditions.
- **Exaltation**. One of the five **dignities**. A sign in which a planet (or sometimes, a **Node**) signifies its matter in a particularly authoritative and refined way. The exaltation is sometimes identified with a particular degree in that sign. See I.6.
- **Face**. One of the five **dignities**. The zodiac is divided into 36 faces of 10° each, starting with the beginning of Aries. See I.5.
- **Facing**. A relationship between a planet and a **luminary**, if their respective signs are configured at the same distance as their **domiciles** are. For example, Leo (ruled by the Sun) is two signs to the **right** of Libra (ruled by Venus). When Venus is **western** and two signs away from wherever the Sun is, she will be in the facing of the Sun. See II.11.
- **Fall** (Gr. *hupsōma*, Ar. *hubūṭ*, Lat. *casus, descensio*). The sign opposite a planet's **exaltation**; sometimes called "descension." See I.6.
- **Falling** (Lat. *cadens*, Ar. *saqaṭa*). Refers to being **cadent**, but sometimes ambiguous as to whether dynamically by **quadrant division** or by **whole sign** (which is also called **declining**).
- **Falling away from** (Ar. *sāqaṭ ʿan*). Equivalent to **aversion**.

GLOSSARY

- **Familiar** (Lat. *familiaris*). A hard-to-define term which suggests a sense of belonging and close relationship. (1) Sometimes it is contrasted with being **peregrine**, suggesting that a familiar planet is one which is a **lord** over a degree or **place** (that is, it has a **dignity** in it): for a dignity suggests belonging. (2) At other times, it refers to a familiar **aspect** (and probably the **sextile** or **trine** in particular): all of the family houses in a chart have a **whole-sign** aspect to the **Ascendant**.
- *Fardār*. See *Firdārīyyah*.
- **Feminine**. See **Gender**.
- **Feral** (Ar. *waḥshiyy*, Lat. *feralis*). Equivalent to **Wildness**.
- **Figure**. One of several polygons implied by an **aspect**. For example, a planet in Aries and one in Capricorn do not actually form a **square**, but they imply one because Aries and Capricorn, together with Libra and Cancer, form a square amongst themselves. See III.8.
- *Firdārīyyah* (pl. *firdārīyyāt*). A **time lord** method in which planets rule different periods of life, with each period broken down into sub-periods (there are also mundane versions). See VII.1.
- **Firm**. In terms of signs, the **fixed** signs: see **Quadruplicity**. For houses, equivalent to the **Angles**.
- **Fixed**. See **Quadruplicity**.
- **Foreign** (Lat. *extraneus*). Usually equivalent to **Peregrine**.
- **Fortunate**. Normally, a planet whose condition is made better by one of the **bearings** described in IV.
- **Fortunes**. See **Benefic/malefic**.
- **Foundations of the Moon**. See **Centers of the Moon**.
- **Free** (Ar. *nazīah*, Lat. *liber*). Sometimes, being **cleansed** of the **malefics**; at other times, being out of the **Sun's rays**.
- **Gender**. The division of signs, degrees, planets and hours into masculine and feminine groups. See I.3, V.10, V.14, VII.8.
- **Generosity and benefits**. Favorable relationships between signs and planets, as defined in III.26.
- **Good ones**. See **Benefic/malefic**.
- **Good places**. Equivalent to **Advantageous places**.
- **Governor** (Ar. *mustawlī*). A planet which has preeminence or rulership over some topic or indication (such as the governor over an eclipse); normally, it is a kind of **victor**.
- **Greater, middle, lesser years**. See **Planetary years**.

- **Ḥalb.** Probably Pahlavi for **sect**, but normally describes a rejoicing condition: see III.2.
- **Ḥayyiz.** Arabic for **domain**, normally a gender-intensified condition of *ḥalb*; but sometimes seems to refer to **sect**. See III.2.
- **Hexagon.** Equivalent to **Sextile.**
- **Hīlāj** (From the Pahlavi for "releaser"). Equivalent to **releaser.**
- **Hold onto.** Hugo's synonym for a planet being in or **transiting** a **sign.**
- **Horary astrology.** A late historical designation for **questions.**
- **Hours (planetary).** The assigning of rulership over hours of the day and night to planets. The hours of daylight (and night, respectively) are divided by 12, and each period is ruled first by the planet ruling that day, then the rest in descending planetary order. For example, on Sunday the Sun rules the first planetary "hour" from daybreak, then Venus, then Mercury, the Moon, Saturn, and so on. See V.13.
- **House.** A twelve-fold spatial division of a chart, in which each house signifies one or more areas of life. Two basic schemes are (1) **whole-sign** houses, in which the **signs** are equivalent to the houses, and (2) **quadrant houses.** But in the context of dignities and rulerships, "house" is the equivalent of **domicile.**
- **House-master.** Often called the *alcochoden* in Latin, from **kadukhudhāh** (the Pahlavi for "house-master"). One of the lords of the longevity **releaser,** preferably the **bound lord.** See VIII.1.3. But the Greek equivalent of this word (*oikodespotēs*, "house-master") is used in various ways in Hellenistic Greek texts, sometimes indicating the **lord** of a **domicile,** at other times the same longevity planet just mentioned, and at other times a kind of **victor** over the whole **nativity.**
- **Humor.** Any one of four fluids in the body (according to traditional medicine), the balance between which determines one's health and **temperament** (outlook and energy level). Choler or yellow bile is associated with fire and the choleric temperament; blood is associated with air and the sanguine temperament; phlegm is associated with water and the phlegmatic temperament; black bile is associated with earth and the melancholic temperament. See I.3.
- **IC.** See *Imum Caeli.*
- **Imum Caeli** (Lat., "lowest part of heaven"). The degree of the zodiac on which the lower half of the meridian circle falls; in **quadrant house** systems, it marks the beginning of the fourth **house.**

- **In the heart.** Often called *cazimi* in English texts, from the Ar. *kaṣmīmī*. A planet is in the heart of the Sun when it is either in the same degree as the Sun (according to Sahl b. Bishr and Rhetorius), or within 16' of longitude from him. See II.9.
- **Indicator.** A degree which is supposed to indicate the approximate position of the degree of the natal **Ascendant**, in cases where the time of birth is uncertain. See VIII.1.2.
- **Inferior.** The planets lower than the Sun: Venus, Mercury, Moon.
- **Infortunes.** See **Benefic/malefic**.
- *'Ittiṣāl*. Equivalent to **Connection**.
- **Joys.** Places in which the planets are said to "rejoice" in acting or signifying their natures. Joys by house are found in I.16; by sign in I.10.7.
- *Jārbakhtār* (From the Pahlavi for "distributor of time"). Equivalent to **Distributor**; see **Distribution**.
- *Kadukhudhāh* (From the Pahlavi for "house-master"), often called the *alcochoden* in Latin transliteration. See **House-master**.
- *Kardaja* (Ar. *kardajah*, from Sanskrit *kramajyā*). An interval used in the rows of astronomical tables such as in the *Almagest*. Each row begins with a value (called an "argument"), and one reads across to find the corresponding value used to correct such things as planetary positions. The increment or interval between each argument is a *kardaja*. A single table may use different increments based on theoretical considerations, levels of accuracy needed, *etc*. Some books of tables defined the *kardajas* in terms of sine functions. According to al-Hāshimī (1981, p. 143), the lower **sectors** of a planet's epicycle (closer to the earth, where it is retrograde) are the "fast" *kardajas*. But this probably also refers to the lower sectors of the eccentric or deferent circle, closer to a planet's **perigee**.
- *Kaṣmīmī*: see **In the heart**.
- **Kingdom.** Equivalent to **exaltation**.
- **Largesse and recompense.** A reciprocal relation in which one planet is rescued from being in its own **fall** or a **well**, and then returns the favor when the other planet is in its fall or well. See III.24.
- **Leader** (Lat. *dux*). Equivalent to a **significator** for some topic. The Arabic word for "significator" means to indicate something by pointing the way toward something: thus the significator for a topic or matter "leads" the astrologer to some answer. Used by some less popular Latin translators (such as Hugo of Santalla and Hermann of Carinthia).

- **Linger in** (Lat. *commoror*). Hugo's synonym for a planet being in or **transiting** through a **sign**.
- **Lodging-place** (Lat. *hospitium*). Hugo's synonym for a **house**, particularly the **sign** which occupies a house.
- **Look, look at** (Lat. *aspicio*, Ar. *naẓara*). Equivalent to **aspect**.
- **Lord of the year.** The **domicile lord** of a **profection**. The Sun and Moon are not allowed to be primary lords of the year, according to Persian doctrine. See VIII.2.1 and VIII.3.2, and Appendix F.
- **Lord.** A designation for the planet which has a particular **dignity**, but when used alone it usually means the **domicile** lord. For example, Mars is the lord of Aries.
- **Lord of the question.** In questions, the lord of the **house** of the **quaesited** matter. But sometimes, it refers to the client or **querent** whose question it is.
- **Lord of the year.** In mundane ingress charts, the planet that is the **victor** over the chart, indicating the general meanings of the year.
- **Lot.** Sometimes called "Parts." A place (often treated as equivalent to an entire sign) expressing a ratio derived from the position of three other parts of a chart. Normally, the distance between two places is measured in zodiacal order from one to the other, and this distance is projected forward from some other place (usually the Ascendant): where the counting stops, is the Lot. Lots are used both interpretively and predictively. See Book VI.
- **Lucky/unlucky.** See **Benefic/malefic**.
- **Luminary.** The Sun or Moon.
- **Malefic.** See **Benefic/malefic**.
- **Malevolents.** See **Benefic/malefic**.
- **Masculine.** See **Gender**.
- **Meeting** (Ar. *ʾijtimāʿ*). The conjunction of the Sun and Moon at the New Moon, which makes it a **connection** by body.
- **Melancholic.** See **Humor**.
- **Midheaven.** Either the tenth sign from the **Ascendant**, or the zodiacal degree on which the celestial meridian falls.
- **Minister.** A synonym for **Governor**.
- **Movable signs.** See **Quadruplicity**.
- *Mubtazz*. See **Victor**.
- **Mutable signs**. Equivalent to "common" signs. See **Quadruplicity**.

- *Namūdār*. Equivalent to **Indicator**.
- **Native.** The person whose birth chart it is.
- **Nativity.** Technically, a birth itself, but used by astrologers to describe the chart cast for the moment of a birth.
- **Ninth-parts.** Divisions of each sign into 9 equal parts of 3° 20' apiece, each ruled by a planet. Used predictively by some astrologers as part of the suite of **revolution** techniques. See VII.5.
- **Nobility.** Equivalent to **exaltation**.
- **Nocturnal.** See **Sect**.
- **Node.** The point on the ecliptic where a planet passes into northward latitude (its North Node or Head of the Dragon) or into southern latitude (its South Node or Tail of the Dragon). Normally only the Moon's Nodes are considered. See II.5 and V.8.
- **Northern/southern.** Either planets in northern or southern latitude in the zodiac (relative to the ecliptic), or in northern or southern declination relative to the celestial equator. See I.10.1.
- **Not-reception.** When an **applying** planet is in the **fall** of the planet being applied to.
- **Number** (Ar. *ᶜadad*). In the context of **house** theory, it refers to **whole-sign** houses (namely, by assigning the house numbers by counting to each sign); it is opposed to **quadrant houses** (by **division** or **equation**).
- **Oblique ascensions.** The **ascensions** used in making predictions by ascensional times or primary **directions**.
- **Obstruction.** When one planet is moving towards a second (wanting to be **connected** to it), but a third one in a later degrees goes **retrograde**, connects with the second one, and then with the first one. See III.21.
- **Occidental.** See **Eastern/western**.
- **Opening of the portals/doors.** Times of likely weather changes and rain, determined by certain **transits**. See VIII.3.4, and *AW1*.
- **Opposition.** An **aspect** either by **whole sign** or degree, in which the signs have a 180° relation to each other: for example, a planet in Aries is opposed to one in Libra.
- **Optimal place.** Also called "good" and "the best" places. These are probably a subset of the **advantageous places**, and probably only those houses which **aspect** the **Ascendant**. They definitely include the Ascendant, tenth, and eleventh houses, but may also include the ninth. They are probably also restricted only to houses above the horizon.

- **Orbs/bodies**. Called "orb" by the Latins, and "body" (*jirm*) by Arabic astrologers. A space of power or influence on each side of a planet's body or position, used to determine the intensity of interaction between different planets. See II.6.
- **Oriental**. See **Eastern/western**.
- **Overcoming**. When a planet is in the eleventh, tenth, or ninth sign from another planet (i.e., in a superior **sextile**, **square**, or **trine aspect**), though being in the tenth sign is considered a more dominant or even domineering position. See IV.4.1 and *PN3*'s Introduction, §15.
- **Own light**. This refers either to (1) a planet being a member of the **sect** of the chart (see V.9), or (2) a planet being out of the **Sun's rays** and not yet **connected** to another planet, so that it shines on its own without being **clothed** in another's influence (see II.9).
- **Part**. See **Lot**.
- **Partner**. The body or ray of any planet which a **directed releaser** encounters while being **distributed** through the **bounds**. But in some translations from Arabic, any of the **lords** of a place.
- **Peregrine** (Lat. *peregrinus*, Ar. *gharīb*), lit. "a stranger." When a planet is not in one of its five **dignities**. See I.9.
- **Perigee**. The position on a planet's **deferent** circle which is closest to the earth; it is opposite the **apogee**. See II.0-1.
- **Perverse** (Lat. *perversus*). Hugo's occasional term for (1) **malefic** planets, and (2) **places** in **aversion** to the **Ascendant** by **whole-sign**: definitely the twelfth and sixth, probably the eighth, and possibly the second.
- **Phlegmatic**. See **Humor**.
- **Pitted degrees**. Equivalent to **Welled degrees**.
- **Pivot**. Equivalent to **Angle**.
- **Place**. Equivalent to a **house**, and more often (and more anciently) a **whole-sign** house, namely a **sign**.
- **Planetary years**. Periods of years which the planets signify according to various conditions. See VII.2.
- **Portion** (Lat. *pars*, *portio*; Ar. *juz'*). Normally equivalent to a degree, but sometimes to the **bound** in which a degree falls.
- **Possess**. Hugo's synonym for a planet being in or **transiting** a **sign**.
- **Post** (Ar. *markaz*). A **stake** or **angle**. (The Arabic verb is virtually equivalent to Ar. *watada*, used for a stake.) Sometimes translated as **center**, as in the centers of the Moon.

- **Posts of the Moon.** See **Centers of the Moon**.
- **Prevention.** See **Conjunction/prevention**.
- **Primary directions.** See **Directions**.
- **Primary motion.** The clockwise or east-to-west motion of the heavens.
- **Profection** (Lat. *profectio*, "advancement, setting out"). A predictive technique in which some part of a chart (usually the **Ascendant**) is advanced either by an entire sign or in 30° increments for each year of life. See VIII.2.1 and VIII.3.2, and the sources in Appendix F.
- **Prohibition.** Equivalent to **Blocking**.
- **Promittor** (lit., something "sent forward"). A point which is **directed** to a **significator**, or to which a significator is **released** or directed (depending on how one views the mechanics of directions).
- **Pushing.** What a planet making an **applying connection** does to the one **receiving** it. See III.15-18.
- *Qasim/qismah*: Arabic terms for **distributor** and **distribution**.
- **Quadrant.** A division of the heavens into four parts, defined by the circles of the horizon and meridian, also known as the axes of the **Ascendant-Descendant**, and **Midheaven-IC**.
- **Quadrant houses.** A division of the heavens into twelve spaces which overlap the **whole signs**, and are assigned to topics of life and ways of measuring strength (such as Porphyry, Alchabitius Semi-Arc, or Regiomontanus houses). For example, if the Midheaven fell into the eleventh sign, the space between the Midheaven and the Ascendant would be divided into sections that overlap and are not coincident with the signs. See I.12 and the Introduction §6.
- **Quadruplicity.** A "fourfold" group of signs indicating certain shared patterns of behavior. The movable (or cardinal or convertible) signs are those through which new states of being are quickly formed (including the seasons): Aries, Cancer, Libra, Capricorn. The fixed (sometimes "firm") signs are those through which matters are fixed and lasting in their character: Taurus, Leo, Scorpio, Aquarius. The common (or mutable or bicorporeal) signs are those which make a transition and partake both of quick change and fixed qualities: Gemini, Virgo, Sagittarius, Pisces. See I.10.5.
- **Quaesited/quesited.** In **horary** astrology, the matter asked about.
- **Querent.** In **horary** astrology, the person asking the question (or the person on behalf of whom one asks).

- **Questions**. The branch of astrology dealing with inquiries about individual matters, for which a chart is cast.
- **Reception.** What one planet does when another planet **pushes** or **applies** to it, and especially when they are related by **dignity** or by a **trine** or **sextile** from an **agreeing** sign of various types. For example, if the Moon applies to Mars, Mars will get or receive her application. See III.15-18 and III.25.
- **Reflection**. When two planets are in **aversion** to each other, but a third planet either **collects** or **transfers** their light. If it collects, it reflects the light elsewhere. See III.13.
- **Refrenation**. See **Revoking**.
- **Regard**. Equivalent to **Aspect**.
- **Releaser**. The point which is the focus of a **direction**. In determining longevity, it is the one among a standard set of possible points which has certain qualifications (see VIII.1.3). In annual predictions one either directs or **distributes** the longevity releaser, or any one of a number of points for particular topics, or else the degree of the **Ascendant** as a default releaser. Many astrologers direct the degree of the Ascendant of the **revolution** chart itself as a releaser.
- **Remote** (Lat. *remotus*, prob. a translation of Ar. *zāyīl*). Equivalent to **cadent**: see **Angle**. But see also *Judges* §7.73, where 'Umar (or Hugo) distinguishes being **cadent** from being **remote**, probably translating the Ar. *zāyīl* and *sāqiṭ* ("withdrawn/removed" and "fallen").
- **Render**. When a planet **pushes** to another planet or place.
- **Retreating** (Ar. *'idbār*). When a planet is in a **cadent** place (but it is unclear whether this is by **whole sign** or **quadrant divisions**); see also **withdrawing**. The opposite of **advancing**. See III.4 and the Introduction §6, and **Angle**.
- **Retrograde**. When a planet seems to move backwards or clockwise relative to the signs and fixed stars. See II.8 and II.10.
- **Return, Solar/Lunar**. Equivalent to **Revolution**.
- **Returning**. What a **burned up** or **retrograde** planet does when another planet **pushes** to it. See III.19.
- **Revoking**. When a planet making an applying **connection** stations and turns **retrograde**, not completing the connection. See III.20.
- **Revolution**. Sometimes called the "cycle" or "transfer" or "change-over" of a year. Technically, the **transiting** position of planets and the **Ascend-**

ant at the moment the Sun returns to a particular place in the zodiac: in the case of nativities, when he returns to his exact natal position; in mundane astrology, usually when he makes his ingress into 0° Aries. But the revolution is also understood to involve an entire suite of predictive techniques, including **distribution, profections**, and *firdārīyyāt*. See *PN3*.
- **Right ascensions**. Degrees on the celestial **equator** (its equivalent of geographical longitude), particularly those which move across the meridian when calculating arcs for **ascensions** and **directions**.
- **Right/left.** Right (or "dexter") degrees and **aspects** are those earlier in the zodiac relative to a planet or sign, up to the **opposition**; left (or "sinister") degrees and aspects are those later in the zodiac. For example, if a planet is in Capricorn, its right aspects will be towards Scorpio, Libra, and Virgo; its left aspects will be towards Pisces, Aries, and Taurus. See III.6.
- **Root**. A chart used as a basis for another chart; a root particularly describes something considered to have concrete being of its own. For example, a **nativity** acts as a root for an **election**, so that when planning an election one must make it harmonize with the nativity.
- **Safe**. When a planet is not being harmed, particularly by an **assembly** or **square** or **opposition** with the **malefics**. See **Cleansed**.
- *Sālkhudhāy* (from Pahlavi, "lord of the year"). Equivalent to the **lord of the year**.
- **Sanguine**. See **Humor**.
- **Scorched**. See **Burned up**.
- **Secondary motion**. The counter-clockwise motion of planets forward in the zodiac.
- **Sect**. A division of charts, planets, and signs into "diurnal/day" and "nocturnal/night." Charts are diurnal if the Sun is above the horizon, else they are nocturnal. Planets are divided into sects as shown in V.11. Masculine signs (Aries, Gemini, *etc.*) are diurnal, the feminine signs (Taurus, Cancer, *etc.*) are nocturnal.
- **Sector** (Ar. *niṭāq*). A division of the **deferent** circle or **epicycle** into four parts, used to determine the position, speed, visibility, and other features of a planet. See II.0-1.
- **Seeing, hearing, listening signs**. A way of associating signs similar to **commanding/obeying**. See Paul of Alexandria's version in the two figures attached to I.9.6.

- **Separation.** When planets have completed a **connection** by **assembly** or **aspect**, and move away from one another. See III.8.
- **Sextile.** An **aspect** either by **whole sign** or degree, in which the signs have a 60° relation to each other: for example, Aries and Gemini.
- **Share** (Ar. *ḥazza*). Equivalent to **dignity**.
- **Shift.** (1) Equivalent to **sect** (Ar. *nawbah*), referring not only to the alternation between day and night, but also to the period of night or day itself. The Sun is the lord of the diurnal shift or sect, and the Moon is the lord of the nocturnal shift or sect. (2) In mundane astrology, it refers to the shift (Ar. *intiqāl*) of the Saturn-Jupiter conjunctions from one **triplicity** to another about every 200 (tropical zodiac) or 220 (sidereal zodiac) years.
- **Sign.** One of the twelve 30° divisions of the **ecliptic**, named after the constellations which they used to be roughly congruent to. In tropical astrology, the signs start from the intersection of the ecliptic with the celestial equator (the position of the Sun at the equinoxes). In sidereal astrology, the signs begin from some other point identified according to other principles.
- **Significator.** Either (1) a planet or point in a chart which indicates or signifies something for a topic (either through its own character, or house position, or rulerships, *etc.*), or (2) the point which is **released** in primary **directions**.
- **Significator of the king.** In mundane ingress charts, the **victor** planet which indicates the king or government.
- **Sinister.** "Left": see **Right/left.**
- **Slavery.** Equivalent to **fall**.
- **Sovereignty** (Lat. *regnum*). Equivalent to **Exaltation**.
- **Spearbearing.** Equivalent to **Bodyguarding.**
- **Square.** An **aspect** either by **whole sign** or degree, in which the signs have a 90° relation to each other: for example, Aries and Cancer.
- **Stake.** Equivalent to **Angle.**
- **Sublunar world.** The world of the four **elements** below the sphere of the Moon, in classical cosmology.
- **Substance** (Lat. *substantia*). Sometimes, indicating the real **essence** of a planet or sign. But often it refers to financial assets (perhaps because coins are physical objects indicating real value).
- **Succeedent.** See **Angle.**

- **Sun's rays** (or Sun's beams). In earlier astrology, equivalent to a regularized distance of 15° away from the Sun, so that a planet under the rays is not visible at dawn or dusk. But a later distinction was made between being **burned up** (about 1° - 7.5° away from the Sun) and merely being under the rays (about 7.5° - 15° away).
- **Superior.** The planets higher than the Sun: Saturn, Jupiter, Mars.
- **Supremacy** (Lat. *regnum*). Hugo's word for **Exaltation**, sometimes used in translations by Dykes instead of the slightly more accurate **Sovereignty**.
- **Synastry.** The comparison of two or more charts to determine compatibility, usually in romantic relationships or friendships. See *BA* Appendix C for a discussion and references for friendship, and *BA* III.7.11 and III.12.7.
- *Tasyīr* (Ar. "dispatching, sending out"). Equivalent to primary **directions**.
- **Temperament.** The particular mixture (sometimes, "complexion") of **elements** or **humors** which determines a person's or planet's typical behavior, outlook, and energy level.
- **Testimony.** From Arabic astrology onwards, a little-defined term which can mean (1) the planets which have **dignity** in a place or degree, or (2) the number of dignities a planet has in its own place (or as compared with other planets), or (3) a planet's **assembly** or **aspect** to a place of interest, or (4) generally *any* way in which planets may make themselves relevant to the inquiry at hand. For example, a planet which is the **exalted** lord of the **Ascendant** but also **aspects** it, maby be said to present two testimonies supporting its relevance to an inquiry about the Ascendant.
- **Tetragon.** Equivalent to **Square.**
- **Thought-interpretation.** The practice of identifying a theme or topic in a **querent's** mind, often using a **victor**, before answering the specific **question**. See *Search*.
- **Time lord.** A planet ruling over some period of time according to one of the classical predictive techniques. For example, the **lord of the year** is the time lord over a **profection**.
- **Transfer.** When one planet **separates** from one planet, and **connects** to another. See III.11. Not to be confused with a **shift** of triplicities in Saturn-Jupiter conjunctions, or the annual **revolutions**, either mundane or natal.
- **Transit.** The passing of one planet across another planet or point (by body or **aspect** by exact degree), or through a particular sign (even in a **whole-**

- **sign** relation to some point of interest). In traditional astrology, not every transit is significant; for example, transits of **time lords** or of planets in the **whole-sign angles** of a **profection** might be preferred to others. See VIII.2.4 and *PN3*.
- **Translation**. Equivalent to **Transfer**.
- **Traverse** (Lat. *discurro*). Hugo's synonym for a planet being in or **transiting** through a **sign**.
- **Trigon**. Equivalent to **Trine**.
- **Trine**. An **aspect** either by **whole sign** or degree, in which the signs have a 120° relation to each other: for example, Aries and Leo.
- **Turn** (Ar. *dawr*). A predictive technique in which responsibilities for being a **time lord** rotates between different planets. See VIII.2.3 for one use of the turn, and *AW2* for an explanation of the mundane Turns. But it can occasionally refer more generally to how the planets may equally play a certain *role* in a chart: for example, if the lord of the Ascendant is Saturn, it means X; but if Jupiter, Y; but if Mars, Z; and so on.
- **Turned away**. Equivalent to **Aversion**.
- **Turning signs**. For Hugo of Santalla, equivalent to the movable signs: see **Quadruplicity**. But *tropicus* more specifically refers to the tropical signs Cancer and Capricorn, in which the Sun turns back from its most extreme declinations.
- **Twelfth-parts**. Signs of the zodiac defined by 2.5° divisions of other signs. For example, the twelfth-part of 4° Gemini is Cancer. See IV.6.
- **Two-parted signs**. Equivalent to the double-bodied or common signs: see **Quadruplicity**.
- **Under rays**. When a planet is between approximately 7.5° and 15° from the Sun, and not visible either when rising before the Sun or setting after him. Some astrologers distinguish the distances for individual planets (which is more astronomically accurate). See II.10.
- **Unfortunate**. Normally, when a planet's condition is made more difficult through one of the **bearings** in IV.
- **Unlucky**. See **Benefic/malefic**.
- **Upright** (Ar. *qāʾim*). Describes the axis of the MC-IC, when it falls into the tenth and fourth signs, rather than the eleventh-fifth, or ninth-third.
- *Via combusta*. See **Burnt path**.
- **Victor** (Ar. *mubtazz*). A planet or point identified as the most authoritative over a particular topic or **house** (I.18), or for a chart as a whole (VIII.1.4).

See also *Search*. Dykes distinguishes procedures that find the most authoritative and powerful planet ruling one or more places (a victor "over" places) or the member of a list of candidates which fulfills certain criteria (a victor "among" places).
- **Void in course.** Equivalent to **Emptiness of the course.**
- **Well.** A degree in which a planet is said to be more obscure in its operation. See VII.9.
- **Western.** See **Eastern/western.**
- **Whole signs.** The oldest system of assigning house topics and **aspects**. The entire sign on the horizon (the **Ascendant**) is the first house, the entire second sign is the second house, and so on. Likewise, aspects are considered first of all according to signs: planets in Aries aspect or regard Gemini as a whole, even if aspects by exact degree are more intense. See I.12, III.6, and the Introduction §6.
- **Wildness** (Ar. *waḥshiyah*, Lat. *feralitas*). When a planet is not **aspected** by any other planet, for as long as it is in its current sign. See III.10.
- **Withdrawing.** In some Latin translations (*recedens*), equivalent to one planet **separating** from another. But in Arabic (*zā'il*), a withdrawing planet is dynamically **cadent**, moving by diurnal motion away from the degree of the axes or **stakes**—a near-synonym of **retreating**, and the opposite of **advancing**.
- **Zīj.** The Arabic for a Persian word meaning a set of astronomical tables for calculating planetary positions and other things. Ptolemy's *Almagest* can be considered a *zīj*.

BIBLIOGRAPHY

Abū Ma'shar al-Balkhi, *On Historical Astrology: The Book of Religions and Dynasties (On the Great Conjunctions)*, vols. I-II, eds. and trans. Keiji Yamamoto and Charles Burnett (Leiden: Brill, 2000)

Al-Bīrūnī, Muhammad bin Ahmad, *The Book of Instruction in the Elements of the Art of Astrology*, trans. R. Ramsay Wright (London: Luzac & Co., 1934)

Al-Bīrūnī, Muhammad bin Ahmad, *The Chronology of Ancient Nations* (Lahore: Hijra International Publishers, 1983)

Bonatti, Guido, trans. Benjamin N. Dykes, *The Book of Astronomy* (Golden Valley, MN: The Cazimi Press, 2007)

Bos, Gerrit and Charles Burnett, *Scientific Weather Forecasting in the Middle Ages: The Writings of al-Kindī* (London and New York: Kegan Paul International, 2000)

Brady, Bernadette, *Brady's Book of Fixed Stars* (Boston: Weiser Books, 1998)

Burnett, Charles, and David Pingree eds., *The Liber Aristotilis of Hugo of Santalla* (London: The Warburg Institute, 1997)

Carmody, Francis, *Arabic Astronomical and Astrological Sciences in Latin Translation: A Critical Bibliography* (Berkeley and Los Angeles: University of California Press, 1956)

Dykes, Benjamin trans. and ed., *Works of Sahl & Māshā'allāh* (Golden Valley, MN: The Cazimi Press, 2008)

Dykes, Benjamin, trans. and ed., *Choices & Inceptions: Traditional Electional Astrology* (Minneapolis, MN: The Cazimi Press, 2012)

Dykes, Benjamin, trans. and ed., *Astrology of the World I: The Ptolemaic Inheritance* (Minneapolis, MN: The Cazimi Press, 2013)

Evans, James, *The History and Practice of Ancient Astronomy* (Oxford: Oxford University Press, 1998)

Ibn Ezra, Abraham, *The Book of the World*, Shlomo Sela trans. and ed. (Leiden and Boston: Brill, 2010)

Hephaistion of Thebes, trans. Eduardo Gramaglia and ed. Benjamin Dykes, *Apotelesmatics Book III: On Inceptions* (Minneapolis, MN: The Cazimi Press, 2013)

Ibn Hibintā, *The Sufficient [Book] on the Judgments of the Stars (al-Mughnī fī ahkām al-nujūm)*, facsimile edition (Frankfurt am-Main: Institute for the History of Arabic-Islamic Science at the Johann Wolfgang Goethe University, 1987).

Ibn Labbān, Kušyār, *Introduction to Astrology*, ed. and trans. Michio Yano (Tokyo: Institute for the Study of Languages and Cultures of Asia and Africa, 1997)

Kennedy, E.S., "A Survey of Islamic Astronomical Tables," in *Transactions of the American Philosophical Society*, New Ser. Vol 46, No. 2 (1956), pp. 123-77.

Kennedy, E.S., "The Sasanian Astronomical Handbook *Zīj-I Shāh* and the Astrological Doctrine of 'Transit' (Mamarr)," in *Journal of the American Oriental Society*, Vol. 78, No. 4 (Oct. – Dec. 1958), pp. 246-62.

Kennedy, E.S., "Ramifications of the World-Year Concept in Islamic Astrology," in *Ithaca (Proceedings of the Tenth International Congress of the History of Science)*, 26 VIII – 2 IX 1962, pp. 23-45.

Kennedy, E.S., "The World-Year of the Persians," in *Journal of the American Oriental Society*, Vol. 83, No. 3 (Aug. – Sep. 1963), pp. 315-27.

Kennedy, E.S. and David Pingree, *The Astrological History of Māshā'allāh* (Cambridge, MA: Harvard University Press, 1971)

Kennedy, E.S. et al., "Al-Battānī's Astrological History of the Prophet and the Early Caliphate," in *Suhayl* Vol. 9 (2009-2010), pp. 13-148.

Kennedy, Hugh, *The Prophet and the Age of the Caliphates: the Islamic Near East from the Sixth to the Eleventh Century* [2nd Ed.] (Harlow, Great Britain: Pearson Education Ltd., 2004).

Kunitzsch, Paul and Tim Smart, *A Dictionary of Modern Star Names* (Cambridge, MA: New Track Media, 2006)

Lucentini, Paolo et al., *Hermetis Trismegisti: Astrologica et Divinatoria* (Turnhout, Belgium: Brepols Publishers, 2001)

Māshā'allāh, *On Reception*, ed. and trans. Robert Hand (ARHAT Publications, 1998)

Maternus, Firmicus, *Mathesis*, trans. and ed. James H. Holden (Tempe, AZ: American Federation of Astrologers, Inc., 2011)

Nykle, A. R., "Libro Conplido en los Juizios de Las Estrellas," *Speculum* Vol. 29, No. 1 (Jan. 1954), pp. 85-99.

Pingree, David, "Astronomy and Astrology in India and Iran," in *Isis* Vol. 54, No. 2 (Jun., 1963), pp. 229-46.

Pingree, David, *The Thousands of Abū Ma'shar* (London: The Warburg Institute and University of London, 1968)

Pingree, David, "The *Liber Universus* of 'Umar Ibn al-Farrūkhān al-Tabarī," in *Journal for the History of Arabic Science*, Vol. 1, No. 1, 1977, pp. 8-12.

Pingree, David, "From Alexandria to Baghdād to Byzantium: The Transmission of Astrology," *International Journal of the Classical Tradition*, Vol. 8, No. 1, Summer 2001, pp. 3-37.

Ptolemy, Claudius, *Ptolemy's Almagest*, trans. and ed. G.J. Toomer (Princeton, NJ: Princeton University Press, 1998)

Al-Qabīsī, *The Introduction to Astrology*, eds. Charles Burnett, Keiji Yamamoto, Michio Yano (London and Turin: The Warburg Institute, 2004)

Sachau, Edward C. trans. and ed., *Albērūnī's India* (New Delhi: Rupert & Co., 2002)

Schmidt, Robert H., trans. and ed. *Definitions and Foundations* (Cumberland, MD: The Golden Hind Press, 2009)

Sezgin, Fuat, *Geschichte des Arabischen Schrifttums* vol. 7 (Leiden: E.J. Brill, 1979)

Stieglitz, Robert R., "The Hebrew Names of the Seven Planets," *Journal of Near Eastern Studies*, Vol. 40, No. 2 (Apr. 1981), pp. 135-137.

Van der Waerden, B.L., "The Great Year in Greek, Persian and Hindu Astronomy," *Archive for the History of Exact Sciences*, Vol. 18, No. 4 (1978), pp. 359-383.

Select Index

Because of the extensive organization of the Introduction, *Comments* to each Section, and footnotes, this select index is comprised mainly of names, especially those names which are only mentioned a few times. Names which appear throughout (such as Māshā'allāh, Sahl, Abū Ma'shar) are omitted.

'A'isha, wife of Muhammad 274
'Abd al-Malik, Caliph 534
'Alī b. Abī Tālib, Caliph 274
'Umar II, Caliph 537, 540
'Uthmān, Caliph 274, 280, 283, 529
Abū 'Aun 497
al-Battānī..10, 21, 30- 32, 202, 359
al-Mughīrah 499, 501
al-Sijzī 11, 61
al-Zubayr, 'Abd Allāh b. 533-34
Antiochus 367
Battle of Siffīn........527-29, 534-35
Battle of the Camel... 178, 273-74, 280, 527, 529, 533
Bonatti, Guido .... .146, 205, 214, 228, 230, 239-40, 242-44, 250- 51, 263, 287, 291, 303, 308, 332, 334, 354
Buzurjmihr 443
Critodemus 6
Dorotheus 6, 111, 232, 484
Hardūn, Sa'īd b. 508
Hāshimī, 'Abd Allāh b. Muhammad..........................501
Hermes....... 82, 130, 159, 211, 303, 356, 370, 384, 387, 389, 413, 416, 451, 489-90

ibn Bishr, 'Abd Allah b. Muhammad 198
ibn Ezra, Abraham......6, 144, 326, 481
ibn Hibintā 7, 28, 56, 90, 92, 93, 156, 158, 160, 165, 169-74, 178-80, 184-86, 188-89, 197, 201-03
ibn Kisūn/Kīsūn 497
ibn Labbān, Kushyar 6, 35, 185
ibn Masrūr, 'Abū 'Abd Allāh..387, 389
Kankah.....2, 4, 29, 74-78, 81, 493, 504, 507, 541
Kisrā Anūshīrwān 15, 91, 496
Mumtahan zīj 31, 45, 202, 504
Ptolemy, Claudius 4, 30-31, 37, 39, 43, 68, 123, 135, 150, 302-03, 329, 333-34, 356, 359, 367, 389, 412, 414, 426, 481, 485, 496-97, 504, 544, 549, 565
Sindhind..........................11, 45, 504
Timocharis...................................6
Valens, Vettius 6, 450
Zarādusht....................................303
Zīj al-Shāh..12, 14, 28, 91, 170, 202